BAUDELAIRE AND NATURE

FOR MY WIFE
in deepest gratitude of all

to the memory of
P. MANSELL JONES

Baudelaire and Nature

by

F. W. LEAKEY

MANCHESTER UNIVERSITY PRESS
BARNES & NOBLE, INC.

© 1969 F. W. LEAKEY
Published by the University of Manchester at
THE UNIVERSITY PRESS
316–324 Oxford Road, Manchester, M13 9NR
G.B. SBN 7190 0345 8

U.S.A.
BARNES & NOBLE, INC.
105 Fifth Avenue, New York, N.Y. 10003
U.S. SBN 389 01053 7

Printed in the Republic of Ireland by
Hely Thom, Limited, Dublin

Contents

Acknowledgements

THE name I must first inscribe under this heading is that of P. Mansell Jones—that fine scholar but above all that wisest and kindest of men, whose warm and unstinted encouragement and ever-sagacious counsel had sustained me in many difficult times. But now deep sorrow has come to cloud this acknowledgement: our beloved 'P.M.' has passed away, and with him the true friend and shrewd, generous mentor of scholars, teachers and students throughout the world. May the dedication of this volume carry its small tribute to the memory of a great and good man.

I am also grateful, looking back over many years devoted to the study of Baudelaire, for the support lent to me in the first instance by Emeritus Professor Jules Dechamps, the supervisor of my London Ph.D. thesis on certain aspects of metaphor in *Les Fleurs du Mal*; by Dr. Enid Starkie, who guided some of my first steps in Baudelaire, and whose subsequent championship of my work I have deeply appreciated; by the late George T. Clapton, that most perceptive and trenchant of Baudelairians, whose judgment on the present book I would so greatly have valued; by Emeritus Professor Harold W. Lawton, from whose helpful suggestions I profited both in the completion of my thesis and in the composition of my first articles on Baudelaire; by Emeritus Professor Alan M. Boase, whose continued advocacy made possible for me the two periods of study leave below-mentioned; by another highly distinguished scholar, both in the Baudelairian and post-Baudelairian fields, for whom I have the most cordial esteem, Professor Lloyd J. Austin; finally, by my deeply admired and respected Baudelairian friends Professors William T. Bandy and Claude Pichois—the first, *doyen* of all specialists within this field, to whom over the past forty years we owe so many brilliant discoveries concerning our poet; the second, worthy 'inheritor' of the great work of Jacques Crépet, who now continues and deepens that work with a precision, authority and penetration that could not better augur for its future.[1]

[1]Concerning Jacques Crépet and his father Eugène (the pioneer Baudelairian of all), I cannot here resist the temptation of quoting an anecdote told many years ago by the then 'Atticus' of the *Sunday Times* (11 November 1956), but which I have not seen reproduced since. The anecdote concerns the poet Jules Supervielle: 'Some time ago . . . I spoke to him of the high merits of Crépet *père et fils* as editors of Baudelaire. "But of course", he replied. "The Crépets have specialised in Baudelaire since the reign of Louis XIV".'

vii

Coming now to the present book, I must first express my most grateful thanks to my friends John H. B. Bennett and Dalibor B. Chrástek, who on more than one occasion have given generously (and respectively) of their time in examining, verifying or copying for me texts, etc., that for geographical reasons I have been unable to consult myself; Dr. Bennett was also kind enough to read through a substantial portion of my final typescript and to offer his helpful comments thereon. Nor must I forget the valuable aid rendered me on specific points of documentation by my friends Professor Alan J. Steele, Dr. George M. Sutherland and Mr. Edward G. Taylor, as equally again, by Professor Bandy and Professor Pichois. My warm thanks are due also to Mrs. Cynthia Carter, for her expert and patient assistance with the typing of my manuscript, and to the courteous and ever-helpful Staff of Glasgow University Library; I would mention particularly, in this latter respect, the facilities so efficiently offered through the Inter-Library Loan Department, without which I should have found it difficult indeed to carry my task through to its conclusion. Lastly, I must record my gratitude to Sir Alexander Cross, Bart., and to the Carnegie Trust for the Universities of Scotland, for financial awards which enabled me to take two periods of study leave of one term and one session respectively, during which I was able to pursue intensively much of the work here presented in its final form, as also to the University of Glasgow for granting me leave of absence on these two occasions and for making various awards for research expenses under the appropriate University Fund.

Key to Abbreviations

Note: For full details of books cited below, see Analytical Bibliography, s.v. Sections A (Baudelaire texts) or C.

AIP   B., *Art in Paris*, trans. and ed. J. Mayne.
AR   B., *L'Art romantique*, ed. J. Crépet (in B., *OCC*).
B.   Baudelaire
BDC   B. *devant ses contemporains*, ed. W. T. Bandy and C. Pichois (1967 reprint).
BDI   B. *Documents iconographiques*, ed. C. Pichois and F. Ruchon.
BJC   W. T. Bandy, *B. judged by his Contemporaries.*
BMFP   P. Mansell Jones, *The Background of Modern French Poetry.*
BNE   *Charles Baudelaire*, Bibliothèque nationale (Catalogue of 1957 Exhibition).
CE   B., *Curiosités esthétiques* (unless otherwise stated, in *OCC*, ed. J. Crépet).
CG   B., *Correspondance générale*, ed. J. Crépet and C. Pichois (in *OCC*).
CLM   B., *Critique littéraire et musicale*, ed. C. Pichois, Cluny.
CML   B., *Œuvres complètes*, Le Club du meilleur livre.
DP   B., *Douze poèmes*, ed. A. van Bever.
EJC   E. and J. Crépet, *Charles Baudelaire*, Vanier-Messein.
FM   B., *Les Fleurs du Mal.*
FMA   B., *FM*, ed. A. Adam, Garnier.
FMC   B., *FM*, ed. J. Crépet (in *OCC*).
FMCB   B., *FM*, ed J. Crépet and G. Blin, Corti.
FMLD   B., *FM. Documents etc.*, ed. Y. G. Le Dantec (*OC*, NRF, vol. II).
FMPP   B., *FM*, ed. J. Pommier and C. Pichois.
FRH   *The French Renaissance and its Heritage. Essays presented to Alan Boase.*
FS   *French Studies.*
HE   Poe, trans. B., *Histoires extraordinaires*, ed. J. Crépet (in *OCC*).
JAAC   *Journal of Aesthetics and Art Criticism.*
JI   *Journaux intimes*, ed. J. Crépet and G. Blin, Corti.
L.   Letter to.
LM   *Letterature moderne.*
LS   B., *Lettres inédites aux siens*, ed. P. Auserve.
MF   *Mercure de France* (journal).
MGC   B. and others, *Mystères galans*, ed. J. Crépet.
MLN   *Modern Language Notes.*
MLR   *Modern Language Review.*
NHE   Poe, trans. B., *Nouvelles Histoires extraordinaires*, ed. J. Crépet (in *OCC*).

OC   *Œuvres complètes.*
OCC   *Œuvres complètes,* Conard.
OCP   B., *Œuvres complètes,* ed. Y. G. Le Dantec and C. Pichois,
         Pléiade. (Note: all references are to the 1966 revision and
         reprint.)
OP   B., *Œuvres posthumes. Reliquiæ,* ed. J. Crépet (in *OCC*).
PA   B., *Les Paradis artificiels*
         (unless otherwise stated, in *OCC,* ed. J. Crépet).
PC   *Poésies complètes.*
Pléiade Pléiade edition (NRF) of works of writer in question.
PPP   B., *Petits poëmes en prose* (unless otherwise stated, in *OCC,* ed.
         J. Crépet).
R.   *Revue.*
RC   *Revue contemporaine.*
RDM   *Revue des Deux Mondes.*
RES   *Revue de l'Enseignement Supérieur.*
RF   *Revue française.*
RHLF   *Revue d'histoire littéraire de la France.*
RLC   *Revue de littérature comparée.*
RLM   *Rivista di Letterature Moderne e Comparate.*
RPa   *Revue de Paris.*
RR   *Romanic Review.*
RSH   *Revue des sciences humaines.*
S45F   B., *Le Salon de 1845,* ed. A. Ferran.
SMFL   *Studies in Modern French Literature presented to P. Mansell
         Jones.*[1]
var(s)   For variant(s) here cited, see also . . .
VR   B., *Vers retrouvés, etc.,* ed. J. Mouquet, Émile-Paul.
YFS   *Yale French Studies.*

---

[1]For details, see Bibliography. Section C, s.v. AUSTIN, L.J.

Preface

Tout poète puise au catalogue de la nature.
(JACQUES CHARPIER, *Saint-John Perse*)

IN the present book I have sought mainly to trace the sequence and evolution of Baudelaire's attitudes towards external Nature, as displayed both in his poetry (i.e. in those poems in which Nature figures as a direct theme, rather than as a source of analogies[1]) and in his critical writings on literature and art. I say 'mainly' advisedly, since it is well known that the word 'Nature' is dangerously ambiguous,[2] and that the notions of 'external Nature' and 'human Nature' tend imperceptibly to shade into one another; indeed, as has been noted,[3] this is often the case with Baudelaire himself. In practice, however (which is to say, in the practical analysis of texts), these problems will be found to resolve themselves in the light of the defining context and theme; while, therefore, I have been obliged to take into account a certain number of texts in which Baudelaire passes without change of terminology from the one conception of Nature to the other, I have nevertheless retained, as my primary and specific concern, his attitudes to the *external* (i.e. material and non-human) universe that surrounds us—sky, sea, woods, fields, lakes, rivers, etc.; in Volney's phrase, 'les objets du ciel et de la terre offerts à nos regards'[4]—and with the concepts formed from those attitudes.

---

[1]Cf., in this connection, my comment, p. 233 n. 1, below.

[2]Cf. the aphorism by Leslie Stephen, cit. B. Willey, *18th-Century Background*, 2: 'Nature is a word contrived in order to introduce as many equivocations as possible into all the theories, political, legal, artistic or literary, into which it enters'. The attempt to define the manifold meanings which have attached themselves to this word, has been made by many scholars, and notably by A. O. Lovejoy (*Essays in the History of Ideas*, 69 ff.; with G. Boas, *Primitivism and Related Ideas in Antiquity*, 447–56); cf. also R. Pomeau, *RES*, 1959, pp. 107–19, and A. Lalande, *Vocabulaire de la philosophie*, II, 503–7. For the distinction between 'Natura naturans' and 'Natura naturata', and its post-mediaeval literary survivals, cf. D. B. Wilson, *Ronsard, Poet of Nature*, vi, 60–1; J. Beach, *Concept of Nature in 19th-Century English Poetry*, 326, 598–9 (Coleridge), 504 (Hardy). For a discussion of these problems of definition as they arise in an important precursor of B.'s, see Béatrice Le Gall, *L'Imaginaire chez Senancour*, I, 362, 371, 377.

[3]By Margaret Gilman, *B. the Critic*, 161–6.

[4]*La Loi naturelle*, Ch. 1 (cit. Lalande, op. cit., II, 506).

To my knowledge, this aspect of Baudelaire's work has nowhere previously been studied in its full and detailed chronological sequence.[1] Indeed one may observe throughout the whole range of Baudelaire studies a curious reluctance to accept and follow what nevertheless for him as for others must remain the fundamental laws of chronology—even though, in disregarding these laws, the critic may reduce his analysis of an author's work to a purely abstract and intellectualized construction, a mere function of the systematizing and rationalizing faculty, divorced from the mobile reality of the actual creative experience. The common assumption that is made, however, in respect of Baudelaire, is that his thought remained consistent and unchanging throughout his whole career, or at least settled at a very early stage into a definite mould which remained unbroken during the rest of his life. Yet not only does this assumption go against all human probability, it also conflicts (as will be amply seen hereafter) with the clear evidence of his writings; these show his ideas to have been in fact, like those of most intelligent people, in perpetual readjustment and correction.[2] It must

---

[1]An excellent (but by its brevity, necessarily incomplete) survey of Baudelaire's concepts of Nature, is given by M. Gilman, *B. the Critic*, 161–6. M. Ruff, in the two pages he devotes to this theme, *Esprit du Mal*, 268–9, effectively descredits the notion that B. lacked true 'Nature-feeling'; against this must be set, however, the pertinent observations made by H. Peyre, *Connaissance de B.*, 83–5, as to the limitations of this same Nature-feeling, and the specific 'areas' in which it manifests itself. J. Prévost, on the other hand, disappoints, in the chapter on 'B. et la nature' which he contributes to what remains nevertheless probably the finest critical study to have been written on B. The monograph by G. Hess, *Die Landschaft in Bs FM*, is essentially concerned with B.'s Nature-*imagery*—the word 'landscape' being taken, in its broadest sense, to include descriptive or pictorial detail of whatever kind. J. P. Sartre, *B.*, 116–34, while recognizing the complexity of B.'s attitude to Nature, nevertheless over-simplifies its psychology by exaggerating (persuasively) the significance of certain chosen texts. Several critics, finally, have drawn attention to the decided 'naturalism' of B.'s philosophies during the first phase of his career (1841–6); cf. G. T. Clapton, *RLC*, 1933, pp. 430–2; L. J. Austin, *Univers poétique de B.*, 87–8; A. Adam, *FMA* 308, 312. I must here add a reference to an unpublished Doctoral dissertation by Liliane M. Welch, *The Problem of Nature in B.*, Pennsylvania State University, 1964, which I have not had the opportunity of consulting.

[2]Cf. this passage from the *Exposition universelle 1855*, in which he gives clear warning to all over-systematizing critics: 'J'ai essayé plus d'une fois, comme tous mes amis, de m'enfermer dans un système pour y prêcher à mon aise. Mais un système est une espèce de damnation qui nous pousse à une abjuration

be admitted, however, that two particular and local factors have in the past combined to impede chronological approaches to Baudelaire's work, and have thus frustrated in his case—needlessly, as I shall go on to argue—what he himself called 'le plaisir qu'on a à lire dans les œuvres d'un artiste les diverses transformations de son art et les préoccupations successives de son esprit'.[1]

The first (and lesser) of these difficulties arises from the *recurrence* of certain ideas or themes at different periods of Baudelaire's life, thus falsely suggesting an unbroken continuity of thought; in most of these instances, however, the examination of intermediate developments—as, equally, the restoration of the text in question to its immediate context—shows the apparent continuity to conceal in fact a normally 'accidented' development. (A frequent explanation of these recurrences, incidentally, lies in Baudelaire's habit of borrowing, when in creative difficulties, from his own previous writings and formulations.[2]) A second and more essential problem of Baudelairian chronology concerns his poetry alone: it is simply that we possess so few dated or datable texts for his numerous early poems. Thus although we know the majority of the 101 poems comprising the 1857 edition of *Les Fleurs du Mal* to have been composed well before 1850, for only six of these do we possess versions clearly belonging to this period, and for only forty-five, versions of earlier date than 1857 itself.[3] We can, however, from external evidence of various kinds (testimonies by contemporaries, biographical or stylistic inferences, analogies with texts by other authors or by Baudelaire himself, etc.) establish or at least plausibly conjecture the approximate date of composition of a considerable

---

perpétuelle; il en faut toujours inventer un autre, et cette fatigue est un cruel châtiment' (*CE* 223). For a further elaboration (and demonstration) of this viewpoint, see my art., 'Les Esthétiques de B.', *RSH*, 1967, pp. 481–96.

[1] *Salon de 1845, CE* 19.

[2] Cf., in this connection, the brilliant and cogent study by C. Pichois, 'B. ou la difficulté créatrice', *B.*, 246–9.

[3] For a discussion of this whole question, see my art. 'Pour une étude chronologique des *FM*', *RHLF*, 1967, pp. 343–6. To the six pre-1850 texts in question (*A une dame créole, A une mendiante rousse, Le Vin des chiffonniers, Le Mauvais moine, Don Juan aux Enfers, Les Chats*) should of course be added various other earlier poems which have survived, but which B. chose to exclude from the 1857 or 1861 editions of his book; these 'discarded' texts I have taken into account wherever appropriate.

number of these 'missing' youthful texts,[1] and such ancillary documentation fully suffices, in my view, to allow the type of *thematic* survey essayed in the present book, in which within the general chronological framework of Baudelaire's career as a poet and critic, poems are studied in close conjunction with prose texts: the latter can almost always be precisely dated, and we are thus able, by combining these specific items of information with others more general, to plot with some degree of accuracy the incidence, recurrence and disappearance of themes and counter-themes. I must add that when dealing with this earlier period of Baudelaire's work I have been careful always, where no original draft of a youthful poem survives, to quote (if possible from the original source) the *earliest subsequent* version available;[2] nor when, in default of the original draft, I have offered detailed comments on these later versions, should this be taken as implying any assumption on my part that earlier and later texts will necessarily have been identical in all respects. Since, however, in the few cases where we do possess a number of successive versions of a poem of Baudelaire's, the main content and imagery tend to remain unchanged,[3] and since without some reference to points of detail one can scarcely adequately convey the 'argument' of any poem, I have felt such strictly anachronistic commentaries to be admissible—the more so in that they are in all cases preceded by a reminder of the actual date of the (later) text under discussion, and are set in the general context of a fully authenticated chronology.

Within this chronology—which as far as possible, then, is governed by Baudelaire's own order of composition—I have discerned a

[1]See, in the present volume, my chronological notes regarding certain texts, and for all other texts, the *Chronological Index* in which I collate in summary form all available information concerning dates of composition.

[2]The date and provenance of each text quoted, are briefly noted either in parentheses at the end of the quotation, or in footnote; for full details of the various texts, consult Chronological Index of Texts. In cases where I quote directly from the original source, I have corrected a few obvious misprints and modernized certain spellings; other citations, with a few (specified) exceptions, are in the case of verse texts, to *FMCB* (from which, for instance, I have attempted to 'reconstruct' the anterior proof versions of certain poems in *FM* 1857, pending the full publication of these variants in the forthcoming revised edition of *FMCB* by G. Blin and C. Pichois; cf. in this connection p. 341 n. 2, below), and in the case of prose texts, to the appropriate vol. of *OCC*.

[3]Cf., in this connection, my art. cit., p. 346.

central division between the two main parts of his career (1841–51; 1852–64); within this again, a number of groupings which have, so to speak, 'imposed themselves' by the very nature of the texts concerned.[1] Here, while keeping an eye to the precise chronological relation of one text with another, I have deviated on occasion from strict sequence of composition in order to trace out the development of a particular theme or preoccupation. As is inevitable in a study of this nature, there are on occasion overlappings from one chapter or sub-chapter to another; where, however, different elements of a same text are examined from distinct and successive standpoints, I have been careful to restore them in each case to their full context, in the hope thereby of mitigating any infringement of the text's artistic unity.

No less important, in my view, than the immediate personal chronology of a writer's work, is that wider European background which requires particularly to be taken into account when the theme, as in the present instance, is so essentially 'of' its (Romantic and pre-Romantic) era. Unfortunately we still lack that comprehensive history of European Nature-poetry which would allow us fully to plot the ramifications of the various antecedent and contemporary ideas on Nature which here emerge in a Baudelaire, there in another writer;[2] my own attempt, therefore (mainly within my footnotes) to fill in this broader perspective, can at best be only partial and unsystematic. Such gleanings will at least, however, serve as a reminder that Baudelaire no more than any other writer, lived or wrote in a 'vacuum', sealed off from other influences and especially from those of his contemporaries. Herein lies, in my view, the particular importance of the investigation of literary sources, which are so often judged solely in their 'genetic' relation to the specific text towards which they point. But a 'source', even if problematic or dubious, presents us at the very least with two minds (often two contemporary minds) grappling with a same idea, together extending its range of connotation, together attesting its widening diffusion; still better, where the source is certain or probable, it may reveal to

[1]Cf., for a summary of this evolution, my Conclusion, pp. 311–17, below, as also my Table of Contents.

[2]Cf., however, the conspectus offered—within the space of 11 pages!—by B.'s contemporary, Villemain, in his study of *Chateaubriand*, 40–51—a 'digression' which earned him, incidentally, for his pains, a heavily ironic commentary from B.; see the latter's *Villemain*, OP I, 325–7, and cf. ibid., 597–8.

us the strange *diversity* of the influences that go to shape a writer's thought and imagination—as when a Baudelaire is seen to borrow, without obvious inhibition, from writers he on more public occasions goes out of his way to condemn or ridicule: Laprade, Musset, George Sand.........[1] Thus without in any way claiming to have enumerated exhaustively all previously discovered sources of the texts I discuss, I have attempted to take into account those which bear specifically on the theme of Nature, while contributing for my own part not only various 'new' sources, but also a number of what I would call 'analogues' (rather than 'analogies') with contemporary or earlier writers; these latter, without necessarily implying a direct influence on Baudelaire, seem to me significantly illustrative of a common background jointly shared, a common tradition jointly inherited.

A substantial proportion of this book being made up of commentaries on individual texts by Baudelaire, I must stress that I have been deliberately selective in my reference to previous 'interpretations'. In the main—in those cases where I do not advance 'new' interpretations of my own—I have confined myself to citing those commentaries by other critics which I myself have followed, or which seem of particular significance from my present standpoint. The sole truly valid test for any literary commentary is in any case that it should be measured against the actual *text* which is its proper basis and starting-point, and thereafter judged according to its humble fidelity to the author's *intentions* as revealed within that text;[2] here as in other respects it may be found useful that I have quoted so liberally, throughout, from Baudelaire's own writings.

I add a final word of explanation, concerning the bibliographical apparatus of the book. References within footnotes or within the Chronological Index of Texts, are given in abbreviated form; for

---

[1]Sources relating to each of these three authors are in fact cited in the ensuing pages; cf. also, for Musset and George Sand, the articles by J. Pommier (*Mélanges Bonnerot*) and L. Cellier (*RHLF*, 1967), respectively.

[2]It will be gathered from this that I subscribe unreservedly to what latterly (following the 'lead' given by W. K. Wimsatt and M. C. Beardsley; see the former's *The Verbal Icon*, 3–18) has been misnamed 'The Intentional Fallacy'—misnamed, because far from being 'fallacious', the concern (or respect) for intention remains surely an essential requirement for all critics . . . Cf., in this connection, my article, 'Intention in Metaphor', *Essays in Criticism*, 1954, pp. 191–2, as also my prudential comment, p. 297 n. 2, below.

these abbreviations, where not self-explanatory, the reader is referred to the Key to Abbreviations which precedes this Preface;[1] full details of all books, articles, etc., cited are given in my Bibliography.[2] To facilitate consultation of the book, I have included, as well as the Chronological Index of Texts aforementioned, a very full system of cross-references within the footnotes, and an Index of Persons.

[1]For the sake of clarity, I have sometimes been inconsistent in my abbreviations. For instance, page-references are normally given as simple numerals; where any possible ambiguity might arise, however, the numeral is preceded by the indication 'p.', 'pp.'. I have likewise been sparing in my recourse to the unsupported formulas 'op. cit.', 'art. cit.', etc., using these only when the item in question has been cited in the immediately preceding footnotes; much frustration, in my experience, arises from the search through several hundred pages of text for the original and only full reference to a particular article or book!

[2]Bibliographical indications for all texts other than those by B., follow the usual conventions: titles of books and periodicals are in italics, titles of articles are within inverted commas, etc. But in the case of texts by B., titles are italicized whenever the text is a work complete in itself, i.e. a poem or a critical article, as well as a whole book; quotation marks are used for titles only when the text in question forms an incomplete part of such a work, i.e. a section of an article or a chapter of a book.

PART ONE
1832-51

Introduction

(1832-41):

A YOUTHFUL NATURE-LOVER

ONE of Baudelaire's earliest surviving letters, in which he recounts
(for the benefit of his step-brother Claude-Alphonse) the journey
he had made from Paris to Lyons on his family's establishment there
at the beginning of 1832, contains a brief description displaying not
only marked literary precocity but also, I suggest, a discriminating
response to the beauties of Nature rare in a ten-year-old. Passing
rapidly over the day's various 'stages', Baudelaire pauses to describe
the *evening* scene:

Le jour étant tombé, je vis un bien beau spectacle: c'était le soleil couchant; cette couleur rougeâtre formait un contraste singulier avec les
montagnes qui étaient bleues comme le pantalon le plus foncé.

(*LS* 45)

The remaining sentence of the letter, while it may return us to the
world of childhood in which one wears a 'little silk cap' and is
plagued by 'accursed' homework, at the same time brings a further
reflection, on the delights of 'endless travel', which holds equally
(as we shall discover) its own prophetic significance:[1]

Ayant mis mon petit bonnet de soie, je me laissai aller sur le dos de la
voiture et il me sembla que toujours voyager serait une vie qui me plairait
beaucoup; je voudrais bien t'en écrire davantage, mais un *maudit thème*
m'oblige de fermer ici ma lettre.

(*LS* 45-6)

And he signs: 'Ton petit frère'. Other passages in these letters
written during his schooldays to his step-brother or mother, attest

[1]See p. 300, below. Cf., within the present period, the disappointment over
a postponed holiday trip with his step-father (*LS* 59-60), and the self-
description: 'amateur de géographie' (*LS* 77-8)—as also these surely autobiographical allusions within two later texts: the opening couplet of *Le Voyage*
(1859: 'Pour l'enfant, amoureux de cartes et d'estampes, / L'univers est égal
à son vaste appétit'); the avowal by the fourth young boy in the prose poem
Les Vocations (1864, *PPP* 116: 'Il m'a souvent semblé que mon plaisir serait
d'aller toujours droit devant moi, sans savoir où, sans que personne s'en
inquiète, et de voir toujours des pays nouveaux').

a similar if sometimes less articulate feeling for Nature;[1] and it is
no doubt significant in this respect that when writing to his mother
in July 1839, he should have instanced among other things that stir
him deeply, a beautiful sunset seen from a window[2]—thus echoing,
at some seven years' remove, the youthful passage quoted above,
as well as prefiguring the theme of one of the most personal of his
subsequent poems, *Je n'ai pas oublié, voisine de la ville*.[3]

May we not, however, in the light of the poem *Bénédiction*, go a little
farther than this, in seeking to measure the intensity of Baudelaire's
youthful feeling for Nature? Here is Baudelaire's picture—sketched
initially, perhaps, during the period 1844–6[4]—of the infant Poet
delighting in his instinctive communion with sun, wind and cloud:

> Pourtant, sous la tutelle invisible d'un Ange,
> L'Enfant déshérité s'enivre de soleil,
> Et dans tout ce qu'il boit et dans tout ce qu'il mange
> Retrouve l'ambroisie et le nectar vermeil.
>
> Il joue avec le vent, cause avec le nuage,
> Et s'enivre en chantant du chemin de la croix,
> Et l'Esprit qui le suit dans son pélerinage
> Pleure de le voir gai comme un oiseau des bois.
>
> (ll. 21–8; 1857 text)

These lines—if one discounts the Messianic note imposed by the
general theme of *Bénédiction* (the Poet, misunderstood and rejected
by his fellow-men, finds his true reward in the Heaven from which
originally, by divine 'decree', he had been sent down on earth)—
might well be taken as an exalted reminiscence of Baudelaire's own

---

[1] Cf. *LS* 46–7 (description of main road leading out from Villeneuve), 61
(the view from the new house in Lyons: 'Tu ne peux pas te figurer comme
c'est beau, comme c'est magnifique, comme c'est beau [sic], comme ce coteau
est riche, comme il est vert'—a veritable torrent of superlatives!), 128 ('im-
prisoned', because of a knee injury, within the school infirmary, he observes
longingly 'un beau ciel, des rayons de soleil').

[2] *CG* I, 6.

[3] See p. 13, below. Cf. also this description—in a letter I would myself (for
reasons I shall hope to make clear in another publication) date as of April 1841—
of the second of his two preferred modes of escape from the 'provincialism'
of Creil (the first being obligingly furnished by 'une femme qui a les mains
blanches, et qui parle français'): 'Le reste du temps je me sauve dans les
champs, et je me chauffe au grand soleil' (*CG* I, 12).

[4] Cf. Chronological Index.

childhood;[1] for in how many other texts, with an insistence which surely argues a basis in personal experience, does he not evoke the generic Child's delighted and wondering apprehension of the world of Nature, his primordial 'intoxication' with its forms and colours— or, again, the related vividness and freshness of the adolescent's perceptions?

L'enfant voit tout en *nouveauté*; il est toujours *ivre*. Rien ne ressemble plus à ce qu'on appelle l'inspiration, que la joie avec laquelle l'enfant absorbe la forme et la couleur.[2]

Tous ceux qui ont réfléchi sur leur propre vie . . . savent quelle part immense l'adolescence tient dans le génie définitif d'un homme. C'est alors que les objets enfoncent profondément leurs empreintes dans l'esprit tendre et facile; c'est alors que les couleurs sont voyantes, et que les sens parlent une langue mystérieuse.[3]

Le beau temps que celui où le matin ne réveilla jamais nos genoux engourdis ou rompus par la fatigue des songes, où nos yeux clairs riaient à toute la nature, où notre âme ne raisonnait pas, mais où elle vivait et jouissait...[4]

> . . . la sainte jeunesse, à l'air simple, au doux front,
> A l'œil limpide et clair ainsi qu'une eau courante,
> Et qui va répandant sur tout, insouciante
> Comme l'azur du ciel, les oiseaux et les fleurs,
> Ses parfums, ses chansons et ses douces chaleurs!
> (*J'aime le souvenir de ces époques nues*, 1857 text, ll. 36–40)

---

[1] Even to the note of uncaring 'gaiety' sounded in certain early letters—a gaiety which in the perspective of later tribulations might well excite any Guardian Angel's compassion! Cf. the charming episode within the ten-year-old B.'s narration of his journey from Paris to Lyons, in which he recounts with naive glee how, having slipped away from the stage-coach and from his mother, he scurries off along the road, delighted to be free of all restraints and to be described, later, as a 'petit *Monsieur*' (*LS* 47–8).

[2] *Le Peintre de la vie moderne* (comp. 1859–60), *AR* 59–60; the context here is that of the mature inspiration of the creative artist. Cf. this description (dated 1863–5? see Chronological Index, below, s.v. ' "*Spleen de Paris*" ') of a projected prose poem: 'L'Auberge du Bocage (souvenir de jeunesse, par l'odeur, la couleur, et le vent frais)' (*OCP* 314).

[3] *Edgar Allan Poe* (pub. 1852), *OP* I, 251.

[4] *La Fanfarlo* (pub. 1847), ed. C. Pichois, 60.

Alors je rêverai des horizons bleuâtres,
Des jardins, des jets d'eau pleurant dans les albâtres,
Des baisers, des oiseaux chantant soir et matin,
Et tout ce que l'Idylle a de plus enfantin.

(*Paysage parisien*, 1857 text, ll. 17–20)

But whatever the force of these analogies, there remains one further text from this early period, which is of quite unmistakable signific-ance from our present standpoint; for it so happens that the very earliest of all Baudelaire's extant poems is specifically a Nature-poem, written when he was only seventeen. This sequence of seven quatrains—which one may now date, quite precisely, from the end of August or the first three weeks of September 1838—describes, under the title *Incompatibilité,* a landscape admired during a holiday spent in the Pyrenees with his mother and stepfather.[1] The whole experience seems to have left a deep impression on him, if we may judge not only from the brief account given to his step-brother (and in which he declares notably: 'Bagnères est un lieu de délices: le plus beau pays de France'),[2] but also from the readiness with which he appears to hark back to it in certain later texts.[3] The specific scene, here, is a mountain lake;[4] after a slow and measured 'ascent'—which the young poet perhaps strove to convey, by 'imitation', in the sustained unwinding of his opening sentence, with its suspensive repetitions and gradual multiplication of detail—

---

[1] Cf. *OP* I, 376 (prefatory note cit. from *L'Idée libre,* 1892); C. Pichois, *MF,* Aug. 1955, pp. 671–2 and note 211; *LS* 160–2 and 164–5. It is this latter text (bringing several letters of B.'s, directly referring to the 1838 holiday) which allows of the precise dating aforementioned.

[2] Letter of 23 October 1838, *LS* 164–5. Two letters written, to his step-brother and mother respectively, convey his excitement at the prospect both of the holiday and of the journey to be accomplished *alone*; see *LS* 160–2.

[3] It is notable, for instance, that in the autobiographical notes drawn up for Duranty c. 1861 (*OP* II, 136), B.'s 'voyages avec [son] beau-père dans les Pyrénées' are among the few events he chooses to recall from his schooldays. Cf. also (pp. 8–9, 95 and n. 2, 192, 257, below) the prose poem *Le Gâteau* (1862), the essay *Edgar Poe, sa vie et ses œuvres* (1856), the poem *Élévation* (pub. 1857), etc.

[4] Now that we have (in the letter to his step-brother, *LS* 164–5) the actual details of B.'s itinerary, it should no doubt be possible to locate the precise site that he here describes! The Baudelairian pilgrim so minded could perhaps best start from Bagnères—if one assumes that the mountain lake in question is among the 'delights' ('Bagnères est un lieu de délices') to be tasted in that region.

we at last reach the dark waters hemmed in by their desolate, snow-capped peaks:

> Tout là-haut, tout là-haut, loin de la route sûre,
> Des fermes, des vallons, par delà les coteaux,
> Par delà les forêts, les tapis de verdure,
> Loin des derniers gazons foulés par les troupeaux,
>
> On rencontre un lac sombre encaissé dans l'abîme
> Que forment quelques pics désolés et neigeux;
> L'eau, nuit et jour, y dort dans un repos sublime,
> Et n'interrompt jamais son silence orageux.
>
> (*OP* i, 8–9)

What is mainly (and not unsuccessfully) conveyed hereafter is the vague disquiet, apprehension even, which colours the traveller's further response—a mood engendered by the remoteness and solitude of the scene, and above all by its extraordinary depth and intensity of silence. The silence is at first only relative: to disturb the obscurely threatening stillness, the 'silence orageux', of the sleeping waters, there still float up vestigial and muted sounds, distantly recalling the activities of Man:

> Dans ce morne désert, à l'oreille incertaine
> Arrivent par moments des bruits faibles et longs,
> Et des échos plus morts que la cloche lointaine
> D'une vache qui paît aux penchants des vallons.

But thereafter, in the succeeding two verses which form the poem's climax (and despite one or two weak lines, its most impressive moment), the silence becomes absolute and overwhelming:

> Sur ces monts où le vent efface tout vestige,
> Ces glaciers pailletés qu'allume le soleil,
> Sur ces rochers altiers où guette le vertige,
> Dans ce lac où le soir mire son teint vermeil,
>
> Sous mes pieds, sur ma tête et partout le silence,
> Le silence qui fait qu'on voudrait se sauver,
> Le silence éternel en la montagne immense,
> Car l'air est immobile et tout semble rêver.

Here no doubt lies the significance of the poem's title: stirred by this vague fear, this desire to *escape*, the onlooker, for all his awareness of the majesty and grandeur of the scene, feels himself to have no part in, no true 'compatibility' with, the vast, brooding, endlessly silent landscape. The next verse suggests a more fundamental, less subjective disharmony:

> On dirait que le ciel, en cette solitude,
> Se contemple dans l'onde, et que ces monts, là-bas,
> Écoutent, recueillis, dans leur grave attitude,
> Un mystère divin que l'homme n'entend pas.

This quatrain is less conventional than its recourse to the 'Pathetic Fallacy' might seem to imply: the 'humanly' self-sufficient and self-absorbed attitudes ascribed to the sky and mountains, serve to make still more complete the total exclusion of Man, the suggestion of mysteries to which he has no access; for him, the silence may be utter and forbidding—but for the mountains, the silence 'speaks' and is pregnant with spiritual meaning. The last verse unfortunately weakens the effect of 'alienation' built up over the rest of the poem, by its facile declension to the realm of conventional fancy:

> Et lorsque par hasard une nuée errante
> Assombrit dans son vol le lac silencieux,
> On croirait voir la robe ou l'ombre transparente
> D'un esprit qui voyage et passe dans les cieux.

The intention is no doubt to heighten by a final image the effect of supernatural majesty conveyed in the previous verses; but this intention is defeated by the very facility of the personification and the too casual phrase 'On croirait'—for if, as the previous verse has declared, the 'divine mystery' of the scene eludes human comprehension, why strive to capture its quality by further all too human images? It is interesting to compare these verses with the more elaborate version of this same youthful experience, given many years later in the opening paragraph of the prose poem *Le Gâteau*; there, Baudelaire more happily (and more accurately?) assimilates the reflection of the passing cloud dipping its shadow in the lake, to the general feeling—joy as well as the earlier 'vague fear'—that the scene arouses in him:

Je voyageais. Le paysage au milieu duquel j'étais placé était d'une grandeur et d'une noblesse irrésistibles. Il en passa sans doute en ce moment quelque chose dans mon âme. Mes pensées voltigeaient avec une légèreté égale à celle de l'atmosphère; les passions vulgaires, telles que la haine et l'amour profane, m'apparaissaient maintenant aussi éloignées que les nuées qui défilaient au fond des abîmes sous mes pieds; mon âme me semblait aussi vaste et aussi pure que la coupole du ciel dont j'étais enveloppé; le souvenir des choses terrestres n'arrivait à mon cœur qu'affaibli et diminué, comme le son de la clochette des bestiaux imperceptibles qui paissaient loin, bien loin, sur le versant d'une autre montagne. Sur le petit lac immobile, noir de son immense profondeur, passait quelquefois l'ombre d'un nuage, comme le reflet du manteau d'un géant aérien volant à travers le ciel. Et je me souviens que cette sensation solennelle et rare, causée par un grand mouvement parfaitement silencieux, me remplissait d'une joie mêlée de peur. Bref, je me sentais, grâce à l'enthousiasmante beauté dont j'étais environné, en parfaite paix avec moi-même et avec l'univers . . . .[1]

The general theme of the prose poem—with its antithesis between the 'beatitude' of the traveller alone amidst the beauties of Nature, and the human discord which irrupts upon him in the shape of two small boys ferociously disputing the 'cake' (i.e. the hunk of bread) offered them—demands that Baudelaire should stress the feelings of serenity and joy aroused by the mountain scene; the youthful verses, on the other hand, in so far as they do reveal the poet's personal emotion, convey awe and admiration, certainly, but at the same time interpose, more distinctly, their note of apprehensive disquiet, their hint of some deeper 'alienation'.[2] The youthful Nature-lover's befitting awe before the grandiose spectacle that here confronts him, thus takes on at the same time a certain *ambivalent* quality we shall find to be strangely prophetic of later and fully characteristic attitudes.

Perhaps implicit, finally, in the concluding verses of *Incompatibi-*

[1]*PPP* 45–6. The analogy with *Incompatibilité* was first noted by G. de Reynold, *B.*, 339; cf. also p. 280, below, and for the further analogy with the poem *Élévation*, p. 192, below. Not all is pure gain, it must be added, in the later (prose-poem) version: is the 'aerial giant' of 1862 really any more convincing than the 'voyaging spirit' of 1838?

[2]These latter are more closely echoed, perhaps, in a text bringing what is obviously a further reminiscence of this same youthful experience; introducing his Poe translations of 1856, B. declares: 'Au sein de cette littérature où l'air est raréfié, l'esprit peut éprouver cette vague angoisse, cette peur prompte aux larmes et ce malaise du cœur qui habitent les lieux immenses et singuliers' (*HE* xxix). Cf. also (p. 257 and n. 2, below) the reference in the *Salon de 1859* to 'ces grands lacs qui représentent l'immobilité dans le bonheur et dans le désespoir' (*CE* 344, var. 498).

lité, is a vein of youthful Nature-*mysticism*, which we may find indirectly attested in certain later and retrospective texts. Thus in the
prose poem *Les Vocations*, the second of the four young boys (each
of whom represents some distinct aspect of Baudelaire's childhood
experience) is presented in these terms:

L'un des quatre enfants, qui depuis quelques secondes n'écoutait plus
le discours de son camarade et observait avec une fixité étonnante je ne
sais quel point du ciel, dit tout à coup: "Regardez, regardez là-bas . . .!
Le voyez-vous? Il est assis sur ce petit nuage isolé, ce petit nuage couleur
de feu, qui marche doucement. *Lui* aussi, on dirait qu'*il* nous regarde."
"Mais qui donc?" demandèrent les autres.
"Dieu!" répondit-il avec un accent parfait de conviction. "Ah! il est
déjà bien loin; tout à l'heure, vous ne pourrez plus le voir. Sans doute il
voyage, pour visiter tous les pays. Tenez, il va passer derrière cette rangée
d'arbres qui est presque à l'horizon . . . et maintenant il descend derrière
le clocher . . . Ah! on ne le voit plus!" Et l'enfant resta longtemps tourné
du même côté, fixant sur la ligne qui sépare la terre du ciel des yeux où
brillait une inexprimable expression d'extase et de regret.[1]

There is a clear analogy between this peripatetic God surveying the
universe from his private cloud, and the 'nuée errante' of *Incompatibilité*, with its cognate 'esprit qui voyage et passe dans les cieux';
and if further confirmation were needed that this young mystic is
indeed to be identified with Baudelaire himself, one might find it
simply by 'leading on', from the description (already quoted) of the
infant Poet of *Bénédiction* 'conversing' with the clouds ('Il joue avec
le vent, cause avec le nuage'), to this explicitly autobiographical
comment furnished many years later: 'Dès mon enfance, tendance
à la mysticité. Mes conversations avec Dieu'.[2] One can of course
scarcely attempt to measure, in the absence of any specific contemporary text, the full range and significance of these early in-
clinations towards a mysticism of Nature; what, however, will

---

[1]*PPP* 114. For the analogy between B. himself and the *fourth* of the young
boys, cf. p. 3 n. 1, above, p. 292 n. 1, below.
[2]*Mon Cœur mis à nu*, XLV, *JI* 101; cf. *Tous imberbes, alors* . . ., *FMA* 228,
l. 45. In his adaptation, under the title *Un Mangeur d'opium*, of De Quincey's
Confessions (*PA* 172–3), B. abridges (to his 'very great regret') a long section
on 'the religion of children'; this includes a statement: 'God speaks to children,
also, in dreams . . . But in solitude, above all things, . . . God holds "communion undisturbed" with children' (ed. M. Elwin, 477), in which, as G. T.
Clapton has observed (*B. et De Quincey*, 93), B. must have discerned 'echoes'
of his own childhood.

readily be seen from subsequent chapters, is that the strain quickly dies out in Baudelaire, never again to recur save in purely reminiscent contexts.[1]

[1]Perhaps its last manifestation is in the sanctimonious verses *Hélas! qui n'a gémi* . . ., dedicated (in 1839–40?) to Henri Hignard; cf. p. 12 and n. 3, below.

Nature Beneficent:
A Religion of Nature?

AFTER 1838, Baudelaire appears to have written no further poems directly descriptive of natural landscapes. This does not mean, however, that he thenceforth turned his back on the external world; on the contrary there is evidence that he subscribed for some years, or especially during the period 1841–6, to something very like a 'cult' or 'religion' of Nature.[1] Certainly the *feeling* for Nature persists, even if the standpoint seems increasingly to become that of the literary-minded townsman. A curious (but no doubt authentic) anecdote retailed by Asselineau is perhaps significant in this respect: when living (from 1843 to 1845) in the Hôtel Pimodan, Baudelaire would explain that the panes of his main window were kept frosted 'afin de ne voir que le ciel'[2]—a preoccupation which is so to speak given its symbolic extension in the edifying verses *Hélas! qui n'a gémi . . .*, abandoned (rightly!) to Hignard during this same period.[3] I have mentioned in my previous chapter the letter of 1839 in which—within a context which speaks of the deeply personal tie that binds him to his mother—Baudelaire recalls, in passing, the

---

[1] As has previously been noted; see p. xii n. 1, above.

[2] *B. et Asselineau,* 67. Asselineau adds: 'Il était plus tard bien revenu de ces mélancolies éthérées, et aima plus que personne les maisons et les rues'; this would seem to imply, during the present period, a certain exaltation of Nature above Man (or his cities). For the authenticity of the anecdote, as also for the dates of B.'s stay at the Hôtel Pimodan, see C. Pichois, *B. à Paris,* 16–17.

[3] 'Alors lassé du monde et de ses vains discours, / Il faut lever les yeux aux voûtes sans nuages . . .' (ll. 5–6, *OP* I, 14; cf. ibid., 382). Hignard declares this poem to have been offered him by B. during a conversation they held at the Hôtel Pimodan, i.e. during the period 1843–5 (cf. previous n.); but he goes on to say: 'elle [cette pièce] date de l'époque où je l'ai vu se débattre entre le bien et le mal' (cit. *OP* I, 382), and this to me suggests rather, as the date of actual composition of the poem, the period 1839–40, when we know B. not only to have had at least one earnest moral discussion with Hignard, but also to have composed a sonnet, *Vous avez, compagnon, dont le cœur est poëte . . .*, of very similar inspiration to the present one—whereas by 1843–5 Hignard seems already to have given up his friend as 'lost'. Cf. *BDC* 52–3; *OP* I, 11–12 and 378–9; *EJC* 37.

emotions stirred in him by a beautiful sunset seen from a window; the particular affective resonance held for him by this image can perhaps best be understood from its recurrence, a few years later, in a poem which though composed originally in 1841-3, no doubt refers back to that delicious interim period (1827-8) in which, after his father's death and before the arrival on the scene of his step-father-to-be, the six-year-old boy had enjoyed his mother's exclusive favours.[1] The poem in question is the miniature 'idyll' *Je n'ai pas oublié, voisine de la ville,* with its brief initial description, in the 'intimate' style of Sainte-Beuve's *Joseph Delorme,* of the little house on the outskirts of Paris, followed in turn by a vivid characterization of the evening sun curiously 'eyeing' the silent diners from behind the glittering window-pane:

> Je n'ai pas oublié, voisine de la ville,
> Notre blanche maison, petite mais tranquille;
> Sa Pomone de plâtre et sa vieille Vénus
> Dans un bosquet chétif cachant leurs membres nus,
> Et le soleil, le soir, ruisselant et superbe,
> Qui, derrière la vitre où se brisait sa gerbe,
> Semblait, au fond du ciel,—en témoin curieux,
> Contempler nos dîners longs et silencieux,
> Et versait doucement ses grands reflets de cierge
> Sur la nappe frugale et les rideaux de serge.

(1857 proofs)

This hinted personification of the sun, becomes explicit in the second and third sections (perhaps originally conceived, in 1841, during Baudelaire's 'enforced' stay at Creil?[2]) of a strangely inconsequent poem, *Le Soleil,* which in its 'complete' form is no doubt of considerably later date:[3]

> Ce père nourricier, ennemi des chloroses,
> Anime dans les champs les vers comme les roses;
> Il fait s'évaporer les soucis vers le ciel,
> Et remplit les cerveaux et les ruches de miel.
> C'est lui qui rajeunit les porteurs de béquilles
> Et les rend gais et doux comme des jeunes filles,
> Et commande aux moissons de croître et de mûrir
> Dans le cœur immortel qui toujours veut fleurir!

---

[1] See *CG* III, 283 and n. 1 (L. Mme Aupick of 6/4/1861), and cf. the comment by F. Porché, *B.*, 18-20.

[2] Where he had spent his days 'sunning' himself, as we have seen, in the open fields; cf. p. 4 n. 3, above.

[3] Cf. pp. 106-8, below.

> Quand, ainsi qu'un poète, il descend dans les villes,
> Il ennoblit le sort des choses les plus viles,
> Et s'introduit en roi, sans bruit et sans valets,
> Dans tous les hôpitaux et dans tous les palais.
>
> (1857 proofs)

The sun here acts as a unifying, as well as a 'nutritive' and re-cuperative force: shining down impartially on all living things, it as it were reminds them of their common origin and continual renewal within Nature's 'immortal heart'.[1] This whole inspiriting message is conveyed, as I have indicated, in terms of personification—or rather of two personifications, appropriate successively to country-side, then town. First, we have the reinvigorating 'foster-father', vaguely god-like in his ministrations to the careworn and crippled, specifically god-like in combining, in his 'commands' to the harvests, the functions of Phoebus and of Pan. (These two deities figure by name, incidentally, but in dissociation, in another poem shortly to be discussed: *La Muse malade*.) Then, in its second guise, we see the sun descending 'poet-like' into the towns, exerting on all things its vaguely 'transfiguring' influence, and claiming, finally, its 'royal' right of entry into hospitals and palaces alike.[2]

For all the intermittent 'piety' of this 'hymn to the sun' (as, again, of the reference to Phoebus, 'le père des chansons', in *La Muse malade*), Baudelaire (perhaps for temperamental reasons) appears more truly responsive to the spell cast by the sister planet.[3] Cer-

---

[1] The sense, syntax and general context of this section alike make clear that the 'cœur immortel qui toujours veut fleurir' must refer to the perpetual rebirth of Nature.

[2] The analogy between sun and poet is purely incidental, be it noted, and does not extend to the two subsequent metaphors. But it is interesting to observe that the sun's gift of transfiguration is also, more specifically, claimed by B. for himself, in a verse fragment on which he was ultimately to draw for the concluding lines of his projected *Epilogue* to the 1861 edition of *FM* (cf. *FMCB* 216), but which dates originally, perhaps, from the present period: 'J'ai pétri de la boue et j'en ai fait de l'or' (*OP* I, 3, 370; for a later *reversal* of this same Midas-type symbol cf. (pp. 246-7, below) the sonnet *Alchimie de la douleur*). It should likewise be noted that in the novella *La Fanfarlo* (1843-6), B. characterizes his *alter ego* Samuel Cramer in terms that recall strongly the final couplet of *Le Soleil*: 'Samuel était hardi comme les papillons, les hannetons et les poètes; il se jetait dans toutes les flammes et *entrait par toutes les fenêtres*' (ed. Pichois, 74; my italics).

[3] Cf. in this respect (pp. 264 and n. 1, below) the two prose poems published many years later, in 1863: *Le Désir de peindre* and *Les Bienfaits de la lune*.

tainly the personifications of *Le Soleil* seem tired and prosaic, when set beside the persuasive 'characterizations' of the moon offered in two sonnets of this period, *Le Vin du solitaire* and *Tristesses de la lune*.[1] In the first of these the moon figures, by analogy with 'le regard singulier d'une femme galante', as the initial element in a cumulative hyperbole celebrating the superior virtues of wine:

> Le regard singulier d'une femme galante
> Qui se glisse vers nous comme le rayon blanc
> Que la lune onduleuse envoie au lac tremblant,
> Quand elle y veut tremper sa beauté nonchalante...
>
> ....
> Tout cela na vaut pas, ô bouteille profonde, etc.
>
> (1857 proofs)

Altogether more elaborate is the 'portrait' sketched in *Tristesses de la lune*:

> Ce soir, la lune rêve avec plus de paresse;
> Ainsi qu'une beauté, sur de nombreux coussins,
> Qui d'une main distraite et légère caresse,
> Avant de s'endormir, le contour de ses seins,
>
> Sur le dos satiné des molles avalanches,
> Mourante, elle se livre aux longues pâmoisons,
> Et promène ses yeux sur les visions blanches
> Qui montent dans l'azur comme des floraisons.
>
> Quand parfois sur ce globe, en sa langueur oisive,
> Elle laisse filer une larme furtive,
> Un poète pieux, ennemi du sommeil,
>
> Dans le creux de sa main prend cette larme pâle,
> Aux reflets irisés comme un fragment d'opale,
> Et la met dans son cœur loin des yeux du soleil.
>
> (1857 text)

For P. Moreau (*Symposium*, v, 1951, p. 99), the moon is one of B.'s 'mythes de prédilection'; for J. P. Sartre (*B.*, 135–6), it is emblematic both of his cult of the frigid, and of his 'Satanism'. I have been unable to consult the article by R. L. Rousseau, 'B. adorateur de la lune', *Synthèses* (Brussels), June-July and August 1964.

[1]For the linked chronology of these two poems, see *FMA* 406–7 and 356, and cf. *FMCB* 491. Cf. also the 'enchantment' lent by the moon to the land-scapes (or townscapes) of *Paysage* (l. 12), *Confession* (ll. 5–6, 37), *Le Jet d'eau* (ll. 11–12 etc., ll. 33–6).

The quatrains of this graceful if somewhat vapid sonnet hold a certain obscurity; one presumes, however, that the 'avalanches' on which the moon 'reclines' (or onto which she 'swoons'), the 'white visions' that swirl up around her, correspond to banks of cloud passing gently across her surface in the night sky.[1] But these vaguenesses of 'scenic' detail are of little real account; Baudelaire's purpose is not truly descriptive, and what matters is the idyllic and melodious characterization of the moon herself: less deity than odalisque, as languidly, voluptuously, she reclines upon her couch; shedding her furtive tear less in true sorrow, perhaps, than through the sheer oppression of her languor; oblivious of the earth over which she almost accidentally shines, and of the admirers (her poet among them) that she numbers there. Even the final reverent gesture that the poet accomplishes, seems more an act of amorous than of religious 'piety': he gathers the 'tear' to his heart, hides it away from the sun, as another man might hide a lock of hair, a miniature, a letter, from the eyes of the world—or of some jealous rival. Some lingering trace of mythological tradition persists, however, in Baudelaire's image of the moon: the pose he evokes by way of comparison, that of the languid beauty dreamily caressing her breasts, is one that in its narcissistic, 'sterile' voluptuousness, he seems more than once to have felt appropriate to the young virgin of authentic 'Diana' or moon-goddess type.[2]

[1] F. Scarfe translates l. 5: 'on the satined pillow of soft drifts of cloud' (ed., B., *Selected Verse,* 14). Cf. the judicious comment by L. J. Austin: 'Les "avalanches" traduisent le mouvement descendant de certains nuages, tandis que d'autres qui s'élèvent sont comme des visions de fleurs blanches qui monteraient lentement à travers le ciel bleu' (*L'Univers poétique de B.,* 204.) But cf. on the other hand, for the 'visions blanches', the *mist*-shapes invoked in *La Fanfarlo* (pub. Jan. 1847) to convey the quality of the eponymous dancer's art: 'Les brouillards mêlent des formes de fées et d'ondines moins vaporeuses et moins nonchalantes' (ed. Pichois, 83).

[2] Cf. *Lesbos,* ll. 16-19; *Bribes,* ll. 18-20 (*FMA* 215); *Tous imberbes . . .,* ll. 33-6 (*FMA* 228)—but cf. also, p. 30 n. 1, below, the rather different and more vital image of 'Diana huntress'. Champfleury, in a satirical novel published many years later, in 1859 (and to which I shall return), might well be thought to be referring to B.'s *Tristesses de la lune,* when enumerating the various types of pantheistic effusion common around 1846—a sly reminder, perhaps, that his friend B., so recently, in 1853-4, the denouncer of pantheism, had once subscribed to something very like this same 'cult': 'La lune, avec sa mine de mélancolique convalescente, reçut nombre de consolations affectueuses . . .' (*Amis de la nature,* 16; cf. pp. 118-19, below). For antecedent eighteenth-century personifications of the moon, see Paul van Tieghem, *Sentiment de la nature dans le préromantisme,* 127-9.

We have seen that in three at least of his earlier poems, Baudelaire was ready to take as his theme certain elemental aspects of Nature; one could scarcely, however, claim for him that he was ever (even during this period) a 'pastoral' poet in any true sense of the word—in the sense in which he himself applies it, for instance, in 1851, when writing of his friend Pierre Dupont in an essay later to be discussed. Yet in *Paysage [parisien]*—a poem which although published only in November 1857 (in a version later to be substantially revised, for the second edition of 1861 of *Les Fleurs du Mal*), may well, originally, have been composed as early as 1841 or 1843–1845[1]—Baudelaire quite explicitly declares his intention of writing a number, even a whole series, of gently idyllic 'eclogues'. The title given to the original version of the poem, '*Parisian* landscape', is in this respect somewhat misleading; it is in fact only in the brief opening section, and then only as a preliminary to the main purpose declared in the first line, that Baudelaire, from the vantage-point of his lofty garret, evokes the muted sights and sounds of the city: ·

> Je veux, pour composer chastement mes églogues,
> Coucher auprès du ciel, comme les astrologues,
> Et, voisin des clochers, écouter en rêvant
> Leurs chants mélodieux emportés par le vent.
> Les deux mains au menton, du haut de ma mansarde,
> Je verrai l'atelier qui chante et qui bavarde,
> Les tuyaux, les clochers, ces mâts de la cité,
> Les grands ciels bleus qui font rêver d'éternité!

> (1857 text, ll. 1–8)

The poet's primary intention, however, is less realistic than imaginative-pastoral; if he has thus retreated to his garret above the city, it is the better (or more 'chastely') to compose his *eclogues*—and these, of necessity, must find their subject-matter not in the urban reality he sees spread out before him, but in some pastoral

---

[1]Cf. J. Pommier, *Dans les chemins de B.*, 177 (analogy with *La servante au grand cœur . . .*, itself composed well before 1843; possible recollection, in l. 21, of the Paris insurrections of, e.g., 1839); P. Citron, *Poésie de Paris*, 11, 361 and n. 3 (l. 2: a reference perhaps, to B.'s lodging, 'sous les combles', at the Hôtel Pimodan, 1843–5? Cf. the description of this lodging by C. Pichois, *B. à Paris*, 16–18). For a (corollary) refutation of the assumption (made by J. Prévost, *B.*, 170–1) that the poem was directly inspired by Meryon's engravings of Paris, see *FMPP* 477–8, and cf. my review of Prévost's book, *MLR*, 1955, p. 86, as also *FMA* 375. For a discussion of the title(s) of the poem, and of its later (1861) version, see pp. 162–5, below.

dream conjured out of the world of his imagination or memory. The remaining and much longer section of the poem thus looks forward to the time when having watched from his window the unfolding and enchanted sequence of the first three seasons of the year, he at last closes his doors and shutters on the snowbound city, and turns away into himself to build, the winter through, his 'enchanted palaces'—to dream his childlike (and stylized) Idyll of blue horizons, gardens, weeping fountains, birdsong, kisses . . .—to fashion from all this, at his solitary desk, the 'fragrantly' bucolic verses he promises anew in his closing line:

C'est plaisir, à travers les brumes, de voir naître
L'étoile dans l'azur, la lampe à la fenêtre,
Les fleuves de charbon monter au firmament
Et, la lune verser son pâle enchantement.
Je verrai les printemps, les étés, les automnes,
Et, quand viendra l'hiver aux neiges monotones,
Je fermerai partout portières et volets
Pour bâtir dans la nuit mes féeriques palais.
Alors je rêverai des horizons bleuâtres,
Des jardins, des jets d'eau pleurant dans les albâtres,
Des baisers, des oiseaux chantant soir et matin,
Et tout ce que l'Idylle a de plus enfantin.
Et l'émeute aura beau tempêter à ma vitre,
Je ne lèverai pas le front de mon pupitre,
Et ne bougerai plus de l'antique fauteuil,
Où je veux composer pour un jeune cercueil
(Il faut charmer nos morts dans leurs noires retraites)
De doux vers tout fumants comme des cassolettes.

(1857 text, ll. 9–26)

It is interesting to speculate on the further experiments within the pastoral genre that Baudelaire might have given us, had he been able to fulfil the poetic 'programme' here set out—or had he not been precluded from doing so, perhaps, by the further development of his ideas on Nature and Art. As it is, the middle lines of the present poem, together with the final section of *J'aime le souvenir de ces époques nues* and the last two verses of *Moesta et errabunda*, must suffice as fragmentary and tantalising specimens of these 'eclogues' that Baudelaire (to our knowledge) never fully composed[1]—however

[1] To call *Rêve parisien* an 'eclogue' (A. Feuillerat, 'Architecture des *FM*', 310) seems to me plainly an abuse of this term. For the two poems aforementioned, cf. pp. 57–60, below.

austerely determined may have been his immediate resolve (conveyed from the outset in that emphatic 'Je veux' which recurs again at the poem's *envoi*[1]) to forswear, as he securely barricades himself against the Parisian winter, the external world whether of politics or of love: 'Je veux, pour composer *chastement* mes églogues'; '. . . *l'émeute* aura beau tempêter à ma vitre . . .'[2]

The four poems so far examined in this chapter, imply a view of Nature as essentially benevolent or at least benign. A similar attitude is vouchsafed, but more explicitly, in certain other texts deriving from our present period. Thus the sonnet *La Mort des artistes,* first published in 1851 but no doubt composed some years earlier, tells in its opening quatrain of the calm haven to which 'kindly Nature' may welcome the creative artist, after his long and arduous pilgrimage:

> Il faut marcher longtemps et par monts et par vaux,
> Broyer bien des cailloux et crever sa monture,
> Pour trouver un asile où la bonne nature
> Invite enfin le cœur à trouver du repos.

(1851 text)

By 'la bonne nature' Baudelaire appears to mean some vaguely beneficent force akin to the traditional 'Mother Nature', and whose bounty likewise extends to all her creatures.[3] This perennial concept, which had been extensively renewed by such contemporary poets as

---

[1]For the aesthetic implications of this phrase, viewed in relation to the 1861 version of the poem, which stresses the notion of 'will' in a more strictly imaginative context ('Car je serai plongé dans cette volupté / D'évoquer le Printemps avec ma *volonté*'—my italics), cf. J. Prévost, *B.*, 200–1 (part of a chap. entitled 'Le "Fiat" poétique'), as also R. B. Chérix, *Commentaire des 'FM'*, 314–15.

[2]Cf., however, the poem *Tout entière,* which in its rather different context would seem to give the lie to the notion that in 'dwelling high' one gains any security from amorous temptation! . . . : 'Le Démon, dans ma *chambre haute,* / Ce matin est venu me voir . . .' (ll. 1–2, first pub. 1857).

[3]In the ensuing quatrain, this hard-won repose is linked with the artist's attainment of a specific ideal, his moulding of an 'idéale figure'; the tercets (to which alone the title strictly applies) recall those other and more tormented artists whose sole hope is that *death* somehow may bring their dreams to fruition. In the subsequent (1857) version of this sonnet, the quatrains are entirely remodelled, and the too naive reference to 'la bonne nature' duly excised.

Hugo and Laprade,[1] informs three further poems by Baudelaire himself: *J'aime le souvenir de ces époques nues, La Caravane des Bohémiens, La Géante*, and it is notable that in the first of these, the instinctual happiness of primitive Man is represented as the direct fruit of the Earth-Mother's overflowing 'tenderness'.[2] More significantly, perhaps, Baudelaire appears to regard Nature (in the wider sense) as being in herself the source of all *morality*, to the extent that Nature and morality become (as he says) one and the same;[3] the further implications of this notion may be traced in a whole series of roughly contemporary texts. Thus in the *Conseils aux jeunes littérateurs* of April 1846, we find Baudelaire saluting comradeship as being one (among many, presumably) of the 'holy manifestations of Nature'.[4] At a more frivolous level, the exactly contemporary *Choix de maximes consolantes sur l'amour* postulates a whole science of natural amorous affinities ('Nature, in food as in love, rarely gives us a taste for what is bad for us'), and by implication equates 'victory over rigorous Nature' (e.g. that gained by the impious 'husband' who turns to amorous account his 'wife's' devoutness) with 'blasphemy against the Gods'.[5] Towards the end of this same article the argument from Nature takes a more sophisticated turn, as Baudelaire ingeniously prescribes his 'simple' remedy

[1]For Hugo, cf. that embarrassing idyll *La Vache* (*Les Voix intérieures*, xv), which ends on this rousing note: 'Ainsi, Nature! abri de toute créature! / O mère universelle! indulgente Nature! / Ainsi, tous à la fois, mystiques et charnels, / Cherchant l'ombre et le lait sous tes flancs éternels, / Nous sommes là, savants, poètes, pêle-mêle, / Pendus de toutes parts à ta forte mamelle!' etc. For Laprade, cf. in the *Odes et poëmes* of 1843, *Invocation sur la montagne, Alma parens, A la terre, La Mort d'un chêne*, etc. Among other contemporary examples may be cited Lacaussade's *A la Nature* and *A Jules de Saint-Félix* (*Poèmes et paysages*, 1852); as for earlier instances, these—ranging from Montaigne ('notre grande et puissante mère nature') and Ronsard, to Rousseau, Herder, Goethe and Schiller—may be abundantly culled, e.g., from R. Pomeau, *Revue de l'enseignement supérieur*, 1959, pp. 108 and 110, as from the two books on the theme *Le Sentiment de la nature* by G. Charlier (p. 31) and Paul van Tieghem (p. 238), respectively.

[2]See, for a further discussion of these three poems, pp. 49–55, below.

[3]'La nature n'a d'autre morale que le fait, parce qu'elle est la morale elle-même . . .' (*Salon de 1846, CE* 177). The context of this passage is a summary dismissal of the whole 'historical landscape' genre; see p. 75, below.

[4]Ch. III, 'Des Sympathies et des antipathies', *AR* 271.

[5]*OP* II, 4–5, 8. Cf., however, ibid., 4, the opening apostrophe addressed to those lovers to whom Nature (in the form of their own innate lethargy?) is 'unkind': 'Vous pour qui la nature est cruelle et le temps précieux'.

for all those who (betrayed by their natural affinities!) find themselves saddled with a wholly ignoble mistress: resolve boldly to *idealize* the very depravity that torments you, and reflect that 'great Nature' alone can know and determine what role truly belongs to so masterfully brazen a trollop.[1]

Significantly, Baudelaire here as in several other texts uses the phrase 'la grande Nature'. This perennial formula, with its tritely eulogistic epithet, is admittedly one that was much favoured within Baudelaire's circle during this period;[2] in thus adopting it, however, he must clearly have accepted its general implications, while at the same time conferring (as in the *Maxims on Love*) a decidedly personal imprint of his own. Thus when echoing, in a quatrain of *Une Charogne*, the perennial theme of the endless cycle of creation, he imparts through his context a ferocious irony that is utterly remote from such more conventional versions of the theme as his friend Banville's *Dans le vieux cimetière*, with its exalted transmutation of a macabre reality only fleetingly touched upon.[3] In *Une Charogne*,

[1]'. . . d'une si puissante coquine la grande Nature seule sait ce qu'elle veut faire' (*OP* II, 9). I would dismiss altogether the further reference to (human) Nature, contained within a scurrilous compilation to which B. is known to have contributed, the *Mystères galans des théâtres de Paris* (*MGC*, 33; cf. ibid., 144-6) —firstly, because it is by no means certain that the passage in question (a dialogue between a worldly gentleman, and a schoolboy admirer of the actress Mlle Plessy, here dubbed 'Célimène') was actually penned by B.; secondly because its ironies at the expense of the proposition 'Beauty is Goodness, Nature cannot lie' (answer, quick as lightning: 'Ah, but *Célimène's* nature lies') are so facile and jejune as to lack all significance whatever in our present context.

[2]Cf., e.g., Esquiros, with his 'religion de la grande Nature' (*Les Chants d'un prisonnier*, 1841, cit. J. P. van der Linden, *Alph. Esquiros*, 175); Banville, in his poem *Dans le vieux cimetière* (dated May 1845, pub. *Les Stalactites*, 1846), sagely acclaiming 'la grande Nature,/Si pleine de raison'; Delacroix lauding, in his *Journal* (cit. *FMA* 312), 'la grande et sublime nature'; Prarond, in a poem of rather later date, saluting the 'ineffable bonté de la grande Nature' (*Les Impressions et Pensées d'Albert*, 1854: *Prologue*, II); and so on. All this no doubt goes back at least to Shaftesbury's famous and influential 'hymn to Nature'; cf. B. Willey, *Eighteenth-Century Background*, 61-5, as also Paul van Tieghem, *Sentiment de la nature dans le préromantisme*, 249-51.

[3]Banville's poem (which likewise speaks of 'la grande Nature', and likewise confronts the poet's companion—if more discreetly!—with the reminder of death in life) may perhaps have been conceived as a 'reply' to B.'s: it is dated May 1845 (pub. 1846, in *Les Stalactites*), and by that time Banville must more than once have heard *Une Charogne*, which B. had begun to recite to his friends around 1843 (see Prarond, *CML* II, 1154). For the analogies and contrasts between the two poems, cf. also E. Souffrin, ed. *Stalactites*, 361-2, 365. Among the

on the other hand, it is this same, yet now brutally dissonant reality—the radiant summer morning disclosing, under its hot sun, the carrion 'roasting to a turn'—that serves to attest the sovereign 'greatness' of Nature:

> Rappelez-vous l'objet que nous vîmes, mon âme,
>   Ce beau matin d'été si doux:
> Au détour d'un sentier une charogne infâme
>   Sur un lit semé de cailloux . . .
> . . . .
> Le soleil rayonnait sur cette pourriture,
>   Comme afin de la cuire à point,
> Et de *rendre au centuple à la grande Nature*
>   *Tout ce qu'ensemble elle avait joint.*
>
> (1857 text, ll. 1-4, 9-12; my italics)

More truly audacious, however, is the concept implied in the *Maxims on Love*, as also in two further, verse texts—that of some vast cosmic design in which evil no less than good has its allotted place, and depravity is seen as necessary and even providential within the scheme of Nature.[1] In the first of the two poems mentioned, *Tu mettrais l'univers entier dans ta ruelle*, the situation is precisely that envisaged (or recollected) in the *Maximes*—with this difference, that while Baudelaire may likewise accord to *this* 'femme impure' a salutary cosmic role of some kind, his admiration (in both senses of the word) is no longer tolerant but stridently censorious:

---

many antecedent versions of this theme, one might cite the final section, beginning: 'Que ta puissance (ô Mort) est grande et admirable!', of Ronsard's *Hymne de la Mort*; cf. also Paul van Tieghem, *Sentiment de la nature dans le préromantisme*, 252.

[1] The decisive influence here would seem to be that of Sade; cf. L. G. Crocker, *Nature and Culture*, 401, and for Sade's general (and persisting) influence on B., G. Blin, *Le Sadisme de B.*, pp. 13–72. It must be stressed that Nature is nowhere *denounced*, in these texts of B.'s, for the evil she fosters; there is thus no reason to suppose that he has, *as yet*, diverged on this point from Sade, and the comment by M. Blin: 'le sadisme du marquis de Sade tend à servir et magnifier la nature, celui de Baudelaire vise, au contraire, à la corriger et à l'étouffer' (ibid., 61), properly applies only to a much *later* phase of B.'s thought. See in this whole connection Part Two, Chapter V, below ('The Repudiation of Nature'). For the general 18th-century notion of 'cosmic harmony', see Paul van Tieghem, op. cit., 253.

Tu mettrais l'univers entier dans ta ruelle,
Femme impure! L'ennui rend ton âme cruelle.
Pour exercer tes dents à ce jeu singulier,
Il te faut chaque jour un cœur au râtelier.
Tes yeux illuminés ainsi que des boutiques
Et des ifs flamboyants dans les fêtes publiques
Usent insolemment d'un pouvoir emprunté,
Sans connaître jamais la loi de leur beauté.

Machine aveugle et sourde en cruautés féconde!
Salutaire instrument buveur du sang du monde,
Comment n'as-tu pas honte, et comment n'as-tu pas
Devant tous les miroirs vu pâlir tes appas?
La grandeur de ce mal où tu te crois savante
Ne t'a donc jamais fait reculer d'épouvante,
Quand la nature, grande en ses desseins cachés,
De toi se sert, ô femme, ô reine des péchés,
—De toi, vil animal,—pour pétrir un génie?

O fangeuse grandeur, sublime ignominie!   (1857 text)

It will be observed that (at least in this 1857 version) Nature's 'secret designs' are linked, subjectively, with the creative experience of the poet ('De toi se sert . . . pour pétrir un génie');[1] in *Allégorie*, on the other hand, we have the purely objective portrait of a woman wholly (and professionally) dedicated to the cult of pleasure:

Elle a dans le plaisir la foi mahométane,
Et dans ses bras ouverts, que remplissent ses seins,
Elle appelle des yeux la race des humains.
Ne croira-t-elle pas ⎫
Elle sent, elle croit, ⎬ cette vierge inféconde
Et pourtant nécessaire à la marche du monde,
Que la beauté du corps est un sublime don
Qui de toute infamie arrache le pardon.

(ll. 10–16; 1857 proofs)

---

[1]There is an interesting analogy here with a sentence which occurs in the opening chapter of Holbach's *Système de la Nature*: '. . . l'ART n'est que la Nature agissante à l'aide des instruments qu'elle a faits' (1770 ed., I, 3; cit. B. Willey, op. cit., 156). Admittedly Holbach is here taking 'Art' in the widest sense to include all that is a modification of Nature, i.e. the whole civilization of Man; but in B.'s poem is it not artifice, precisely (the woman's enhancement, through a 'pouvoir emprunté', of the beauty of her eyes), which is among the wiles whereby she ensnares (and 'moulds') the hapless 'genius'? For the very different role that B. was ultimately to assign to Art and artifice in relation to Nature, see pp. 139–45, below; for a further possible echo, during the present period, of 18th-century philosophies of Nature, p. 76 n. 2, below.

In what sense exactly the woman is deemed 'necessary' to the functioning of the world, Baudelaire does not make clear: perhaps because although she may choose to abdicate her maternal role as propagator of the species, she none the less plays her part in the universal scheme by ensuring the gratification of certain imperious and *promiscuous* sexual needs.

For a fully explicit revelation of Baudelaire's youthful cult of Nature, we must turn, however, to the scathing review, published in February 1846, of the elaborate 'philosophical' poem *Prométhée délivré* by his friend Louis Ménard. (The friendship, needless to say, did not long survive the review.) Baudelaire takes Ménard to task for having (among other things) 'eluded' what he calls 'le culte de la Nature, cette grande religion de Diderot et d'Holbach, cet unique ornement de l'athéisme'. By this he means that Ménard's atheism (which would have been entirely acceptable, had it been 'gai, aimable, séduisant et nourrissant' in the authentic pagan tradition[1]) is of the wrong kind: instead of offering this drab cult of Science, he would have done far better to have developed the *pantheistic* and *naturalistic* side of his theme, thus fulfilling the expectations aroused earlier in the poem by certain 'noble and great verses' (no doubt within the section hymning the 'mysteries and secrets of Nature').[2]

[1] Cf. the phrase used in Jan. 1846 to describe an imagined painting by Ingres: 'robuste et nourrissant comme l'amour antique' (*Le Musée classique du Bazar Bonne-Nouvelle*, CE 213).

[2] *OP* I, 238–41. For a full appreciation (more accurate and charitable than B.'s!) of Ménard's poem, cf. H. J. Hunt, *The Epic in Nineteenth-Century France*, 259–64, and H. Peyre, *Louis Ménard*, 38–46; for the relations between the two poets during this period, see ibid., 23–9, 46–8, and *OP* I, 561–2. In the foregoing account of B.'s vaguely adumbrated 'Religion of Nature' I have, for reasons to be explained in a later chapter, left entirely out of account the sonnet *Correspondances*—despite the fact that this may well have been originally composed around 1845, and that its opening phrase: 'La Nature est un temple . . .' might well seem of particular significance in the present context. Cf. pp. 196–7, below.

III

The Nostalgic Primitivist:

A Pagan 'Elsewhere'

THE admiration Baudelaire implies, in his article on Ménard, for eighteenth-century 'religions of Nature', while it may not necessarily be founded on a close first-hand knowledge of these philosophies,[1] is none the less a good deal more central to his whole thought during this period than is generally supposed; certainly it is from the current of ideas set in motion by Diderot, Rousseau and others, that are derived the wider perspectives, historical and geographical, that his Nature-cult equally demands. The essential concept here is of a Nature wild, free, vigorous, untamed, and of a Natural Man endowed, by harmonious assimilation, with the same qualities. Such an ideal—being by definition the antithesis of modern European civilization, with its constraints, artificialities and corruptions— could only, if it existed at all, be located in primitive communities, or in a remote Golden Age.[2]

Both these migrations—in time as well as in space—are carried through in Baudelaire's writings during this period. Here we must

[1]The formula he uses is in fact prefigured almost textually in a passage of Sainte-Beuve's *Joseph Delorme* (1829), which speaks, in the context of the eponymous hero's moral evolution, of 'cette adoration sombre et mystique de la nature qui, chez Diderot et d'Holbach, ressemble presque à une religion' (ed. Antoine, 6). For the role played by this work in B.'s general literary development, see ibid., cviii-cxx; for a general conspectus of eighteenth-century 'religions of Nature', see B. Willey, *The Eighteenth Century Background*, passim. The phrase 'the religion of Nature' recurs, incidentally, with the same admirative implication, in an art. pub. Jan. 1848, *Les Contes de Champfleury*; cf. p. 86, below.

[2]This cult of the primitive goes back, of course, far beyond the eighteenth century; cf., in this connection, A. O. Lovejoy and G. Boas, *Primitivism and Related Ideas in Antiquity*, and for the more recent history of the subject, G. Chinard, *L'Exotisme américain dans la littérature française au XVIe siècle* and *L'Amérique et le rêve exotique dans la littérature française au XVIIe et au XVIIIe siècle*; G. Atkinson, *Les Relations de Voyages du XVIIe siècle* (chap. IV: 'Le bon sauvage'); H. N. Fairchild, *The Noble Savage. A Study in Romantic Naturalism*. For the strictly relative nature of both Rousseau's and Diderot's primitivism, cf., respectively: A. O. Lovejoy, 'The Supposed Primitivism of Rousseau's *Discourse on Inequality*', *Essays in the History of Ideas*, 14-37; P. Hermand, *Les Idées morales de Diderot*, 117-19.

take into account not only the example and influence of his contemporaries, but also a local and personal factor of the greatest
importance. In early June 1841, as a remedial or disciplinary
measure, he had been despatched by his step-father, General
Aupick, on a long sea voyage aboard a schooner (the *Paquebot-des-
mers-du-sud*) bound for India; having got as far as Mauritius and
Réunion, however, Baudelaire (whose mood had remained one of
unbending truculence) had insisted on transferring to a homeward-
bound vessel, the *Alcide*, and had thus found himself back in
Bordeaux in mid-February 1842.[1] Yet this voyage, although fiercely
resented at the time, proved in retrospect (as Baudelaire himself
must sometimes have conceded) one of the few unquestionable
services rendered him by his step-father; certainly he made copious
indirect acknowledgement of his gratitude, in the frequency with
which in imagination he retraced the journey.[2] The fullest testimony
to the profound and endless *nourishment* brought by the voyage to
Baudelaire's mind and art, is perhaps that furnished in an article of
1855, on the Paris Universal Exhibition of that year. He is here
arguing the relativity, the protean diversity, of Beauty, and there
can be no doubt that the experiences he here imputes to his intelligent and worldly 'traveller', must have been closely modelled on
those of the young Baudelaire of 1841-2:

Si, au lieu d'un pédagogue, je prends un homme du monde, un intelligent,
et si je le transporte dans une contrée lointaine, je suis sûr que, si les
étonnements du débarquement sont grands, si l'accoutumance est plus
ou moins longue, plus ou moins laborieuse, la sympathie sera tôt ou
tard si vive, si pénétrante, qu'elle créera en lui un monde nouveau d'idées,
monde qui fera partie intégrante de lui-même, et qui l'accompagnera,
sous la forme de souvenirs, jusqu'à la mort. Ces formes de bâtiments,
qui contrariaient d'abord son œil académique (tout peuple est académique
en jugeant les autres, tout peuple est barbare quand il est jugé), ces
végétaux inquiétants pour sa mémoire chargée des souvenirs natals, ces
femmes et ces hommes dont les muscles ne vibrent pas suivant l'allure
classique de son pays, dont la démarche n'est pas cadencée selon le

---

[1] See *LS* 207-12; *CML* II, 1167-9 (letter from Captain Saliz to Aupick); *EJC*
255-6 (letter from Mme Aupick to Asselineau); C. D. Hérisson, *MF*, Oct. 1956,
pp. 288-94, and March 1960, pp. 449-63; C. Pichois, *RHLF*, 1957, pp. 568-70.
[2] As far as the *reality* was concerned, however, such a return journey seems to
have been envisaged (in Dec. 1847) only as a last desperate expedient whereby to
'expiate' his financial improvidence . . . See *CG* I, 93-4.

rythme accoutumé, dont le regard n'est pas projeté avec le même magnétisme, ces odeurs qui ne sont plus celles du boudoir maternel, ces fleurs mystérieuses dont la couleur profonde entre dans l'œil despotique-ment, pendant que leur forme taquine le regard, ces fruits dont le goût trompe et déplace les sens, et révèle au palais des idées qui appartiennent à l'odorat, tout ce monde d'harmonies nouvelles entrera lentement en lui, le pénétrera patiemment, comme la vapeur d'une étuve aromatisée; toute cette vitalité inconnue sera ajoutée à sa vitalité propre; quelques milliers d'idées et de sensations enrichiront son dictionnaire de mortel, et même il est possible que, dépassant la mesure et transformant la justice en révolte, il fasse comme le Sicambre converti, qu'il brûle ce qu'il avait adoré, et qu'il adore ce qu'il avait brûlé.[1]

This slow infiltration of exotic images, this gradual enrichment of sensibility, is of course something that can be confirmed from a dozen or more of Baudelaire's poems, to say nothing of all the other writings in which we encounter echoes, direct or indirect, of his voyage;[2] what is here, for the poet, a vast storehouse of themes and images on which he may endlessly draw, there becomes, for the critic, a constant yardstick of aesthetic measurement. Thus by an accident of circumstance, Baudelaire was drawn into the great wave of exoticism and orientalism that swept through France, as through other European countries, in the wake of Romanticism. Yet Baudelaire's gain from his voyage was not merely imaginative and literary, but philosophical as well; through it, he acquired a com-mitment to primitivism which to some extent remained with him to the end of his life, surviving even his most vehement subsequent denunciations of the Nature-cult in general.[3] Nor can this commit-ment be explained away simply in terms of literary influence, of intermediaries or 'intercessors' such as Bernardin de Saint-Pierre;

[1] *CE* 221-2; cf. ibid., 483.

[2] Cf. Gautier, Preface to *FM* 1868, xiii; *FMC* xix-xx; Prévost, *B.*, 27-31.

[3] One might almost, remembering the analogy with Clovis the Sicambrian in the passage quoted above, speak of a *conversion* to primitivism. For an example of the persistence with which B. clings to this doctrine, and of the contradictions which thereby ensue, cf. (pp. 154-5, below) the famous 'Éloge du maquillage' (from *Le Peintre de la vie moderne,* 1859-60). B. himself, however (it must be added), might be thought to have issued his own warning against any too-sweep-ing exaggeration of the influence on him of his voyage, when thus dismissing (with an ironic adaptation of Molière) Villemain's judgment on Chateaubriand: 'Et voilà ce qui explique pourquoi votre fille est muette, c'est-à-dire pourquoi, si Chateaubriand n'était pas allé en Amérique, il n'eût pas été Chateaubriand' (*Villemain, OP* 1, 327; comp. 1862) . . .

surely if, on his return from his voyage, the vision of a way of life at once primitive and idyllic so strongly imposed itself on Baudelaire's imagination as to blot out all other more sombre recollections, it must be because such a vision drew out, and at the same time fulfilled, a deep atavistic longing.[1] (The Rousseau-esque cult of the primitive owes its enduring and obstinate success—so baffling to those rationalists who dispute, quite legitimately, its authentic basis in reality—precisely to the fact that this same longing or nostalgia is incurably widespread throughout the civilized world, and must therefore have profound roots within the human psyche.) Perhaps if Baudelaire's stay in Mauritius or Réunion had been less brief—or, better, if like his fellow-poets Leconte de Lisle and Lacaussade he had spent all or a part of his childhood there—perhaps then he might have retained the same vivid store of images but without falling victim to the primitivist myth; as it is, his brief experience of the tropics was sufficient both to crystallize certain vague hankerings of the heart, and to confirm and 'document' what he would already have gleaned from his eighteenth-century readings[2]—namely that Natural Man still survived and flourished, for the admiration and edification of civilized man, in certain more primitive present-day societies.[3]

Three verse texts dating specifically from this period, offer glimpses of what Baudelaire was later to remember as the 'beauty and magic' of the tropics, with their 'mysterious graces' unexampled in any other clime.[4] All three poems appeared in *L'Artiste* during 1845–

[1] I am here arguing against J. Prévost (*B.*, 29–30).

[2] Such readings would in this instance be of *travellers* as much as (or more than) of philosophers; cf. the letter to Poulet-Malassis, of 28 March 1857, in which B. draws up a comprehensive list of eighteenth-century texts, based on what he calls 'les souvenirs de mes lectures, du temps [i.e. our present period?] que je lisais le 18e siècle', and particularly stresses the importance of travel-writings: 'VOYAGEURS (*très importants*)' (*CG* II, 35–6), as also the reference in his *Salon de 1846*, *CE* 183, to 'le charme des lectures de voyages'. For other related texts, cf. pp. 3 n. 1, 300 n. 2, below; for the part played by eighteenth-century travel-writings in the general development of the primitivist cult, see G. Chinard, *L'Amérique et le rêve exotique*, passim.

[3] Cf. for this notion (crystallized, as it were, in the Jesuit father Lafitau's title *Mœurs des Sauvages américains comparées aux Mœurs des premiers temps*), G. Chinard, *L'Amérique et le rêve exotique*, 431 and passim; for B.'s own affirmation of the presumed continuity, p. 49, below.

[4] *AR* 375–6; the context is a eulogy of Leconte de Lisle's poem *Le Manchy*. Cf., during the present period, in the *Salon de 1846*, the description of a seascape by Jules Noël: '. . . un grand port, où circule et nage toute la lumière de l'Orient' (*CE* 185).

6: the first, a sonnet, in January 1845, under the title *A Ivonne Pen-Moore* and the signature of Baudelaire's friend, Privat d'Anglemont;[1] the second, another sonnet, *A une Créole,* in May of that year but under the poet's own name ('Baudelaire Dufays'); the third and most elaborate, *A une Indienne* (which I must reserve for discussion later in this chapter), in December 1846 and under the variant *nom de plume* 'Pierre de Fayis'. *A une Créole* (probably the first-composed of the three) was addressed originally, in October 1841, to a distinguished Mauritian lady, Mme Autard de Bragard, at whose home Baudelaire had been received a month or so earlier.[2] It opens with a 'portrait' which combines a glimpse of the far-off land itself—its warmth, idleness and strange, sweet-scented vegetation each perfectly setting off the lady's faintly exotic beauty:[3]

> Au pays parfumé que le soleil caresse,
> J'ai vu dans un retrait de tamarins ambrés
> Et de palmiers d'où pleut sur les yeux la paresse,
> Une dame créole aux charmes ignorés.
>
> Son teint est pâle et chaud; la brune enchanteresse
> A dans le cou des airs noblement maniérés;
> Grande et svelte en marchant comme une chasseresse,
> Son sourire est tranquille et ses yeux assurés.
>
> (MS. 1841, *CG* i, 16)

The tercets of this respectfully gallant sonnet, as it were remedy in the poet's imagination the 'neglect' of which he had spoken in the fourth line: if the 'unknown' Creole lady were to visit France—the land of poets, the true 'pays de gloire'—her charms would inspire not one sonnet merely (the present one) but a thousand . . .

It will be seen that, in the interests of hyperbole, France (or a highly stylized 'vieille France', with feudal domains set among green rivers and besieged by eager poets[4]) is 'recommended' by the poet even above the 'pays parfumé' of the first quatrain. A quite contrary 'lesson' emerges from the companion sonnet, *A Ivonne Pen-Moore*:

[1] For the attribution to B., see *OP* i, 419–20, 414 and n. 1.

[2] With studied propriety, B. had in the first instance addressed his (then untitled) verses to the lady's *husband*; see *CG* i, 15, and cf. *FMCB* 405–6 (Daruty de Grandpré cit.). Ultimate title (1857 onwards): 'A une *dame* créole'.

[3] A contemporary portrait in oils, shown at the Baudelaire Exhibition of 1957 (BNE, p. 18, item 47; reprod. *FMA*, and *FMPP* facing p. 189), reveals her to have been unquestionably a most dazzling charmer.

[4] A very similar background appears in another poem of the same period, *A une mendiante rousse*.

Te souvient-il, enfant, des jours de ta jeunesse,
Et des grandes forêts où tu courais pieds nus,
Rêveuse et vagabonde, oubliant ta détresse
Et laissant le zéphir [sic] baiser tes bras charnus?

Tes cheveux crespelés, ta peau de mulâtresse
Rendaient plus attrayants tes charmes ingénus:
Telle avant ses amours Diane chasseresse
Courait dans la bruyère et sur les monts chenus.

Il ne reste plus rien de ta beauté sauvage;
Le flot ne mordra plus tes pieds sur le rivage,
Et l'herbe a recouvert l'empreinte de tes pas.

Paris t'a faite riche entre les plus hautaines.
Tes frères les chasseurs ne reconnaîtraient pas
Leur sœur qui, dans ses mains, buvait l'eau des fontaines.

(*L'Artiste*, 1845)

The situation imagined in the tercets of *A une Créole* has here in
fact come about (with this difference, of course, that the lady is
coloured—a mulatto—and moves in a rather different social milieu
from that envisaged for Mme Autard de Bragard); the poet's attitude, however, is now one of poised, somewhat stilted *regret*—regret
at the completeness with which the acquisitive and artificial stan-
dards of 'civilized' society have transformed the 'child of Nature',
running free among her native forests and shores like Diana the
huntress before she had known love,[1] into a creature wealthy among
the haughtiest, whose former wild beauty has become changed (and
corrupted?) to a pattern that her brother hunters would no longer
recognize.

In this sonnet the exotic background is no more than faintly, even
perfunctorily, sketched in (the vast forests, the 'kiss' of the breeze,
the lapping tide, the mountain or woodland springs); altogether
more explicit are the two texts—unfortunately available only in considerably later versions— which most memorably enshrine Baude-

[1]The Creole lady, it will be recalled, was also compared to a huntress; this
image, as we may see again from the later poem *Sisina* (pub. 1859; ll. 1–4), seems
frequently to be called up in B.'s mind, when he seeks to characterize qualities of
ingenuous yet graceful vitality that are admired from an essentially primitivist
standpoint. For the moon-goddess 'après les amours', cf. (pp. 62–8, below)
the sonnet *La Lune offensée*.

laire's 'exotic dream'. These texts are the linked love poems *Parfum exotique* and *La Chevelure*[1]—if 'love poem' is the right term for a genre that so curiously blends amorous homage with a nostalgia which strictly has nothing whatever to do with love. The woman to whom both poems are dedicated—no doubt Jeanne Duval, herself an exotic by virtue of her dark pigmentation—in truth serves no more than to set the poet's imagination astir, as with closed eyes, 'guided' by her perfume, he sails out over the 'dark ocean' of her hair.

In *Parfum exotique*, the claims of nostalgia are so despotic that within two lines the poet's whole mind is absorbed in the vision of sun-drenched shores; at the tercets, it is true, Jeanne's presence is fleetingly recalled, but only to yield anew to a still more haunting evocation:

> Quand, les deux yeux fermés, en un soir chaud d'automne,
> Je respire l'odeur de ton sein chaleureux,
> Je vois se dérouler des rivages heureux
> Qu'éblouissent les feux d'un soleil monotone:
>
> Une île paresseuse où la nature donne
> Des arbres singuliers et des fruits savoureux;
> Des hommes dont le corps est mince et vigoureux,
> Et des femmes dont l'œil par sa franchise étonne.

---

[1] *Parfum exotique* was first published in *FM* 1857, *La Chevelure* in 1859 ; the two poems figure together, however, on Prarond's 'second list' of the poems he recalled (though not with absolute certainty) as having heard recited by B. in 1846 if not before; see *CML* II, 1155, and for the whole question of the (attested) reliability of Prarond's testimony, my art. cit., 'Pour une étude chronologique des *FM*', pp. 344–5. I would presume that B.'s reason for not including *both* poems in *FM* 1857, was that he wished at that time to avoid offering two versions of the same theme, and therefore chose the one which seemed the more 'finished', etc.—thereby leaving himself free, incidentally, to publish in Aug. 1857 a (newly composed?) prose poem drawing upon the same material, and initially given this same title *La Chevelure*, before becoming, ultimately, *Un Hémisphère dans une chevelure*. (Where B.'s 'doublet' versions are concerned, the verse text seems normally to have preceded that in prose; cf., on this general question, G. Blin, *Sadisme de B.*, 161 and n. 3, and C. Pichois, ed. *Fanfarlo*, 105.) By 1859, however, the urgent need had arisen for further poems to replace, in the forthcoming 2nd edition of *FM*, those 'condemned' in 1857; B. would thus no longer have scrupled to press into service *La Chevelure* in its verse text. I would add, as further confirmation of the early composition of both *Parfum exotique* and *La Chevelure*, the fact that both are clearly written for a woman in her prime of beauty, and that both clearly arise from a relationship that is still in its heyday; if (as is by common consent agreed) this woman is Jeanne, the corresponding dates would be precisely those indicated by Prarond: 1842–6. Cf., in this connection, the tentative comment by M. Turnell, *B.*, 79.

Guidé par ton odeur vers de charmants climats,
Je vois un port rempli de voiles et de mâts
Encor tout fatigués par la vague marine,

Pendant que le parfum des verts tamariniers,
Qui circule dans l'air et m'enfle la narine,
Se mêle dans mon âme au chant des mariniers.

(1857 text)

The structure of this sonnet is as balanced and symmetrical as is
its verse-form. Thus in quatrains and tercets alike, a brief prelude
recalls both the amorous occasion and the particular imaginative
stimulus it affords (the warm autumn evening, the warmth and
fragrance of her breast, the 'guiding' perfume); then, as the mind
casts back, comes the general vista ('rivages heureux' or 'charmants
climats') succeeded in each case by a single more detailed scene (in
the quatrains, the 'lazy' island with its strange trees and luscious
fruits, its graceful men and bold-eyed women; in the tercets, the
bustling port with its throng of ships)—a 'cinematic' technique, one
might say, with the 'camera' slowly 'travelling' along the unfolding
shores before it pauses, settles upon a particular point, slides in to
examine it more closely. But Baudelaire adds the refinement not only
of a 'sound-track' (the sailors' shanties laying their spell over his
heart), but also of the pervasive perfume that wafts in from the shore
and that will, when he re-opens his eyes, resolve back into another,
more real fragrance: that of Jeanne's 'sein chaleureux'. Significantly,
from our present standpoint, Baudelaire in his second quatrain
implies both the beneficence of Nature and its primal harmony: the
trees and fruits are 'gifts' bestowed by Nature on a primitive com-
munity which in its ease and relaxed vigour, its poise and serenity,[1]
might seem (as the jargon has it) truly to have 'mastered the art of
living'.

Though sharing with *Parfum exotique* the same general theme (the
exotic visions conjured up in the poet's mind by Jeanne's perfume),
La Chevelure differs strikingly in almost every detail of the theme's
development. Clearly this long sequence of seven five-line stanzas
cannot reproduce the symmetry, balance and economy of its sonnet
companion; but it holds a subtle pattern and persuasive impetus of
its own, and unfolds, like the imagined ocean of Jeanne's hair, in a

---

[1] In certain others of B.'s love poems (*Avec ses vêtements* . . ., *Le Serpent qui
danse*, *Les Bijoux*), these qualities are observed, and admired, in Jeanne herself.

succession of smoothly overlapping waves.[1] The title, and the opening verse, with its passionate invocation to the 'chevelure' itself, are deceptive, in that they suggest a rapturous tribute to sensual delights both present and past; for would one not suppose, within this context, that the 'sleeping' memories were shared memories of *love*?

> O toison, moutonnant jusque sur l'encolure!
> O boucles! O parfum chargé de nonchaloir!
> Extase! Pour peupler ce soir l'alcôve obscure
> Des souvenirs dormant dans cette chevelure,
> Je la veux agiter dans l'air comme un mouchoir!
>
> (1859 text)

The next verse brings a first, sudden glimpse of other climates and continents; as abruptly banishes them to a distant past which we infer to be personal to the poet (since how else should it be 'almost defunct' as well as 'absent'?); then, by a further, still more calculated contrast (the slight pause on 'défunt' at the end of one line, immediately followed by the emphatic statement of its antithesis 'vit'), recalls the vanished world to life, or shows it quickening within the forest of her hair—all this within a few lines that may be said to hold the poem's quintessence:

> La langoureuse Asie et la brûlante Afrique,
> Tout un monde lointain, absent, presque défunt,
> Vit dans tes profondeurs, forêt aromatique!
> Comme d'autres esprits voguent sur la musique,
> Le mien, ô mon amour, nage sur ton parfum.

The last two lines show the poet firmly launched on the tide of memory—or rather, of the perfume that with Baudelaire is almost a form of memory: 'parfum, donc souvenir'.[2] The two ensuing verses are those that in spirit and imagery most nearly recall *Parfum exotique*:

> J'irai là-bas où l'arbre et l'homme, pleins de séve,
> Se pâment longuement sous l'ardeur des climats;
> Fortes tresses, soyez la houle qui m'enlève!
> Tu contiens, mer d'ébène, un éblouissant rêve
> De voiles, de rameurs, de flammes et de mâts:

---

[1] For a subtle analysis of the rhythmic (or 'respiratory') structure of this poem, see J. Prévost, *B.*, 292–5.

[2] I borrow the striking formula coined by J. Prévost (*B.*, 217).

> Un port retentissant où mon âme peut boire
> A grands flots le parfum, le son et la couleur;
> Où les vaisseaux, glissant dans l'or et dans la moire,
> Ouvrent leurs vastes bras pour embrasser la gloire
> D'un ciel pur où frémit l'éternelle chaleur.

Here, once again, the indolent vigour of tropical life, the teeming harbour-scene, are alike conjured up out of that distant 'là-bas'. But where previously Baudelaire had given us only the rapid tracery of sails and masts, he now adds the further dimension of colour, together with an added richness of detail: oarsmen, pennants, the gold and shot silk of the harbour waters, the sailing-vessels straining their 'arms' towards the eternal shimmering blue—a 'tableau' that in its authenticity and careful composition recalls, rather, the interiors and landscapes of that other poem of departure, *L'Invitation au voyage*. Thus far (as in *L'Invitation au voyage*) the appeal is almost exclusively to the visual sense; but Baudelaire has claimed to 'drink in' from the scene not only colour but perfume and sound, and in the remaining verses the range of sensory impression becomes wider, the exotic evocations are more continuously and variously related to the physical sensations (the colour,[1] feel and scent of Jeanne's hair) from which they arise; we are given not only the vast azure dome of the tropical sky (the 'ciel pur où frémit l'éternelle chaleur' of the previous verse), but also the whole subtle amalgam of odours (tar, coco-nut oil, musk), and even the caressing movement of the ship as it lies at anchor:[2]

[1] Ebony-black in the third and fifth verses, then in the sixth verse 'midnight blue' ('Cheveux *bleus*, pavillon de *ténèbres* tendues'; 'un noir tournant au bleu', as L. J. Austin notes, *L'Univers poétique de B.*, 227)—blue, to allow the associative transition ('bleus'—'azur') which leads back to the tropical sky of the previous verse. Cf. *Le Serpent qui danse*, ll. 5–8: 'Sur ta chevelure profonde/Aux âcres parfums,/Mer odorante et vagabonde/Aux flots *bleus et bruns* . . .' (1857 text; my italics).

[2] Cf., for the recurrence of these various details, the two 'exotic' prose poems published together in August 1857: 'Dans l'atmosphère, une odeur flottante d'huile de coco, et partout un parfum indescriptible de musc' (*Les Projets, PPP* 307–8); 'Dans les caresses de ta chevelure, je retrouve les langueurs des longues journées passées sur le divan, dans la chambre d'un beau navire, bercées par le roulis imperceptible *du port* . . . dans la nuit de ta chevelure, je vois resplendir *l'infini de l'azur tropical*; sur les rivages duvetés de ta chevelure, je m'enivre des odeurs combinées du goudron, du musc et de l'huile de coco' (*La Chevelure*, later to be re-entitled *Un Hémisphère dans une chevelure, PPP* 52 and var. 291). Since this latter text may in effect be considered the prose 'doublet' of our

Je plongerai ma tête amoureuse d'ivresse
Dans ce noir océan où l'autre est enfermé;
Et mon esprit subtil que le roulis caresse
Saura vous retrouver, ô féconde paresse,
Infinis bercements du loisir embaumé!

Cheveux bleus, pavillon de ténèbres tendues,
Vous me rendez l'azur du ciel immense et rond;
Sur les bords duvetés de vos mèches tordues
Je m'enivre ardemment des senteurs confondues
De l'huile de coco, du musc et du goudron.

In the final verse, Baudelaire turns at last from the exotic past to
speak directly to Jeanne (rather than merely to her hair)—and in so
doing sets upon the poem the seal of a fervent yet (as we shall see)
curiously ambiguous tribute:

Longtemps! toujours! ma main dans ta crinière lourde
Sèmera le rubis, la perle et le saphir,
Afin qu'à mon désir tu ne sois jamais sourde.
N'es-tu pas l'oasis où je rêve, et la gourde
Où je hume à longs traits le vin du souvenir?

Through the whole complex structure of this poem there runs a
metaphoric pattern of equal intricacy, and here the contrast with the
companion sonnet is still more striking. The imagery of *Parfum
exotique* is almost wholly literal;[1] in *La Chevelure*, on the other hand,
the texture is continuously figurative, and the title-image in particular undergoes a series of elaborate and audacious metaphoric transformations (fleece, dark alcove, handkerchief, forest, ebony sea or
black ocean, tent or banner of darkness,[2] mane!) which might almost

---

present poem, the phrases italicized (by me) would confirm that in the verse
text also, the ship is thought of as lying in harbour, and that the 'ciel pur où
frémit l'éternelle chaleur' of the previous verse, like the 'azur du ciel immense et
rond', refers simply and literally to the tropical sky.

[1] Even the word 'fatigués' (l. 11) is less a metaphorical 'coinage' than a term
borrowed from the technical vocabulary of sailors.

[2] The second of these two alternative interpretations—with 'pavillon' taken in
its other and appropriately nautical sense ('cf. 'flammes' designating 'pennants' in
l. 15)—seems to me the more plausible: the hair streaming out like a dark flag
stretched in the wind ('pavillon de ténèbres *tendues*'), and continuing the idea of
l. 5: 'je la veux agiter dans l'air comme un mouchoir'. I am grateful to Claude
Pichois for his comments on this particular point of interpretation.

be designed to demonstrate the validity of the self-description 'mon esprit subtil' . . . These metaphors are by no means solely descriptive or impressionistic; as well as the pure analogies of colour and shape (the darkness and flow common to both sea and 'chevelure'), we have also those images which mark the transition from present to past, from here to elsewhere, from immediate stimulus to remote, determining memory: 'Fortes tresses, *soyez* la houle qui m'enlève'; 'Tu *contiens*, mer d'ébène, un éblouissant rêve . . .'; 'ce noir océan où l'autre *est enfermé*'.

I have referred above to the curiously ambiguous nature of Baudelaire's tribute to Jeanne in *La Chevelure*. The tone is ardent, even exalted, and magnificently sustained through all the various metaphoric transformations; however vivid and compulsive may be the poet's imaginative migration to 'la langoureuse Asie et la brûlante Afrique', he remains, in the fullest and most immediate sense, in continuous *touch* with the flowing mane of her hair—raising it in his hands, running it through his fingers, burying his face in its aromatic depths. As to the final verse, its homage might at first be thought to be as generous and unstinted as its hyperbole is extravagant. And yet, although in this respect the tone may appear to differ from that of *Parfum exotique*, the poet's attitude to his mistress remains essentially the same—essentially self-absorbed, and to that extent ungallant, unflattering even. Is the compliment not decidedly double-edged, when the lover says in effect: 'As I lie in your arms, as I savour the fragrance of your body, as I plunge my head into your beautiful hair, my thoughts are of . . . other things!'?[1] Almost it might seem as if Jeanne's presence served as a mere pretext for luxuriant reminiscence, a springboard for the elastic bounds of

---

[1]Cf. the more explicit exclamations in the prose-poem doublet aforementioned, *Un Hémisphère dans une chevelure*: 'Si tu pouvais savoir tout ce que je vois! tout ce que je sens! tout ce que j'entends dans tes cheveux! . . . Quand je mordille tes cheveux solides et crépus, il me semble que je mange des souvenirs' (1857 text; *PPP* 51–2 var. 291)—as also the lines from *Le Serpent qui danse*: 'Sur ta chevelure profonde/Aux âcres parfums,/Mer odorante et vagabonde/Aux flots bleus et bruns,/Comme un navire qui s'éveille/Au vent du matin,/Mon âme rêveuse appareille/Pour un ciel lointain' (1857 text, ll. 5–12). The reiteration, incidentally, of this same theme in four texts of differing dates (see the respective entries in my Chronological Index), illustrates strikingly the extent to which B.'s imagination continued to be haunted by the 'exotic dream'. Cf. also, in this connection the prose poem above-mentioned *Les Projets*, and the later texts cit. p. 303 n. 1, below.

his imagination;[1] or to take Baudelaire's own analogy from music ('Comme d'autres esprits voguent sur la musique,/Le mien, ô mon amour, nage sur ton parfum'), what composer would be flattered to hear, from a self-styled 'admirer', some such tribute as this: 'I just *adore* your music—I get such *beautiful* day-dreams as I listen to it!'?[2] But there is, of course, more to the psychology of this final verse than a mere tactless abstractedness;[3] when Baudelaire asks: 'N'es-tu pas l'oasis où je rêve, et la gourde/Où je hume à longs traits le vin du souvenir?', is he not confessing openly that what he prizes *above all else* in Jeanne is her power to summon up the past—*his* past, a past to which she belongs only in the vaguest and most general sense, by the accident of race and colour (and perfume)? And this past he values not only for the intrinsic beauty of its tropical scenes, but for its poignant embodiment of those very qualities that constitute the eternal primitivist ideal, and that by implication are wholly absent from the real (and sophisticated) present within which he lives: '*There,* Man and Nature alike share a rich vitality and freedom; *there,* the sun shines eternally from a sky eternally blue; *there,* leisure is infinite, fragrant and self-rewarding—whereas here . . .?' The exotic dream, in fact, outshines in glamour Jeanne herself, for all her (acknowledged) charms—and perhaps in a sense it stirs the poet's emotions still more profoundly.

This almost therapeutic virtue of the exotic, as a cure for the 'sickness' of modern civilization, is made explicit in certain verses (the first four out of six, to be precise) of a poem which may equally, in its original draft, belong to the present period: *Moesta et erra-bunda.*[4] This, like several others among Baudelaire's most original

---

[1]Cf. the observation by M. Turnell, *B.*, 114: '. . . when we reach the heart of the poem—the sense of beatitude described in the fourth verse—we find that the woman has vanished from the scene altogether . . .'

[2]As it happens Baudelaire (whose musical sensibility was strictly limited, though genuine enough within those limits) did say something not very different from this, when striving (*AR* 206-7) to express his admiration for Wagner's *Lohengrin* Prelude. But that is another story.

[3]Cf. the ribald commentary (in this sole respect perhaps not wholly without point) that the poem drew, on its first publication, from the critic of *Le Figaro*, Alph. Duchesne: 'Pour ma part, j'avoue que je n'aime pas à rencontrer tant de monde dans les cheveux d'une femme. Car, enfin, quel est le monde? d'où est-il venu et que fait-il là?' (cit. *FMCB* 338).

[4]For this dating, cf. my art. cit., 'Pour une étude chronologique des *FM*', pp. 349-50, 351 n. 4; for the remaining two verses, see pp. 59-60, below

love poems, is in effect a sort of 'conversation-piece':[1] even though he may here be 'musing aloud', and following the sequence of his thoughts wherever they may lead him, the remembered or imagined presence of the 'Agathe' to whom he speaks, is by no means unimportant to him (or to the poem); it is she ('the sad and wandering one' of the title) who, directly or indirectly, sets his thoughts in train, and she who prompts their direction by the *sadness* of her face and heart, by her *wandering* bent or perhaps (less literally) by the sympathetic *vagrancy* of her mind.[2] The whole poem, as will be seen, is built up on a pattern which alternates rhetorical questions with exclamatory digressions, according as the poet withdraws into his reverie, or emerges to seek support and sympathy from his companion; the capriciousness of this pattern is enhanced by the repeated lines which, stanza by stanza, interrupt or suspend the successive stages of the 'argument'. The first verse juxtaposes, and opposes, two 'oceans': the figurative ocean, dark and hideous, of the engulfing city; the 'other' and real ocean, dazzling and blue, which unfurls its known splendours on the far side of the earth:[3]

> Dis-moi, ton cœur parfois s'envole-t-il, Agathe,
> Loin du noir océan de l'immonde cité,
> Vers un autre océan où la splendeur éclate,
> Bleu, clair, profond, ainsi que la virginité?
> Dis-moi, ton cœur parfois s'envole-t-il, Agathe?

(1855 text)

The question framing this antithesis—a question that will be echoed in the third stanza—is perhaps more strictly a plea; the questioner here speaks from his *own* heart, hoping to find its counterpart in another's. 'Does your heart too, *like mine*, long to escape?' But the

---

[1]Cf. *L'Invitation au voyage, Réversibilité, L'Irréparable, Chant d'automne, Sonnet d'automne, Causerie.*

[2]Cf. (p. 30, above) the description of Ivonne Pen-Moore (as a young girl): 'rêveuse et vagabonde', and of himself in the lines, already quoted, from *Le Serpent qui danse*: 'Sur ta chevelure profonde ... Mon âme rêveuse appareille/Pour un ciel lointain'. And no doubt he is thinking, once again, of such as Agathe and himself when, in his *Salon de 1846*, he says of Delacroix: '[il] ouvre dans [ses "poëmes"] de profondes avenues à l'imagination la plus voyageuse' (*CE* 106), or, in a later chapter, discerns in the paintings of Joyant, Chacaton, Lottier and Borget 'le charme des lectures de voyages' (*CE* 182–3; cf., for Borget, *CE* 61).

[3]The metaphoric design (like the verse-form) resembles that of *La Chevelure*; in that poem, however, as will be recalled, the real ocean *continues* (rather than contrasts with) the figurative ocean (Jeanne's hair).

speculation implies no active sequel; this is no 'invitation to a journey', and the question posed, in the ensuing verse, within a miniature hymn to the vast, consoling sea, no more than echoes, rhetorically, the musings of one who himself has many times been cradled by the soothing tumult of wind and waves:

> La mer, la vaste mer, console nos labeurs.
> Quel démon a doté la mer,—rude chanteuse
> Qu'accompagne l'immense orgue des vents grondeurs,—
> De cette fonction sublime de berceuse?
> La mer, la vaste mer, console nos labeurs.

All these memories (specific memories, I believe) crystallize into the heartfelt cry of the next verse: a movement of impatient longing (as if in answer to that final 'chant des mariniers' of *Parfum exotique*) rather, perhaps, than a true resolve. 'Oh to be carried over land and sea, far, far away . . . far from all that we see around us, and must endure!'

> Emporte-moi, wagon! enlève-moi, frégate!
> Loin!—loin!—ici la boue est faite de nos pleurs!
> —Est-il vrai que parfois le triste cœur d'Agathe
> Dise: Loin des remords, des crimes, des douleurs,
> Emporte-moi, wagon, enlève-moi, frégate?

The reminder of the city's squalor and suffering, of its 'mud and tears', has brought a reminder also of Agathe, and a renewal of the opening question: sharing his exile within the city's crime and remorse and pain—sharing his sadness of heart—does she not also share, at times, his yearning to depart? But the plea has already begun to fade—with the renewed image of departure, the renewed 'loin', sounding (as throughout the poem) its irresistible call, and drawing the poet's imagination away over the sea once again, to the 'perfumed Paradise' lying beneath skies of the same translucent blue as the ocean that surrounds it:

> Comme vous êtes loin, paradis parfumé,
> Où sous un clair azur tout n'est qu'amour et joie,
> Où tout ce que l'on aime est digne d'être aimé,
> Où dans la volupté pure le cœur se noie!
> Comme vous étes loin, paradis parfumé!

Significantly, the distant Paradise is now figured in terms (purity, joy, delight, love and the dignity of love) that make it the *moral* antithesis of all the squalor, suffering and guilt that darken the poet's present horizons.

The same antithesis is presented, in more obvious and sentimental terms, in the third of the three 1845-6 texts aforementioned, *A une Indienne*. The 'Indian girl' of the original title (in the definitive version of 1857, the poem is re-named *A une Malabaraise*) was apparently the foster-sister of the 'dame créole', and had thus attended Baudelaire during his visits to the Bragard household in Mauritius.[1] The first section, after its initial compliment to the girl's beauty, goes on to 'remind' her of the freedom, warmth and colour, the idyllic and unexacting simplicity, of the life that she so happily leads in her native 'climats chauds et bleus':

> Tes pieds sont aussi fins que tes mains, et ta hanche
> Est large à faire envie à la plus fière blanche;
> A l'artiste pensif ton corps est doux et cher,
> Tes grands yeux indiens sont plus noirs que ta chair.
> Aux climats chauds et bleus où ton Dieu t'a fait naître,
> Ta tâche est d'allumer la pipe de ton maître,
> De pourvoir les flacons d'eaux fraîches et d'odeurs,
> Et de chasser du lit les moustiques rôdeurs,
> Et, dès que le matin fait chanter les platanes,
> D'acheter au bazar ananas et bananes.
> Tout le jour où tu veux tu mènes tes pieds nus,
> Et fredonnes tout bas de doux airs inconnus;
> Et, quand descend le soir au manteau d'écarlate,
> Tu poses doucument ton corps sur une natte,
> Où tes rêves flottants sont pleins de colibris,
> Et toujours comme toi gracieux et fleuris.

(1846 text: ll. 1-16)

---

[1]According to S. Rosenmark, cit. *FMCB* 543; cf., however, J. Pommier, *Dans les chemins de B.*, 345-8, who shows that the 'Indian girl' in question cannot *also* have been the 'Dorothée' of *Bien loin d'ici* and *La Belle Dorothée*. As to the chronology of the poem, no conclusion can in my view be drawn from the indication '1840' given in *Les Épaves*, in view of the fact that the date assigned to another text within this volume, *Sur 'Le Tasse en Prison'* . . ., is manifestly erroneous —'1842' for 1844; see *FMCB* 577, and cf. likewise certain other inaccuracies of annotation in *Les Épaves*, cited p. 275 n. 2, below (in respect of the sonnet *Le Coucher du soleil romantique*). Nor need the fact that B. is certainly here drawing on various literary models (not only on Hugo and Gautier, as noted *FMCB* 543-4, but also on another, still more immediate source, as I hope shortly to have the opportunity of showing) in any way invalidate the assumption that the poem was composed during or after the voyage of 1841-2: B. could, after all, just as

The second part, however, reveals this whole charming portrait to have an ulterior purpose, a 'moral' in the form of an eloquent and 'paternal' warning:

> Pourquoi, l'heureuse enfant, veux-tu voir notre France,
> Ce pays trop peuplé que fauche la souffrance,
> Et, confiant ta vie aux bras forts des marins,
> Faire de grands adieux à tes chers tamarins?
> Toi, vêtue à moitié de mousselines frêles,
> Frissonante là-bas sous la neige et les grêles,
> Que tu regretterais tes loisirs doux et francs,
> Si, le corset brutal martyrisant tes flancs,
> Il te fallait glaner ton souper dans nos fanges,
> Et vendre le parfum de tes charmes étranges,
> L'œil errant et suivant dans nos vastes brouillards
> Des cocotiers natifs les fantômes épars!

Beyond the purely personal admonition (aimed at the Indian girl herself), the reader cannot fail to perceive, in the antithesis between the first and second parts of the poem, a more general if implicit 'message': on the one hand, the poet exalts the primitive way of life (the girl's way of life, which is also that of her fellows); on the other, he indicts, through her imagined predicament, the whole ethos and social order of 'this France of ours'[1]—crowded and shivering within its fog-bound cities, answering hunger with prostitution, sorrow with squalor and filth. (Here too, as in *Moesta et errabunda*, the very mud is compounded of 'our tears'.)

Now it might seem that the haunting final image above-quoted— with its distant, forsaken palm-trees emerging, as a 'ghostly' memory, from behind the fog that blots out all nearer objects—would form, in its imaginative 'resonance' and drawing-together of all the various threads, the perfect and inevitable conclusion to the poem; and so in fact Baudelaire decided, when he came to reprint the poem in 1857 and thereafter. But in 1846 he was not content to end on this note; he must needs add, by way of coda, six further lines in which the

---

well imitate Hugo, Gautier, etc., in 1842, as in 1840. All that one can with certainty affirm is that the poem had already, by 1843, been heard by Prarond (see *CML* II, 1154), in some version which may or may not have been identical with that published in 1846 in *L'Artiste*; cf. in this connection my art. cit., 'B.: The Poet as Moralist', p. 199.

[1] The same indictment-by-antithesis is of course implicit within Bernardin de Saint-Pierre's *Paul et Virginie*. Cf. pp. 42–3, below.

girl's imagined misfortune is turned (not altogether unpoetically, yet from a modern reader's standpoint, how gratuitously!) to expressly edifying account:[1]

> Amour de l'inconnu, jus de l'antique pomme,
> Vieille perdition de la femme et de l'homme,
> O curiosité, toujours tu leur feras
> Déserter comme font les oiseaux, ces ingrats,
> Pour un lointain mirage et des cieux moins prospères,
> Le toit qu'ont parfumé les cercueils de leurs pères.

Vicarious nostalgia has here turned to banal sententiousness; moreover, the force of the contrast between primitive and 'civilized' modes of life has been lost, since logically the same moral could equally well be applied, in reverse, to the Parisian deserting *his* 'native roof' for some distant *tropical* mirage . . .[2] Taken as a whole, however, the poem even in its 1846 version does not fail to make its persuasive (even if indirect) plea for that 'other world' which Gautier equally, in an earlier poem, had set against the sad, grim, urbanized reality of nineteenth-century France.[3]

A final and more specialized instance of this antithesis between two 'worlds', brings in that archetypal figure of the 'primitive innocent', Bernardin de Saint-Pierre's Virginie. In an essay which in 1845 was to bear the title 'De la Caricature', but which ultimately, some ten years later, became the famous *De l'Essence du rire*, Baudelaire seeks to demonstrate his assertion (borrowed from his friend Chennevières) that laughter, being a product of human sin, was unknown in the first Garden of the world—has no place indeed in *any* Earthly Paradise whether past or future, theological or Utopian.[4] Accordingly— as a 'poetic' instance whereby to rebut any charge of a-prioristic 'mysticism'—he devizes a new and intriguing complement to Virginie's long (yet essentially uninformative)

---

[1]For a discussion of the aesthetic implications of this plunge into didacticism, see my art. cit., 'B.: The Poet as Moralist', in *SMFL*, 198-9—from which I borrow, incidentally, certain of the foregoing comments.

[2]It could indeed be applied to the Parisian B.—who in Dec. 1847 was to contemplate, as a last desperate resort, returning to Mauritius to try his fortune there; see *CG* I, 93-4.

[3]My reference is to *Ce monde-ci et l'autre* (1833), written by Gautier for the Creole poetess Louise Arbey; see his *PC*, ed. Jasinski, II, 141-3 and I, xlvii.

[4]*CE* 373-4. For the borrowing from Chennevières, as also for the detailed chronology of the essay, see C. Pichois, *B.*, 80-94.

letter from France, and imagines her confronted, here in Paris, with some truculent specimen or other of the modern art of *caricature*. It will be observed once again how strongly, how lyrically, in this 1855 version (which in Claude Pichois' expert view,[1] will have differed little from the original text), Baudelaire accentuates the contrast between the solemnity and grandeur of elemental Nature on the one hand, and the turbulence and squalor of urban civilization on the other:

Essayons, puisque le comique est un élément damnable et d'origine diabolique, de mettre en face une âme absolument primitive et sortant, pour ainsi dire, des mains de la nature. Prenons pour exemple la grande et typique figure de Virginie, qui symbolise parfaitement la pureté et la naïveté absolues. Virginie arrive à Paris encore toute trempée des brumes de la mer et dorée par le soleil des tropiques, les yeux pleins des grandes images primitives des vagues, des montagnes et des forêts. Elle tombe ici en pleine civilisation turbulente, débordante et méphitique, elle, tout imprégnée des pures et riches senteurs de l'Inde; elle se rattache à l'humanité par la famille et par l'amour, par sa mère et par son amant, son Paul, angélique comme elle, et dont le sexe ne se distingue pour ainsi dire pas du sien dans les ardeurs inassouvies d'un amour qui s'ignore. Dieu, elle l'a connu dans l'église des Pamplemousses, une petite église toute modeste et toute chétive, et dans l'immensité de l'indescriptible azur tropical, et dans la musique immortelle des forêts et des torrents. . . . Or, un jour, Virginie rencontre par hasard, innocemment, au Palais-Royal, aux carreaux d'un vitrier, sur une table, dans un lieu public, une caricature!

(1855 text; *CE* 374-5)

Baudelaire's Virginie (predictably) is taken aback; she hardly knows what to make of this strange product of a 'perspicacious and bored civilisation,' but at the same time feels a certain apprehensive disquiet:

L'ange a senti que le scandale était là. Et, en vérité, je vous le dis, qu'elle ait compris ou qu'elle n'ait pas compris, il lui restera de cette impression je ne sais quel malaise, quelque chose qui ressemble à la peur. Sans doute, que Virginie reste à Paris et que la science lui vienne, le rire lui viendra; nous verrons pourquoi.

(*CE* 376)

What in fact it would be, as we learn on the following page, that would bring laughter to her lips (and within her ken), would be the

[1]Op. cit., p. 92.

sense of her own superiority, growing in proportion as her 'purity' diminishes (a sense of superiority being the first and most obvious motive for laughter). Thereafter, Baudelaire develops an argument of increasing subtlety, distinguishing (with subdivisions) 'le comique absolu'—i.e. the grotesque—from 'le comique significatif', and so on. But the part played in the original elaboration of these theories, by Baudelaire's assumptions as to the primordial goodness of Nature and of Man in Nature, can be further divined from this next passage, which envisages a 'superior' and laughter-free mode of poetry, sharing (and returning to) the 'limpidity and profundity' of Nature herself:

... si dans ces mêmes nations ultra-civilisées, une intelligence, poussée par une ambition supérieure, veut franchir les limites de l'orgueil mondain et aspirer sincèrement à la poésie pure, dans cette poésie, *limpide et profonde comme la nature*, le rire fera défaut comme dans l'âme du Sage.[1]

Perhaps the most haunting of all Baudelaire's visions of the tropical 'elsewhere', is that offered in *La Vie antérieure*:

> J'ai longtemps habité sous de vastes portiques
> Que les soleils marins teignaient de mille feux,
> Et que leurs grands piliers droits et majestueux
> Rendaient pareils le soir aux grottes basaltiques.
>
> Les houles, en roulant les images des cieux,
> Mêlaient d'une façon solennelle et mystique
> Les tout-puissants accords de leur riche musique
> Aux couleurs du couchant reflété par mes yeux.
>
> C'est là que j'ai vécu dans les voluptés calmes,
> Au milieu de l'azur, des flots et des splendeurs,
> Et des esclaves nus tout imprégnés d'odeurs,
>
> Qui me rafraîchissaient le front avec des palmes,
> Et dont l'unique soin était d'approfondir
> Le secret douloureux qui me faisait languir.

(1855 text)

The quatrains of this sonnet surely derive from certain specific impressions culled from the voyage of 1841–2[2]—the very setting, perhaps (the vast, undulating seascape, under its shimmering tropi-

---

[1] *CE* 380, var. ibid. 501; my italics.
[2] Cf. A. Cassagne, *La Théorie de l'art pour l'art*, 379; J. Prévost, *B.*, 220–1.

cal sun) that is more briefly conjured up towards the end of the long
verse epistle (*Tous imberbes alors* . . .) addressed in 1843–5 to Sainte-
Beuve; Baudelaire is here describing the diverse places and occasions
that still find him returning to that author's 'magical' (and influential) novel *Volupté*:

> Soit que, sous les soleils des zones différentes,
> L'éternel bercement des houles enivrantes,
> Et l'aspect renaissant des horizons sans fin
> Ramenassent ce cœur vers le songe divin[1] . . .

We might further suppose, as a determining factor in the composition of *La Vie antérieure*, some such wave of 'nostalgia' as swept over
him many years later, as he stood before the canvases of Fromentin
at the 1859 Salon:

> . . . la lumière et la chaleur, qui jettent dans quelques cerveaux une
> espèce de folie tropicale, les agitent d'une fureur inapaisable et les
> poussent à des danses inconnues, ne versent dans son âme qu'une
> contemplation douce et reposée. C'est l'extase plutôt que le fanatisme.
> Il est présumable que je suis moi-même atteint quelque peu d'une
> nostalgie qui m'entraîne vers le soleil; car de ces toiles lumineuses
> s'élève pour moi une vapeur enivrante, qui se condense bientôt en
> désirs et en regrets. Je me surprends à envier le sort de ces hommes
> étendus sous ces ombres bleues, et dont les yeux, qui ne sont ni éveillés
> ni endormis, n'expriment, si toutefois ils expriment quelque chose, que
> l'amour du repos et le sentiment du bonheur qu'inspire une immense
> lumière.

$$(CE\ 317\text{--}18)$$

In *La Vie antérieure*, Baudelaire gives us a landscape that combines
both the subjective and objective qualities ascribed to Fromentin's
paintings:[2] the contemplative 'ecstasy' of the artist as, nostalgically,
he 'feels himself into' the blissful inertia of tropical man.[3] But the

---

[1]*OCP* 199. *La Vie antérieure* is among the poems on Prarond's 'second list',
i.e. those he was inclined to date, from his own recollections, as of 1844–6 if not
of 1841–3; see *CML* II, 1155, and cf. my art. cit., 'Pour une étude chronologique
des *FM*', *RHLF*, 1967, pp. 344–5.

[2]This is not of course to say that an actual painting by Fromentin would offer
the truest analogy with B.'s poem; G. Blin (*B.*, 121) perceptively suggests
Claude for the quatrains, Gauguin for the tercets.

[3]Ironically enough, what in 1841 seems to have driven B. to *forsake* the exotic
paradise attained in Bourbon and Mauritius, was (among other things) his
nostalgia for his *true* native land, i.e. France; see *CML* II, 1168 (letter from
Captain Saliz to Aupick), and cf. *CG* I, 15.

poet's sense of nostalgia goes deeper than the critic's, is indeed
nostalgia in the true and etymological sense of the word: by sheer
force of affinity, he here transforms the tropical paradise into his
own native—or pre-natal—land. Such surely is the implication of
the title, and of the almost identical phrases that in turn launch
quatrains and tercets; by thus projecting his exotic dream backwards
into time, as well as outwards into space, Baudelaire is in effect
claiming kinship with those spiritual 'exiles' whom Théophile Gautier had described in 1843, in a text which the younger poet will
very probably have read:

On n'est pas toujours du pays qui vous a vu naître, et, alors, on cherche
à travers tout sa vraie patrie; ceux qui sont faits de la sorte se sentent
exilés dans leur ville, étrangers dans leurs foyers, et tourmentés de
nostalgies inverses. C'est une bizarre maladie: on est comme des oiseaux
de passage encagés. Quand arrive le temps du départ, de grands désirs
vous agitent, et vous étes pris d'inquiétudes en voyant les nuages qui
vont du côté de la lumière.—Si l'on voulait, il serait facile d'assigner à
chaque célébrité d'aujourd'hui nonseulement le pays, mais le siècle où
aurait dû se passer son existence véritable: Lamartine et de Vigny sont
Anglais modernes; Hugo est Espagnol-Flamand du temps de Charles-
Quint; Alfred de Musset, Napolitain du temps de la domination es-
pagnole; Decamps, Turc asiatique; Marilhat, Arabe; Delacroix,
Marocain. On pourrait pousser fort loin ces remarques, justifiables
jusque dans les moindres détails, et que viennent confirmer même les
types de figure.—Toi, tu es Allemand; moi, je suis Turc, non de
Constantinople, mais d'Égypte. Il me semble que j'ai vécu en Orient;
et, lorsque, pendant le carnaval, je me déguise avec quelque cafetan et
quelque tarbouch authentique, je crois reprendre mes vrais habits. J'ai
toujours été surpris de ne pas entendre l'arabe couramment; il faut que
je l'aie oublié.[1]

So, too, George Sand, in a text reprinted in the same year, 1843,

[1]*La Presse*, 25 July 1843; reprod. in: *Histoire de l'art dramatique*, III, 76–7.
Gautier is here reviewing, in a 'letter' addressed to his friend Nerval (then in
Cairo), his own ballet *La Péri*! See Lovenjoul, *Histoire des œuvres de Gautier*, I,
256, no. 623. That B. was a close reader of Gautier's *feuilletons* is attested by
certain uncomplimentary references to them during this period; cf. *OP* I, 117,
124, 125; *CE* 152–3; *AR* 276. The notion of a 'double' nostalgia recurs in a
remark attributed to Gautier by Edmond de Goncourt, in his preface to
Bergerat's *Gautier. Entretiens, souvenirs et correspondance*, p. iii: 'Nous ne
sommes pas Français, nous autres; nous tenons à d'autres races. Nous sommes
pleins de nostalgies. Et puis, quant [sic] à la nostalgie d'un pays se joint la
nostalgie d'un temps . . . oh! alors c'est complet . . .'

declares, for that exotic among European countries, Bohemia, her own haunting intuition of remote, spiritual 'nationality':

O verte Bohême! patrie fantastique des âmes sans ambition et sans entraves, je vais donc te revoir! J'ai erré souvent dans tes montagnes et voltigé sur la cime de tes sapins; je m'en souviens fort bien, quoique je ne fusse pas encore né parmi les hommes, et mon malheur est venu de n'avoir pu t'oublier en vivant ici.

(Lettres d'un voyageur, 1843, p. 231)

Other and later texts of Baudelaire's own could equally be cited, in which this same compelling sense of *déjà-vu* is linked, explicitly or implicitly, with the postulate of an 'anterior existence'.[1] We have thus no need, in order to explain the title of our present sonnet, to invoke what in the context would be purely gratuitous doctrines of metempsychosis or palingenesis; at the very most one might suppose that in offering a hint of such doctrines, Baudelaire may have sought to accentuate, by the suggestion of an impressively remote heredity, the note of lingering satiety, of *troubled* languor, sounded in the concluding couplet.[2] It is in fact this element precisely—the disquieting intrusion of the mysterious and corroding 'secret'—that constitutes the distinctive originality of Baudelaire's exotic vision. The 'calm delight' breathed by the magical seascape—the eternal blue; the evening sun shining through vast pillared porticoes, its colours (themselves reflected in the onlooker's eyes) borne to and fro in the swell of the waves as they boom their rich (chromatic?)

---

[1]Cf. *Salon de 1859, CE* 344 (of Eduard Hildebrandt's water-colours): 'En parcourant ces amusants albums de voyage, il me semble toujours que je *revois,* que je reconnais ce que je n'ai jamais vu'; *Le Joueur généreux* (first pub. 1864), *PPP* 102: 'Il y avait là [i.e. in the subterranean dwelling-place of the Devil] des visages étranges d'hommes et de femmes, marqués d'une beauté fatale, qu'il me semblait avoir vus déjà à des époques et dans des pays dont il m'était impossible de me souvenir exactement, et qui m'inspiraient plutôt une sympathie fraternelle que cette crainte qui naît ordinairement à l'aspect de l'inconnu'. Cf. also these lines from Maxime Du Camp's *Avataras,* published in 1855 in *Les Chants modernes*: 'J'habitais, je le sais, dans d'autres existences, / Ces pays radieux, et je suis convaincu / Que je sais retrouver, à travers les distances, / Tous les endroits certains où j'ai déjà vécu' (cit. Y. Abé, *RHLF,* 1967, p. 279, and J. Pommier, *Dans les chemins de B.,* 182).

[2]Cf. the observation by G. Blin, *B.,* 121: 'Même par delà sa naissance il se trouve lui-même avec "son secret douloureux".'

chords;[1] the luxurious indolence fostered and guarded by slaves who are the servants of desire or caprice—this whole hedonist's paradise is revealed to be subtly flawed, to conceal a canker: 'then' as by implication now, the poet knows an inner grief so familiar, so welcome almost in its familiarity, that he has no thought but to maintain and 'deepen' it.[2] Thus whereas in *Moesta et errabunda* the 'other ocean' may be presented as a means of escape from, an antidote to, the sorrows of civilization, here these sorrows are merely muffled or dulled, sheltered within a soft cocoon of graceful ease and sensuous delight. (In a more realistic sense, the final couplet could of course be taken simply as the tacit recognition of a truth elsewhere admitted by Baudelaire[3]—that the tropics, no less than our more temperate zones, breed their own endemic and stultifying forms of *ennui.)*

The past of *La Vie antérieure* is, of course, a purely personal past. In other texts of the period, Baudelaire's nostalgic primitivism is set in that more general, historical perspective which assumes a direct continuity between the present-day 'savage', and the prehistoric Natural Man whose way of life he supposedly perpetuates—the scope of 'prehistoric' being moreover extended, by a convenient rationalization, to include subsequent 'Golden Ages', Hellenic antiquity in general, even the whole pagan and pre-Christian world. The presumed solidarity between the modern primitive and the classical,

---

[1]The epithet 'mystique', as applied here to the 'music' of the waves, has surely simply the meaning 'mysterious'; cf., for instances of its similar use by B. in this sense (or in the cognate sense of 'mysteriously ideal'), *L'Ennemi*, l. 11; *Je te donne ces vers . . .*, l. 7; *Tout entière*, l. 21; *Les Chats*, l. 14; *La Mort des artistes* (1857), l. 3; *Femmes damnées: A la pâle clarté . . .*, l. 65; and see also the art. by R. L. Wagner, in *Gedenkschrift für Eugen Lerch*, 424–30. The resolute hedonism of the whole tableau is in any case such as to exclude even the most diffuse spirituality.

[2]Cf. (p. 268, below) the almost tender invocation to his Suffering, in the later sonnet *Recueillement* (pub. 1861). I must add that for J. Prévost—as more elaborately, for C. R. François, *MLN*, 1958, 194–200—B.'s tropical vision owes its qualities of remoteness, of 'amplification', of 'dilatation in space', to the presumed effects of opium or hashish; such also is therefore the implication of the 'secret douloureux' of the final line: 'les langueurs causées par la drogue sont senties comme une expiation mystérieuse' (Prévost, *B.*, 221). Cf. also, for a literary analogy (with Dumas père) which would tend to confirm the 'hashish' interpretation, C. Pichois (with J. Dagens), *B.*, 150–5.

[3]E.g. in the letter (to his mother) of Dec. 1847, in which he canvasses the possibility of returning (i.e. of emigrating) to Mauritius: 'j'y trouverai . . . *l'ennui, l'ennui horrible et l'affaiblissement intellectuel des pays chauds et bleus'* (*CG* I, 94; B.'s italics). Cf. p. 42 n. 2, above.

is so to speak crystallized in a sentence of the *Salon de 1846*, describing the aesthetic consequences for Delacroix of his voyage to Morocco in 1832:[1]

Un voyage à Maroc laissa dans son esprit, à ce qu'il semble, une impression profonde; là il put à loisir étudier l'homme et la femme dans l'indépendance et l'originalité native de leurs mouvements, et comprendre la beauté antique par l'aspect d'une race pure de toute mésalliance et ornée de sa santé et du libre développement de ses muscles.[2]

The approach is not always, however, from the contemporary-exotic 'end' of the space-time continuum; thus the first part of *J'aime le souvenir de ces époques nues* offers a fervent eulogy of a Golden Age of *antiquity*, in which men and women walked innocent and unashamed in all the natural grace and beauty of their nakedness:

> J'aime le souvenir de ces époques nues,
> Dont le soleil se plaît à dorer les statues.
> Alors l'homme et la femme en leur agilité
> Jouissaient sans mensonge et sans anxiété,
> Et, le ciel amoureux leur caressant l'échine,
> Exerçaient la santé de leur noble machine.
> Cybèle alors, fertile en produits généreux,
> Ne trouvait[3] point ses fils un poids trop onéreux,
> Louve au cœur ruisselant de tendresses communes
> Suspendait l'univers à ses tétines brunes.
> L'homme élégant, robuste et fort, avait le droit
> D'être fier des beautés dont il était le roi,
> Fruits purs de tout outrage et vierges de gerçures,
> Dont la chair lisse et ferme appelait les morsures!
>
> (1857 proofs, ll. 1–14)

---

[1]Consequences strikingly analogous to those for B. of his own voyage—cf. the comment by M. Sérullaz: 'Delacroix recueillit un répertoire inépuisable de thèmes, de portraits ou paysages, de formes ou de couleurs, d'images lumineuses . . .' (in: *Delacroix. Aquarelles du Maroc*, xv). The 'journey to the Orient' had for Romantic artists and writers become something of a ritual pilgrimage; cf. P. Dorbec, *L'Art du paysage*, 133-9; A. Cassagne, *Théorie de l'art pour l'art*, 376-8.

[2]*CE* 104; this statement is confirmed by Delacroix' own observations, as quoted by J. Alazard, *L'Orient et la peinture*, 52, and R. Canat, *Hellénisme des romantiques*, ii, 81. Cf. also B.'s comments, on a later page of this same *Salon*, on Catlin's portraits of Red Indians: 'Par leurs belles attitudes et l'aisance de leurs mouvements, ces sauvages font comprendre la sculpture antique' (*CE* 128, cf. 318-19); similar affinities had earlier been discerned by the Jesuit missionaries to Canada—see G. Chinard, *L'Amérique et le rêve exotique*, 139-40.

[3]Sic (*FMCB* p. 10)—for 'trouvant'?

We re-encounter here the very qualities (beauty, natural elegance and grace, vigour, spontaneity, joyful simplicity and 'frankness') that inform the exotic way of life pictured in *Parfum exotique, La Chevelure, Moesta et errabunda, A une Indienne*; moreover, the harmony which there was implied between Man and Nature, is here made fully explicit.[1] Baudelaire stresses, it will be observed, the *moral* (as well as physical) health enjoyed in primitive times by Man, the easy frankness of relationship between Man and Woman;[2] this serves the better to point the contrast with the anxieties and tensions of modern life that are the subject of the second part of the poem (to be discussed below).

In *La Muse malade*, a similar antithesis is presented, but in more directly personal and professional terms—'professional', in the sense that the poet is here deploring (in a poem) the 'morbidity' of his poetic inspiration:

> Ma pauvre muse, hélas! qu'as-tu donc ce matin?
> Tes yeux creux sont peuplés de visions nocturnes,
> Et je vois tour à tour réfléchis [sic] sur ton teint
> La folie et l'horreur, froides et taciturnes.
>
> Le succube verdâtre et le rose lutin
> T'ont-ils versé la peur et l'amour de leurs urnes?
> Le cauchemar, d'un poing despotique et mutin,
> T'a-t-il noyée au fond d'un fabuleux Minturnes?

---

[1]Through the image of the 'amorous' sky bestowing her 'caresses', but more especially through that (adapted from Hugo's *La Vache*? cf. p. 20 n. 1, above) of Cybele as the she-wolf suckling her human progeny. It is interesting to note that B.'s (Golden) Age of Nakedness conforms in almost every respect with the long tradition of so-called 'soft primitivism', as thus summarized by G. Chinard (ed. Diderot, *Supplément au Voyage de Bougainville*, 43; cf. A. O. Lovejoy and G. Boas, *Primitivism in Antiquity*, 9-11): '. . . d'autres moins préoccupés de vertu que de bonheur, avaient devant les yeux la vision d'un âge d'or, d'un état édénique où, sans travail et sans maître, libre de satisfaire ses appétits sans inquiétude métaphysique ou morale et de développer son corps sans la gêne des vêtements, l'homme des premiers temps passait sa vie ignorant des contraintes qui se multiplient à mesure que la civilisation augmente'. (For these latter 'constraints', cf. the second part of B.'s poem, shortly to be discussed.)

[2]Cf. the phrase he uses (in the context of an imagined painting by Ingres, at the 'commission' of the island of Cythera) in his article of Jan. 1846 on *Le Musée classique du Bazar Bonne-Nouvelle*: 'robuste et nourrissant comme l'amour antique' (*CE* 213).

Je voudrais qu'exhalant l'odeur de la santé
Ton sein de pensers forts fût toujours fréquenté,
Et que ton sang chrétien coulât à flots rythmiques,

Comme les sons nombreux des syllabes antiques,
Où règnent tour à tour le père des chansons,
Phœbus, et le grand Pan, le seigneur des moissons.

(1857 text)

From the subjective standpoint, the admonitions here framed are in effect precisely those levelled by Mme Cosmelly, in the novella *La Fanfarlo* (published January 1847), at Baudelaire's *alter ego* Samuel Cramer. Why, she asks, having perused the latter's volume of sonnets, *Les Orfraies*, should he prefer, when in the full flower of his youth and talent, to hymn the sinister and perverse aspects of life, rather than its vigorous joys?[1] But in the present instance, the question takes the form of an ironic enquiry, by the poet himself, into his Muse's 'state of health', the effect of which is to 'debunk' effectively (if incidentally) a whole Romantic convention: nothing surely could be more remote from the glamorous hoyden who by turns rallies or consoles 'her' poet in Musset's *Nuits* sequence, than the haggard, tormented creature of Baudelaire's sonnet, with her sunken eyes and deathly, haunted pallor. The tercets, however, carry a moral that is more serious and less purely personal in its application. In craving a renewal and reinvigoration of his talent, Baudelaire invokes the dream (so remote from the *nightmares* of his own Muse!) of that ideal classical mode whose strong and fluent rhythms seem the direct embodiment of the beneficence of Nature, seem directly inspired by the great gods Phœbus and Pan.[2] (Or does Baudelaire, when speaking here of Phœbus and Pan as 'presiding' in turn over the 'harmonious cadences' of antiquity, have in mind odes or hymns expressly dedicated to these deities?) We are reminded, in this conception of a Sun God who is at the same time the 'father of song', of the poet-like 'foster-father' who in *Le Soleil* sets all Nature rejoicing; as for the 'lord of the harvests', we see his female counterpart not only in the Cybele who is invoked both in *J'aime le souvenir de ces époques nues* and in *La Caravane des Bohémiens*, but also in the image, sketched in the

[1] *Fanfarlo*, ed. Pichois, 58.
[2] Ironically enough, B. in his quatrains had drawn on this same pagan tradition, when characterizing the nightmares of his own too-*Christian* Muse: succubus, sprite, urns, Minturnae . . .

opening lines of a further sonnet, *La Géante*, of an exuberantly
prolific 'Mother Nature':

> Du temps que la Nature en sa verve puissante
> Concevait chaque jour des enfants monstrueux . . .
>
> (1857 text)

But beyond these rather formal, even stiff personifications, do we
not catch a further glimpse, in *La Muse malade*, of that whole
harmonious scheme of Nature, that unflawed primitive cosmos, we
have seen pictured in *J'aime le souvenir de ces époques nues*—with all
mankind there enjoying that intimate *rapport* with the sun and the
fruits of the earth here accorded to the poet alone? Thus envisaged,
Baudelaire's desire for a transfusion of pagan vitality into the debili-
tated Christian bloodstream of his Muse, holds something of a more
general nostalgia and regret—nostalgia, for an epoch to which, however remotely, he feels himself by temperament to belong; regret,
that as a *modern* poet he cannot somehow recapture that honest
fluency and vigour known to earlier and less decadent eras. At the
same time, there is no doubt an element of more immediate and
contemporary jealousy: the backward look over the centuries does not
exclude a sidelong glance at his friend (and rival) Banville, whose
cheerful facility within the mythological and Hellenistic mode he
must often have envied, as he strenuously battled with his own less
compliant (and astringently 'modern') Muse. This contrast between
the two poets emerges very clearly in the paragraph—in certain
respects almost a paraphrase of our present poem, but with the note
of self-accusation latent rather than openly sounded—with which
Baudelaire, in 1861, chose to conclude his essentially generous
tribute to his friend:

. . . Théodore de Banville refuse de se pencher sur ces marécages de
sang, sur ces abîmes de boue. Comme l'art antique, il n'exprime que ce
qui est beau, joyeux, noble, grand, rhythmique. Aussi dans ses œuvres,
vous n'entendrez pas les dissonances, les discordances des musiques du
sabbat, non plus que les glapissements de l'ironie, cette vengeance du
vaincu. Dans ses vers, tout a un air de fête et d'innocence, même la
volupté. Sa poésie n'est pas seulement un regret, une nostalgie, elle est
même un retour très-volontaire vers l'état paradisiaque. A ce point de
vue, nous pouvons donc le considérer comme un original de la nature
la plus courageuse. En pleine atmosphère satanique ou romantique, au
milieu d'un concert d'imprécations, il a l'audace de chanter la bonté

des Dieux, et d'être un parfait *classique*. Je veux que ce mot soit entendu ici dans le sens le plus noble, dans le sens vraiment historique.

(1862 text, *Les Poëtes français*, IV, 586)

Baudelaire's own neo-pagan aspirations, however, though sharing something of the essential hedonism of Banville's, are much less firmly rooted in the literature and mythology of Greek antiquity, and indeed are perhaps nearer to the eclectic and 'mystical' polytheism of a Nerval.[1] Most important of all, Baudelaire in his assimilation of pagan values remains a true Romantic rather than a Classicist; throughout this period, he declares his strong (and eloquent) opposition to neo-classicism whether in literature or in art,[2] and it would be entirely misleading to conceive of the tercets of *La Muse malade* as being in any strict aesthetic sense a gloss on Goethe's dictum 'Classicism is health, Romanticism sickness'.

Before turning back to discuss the second part of *J'aime le souvenir de ces époques nues*, I must mention a poem, *La Caravane des Bohémiens* (ultimately to be entitled *Bohémiens en voyage*), which demonstrates that the admired harmony between Man and Nature need not be the exclusive prerogative of primitive societies, but is still to be found, even within the Western world, among such ethno-

---

[1] Cf. Prarond, *CML* II, 1158. For further evidence of B.'s paganism or atheism during this period, and of his admiration for pagan peoples and cultures, cf.: Le Vavasseur, cit. *EJC*, 20 ('païen par révolte'); Chennevières, *L'Artiste*, March, 1889, p. 211: ('Baudelaire et Banville étaient avant tout des artistes, des payens [sic] néo-grecs ou plutôt néo-latins, de la meilleure décadence'); *La Fanfarlo*, ed. Pichois, 50 (of Samuel Cramer: 'il était athée avec passion'); ibid. 82, 87; *Salon de 1846*, *CE* 196 ('La vie ancienne ... était faite surtout pour le plaisir des yeux ; et ce paganisme journalier a merveilleusement servi les arts'); his choice of *The Young Enchanter* (subtitled 'From a Papyrus of Herculaneum') for trans. and publication under his own name in Feb.1846 (see W. T. Bandy, *MF*, Feb. 1950, 233–47). For a brief general account of contemporary 'paganism', see *FMA* 277–8; for the general kinship, during this period, between B. and Banville, see J. Pommier, *Dans les chemins de B.*, 196–200, 205–9.

[2] Cf. *Un Soutien du valet de trèfle*, 1841 (anonymous verse satire, written in collaboration with Le Vavasseur, and aimed, through Cas. Delavigne, at Ancelot; see *OCP* 1590–1); *L'École païenne* (1852; p. 97, below); the chap. 'Ponsard', in the *Mystères galans* of 1844 (*OP* I, 105–13; cf. ibid. 482–3); *Salon de 1846*, *CE* 177–9, 201; the paragraph under the heading 'Réouverture des théâtres' in the short-lived Republican journal launched in 1848 by B., Champfleury and Toubin (*OP* I, 198; 'Ne sommes-nous pas plus grands aujourd'hui que *Brutus*, etc.?'). Cf. also, *AR* 361, the retrospective opening paragraph of the 1861 art. on Pierre Dupont.

logical 'sports' as the gipsies — those surviving 'primitives' who
somehow have contrived to evade the deadening conformity and
sophistication of the societies through which, elusively, they move.[1]
The quatrains of this sonnet are for the most part the faithful
'transposition' of an engraving by Callot—the first in his series of
four, Les Bohémiens:[2]

> La tribu prophétique aux prunelles ardentes
> Hier s'est mise en route emportant ses petits
> Sur son dos ou livrant à leurs fiers appétits
> Le trésor toujours prêt des mamelles pendantes.
>
> Les hommes vont à pied sous leurs armes luisantes
> Le long du chariot où les leurs sont blottis,
> Promenant sur le ciel des yeux appesantis
> Par le morne regret des chimères absentes.

(MS. 1851–2)

The sole respect in which Baudelaire here diverges from his graphic
'model', is in the stress he lays on the gipsies' gift of prophecy: thus
in Callot's gipsies we find no trace of that mournful longing for a
chimerical 'elsewhere' here lent to them by Baudelaire, nor even of
the ardent, *searching* intensity of glance ('La tribu prophétique aux
prunelles ardentes') he imputes to them in his opening line.[3] In the
tercets, on the other hand, Baudelaire departs more radically from
his model, and in so doing broaches the true and *immediate* theme of

---

[1]For B.'s perennial sense of kinship with gipsies, his feeling for the nomadic
way of life, cf. the following texts (listed in roughly chronological order):
OP I, 80–1 (*La Fin de don Juan*: 'Cette race bizarre a pour moi le charme de
l'inconnu'), 101 (project for *Un drame sur les Bohémiens*); *JI* 94 (*Mon Cœur
mis à nu* XXXVIII: 'glorifier le vagabondage et ce qu'on peut appeler le Bohémian-
isme'); *PPP* 116–18 (*Les Vocations,* the whole final section).

[2]The *first,* rather than the *first two* (*pace* K. Gallas, cit. *FMCB* 615)—as I
hope elsewhere to have the opportunity of showing. See also, for this source:
FMCB 318 (E. Bernard cit.); J. Pommier, *Dans les chemins de B.*, 293; J.
Prévost, *B.*, 163; *FMA* 289–90 and reprod.; *FMPP*, reprod. facing p. 81.

[3]I say 'in *Callot's* gipsies' advisedly, since the verse legend accompanying the
print does admittedly stress (but ironically, as J. Prévost has observed, *B.*, 163)
the gipsies' preoccupation, as fortune-tellers, with 'future things': 'Ces pauvres
gueux pleins de bonadventures / Ne portent rien que des Choses futures'. As
to the further 'subtle' and 'significant' modifications of the Callot original,
detected by Mme M. Menemencioglu in the sonnet's quatrains (see her art. in
Cahiers de l'Association des Études françaises, 1966, pp. 228–30), these in my
view go beyond anything that is even implied, let alone stated, in B.'s (unforced)
text.

the poem, to which the quatrains (or at least the first quatrain, with its retrospective 'hier') had formed merely the antecedent. Yesterday the gipsies set off—and today (or any day, henceforward):

> Du fond de son palais verdoyant, le grillon
> En les voyant passer, redouble sa chanson.
> Cybèle qui les aime augmente ses verdures,
>
> Fait couler les rochers et fleurit le désert
> A ces chers voyageurs pour lesquels est ouvert
> L'empire familier des ténèbres futures.

Callot's swashbuckling rogues have here, in Baudelaire's version, become a race apart, a tribe of brooding seers who as nomads enjoy the special favours of Nature: for them the cricket 'redoubles' his song, for them Cybele 'fondly' refreshes and fructifies the desert.[1] The concluding couplet, by its renewed emphasis on their gift of prophecy, serves at once to explain this privileged status, and to relate it to Baudelaire's whole Nature-philosophy during this period: if Nature (in the form of the chirping cricket, the bounteous Earth-Goddess) thus extends its protection and encouragement to the gipsies, it is because by virtue of their intuitions these 'cherished' travellers also—like the primitive communities of *J'aime le souvenir de ces époques nues* and of Baudelaire's 'exotic' poems—reveal themselves to be in harmonious communion with the true elemental forces of the universe.[2]

The negative counterpart to the cult of the primitive is, as we have seen from *Moesta et errabunda* and *A une Indienne*, the denunciation of modern civilization—a denunciation that becomes fully explicit in the second part of *J'aime le souvenir de ces époques nues*. The con-

---

[1]M. Menemencioglu, in her art. cit., pp. 231-5, shows that in presenting the gipsies in this light, B. has elected to follow a *literary* tradition going back at least to Cervantes. I see no textual or other justification for the common assumption that B. intends his gipsies to symbolize the Poet or the creative artist.

[2]Perhaps also because, as nomads, they are brought into a more continuous and sympathetic relationship with Nature—and happily have no roots in the decadent civilization of the towns? Cf. in this connection the anecdote concerning Paganini and the Spanish guitarist, recounted by B. in *Du Vin et du hachish* (pub. 1851): 'Ils menaient à eux deux la grande vie vagabonde des bohémiens, des musiciens ambulants, des gens sans famille et sans patrie . . . . Mon Espagnol avait un talent tel, qu'il pouvait dire comme Orphée: "Je suis le maître de la nature." ' (*PA* 210).

text here, it will be remembered, is the poet's admiring evocation of the far-distant 'ages of nakedness'; against this idyllic picture, he now sets the sorry decadence into which, in our own age, the human body has fallen—the grotesque and chilling spectacle that confronts the Poet seeking some modern equivalent of the 'native grandeurs' of the pagan nude:

> Le poète aujourd'hui, quand il veut concevoir
> Ces natives grandeurs, aux lieux où se peut voir
> La nudité de l'homme et celle de la femme,
> Sent un froid ténébreux envelopper son âme
> A l'aspect du tableau plein d'épouvantement
> Des monstruosités que voile un vêtement;
> Des visages manqués et plus laids que des masques;
> De tous ces pauvres corps, maigres, ventrus ou flasques,
> Que le Dieu de l'utile, implacable et serein,
> Enfants, emmaillotta dans ses langes d'airain,
> De ces femmes, hélas! pâles comme des cierges,
> Que ronge et que nourrit la honte, et de ces vierges,
> Du vice maternel traînant l'hérédité
> Et toutes les hideurs de la fécondité!

(1857 proofs, ll. 15–28)

Just as the eulogy of pagan nakedness implied the larger concept of a harmonious natural order, so too the diatribe against the modern 'body unbeautiful'[1] implies a critique (sketched out already in *A une Indienne*) of the whole social and moral order from which such ugliness springs. Thus it is not merely that our modern garments restrain true freedom of movement and prevent us from delighting fitly in the caresses of sun and air; nor, still worse, that swaddling-clothes in infancy, the 'brutal corset' (deplored in *A une Indienne*) in girlhood, may actually cripple and deform our bodies;[2] more signif-

---

[1] Very probably, when B. here speaks of the 'lieux où se peut voir / La nudité de l'homme et celle de la femme', he has in mind the particular occasions or places (bed, bath, surgical amphitheatre) named, in the identical context, in a passage (cit. p. 58, below) from the *Salon de 1846*. Cf., however, the suggestion made by J. Prévost, *B.*, 188–9, concerning the presumed influence of Daumier.

[2] Cf. the comment by Bougainville on the women of Oceania: 'ce qui les distingue, c'est la beauté de leur corps, dont les contours n'ont pas été défigurés par quinze ans de tortures' (*Voyage autour du monde*, 214, cit. G. Chinard, *L'Amérique et le rêve exotique*, 381). Or again Delacroix, in the concluding entry of his Moroccan Journal of 1832: 'Ils [les Maures] sont plus près de la nature de mille manières: leurs habits, la forme de leurs souliers. Aussi, la beauté s'unit à tout ce qu'ils font. Nous autres, dans nos corsets, nos souliers

icant still is that this should be done in the name of that stern modern God of 'Utility' whom we have substituted for the bounteous
Earth-Goddess of our ancestors. Or again, the infirmities of our
virgins, the waxen pallor of our women, even by implication the
'hideousness' of their 'pregnancies'[1]—all are stigmatized as the
product of our corroding modern shames or 'hereditary' modern
vice. In short, in abjuring our pristine nakedness, we have donned
the garments of anxiety and guilt—those encumbrances from which
primitive man and woman were so notably free: 'Alors l'homme et la
femme en leur agilité/Jouissaient sans mensonge et sans anxiété'; the
curse we have condemned ourselves to live under, is that of *acquired*
(rather than original) sin.[2]

   This severe indictment is unexpectedly qualified in the third and

---

étroits, nos gaines ridicules, nous faisons pitié. La grâce se venge de notre
science'. (*Journal,* ed. Joubin, I, 152). The same antithesis is made by Diderot,
in more comprehensive terms, in certain *Salons* which B. is likely to have
read during this period; cf. J. Pommier, *Dans les chemins de B.*, 281–2. As for
B.'s implied (and enlightened) condemnation of swaddling-clothes, this seems
to me to derive from the first book of Rousseau's *Émile*; cf. Garnier ed., 13–16,
38–9.

   [1]This particular stricture might appear to contradict the earlier reference,
in the first part of the poem, to the 'tender' fecundity of Cybele; but presumably what now, in B.'s eyes, makes fecundity hideous, is that it *intensifies*
the ugliness assumed to be endemic in the modern female body. The revulsion
from pregnancy ascribed to Samuel Cramer (*Fanfarlo,* ed. Pichois, 89: 'l'amour
était chez lui . . . surtout *l'admiration et l'appétit du beau*; il considérait la
reproduction comme un vice de l'amour, la grossesse comme une maladie
d'araignée'—my italics) can likewise be seen, if replaced in its proper context,
to be essentially aesthetic in origin, rather than indicative of that 'revolt against
the laws of Nature' (*FMCB* 302; cf. ibid. 345), which we shall find to belong
to a much later phase of B.'s thought. Cf., however, in the context of B.'s
youthful 'cult of depravity', the admired sterility of the 'femme belle' of
Allégorie (pp. 23–4, above), of the eponymous *Deux bonnes sœurs* (ll. 3–4), of Jeanne
herself in *Avec ses vêtements* (l. 14), of the 'prêtresse de débauche' in the verse
fragment *Noble femme au bras fort . . . (FMA* 226, ll. 8–12). As to Cramer's
wayward preference, expressed on the previous page of B.'s novella (ed. Pichois,
88), for 'La Fanfarlo' in her dancer's costume rather than in the state of nature
more truly warranted by the actual situation, this is surely to be explained on
psychological rather than aesthetic or philosophical grounds.

   [2]The poet's whole context being resolutely pagan rather than Christian, I
assume the chronology of B.'s 'naked ages' to be *post*-lapsarian—this despite
the obvious echo of the 2nd chap. of *Genesis,* v. 25: 'And they were both naked,
the man and his wife, and were not ashamed'. For a pertinent general comment
on this continuity between pagan and Christian mythologies, see H. N. Fairchild,
The Noble Savage, 7.

concluding section of the poem—so unexpectedly, indeed, that one suspects these lines to have been intended originally for some quite separate poem (or poems). The new concession to modernity involves, moreover, the abandonment of the poem's basic antithesis between the two forms, ancient and modern, of the human nude; the focus of interest now shifts from the grotesquely tortured modern body to the intriguingly ravaged modern face, and to certain qualities of posture and demeanour summed up in the telling phrase 'des beautés de langueur':

> Nous avons, il est vrai, nations corrompues,
> Aux peuples anciens des beautés inconnues:
> Des visages rongés par les chancres du cœur,
> Et comme qui dirait des beautés de langueur;
>
> (ll. 29–32)

This recognition (however grudging) of the authentic beauty that may after all be discerned in modern life, finds its more explicit echo in certain other texts of the period. Thus in the quatrains of the sonnet *L'Idéal*, the poet specifies (albeit dismissively) the type of 'twittering', etiolated beauty captured by the contemporary draughtsman Gavarni. Or again, after characterizing, in a passage of the *Salon de 1846*, that inveterate 'melancholy' of Delacroix' which makes of him 'the true painter of the nineteenth century', Baudelaire notes as a corollary that the women Delacroix portrays have nearly all a certain *ailing* quality, a *morbid* beauty that as it were shines from within.[1] Finally, and most relevant of all, there is the concluding chapter of this same *Salon de 1846*, in which, precisely, Baudelaire sets out to define and exemplify the 'heroism', the 'epic' beauty, of modern life; having singled out the *frock-coat* as being (of all things) the characteristic emblem of modern beauty, he goes on to make this highly pertinent observation:

La vie parisienne est féconde en sujets poétiques et merveilleux. Le merveilleux nous enveloppe et nous abreuve comme l'atmosphère; mais nous ne le voyons pas.

Le *nu*, cette chose si chère aux artistes, cet élément nécessaire de succès, est aussi fréquent et aussi nécessaire que dans la vie ancienne:—au lit, au bain, à l'amphithéâtre. Les moyens et les motifs de la peinture sont également abondants et variés; mais il y a un élément nouveau, qui est la beauté moderne.   (*CE* 200–201)

---

[1] *CE* 119–20; cf. ibid., 124: 'les mornes beautés de Delacroix, telles qu'on peut se les figurer: de grandes femmes pâles, noyées dans le satin!'

It will be noted that this passage in effect refutes the second part
of the present poem, by invoking the argument of its third part!
(Nothing could better demonstrate the signal incoherence of the
poem's structure.) But the concluding lines of all hold a still further
surprise in store. What seemed to begin as a reluctant enumeration
of modern forms of beauty, turns out to be the mere pretext for a
further nostalgic tribute—this time to the simplicity and gentle
innocence of *youth*, imaged in the 'corresponding' forms of Nature
(blue sky, birds, flowers) and thus once more attesting, indirectly,
the renewed harmony of Man and his environment:

> Mais ces inventions de nos muses tardives
> N'empêcheront jamais les races maladives
> De rendre à la jeunesse un hommage profond,
> —A la sainte jeunesse, à l'air simple, au doux front,
> A l'œil limpide et clair ainsi qu'une eau courante,
> Et qui va répandant sur tout, insouciante
> Comme l'azur du ciel, les oiseaux et les fleurs,
> Ses parfums, ses chansons et ses douces chaleurs!

> (ll. 33–40)

This idyllic vision of youth has been thought so uncharacteristic
of Baudelaire as to suggest a conscious imitation of Hugo in his
rhapsodic vein.[1] Certainly he appears at one time to have thought
poorly enough of it himself, if it is indeed to these verses that he is
referring when, in *La Fanfarlo*, he offers his 'prose translation', in
very similar vein, of what he calls 'quelques mauvaises stances' in
Cramer's (i.e. his own) earlier manner.[2] Yet both this prose passage
within *La Fanfarlo*, and the verses it putatively 'transposes' (i.e. the
concluding lines of *J'aime le souvenir de ces époques nues*), have, as
I suggested in an earlier chapter, a clear relevance to Baudelaire's
own childhood; moreover, childhood and adolescence would seem
for him during the present period to be linked not only (as in
J'aime le souvenir de ces époques nues) with the original Eden of
primitive Man, but also with the tropical paradise evoked in the
'exotic' poems. Thus in the final verses of a poem already discussed,
Moesta et errabunda, the poet's mind seems drawn as if compulsive-

---

[1]*FMCB* 303, *FMC* 413. For a similar association of youth ('tout ce que
l'Idylle a de plus enfantin') with a gently harmonious pastoral background,
cf. (p. 18, above) the poem *Paysage [parisien]*.
[2]Pichois ed., 59–60 (cit. p. 5, above); cf. ibid., 105.

ly from the one lost paradise to the other—back over the years to
the far-distant idylls of adolescent or 'childish' love:

> Comme vous êtes loin, paradis parfumé!
>
> Mais le vert paradis des amours enfantines,
> Les courses, les chansons, les baisers, les bouquets,
> Les violons mourants derrière les collines
> Avec les pots de vin, le soir, dans les bosquets,
> —Mais le vert paradis des amours enfantines,
>
> L'innocent paradis, plein de plaisirs furtifs,
> Est-il déjà plus loin que l'Inde et que la Chine?
> —Peut-on le rappeler avec des cris plaintifs,
> Et l'animer encor d'une voix argentine,
> L'innocent paradis plein de plaisirs furtifs?

(1855 text, ll. 20–30)

The 'Elsewhere' of Time here merges almost imperceptibly into the
'Elsewhere' of Space—an altogether smoother transition, it will be
noted, than that which brings in the cognate final section of *J'aime
le souvenir de ces époques nues*. For whatever the 'natural' continuity
of idea linking the youth of the world with the youth of individual
Man,[1] the fact remains that between the first and third parts of this
latter poem there is interposed a section—the contrasting diatribe
against the moderns—which is at total variance with the naïvely
exalted tone of the concluding lines; moreover the syntactical
expedient whereby Baudelaire passes, concessively, from the one
theme to the other ('But decadent though our modern forms of
beauty may be, we nevertheless cannot withhold our admiration for
the irresistible charm of youth, etc'.), is surely perfunctory in the
extreme. I would thus (as I have said) hazard the view that these
final lines were originally destined for some quite different poem
(an ode to youth? an 'ecologue' of the type envisaged in *Paysage
[parisien]*? an idyll of young love, such as is fleetingly sketched
in *Moesta et errabunda*?), and are here brought in merely because
by their convenient if incongruous 'finality' they enable Baudelaire
to round off (after a fashion) this whole somewhat rambling
composition.

I must here mention once again a text already cited, for its autobiographical implications, in my introductory chapter:

[1]Cf. G. Blin, *B.*, 121: 'Par un glissement naturel de l'imagination, Baudelaire
transporte dans l'enfance la splendeur irrémédiable de l'âge d'or'.

Pourtant, sous la tutelle invisible d'un Ange,
L'Enfant déshérité s'enivre de soleil,
Et dans tout ce qu'il boit et dans tout ce qu'il mange
Retrouve l'ambroisie et le nectar vermeil.

Il joue avec le vent, cause avec le nuage,
Et s'enivre en chantant du chemin de la croix,
Et l'Esprit qui le suit dans son pélerinage
Pleure de le voir gai comme un oiseau des bois.

(Bénédiction, 1857 text, ll. 21–8)

In the second of these two verses, Baudelaire might well seem to be renewing the stock Romantic convention of the 'Child of Nature'— a convention, closely allied to that of the 'Noble Savage', which has been well defined in these terms by H. N. Fairchild:

Every reader of romantic literature is familiar with the child of nature— generally, though not always, a girl—who is born and grows to maturity in the heart of some wild region untouched by civilization, and who imbibes beauty, innocence and an unerring moral sense from the scenery which surrounds her. It is the heroine of Wordsworth's *Three Years She Grew* who best represents the type.[1]

Baudelaire's previous verse, however, with its hints of pre-natal felicity and of an anterior 'heritage' of which the child has now been divested ('L'Enfant *déshérité*', ' *Retrouve* l'ambroisie et le nectar vermeil'), suggests a conception closer to that of another poem of Wordsworth's, the ode on *Intimations of Immortality* ;[2] and indeed

[1] *The Noble Savage,* 366. Rather than Wordsworth's Lucy, B.'s own model is more likely to have been Laprade's eponymous *Hermia*; cf. especially these lines, which are interpolated within the long description (*Odes et poëmes*, 1843, pp. 72–92) of the 'enfant béni' gently communing with each element of Nature. Cf. also, however, Balzac's *L'Enfant maudit* (*FMCB* 286: R. Hughes cit.)—as equally B.'s own sonnet *A Ivonne Pen-Moore* (p. 30, above); for a later reference, in the context of Banville's 'lyricism', to the 'lost Eden' of childhood, cf. the art. of 1861 on this poet, *AR* 355.

[2] This suggestive analogy has been made by L. J. Austin, *Univers poétique de B.*, 324–5; cf. especially Wordsworth's opening lines: 'There was a time when meadow, grove and stream, / The earth and every common sight, / To me did seem / Apparelled in celestial light . . .' A no less striking affinity would be with the rapturous evocation of childhood in Traherne's *Centuries of Meditations*: 'All appeared new, and strange at first, inexpressibly rare and delightful and beautiful . . . The corn was orient and immortal wheat, which never should be reaped, nor was ever sown. I thought it had stood from everlasting to everlasting . . . The green trees when I saw them first . . . transported and ravished me, their sweetness and unusual beauty made my heart to leap, and almost mad with ecstasy, they were such strange and wonderful

the celestial origins claimed for this Child seem his not so much (as in Wordsworth's poem) by generic right,[1] as by unquestioned Messianic privilege: sent down on earth by God, almost as if His emissary,[2] this Poet is by clear analogy assimilated to that other Saviour of Whom, with prophetic irony (and to his Guardian Angel's compassionate sorrow), he so exultantly sings: 'Il s'enivre en chantant du chemin de la croix . . .'

A final text, *La Lune offensée*, offers a rather more subtle denunciation of the modern age than any we have hitherto encountered in Baudelaire.[3] The tone and attitude of this sonnet differ markedly

---

things . . . The skies were mine, and so were the sun and moon and stars, and all the World was mine; and I the only spectator and enjoyer of it' (Dobell ed., 156–8). This passage has previously been invoked in respect of B. by P. Quennell, *B. and the Symbolists*, 24–5, but in the context of a passage (cit. p. 5, above) from *Le Peintre de la vie moderne,* rather than of the present verses from *Bénédiction.*

[1]Cf. Part V: '. . . trailing clouds of glory do *we* come / From God who is *our* home . . .', etc.

[2]Cf. ll. 1–2: 'Lorsque, par un décret des puissances suprêmes, / Le Poète apparaît en ce monde ennuyé . . .'

[3]This poem, though published only in 1862, is among those figuring on Prarond's 'second list' of poems composed if not by 1843, then between 1843 and 1846; he says specifically: 'j'ai quelque souvenir du second tercet' (*CML* II, 1155). If, as J. Mouquet has supposed, *VR* 12–14, Le Vavasseur's poem *Pastel,* dated Jan. 1843 and published a few months later in the collection *Vers,* is a *reply* to B.'s sonnet, then December 1842 would be the latest date at which the latter could have been composed. But this whole assumption seems to me a dubious one: the sequence of texts could just as well have been reversed, with *La Lune offensée* as a reply to *Pastel,* and in any case the analogies between the two poems are a good deal less comprehensive than those which link B.'s sonnet with some verses by Gautier, first published by him in *RPa,* 14/4/1844, under the title *Le Soleil et la lune*; these latter analogies (detailed hereunder, p. 64 n. 1) are indeed so striking as to suggest that we have here an unmistakable source. If this, together with Prarond's chronology, be accepted, we could presume the poem to have been composed in its first draft between March 1844 and the end of 1846; further support would be lent to such a dating by the presumed 'autobiographical' interpretation of the first tercet (see below), since it was precisely in 1844–5, after the appointment of Ancelle as 'conseil judiciaire', that B.'s hostility to his mother was at its greatest; cf. in this connection the savage letter of Oct. 1844, *LS* 213–14. If, finally, it is agreed, with J. Prévost, *B.,* 150–1 that this second tercet derives from Goya's engraving *Hasta la muerte* (*Caprichos,* no. 55), then it should be noted that this engraving is among those described in the 'Catalogue raisonné de l'œuvre gravé de . . . Goya . . .' annexed by Eug. Piot, in the *Cabinet de l'amateur* of Sept. 1842, to Gautier's article on this artist—an article (expanded from an earlier essay

from those we have noted in Baudelaire's other sonnet concerning
the moon, *Tristesses de la lune*: here, in place of the gently idyllic
fantasia, with its 'pious poet' carefully storing away the moon's
'furtive' (and cherished) tear, we have a satirical dialogue in which
an 'offended', even scandalized moon is teasingly interrogated by a
wholly *im*pious poet. Nothing indeed could be more irreverent than
the jocular familiarity with which he now apostrophises his 'vieille
Cynthia' (as he presumes to call her):

> O Lune qu'adoraient discrètement nos pères,
> Du haut des pays bleus où, radieux sérail,
> Les astres vont te suivre en pimpant attirail,
> Ma vieille Cynthia, lampe de nos repaires,
>
> Vois-tu les amoureux, sur leurs grabats prospères,
> De leur bouche en dormant montrer le frais émail?
> Le poëte buter du front sur son travail?
> Ou sous les gazons secs s'accoupler les vipères?
>
> Sous ton domino jaune, et d'un pied clandestin,
> Vas-tu, comme jadis, du soir jusqu'au matin,
> Baiser d'Endymion les grâces surannées?

> (1862 text)

It is the moon, however, who has the final word:

> —'Je vois ta mère, enfant de ce siècle appauvri,
> Qui vers son miroir penche un lourd amas d'années,
> Et plâtre artistement le sein qui t'a nourri!'

After which, we may presume, the poet retires discomfited—not
only by the uncomfortable pungency of the moon's riposte, but also
by the very precision with which his own half-affectionate raillery

---

of 1838 on the *Caprichos* alone; see Spoelberch de Lovenjoul, *Gautier*, I,
pp. 165 no. 359 bis, and 245 no. 578 bis) to which B. explicitly refers in his
own *Quelques caricaturistes étrangers*, *CE* 436; Piot's description runs, notably:
'Une vieille étique, assise devant son miroir, ajuste un ornement sur sa tête
déjà couverte d'une perruque noire. Devant elle, deux hommes dans l'attitude
admirative . . . Il est ici question de l'éternelle coquetterie de certaines grandes
dames de la cour' (p. 353). Thus it may well be that B. owed both his introduction to the world of the *Caprichos*, and one immediate stimulus, at least,
for the composition of the present sonnet, to the Gautier-Piot article of 1842.

has been turned against him.[1] For the moon, in the second quatrain, is in effect shown as prying into all the secret haunts and intimate activities of man and beast; the first tercet even imputes to her a certain unbecoming coquetry, as the aged pursuer of a 'faded' and decrepit lover (Endymion, with his 'grâces surannées'). The moon's rejoinder takes up these oblique taunts: is not her coquetry, she would seem to imply, far surpassed by that of the poet's mother, 'surprised' at her mirror as she labours to 'rejuvenate' her faded charms?[2] And in thus 'exposing' these womanly artifices, does the moon not show herself able to *pry* still more searchingly and disconcertingly than the

---

[1] I would here note the particularly marked analogy of *structure* with the Gautier poem aforementioned. It is of course true that in Gautier's case the two protagonists are the moon and the sun (hence the poem's successive titles from 1845: *Le Soleil et la lune*, *La Lune et le soleil*), rather than the moon and the poet. But with Gautier, too, we have an 'invocation' to the moon ranging over the greater part of the poem (i.e. over 5 of its 6 quatrains); a 'planet's-eye view' of the multifarious activity of night; the moon's discouraging and tart reply compressed within a single stanza. It is Gautier's fourth verse, however, with its 'pas clandestins' anticipating B.'s 'pied clandestin', and its similar, if less poetic, suggestion of an amorous retinue of stars ('astres libertins' in the one case, 'radieux sérail' in the other), that offers the most specific verbal analogy with *La Lune offensée*: 'Des planètes équivoques / Et des astres libertins, / Croyant que tu les provoques, / Suivront tes pas clandestins' (*España*, ed. Jasinski, 193). The divergences between the two poems are of course no less clearly marked, and the tone, phrasing and verse-form of *Le Soleil et la lune* are of a flippancy quite alien to B.'s satiric purposes as I shall analyse these hereunder. (Certain details of this analysis, I would add, are borrowed from my article 'Two Poems of B.', *LM*, 1956, pp. 485–6.)

[2] This is the image which J. Prévost has derived from Goya's engraving (*Hasta la muerte*) of the hideous old lady 'beautifying' herself before her mirror (and her 'little friends') on her 75th birthday; cf. pp. 62–3 n. 3, above. But it should be noted that B. could equally well have gone, for this image, to a literary model, viz. the famous lines from Racine's *Athalie* (494–6), in which the queen describes her mother Jezebel's appearance to her in a dream: 'Même elle avait encor cet éclat emprunté / Dont elle eut soin de peindre et d'orner son visage, / Pour réparer des ans l'irréparable outrage'. These lines would seem to have held for B. a fascination equal to that of the Goya print; thus he borrows them as his epigraph for the original version of 1860 of *L'Amour du mensonge*, and might seem to be echoing them in this phrase from his early poem *Tu mettrais l'univers entier dans ta ruelle* (cit. *in toto* p. 23, above): 'Tes yeux . . . / Usent insolemment d'un pouvoir emprunté . . .' (ll. 5, 7). Of the same woman, be it noted, he goes on to say (ll. 11–12): 'Comment n'as-tu pas honte, et comment n'as-tu pas / Devant tous les miroirs vu pâlir tes appas?'—a further analogy with *La Lune offensée* suggesting that both poems were completed during the same (early) period.

poet had supposed?[1] Nor is this the only sense in which the latter finds the tables to be turned on him at the last. The various intimate activities catalogued in the second quatrain are chosen with no particular indulgence towards mankind; indeed, the antecedent word 'repaires', with its suggestion of a criminal's or a wild animal's 'lair', carries a distinctly depreciative implication.[2] Yet these activities have at least a certain primal creative energy in common: the lovers prospering in sleep, despite the poverty of their 'grabats'; the poet striving to complete or to perfect his work; the vipers in their sinister couplings beneath the dry grass. What the moon 'really' sees, however, from the judicial remoteness of her 'pays bleus', is an act not of spontaneous vigour but of sterile artifice; in her description of the mother seeking to repair and disguise the ravages of the years, in her scathing allusion to the 'siècle appauvri', she in effect substitutes for the crude dynamism of the poet's world, a very different and wholly unflattering picture. '*This*, rather than *that*, is what truly goes on in your impoverished nineteenth-century world!'[3]

This brings me to the question of the poem's anti-modernism—explicit in the derisive formula of the final tercet, 'enfant de ce siècle appauvri',[4] implicit (as I shall suggest) throughout the poem as a

[1] Cf. her altogether more benign counterparts in other poems of B.'s: the incurious moon of *Tristesses de la lune* (p. 15, above), the 'discreet' moon of *Le Désir de peindre* (*PPP* 132: 'la lune paisible et discrète visitant le sommeil des hommes *purs*'—my italics). In *La Lune offensée*, incidentally, it is the moon-worshippers our 'fathers' who are 'discreet': a reference to covert eighteenth-century paganism? or are these our *remote* ancestors, rather ('pères' in the sense of 'aïeux')?

[2] Cf. J. Crépet, *FMCB* 564, who glosses: '*Repaires*, peut-être pour traduire la haine de l'auteur à l'égard de l'homme, assimilé par là aux bêtes malfaisantes' —but adds: 'ou pour les besoins de la rime?' The first of these comments, however, assumes a generalized misanthropy on B.'s part, such as belongs only in my view (cf. Part Two, Chap. VII, below, 'Nature without Man') to a much later phase of his thought.

[3] I have left wholly out of account—since it does not affect the present issue—the question of the identity of the 'mother' here cruelly ridiculed. Did B. really here have in mind his own mother, Mme Aupick? (See *FMCB* 563; Prévost, *B.*, 150.) I am now disposed to accept this view, rather than to argue (as, previously—*mea culpa*—in my art. cit., *LM* 1956, pp. 482–4) that the 'mother' is herself to be identified with the 'siècle appauvri'; cf., however, M. Ruff, *L'Esprit du mal*, 448 n. 11.

[4] It should be stressed that it is this final, explicitly anti-modern section of the poem that Prarond remembers (vaguely) as having heard around 1843 or in 1846: 'j'ai quelque souvenir du second tercet' (*CML* II, 1155). Cf. the similar phrase, 'un siècle vaurien', which occurs in the first extant version pub. 1851) of another sonnet composed during this period, *L'Idéal*.

whole. Baudelaire has in effect reproved his impious 'self' for thus 'blaspheming' against a deity of Nature—against the moon. But this moon, with her retinue of stars, her flock of (discreet) worshippers, her legendary courtship of Endymion, is a 'classical' and pagan moon; the poet she rebukes, and whom she worsts in argument, is by contrast a child of his (impoverished) century, an effete 'modern'. And thus by implication, as more explicitly in *La Muse malade* or *J'aime le souvenir de ces époques nues* . . ., the decadence and morbidity of the present century are set contemptuously in relation with the exemplary vigour of antiquity.[1] But what in the present poem gives specific pungency to Baudelaire's anti-modernism, is, as I have indicated, his use of the vocative phrase 'enfant de ce siècle appauvri'[2]—a phrase which for his contemporary readers could scarcely fail to carry a certain *representative* implication: since the publication in 1836 of Musset's *La Confession d'un enfant du siècle*, the cliché of the 'child of our time' had increasingly imposed itself, and with it the facile assumption that the typical young man of the 1830's or 1840's was a restless debauchee tormented, among other things, by the desire to *know*, the compulsion to probe and analyse endlessly every motive and action.[3] Baudelaire himself, during the present phase of his career, seems certainly to have subscribed to this psychology;

[1]An idea perhaps explicitly voiced some years later, in the Introductory article on the *Exposition universelle 1855*: 'Nous vivons . . . dans un siècle orgueilleux qui se croit au-dessus des mésaventures de la Grèce et de Rome' (*CE* 230).

[2]To be read, in this context, 'O enfant de ce siècle appauvri, je vois ta mère', etc.

[3]Cf. in this connection the reference by Balzac, in *La Muse du Département*, to 'une de ces longues et monotones tragédies conjugales qui demeureraient éternellement inconnues, si l'avide scalpel du Dix-Neuvième siècle n'allait pas, conduit par la nécessité de trouver du nouveau, fouiller les coins les plus obscurs du cœur, ou, si vous voulez, ceux que la pudeur des siècles précédents avait respectés' (cit. J. B. Barrère, *RHLF*, 1967, p. 338)—or, again, the comment by Sainte-Beuve on Chateaubriand's René: 'René est le fils d'un siècle qui a tout examiné, tout mis en question' (*Chateaubriand et son groupe littéraire*, 1861 ed., I, 340). For this *'fils* du siècle' variant of the 'child' metaphor, cf. also the accusation levelled in Gautier's *Comédie de la mort* (1838), by the skull [sic] of the painter Raphael, against the 'sons' of an 'infamous' century which is declared to be in its 'death-throes' (*PC* ed. R. Jasinski, II, 22)—or the complaint made, a few years later, by Nerval: '. . . ne suis-je pas toujours, hélas! le fils d'un siècle déshérité d'illusions, qui a besoin de toucher pour croire, et de rêver le passé sur ses débris?' (*L'Artiste*, 11 Aug. 1844, p. 225; *Voyage en Orient*, ed. G. Rouger, I, 216).

thus the poet Samuel Cramer, in *La Fanfarlo*, describes his malady, and that of his fellows, in terms that strongly recall the self-accusations of Musset's Octave:

Nous nous sommes tellement appliqués à sophistiquer notre cœur, nous avons tant abusé du microscope pour étudier les hideuses excroissances et les honteuses verrues dont il est couvert, et que nous grossissons à plaisir, qu'il est impossible que nous parlions le langage des autres hommes. Ils vivent pour vivre, et nous, hélas! nous vivons pour savoir.[1]

Samuel Cramer is, by common consent, a self-portrait; but here is Baudelaire writing a few years later, in his article of 1852 on *Edgar Allan Poe, sa vie et ses ouvrages*, of the whole tribe of 'mystics':

Si vouloir à tout prix connaître la vérité est un grand crime, ou au moins peut conduire à de grandes fautes, si la niaiserie et l'insouciance sont une vertu et une garantie d'équilibre, je crois que nous devons être très-indulgents pour ces illustres coupables, car, *enfants du XVIIIᵉ et du XIXᵉ siècles*, ce même vice nous est à tous imputable.

(*OP* I, 292–3; my italics)

These connotations of the phrase 'enfant du siècle' cannot, I think, have been absent from Baudelaire's mind when he wrote *La Lune offensée*; indeed, the reproof uttered by the offended moon may be designed not merely to wound the poet by profaning a sacred object (i.e. his mother), but also to indict him, obliquely, for having exhibited the typical and pathological *curiosity* of his generation. For, after all, it is really the poet (and not the moon) who imagines those secret activities into which she is presumed to be 'prying'; it is not she, truly, who is the 'peeping Cynthia', but he who is the peeping Tom (or Charles)—the voyeur who by this same vicarious curiosity

[1] Pichois ed., 58–9; cf. Musset, *Confession d'un enfant du siècle, OC en prose*, Pléiade, 246–8, 252. B. borrows from this work for other episodes of his novella, as well as for various poems (see my art. cit., 'Pour une chronologie des *FM*', *RHLF*, 1967, pp. 352–4, as also p. 109 n. 1, below); its general theme was in any case well calculated to interest him during this period. In two further contemporary texts, B. is at pains to stress the primordial *innateness* of the spirit of curiosity: thus in the *Choix de maximes consolantes sur l'amour* (pub. March 1846), he declares 'la soif de l'inconnu' to be a 'sentiment . . . dont chacun porte en soi le germe plus ou moins développé' (*OP* II, 6–7); while again, in the prefatory Note to his translation of Poe's *Mesmeric Revelation* (pub. July 1848), he refers to 'cet esprit primitif de *chercherie*, . . . cet esprit inquisitorial, esprit de juge d'instruction, qui a peut-être ses racines dans les plus lointaines impressions de l'enfance' (*HE* 457).

reveals himself to be a true 'enfant du siècle'. By her use of this phrase, the moon thus implies an additional and covert accusation: 'You who *must* know everything, child of your century that you are— you ask me what I see as I shine down on your world?'

The poet who speaks in the first three verses is accordingly not so much Baudelaire alone, as Baudelaire the representative young poet of his time. Or should we rather say, Baudelaire-Musset? For Musset, as well as being the prime disseminator (if not the actual inventor[1]) of the 'enfant du siècle' myth, was also the author of the famous *Ballade à la lune*—the poet who in 1830 had dared to tease the 'moribund' moon with a whole series of disrespectful analogies, and to impute to her, in a concluding sequence of verses that was deemed publishable only in 1840,[2] curiosities still more scabrous than Baudelaire's sonnet was later to credit her with. Since Musset fails, in his poem, to accord the moon the right of reply, Baudelaire may have felt it only proper that he should repair this omission, and allow her a counter-attack aimed not only at the original 'enfant du siècle' and mocker of the moon (i.e. Musset),[3] but also at his poetic fellows, including the author of *La Lune offensée* . . .[4] Be this as it may, the Baudelaire who here tilts at his 'impoverished' century, is recognizably the same Baudelaire as throughout this period pursues —into childhood, into the remote classical past, across the oceans to far-distant tropical 'paradises'—his dream of an ideal 'elsewhere'. At the same time, he is clear-sighted enough to perceive that the dream is nothing more *than* a dream, that it has no true relevance to modern life; even at this stage of his career, he is unlikely to have shared the naive belief, held by certain of his neo-pagan friends, that modern man can still re-learn the lessons of classical or oriental antiquity, can still rediscover, from the example of primitive peoples, the vanished

---

[1]See, in this connection, A. Hoog, *YFS*, No. 13, pp. 42–3.

[2]See Musset, *PC*, Pléiade, 86–7 and 631 n. 7, and cf. ibid., ix, x.

[3]Cf. J. Pommier, *Mélanges Bonnerot*, 362: 'Les interrogations de la *Ballade à la lune* n'ont-elles pas commandé celles de *la Lune offensée*?'

[4]It is true that the Moon derided (wholly flippantly) by Musset, is the moon of his *own* day, and that he goes on to sigh, nostalgically, for the 'true' Moon of legend and story—for the virgin Diana unleashing her hounds after the stag, for Phœbe 'surprised' at her pool or bestowing upon 'a shepherd's lips' the gentlest of kisses (*PC* ed. Allem, 85). Musset, incidentally—more 'discreet' in this than B.—does not directly name Endymion . . . (or indeed Actæon).

art of living.[1] The modern poet, for his part, sigh though he may for the days when the great Pan ruled over harvests and verses alike, must nevertheless accept that (as the legend tells us) the great Pan is dead and has long been dead; must accept, likewise, that the island of Venus has become an arid waste symbolising (in its solitary 'inhabitant') the horrors of modern love—that the exotic paradise (like the paradise of childhood) is now lost beyond all recall—that the age-old harmony between Man and Nature has been finally and fatally disrupted.[2] Indeed, since Romanticism is by definition simply 'the most recent and topical expression of the beautiful', to call oneself a Romantic (as by implied allegiance does Baudelaire) while turning systematically towards the past, is nothing but a contradiction in terms.[3] Faced with the admitted corruptions and 'impoverishments' of his own century, the modern artist should thus resolve not merely to profit boldly, even cynically, from the opportunities it offers,[4] but also, more nobly, to seek out the latent beauty and 'heroism' its distinctive 'passions' may hold.[5] We shall see, in the ensuing

[1]Cf. (pp. 97–8, below) his later art., *L'Ecole païenne* (pub. Feb. 1852), with its satirical dialogue in which one ardent votary of the god Pan declares that Paganism alone, with its return to the 'true doctrines', can 'save the world' (*AR* 289–91). This particular passage is no doubt aimed at Nerval, as I hope to demonstrate fully on another occasion; other 'pagans', however, are no doubt incriminated elsewhere in the article. Cf. *AR* 533–4, and pp. 120 n. 1, 123 and n. 1, below.

[2]My references are, successively, to: *La Muse malade*; *L'Ecole païenne* (loc. cit.); *Voyage à Cythère*; *Moesta et errabunda*; *J'aime le souvenir de ces époques nues* . . .

[3]*CE* 89–90; cf. p. 53 and n. 2, above, as also my article, 'Les Esthétiques de B.', *RSH*, 1967, pp. 485–6.

[4]*OP* I, 241, brief notice (tagged on to the review of Ménard's *Prométhée délivré*, and therefore dated Feb. 1846) of a verse satire, *Le Siècle*, by one Bouniol: 'True, my good sir, these *are* corrupt and wicked times we live in; but the wise philosophy is to profit covertly from such a situation and to snatch at the opportunities if offers, rather than waste time on anathemas'— i.e. rather than imitate the author of *J'aime le souvenir de ces époques nues*, *La Lune offensée* and *L'Idéal*! Cf. this aside, that B. lets fall a month later in his *Choix de maximes consolantes sur l'amour*: 'Bien qu'il faille être de son siècle . . . (*OP* II, 10).

[5]*CE* 90, 196–201; cf. p. 58, above. A. Adam, *FMA* 278, relates B.'s newfound 'modernism' specifically to his meeting with Delacroix in 1845–6 (see, for this date, G. Gendreau and C. Pichois, *RHLF*, 1957, p. 578), which would thus mark the end of the poet's 'pagan period'; this, however, scarcely takes account of the fact that certain specifically 'pagan' texts (*Le Jeune enchanteur*;

chapters, that it is precisely within the context of such *aesthetic* formulations as these that Baudelaire is led to develop certain more subtle and challenging conceptions of Man's relationship to Nature.

Salon de 1846, *CE* 196; *La Fanfarlo,* ed. C. Pichois, 82, 87—cf. p. 53 n. 1, above) are of somewhat later date, i.e. 1846–7.

IV

Nature, Art and Man:
Nature idealized and moralized

FROM certain appreciative references encountered within Baudelaire's critical writings during the period 1845-7, one might be
tempted to conclude that the vague 'cult of Nature' described in my
second chapter, extended equally to the aesthetic sphere. Thus he
by implication classes himself among the 'sincere lovers of Nature',[1]
and it is for this same 'sincere' (or 'profound', or 'serious', or 'passionate') love of Nature—a quality linked expressly with the 'naivety'
of the true artist—that he commends not only the painters Corot,
Français and Rousseau, the caricaturist Daumier, but also his literary
friend Philippe de Chennevières.[2] What Baudelaire understands,
however, by this sentiment, as applied to the creative artist, turns
out to be considerably more complex and circumstantial than anything his fellow 'pagan' Banville, for instance, could have envisaged,
when offering such facile injunctions as these:

> Gardons soigneusement dans nos cœurs extatiques
> *L'amour de la Nature et des beautés antiques,*
> Pour voir briller toujours, même à notre couchant,
> Le Chant, cet autre Amour! l'Amour, cet autre Chant![3]

We may glimpse something already of Baudelaire's reservations on
this question, from the comment he makes on the work of another

[1]*Salon de 1846*, CE 97: 'un passage d'Hoffmann qui exprime parfaitement
mon idée, et qui plaira à tous ceux qui aiment sincèrement la nature'.

[2]*Salon de 1845*, CE 55, 57; *Salon de 1846*, CE 184; *Quelques caricaturistes
français*, CE 412, 418; *Les Contes normands et Historiettes baguenaudières*
(review, dated Nov. 1845, of two books by Chennevières, alias 'Jean de Falaise'),
OP I, 237. In Jan. 1848, Chennevières and Champfleury are jointly praised for
their 'dedication' to the 'religion of Nature' (*OP* I, 242; cf. pp. 85-6, below).
For B.'s conception of 'naivety' (that criterion drawn from Nature itself, and
defined as 'la science du métier . . . laissant le beau rôle au tempérament'),
see *Salon de 1846*, CE 87-8 and 106 n.1, and cf. M. Gilman, *B. the Critic*,
23, 32-3.

[3]*A Victor Perrot et Armand Dumesnil*, in: *Les Cariatides*, 1842, p. 370
(my italics).

artist who (like Corot and Français) exhibited at the 1845 Salon. Speaking of the statue *L'Enfant à la grappe* by David d'Angers, Baudelaire declares:

. . . c'est de la chair, il est vrai; mais c'est bête comme la nature, et c'est pourtant une vérité incontestée que le but de la sculpture n'est pas de rivaliser avec des moulages.

(*CE* 73)

The phrase 'bête comme la nature' should not be taken as implying any outright condemnation of Nature, such as Baudelaire was later so dogmatically to voice. Here, what he means is not so much that all Nature is by definition stupid, but rather that in the case of David's statue, the work of art has blindly and needlessly *imitated* Nature, to the extent of reproducing exactly (as in a plaster cast) the 'stupidity' of the original (i.e. of the child with her bunch of grapes).[1] The truest artists, on the other hand, while remaining entirely faithful to their model,[2] strive to render certain more 'general' and 'atmospheric' qualities of Nature. Thus of a botanical painting by Chazal Baudelaire remarks:

. . . ce tableau est très-bien, non parce que tout y est, et que l'on peut compter les feuilles, mais parce qu'il rend en même temps le *caractère général de la nature*—parce qu'il exprime bien l'aspect vert cru d'un parc au bord de la Seine, et de notre soleil froid; bref, parce qu'il est fait avec une profonde naïveté . . .

(*S45F,* 191; my italics)

So, too, the type of draughtsmanship (analogous to that of Rubens) exhibited in Delacroix' *Dernières paroles de Marc-Aurèle*, is deemed to render perfectly Nature's very 'movement' and 'physionomy', her

[1]The justice of this verdict may be gauged from a glance at the engraving after David's statue, reprod. *S45F,* facing p. 196; cf., none the less, the admiring comments by other critics, cit. ibid. 279. B.'s views here seem incidentally, even in their actual formulation, to be very close to those expounded by Balzac's Frenhofer to his fellow-artist Porbus: ' "La mission de l'art n'est pas de copier la nature, mais de l'exprimer! Tu n'es pas un vil copiste, mais un poëte! . . . Autrement un sculpteur serait quitte de tous ses travaux en moulant une femme! . . ." ' (*Le Chef-d'œuvre inconnu, OCC,* [XXVIII], 9; cf. P. Laubriet, *Intelligence de l'art chez Balzac,* 48–9).

[2]Cf. his criticism (noted by G. T. Clapton, *RLC* 1933, pp. 296–7) of the 'poor likeness' of certain portraits: *CE* 42 (Pérignon), 43 (Flandrin, portrait of M. Chaix d'Est-Ange), 44 (Scheffer, *Portrait du Roi*)—as also the comment on Saint-Jean, *CE* 62 (cit. p. 76 n. 4, below).

'tremulous elusiveness'; the companion painting of the *Sultan de Maroc entouré de sa garde* likewise holds, by its very 'truth' and 'naturalness' of composition, a certain quality of 'unexpectedness'.[1] Decamps, finally, delights in capturing aspects of Nature that are at once 'fantastic' yet 'real', 'sudden' and (here again) 'unexpected'.[2] These various scattered comments within the *Salon de 1845*, taken together with the eulogies of Corot and Français, imply that while it may be the first duty of the artist to 'love Nature sincerely', he is not by that token justified in assuming that his sole task is to transcribe meticulously, to 'imitate', each detail of his model; rather should he seek to convey its more 'general' and essential qualities, its more elusive and 'surprising' aspects, while at the same time 'naively' infusing into his painting something of his own idiosyncratic response to Nature, something, indeed, of his *own* nature.

Altogether more explicit are the indications furnished the following year in the elaborate and discursive *Salon de 1846*. This, as Baudelaire's contemporaries were quick to realise, is in effect a treatise on the fine arts, smuggled into a review of a contemporary exhibition,[3] and indeed behind its dazzling generalizations a whole doctrine of Nature may be intermittently glimpsed.[4] An attentive reading reveals Baudelaire to have here distinguished three main artistic attitudes towards Nature; from his comments and judgments on these we may discern clearly the direction in which his own philosophy was evolving. The first group of artists are the 'naturalists'. As landscape painters these command (or compel) Baudelaire's

[1]*CE* 11, 13.

[2]*CE* 20.

[3]Cf. Prarond, *De quelques écrivains nouveaux*, 7: 'tout un catéchisme de la peinture moderne'; Banville, cit. *CE* 474: 'Le *Salon de 1846* . . . exposait toute une théorie de la couleur . . . etc.'. In a contemporary 'gossip column' (cit. *BJ* 15), B. is shown as bragging about the 'incredible number of new ideas' he has introduced into his book (i.e. the present *Salon*). Cf., finally, the comment by Crépet (*CE* 450): 'un compte rendu d'actualité introduit dans un traité didactique'.

[4]The question of B.'s sources for the ideas on Nature and Art developed in the *Salon de 1846*, is unfortunately too complex to allow of full discussion within the present context; cf., in this connection, M. Gilman, *B. the Critic*, 34–54, and A. Ferran, *Esthétique de B.*, 138–53, as also the two monographs by L. Horner and G. May respectively, *B. critique de Delacroix* and *Diderot et B. critiques d'art*. For an account of the whole 'aesthetic system' to which B. appears to have subscribed during this period, see my art., 'Les Esthétiques de B.: le "système" des années 1844–7', *RSH*, 1967, passim.

esteem and admiration—partly by virtue of that same *dedication* to
Nature, that same 'sincerity', applauded in 1845 in Corot and Français, partly in recognition of the elements of idealism and personal
emotion that willy-nilly creep into their compositions.[1] Baudelaire's
theoretical objections to naturalistic art—voiced, in the name of
Romanticism, in an opening chapter of this *Salon*[2]—find, however,
their practical application when he comes to discuss other genres.
Thus he declares a certain type of 'negative' draughtsmanship to be
'incorrect' by its very realism (or excess of realism); exact imitation,
as practised for instance by the type of portrait painter who seizes
delightedly upon every wart, hampers the work of memory which is
the truest criterion of art.[3] As for sculpture, this is condemned *en
bloc* (the pun seems unavoidable): firstly because in comparison with
painting, which demands 'profound reflection' and for its enjoyment
a special initiation, it is crude and primitive (i.e. primaeval; in other
contexts, as we have seen, such an ancestry might have seemed to
Baudelaire a recommendation rather than a cause for disparagement); secondly, because it at one and the same time has the 'brutal
positiveness' of Nature herself (by which is meant that it reproduces
Nature 'in the raw' too directly and immediately), yet also the vague
elusiveness of an art that can be seen from a hundred different angles
and thus cannot impose a single viewpoint on the spectator.[4] The

[1]*CE* 176-7, 181 (the modern school of landscape painters: wholly giving
themselves up, with 'admirable servility', to the study of Nature and to the
'eternal adoration of the visible world' in all its aspects and details, sincerely
accepting everything that Nature offers and owing to all this the singular
brilliance of their achievement, yet counting among their number 'des naturalistes
idéalisant à leur insu'); 184 (Th. Rousseau: 'un amour profond et sérieux de
la nature . . . Il . . . mêle [à ses tableaux] beaucoup de son âme, comme
Delacroix; c'est un naturaliste entraîné sans cesse vers l'idéal'). Cabat (180) is
reproached for no longer 'putting his trust in Nature'; cf. the comment on
Decamps (131): 'le goût minutieux de la nature . . . l'avait toujours sauvé et
maintenu dans une région supérieure'.

[2]*CE* 89-90: 'La vérité dans l'art et la couleur locale . . . ont égaré beaucoup
d'autres . . . Le romantisme n'est précisément ni dans le choix des sujets
ni dans la vérité exacte, mais dans la manière de sentir. Ils l'ont cherché en
dehors, et c'est en dedans qu'il était seulement possible de le trouver.'

[3]*CE* 110-11, 142. Cf. the comments on H. Vernet (163: 'nulle passion et une
mémoire d'almanach!') and on V. Hugo (106-7: 'un peintre en poésie', 'Trop
matériel, trop attentif aux superficies de la nature').

[4]*CE* 187-8; cf. 110, and the comment (cit. p. 72, above) on David's statue
L'Enfant à la grappe at the 1845 Salon. On an earlier page of the present *Salon*,
however (*CE* 91), B. does allow himself certain regional discriminations in

second group of artists are at the other extreme, and might be called the 'false idealists': their elected medium is the so-called 'historical landscape', a strange genre which conventionalizes and 'moralizes' the forms of Nature into ideal 'patterns' or archetypes of trees, fountains, tombs, urns, etc., and arranges these into a composition which bears no relation whatsoever to any existing landscape. (Indeed, any 'immoral' tree surprised in the act of spontaneous growth must of necessity be 'felled' by these austere classicists; Hell, for them—as they picture it in their moments of remorse at having committed certain 'natural'. . . peccadillos—no doubt takes the form of some wild, free, alarmingly *real* landscape: a savanna, say, or a virgin forest . . .) Significantly enough—having announced that he proposes to intone a form of 'funeral service' for the historical landscape—Baudelaire invokes by way of analogy that 'forgotten' genre surviving only, he declares, within the 'deserted' auditorium of the Comédie-Française, i.e. classical tragedy.[1]

The third and final group—the 'true idealists', one might call them, including not only Delacroix and the 'colourists', but also the 'harmonist' Rembrandt, Rubens and Watteau with their 'landscapes of fantasy', Michelangelo even[2]—occupy an intermediate position between the two extremes of over-particularization and over-generalization;[3] it is they who command Baudelaire's warmest sympathy, and in describing their methods, he is in effect expounding his own aesthetic. The artist must, he agrees, observe and follow Nature closely;[4] but this is only a starting-point, and thereafter begins the

his judgment of sculpture: the phrase 'as brutal and positive as a sculptor' recurs, but is applied only to Mediterranean art; it is conceded that *Northern* sculpture will tend to be 'picturesque' and imaginative, rather than 'classical'. Cf. also the comment (191) on the portrait bust by Lenglet: 'Ce petit buste . . . a le magnifique caractère des bonnes œuvres romaines, qui est l'idéalisation trouvée dans la nature elle-même'.

[1] *CE* 176, 177-9.

[2] *CE* 91-2, 177, 145-6. For Delacroix and the colourists, see my further refs., below.

[3] Cf. *CE* 142: 'Trop particulariser ou trop généraliser empêchent également le souvenir'.

[4] Cf., in addition to the comments already cit., the injunction to Vidal: 'Regardez la nature, monsieur' (*CE* 153); the definition of *chic:* 'absence de modèle et de nature' (160); the modernist prescription: 'Il faut . . . avant tout, connaître les aspects de la nature et les situations de l'homme, que les artistes du passé ont dédaignés ou n'ont pas connus' (90); the commendation (187) of P. Rousseau's convincingly lifelike ducks. So, too, in the *Salon de 1845*, B. had

work of imaginative transposition and modification—or (as he himself variously terms it) of 'idealization', 'interpretation' or 'generalization'. The latter demands (as he has already intimated in the *Salon
de 1845*[1]) that the artist's primary concern should be with the *whole*
—with the total effect, with the translation of Nature's 'intentions'
into a simpler and more 'luminous' language; to this end, he must be
willing to 'sacrifice' detail, to invent or to 'tell lies', even; so, too,
the 'melodiousness' or colour-unity of a painting can best be judged
if one steps back from it and surveys it, as a whole, from a certain
distance.[2] Linked with this is the essential process of idealization;[3]
but this term has for Baudelaire a rather specialized and personal
meaning, and it is here in particular that he parts company with
traditionalist and classical theory. There is no single, general,
absolute ideal of beauty (as the historical landscape, for instance,
assumes); on the contrary, there are as many ideals as there are subjects and painters; each artist creates his own appropriately idealized
(and generalized) version of the forms of Nature.[4] But what determines the nature of this personal 'ideal'? Simply the artist's own
'temperament', which is to say his intuitive, imaginative, 'poetic'
or 'naïve' response to the model he has chosen and studied.[5] Thus a

said of the paintings of Saint-Jean: 'Nous préférons les fleurs et les fruits de
Rubens, et les trouvons plus *naturels*' (*CE* 62; my italics).

[1] Cf. pp. 72–3, above.

[2] *CE* 95–9, 144, 110 ('les chefs-d'œuvre ne sont jamais que des extraits divers
de la nature'). Cf., for the 'poetry' of Nature, 181, 182 (Héroult), 134 (Decamps);
for the rendering of 'character' in a portrait, 158 (V. Robert), 189 (Feuchère);
for the idealist artist's obligation to abjure the 'improbabilities' of Nature, 174;
for the 'distance test' as applied to Delacroix, 109. The phrase 'les intentions
de la nature' (144) may carry an echo of 18th-century philosophies of Nature;
cf. R. Pomeau, *RES*, 1959, p. 114.

[3] '. . . l'art, pour être profond, veut une idéalisation perpétuelle' (*CE* 167).

[4] *CE* 141–5; cf. 108 (Heine cit.), and the definition, in the contemporary
article (dated Jan. 1846) on *Le Musée classique du Bazar Bonne-Nouvelle*, of
the 'true portrait': 'la reconstruction idéale des individus' (*CE* 212). The
colourist who chooses to 'dispense with' Nature, but without regard for the
ideal, may lapse into mere picturesque showmanship; this is the error of certain
of Delacroix' disciples (*CE* 121–2), and specifically of Troyon (181; cf. *Salon
de 1845*, *CE* 58).

[5] *CE* 87–8. Cf. 90: true Romanticism is a 'mode of feeling', and can come only
from *within* the artist's self. One might cite from B.'s own poem *La Fontaine
de sang*, as an extreme instance (in another, cognate, medium) of this tendency
towards the personal assimilation or *appropriation* of landscape, these lines
describing the terrible progress of the poet's obsession: 'Il me semble parfois

beautiful painting is defined as 'Nature reflected by (or in) an artist';[1]
Delacroix, whose works are 'great poems, naively conceived and carried through with all the accustomed insolence of genius', starts out
from the principle that a painting must above all reproduce the
artist's 'intimate thought', and conceives Nature simply as a 'vast
dictionary', to be searchingly consulted and then drawn on from
memory;[2] a portrait, if painted by a colourist, will allow scope for
purely imaginative and 'atmospheric' touches;[3] a great historical
painting, such as Louis David's *Marat*, will heighten the sombre
realism of its detail by some subtle spirituality of 'atmosphere'.[4]
Similarly emotive and 'poetic' should be the spectator's response, and
Delacroix' paintings in particular give wide scope to the vagrant

que mon sang coule à flots . . . / A travers le marché, comme dans un champ
clos, / Il s'en va transformant les pavés en îlots, / Désaltérant la soif de chaque
créature, / Et partout *colorant en rouge la nature*' (MS. 1851-2, ll. 1, 5-8; my
italics).

[1]*CE* 87.

[2]*CE* 106, 108, 109. Recollecting, in a passage of the *Salon de 1859* (*CE* 279-
80), his first meeting with Delacroix in 1845-6, B. there explains in detail
what exactly the great painter intended by this idea of Nature as a 'dictionary';
cf. p. 131, below. B. himself seems quickly to have adopted the metaphor to
his own purposes, if we may judge from an anecdote of Champfleury's, cit.
BDC 68-70, recording a conversation (which I myself would date as of this same
period 1845-6) between the poet and the caricaturist Henry Monnier: the
latter's drawings, B. gravely opined, were 'useful *dictionaries*' but no more,
since 'l'idéalisation manquait à ces types qui restaient seulement à l'état de
croquis d'après nature'. (B. was perhaps here quoting from the first draft of
what was later to become his essay *Quelques caricaturistes français*; cf. the very
similar judgement on Monnier, *CE* 419-20, in which, however, he substitutes
for the 'dictionary' metaphor that of a 'miroir qui ne pense pas et qui se
contente de réfléchir les passants'. For the analogy between this text and the
Champfleury anecdote, cf. *CE* 506-7; for the chronology of B.'s various essays
on caricature, see C. Pichois, *B.*, 92-4). Delacroix for his part seems only once
to have set down in print his 'dictionary' concept—in a note on 'la question
du réalisme' (*Œuvres littéraires*, I, 58; cit. M. Gilman, *B. the Critic*, 38);
L. Horner is thus in error when she states, *B. critique de Delacroix*, 152 (cf. ibid.,
85), that 'l'image . . . du dictionnaire . . . ne se trouve nulle part chez Delacroix'.

[3]*CE* 154-5.

[4]*Musée classique du Bazar Bonne-Nouvelle* (pub. Jan. 1846): 'Tous ces détails
sont historiques et réels, comme un roman de Balzac; le drame est là, vivant
dans toute sa lamentable horreur, et par un tour de force étrange qui fait de cette
peinture le chef-d'œuvre de David et une des grandes curiosités de l'art moderne,
elle n'a rien de trivial ni d'ignoble . . . Ceci est le pain des forts et le triomphe
du spiritualisme; cruel comme la nature, ce tableau a tout le parfum de l'idéal'
(*CE* 208).

fancy.[1] But from this creative (or re-creative) relationship between the artist and his model, between the artist and Nature, there must necessarily arise certain contradictions and tensions. Thus the colourist may be led, by his very 'study' of Nature, to results which differ markedly from the original model; the art of drawing may seem a 'struggle' between Nature and the artist, whereby the latter strives to understand and interpret Nature's 'intentions'; certain types of draughtsman may deal in more or less cavalier fashion with Nature —the 'physionomic' draughtsman, if imbued with the genius of an Ingres, may select, arrange, correct, guess, even 'rebuke' or 'bully', whilst the 'creative' draughtsman may invent a Nature of his own, which ignores the external model and solely reflects his own temperament; or again, there is the landscape of fantasy, as exemplified in Rembrandt, Rubens, Watteau (as also, incongruously, in certain illustrated English gift-books or annuals!), in which Nature is ousted in favour of human reverie and 'egoism'.[2] It is in the light of such specialized cases as these that we should interpret Baudelaire's resounding declaration, made elsewhere in this same *Salon*, that the artist's first concern is to substitute Man for Nature, as an act of 'naive' and passionate protest.[3] The immediate context here, it must be noted, is polemical: Baudelaire is denouncing the benighted 'eclectic' artist for (among other things) his lack of 'temperament', and his refusal to commit himself to a specific ideal. If we take this

[1] *CE* 169, 106 (Delacroix). Cf. in this connection my art. cit., 'Les Esthétiques de B.', *RSH*, 1967, p. 492 and n. 67.

[2] *CE* 96, 144, 110–11, 177. Cf. this comment on the caricatures of Grandville: 'Cet homme, avec un courage surhumain, a passé sa vie à refaire la création. Il la prenait dans ses mains, la tordait, la rarrangeait, l'expliquait, la commentait; et la nature se transformait en apocalypse. Il a mis le monde sens dessus dessous' *(Quelques caricaturistes français, CE* 421)—as also B.'s own amusing literary example of the 'landscape of fantasy', in this gloss of a passage quoted from Heine's *Die romantische Schule:* 'Les tableaux de M. Borget nous font regretter cette Chine où le vent lui-même, dit H. Heine, prend un son comique en passant par les clochettes,—et où la nature et l'homme ne peuvent pas se regarder sans rire' *(Salon de 1845, CE* 61; cf. *S45F* 265–6). For B.'s (largely admiring) attitude to Ingres during this period, cf. my art. cit., 'Les Esthétiques de B.), *RSH*, 1967, pp. 487, 489 n. 36 and 493–4.

[3] *CE* 168. Cf. equally the distinction made in the essay *De l'essence du rire* (and in a precisely similar context, be it noted) between the two types of humour: 'ordinary', 'significative', 'imitative', on the one hand—'grotesque', 'absolute', 'creative' on the other; in the latter type, 'le rire est l'expression de l'idée de supériorité, non plus de l'homme sur l'homme, mais de l'homme sur la nature' (*CE* 384).

into account, and bear in mind also the general argument pursued throughout the *Salon de 1846*, we see clearly that what is being asserted is simply the artist's right to generalize, idealize, interpret, modify or re-arrange Nature in accordance with his own temperament and feeling;[1] conversely, what by implication is being *denied*, is his obligation to reproduce mechanically and unimaginatively whatever Nature may place before his eyes.

Any notion that these decidedly circumstantial 'audacities' might constitute a fully-fledged *rebellion* against Nature, is in any case belied not only by those passages within the *Salon de 1846* in which, as we have seen, Nature remains the ultimate guide and criterion of artistic endeavour, but also and more indirectly by various contemporary texts attesting Baudelaire's particular and continuing sensitiveness to natural beauty. Of these the most striking and explicit is the rapturous 'colour symphony'—a prose poem in itself, as has been remarked—that introduces the third chapter, 'De la Couleur', of this same *Salon de 1846*:[2]

[1] To the extent even of 'repainting the trees and the sky'!—if, that is, we are to ascribe to B. himself the hankering attributed to his contemporary *alter ego* Samuel Cramer (*La Fanfarlo*, ed. Pichois, 88), but voiced originally by Petrus Borel's *Champavert* (cf. E. Starkie, *B.*, 294, and *Petrus Borel*, 119–20). Cf. also, in this connection, the hypothesis put forward in the *Salon de 1846*, by way of demonstrating the true colourist's intuitive perception of colour harmonies: 'si un propriétaire anticoloriste s'avisait de repeindre sa campagne d'une manière absurde et dans un système de couleurs charivariques, le vernis épais et transparent de l'atmosphère et l'œil savant de Veronèse redresseraient le tout et produiraient sur une toile un ensemble satisfaisant, conventionnel sans doute, mais logique' (*CE* 96). There is a curious echo, incidentally, of these notions of Borel's and B.'s, in a passage of Gautier's *Salon de 1847* (pub. a few months after *La Fanfarlo*): 'Il est . . . incontestable que les feuillages et les prés, au printemps et au commencement de l'été, sont d'un vert très-prononcé, très-cru, très-vif. Il se peut que la nature ait tort, mais les choses se passent ainsi. Comment se fait-il que le bon Dieu n'ait pas pensé à faire des arbres gris, roses, bleu de ciel et lilas, pour la plus grande commodité des amateurs de l'harmonie?' (pp. 187–8). Cf., finally, at the level of pathological obsession, the lines from *La Fontaine de sang*, cit. pp. 76–7 n. 5, above—as also the later dismissals of Karr's and Fournel's gibes at Delacroix' 'improbabilities' of colour (*CE* 244–5, 291; cf. L. Horner, *MLN*, 1958, pp. 432–4).

[2] Cf. A. Ferran, *Esthétique de B.*, 140: 'Baudelaire chante, en une sorte de poème en prose, la symphonie colorée du monde sous le soleil'. For a full analysis of the technical basis and antecedents of B.'s theory of colour, see ibid., 140–8. For other, no less eloquent if less extended Nature-descriptions, cf. the comments (*CE* 184, 117, 118) on Th. Rousseau and on certain paintings by Delacroix (the ceiling for the Senate Library at the Luxembourg, the *Adieux de Roméo et Juliette*).

Supposons un bel espace de nature où tout verdoie, rougeoie, poudroie et chatoie en pleine liberté ... Une immensité, bleue quelquefois et verte souvent, s'étend jusqu'aux confins du ciel: c'est la mer. Les arbres sont verts, les gazons verts, les mousses vertes; le vert serpente dans les troncs, les tiges non mûres sont vertes; le vert est le fond de la nature, parce que le vert se marie facilement à tous les autres tons. Ce qui me frappe d'abord, c'est que partout,—coquelicots dans les gazons, pavots, perroquets, etc.,— le rouge chante la gloire du vert; le noir,—quand il y en a,—zéro solitaire et insignifiant, intercède le secours du bleu ou du rouge. Le bleu, c'est-à-dire le ciel, est coupé de légers flocons blancs ou de masses grises qui trempent heureusement sa morne crudité,—et, comme la vapeur de la saison,—hiver ou été,—baigne, adoucit, ou engloutit les contours, la nature ressemble à un toton qui, mû par une vitesse accélérée, nous apparaît gris, bien qu'il résume en lui toutes les couleurs.

La séve monte et, mélange de principes, elle s'épanouit en *tons mélangés*; les arbres, les rochers, les granits se mirent dans les eaux et y déposent leurs *reflets*; tous les objets transparents accrochent au passage lumières et couleurs voisines et lointaines. A mesure que l'astre du jour se dérange, les tons changent de valeur, mais, respectant toujours leurs sympathies et leurs haines naturelles, continuent à vivre en harmonie par des concessions réciproques. Les ombres se déplacent lentement, et font fuir devant elles ou éteignent les tons à mesure que la lumière, déplacée elle-même, en veut faire résonner de nouveau. Ceux-ci se renvoient leurs reflets, et, modifiant leurs qualités en les *glaçant* de qualités transparentes et empruntées, multiplient à l'infini leurs mariages mélodieux et les rendent plus faciles. Quand le grand foyer descend dans les eaux, de rouges fanfares s'élancent de tous côtés; une sanglante harmonie éclate à l'horizon, et le vert s'empourpre richement. Mais bientôt de vastes ombres bleues chassent en cadence devant elles la foule des tons orangés et rose tendre qui sont comme l'écho lointain et affaibli de la lumière. Cette grande symphonie du jour, qui est l'éternelle variation de la symphonie d'hier, cette succession de mélodies, où la variété sort toujours de l'infini, cet hymne compliqué s'appelle la couleur.

(*CE* 92–4)

Although the diverse aspects of Nature may here figure essentially as elements within a complex scheme of colour-values (the *blue* of the sea and sky; the ubiquitous *green* of the trees and grass and moss, set off by the 'singing' *reds* of the poppies and parrots; and so on), they do so, after all, by virtue of some determining visual or imaginative experience; implicit throughout, moreover, is the delighted, even reverent, acceptance of a natural order which yields to the artist such *gifts* of Beauty. But the colours of Nature are admired—and commended to painters—not merely for their intrinsic harmoniousness or 'poetry',[1] but equally for their emotive or 'moral' associations: red, we are reminded, is 'the colour of blood, the colour of life', green the 'calm, gay, smiling colour of Nature'.[2] Similar associations attach to a particular painter's use of colour. Thus of Decamps, Baudelaire declares: 'Sa couleur splendide et rayonnante . . . était, pour me servir de mots empruntés à l'ordre moral, sanguinaire et mordante';[3] recalling the nervous reaction of a young artist friend of his, to Delacroix' *Pietà* ('peinture de cannibale'), he likewise exclaims:

A coup sûr, ce n'est point dans les curiosités d'une palette encombrée, ni dans le dictionnaire des règles, que notre jeune ami saura trouver cette sanglante et farouche désolation, à peine compensée par le vert sombre de l'espérance!   (*CE* 113)

Again, more comprehensively, he notes that where in Veronese the colour is 'calm and gay' (i.e. predominantly green?), in Delacroix it may be 'plaintive', in Catlin 'awe-inspiring', in others again, 'playful', 'sad', 'rich', etc.[4] These observations occur towards the end of the chapter 'De la Couleur'; before going on thereafter to cite a passage from Hoffmann—in which is asserted and illustrated (to the satisfaction, Baudelaire opines, of all 'sincere lovers of Nature') the intimate connection that for the German writer obtains between colours, sounds and scents—Baudelaire ventures the speculation as to whether any analogist has yet worked out a complete 'scale' of colours and feelings.[5] Baudelaire seems, around 1846, to have been

[1] For this alternative metaphor, cf. the enumeration (*CE* 181) of the elements composing the 'poetry of Nature': 'light, shade, reflections, atmospheric coloration' ('l'atmosphère colorante').

[2] *CE* 128 (of Catlin's portraits of Red Indians).

[3] *CE* 132. I cannot agree with P. Laubriet, *Intelligence de l'art chez Balzac*, 316 n. 148, in finding this comment on Decamps to be a 'somewhat ironic' application of the Hoffmann text hereunder cited.

[4] *CE* 97. 'Terrible' is the actual word used to describe Catlin's palette; what this means, however, is shown in the subsequent appreciation of this artist (127–8).

[5] *CE* 97. Cf. in this connection, as well as the theories of Fourier (J. Pommier, *Mystique de B.*, 62 and 73), the treatise published in 1837 by F. Portal, *Des Couleurs symboliques*; while largely concerned with the religious aspects of colour-symbolism, Portal has an interesting passage, p. 33, in which he speaks of the 'rule of (emotive) oppositions': '. . . le rouge signifie l'amour, l'égoïsme et la haine; le vert, la régénération céleste et la dégradation infernale, la sagesse et la folie', etc. For the Hoffmann passage (from *Kreisleriana*), see J. Pommier, op. cit., 8, 164 n. 20, and cf. ibid., 7.

particularly intrigued by this whole question of colour symbolism; in *La Fanfarlo* (published January 1847) he returns to the charge, imagining his *alter ego* Cramer to have in fact (or rather, in fiction) answered the need specified a few months earlier, by producing a book on . . . 'la symbolique des couleurs'.[1]

At a more subjective, less systematic, level, we encounter in the *Choix de maximes consolantes sur l'amour* of March 1846, a passage that is surely a self-description:

Vous tous qui nourrissez quelque vautour insatiable,—vous poètes hoff-maniques que l'harmonica fait danser dans les régions du cristal, et que le violon déchire comme une lame qui cherche le cœur,—contemplateurs âpres et goulus à qui le spectacle de la nature elle-même donne des extases dangereuses,—que l'amour vous soit un calmant.[2]

Now among these 'Hoffmannesque poets', these 'greedy contemplatives' who before the spectacle of Nature fall into 'dangerous ecstasies', and whom the sound of the violin 'pierces like some blade seeking the heart'—among these must certainly be numbered the poet of *Harmonie du soir*: not only because here too, in a similar atmosphere of ecstatic or 'vertiginous' languor, the violin bespeaks (by analogy) the wounded heart, but also because, as I have shown elsewhere,[3] it is precisely to Hoffmann that the poem owes its theme and perhaps its initial inspiration:

> Voici venir les temps où vibrant sur sa tige
> Chaque fleur s'évapore ainsi qu'un encensoir;
> Les sons et les parfums tournent dans l'air du soir,
> —Valse mélancolique et langoureux vertige!—

[1]Pichois ed., 93. A fragmentary jotting, undated and under the general heading 'Romans', suggests that B. may actively have toyed with some such project: 'Pénétrer le sens (vague et général) des couleurs. Divisions et subdivisions.' (*OP* III, 10). Cf., for various later instances of colour symbolism in B., J. Pommier, op. cit., 72–4 (p. 213 n. 2, below); for the influence, in this respect, of Balzac, C. G. Castex, *RSH*, 1958, p. 143; for B.'s parallel interest in the 'science' of 'physionomic signs', the *Choix de maximes consolantes sur l'amour* of March 1846 (*OP* II, 4–5).

[2]*OP* II, 3–4. B. seems to be recalling this passage when summarizing, many years later, the disquisition on Grief in De Quincey's *Suspiria*; the phrase italicized (by me) is a free rendering indeed of the English writer's 'these were fascinations as of witchcraft': 'Les vastes silences de la campagne, les étés criblés d'une lumière accablante, les après-midi brumeuses, le *remplissaient d'une dangereuse volupté*' (*Mangeur d'opium*, *PA* 172; cf. De Quincey, *Confessions*, ed. M. Elwin, 474).

[3]In my article, 'Pour une étude chronologique des *FM*', *RHLF*, 1967, p. 347.

Chaque fleur s'évapore ainsi qu'un encensoir;
Le violon frémit comme un cœur qu'on afflige;
—Valse mélancolique et langoureux vertige!—
Le ciel est triste et beau comme un grand reposoir.

Le violon frémit comme un cœur qu'on afflige,
Un cœur tendre, qui hait le néant vaste et noir!
—Le ciel est triste et beau comme un grand reposoir;
Le soleil s'est noyé dans son sang qui se fige.

Un cœur tendre qui hait le néant vaste et noir
Du passé lumineux recueille tout vestige;
—Le soleil s'est noyé dans son sang qui se fige;
Ton souvenir en moi luit comme un ostensoir!

(1857 text)

Do we not have here a 'generalization' or 'interpretation' of Nature, precisely in the sense specified for the true artist in the *Salon de 1846*[1]—a landscape coloured by personal emotion, a composition subtly interfusing descriptive and subjective elements? Of the actual scene and moment of the poem, we are given only the vaguest indications: the evening coming on, the wide sky, the sun setting (or 'congealing') in its 'blood-red' glow,[2] the flowers (in a garden?), the sound of the violin, other unspecified sounds and scents. But the main concern, implicit within the title and explicit in the third and fourth lines, is with the imagined *fusion* of these scents and sounds, in a 'dance' that is not merely pictured for us ('Les sons et les parfums *tournent* dans l'air du soir'), but can be *heard* also in the lilt— assuming almost, at times, the slow yet strongly accented rhythms of the 'melancholy waltz' itself—of certain metrical phrases:

[1]Cf. pp. 75–7, above.

[2]The image is less melodramatic in its context than might seem, and indeed has its exact counterpart in the description already quoted from the chapter 'De la couleur' of the *Salon de 1846*: 'Quand le grand foyer descend dans les eaux . . . une *sanglante harmonie* éclate à l'horizon . . .' (*CE* 94)—another 'evening harmony', be it noted. Certainly, there is no more than a hint here of the studied complicity informing this similar image from a probably earlier poem, *Une Martyre*: 'Un cadavre sans tête épanche, comme un fleuve, / Sur l'oreiller désaltéré/Un sang rouge et vivant, dont la toile s'abreuve/Avec l'avidité d'un pré' (1857 text). The title 'Harmonie du soir', incidentally (like the almost identical title, 'Harmonies du soir', given by Liszt to the eleventh of the *Etudes d'exécution transcendante* published by him in 1852), may well have derived from a curious passage in Musset's *La Confession d'un enfant du siècle*; see my art. cit., pp. 352–3 and n. 2.

Voici/venir les temps / où vibrant / sur sa tige
Chaque fleur / s'évapo/re ainsi / qu'un encensoir;
Les sons / et les parfums / tour/nent dans l'air du soir,
Val/se mélancoli/que et langoureux / vertige!

The stanza-pattern adopted by Baudelaire—a modification of the Malayan 'pantoum', with the second and fourth lines becoming the first and third of the next[1]—confers, by its symmetrical reiterations, a certain haunting solemnity of 'incantation'. A further requirement of the pantoum genre is that two independent groups of ideas should throughout alternate, couplet by couplet. *Harmonie du soir*, while scarcely conforming to this convention, may yet be called 'binary' in its structure, in the sense that a single moment or impression of Nature is rendered through two distinct series of images: the one series (the flowers as 'fuming' censers, the sky as a vast altar, the memory of the loved one as a monstrance shining against the dark) drawn from the Catholic liturgy and gaining, from their invariable recurrence at the rhyme-word ('encen*soir*': 'repo*soir*': 'osten*soir*'), an added 'resonance' and depth of perspective; the other, no less insistent, evoking personal emotion of a sad or troubled kind ('Valse *mélancolique*,' 'un cœur qu'on *afflige*', 'Le ciel est *triste* et beau', 'Un cœur *tendre* qui *hait le néant*'). The two image-sequences are at last brought together, as Jean Prévost has observed,[2] in the concluding line of the poem: 'Ton souvenir en moi luit comme un ostensoir!'; already at the outset of the final quatrain, however, the 'sentimental' imagery has begun to detach itself from the general landscape impression, the 'cœur tendre' has ceased to be a mere term of comparison ('Le violon frémit *comme* un cœur qu'on afflige') and has begun to assume an independent 'personality' of its own:

> Un cœur tendre, qui hait le néant vaste et noir,
> Du passé lumineux recueille tout vestige!

---

[1] For the 'rules' governing the pantoum genre, see Banville, *Petit traité de poésie française*, 1883, pp. 243–8, but cf. I. Feuerlicht, 'B.'s *Harmonie du soir*', *French Review*, Oct. 1959, pp. 18–19; for B.'s supposed 'infringements' of these rules, cf. on the one hand Cassagne, *Versification et métrique de B.*, 106, and on the other, Feuerlicht, ibid., 19–20. For further details concerning the history of the genre in France, see: C. Pichois, *MF*, March 1955, pp. 548–51; my art. cit., p. 356 n. 2; H. Heiss, 'Die Pantouns Malais', in: *Festschrift für Oskar Walzel*, pp. 145–7.
[2] *B.*, 341.

This couplet confirms that the tremulous 'lament' previously discerned in the violin's 'sad waltz', answers to a real (and not merely to a figurative) affliction—that the landscape is truly a *paysage d'âme*.[1] Yet is the ultimate revelation ('Ton souvenir *en moi* luit . . .') that this all-too tender heart is indeed the poet's own, that the 'luminous' vestiges of the past he has shored up against the gathering dark, are indeed memories of his own beloved—is this enough to make of *Harmonie du soir* a *love* poem in any true sense of the word? In the sense, even, that *Parfum exotique* and *La Chevelure* can be termed love poems? Like them, *Harmonie du soir* stands at a certain remove from amorous reality[2]—but with this further difference (or reversal), that here it is the landscape which is present, the woman who is absent but remembered. The fact that ultimately, in the 1857 edition of *Les Fleurs du Mal*, Baudelaire chose to include this poem within a cycle of poems largely dedicated to Mme Sabatier (which is not to say that the poem was necessarily composed for her in the first instance[3]) should not in any case mislead us into conceiving it solely as 'an offering to the beloved of a spectacle of Nature linked with a memory' (i.e. of her).[4] For what emerges most strongly of all from these verses—more strongly than any image or memory of a loved one—is precisely the actual spectacle or impression of Nature, the evocation of that 'evening harmony' that for the 'Hoffmannesque poet' steals so insidiously and 'dangerously' upon the ear.

The three years following the appearance, in January 1847, of *La Fanfarlo*, seem to have been particularly lean ones for Baudelaire, as far as actual publication of his writings was concerned: if we discount the various (and trivial) journalistic products of his involvement in the political events of 1848,[5] and the *re*publication of his novella in 1849, no more than a dozen or so pages from his pen appear to have found their way into print during the three years in question. One interesting gleaning, however, from this meagre harvest, is the review, contributed in January 1848 to *Le Corsaire-Satan*, of three books of 'Tales' by Champfleury.[6] Champfleury is

---

[1] For a further discussion of this form of Nature-symbolism, cf. pp. 238–40, below.
[2] Cf. p. above.
[3] Cf. my art. cit., pp. 355–6.
[4] J. Prévost, *B.*, 342.
[5] See p. 86 n. 4, and p. 88, below.
[6] *Chien-Caillou, Pauvre Trompette, Feu Miette*; all three vols. pub. 1847 by Martinon (a subsidiary of Michel Lévy). Certain of these tales were reprinted in

here praised for having 'dared', in these maiden publications of his, to 'content himself with Nature' and accord her his 'unlimited trust';[1] in this (as in his excellent knowledge of provincial life) he is declared to resemble that other friend and writer of tales, Philippe de Chennevières, whom Baudelaire had already commended a few years earlier for his 'sincere love of Nature',[2] and who is now described as a 'brave soul' wholly dedicated (like Champfleury) to the 'religion of Nature'. Of the third volume, *Feu Miette*, which is dedicated to Balzac, Baudelaire remarks specifically that no more august and appropriate patron could have been found for stories as judicious, as simple, as *natural* as these, than the great novelist who is at once observer and inventor—the *naturalist* who at the same time can perceive the 'laws' governing the 'generation of ideas and of visible beings'. Even Champfleury's style has, in its breadth, bold immediacy and 'poetry', something of Nature herself . . .[3] Much of Baudelaire's charitable indulgence towards Champfleury can, of course, be explained in terms of friendship, gratitude, political solidarity;[4] yet this is no reason for dismissing as wholly insincere the naturalist credo here by implication professed, the less so since certain of the statements above-quoted have their exact counterpart in other texts of the period. It is particularly significant, in this respect, that on the very page of the *Salon de 1846* in which

---

1852, under the title *Contes vieux et nouveaux*, this time directly under the Lévy imprint. Title of B.'s review: *Les Contes de Champfleury*.

[1] *OP* I, 242. This is precisely, it will be recalled, what Cabat in his paintings of 1846 was reproached for *not* doing (*CE* 180).

[2] In Nov. 1845, and likewise in the columns of the *Corsaire-Satan*, albeit anonymously and more briefly; see *OP* I, 237, and cf. p. 71 n. 2. It is significant, incidentally, that as C. Pichois points out (*B.*, 88), B. should have singled out this quality, together with Chennevières' 'naivety' and epicureanism, while making no mention whatever of the 'Christian-philosophical' passages in his friend's *Tales*, on which nevertheless he must already have begun to draw for the first draft of his essay *De l'essence du rire*.

[3] *OP* I, 242, 243-4, 244.

[4] Cf. M. Gilman, *B. the Critic*, 67: 'obviously a blurb for a friend'. Champfleury had obligingly (if anonymously) contributed to the *Corsaire-Satan* a favourable notice of B.'s *Salon de 1845*—see *CE* 466-7; as for 'political solidarity', B.'s art. on Champfleury was published only a few weeks before the outbreak of the Revolution of Feb. 1848, in which both writers were to be closely and fraternally involved (e.g. as joint editors of a short-lived Republican journal, *Le Salut public*; see *OP* I, 191-207, 528-35, as also J. Mouquet and W. T. Bandy, *B. en 1848*, 6-19).

Baudelaire dismisses as an aberration the search for 'exact truth' (e.g. through 'local colour'), he should go on to make, in the name of Romanticism, what is almost a Realist declaration of principle:

Il faut donc, avant tout, connaître les aspects de la nature et les situations de l'âme, que les artistes du passé ont dédaignés ou n'ont pas connus.[1]

New aspects of Nature, human situations hitherto unexplored: such is, by definition, the very subject-matter of Realist art, and Baudelaire, in his account of certain of Champfleury's Tales, recurs continually, almost mechanically, to the qualities of 'truth' and authenticity they display in their observation of human behaviour.[2] No doubt in his *Salon de 1846* Baudelaire has been careful to distinguish between the artist's obligation to 'know' and 'study' Nature, and the work of 'interpretation' (rather than of exact transcription or 'imitation') that should properly follow. But in practice (e.g. in the eulogy of Decamps) the distinction is not always consistently applied; we may thus feel not only that Baudelaire had as yet lacked the opportunity or the incentive to work out the full *literary* implications of his doctrine,[3] but also that even in its general aesthetic formulation, this still remained somewhat fluid—fluid enough to allow a Champfleury, for instance, on the one hand to earn praise as a 'sincere lover of Nature', but on the other to escape censure for having in fact served up just such raw, ungarnished 'slices of life' as his friend would certainly have condemned had they been proffered by a painter or a sculptor. As it happens, Baudelaire unwittingly demonstrates, within the Champfleury article, the operation of this curious 'double standard', by seizing upon the opportunity—afforded by the particular theme of the tale *Van Schaendel, père et fils*—of sniping at

---

[1]*CE* 90, 476. I reproduce the 1846 text of this passage; the 1868 text reads (more clearly) 'les situations de *l'homme*'.

[2]'Histoire *vraie comme les précédentes*'; 'On ne saurait imaginer ce que Champfleury sait mettre ou plutôt sait *voir* là-dessous de douleur et de mélancolie *vraies*'; '*peinture au naturel*'; 'histoire . . . *véridique* comme toujours'; 'Il est difficile de *mieux peindre* et de *mieux dessiner* les automates ambulants, etc.'; 'L'auteur, de même qu'il s'applique à *bien voir* les êtres et leurs physionomies toujours étranges pour qui sait bien voir, s'applique aussi à *bien retenir* le cri de leur animalité' (*OP* I, 243–4; my italics).

[3]Cf., for this question of the literary applications (or applicability) of B.'s 'aesthetic system' of 1844–7, my art. cit., 'Les Esthétiques de B.', p. 495; for the direct reference to this system, made within the Champfleury review, ibid., pp. 483–4.

certain 'rabidly' naturalist painters: those whose mania for exactitude leads them to feed on carrots the better to draw them, etc. . . .[1] Baudelaire does admittedly speak appreciatively of Champfleury's 'involuntary and persistent *irony*' (recalling that of certain German and English writers),[2] and this might well be taken as an instance of temperament duly modifying (as the *Salon de 1846* had recommended) the 'unprocessed' data of reality; as a further possible echo, however, of the subtle discriminations pursued in that same *Salon*, could be mentioned Baudelaire's gentle complaint that Champfleury should in these stories have denied himself so stringently all element of personal commentary or expansive elaboration[3]—which is in effect to say, of 'interpretation'.

A more consistent literary application of the aesthetic outlined in the *Salon de 1846*, is to be found in the prefatory Note which preceded Baudelaire's translation, under the title 'Révélation magnétique', of Poe's *Mesmeric Revelation*. This brief article, though it appeared only in July 1848 (in the columns of *La Liberté de Penser*), is likely, I suggest, and for the following reasons, to have been composed some six or seven months earlier. There is first of all the fact that from February to June 1848 Baudelaire seems to have been wholly immersed in political activity and journalism,[4] and would thus have had little time for what were always for him (but particularly

---

[1]*OP* I, 244. Champfleury's Van Schaendel the elder, when commissioned to paint a still life or a portrait, felt obliged, initially, to *eat* the actual vegetables, or *wear* the actual clothes, which were to figure in the painting: '. . . pendant toute la durée du tableau, le Malinois, fidèle à son système, ne se nourrissait que des légumes qu'il peignait. Il appelait cela "se nourrir de son modèle"; et il exécrait les légumes!' (*Contes vieux et nouveaux*, 181).

[2]*OP* I, 243, 244. According to E. Bouvier, *Bataille réaliste*, 130, B. is here thinking of Sterne, Jean-Paul Richter and Heine. Cf. also the comment by C. Pichois, *Image de Jean-Paul Richter*, 223, 225: what B. has in mind may be simply the various *humorous* effects borrowed by Champfleury from the writers in question.

[3]'La seule chose que je reprocherais volontiers à l'auteur est de ne pas connaître peut-être ses richesses, de n'être pas suffisamment rabâcheur, de trop se fier à ses lecteurs, de ne pas tirer de conclusions, de ne pas épuiser un sujet . . .' (*OP* I, 245). But B. quickly adds that he 'may be wrong' in making this (one) reproach, and indeed in an article published only a few months later, he implicitly criticizes (as we shall see) those naturalistic novelists who strive unavailingly to detect (and explain) the 'inner mechanism' of the minds they so meticulously explore; see p. 90, below.

[4]See J. Mouquet and W. T. Bandy, *B. en 1848*, 6-42.

at this early stage of his career) the arduous labours of translation[1] —or indeed, for that matter, for the writing of this introductory Note. A further consideration is that Baudelaire's 'discovery' of Poe goes back, almost certainly, to early 1847;[2] in view of the 'singular commotion' that this engendered in him,[3] it appears probable that very shortly thereafter he would have embarked on a first translation of one of the American writer's *Tales*.[4] Finally, it is surely significant that while the *Révélation magnétique* 'Notice' bears no trace whatsoever of the social doctrines to which, from February 1848, he for a brief period became ardently committed, it does on the contrary echo specifically several texts belonging to the period immediately preceding: the long letter to his mother of 4th December 1847, with its (deceptively) resolute 'declaration of intent' betraying exactly those general preoccupations with the novel as a genre, that find their outlet in the present article;[5] the review of Champfleury's *Tales*, with its derisive comments, above-noted, on naturalistic painters;[6] the *Salon de 1846*, above all, with its underlying 'aesthetic system' which he was so soon to discard in favour of a frankly utilitarian, even didactic theory,[7] but on which he here still continues to draw freely. Thus we find Baudelaire now asserting—as previously of the 'creative' draughtsmanship of artists such as Delacroix—that certain more 'powerful' or 'surprising' novelists (the list of 'romanciers forts' includes Diderot, Laclos, Hoffmann, Goethe, Jean-Paul,

[1]His proofs for this particular translation (conserved by Champfleury) showed numerous corrections; see *HE* 458, and cf., for the whole history of his labours on Poe's behalf, P. F. Quinn, *The French Face of Edgar Poe*, 88–108.

[2]See ibid., 71–2, and cf. Asselineau, in *B. et Asselineau*, 175.

[3]*CG* III, 41 (letter to Arm. Fraisse of 18 Feb. 1860).

[4]Cf. the letter to his mother, written at the end of Oct. 1847, in which he mentions having spent all his available resources on certain books he required (*LS* 215); perhaps one of these was the 1845 edition of Poe's *Tales*, which he must certainly have had in his possession when translating, from it, *Mesmeric Revelation*? Cf. L. Lemonnier, *Traducteurs de Poe*, 167; *HE* 456.

[5]'A partir du jour de l'an, je commence un nouveau métier,—c'est-à-dire la création d'œuvres d'imagination pure,—le Roman. Il est inutile que je vous démontre ici la gravité, la beauté, et le côté infini de cet art-là.' (*CG* I, 95). As in the case of the projected 'Eclogues' (p. 18, above), circumstances conspired (with B.'s own temperament) to thwart these impressive literary ambitions.

[6]Cf. pp. 87–8, above. The reference to 'naturalistes enragés' is in fact carried over almost bodily to the 'Note' introducing *Révélation magnétique*; see p. 90 n. 2.

[7]Cf., for these two phases of B.'s aesthetic, my two arts. cit., 'B.: the Poet as Moralist' pp. 197–204, and 'Les Esthétiques de B.', pp. 482–4 and passim—as also p. 94, below.

Maturin, Balzac, Sterne, as well as Poe) 'copy' Nature only in the sense that they refashion it in their own image.[1] In this, they differ on the one hand from the merely 'imaginative' writers, who accumulate and align events without attempting to explain their 'mysterious meaning', on the other from the 'rabid' naturalists (the epithet is identical, be it noted, with that applied to naturalistic *painters* in the *Contes de Champfleury*) who bring to bear on the human mind the same meticulous scrutiny as is accorded by doctors to the human body, in a vain attempt to 'find the (invisible) mainspring'.[2] Another point of interest is that Baudelaire here once again brings in the notion of 'supernaturalism', which in the *Salon de 1846* he had invoked in respect of Delacroix—albeit in a rather specialized connotation, borrowed from a text of Heine's in which the German writer, after roundly declaring that where art was concerned, he was a 'surnaturaliste', had gone on to affirm that the types required by the artist were to be found not only in Nature but also (and these were the most remarkable) within the artist's own mind or soul, 'comme la symbolique innée d'idées innées'.[3] But in the 1848 article on Poe, the term appears to retain its more conventional meaning, and to denote simply any system of ideas, or system of enquiry, that seeks to go beyond (or 'above') natural law. Thus Baudelaire

[1]'Tous ces gens, avec une volonté et une bonne foi infatigable, décalquent la nature, la pure nature.—Laquelle?—La leur.' (*HE* 457). Cf. *Salon de 1846*, *CE* 111:'. . . le troisième [dessin] . . . peut négliger la nature; il en représente une autre, analogue à l'esprit et au tempérament de l'auteur'. The sole change, it will be observed, is in the more vivid image contained in the word 'décalquer'— which means, literally and technically, to 'transfer' a design from one piece of paper to another. Cf. equally, for this notion of the re-creation of Nature, the texts from *Quelques caricaturistes français* and *De l'essence du rire*, cit. p. 78 n. 2 and 3, above.

[2]'D'autres, naturalistes enragés, examinent l'âme à la loupe, comme les médecins le corps, et tuent leurs yeux à trouver le ressort' (*HE* 457). Cf. p. 88, above.

[3]*CE* 108. The quotation (from Heine's *Salon de 1831*) is introduced with the words: 'Voici quelques lignes de M. Henri Heine qui expliquent assez bien la méthode de Delacroix, méthode qui est, comme chez tous les hommes vigoureusement constitués, le résultat de son tempérament...' Inasmuch as Delacroix himself was wont to use the expression 'le surnaturel' in the sense simply of 'le merveilleux' or 'le miraculeux' (see L. Horner, *B. critique de Delacroix*, 137 n. 200), B.'s application to him of Heine's formula, might well give rise to some ambiguity. The actual notion expressed by Heine is, incidentally, to be found already in Byron's *Childe Harold's Pilgrimage*, Canto IV, verse cxxii: 'Where are the forms the sculptor's soul hath seized? /In him alone. Can Nature show so fair?' (Everyman ed., p. 130).

observes that in several of these 'romanciers forts', one may discern 'la préoccupation d'un perpétuel surnaturalisme'; and this is linked, in the cases especially of Balzac and Poe, with the search for some 'unitary system', some spiritual principle which could be presumed to underlie and explain the material universe.[1]

A phrase used by Baudelaire in defining these preoccupations, suggests strongly that he too may have shared them in some degree.[2] This is confirmed not only by the testimony of his friends Champfleury[3] and Prarond,[4] but by certain oblique references made in two prose texts of slightly later date: the essay *Du Vin et du hachish* (March 1851), the study of *Edgar Allan Poe, sa vie et ses ouvrages* (March–April 1852); in these, Baudelaire implies his decided sympathy with those 'spiritualists' who seek to raise themselves to a 'supra-natural existence',[5] those 'mystics' who aspire towards the Infinite and strive 'ardently' to discover 'the laws of their being'.[6] More difficult to determine, however, is the precise effect this new-found 'spiritualism' may have had on Baudelaire's attitudes to Nature. Thus for the period 1847–50, our sole evidence is that

---

[1] *HE* 457–8. B. has here a good deal more to say about Balzac's 'system' than about Poe's, of which at this stage, indeed, he had little knowledge; cf., however, the brief comment in his 1852 article on Poe: 'Il a, comme les conquérants et les philosophes, une entraînante aspiration vers l'unité; il assimile les choses morales aux choses physiques' (*OP* 1, 287). Cf., for Balzac's 'unitary' aspirations, P. Laubriet, *Intelligence de l'art chez Balzac*, 45–8.

[2] '. . . toutes ces théories récentes sont quelquefois tombées par un accident singulier dans la tête des poètes, en même temps que dans les têtes savantes' (*HE* 457). To which Claude Pichois, *B.*, 117, justly adds this comment: 'Dans la tête des poètes, donc dans la tête de Baudelaire qui dut alors se transformer en volcan d'idées'.

[3] Who describes him, around 1846, as forever speaking of 'things supernatural': 'Ses adversaires l'accusaient de chercher à ne pas paraître *naturel*; en effet il ne parlait guère que de choses surnaturelles' (*Souvenirs*, 135).

[4] Who says, of B.'s undogmatic 'spiritualism': 'Il était, j'en suis sûr, et on en trouverait la trace dans ses œuvres, attiré par le surnaturalisme' (*CML* 11, 1158). These recollections of Prarond's mostly concern the period 1841–6.

[5] *Du Vin et du hachish*, *PA* 228, 233. (To avoid tiresome recourse hereafter to a qualifying 'sic', I specify, once and for all, that the spelling 'hachish'—as C. Pichois, in his edition of *PA*, was the first to note—is that adopted by B. himself.) Cf. this approving declaration (attributed to B.), in the second (and final!) number of *Le Salut public*: 'En 89, la société était rationaliste et matérialiste.— Aujourd'hui elle est foncièrement spiritualiste et chrétienne' (*OP* 1 205; cf. 529, 534).

[6] *Edgar Allan Poe, OP* 1, 292–3.

furnished by the contemporary versions of two poems, *Le Vin des chiffonniers* and *Le Vin des honnêtes gens*, both of which were originally composed in 1841–3. To take first *Le Vin des chiffonniers*, this concludes with a grateful homage to a Deity whose gifts to suffering Mankind include wine no less than sleep, and whom all things in Nature humbly combine to 'name':

> Grandeur de la bonté de *Celui que tout nomme*,
> Qui nous avait déjà donné le doux sommeil,
> Et voulut ajouter le vin, fils du soleil,
> Pour réchauffer le cœur et calmer la souffrance
> De tous les malheureux qui meurent en silence.[1]

The concept implied in the phrase italicized appears less pantheistic than deistic: the objects of creation, that is to say, do not so much directly 'embody' God, as collectively *attest* His existence and thereby 'declare' and glorify His name.[2] If, however, we now turn to the poem published by Baudelaire in June 1850, under the title *Le Vin des honnêtes gens* and the general heading (jointly with *Châtiment de l'orgueil*) 'Poésies de la famille',[3] we perceive that this form of 'testimony' may be active rather than merely passive, and in that sense be said to constitute a 'natural' (i.e. spontaneous) form of worship; God in his goodness having 'engendered' wine and bestowed its consolations upon Man, Man and wine now in their turn declare their gratitude through the 'poems' they jointly create and

---

[1]MS. Godoy (reprod. *OCP* 1551, and in facsimile in *CML* II, pl. i); my italics. The following two considerations allow this MS. to be dated as of 1848–51: (a) it is signed 'Charles Baudelaire'—a form that B. employed only from Jan. 1848 onwards (cf. *OP* I, 563; *FMA* 402); (b) what is obviously a later version of the poem, is also extant, and this (reprod. *DP*) must be dated as of 1851–2. For the presumed differences between the (missing) 1841–3 version and the present one, cf. *FMA* 402–3.

[2]In short, not *Deus sive Natura* but *Cœli enarrant gloriam Dei*. B. may of course simply here have intended to transpose—but to his own humanitarian context—the actual form of words of the first verse of the 19th Psalm. Cf., for a comment on B.'s phrase in its relation both to his own later philosophy and to that of Lamartine, J. Pommier, *Mystique de B.*, 148—as also pp. 200–1 and n. 4, below. For B.'s (inferred) attitude to pantheism around 1851, cf. p. 122 and n. 5.

[3]This highly un-Baudelairian phrase may perhaps be a concession to the general tone of the journal (*Le Magasin des familles*) in which the two poems appeared—a tone sufficiently conveyed by the title of the fairy-tale immediately following: 'Contes des veillées de famille. Le Soldat de plomb, tendre et constant. Conte d'enfant' . . .

that 'rise upwards' towards God.[1] In the preceding verses, however, the gratitude directly expressed is that of wine itself—delighting to refresh not only the honest tiller of the soil, but also (in this true 'Poésie de la famille') his wife and son; implicitly at least, therefore, Nature and Man are here harmoniously at one:

> Le soir, l'âme du vin chante dans les bouteilles:
> Homme, je pousserai vers toi, mon bien-aimé,
> Sous ma prison de verre et mes cires vermeilles
> Un chant plein de lumière et de fraternité.
>
> Je sais combien il faut, sur la colline en flamme,
> De peine, de sueur, et de soleil cuisant
> Pour engendrer ma vie et pour me donner l'âme;
> Mais je ne serai point ingrat ni malfaisant,
>
> Car j'éprouve une joie extrême quand je tombe
> Dans le gosier d'un homme usé par les travaux,
> Et sa poitrine honnête est une chaude tombe
> Où je me plais bien mieux que dans mes froids caveaux.
>
> Entends-tu retentir les refrains des dimanches
> Et l'espoir qui gazouille en mon sein palpitant?
> Les coudes sur la table et retroussant tes manches,
> Tu me glorifieras, et tu seras content.
>
> J'allumerai les yeux de ta femme attendrie,
> A ton fils je rendrai sa force et ses couleurs,
> Et serai pour ce frêle athlète de la vie
> L'huile qui raffermit les muscles des lutteurs.
>
> En toi je tomberai, végétale ambroisie,
> Comme le grain fécond tombe dans le sillon,
> Et de notre union naîtra la poésie
> Qui montera vers Dieu comme un grand papillon![2]

It might almost seem, then, from these two verse texts of 1848–51, that having earlier expelled God from Nature, in the tradition of eighteenth-century 'natural religion', Baudelaire now felt obliged to restore Him to His rightful place both as Creator and as supreme object

---

[1] A cognate expression of this notion of 'testimony', but this time exclusively limited to the sphere of Art, is to be found in the final verse of Les Phares (a poem which may well have been conceived in first draft during the present period); cf. FMA 282–3, 279–80, as also my art. cit. 'Les Esthétiques de B.', pp. 486–7 n. 24.

[2] Magasin des familles, June 1850, pp. 336–7.

of worship. Yet if we now go on to examine three important prose texts of 1851–2, we shall find the change of standpoint, though unquestionable, to be essentially moral rather than religious. We must, of course, here reckon with Baudelaire's decided espousal, as the direct result or by-product of his involvement in the events of 1848, of certain humanitarian and utilitarian doctrines of art.[1] This new affiliation for the first time becomes evident in the essay on *Pierre Dupont* which was to form, towards the end of August 1851, one of the later instalments of the *Chants et chansons* at that time being issued by this friend of some seven or eight years' standing. Baudelaire begins by offering a 'broad and rapid' conspectus of the recent development of poetry in France: affirming his preference for the type of poet who freely expresses his own personal emotions or who, better, 'incarnates' those of his fellow-men, he sums up his general position by declaring boldly that with the publication of certain poems by Auguste Barbier,[2] 'la question fut vidée, et l'art fut désormais inséparable de la morale et de l'utilité'.[3] It is interesting, in the light of the similar ideas soon to be expressed more fully (as we shall see) in the other two prose texts of this period, to note Baudelaire's reasons for condemning the whole Romantic 'deviation' into aestheticism:

La puérile utopie de l'école de *l'art pour l'art*, en excluant la morale, et souvent même la passion, était nécessairement stérile. Elle se mettait en flagrante contravention avec le génie de l'humanité. *Au nom des principes supérieurs qui constituent la vie universelle*, nous avons le droit de la déclarer coupable d'hétérodoxie.[4]

Predictably enough, after this preamble, Baudelaire shows himself hereafter mainly concerned with Dupont's 'political and socialist songs'; he does, however, salute in passing (and from an implicitly primitivist standpoint) the appearance, in 1849, of Dupont's *Le Chant des paysans*,[5] while stressing above all, in his friend that same deep (or 'fanatical') love of Nature he had so often previously discerned,

[1] See in this connection my art. cit., 'B: the Poet as Moralist', pp. 197–204.

[2] The reference is to Barbier's *Iambes* and *Lazare*, first published during the 1830's.

[3] *AR* 185.

[4] *AR* 184; my italics in the second case. Cf. pp. 96–8, below.

[5] *AR* 190: 'Tout le monde sut gré au poëte d'avoir enfin introduit un peu de vérité et de nature dans ces chants destinés à charmer les soirées . . . C'était un mélange véridique d'une mélancolie naïve avec une joie turbulente et innocente, et par-ci par-là les accents robustes de la virilité laborieuse'.

as we have seen, in admired artists and writers.[1] Not that the 'pastoral Muse' (he adds) is to be found only in Dupont's 'rustic songs'; even in his political poems, or in those 'chants symboliques' which express his essential philosophy, the voice of Nature is still to be heard—for all the world like some mountain stream, fresh from the 'high snows', murmuring gently yet persistently beside a busy, characterless road.[2] To illustrate this point further, Baudelaire goes on, significantly, to invoke the passage from Calderón's *El Mágico prodigioso* in which Nature sings, with one voice, the message of universal Love; this same mysterious voice, this same 'universal remedy', is heard (Baudelaire claims) throughout Dupont's work.[3] Thus even when the song to be composed is a dirge or an elegy on the 'abominable civil war', the first images that come into a mind deeply imprinted with the 'melancholy beauty of Nature', are those of pale lilies and of grey verbena:

> La France est pâle comme un lys,
> Le front ceint de grises verveines.[4]

In all this praise of Dupont's qualities, there enters, no doubt (as equally in the companion texts next to be considered), a certain element of covert, almost 'therapeutic' self-admonition; to whom after all, if not to the critic himself, is the following reproachful exhortation addressed?

En effet, la nature est si belle, et l'homme est si grand, qu'il est difficile, en se mettant à un point de vue supérieur, de concevoir le sens du mot: irréparable. Quand un poëte [i.e. Dupont] vient affirmer des choses aussi bonnes et aussi consolantes, aurez-vous le courage de regimber?[5]

[1]Among artists, Corot, Français, Th. Rousseau, Decamps, Daumier, the Romantic landscape-painters in general; among writers, Chennevières, Champfleury and (by implication) Hoffmann. See pp. 71, 86, above; for Dupont, see *AR* 192.

[2]*AR* 192. Cf., in this connection, the article on Dupont by D. Higgins, *FS*, 1949, pp. 131–2. As to B.'s image this, as I have suggested above (p. 6 n. 3), may derive from his recollections of the Pyrenean holiday of 1838.

[3]*AR* 192–3; cf. 506–7. Equally with Calderón, could not B. here have instanced the Shelley of *Love's Philosophy*?

[4]*AR* 1930. The lines quoted are from Dupont's 'chant funèbre', *Les Journées de juin*.

[5]*AR* 195. Cf. this almost exactly contemporary observation, in a letter to Ancelle dated 10 Jan. 1850; B. has just expressed the desire that relations between the two of them should henceforth improve: 'D'ailleurs, *à tout péché miséricorde*, ce que vous savez que je traduis ainsi: il n'y a rien d'irréparable' (*CG* I, 123).

Baudelaire himself, alas, was to prove only too 'courageously' recalcitrant: not only, within the next few years, was he to profess dogmatically his total *un*concern for the beauty of Nature, but he was to proclaim, by the very titles of two of his most tragic poems, *L'Irréparable* and *L'Irrémédiable* (published respectively in 1855 and 1857), the all too real significance of the word he here so confidently rejects . . .

Of our other two prose texts of 1851–2: *Les Drames et les romans honnêtes, L'École païenne*, the second is by far the more important for our present purposes. But the two articles remain closely linked both in their publication and conception (they appeared, within a few weeks of each other, in a journal with which Baudelaire was to be closely associated throughout the whole of its short life[1]), and to some extent—at any rate in the moral sphere—they pursue a single, continuous argument. I would single out initially in this respect, in *Les Drames et les romans honnêtes*, the paragraph in which Baudelaire passes, from an attack on specific dramatists and novelists of the 'virtuous' school incriminated, to a consideration of the whole question of morality in art:

L'art est-il utile? Oui. Pourquoi? Parce qu'il est l'art. Y a-t-il un art pernicieux? Oui. C'est celui qui dérange *les conditions de la vie*. Le vice est séduisant, il faut le peindre séduisant; mais il traîne avec lui des maladies et des douleurs morales singulières; il faut les décrire . . . Le crime est-il toujours châtié, la vertu gratifiée? Non; mais, cependant, si votre roman, si votre drame est bien fait, il ne prendra envie à personne de violer *les lois de la nature*. La première condition nécessaire pour faire un art sain est la croyance à *l'unité intégrale*. Je défie qu'on me trouve un seul ouvrage d'imagination qui réunisse toutes les conditions du beau, et qui soit un ouvrage pernicieux.[2]

After which, Baudelaire goes on to invoke the magisterial 'open letter' addressed by Balzac to Hippolyte Castille in October 1846, in which, according to Baudelaire, the great novelist had enumerated

---

[1]Cf., in this connection, *OP* I, 536–7; *CLM* 455 n. 57; my art. cit., 'Les Esthétiques de B.', p. 483.

[2]*Semaine théâtrale*, 27 November 1851, p. 27 (*AR* 284; my italics). This argument was to be taken up again by B., and adapted to his own case, in the 'Notes' he prepared in 1857 for his defence counsel; see my art. cit., 'B.: The Poet as Moralist', pp. 205–6.

tous les châtiments qui suivent incessamment les violateurs de la loi morale et les enveloppent déjà comme un enfer terrestre . . .[1]

The argument in *L'École païenne* is less subtle, yet at the same time more deeply felt. The initial denunciation, as the title implies, is of the nostalgic 'pagans' whose worldly innocence is matched by their political irresponsibility:

La ville est sens dessus dessous. Les boutiques se ferment. Les femmes font à la hâte leurs provisions, les rues se dépavent, tous les cœurs sont serrés par l'angoisse d'un grand événement. Le pavé sera prochainement inondé de sang.—Vous rencontrez un animal plein de béatitude; il a sous le bras des bouquins étranges et hiéroglyphiques.—Et vous, lui dites-vous, quel parti prenez-vous?—Mon cher, répond-il d'une voix douce, je viens de découvrir de nouveaux renseignements très curieux sur le mariage d'Isis et d'Osiris.[2]

This same paganism, albeit in a less specific (and incongruous) form, had been professed by Baudelaire himself a few years earlier;[3] but what he goes on to repudiate, in the second half of this article of January 1852, is something altogether more integral to his own literary inspiration, to his own personal philosophy, to his own way of life: the cult of images, the 'immoderate' and passionate pursuit of beauty, form, art. In the ardour of his self-denunciation, Baudelaire reverts indeed to the utilitarian position taken up some months previously in the article on *Pierre Dupont*—quite forgetting, it would seem, his more recent condemnation, in *Les Drames et les romans*

---

[1]Loc. cit. (*AR* 285). The reference here imputed to Balzac being to the *moral* sufferings endured by the miscreants, need not be taken as contradicting the rhetorical dialogue (above-quoted) in the paragraph immediately preceding, in the course of which, no doubt with purely *legal* sanctions in mind, B. had (as we have seen) returned a negative answer to the question 'Le crime est-il toujours châtié, la vertu gratifiée?'—I say 'imputed to Balzac', and 'according to B.', advisedly: there is in fact nothing in Balzac's 'letter' (which appeared in the journal *La Semaine*; cf. *Œuvres diverses* III, *OCC*, [XL], 646–52) that could be said to correspond with the 'enumeration' in question. On another occasion I hope to return to this whole question of the influence on B. of Balzac's letter to Castille; cf., in the meantime, *OP* I, 127–8 (text of a *Causerie* attrib. B. by J. Crépet, ibid., 503, and pub. in *Le Tintamarre* towards the end of October 1846).

[2]*Semaine théâtrale*, 22 Jan. 1852, p. 18 (*AR* 292). For the identity of certain of the 'pagans' in question, cf. 69 n. 1, 120 n. 1, 123 and n. 1, below.

[3]Cf. pp. 48–53, above.

honnêtes, of all 'moralizing' or 'propagandist' schools.[1] But although in *L'École païenne* the aesthetic standpoint may have shifted, the underlying moral doctrine, as may be seen from the ensuing quotation, remains substantially unchanged, or is simply carried a stage further in the same direction. Thus Baudelaire here asserts, once again, the integral 'unity' of the world and hence of the moral order obtaining within it, but at the same time he amplifies considerably the notion of retribution briefly affirmed in *Les Drames et les romans honnêtes,* whereby each 'violation' of Nature's 'laws' infallibly exacts its due punishment from her.[2] The spirituality of the universe, finally, the 'hidden' and immaterial forces which govern its 'movement'—these are now clearly affirmed:

S'environner exclusivement des séductions de l'art physique, c'est créer de grandes chances de perdition... Le monde ne vous apparaîtra que sous sa forme matérielle. *Les ressorts qui le font se mouvoir* vous resteront longtemps cachés.

Puissent la religion et la philosophie venir un jour, comme forcées par le cri d'un désespéré. Telle sera toujours la destinée des insensés *qui ne voient dans la nature que des rhythmes et des formes.* Encore la philosophie ne leur apparaîtra-t-elle d'abord que comme un jeu intéressant, une gymnastique agréable, une escrime dans le vide. Mais combien ils seront châtiés! Tout enfant dont l'esprit poétique sera surexcité, dont le spectacle excitant de mœurs actives et laborieuses ne frappera pas incessamment les yeux, qui entendra sans cesse parler de gloire et de volupté, dont les sens seront journellement caressés, irrités, effrayés, allumés et satisfaits par des objets d'art, deviendra le plus malheureux des hommes et rendra les autres malheureux... Tout ce qui peut lui arriver de plus heureux, c'est que *la nature le frappe d'un effrayant rappel à l'ordre.* En effet, telle est la loi de la vie, que qui refuse les jouissances pures de l'activité honnête ne peut sentir que les jouissances terribles du vice. Le péché contient son

---

[1]Cf., on the one hand, this passage from *Les Drames et les romans honnêtes*: 'Il est douloureux de noter que nous trouvons des erreurs semblables dans deux écoles opposées: l'école bourgeoise et l'école socialiste. Moralisons, moralisons, s'écrient toutes les deux avec une fièvre de missionnaires. Naturellement l'une prêche la morale bourgeoise, et l'autre la morale socialiste. Dès lors l'art n'est plus qu'une question de propagande' (*Semaine théâtrale*, 27 Nov. 1851, p. 27; *AR* 284)—and on the other, this fervent rallying cry which conclut *L'École païenne*: 'Il faut que la littérature aille retremper ses forces dans une atmosphère meilleure. Le temps n'est pas loin où l'on comprendra que toute littérature qui se refuse à marcher fraternellement entre la science et la philosophie est une littérature homicide et suicide' (ibid, 22 Jan. 1852, p. 18; *AR* 297).

[2]Cf. p. 96, above.

enfer, et *la nature dit de temps en temps à la douleur et à la misère: Allez convaincre ces rebelles.*[1]

In a sense, this might still be termed a 'cult of Nature': Baudelaire has by no means entirely parted company with those eighteenth-century philosophers of Nature invoked, as will be recalled, in the 1846 article on Ménard,[2] and indeed in at least one passage of *Le Neveu de Rameau* we may find Diderot's eponymous 'amoralist' professing something very like Baudelaire's notion that vice carries within itself the seeds of its own perdition.[3] The fact remains, nevertheless, that in these three texts of 1851–2 Baudelaire has clearly abandoned his earlier belief that evil, within the scheme of Nature, enjoys and should enjoy a privileged and providential status.[4] Nothing perhaps could better illustrate this whole change (or reversal) of standpoint, than a comparison between the two poems *Allégorie* (composed in first draft around 1843), and *Châtiment de l'orgueil* (published in 1850, written perhaps two or three years earlier): in the one case, the courtesan, deemed 'necessary' to the functioning of the world, who believes the gift of beauty to absolve her from all infamy; in the other, the mediaeval doctor punished (as a principle of Nature: 'thus is *all* pride punished', implies the title) for the arrogance of his *furor theologicus*: he had dared to challenge Jesus, in

[1]*Semaine théâtrale*, 22 Jan. 1852, p. 18 (*AR* 294–6; my italics). An erratum in this passage ('de grandes *chaînes* de perdition' for 'de grandes chances') was corrected in the following no., 1 Feb. 1852, p. 32; see *AR* 535. But J. Crépet, *AR* 536, has failed to note that the reading 'Allez *convaincre* ces rebelles' (corrected in the 1869 edition of *L'Art romantique* to 'Allez vaincre . . .') figured as such in the original text as well as in the 1866 reprint. Nature being here viewed as a (chastising) force for good, rather than as a propensity to evil, I cannot agree with Margaret Gilman, *B. the Critic*, 72 (cf., however, the more cautious observation by Mother Mary Alphonsus, *Influence of J. de Maistre on B.*, 16) in detecting the influence of Maistre in this passage: if not Balzac (directly named in this connection, it will be recalled, in *Les Drames et les romans honnêtes*), then Diderot, would seem here to be a more likely mentor for B.—cf. pp. 96–7, and n. 3, below.

[2]Cf. p. 24, above.

[3]Rameau's system of 'punishments' is admittedly of a more purely material order than Baudelaire's: 'Tout a son vrai loyer dans ce monde. Il y a deux procureurs-généraux, l'un à votre porte, qui châtie les délits contre la société; la nature est l'autre. Celle-ci connaît de tous les vices qui échappent aux lois. Vous vous livrez à la débauche des femmes, vous serez hydropique; vous êtes crapuleux, vous serez pulmonique; vous ouvrez votre porte à des marauds et vous vivez avec eux, vous serez trahi, persifflé, méprisé . . .' (Diderot, *Le Neveu de Rameau*, in *Œuvres*, Brière, 1821, XXI, 95; cf. ed. J. Fabre, 212–13 n. 237.

[4]Cf. p. 22, above.

an instant his towering intellect is made to crumble into imbecility.[1]

Viewed in relation to the subsequent development of his thought, Baudelaire's new-found didacticism could not but weaken, even undermine, his allegiance to Nature; the naive optimism of the Dupont article, the *simpliste* moral determinism of *Les Drames et les romans honnêtes* and *L'École païenne*—such beliefs could scarcely for long maintain themselves against the manifold discouragements, personal no less than political, that were now crowding in upon the beleaguered poet.

[1]For *Allégorie*, cf. also pp. 23–4, above; for *Châtiment de l'orgueil*, my art. cit., 'B. The Poet as Moralist', p. 203. No aesthetic conclusion, incidentally, can be drawn from this contrast: *both* poems must be counted among the weakest that B. wrote!

PART TWO
1852–65

V

The Repudiation of Nature

1. NATURE VERSUS MAN

THE year 1852 was something of a climacteric for Baudelaire. Predictably, the Bonapartist *coup d'état* of 2 December 1851 had induced a revulsion from politics or at least from all political action; with the jettisoning of his project for a verse-collection under the title *Les Limbes*, he seems for a time to have considered abandoning poetry altogether, in order to devote himself to the writing of 'metaphysical' novels; the preparation of his long article of March–April 1852 on *Edgar Allan Poe, sa vie et ses ouvrages*, will have impelled him to ponder, and to begin to assimilate to himself, Poe's firmly anti-didactic and anti-utilitarian theories; and finally, it was in March 1852 that he resolved—emphatically if (as it turned out) prematurely—to bring to an end his long and chequered relationship with Jeanne Duval.[1] It is perhaps no accident that this general volte-face, manifested in so many domains, should have led in due course to a new phase of active (if not always consistent) *hostility* towards Nature—a repudiation, for the first time, of that belief in Nature as ultimate guide or arbiter which Baudelaire had retained, as we have seen, through all the transformations of his moral and aesthetic thought. Now, however, the sally which he had allowed himself in his *Salon de 1846*: 'la première affaire d'un artiste est de substituer l'homme à la nature et de protester contre elle'—a sally which in its original context had carried certain quite specific

---

[1] Cf. the comments made in two letters of March 1852, to Ancelle and Poulet-Malassis respectively: '*Le 2 Décembre m'a physiquement dépolitiqué*'; '. . . je suis décidé à rester désormais étranger à toute la polémique humaine, et plus décidé que jamais à poursuivre le rêve supérieur de l'application de la métaphysique au roman' (*CG* I, 152, 157). In the same month, he writes to his mother (ibid., 168) of the 'influence foudroyante' that recent political events have had on him, and this 'shattering impact' may well be reflected in the final verse of *Le Reniement de Saint-Pierre* (written out in MS. at some time before the beginning of April 1852, and first published in Oct. of that year; see ibid., 153–4, and cf. *FMA* 420–1). For the abandonment of the *Limbes* project, see *FMC* 302–4; for the reference, in the 1852 essay, to Poe's literary theories, *OP* I, 262–3; for the 'break' with Jeanne, *CG* I, 162–5 and 193–4.

(and limiting) polemical connotations[1]— begins for the first time to acquire a truly comprehensive relevance.

On the evidence of several texts shortly to be discussed, we may perhaps date more or less exactly, from the early months of 1852, Baudelaire's entry into the new phase of *anti*-naturalism. Before coming to these texts, however, I must first mention in the same connection two further poems of more uncertain date and implication. The first of these, *L'Homme libre et la mer* (later to be entitled simply: *L'Homme et la mer*), appeared in the *Revue de Paris* in October 1852, but was perhaps written several years earlier:

> Homme libre, toujours tu chériras la mer;
> La mer est ton miroir; tu contemples ton âme
> Dans le déroulement infini de sa lame,
> Et ton esprit n'est pas un gouffre moins amer.
>
> Tu te plais à plonger au sein de ton image,
> Tu l'embrasses des yeux et des bras, et ton cœur
> Se distrait quelquefois de sa propre rumeur
> Au bruit de cette plainte indomptable et sauvage.
>
> Vous êtes tous les deux ténébreux et discrets;
> Homme, nul ne connaît le fond de tes abîmes;
> O mer, nul ne connaît tes richesses intimes,
> Tant vous êtes jaloux de garder vos secrets.
>
> Et cependant, voilà des siècles innombrables
> Que vous vous combattez sans pitié ni remord,
> Tellement vous aimez le carnage et la mort,
> O lutteurs éternels, ô frères implacables!
>
> (1852 text)

It would be misleading to regard these rather mechanical verses as being in any way expressive of a general attitude to Nature: the purely abstract, even intellectual analogies they pursue, imply no personal commitment on the poet's part.[2] Thus in the first two quatrains the affinity between Man (or between certain 'free' men) and the sea, is ingeniously argued from his physical delight in merging into it—as if, when plunging into waters that reflect back his own image, he were really drawn by the desire to explore and

---

[1]See pp. 78–9, above.
[2]Cf. the judgment by H. Peyre, *Connaissance de B.*, 84: 'assez faible pièce, trop laborieuse dans son parallélisme entre les abîmes de l'homme et ceux de l'océan'.

'embrace' his own mirrored likeness. The third stanza takes up a further analogy, that of secretiveness and 'depth', and re-states this in terms first of one, then the other, partner—making the same point three times but in different words. Such analogies have of course little real significance, even at the purely psychological level; they lack altogether the vivid emotive truth, as well as the haunting imagery, of that cognate stanza from *Moesta et errabunda*, in which (as will be remembered) the same wild, consoling voice takes on the harshly 'sublime' accents of a 'lullaby':

> La mer, la vaste mer, console nos labeurs.
> Quel démon a doté la mer,—rude chanteuse
> Qu'accompagne l'immense orgue des vents grondeurs,—
> De cette fonction sublime de berceuse?
> La mer, la vaste mer, console nos labeurs.[1]

(Nor, again, is it necessarily the case that we cherish in others the exact reflection of ourselves . . . .) As to the paradox implicit in the poem's closing words ('ô frères implacables!'), this is effective only if one accepts that the 'brothers' are *true* brothers, and that, as such, their antagonism gives any cause for surprise . . . .[2] There is also the profounder paradox—which Baudelaire scarcely brings out, and may therefore not have intended—that what actually causes this strife is a still further affinity between Man and sea: their shared love of carnage and death. It is true that this final stanza brings a certain *contradiction* of the affinity previously argued. Yet even if it could be proved that the poem was in fact composed during the months immediately preceding its publication, we would still have no grounds for supposing that the particular conflict here dramatized partakes in any sense of that wider and more fundamental hostility between Nature and Man, that Baudelaire was beginning to express in certain texts (as we shall see) from 1852 onwards; the 'game' of analogies here illustrated is on the contrary one that could be

---

[1] 1855 text, ll. 6–10. Here surely, rather than in *L'Homme et la mer*, is that 'Réthorique [sic] de la mer', to which B. mysteriously alludes in his 'Notes' for the unpublished essay of 1857–60 on *L'Art philosophique* (*OCP* 1107).

[2] In his essay *Du Vin et du hachish* (pub. March 1851), B. uses a similar but more vivid and felicitous image, to characterize the 'struggle' between Man and *wine*: 'Le vin et l'homme me font l'effet de deux lutteurs amis sans cesse combattant, sans cesse réconciliés. Le vaincu embrasse toujours le vainqueur' (*PA* 215; cf. *FMLD* 370).

played by *any* writer, having whatever attitude to Nature (or none).[1] In short, except inasmuch as it attests the abiding fascination exerted by the sea over Baudelaire's imagination, *L'Homme et la mer* has little real significance for our purposes, i.e. as a pointer to his developing attitudes to Nature.

The other text I would here cite is the opening section (but the opening section only[2]) of *Le Soleil*:

> Au fond des carrefours où pendent aux masures
> Les persiennes, abri des secrètes luxures,
> Quand le soleil cruel frappe à traits redoublés
> Sur la ville et les champs, sur les toits et les blés,
> Je vais m'exercer seul à ma fantasque escrime,
> Flairant dans tous les coins les hasards de la rime,
> Trébuchant sur les mots comme sur les pavés,
> Heurtant parfois des vers depuis longtemps rêvés.
>
> (1857 proofs)

The sun, it will be noted, here figures as one element only within a wider description—a determining element, it is true, since it fixes roughly the time of day (high noon? the siesta time of the early afternoon?) and explains, partly, the closed shutters past which the poet treads his way. In its 'cruel' intensity,[3] this sun is very

---

[1] For certain more illustrious antecedents (Byron, Heine, Balzac), which may or may not be 'sources', see *FMCB* 319. Cf. also, from Laprade's *Eleusis* of 1841, this apostrophe to the sea uttered by the Chorus of pilgrims grouped on the shore: 'La Terre et toi *luttez*; tu bats son vieux rempart;/Vous avez toutes deux votre existence à part./. . . comme chez un roi, *dans tes profonds domaines,/Des trésors inouïs bravent les mains humaines* . . ./L'homme cueille en tremblant la nacre sur tes plages,/Dérobe le corail à tes murs de granit,/Mais *nul n'a vu* les bords où ton palais finit;/*L'esprit seul peut plonger plus loin que ta surface* . . .! (*Odes et poëmes*, 1843, pp. 265-7; my italics).

[2] For the other two sections, cf. pp. 13-14, above.

[3] Cf., for a later reminiscence (conscious or unconscious) of these lines, the passage from the essay of 1859-60, *Le Peintre de la vie moderne*, describing the presumed matutinal activities of the illustrator Constantin Guys: 'Quand M. G., à son réveil, ouvre les yeux et qu'il voit *le soleil tapageur donnant l'assaut aux carreaux des fenêtres*, il se dit avec remords, avec regrets: "Quel ordre impérieux! quelle fanfare de lumière! . . ." Il contemple les paysages de la grande ville, paysages de pierre . . . *frappés par les soufflets du soleil*' (*AR* 63, my ital.; cf. *Salon de 1859*, *CE* 344). Curiously enough, a phrase almost identical to B.'s 'le soleil tapageur', is ascribed by C. Roger-Marx (*Le Paysage français*, 34) to a painter B. greatly admired, Corot; for the latter also, it seems, the sun was 'le grand tapageur', its noonday exuberance driving him to exclaim: 'Fuyons: on voit tout!' For analogous references by B. to the 'cruelty' or 'irony' of the sun or summer sky,

different from the kindly 'foster-father' who, in the succeeding second and third parts of the poem, displays (it will be recalled) the most tender concern for all that grows within the fields or that walks at large there;[1] here, on the contrary, the main focus is on the poet (i.e. the individual poet: Baudelaire), as he pursues his solitary way through the city streets, wholly absorbed in his endless running-battles with words. But the contradiction between the two main parts of the poem goes in fact considerably farther than this. In his third and final section, Baudelaire will declare of the sun: 'Quand ainsi qu'un poète, il descend dans les villes, / Il ennoblit le sort des choses les plus viles'. But this could scarcely be taken to apply to the first part of the poem; there, on the contrary, in a town which harbours squalors and secret lusts, we see the shutters pulled down, defensively, *against* the intruding sun. Moreover since (despite the fields and wheat mentioned in the fourth line) the first part as a whole remains clearly and graphically a *town*scape,[2] shall we not find strictly redundant a third section which carefully leads us back *from* the countryside of the second, into an urban world we have already visited in the first? Even at the stylistic level, the discrepancy between the two parts is apparent: the opening lines—with their graphic and telling evocation, within the space of two lines, of a whole 'closed' world of urban vice, and their brilliant portrait of the 'poet at work', his very progress through the streets shaped by (or shaping) the 'lyrical movements' of his mind[3]—have an assurance and individuality of vision that is quite lacking from the rest of the poem, with its prosaic sententiousness and flatly symmetrical enumeration of the 'services rendered' by the sun (to say nothing of the quite singular flatness of its concluding line).

---

cf. (in addition to *Une Charogne*, p. 22, above): *A Celle qui est trop gaie*, ll. 19–20 (p. 108, below); the prose poems of 1859–65 *Le Fou et la Vénus, La Belle Dorothée, Le Tir et le cimetière* (*PPP* 17, 83–4, 156); *Quelques caricaturistes français*, *CE* 414, and *Le Cygne*, l. 26 (p. 110 n. 1, below); *Mangeur d'opium*, *PA* 169–70, 172 (the respective phrases 'un magnifique été débordant *cruellement* dans la chambre mortuaire', 'les étés *criblés* d'une lumière *accablante*'—my italics—are both additions to De Quincey's text; cf. *Confessions* ed. M. Elwin, 467, 474); letter to Gautier of [July 1863], *CG* IV, 174.

[1] Cf. pp. 13–14, above.

[2] Hence, of course, the poem's inclusion within the new *Tableaux parisiens* chapter of the 1861 *FM*; cf. p. 122 n. 2, below.

[3] The phrase is borrowed from Baudelaire's own description, some years later, of the effects he was seeking to convey in his *Petits poëmes en prose* (*PPP*, vi).

All these inconsistencies seem to me proof that the two parts of the poem were, in their first composition, chronologically no less than logically separate from one another—with the opening lines, more-over, written many years later and most probably during the present period.[1] No doubt what induced Baudelaire (in 1856, when preparing the first edition of *Les Fleurs du Mal?*) to bring the two fragments together, was the convenient link furnished by the re-currence in each of certain figures and details: sun, poet, town, fields, corn. But in exploiting these common details, he has failed signally to resolve the inconsistencies that also ensue. It could, I suppose, be argued that the space left between the two parts was intended to imply a certain lapse of time, a certain change of stand-point: as the poet in his turn eventually 'awakens', like the roses and the earthworms in the fields, to the sun's influence, then *his* anxieties, too—perhaps even the preoccupations of his craft—'evaporate' towards the sun; he is brought to see the world in a new light—to 'ennoble' it, in fact (in the process of writing his poem), by virtue of the transfiguring power he shares with, and borrows from, the sun. But in truth nothing of all this is even faintly implied in the text; one must conclude that here as in *J'aime le souvenir de ces époques nues*, Baudelaire was simply unable to weld his two con-stituent fragments into a coherent unity, to 'paper over' the clearly visible 'crack' between them.

From the standpoint of our present chapter, the significant element of this text is of course its allusion, in lines 3–4, to the noonday 'cruelty' of the sun; this detail we re-encounter—but in a *specifically* anti-naturalist context—in the fifth and sixth verses of a poem addressed (anonymously) to Mme Sabatier in December 1852, under the title *A une femme trop gaie*:

> Quelquefois dans un beau jardin
> Où je traînais mon agonie,
> J'ai senti comme une ironie
> Le soleil déchirer mon sein.

---

[1] Other indications to this same effect would be the analogy between the open-ing couplet, and the whole 'anatomy' of urban depravity presented in *Le Crépus-cule du soir* (first text: 1851–2); or again, the reference in l. 8 to 'vers *depuis longtemps* rêvés', suggesting a writer of some maturity rather than the prentice poet of 1841–5.

> Et le printemps et la verdure
> Ont tant humilié mon cœur
> Que j'ai puni sur une fleur
> L'insolence de la Nature.
>
> (1852 MS., ll. 17–24, *CG* I, 181–2)

Within the poem as a whole, it should be explained, these two quatrains have a demonstrative, almost polemical function: they serve to explain, obliquely and retrospectively, the sudden outburst of the preceding line: 'Je te hais autant que je t'aime';[1] they also prepare, more directly, the fantasied 'punishment' described (with singular complicity) in the last part of the poem, whereby the poet 'revenges' himself in imagination upon the woman's body (as previously, in reality, upon a flower) for the 'insulting' exuberance and health of her beauty—for the insufferable and provocative *gaiety* specified in each of the poem's successive titles: *A une femme trop gaie*; *A Celle qui est trop gaie*.

In speaking of the 'irony' of the sun, and of the 'insolence' of Nature, Baudelaire, here as elsewhere, is no doubt simply taking a

---

[1]The sentiment no doubt goes back to Catullus ('Odi et amo'), but the exact phrase would seem to me, like much else in the poem, to derive from an important episode in Musset's *Confession d'un enfant du siècle*. Octave (the narrator of the story, the 'enfant du siècle' of the title) is visited at night by the mistress who has betrayed him; he warns her: 'Devant Dieu, devant Dieu . . . je ne vous reprendrai pas pour maîtresse, car *je vous hais autant que je vous aime*. Devant Dieu, si vous voulez de moi, je vous tue demain matin' (*Œuvres en prose*, Pléiade, 86; the phrase italicized—by me—varies another previously used, ibid., 84: 'Enfin, je l'abhorrais et je l'idolâtrais'). A page or so later (88) recalling his past happiness with this woman, Octave evokes (like B. in his poem) 'le spectacle de la nature dans sa splendeur'—then felt by him, however, not as an 'irony', but on the contrary as 'le plus puissant des aphrodisiaques'. Finally, one may note that the 'punishment' devized by B. for the 'femme trop gaie', is in effect the fantasied extension of certain actions and threats of Octave's—as if B., for his part, in explaining his perverse desire to inflict upon his own beloved (?) 'une blessure large et creuse' (ll. 31–2), had in imagination armed himself with that same kitchen-knife which Octave had melodramatically laid beneath his pillow, swearing 'je te jure que je te tue tout à l'heure et moi aussi' (op. cit., 85); cf. also the earlier paragraph, on this same page, in which Octave strikes his mistress's neck with his hand—revenging himself thereby upon her 'impudent beauty', just as B. was to revenge himself both upon that of the springtime garden ('. . . j'ai *puni* sur une fleur/L'*insolence* de la Nature') and (in imagination) upon that of the woman herself (l. 29: 'Pour *châtier* ta chair *joyeuse* . . .'). For other borrowings by B. from this text of Musset's, see my art. cit., 'Pour une chronologie des *FM*', pp. 352–4 and notes.

stage further the stock Romantic and pre-Romantic theme of Nature's 'callous' disregard of Man's suffering.[1] But this theme is itself the inversion of that far more ancient convention which Ruskin was to dub the 'Pathetic Fallacy'[2]—a convention we may, as it happens, find directly (if incidentally) satirized in a poem, *La Béatrice,* which though published only in 1857, was perhaps composed some ten years earlier:[3]

[1]Cf., in addition to the phrase (discussed below) from the letter to Desnoyers, the second quatrain of the sonnet *Avec ses vêtements ondoyants et nacrés* . . .: 'Comme le sable morne et l'azur des déserts,/Insensibles *tous deux à l'humaine souffrance,*/Comme les longs réseaux de la houle des mers,/Elle se développe avec indifférence' (my italics); the description, in the essay *Quelques caricaturistes français* of a drawing from a 'medical' series by Daumier: 'L'un [de ces dessins], qui a trait au choléra, représente une place publique inondée, criblée de lumière et de chaleur. Le ciel parisien, fidèle à son habitude ironique dans les grands fléaux et les grands remue-ménages politiques, le ciel est splendide; il est blanc, incandescent d'ardeur' (*CE* 414); the later reference, in the poem *Le Cygne* (l. 26), to the 'ironic' and 'cruelly blue' sky that mocks the 'exiled' swan. Cf. on the contrary, the earlier *Une Charogne,* in which, as we have seen (p. 22, above), the 'irony' of Nature is sardonically *admired* rather than resented. Among the various antecedent examples from other writers (Mme de Staël, Byron, Leopardi, Lamartine, George Sand, Mme Ackermann) noted by V. L. Saulnier (ed. Vigny, *Destinées,* 28 n. 3 and 30 n. 1 and E. Lauvrière, *Vigny,* 354–5 and n.s), I would single out as of particular interest these lines from Chênedollé's ode *L'Indifférence de la Nature* (*Études poétiques,* 1820): 'Ainsi la Nature insensible/Est sans pitié pour nos douleurs,/Et, dans sa rigueur inflexible,/Nous est cruelle et sourde, et se montre impassible/A notre mort comme à nos pleurs' (in: A. J. Steele, *Three Centuries of French Verse,* 279). Cf. also, apart from Vigny's own *Maison du Berger* (pub. 1844), ll. 281–301, Lamartine's *Les Pavots* (pub. 1849), ll. 1–4; Hugo's *Tristesse d'Olympio* (1840: 'L'impassible nature a déjà tout repris'); the texts by Boyer and Castille cit. p. 114, and n. 2 to p. 117, below. One could of course find innumerable still earlier versions of this theme, if one were to regard it simply as an accentuated version of the traditional contrast or dissonance (going back at least to Petrarch) between the beauty and serenity of Nature on the one hand, and the unhappiness of the poet on the other.

[2]Cf., in this connection, pp. 239–40 n. 2, below.

[3]Cf. (*FMCB* 499) the similarities of theme and detail with the two poems *De profundis clamavi* (first pub. 1851; original title: *La Béatrix*) and *Le Vampire* (first pub. 1855; original title: *La Béatrice*); if like these two others the present poem may be presumed to concern Jeanne Duval, it is likely to have been drafted, if not finally composed, during the heyday of B.'s relationship with his coloured mistress, i.e. between 1842 and 1848. More specifically, there is the analogy between the final section of the poem, and the 'hypothetical' (but no doubt all too real) situation described in the *Choix de maximes consolantes sur l'amour* of March 1846: 'De nombreuses et ignobles infidélités, des habitudes de bas lieu, de honteux secrets découverts mal à propos vous inspirent de l'horreur pour l'idole . . .' (*OP* II, 8).

Dans des terrains cendreux, calcinés, sans verdure,
Comme je me plaignais un jour à la nature,
Et que de ma pensée, en vaguant au hasard,
J'aiguisais lentement sur mon cœur le poignard,
Je vis en plein midi descendre sur ma tête
Un nuage funèbre et gros d'une tempête,
Qui portait un troupeau de démons vicieux,
Semblables à des nains cruels et curieux.
A me considérer froidement ils se mirent,
Et, comme des passants sur un fou qu'ils admirent,
Je les entendis rire et chuchoter entre eux,
En échangeant maint signe et maint clignement d'yeux

—"Contemplons à loisir cette caricature
Et cette ombre d'Hamlet imitant sa posture,
Le regard indécis et les cheveux au vent.
N'est-ce pas grand'pitié de voir ce bon vivant,
Ce gueux, cet histrion en vacances, ce drôle,
Parce qu'il sait jouer artistement son rôle,
Vouloir intéresser au chant de ses douleurs
Les aigles, les grillons, les ruisseaux et les fleurs,
Et même à nous, auteurs de ces vieilles rubriques,
Réciter en hurlant ses tirades publiques?"

(1857 text, ll. 1–22; my italics)

When set beside the lines here italicized, the two verses previously quoted from *A une femme trop gaie* may well seem no more than the reverse side of the same coin. Thus if the poet's mood there turns to 'anger', if he there seeks to 'punish' Nature by striking down a flower, is this not simply because his surroundings now afford him no longer the direct reflection, but on the contrary the flagrant *contradiction*, of his despair; no longer the bare, bleached, treeless landscape of *La Béatrice,* but on the contrary the springtime garden, blazing with sunshine, 'bursting all over' with colour, vigour and life?[1] It must also be observed, as a further limiting factor from our wider standpoint, that in *A une femme trop gaie* Baudelaire's attitude to Nature, in so far as it is expressly set in parallel with his

[1]Cf. Vigny's personified Nature, in *La Maison du Berger*—compelling (and indifferently acknowledging) human admiration for her springtime splendours: 'Mon printemps ne sent pas vos adorations'. We shall see that for all B.'s ironies in *La Béatrice,* the 'paysage d'âme' is a mode to which he has frequent recourse in his poetry; cf. especially, in this connection (pp. 248–50, below), the sonnet *Horreur sympathique.*

attitude to his mistress, conserves a certain implicit ambivalence: even though he may, at this particular moment, claim to hate Nature for its 'insolence', he still (by analogy) loves it for its beauty. (So too, in *L'Homme et la mer,* he had shown Man locked in continual strife with a sea none the less 'cherished' as a brother.[1]) In short, the words 'Je te hais autant que je t'aime' (as equally, of course, the reverse proposition 'Je t'aime autant que je te hais') may be taken to apply no less to Nature than to the woman herself.[2] I would stress, finally, that the two verses in question are wholly *incidental* to a main poetic 'argument' which to that extent, therefore, predetermines their character: given the analogy with Nature, could the poet who in the final stanzas wreaks an imagined revenge upon his mistress, do other than likewise denounce and 'humiliate' the natural beauty that (as he earlier tells us) she so provocatively evokes?

> Ta tête, ton geste et ton air
> Sont beaux comme un beau paysage,
> Le rire joue en ton visage
> Comme un vent frais dans un ciel clair.
>
> (1852 MS., ll. 1–4; *CG* I, 181)

It seems clear, nevertheless, from the evidence of another and more significant text, that Baudelaire must in fact have begun well by the end of 1852 to take up his new position of decided and thoroughgoing (if not always consistent) hostility to Nature. The text in question is the famous 'open' letter to Fernand Desnoyers, published in May 1855 in the collective volume *Fontainebleau,* but dating in all probability (as I have argued elsewhere[3]) from the second half of 1853 or at the latest from early 1854. Now from a phrase in this letter: '. . . *vous savez bien* que je suis incapable de m'attendrir sur les végétaux', etc., we perceive that within his immediate circle Baudelaire must already for some time have been giving vigorous utterance to his new ideas on Nature; and this would seem to be corroborated by a passage in another letter, written many years later to his mother, in which he recalls an excursion he had made with her to Versailles, probably during the spring or early summer of 1853:

[1]Cf. p. 104, above.
[2]And indeed when thus applied, might be said to sum up the whole 'history' of B.'s attitudes towards Nature; cf. my Conclusion, p. 320, below.
[3]In my article, 'A *Festschrift* of 1855', p. 189 and n. 33.

Tu revenais alors de Madrid ou de Constantinople. Je reconnaissais les points de vue devant lesquels tu criais avec ton emphase habituelle: "Que c'est beau!" et puis tu ajoutais: "*Mais toi, tu ne sens pas les beautés de la nature, ce n'est pas de ton âge*".[1]

Mme Aupick's remark leads one to suppose that Baudelaire had previously expressed to her the anti-naturalist sentiments he had no doubt begun (since the previous year?) to voice on every possible occasion—even though she herself, in the naive fashion he affectionately mocks in this same letter of 1862, may have preferred to attribute these to his 'youth' ('ce n'est pas de ton âge'). As a final indirect confirmation of these attitudes in Baudelaire, I would cite (with due caution) the account later to be given by Jules Levallois, of the Bohemian circle of 1852–55. The members of this group, Levallois relates, would in the summer walk out 'interminably' into the country—to Meudon, to Fontenay-aux-Roses, to Châtenay; Baudelaire for his part, however, would rarely join in these 'rustic diversions':

Baudelaire prenait rarement part à nos divertissements champêtres, trouvant le vert des arbres trop fade. "Je voudrais, disait-il avec son air de pince-sans-rire, les prairies teintes en rouge, les rivières jaune d'or et les arbres peints en bleu. La nature n'a pas d'imagination".[2]

It should by no means be supposed that Baudelaire's was the sole voice to be raised, within this Bohemian circle, against the dominant 'Nature-cult'. On the contrary several texts of this period (all but

---

[1]*CG* IV, 133–4, L. of 13/12/1862. The Aupicks had returned to Paris from Constantinople at the beginning of June 1851 (*CG* I, 133; C. Pichois, *MF*, July 1955, p. 483), from Madrid at the end of April 1853 (*CG* I, 196; C. Pichois, *MF*, Aug. 1955, p. 664 and n. 188); for reasons I hope to explain fully in another publication, I would think the latter of these two dates to be the more plausible, for the Versailles excursion in question. Cf., however, A. Feuillerat, *B. et sa mère*, 49–50.

[2]Levallois, *Mémoires d'un critique*, 93; for the dating of the episode, cf. ibid., 89. We need incidentally attach no particular importance, in the present context, to Baudelaire's extravagant desire to see Nature's colour-scheme changed or 'improved upon'; the paradox is one that he had already attributed, in 1847, to the Samuel Cramer of *La Fanfarlo*—borrowing or adapting, then as no doubt now, from one of Petrus Borel's *Champavert* tales (cf. p. 79 n. 1, above). But the rider: 'Nature has no imagination', intriguingly anticipates, by its formulation, the preamble (to be discussed below, pp. 133–9) to the chapter on landscape in the *Salon de 1859*.

one of which derive from the aforementioned collective volume *Fontainebleau*), show that in three at least of his friends his ideas appear to have found a ready echo—if indeed in the first instance they were not jointly evolved in common (Bohemian) debate; a brief examination of these various texts may thus serve to bring Baudelaire's own personal attitudes into a truer contemporary perspective—may show them to be less purely personal, more circumstantial and representative in their incidence, than has commonly been allowed. As a first instance, then, I take the poem *A une patricienne*, by Philoxène Boyer; this, although published only in 1867 in the collection *Les Deux Saisons*, was dated by Boyer '26 juin 1854'. The poem is launched on this striking personal 'manifesto':

> Je ne suis pas celui qui s'éprend des fontaines,
> Des sables d'or, des lacs, des lueurs incertaines
> Que l'aurore répand sur les bois,—et mon cœur
> Ne s'éparpille pas dans les notes du chœur
> Qu'avec ses fleurs, ses eaux et ses firmaments chante
> La nature brutale, ironique et méchante.
> Car l'esprit n'est pas là. L'univers cache Dieu,
> Le décor ne dit rien du drame, et ce milieu
> De rayons aveuglants, d'éphémère verdure,
> Ne contient pas l'essence invisible et qui dure.
> Aussi, les jours de lutte et d'ennui, si je vais,
> Dolent, meurtri, navré d'avoir été mauvais,
> Cherchant la foi qui sauve et l'art qui tranquillise,
> Ce ne sont pas les champs qui me tentent.—L'église
> Petite, et froide, et sombre, et sans tableaux au mur,
> M'est d'un attrait plus haut et d'un pouvoir plus sûr.[1]

Thereafter, however, Boyer descends all-too swiftly to the most facile post-Petrarchan clichés. When night falls over Paris, when tapers are extinguished and organ and choir are stilled, the poet turns gratefully to that other and secular 'cult' which is the true theme of the poem or at least of its second part: 'Pour être fort, pour être humain, pour être doux, / Il me faut une église encor! . . . Je vais à vous!'[2]

---

[1]*Les Deux Saisons*, pp. 82–3; cit., in part, P. Citron, *Poésie de Paris*, II, 360 n. 2. For B.'s relations with Boyer during this period, see the 'Notes d'Asselineau sur Philoxène Boyer et B.', in: *B. et Asselineau*, 192–215.

[2]*Les Deux Saisons*, p. 84.

Rather different reservations before the spectacle of Nature, are voiced by Champfleury in his brief contribution to the volume *Fontainebleau* above-mentioned. I must explain that this volume—as its sub-title indicates: 'Hommage à C. F. Denecourt'—was designed to honour (as well as materially assist) the legendary 'Sylvan' of the forest of Fontainebleau;[1] this being so, its authors (some 42 in all) duly contributed for the most part items of an appropriately bucolic nature. A few 'dissident' spirits, however—Baudelaire and Champfleury among them—chose rather to send in poems or articles in which the note of admiration for the beauties of the forest, or of Nature generally, was in some way qualified or withheld. Thus Champfleury's item, which bears the ironically misleading title 'Vision dans la forêt', begins with a characterization of those 'esprits satiriques'—a category within which he would no doubt have agreed to include Baudelaire as well as himself—who seem constitutionally incapable of responding freely and expansively to the beauties of Nature:

Les esprits satiriques savent rarement chanter la nature: pour eux les côtés plaisants de l'homme se dessinent seulement dans la chambre noire de leur cerveau. La nature, n'ayant pas de côtés grotesques, trouble les esprits satiriques par sa grandeur pleine de calme, par sa tranquillité et son recueillement, qui font qu'on a pu comparer la forêt à une cathédrale. Conduisez dans la forêt un de ces êtres moqueurs, et il sera sans doute impressionné par les immenses verdures, les chants des oiseaux et les fraîcheurs rafraîchissantes qui lui feront oublier sur l'instant l'atmosphère morbide des grandes villes; mais, le premier moment passé, l'esprit satirique reprendra son vol vers les sujets familiers qui ont pincé ses lèvres de bonne heure; et là où vous le croirez s'enthousiasmer sur un site pittoresque, il sera occupé à creuser des souvenirs qui n'auront rapport ni aux arbres, ni aux plantes, ni à la verdure.[2]

(*Fontainebleau*, pp. 102–3)

It is true that Champfleury goes on to regret, by implication, the repression in urban man of that primordial faculty whereby the

[1] For a full account of the nature and inception of the volume, as also for a a short biography of Denecourt, see my article 'A *Festschrift* of 1855' (art. cit.).

[2] *Fontainebleau*, 102–3. The analogy between the forest and the cathedral recurs equally, with similar reference to the 'atmosphère . . . des grandes villes', in B.'s letter to Desnoyers within the same volume; see p. 121, below. For the general 'satirical' affinity between the two writers, cf. my suggestions, p. 120 and n. 3, below, concerning the character 'Bigle' in Champfleury's *Amis de la nature* of 1859.

country-dweller learns, for his part, to understand and master the 'language' of Nature.[1] All this, however, turns out to be no more than an elaborate preamble to the story of how, on the dutifully 'remedial' visit he had paid to Fontainebleau, Champfleury had eventually found himself unable (so to speak) to see the wood for the *pâté* . . . :

J'appliquai mes sens à saisir la forme des arbres, la coloration des plantes, à écouter les bruits des insectes, des oiseaux, à aspirer les fraîcheurs embaumées; mais, vers les deux heures de l'après-midi, le soleil perça les nuages, et des rayons brillants et gais allèrent tomber, j'ose à peine l'avouer, sur un gros pâté.

(*Fontainebleau*, p. 105)

This enormous, shining *pâté* sets Champfleury's 'satirical' imagination in train: he sees it lovingly transported from Paris by the worthy bourgeois and his family, who for a whole month have been dreaming of ceremoniously consuming it within the depths of the forest, but who at the last contrive, disastrously, to mislay it en route ('Malheureuse! . . . tu as oublié le pâté!') . . .[2] Champfleury's final comment underlines by implication both the essential irreverence of his attitude to Nature, and his decided preference for the inveterately (even if trivially) human, as against all the solemn tranquillities of Nature:

Telle fut la vision qui m'assaillit en pleine forêt . . . et je n'ai pas le courage de dire tous les détails capricieux de cette farce bourgeoise qui se jouait dans l'intérieur de mon cerveau, et qui, à partir de ce moment, me cacha les arbres, la verdure, le soleil.

(*Fontainebleau*, p. 106)

Such, certainly, was the general impression taken from Champfleury's article by Hippolyte Babou, when reviewing the *Fontainebleau* volume for *L'Athenæum français*. This whole review is of considerable interest for our purposes, as a further reflection of the views of what might almost be termed the 'anti-naturalist' or 'humanist' faction within the Bohemian-Realist group.[3] A curious feature of Babou's comments on the volume, is that he nowhere

[1] *Fontainebleau*, 103–5.
[2] Ibid., 105–6.
[3] For B.'s relations with Babou during this period, see J. S. Patty, *RHLF*, 1967, pp. 261–6.

mentions the one text, Baudelaire's letter to Desnoyers, which one would have thought most relevant to his argument (and which he may well, none the less, have been echoing, consciously or un-consciously). Babou does admittedly refer briefly to two other texts of Baudelaire's, the poems *Le Matin* and *Le Soir* (*Les Deux Cré-puscules*);[1] this, however, is to do but scant justice to the one writer who, within the volume, had in fact spoken out with true vigour for the ideas here more urbanely advocated by the critic:

Si nous pouvions hasarder un mot de critique, nous reprocherions aux prosateurs aussi bien qu'aux poëtes d'avoir trop exclusivement célébré la nature à propos de Fontainebleau. La nature est belle et bonne, j'en conviens; mais il me semble qu'il faudrait se garder de la *nature naturante* comme du *Breton bretonnant*. Par patriotisme, je n'aime que les Bretons francisés; par goût littéraire, je n'aime que la *nature humanisée*. Qu'est-ce qu'un arbre en tant qu'arbre, une forêt en tant que forêt? Mettez, comme les païens, une âme sous l'écorce, ou livrez les beaux arbres aux scieurs de long, et laissez la forêt aux forestiers . . . Mais le sujet voulait absolument qu'on adorât la Nature en vers et en prose, dans ce joli volume. Quelques esprits bizarres ont résisté pourtant, je dois le dire, à la tyrannie du sujet. M. Champfleury, par exemple, à propos de la forêt de Fontainebleau, ne nous parle que des infortunes d'un bourgeois parisien à qui on a dérobé un superbe pâté. L'article est amusant: il repose *des grands chênes et des grandes verdures*. M. Charles Asselineau a tourné carrément le dos aux *beaux arbres* pour écrire une sérieuse étude historique: *Fontainebleau avant François Ier*. Quant à M. Charles Baudelaire, il a donné deux pièces de vers, *le Soir et le Matin* [sic] qui ont, outre leur valeur poétique, le mérite de ne pas prononcer une seule fois le grand mot Nature.[2]

---

[1]Better known under their ultimate titles: *Le Crépuscule du matin* and *Le Crépuscule du soir*; cf. p. 121, below.

[2]*L'Athenæum français*, 7 July 1855, pp. 562–3. A. Largent, reviewing the same volume for *L'Artiste*, 15 July 1855, p. 152, singles out, as *his* two 'non-conformists' among the contributors, Champfleury and George Bell; the latter, certainly, one would have expected also to find on Babou's list (in place of Asselineau, whose historical study is only one of several within the volume); but on the other hand Largent makes no mention at all of B. in this connection! See, for this whole question, my art. cit., 'A *Festschrift* of 1855', pp. 190, 193, 201 n. 42a. I there cite also a further *Fontainebleau* text, the essay 'Sur la solitude' by Hippolyte Castille, which has the following interesting comment on the bitterness that may at certain times spring from solitude in Nature: 'Elle [la solitude] se dresse comme une ironie en face de la société vivante et agissante. Elle lui envoie dans ses sauvages parfums comme un soupir de sa haine' (p. 86; cf., for the 'irony' of Nature, the examples cit. p. 110 n. 1, above).

The form and conception of the *Fontainebleau* volume were of course precisely such as to *provoke* anti-naturalist reaction—even (illogically enough) in those who had actually contributed to it. This we may see further confirmed in a curious sequel to the *Fontainebleau* volume, Champfleury's novel *Les Amis de la Nature* (first published, in 1859, in *Le Moniteur universel*), which we may at the same time regard as an ultimate prolongation of the anti-naturalist ideas earlier professed by Champfleury, Baudelaire and their group. *Les Amis de la Nature* interweaves a malicious satire of the good Denecourt (transparently caricatured, under the name 'Gorenflot', as a retired haberdasher who at the beginning of the story has just acquired a small property near Grateloup, i.e. Fontainebleau[1]), with a more amiably ironic account of the activities of a group of Bohemian artists and writers who, around 1846,[2] constitute themselves the adoring and pantheistic 'friends of Nature':

Il n'y a pas plus d'une quinzaine d'années, quelques esprits inquiets tournèrent leurs affections vers la nature, qui n'en avait pas absolument besoin. Ce furent des hymnes sans fin, des adorations et des encens prodigués en pure perte pour les arbres, les plantes, les flots de la mer, les insectes, les animaux, le soleil et la lune. L'homme fut jeté de côté momentanément, mais le brin d'herbe reçut de nombreux hommages. On crut entendre de réels gémissements dans les feuilles des arbres secoués par les vents; le craquement du bois de chauffage dans la cheminée ne parut pas si naturel qu'on se l'était imaginé jusqu'alors, et la colère des flots, jadis regardée comme une image poétique, fut prise tout à fait au sérieux. La lune, avec sa mine de mélancolique convalescente, reçut nombre de consolations affectueuses; quelques-uns appélèrent le soleil

---

[1]This transformation of the ex-N.C.O. in Napoleon's army, into a Parisian bourgeois, must be accounted a stroke of singular perfidy on Champfleury's part, inasmuch as it must clearly have been suggested to him in the first instance by the very article he himself had written in 1855 in *homage* to Denecourt! Thus the monster pâté which in the latter text the tradesman from the rue Grenétat brings (with his family) to the forest of Fontainebleau (*Fontainebleau*, 105–6; cf. p. 116, above), becomes in the novel one of the 'ideas' that stray into the mind of the tradesman from the rue Saint-Denis, as he wanders for the first time in the forest (*Les Amis de la Nature*, 1861, p. 6); in other words, Champfleury has not shrunk from identifying, in his own mind, Denecourt the long-established guardian of the forest of Fontainebleau, with the bourgeois trippers and picnickers who flock from Paris at weekends. . . . For Denecourt's outraged *riposte* to the publication of Champfleury's book, see A. Billy, *Fontainebleau délices des poètes*, 113–14.

[2]For a comment on this date, see my next footnote, below.

mon ami, et poussèrent l'audace jusqu' à le tutoyer; d'autres, plus délicats, qui aimaient les premières violettes, jurèrent que le *chevalier* Printemps s'avançait. Ce fut une drôle de comédie, dans laquelle la brise causait avec la prairie, et le tison avec les étincelles de la cheminée. La littérature affecte quelquefois de ces modes bizarres qui ne prennent pas . . .

Comment se produisit cette religion? qui en fut l'inventeur? Rien n'est plus difficile à constater. Ce fut une mode inventée par un homme qui trouva quelques imitateurs, heureux de se raccrocher à une doctrine qui parut nouvelle sur le moment.[1]

---

[1]*Amis de la Nature*, 15–16; cf. ibid., 28 ('l'âme des pierres'). Consciously or unconsciously, Champfleury seems here to be recalling the very terms in which a few years earlier, B. in his letter to Desnoyers (to be discussed shortly) had dismissed this same 'religion of Nature'; there may also, in the reference to the 'convalescent' moon, be implied (as I have suggested already, p. 16 n. 2, above) a reference to B.'s sonnet *Tristesses de la lune*. Champfleury's satire on anthropomorphism is extended a stage further in his account, in a later chapter, of the speech made in Gorenflot's defence by the counsel Corbin, a former member of the 'Amis de la Nature' group, who enters the plea that Gorenflot, as an '*Amant* de la forêt' in the most literal sense, had embarked on an ardent if 'illicit' relationship with a forest which by its specifically feminine seductions positively solicited his advances (*Amis de la Nature*, 96–105; this whole episode, as could be shown by a detailed comparison of the two texts in question, is in fact an unacknowledged appropriation and transposition of the charming fantasy 'Sylvain' which Gautier had contributed to the *Fontainebleau* volume; cf. in this connection my art. cit., pp. 187–8). For the imputation of pantheism to these 'friends of Nature', cf. also the reference (*Amis de la nature*, p. 126) to the solemn German monograph, and the related periodical articles, in which was supposedly discussed the question of [*L*]*es tendances panthéistes de la nation française en 1846*. As to this latter date, finally, one wonders whether Champfleury may not have hoped to counter the protests, both personal and legal, which his book would arouse, by making the events of his story take place some five or six years *before* Denecourt (as the latter tells us in an Appendix, p. 316, to the 1856 edition of his *Guide* to Fontainebleau; cf. my art. cit., pp. 179, 197 n 14) had actually made the acquaintance of the 'Bohème chantante' group on whom no doubt the 'amis de la Nature' are modelled; if so, the manœuvre could scarcely hope to be successful, since the further episode in which the title 'Sylvain' is bestowed on Gorenflot (*Amis de la Nature*, pp. 123–6), would in itself be sufficient to establish beyond all doubt that Gorenflot = Denecourt. In the passage quoted above there are, I would add, direct allusions not only to B. but to other members of the 'Bohème chantante' group; thus to take but one example, the phrase 'quelques-uns appelèrent le soleil *mon ami*' is clearly a reference to Édouard Plouvier's *L'Ami Soleil*—a poem which had appeared in the *Chants et Chansons de la Bohème* of 1853 and which incidentally may owe something of its inspiration to B.'s *Le Soleil*, or rather to the no doubt earlier-composed 2nd and 3rd sections (cf. pp. 13, 108, above).

The group includes a 'Greek' or 'pagan' poet, one Godard (based no doubt mainly on Banville, but having something in him also of Gautier), who worships the sun, displays a frantic enthusiasm for wood-nymphs and satyrs, imparts a pseudo-scientific gloss to his verses by smuggling in various Greek words, and in general shows himself to be more interested in melodious rhymes than in ideas;[1] a blinkered and maniacal painter of crassly literal 'still lives', Lavertujeon, who recalls somewhat the egregious van Schaendel the elder, of the 'tale' reviewed by Baudelaire in 1848; a philosopher, Bougon, whose self-appointed task it is to cram 'ideas' and 'symbols' into the heads—and paintings—of artists such as Lavertujeon.[2] A slight corrective to these excesses, however, is offered in the person of the sceptical and mocking Bigle—a character who stands on the fringe of the group and would appear to some extent to be modelled both on Champfleury himself and on Baudelaire:

> Dans ce groupe, Bigle était seulement toléré. Il ne traitait pas la nature avec assez de considération: jamais on me l'avait entendu parler d'arbres ni de verdure. Quand un poète commençait à parler des relations de la brise avec le ruisseau, Bigle prenait son chapeau et s'enfuyait. On sut qu'il avait tenu quelques mauvais propos sur le compte des grillons, et il passa pour un sceptique d'une espèce dangereuse.[3]

---

[1] Ibid., 39–40; the latter trait in particular would apply, rather, to Banville. Cf. also the fact that 'Godard' is said (loc. cit.) to be unable to forgive his fellow-Bohemian 'Bigle' for his 'attacks against antiquity'; this would seem to be a reference to B.'s article of 1852, *L'École païenne*—an article we know (from another text of the same date, the 'Notes' concerning the projected journal *Le Hibou philosophe*, *OP* I, 211) to have been aimed in part at Banville. Yet it is of Gautier that we are reminded when reading (pp. 123–6) that Godard 'launches' Gorenflot by inventing for him the soubriquet 'Sylvain'—this being of course, as I have mentioned, the title of Gautier's 'portrait' of Denecourt in the *Fontainebleau* volume.

[2] *Amis de la Nature*, 17–23, 40–3, 53–5, 111–16. For Champfleury's *Van Schaendel, père et fils*, cf. pp. 87–8 and n. 1, above.

[3] *Amis de la Nature*, 25; cf. ibid., 19, 22–3, 47. For the analogy with Champfleury and B., cf. their respective contributions to the *Fontainebleau* volume: like the Champfleury of 'Vision dans la forêt', like the B. of the prose poems *Le Crépuscule du soir* and *La Solitude* and of the letter to Desnoyers, Bigle pays a solitary and 'recuperative' visit to the forest, and is there 'pursued' by the reminder of Man; cf., on the one hand *Amis de la Nature*, 26, 29, 54–55, and on the other, pp. 121–2, 160, below. A further reminder of B. (Bigle's 'attacks on antiquity') has already been noted, p. 120 n. 1, above; cf. also the concluding sentence of the book (p. 141) in which, offered the opportunity of having a

These anti-naturalist railleries of Champfleury's seem shallow indeed, however (as André Billy has remarked[1]), when set beside the vigorous 'profession of faith' Baudelaire himself had offered, a few years previously, in his letter to Desnoyers. For reasons I have discussed fully in another publication,[2] Baudelaire had chosen to contribute to the *Fontainebleau* volume two poems on avowedly *urban* themes (the two *Crépuscules* aforementioned); in justification, he had annexed a letter which to his credit Desnoyers had decided must equally be reproduced. The letter is so trenchant and closely-argued that it demands to be quoted in full:

Mon cher Desnoyers, vous me demandez des vers pour votre petit volume, des vers sur la *Nature*, n'est-ce pas? sur les bois, les grands chênes, la verdure, les insectes,—le soleil, sans doute? Mais vous savez bien que je suis incapable de m'attendrir sur les végétaux, et que mon âme est rebelle à cette singulière Religion nouvelle, qui aura toujours, ce me semble, pour tout être *spirituel* je ne sais quoi de *shocking*. Je ne croirai jamais que l'*âme des Dieux habite dans les plantes*, et, quand même elle y habiterait, je m'en soucierais médiocrement, et considérerais la mienne comme d'un bien plus haut prix que celle des légumes sanctifiés. J'ai même toujours pensé qu'il y avait dans la *Nature*, florissante et rajeunie, quelque chose d'affligeant, de dur, de cruel,—un je ne sais quoi qui frise l'impudence. Dans l'impossibilité de vous satisfaire complétement suivant les termes stricts du programme, je vous envoie deux morceaux poétiques, qui représentent à peu près la somme des rêveries dont je suis assailli aux heures crépusculaires. Dans le fond des bois, enfermé sous ces voûtes semblables à celles des sacristies et des cathédrales, je pense à nos étonnantes villes, et la prodigieuse musique qui

---

tree, bush or rock 'named' after him, Bigle (like the 'heroes' of B.'s two later prose poems, *L'Étranger* and *La Soupe et les nuages*; cf. pp. 262–3, below) replies simply and grandly: 'Monsieur Gorenflot, donnez-moi le nuage qui passe!' The epithets 'railleur', 'sceptique', finally (ibid., 19, 25, 47), recall Champfleury's earlier (and self-characterizing) phrases 'esprits satiriques' and 'êtres moqueurs' (*Fontainebleau*, 102–3; p. 115, above), and at the same time describe exactly B.'s reputed attitudes towards his fellow-artists. As a final comment on Champfleury's novel, I would add that it in fact draws almost entirely, for its plot and characterization, on various contributions to the *Fontainebleau* volume—i.e. not only on those of Gautier and B. as well as on his own, but also (as could be shown in detail) on those by Luchet, Audebrand and Busquet. . . . From which one could argue that the ungrateful Champfleury owed much (even if indirectly) to Denecourt!

[1] *Fontainebleau délices des poètes*, 110.
[2] 'A *Festschrift* of 1855' (art. cit.), pp. 190–3.

roule sur les sommets me semble la traduction des lamentations humaines.[1]

It is amusing, in the light of such earlier texts as *Le Soleil*, to observe Baudelaire's indignant recoil here from the very notion that he should write a poem on the theme of . . . the sun![2] Equally surprising, in the critic who had taken it upon himself to *recommend* to Ménard that the latter should develop the 'pantheistic and naturalistic side' of his Promethean theme,[3] is the comprehensive repudiation of pantheism implied in the declaration 'Je ne croirai jamais que *l'âme des Dieux habite dans les plantes*'—the phrase italicized being an approximate quotation of the opening line ('L'esprit calme des dieux habite dans les plantes') of Laprade's poem *A un grand arbre*, which had figured in the supposedly pantheistic *Odes et poëmes* of 1843.[4] Perhaps for Baudelaire's 'never' we should read 'never again'; certainly a comment made in the course of the essay of March–April 1852 on *Edgar Allan Poe, sa vie et ses ouvrages*, suggests that by that time the term 'pantheist' had begun to acquire for him a somewhat pejorative implication;[5]

[1]*Fontainebleau,* pp. 73–4. For the original draft of the letter, as sent in the first instance to Desnoyers, see *CG* I, 321–3, and *BDI* No. 199a (facsimile reprod.).

[2]For a further discussion of this paradox, and of the whole question of B.'s motives in making the particular contribution he did to the Denecourt volume, see my art. cit., A *Festschrift* of 1855', p. 191. No doubt precisely because of his changed views on Nature, B. seems to have experienced some difficulty in finding, within *FM*, an appropriate place for *Le Soleil*; thus in 1857 it is assigned to the opening group of poems dealing, broadly, with the Poet's vocation and lot, and in 1861, to the newly constituted 'Parisian' chapter; yet as we have seen, neither Paris nor the Poet can be considered a *main* theme of the poem.

[3]*OP* I, 241; cf. p. 24, above.

[4]P. 7; cf., for this allusion, *AR* 534. For the imputation of pantheism, cf. the more explicit reproach made by Paul Mantz when reviewing Laprade's volume: 'A force de faire vivre la nature de la vie de l'esprit, on arrive tout droit au panthéisme, résultat poétique, j'en conviens, mais qui amoindrit l'homme et l'efface' (*L'Artiste,* 27 March 1844, p. 174; cit. P. Séchaud, *Laprade,* 179). For Laprade's later reply to this charge, see Séchaud, ibid., n. 2.

[5]*OP* I, 291–2; cf. also, in the letter to Du Camp of 3 Jan. 1853: 'Quant au panthéisme, j'espère toujours que les hommes dont le talent m'est sympathique, et qui se disent panthéistes, entendent le mot *dans un sens nouveau*—car il me serait trop désagréable, me sentant souvent semblable à eux, de croire que j'ai longtemps été panthéiste sans le savoir' (*CG* I, 183). No disparagement of pantheism seems implied, however, in this account of the effects of hashish, published exactly a year earlier (i.e. in March 1851): 'De temps en temps la

and it may also be (although this seems to me far from proven) that Laprade was among those members of the so-called *École païenne,* whom Baudelaire had attacked in his article of that name published earlier the same year.[1] No less rashly categorical, finally, is his

---

personnalité disparaît. L'objectivité *qui fait certains poètes panthéistiques* et les grands comédiens devient telle que vous vous confondez avec les êtres extérieurs. Vous voici arbre mugissant au vent et racontant à la nature des mélodies végétales. Maintenant vous planez dans l'azur du ciel immensément agrandi' (*Du Vin et du hachish, PA* ed. C. Pichois, 88; my italics). Indeed, there is a marked analogy of imagery between this passage of B.'s, and the pantheistic text by Herder, cit. (in trans.) by Paul van Tieghem, *Sentiment de la Nature dans le préromantisme,* 234: 'Je souffle avec le vent, j'embaume avec les fleurs, je coule avec les ruisseaux, je plane dans le bleu du ciel'; and one may note also, in this same article of 1851, the entire approval accorded to this 'reading' from Hoffmann's 'psychological barometer': 'aspiration à sortir de mon *moi,* objectivité excessive, fusion de mon être avec la nature' (*PA* 202). Here again, therefore, the evidence from B.'s texts would support the assumption that it was during *the early months of 1852* that he began, actively and systematically, to condemn all aspects of the Nature-cult (including pantheism). For a certain continuing pantheism or 'objectivity' in B., cf. pp. 171–2, below.

[1]Cf. *AR* 533–4, as also pp. 69 n. 1, 120 n. 1, above. It is an interesting fact that B. at no time publicly or explicitly denounces Laprade. The nearest he comes to doing so is in the present letter, with its quotation of what is perhaps Laprade's best-known line. But in his article of 1861 on Auguste Barbier (see *CG* III, 83 and n.), B. seems in the end to have decided to exclude any direct mention of Laprade's name; as for the article on *L'Art philosophique,* on which he perhaps began work in 1857 and in which Laprade is specified as a typical product of the Lyonnais school (*AR* 124: 'Tout ce qui vient de Lyon est minutieux, lentement élaboré et craintif'), this was published only after B.'s death (see *AR* 470–1). In his letters, B. admittedly does not spare Laprade, describing him as a 'virtuous pedant', a 'simpleton' (*CG* II, 302; III, 83); such opinions must have rendered all the more delicate the writing of the letter (*CG* IV, 12–16) in which he awkwardly canvasses Laprade's support for his (B.'s) candidature to the Academy! . . . Laprade for his part seems to have taken due note of what in his view were clearly B.'s objectionable opinions, the crux of their disagreement being no doubt (cf. below) the question of morality in art. It is amusing to note, however, that despite their generally opposed viewpoints, they in fact pursued a rather similar evolution in their respective attitudes to Nature. Thus in the very book in which Laprade seeks, at one point, to refute B.'s anti-didacticism of 1861 (*Le Sentiment de la nature chez les modernes,* p. 496; cf. *CG* III, 83 n. 1), he elsewhere professes views which in some respects (condemnation of naturalism in art and especially of 'photographic' realism; depreciation of landscape painting; etc.) are not unlike those voiced by B. in the *Salon de 1859* (cf. in this connection pp. 131–4, below). In his later works, moreover, having (like B.) 'repudiated all allegiance to the idea of inevitable and collective progress', Laprade comes, with the deepening of his Catholicism, to regard Nature as a 'humiliating and hostile

assertion, in the ensuing sentence, that the vernal ebullience of Nature has 'always' seemed to him to border distressingly on the 'impudent'—this from the writer who in his *Salon de 1845* had said of Camille Flers' Norman landscapes: 'tous ces paysages . . . donnaient envie de connaître *ces éternelles et grasses verdures* qu'ils exprimaient si bien';[1] or who in describing, in the 1861 version of *Paysage*, the delights and compensations of a poetic winter, was to declare:

> Car je serai plongé dans cette volupté
> D'évoquer le Printemps avec ma volonté,
> De tirer un soleil de mon cœur, et de faire
> De mes pensers brûlants une tiède atmosphère.

(ll. 23–6);

or who in 1859, finally, in that most searingly expressive of all his poems: *Le Goût du néant*, was to take the perfume of spring as the perfect symbol of a world of sensuous pleasures now irretrievably lost: 'Le Printemps *adorable* a perdu son odeur!'[2] Such self-repudiations constitute, however, as he himself implicitly recognized on occasion, a recurrent pattern within his intellectual development,[3] and indeed one is tempted to claim that the more positive and dogmatic the tone that Baudelaire assumes in any given situation, the more likely it is that he will be contradicting, as self-evidently fallacious, ideas that he has previously professed with quite equal confidence . . . . What concerns us particularly, however, in the passage under discussion, is its relation to the verses above-quoted from *A Celle qui est trop gaie*: the impatience or anger with Nature here reiterated with equal force, but within a

---

principle', and even denounces her, in one of his last poems, *Deo Optimo Maximo* (1881), as an 'implacable marâtre'; see H. J. Hunt, *Epic in Nineteenth-Century France*, 254.

[1] *CE* 59; my italics.

[2] Cf., for a further discussion of this poem, pp. 288–9, below.

[3] Cf. the remark he inscribes within an album of Boyer's: 'Parmi les droits dont on a parlé dans ces derniers temps, il y en a un qu'on a oublié, à la démonstration duquel *tout le monde* est intéressé,—le droit de se contredire' (*OP* II, 140); for similar, if more cryptic assertions, cf. also *OP* I, 291 and *HE* xviii, the two essays on Poe of 1852 and 1856 respectively. We have already encountered, incidentally, one such instance of self-contradiction in B., in discussing (pp. 97–8, above) *L'École païenne*; for another, arising precisely from the present text, see p. 126, below.

context lending a new generality and depth, and at the same time suggesting a fuller explanation of the poet's extravagant irritation.[1] What is it, precisely, in the exuberant efflorescence of Nature, that Baudelaire finds so exasperating—so 'hard', 'cruel', 'impudent'; that causes him to bridle in outrage and spring, as it were, to the attack?[2] Surely its utter self-sufficiency, its total independence and disregard of Man—the eternal indifference from which Vigny had turned aside in *La Maison du Berger*, the indifference that in certain human situations may well seem a positive and cruel 'irony', a calculated taunt. Such situations are admittedly by their nature occasional and extreme, and may depend, for instance (as in *A une femme trop gaie*), on the disheartening coincidence of human sorrow with the aggressive 'triumph' of Spring. The wider 'humanist' significance of the letter to Desnoyers is none the less clear enough: what excites Baudelaire's particular derision in the new and 'shocking' Religion of Nature (not so new, incidentally, as to preclude him from having himself subscribed to one version of it, some ten years earlier!), is its implicit depreciation of Man—its failure to recognise Man's spiritual primacy and *priority*, as against the doubtful spirituality of the vegetable world. It is true that these notions are here framed in purely subjective terms ('My *own* soul I value altogether more highly than that of any sanctified vegetables'); the final sentence, however, with its observation that even on those occasions when the poet does chance to find himself within the heart of Nature (as it might be, within Denecourt's own forest of Fontainebleau[3]), his thoughts and reveries still obstinately

---

[1]It is significant that the sole alteration made by B., when revising his letter for publication in the volume, should have concerned this very point; thus he had originally written 'quelque chose d'impudent et d'affligeant', but later corrected this to the much more forceful 'quelque chose d'affligeant, *de dur, de cruel*,—un je ne sais quoi qui frise l'impudence' (my italics). See *CG* I, 323 and n. 1.

[2]Vigny also, in various (posth.) texts (cit. V. L. Saulnier, ed. *Destinées*, 29 n. 3, 30 n. 3-4; Lauvrière, *Vigny*, 353) speaks of Nature's 'éternité impudente' and 'durée insolente', or again of her beauty as an 'insolente décoration'; but he goes even beyond this (and B.) when exclaiming that 'la nature stupide nous insulte assez'. Cf. also the line from Boyer's *A une patricienne* (cit. p. 114, above): 'La nature brutale, ironique et méchante'. For a general discussion of Vigny's attitude to Nature, see V. L. Saulnier, op. cit., 28-30 and notes, and E. Lauvrière, op. cit., 277-8, 285-7, 349-57; for a further comparison with B. (rather differently conceived from my own), cf. M. Ruff, *Esprit du mal*, 269, as also J. Prévost, *B.*, 271.

[3]Cf., in this connection, my art. cit., 'A *Festschrift* of 1855', p. 189.

turn towards Man, and indeed towards *urban* Man[1]—this brings a more explicit and at the same time more emotive commitment to Mankind in general, akin in spirit to that of the Vigny of *La Maison du Berger*.[2]

It would be imprudent to take the letter to Desnoyers as being in any sense a representative statement of Baudelaire's later attitudes towards Nature; for various circumstantial reasons I have examined elsewhere,[3] he appears here to have been *provoked*, as it were, into making an utterance not only extreme in itself, but which seems very rapidly to have been overtaken by other and contradictory developments in his Nature-philosophy. Thus the sardonic gibes at the expense of the 'légumes sanctifiés', are contradicted (and thereby in effect nullified) almost before they appear in print: in an article (the first of the three devoted to the *Exposition universelle 1855*) which came out within a few days only of the publication of the *Fontainebleau* volume,[4] Baudelaire so far rehabilitates the despised vegetable kingdom as to recognize that there exist in Nature plants *singled out by the Creator* as 'holy', and having their due and 'miraculous' role within the vast harmony of the universe. . . .[5]

[1] Cf. the comment, on this same text, by J. Pommier, *Mystique de B.*, 149: '. . . la comédie ou plutôt la tragédie humaine, voilà ce dont le spectacle de la nature ne distrait pas Baudelaire, mais ce qu'au contraire il lui rappelle sans cesse'. For a discussion of B.'s implicit claim, within the letter to Desnoyers, to have substituted for the poetry of Nature a poetry of Man and of his cities, see pp. 160–2, below. As to the actual situation described by B. ('Dans le fond des bois . . . je pense à nos étonnantes villes'), there is an intriguing analogy here with the comment on Jean-Jacques Rousseau made by Diderot, in his *Salon de 1765* (a text B. no doubt knew well; see Pommier, *Dans les chemins de B.*, 249 ff.): 'Il a beau fermer la fenêtre de son hermitage qui regarde la capitale, c'est le seul endroit du monde qu'il voie. Au fond de sa forêt, il est ailleurs. Il est à Paris' (*Salons*, ed. J. Seznec and J. Adhémar, II, 207; cf., however, P. Citron, *Poésie de Paris*, I, 99–103).

[2] What B. hears in the 'music' resounding from the heights above, i.e. the note of 'human lamentation' from the cities, is essentially that same 'majesty of human suffering' which Vigny had preferred to all the 'vain splendours' of Nature (ll. 320–2: 'Plus que tout votre règne et que ses splendeurs vaines,/J'aime la majesté des souffrances humaines'). B.'s actual image, however, no doubt derives from a passage of Chateaubriand's *Génie du Christianisme*; see *FMCB* 425, and cf. p. 202, below.

[3] In my art. cit., p. 192.

[4] The article appeared (in *Le Pays*) on 26 May 1855; the volume was entered in the *Journal de la Librairie* under the date 2nd June, and was no doubt on sale a week or so earlier.

[5] *CE* 219–20; cf. pp. 173–4, below.

In any case, as we shall perceive in the ensuing chapter, Baudelaire's whole concept of Nature-symbolism during this period is such as to preclude any implicit relegation of the 'vegetable' to the status of mere 'object': even where not 'sanctified' by a direct relationship with God, the objects of Nature may still retain the intrinsic 'spirituality' of a privileged and symbolic 'correspondence' with Man.[1]

2. AESTHETIC ANTI-NATURALISM: NATURE, ART AND ARTIFICE

The contradiction aforementioned, between the letter to Desnoyers and the opening pages of the *Exposition universelle 1855* (the one with its sarcastic reference to 'sanctified vegetables', the other with its solemn affirmation of the 'holiness' of certain plants), could well be said to extend to all three of the articles that make up this latter work[2]—in the broad sense that when writing here about Nature and Art, Baudelaire as yet gives no indication whatsoever of any conversion to anti-naturalist doctrines. Thus while reaffirming the admiration or 'respect' inspired in him, around 1846, by the paintings of Louis David and his school,[3] Baudelaire goes on to emphasize the essential *artificiality* of the world they depict.[4] Similarly, he now *criticizes* in Ingres the too systematic 'amendments' or 'corrections' of Nature that earlier, in the *Salon de 1846*, he had seemed either to admire, or at least to denounce only in the master's more degenerate followers:

. . . le dessin de M. Ingres est le dessin d'un homme à système. Il croit que la nature doit être corrigée, amendée; que la tricherie heureuse,

---

[1] Such a 'correspondence' is indeed implicit already within the final sentence of the letter to Desnoyers; cf. p. 202 and n. 2, below.

[2] Although doubtless composed, together, during the middle part of May 1855, the articles were published in the following somewhat erratic sequence: I, 'Méthode de critique', *Le Pays*, 26 May 1855; II, 'Ingres', *Le Portefeuille*, 12 Aug. 1855; III, 'Eugène Delacroix', *Le Pays*, 3 June 1855. See *CE* 482–3, and cf. *CG* I, 332–3, 339.

[3] Cf. *Musée classique du Bazar Bonne-Nouvelle* (pub. Jan. 1846), *CE* 205–11.

[4] *CE* 232: 'Tout ce monde, véritablement hors nature, s'agitait, ou plutôt posait sous une lumière verdâtre, traduction bizarre du vrai soleil'. On the previous page, David, Guérin and Girodet are described as 'espèces d'abstracteurs de quintessence dans leur genre', their progress illumined by a 'soleil artificiel' of their own making.

agréable, faite en vue du plaisir des yeux, est non-seulement un droit, mais un devoir. On avait dit jusqu'ici que la nature devait être interprétée, traduite dans son ensemble et avec toute sa logique; mais dans les œuvres du maître en question il y a souvent dol, ruse, violence, quelquefois tricherie et croc-en-jambe. Voici une armée de doigts trop uniformément allongés en fuseaux et dont les extrémités étroites oppriment les ongles, que Lavater, à l'inspection de cette poitrine large, de cet avantbras musculeux, de cet ensemble un peu viril, aurait jugés devoir être carrés . . .[1]

In the ensuing paragraph, the standpoint is still more explicitly naturalistic; thus after describing the formalized yet unrealistic 'correctness', so wholly 'alien to the human organism', of Ingres' figures, Baudelaire goes on 'mischievously' to attribute the occasional lively and charming detail to some involuntary impulse of nature in the painter; it is thus not the latter who has 'sought Nature', but she who willy-nilly has overpowered (or 'ravished') him:

Il arrive quelquefois que l'œil tombe sur des morceaux charmants, irréprochablement vivants; mais cette méchante pensée traverse alors l'esprit, que ce n'est pas M. Ingres qui a cherché la nature, mais la nature qui a violé le peintre, et que cette haute et puissante dame l'a dompté par son ascendant irrésistible.

(CE 238)

Delacroix in turn—or rather, by contrast—is praised for the solemn 'truthfulness' of gesture revealed in the figure painting of the *Prise de Constantinople par les Croisés*, as again for his recognition of the principle that good draughtsmanship must model itself not on the 'hard', 'cruel', 'despotic', over-simplified and entirely arbitrary *straight* line that has latterly made such disastrous inroads into painting and sculpture, but on the *curved* line—lively, mobile, sinuous, fleeting—that alone is truly characteristic of the actual forms of Nature.[2] Even when interpolating, in the course of the

[1] CE 237; cf. *Salon de 1846*, CE 111, 149–50. It will be observed that B. here invokes (as previously in the *Salon de 1846*, CE 143) the 'physionomic' and essentially *naturalistic* findings of Lavater; cf., in this whole connection, G. T. Clapton, *RLC*, 1933, pp. 291–8, 429–34. The complaint against Ingres is renewed, from the same standpoint, in the essay of 1859–60, *Le Peintre de la vie moderne*, *AR* 68.

[2] CE 245, 249–50; for Delacroix' own disavowal of the straight line in painting, see L. Horner, *B. critique de Delacroix*, 134. I would add in this connection that while it may be true that in a *land*scape (in the strict sense), the straight lines are

article on Ingres, a somewhat gratuitous critique of the Realist Courbet, Baudelaire contents himself with remarking that where Ingres sacrifices imagination and movement in the name of 'la tradition et . . . l'idée du beau raphaélesque', Courbet for his part, as an 'anti-surnaturaliste', does so in the interests of 'la nature extérieure, positive, immédiate'.[1] Now in all this there is to be found no condemnation of naturalism *per se*; the artist is still in effect enjoined, as earlier in the *Salon de 1846*, to take Nature as his starting-point and ultimate criterion, but is now further required, during the actual process of creation, to give full expression to the shaping *imagination* (which thus takes over something of the role previously assigned to the faculty of 'idealization').[2]

It seems clear, then—even if we take duly into account the rather special circumstances surrounding the composition of these articles on the *Exposition universelle 1855*[3]—that Baudelaire had yet to apply himself to working out the full aesthetic implications of his new anti-naturalist philosophies. An opportunity to develop the specific critique of Courbet's naturalism might, it is true, have been offered by the projected article *Puisque Réalisme il y a*. But these jottings (which date no doubt from the later months of 1855[4]) are concerned largely with the 'history' of the Realist movement, and with the major role played therein by Champfleury—Champfleury whose 'excusable' determination to seek a 'rallying-sign for lovers of truth' is declared to have 'misfired' ('tout cela a mal tourné'), to have become indeed a mere *blague*, and so on.[5] In such a context, the question of external Nature arises scarcely at all, the less so since Champfleury's personal indifference to Nature was well known,

---

nearly always man-made or the by-product of man's activities, Delacroix' (and Baudelaire's) principle does not, in my observation, extend to *all* forms of Nature: a sunset, for instance (or at least a sunset over the Gareloch), may present a black cloud separated from the pinkish glow of the horizon itself by a line of uninterrupted and quite mathematical *straightness*.

[1] *CE* 234–5.

[2] Cf. pp. 75–9, above. The epithet 'positive', be it noted, had equally been applied to Nature (and the naturalist South) in the *Salon de 1846*; cf. *CE* 187, 91. But there, B. had coupled it with the stronger adjective 'brutale'; in this respect at least, therefore, he must be deemed *more* respectful towards Nature in 1855 than in 1846!

[3] I hope to discuss this question fully in a forthcoming publication; cf. in the meantime my art. cit., 'Les Esthétiques de B.', pp. 481–3.

[4] See *OP* I, 579–80.

[5] *OP* I, 298–9.

and indeed is attested, as we have seen, in his contribution to the very volume in which Baudelaire's own anti-naturalist text had figured.[1] The latter does, however, offer this parenthetical comment on the 'minuteness' of Champfleury's realism:

Comme il étudie minutieusement, il croit saisir une *réalité* extérieure.

(*OP* I, 298)

To understand the significance of Baudelaire's underlining of the word 'réalité', we must relate this to two subsequent and equally cryptic passages:

Tout bon poëte fut toujours *réaliste*.
Équation entre l'impression et l'expression.
Sincérité.
Prendre Banville pour exemple . . .

La Poésie est ce qu'il y a de plus réel, c'est ce qui n'est complètement
     vrai que dans *un autre monde*.
Ce monde-ci, dictionnaire hiéroglyphique.   (*OP* I, 298, 299)

Thus against the so-called 'reality' which the Realist claims to capture by the meticulous study of the external world, Baudelaire sets the *true* reality which for him lies in the 'equation' between 'impression' and 'expression', between the outer world and the inner world, between the object and its 'hieroglyphic' or symbolic meaning.[2] A final tantalising heading indicates the further aspects of the question that Baudelaire had proposed, at the time, to go on to treat:

(*Analyse de la Nature, du talent de Courbet, et de la morale.*)
Courbet sauvant le monde.

(*OP* I, 299)

Except briefly, in the similarly unfinished *Pauvre Belgique*, drafted in the final years of the poet's life,[3] the promised study of Courbet seems, regrettably, never to have materialized; the 'analysis of Nature', on the other hand, may very well, as we shall see, have been carried over into certain passages of the *Salon de 1859* next to be discussed.

In this *Salon*, published some four years later, Baudelaire shows himself to have come to full aesthetic realization of the new anti-naturalist credo; indeed he misses no opportunity of proclaiming

[1]Cf. pp. 115–16, above.
[2]For a further discussion of these ideas, see pp. 176–7, below.
[3]See pp. 148–9, below.

this forcibly, whether in his generalizations concerning Art or in his judgments on particular painters. And yet, when we come to examine Baudelaire's specific ideas on the relationship between Nature and Art, we find these still to derive essentially from those previously expounded, with such dazzling cogency, in the *Salon de 1846*. Thus he now gives a fully elaborated version of Delacroix' metaphor—which in 1846, as we have seen, he had cited only in passing—of Nature as a 'dictionary'. Baudelaire is here recalling, from his first conversations with Delacroix (dating precisely from 1845–6), the latter's explanations of the whole question of Nature:

'La nature n'est qu'un dictionnaire', répétait-il fréquemment. Pour bien comprendre l'étendue du sens impliqué dans cette phrase, il faut se figurer les usages nombreux et ordinaires du dictionnaire. On y cherche les sens des mots, la génération des mots, l'étymologie des mots; enfin on en extrait tous les éléments qui composent une phrase et un récit; mais personne n'a jamais considéré le dictionnaire comme une composition dans le sens poétique du mot. Les peintres qui obéissent à l'imagination cherchent dans leur dictionnaire les éléments qui s'accordent à leur conception; encore, en les ajustant avec un certain art, leur donnent-ils une physionomie toute nouvelle. Ceux qui n'ont pas d'imagination copient le dictionnaire.[1]

A few pages later, varying the metaphor, Baudelaire declares the whole 'visible universe' to be no more than a 'store' of images and signs which the imagination must arrange and interpret, a pabulum it must 'digest' and transform.[2] It will be observed that in both these formulations a new and privileged role (briefly foreshadowed already, as we have seen, in the article of 1855 on Ingres[3]) is accorded to the creative imagination; thus it is precisely because the artist who is content to 'copy the dictionary', i.e. to imitate Nature exactly, shows himself thereby to *lack* all imagination, that the philosophy he represents constitutes so grave a threat to all true art of whatever

---

[1] *CE* 280; for the earlier reference to this notion, cf. *CE* 109 and p. 77 and n. 2, above. For the date of B.'s first meetings with Delacroix, cf. p. 69 n. 5, above.

[2] *CE* 283. An earlier passage (*CE* 276) concedes that the truly powerful imagination will benefit proportionately from having built up its own vast 'store' of 'observations' taken from Nature: 'ce qu'il y a de plus fort dans les batailles avec l'idéal, c'est une belle imagination disposant d'un immense magasin d'observations'. Cf. also, *CE* 340, the reference to the 'prodigieuses rêveries continues dans les spectacles de la nature présente'.

[3] *CE* 234; cf. p. 129, above.

kind.[1] In principle, therefore, all naturalistic art must *ipso facto* be condemned; conversely, no painting that is admired can possibly be admitted to be of wholly naturalistic inspiration. Thus Baudelaire cannot bring himself to agree that a certain painting by Amand Gautier (depicting an *Hôpital de folles*), could in fact have been 'copied' exactly and minutely from life—firstly, because he detects other than purely realistic concerns in the actual composition or 'arrangement' of the picture, but also, and secondly, because *by definition* 'what is positively and universally exact is never admirable'.[2]

But it is in the chapter on landscape painting that the new criterion receives its most substantial—and, for our purposes, its most relevant—application. Already, in a previous chapter, Baudelaire had from this standpoint implied the relative *inferiority* of landscape painting as a genre: it attracts 'lazy' or sluggish minds (the man of active imagination preferring rather the spheres of religious painting and 'fantasy'),[3] and moreover its practitioners, who tend

[1]Cf. the opening sentences of the chapter significantly entitled 'La Reine des facultés' (a title already accorded to the imagination in the passage aforementioned, from the article of 1855): 'Dans ces derniers temps nous avons entendu dire de mille manières différentes: "Copiez la nature; ne copiez que la nature. Il n'y a pas de plus grande jouissance ni de plus beau triomphe qu'une copie excellente de la nature." Et cette doctrine, ennemie de l'art, prétendait être appliquée non-seulement à la peinture, mais à tous les arts, même au roman, même à la poésie' (*CE* 272-3). In the previous chapter, B. had complained that the exclusive pursuit of the 'True' is 'oppressing' and 'stifling' the taste for the Beautiful, and that Art was daily losing in self-respect as it 'prostrated itself' before external reality; the deplorable and insidious vogue for photography was in this respect all-too symptomatic (*CE* 267, 272, 268-71).

[2]*CE* 289. B.'s comments on another painting by this artist, *Les Sœurs de Charité*, stress the manner in which Gautier has developed his 'pensée principale' and brought out the intrinsic 'poetry' of his subject—has in short 'idealized' it, as B. would have said in 1846 (*CE* 289-90; cf. also, 339, the appreciation of the 'caractère amoureusement poétique' of Paul Huet's landscapes and seascapes). It must be added that B.'s insistence on the need for imagination even in the domain of portrait painting, does not prevent him from criticizing Ingres and his school (no doubt for the same polemical reasons as in 1855; cf. pp. 127-8, above) for their lack of fidelity to their model! (*CE* 324-9)—while at the same time tacitly recognising, *CE* 328, the contradiction in his own attitude . . .

[3]*CE* 284-5. Cf. the remark ironically imputed by Champfleury, in his anti-naturalist satire *Les Amis de la Nature* published in this same year 1859, to the philosopher 'Bougon': '. . . vous reconnaîtrez la vanité des sujets historiques et religieux, qu'il est impossible de peindre, puisque le peintre ne les a pas vus' (p. 22; cf. p. 120, above).

to pride themselves on the very success with which they conceal their own personalities, are particularly prone to the vice which threatens all those whose speciality brings them into close contact with external Nature: the vice of 'banality'.[1] In his actual chapter 'Le Paysage', Baudelaire goes further than this. A landscape is beautiful not in itself, he declares, but by virtue of the ideas or feelings it inspires in the onlooker; it thus follows that a painter who is unable to convey personal emotion through an 'arrangement' of natural objects, is not properly an *artist* at all.[2] Moreover, while conceding the indisputable strength and skilfulness of the modern school of landscape painting, he nevertheless discerns in the whole 'stupid' cult of Nature (stupid, because dedicated to Nature-in-itself, Nature in the raw, rather than to Nature 'purified' and interpreted by the imagination) an 'obvious' sign of general degradation.[3]

[1] *CE* 280; the passage concludes: 'A force de contempler [a later variant adds: "et de copier"], ils oublient de sentir et de penser'. (The variant is brought, *AR* 10, by the 1863 obituary article on Delacroix, which reproduces the greater part of the present chapter.) Cf. also *CE* 272: 'le peintre [contemporain] devient de plus en plus enclin à peindre, non pas ce qu'il rêve, mais ce qu'il voit'—a statement one might link with the implicit definition of Art offered in this text of 1857 (the poet is describing his ideal 'pays de Cocagne'): 'Pays singulier, supérieur aux autres, comme l'Art l'est à la Nature, où celle-ci est réformée par le rêve, où elle est corrigée, embellie, refondue' (*L'Invitation au voyage*, *OCP* 254; for the 'superiority' of Art to Nature, cf. the passage from Gautier's 'Salon de 1837', cit. F. Luitz, *Ästhetik von Gautier*, 135 n. 35: '. . . la nature est stupide, sans conscience d'elle-même, sans pensée ni passion . . . l'art est plus beau, plus vrai, plus puissant que la nature').

[2] *CE* 332–3 (text cit. p. 137, below); cf. the earlier 'credo' (cit. in its full context p. 138 n. 1, below) imputed to the 'imaginative' artist: ' "Je veux illuminer les choses avec mon esprit et en projeter le reflet sur les autres esprits" ' (*CE* 284). B. may perhaps in all this be echoing a passage from Poe's *Marginalia*, LXXXVI: 'Were I called on to define, *very* briefly, the term "Art", I should call it "the reproduction of what the Senses perceive in Nature through the veil of the soul". The mere imitation, however accurate, of what *is* in Nature, entitles no man to the sacred name of "Artist" . . . We can, at any time, double the true beauty of an actual landscape by half closing our eyes as we look at it' (*Literati, etc.*, 1850, p. 525). But already in his *Salon de 1846* (as will be recalled), B. had advocated the 'interpretation' or 'idealization' of Nature by the artist; cf. pp. 75–9, above.

[3] *CE* 333. Cf. the comment, *CE* 359, on the 'mysterious and abstract beauty' of the human skeleton, as rendered by the mediæval and post-mediæval sculptors: '. . . cette grâce, caressante, mordante, presque scientifique, se dressa à son tour, claire et purifiée des souillures de l'humus, parmi les grâces innombrables que l'Art avait déjà extraites de l'*ignorante Nature*' (my italics); for this latter contrast between Art and 'ignorant' Nature, cf. the Gautier passage above-cited (p. 133 n. 1).

Here he significantly reverts to the notion of Nature as a 'dictionary':
the majority of these artists, he goes on to say, mistake the dictionary
of art for art itself, and believe themselves to have composed a
'poem' by the mere act of copying a word from a dictionary,
of throwing open a window which within its square (or frame)
happens to enclose certain objects (trees, sky, a house). Others may
go further still, and offer as a finished composition a mere 'study',
a sketch taken from life.[1] Now it is significant that among the painters
falling under this latter criticism (which clearly strikes at the whole
fundamental aesthetic of the Barbizon school), should be not only
Français but Théodore Rousseau—both of whom, it will be recalled, Baudelaire had praised in 1846, together with other Romantic
and post-Romantic *paysagistes,* for their 'sincere love of Nature'.[2]
But in Théodore Rousseau (for whom Baudelaire still conserves a
certain esteem hedged round with 'respectful' reservations), this
quality has now become diminished to a 'sincere love of *light*' (i.e.
an expert delight in rendering its qualities), together with a shared
participation in the general 'amour *aveugle* de la nature, de rien que
la nature';[3] Français, for his part, simply shows us a tree—an
enormous and venerable tree, it is true—and declares: 'Here is a
landscape'.[4]

It is at this point that a certain inconsistency begins to manifest
itself within Baudelaire's anti-naturalist argument. Regretting the
reluctance of modern landscape painters to 'abandon themselves' to
the 'prodigious reveries' contained within the (remembered) spectacle of Nature, he goes on to recall, after a brief reference to the
sole painting sent in by Boudin to the 1859 Salon, the several
hundred pastel studies he had seen recently in this artist's studio
at Honfleur:[5]

S'ils [les paysagistes] avaient vu comme j'ai vu récemment, chez M.
Boudin qui, soit dit en passant, a exposé un fort bon et fort sage tableau

---

[1]*CE* 333-4.
[2]Cf. pp. 73-4 and n. 1, above.
[3]'. . . il prend une simple étude pour une composition . . . un petit bout de
nature . . . devien[t] . . . à ses yeux amoureux un tableau suffisant et parfait' (*CE*
336; my italics).
[4]*CE* 334.
[5]Where he had been staying, at his mother's house, for most of the past three
or four months, and from which, in fact, he had written the present *Salon.* Cf.,
for the significance of Honfleur in B.'s life, pp. 254-6, below.

(le *Pardon de sainte Anne Palud*), plusieurs centaines d'études au pastel improvisées en face de la mer et du ciel, ils comprendraient ce qu'ils n'ont pas l'air de comprendre, c'est-à-dire la différence qui sépare une étude d'un tableau. Mais M. Boudin, qui pourrait s'enorgueillir de son dévouement à son art, montre très-modestement sa curieuse collection. Il sait bien qu'il faut que tout cela devienne tableau par le moyen de l'impression poétique rappelée à volonté; et il n'a pas la prétention de donner ses notes pour des tableaux. Plus tard, sans aucun doute, il nous étalera dans des peintures achevées les prodigieuses magies de l'air et de l'eau.

(*CE* 340–1)

Now it might clearly seem, from these observations, that Baudelaire was far from sharing (or anticipating) our modern veneration of the fugitive 'impression', the inspired and authentic 'jotting';[1] on the contrary, he is careful to explain (as his argument requires) that Boudin's pastels are of interest only as *preparatory* studies for some ultimate and finished work of art. Yet does not this next (and immediately ensuing) description convey, by its eager vividness, Baudelaire's keen delight in the actual sketches themselves—in what he (rightly) calls 'these astonishing studies'?[2] (His eloquence and enthusiasm appear all the more striking, incidentally, in that he had previously, as we have seen, accorded so perfunctorily appreciative

[1] It is amusing, in this connection, to note that in discussing the very painting sent in by Boudin to the 1859 Salon (*Le Pardon de Sainte-Anne la Palud*, to give it its correct title), G. Jean-Aubry expresses his decided preference for the *sketch* of the same subject made either directly from life or (more probably) from the actual painting; see his *Boudin*, 134, and cf. ibid., 34–5, 173, 178, 179. For a reproduction of the painting, see ibid., facing p. 32.

[2] I say 'rightly', on the evidence of the five magnificent 'études de ciels', probably from this same sequence, conserved at the Musée de Honfleur and shown, in 1957, at the Bibliothèque Nationale's B. Centenary Exhibition; see *BNE* p. 80 No. 361, and cf. also G. Jean-Aubry, *Boudin*, 133–4, 178. The Musée du Havre also contains (or contained in 1922; see ibid., 179) some ten 'études de ciels'; could not these likewise have been drawn from the 'collection' seen by B.? In this whole connection, one should quote the apt comment made by J. Pommier and C. Pichois, when reproducing one of these pastels in the context of the poem *Horreur sympathique* (cf. p. 248 n. 1, below): 'Ce n'est pas une seule étude de Boudin qu'il faudrait reproduire . . . c'est *le film de leur ensemble* qu'il conviendrait de dérouler aux yeux du lecteur, afin de recréer dans son esprit l'impression qui fut celle de Baudelaire' (*FMPP* 475–7; my italics).

a mention to a work by Boudin which did truly represent a composed and finished *painting*.[1])

Ces étonnantes études, si rapidement et si fidèlement croquées d'après ce qu'il y a de plus inconstant, de plus insaisissable dans sa forme et dans sa couleur, d'après des vagues et des nuages, portent toujours, écrits en marge, la date, l'heure et le vent; ainsi, par exemple: 8 *octobre, midi, vent de nord-ouest*. Si vous avez eu quelquefois le loisir de faire connaissance avec ces beautés météorologiques, vous pourriez vérifier par votre mémoire l'exactitude des observations de M. Boudin. La légende cachée avec la main, vous devineriez la saison, l'heure et le vent. Je n'exagère rien. J'ai vu. A la fin tous ces nuages aux formes fantastiques et lumineuses, ces ténèbres chaotiques, ces immensités vertes et roses, suspendues et ajoutées les unes aux autres, ces fournaises béantes, ces firmaments de satin noir ou violet, fripé, roulé ou déchiré, ces horizons en deuil ou ruisselants de métal fondu, toutes ces profondeurs, toutes ces splendeurs, me montèrent au cerveau comme une boisson capiteuse ou comme l'éloquence de l'opium. Chose assez curieuse, il ne m'arriva pas une seule fois, devant ces magies liquides ou aériennes, de me plaindre de l'absence de l'homme. Mais je me garde bien de tirer de la plénitude de ma jouissance un conseil pour qui que ce soit, non plus que pour M. Boudin. Le conseil serait trop dangereux. Qu'il se rappelle que l'homme, comme dit Robespierre, qui avait soigneusement fait ses *humanités*, ne voit jamais l'homme sans plaisir; et, s'il veut gagner un peu de popularité, qu'il se garde bien de croire que le public soit arrivé à un égal enthousiasme pour la solitude.[2]

I have quoted in full this whole 'Boudin' section of Baudelaire's 1859 *Salon*, since it is, for our purposes, of such varied and striking interest. One notes first of all the sidelong and characteristically perceptive tribute to a great artist who at that time was still unknown and struggling.[3] More specifically, however, in its relation to the general anti-naturalist argument pursued throughout this *Salon*, the passage presents several intriguingly discrepant features. One such I have indicated already: having denounced as aesthetically inferior

---

[1]This may of course simply be because he had lacked the time to give any *but* the most perfunctory attention to the picture in question, when paying what was apparently his one and only visit to the Salon! See the letter to Nadar of 16 May 1859, *CG* II, 317.

[2]*CE* 341–2. The epithet 'étonnantes' ('ces étonnantes études') appears only in this (1859) text; perhaps B. later felt it to conflict with his insistence on the fact that these were, after all, 'mere' preparatory studies?

[3]Cf. G. Jean-Aubry, *Boudin*, 41–2.

the 'study' taken directly from life, Baudelaire than goes on to express (in strongly aesthetic terms) his unstinted admiration for Boudin's . . . studies taken directly from life![1] Again, his initial regret that present-day landscape painters should have failed so signally to respond to the 'prodigieuses rêveries contenues dans les spectacles de la nature présente'; his reference to the (likewise 'prodigious') 'magies de l'air et de l'eau', the 'beautés météorologiques', captured, or ultimately to be captured, by Boudin[2]—these, together with numerous other texts (including several from this same chapter 'Le Paysage') that could equally be cited, confirm that for all his polemical assertions to the contrary,[3] Baudelaire's sensibility to Nature, or at least to certain aspects of Nature, remains as keen and as delicate as ever before. Finally and most important (to return to the section on Boudin), there is the curious passage in which Baudelaire seems tacitly to *approve* the 'absence of Man' from these pastels, and goes on to depreciate, almost sneeringly, Man's liking for the society of his fellows.[4] Yet this same chapter of the *Salon de 1859* had opened with a long explanation—marking a quite new development of Baudelaire's thought in this domain—of the aesthetic '*necessity*' of Man's presence in Nature, the aesthetic *nullity* of Nature in the absence of Man!

Si tel assemblage d'arbres, de montagnes, d'eaux et de maisons, que nous appelons un paysage, est beau, ce n'est pas par lui-même, mais par moi, par ma grâce propre, par l'idée ou le sentiment que j'y attache. C'est dire suffisamment, je pense, que tout paysagiste qui ne sait pas traduire un sentiment par un assemblage de matière végétale ou minérale n'est pas un artiste. Je sais bien que l'imagination humaine peut, par un effort singulier, concevoir un instant la nature sans l'homme, et toute la masse suggestive éparpillée dans l'espace sans un contemplateur pour en extraire la comparaison, la métaphore et l'allégorie. Il

---

[1] If further confirmation were needed of this admiration, one could find it in Boudin's letter to Soudan de Pierrefitte, recalling his days at Honfleur (where he lived as a close neighbour of B.'s): 'J'y "régalais" Baudelaire de la vue de mes ciels au pastel' (cit. G. Jean-Aubry, *Eugène Boudin*, 41 cf. the same author's *B. et Honfleur*, 26 and n. 3.)

[2] *CE* 340, 341.

[3] Cf. especially, e.g., the retort imputed to an 'homme imaginatif' whom we may readily identify with B. himself: 'La nature est *laide*, et je préfère les monstres de ma fantaisie à la trivialité positive' (*CE* 273; my italics).

[4] Cf., for a further discussion of this attitude (as also of the Nature-feeling previously mentioned), my penultimate chapter, 'Nature without Man'.

est certain que tout cet ordre et toute cette harmonie n'en gardent pas moins la qualité inspiratrice qui y est providentiellement déposée; mais, dans ce cas, faute d'une intelligence qu'elle pût inspirer, cette qualité serait comme si elle n'était pas. Les artistes qui veulent exprimer la nature, moins les sentiments qu'elle inspire, se soumettent à une opération bizarre qui consiste à tuer en eux l'homme pensant et sentant . . . presque tous [les paysagistes modernes] oublient qu'un site naturel n'a de valeur que le sentiment actuel que l'artiste y sait mettre.[1]

Baudelaire's originality in this passage is to have transposed into explicitly *aesthetic* terms the notion of a Man-centred universe—a notion which in one form or another is no doubt as old as human egoism itself, but to which Diderot, a century earlier, had given a specific formulation that consciously or unconsciously Baudelaire may well here have had in mind:

. . . si l'on bannit l'homme ou l'être pensant ou contemplateur de dessus la surface de la terre, ce spectacle pathétique et sublime de la nature n'est plus qu'une scène triste et muette. L'univers se tait; le silence et la nuit s'en emparent. Tout se change en une vaste solitude où les phénomènes inobservés se passent d'une manière obscure et sourde. C'est la présence de l'homme qui rend l'existence des êtres intéressante . . . [2]

Baudelaire, for his part, while conceding that Nature may, by a 'singular' effort of the imagination, be conceived 'without Man',

---

[1]*CE* 332–3. Cf., in an earlier chapter, *CE* 284, the distinction made between the two kinds of artist—the 'realist' (or 'positivist') on the one hand, the 'imaginative' on the other: 'Celui-ci . . . dit: "Je veux représenter les choses telles qu'elles sont, ou bien qu'elles seraient, en supposant que je n'existe pas". L'univers sans l'homme. Et celui-là . . . dit: "Je veux illuminer les choses avec mon esprit et en projeter le reflet sur les autres esprits"'.

[2]*Encyclopédie*, ed. J. Lough, 55–6, art. 'Encyclopédie'. Cf. B.'s comment (above-quoted): 'l'univers sans l'homme', on the credo attributed to the 'realist' or 'positivist' artist: 'Je veux représenter les choses telles qu'elles sont, ou bien qu'elles seraient, en supposant que je n'existe pas' (*CE* 284). Among antecedent *literary* versions of this theme, the most striking, perhaps, from our present standpoint, would be the passage from Senancour's *Oberman* (Letter XXXVI; cit. G. Charlier, *Sentiment de la nature chez les romantiques français*, 251) which ends in these terms: 'La nature sentie n'est que dans les rapports humains, et l'éloquence des choses n'est rien que l'éloquence de l'homme'. Cf. also these lines from Delille's *L'Homme des champs*, cit. Paul van Tieghem, *Sentiment de la nature dans le préromantisme*, 218: 'Oui, l'homme aux yeux de l'homme est l'ornement du monde; / Les lieux les plus riants sans lui nous touchent peu; / C'est un temple désert qui demande son dieu'.

goes on (as we have seen) to stress the crucial importance of the *subjective* element in the aesthetic perception of Nature: a landscape is beautiful by sole virtue (so he affirms) of the idea or feeling which the human spectator reads into it. (This is not quite the same thing as saying that 'Beauty is in the eye of the beholder'; rather that in the absence of a beholder, there can be no true beauty.) In its practical applications within the sphere of art criticism, this notion simply confirms the preference—already voiced in 1846, but now renewed more strongly in the name of the sovereign creative imagination—for those forms of art which subjectively 'interpret' rather than objectively transcribe Nature.[1] Viewed, however, within the larger perspective of Baudelaire's developing aesthetic theory, the passage as a whole is of interest less for its determined subordination of Nature to Man (a principle nowhere subsequently, as it turned out, to be explored or even reaffirmed[2]), than for its cryptic allusion to the *literary* theory of correspondences (the 'extraction' from Nature, by the human 'contemplator', of simile, metaphor, allegory) that Baudelaire had by now, as will be seen from my next chapter, begun to elaborate.

The notion, fleetingly adumbrated in the *Salon de 1859* as in one earlier prose poem, that the proper function of Art is the 'correction' or 'improvement' of Nature,[3] has as its further corollary a dogmatic or temperamental preference for the *artificial* over the real. But the importance of this aspect of Baudelaire's aesthetic has been much

---

[1] A clear illustration, *CE* 296–7, would be Delacroix' *Ovide chez les Scythes*. Cf., however, in the art. of 1861, *Peintures murales d'Eugène Delacroix à Saint-Sulpice*, this further application of B.'s 'humanist' aesthetic to the technical question of colour and line in painting: 'La nature extérieure . . . n'est qu'un amas incohérent de matériaux que l'artiste est invité à associer et à mettre en ordre, un *incitamentum,* un réveil pour les facultés sommeillantes. Pour parler exactement, il n'y a dans la nature ni ligne ni couleur. C'est l'homme qui crée la ligne et la couleur. Ce sont deux abstractions qui tirent leur égale noblesse d'une même origine' (*AR* 15). It will be observed that this in effect refutes the (implied) past assertion, in the chapter 'De la Couleur' of the *Salon de 1846*, of the *innate* and *pre-existing* colour-harmony of Nature; cf. pp. 79–81, above.

[2] A year later, on the contrary, when writing to Wagner, B. does not hesitate to conjoin, within a single musical impression, the grandeur of Nature and the grandeur of human passions: 'J'ai retrouvé partout dans vos ouvrages la solennité des grands bruits, des grands aspects de la Nature, et la solennité des grandes passions de l'homme' (*CG* III, 33).

[3] *Salon de 1859*, *CE* 359; *L'Invitation au voyage*, *PPP* 55. (See pp. 133 n. 1 and n. 3, above.)

exaggerated by critics[1]—on the strength largely of two further texts dating both from this same period 1859–60: the poem *Rêve parisien*; the section 'Éloge du maquillage' of the long essay, *Le Peintre de la vie moderne*, devoted to the draughtsman Constantin Guys. Indeed, in the first of these two texts (i.e. *Rêve parisien*) the element of the 'artificial' is no more than incidental and secondary to the poem's main theme and structure.[2] The 'Éloge du maquillage', on the other hand, does present this notion to us within a fully developed and elaborated argument—while yet remaining by definition within the sphere of what in the most literal sense, perhaps, one should term an *applied* art . . . Baudelaire takes as his starting-point here a phrase from a 'vaudeville' of the day—a phrase, 'La nature embellit la beauté', which to him seems as inept as it is self-contradictory:

Il est une chanson . . . qui traduit fort bien, en style vaudevilliste, l'esthétique des gens qui ne pensent pas. *La nature embellit la beauté*! Il est présumable que le *poëte*, s'il avait pu parler en français, aurait dit: *La simplicité embellit la beauté*! ce qui équivaut à cette *vérité*, d'un genre tout à fait inattendu: Le *rien* embellit ce qui est.[3]

These current misconceptions regarding beauty, Baudelaire goes on to derive from what he now regards as the 'false' naturalistic ethic of the eighteenth-century *philosophes*, with its denial of original sin and its (supposed) glorification of Nature as the one 'source, basis and type' of all that is beautiful and good. In actual fact, Baudelaire protests, Nature 'teaches' us nothing of moral value: it merely obliges us to satisfy certain basic needs, and encourages us to kill, imprison, torture, even devour our fellow-men; parricide and cannibalism are its typical and conspicuous fruits. Evil and crime, being 'natural' to Man ('la nature ne peut conseiller que le crime'; 'Le crime, dont l'animal humain a puisé le goût dans le ventre de sa mère, est originellement naturel'), are accomplished without effort, as if by some fatal compulsion; virtue, on the other hand is

[1]E.g. by A. Cassagne, *Théorie de l'art pour l'art*, 324–6.
[2]Cf. my comments on this poem, pp. 165–70, below.
[3]*AR* 95. The abstrusely ironic quatrain addressed to an unknown lady, *Je vis, et ton bouquet est de l'architecture* (*OP* I, 22), in which B. plays a further variation on the phrase in question (actually a couplet: 'Et toujours la nature / Embellit la beauté', of which the unfortunate perpetrator was one Planard; see *OP* I, 396), has, I believe, no relevance to the present context, being intended purely as a *jeu d'esprit*. (I hope to return more fully to this question in a future publication).

artificial and 'supernatural', and everything that is noble and beautiful is the product of reason and calculation.[1] All this one might think to be aimed less at Rousseau than at Diderot—at the Diderot who in his *Supplément au Voyage de Bougainville* had offered this lapidary formula, which Baudelaire in his turn seems almost symmetrically to be reversing:

Voulez-vous savoir l'histoire abrégée de presque toute notre misère? la voici. Il existoit un homme naturel: on a introduit au dedans de cet homme un homme artificiel, et il s'est elevé dans la caverne une guerre civile qui dure toute la vie.[2]

But for Baudelaire, as we have seen, it is with 'artificial man' that all virtue lies: 'le bien est toujours le produit d'un art'. And this word 'art' now allows him, by a convenient transition, to transfer his argument first to the primitive *arts* of adornment, as practised by the baby and the savage,[3] and then to certain more specifically feminine arts. Thus of fashion he declares:

La mode doit . . . être considérée comme un symptôme du goût de l'idéal surnageant dans le cerveau humain au-dessus de tout ce que la vie naturelle y accumule de grossier, de terrestre et d'immonde, comme une déformation sublime de la nature, ou plutôt comme un essai permanent et successif de réformation de la nature . . .

---

[1] *AR* 95–7. B.'s position is here Johnsonian (as well as Maistrian); cf. (cit. Fairchild, *Noble Savage*, 331): 'Pity is not natural to Man. Children are always cruel. Savages are always cruel. Pity is acquired and improved by the cultivation of reason'. But we shall see (pp. 153–6, below) that as far as 'children and savages' are concerned, B. shows himself less consistent than either Johnson or Maistre; for the latter's influence on the present text, see (Mother) Mary Alphonsus, *Influence of J. de Maistre on B.*, 17–19.

[2] G. Chinard ed., 58 (=published text of this passage; for MS. version, see ibid., 190). Prof. Chinard points out (ibid., 57–8) that Diderot is here in effect refuting Buffon's 'prudent' assertion of the superiority, over the physical, of Man's moral nature—that very dualism (*homo duplex*) which B. was ultimately to invoke, in Buffon's name, when reviewing in 1859 his friend Asselineau's book *La Double vie* (*AR* 409). Thus B., who in his early art criticism owed so much to Diderot (see J. Pommier, *Chemins de B.*, 249–87; M. Gilman, *B. the Critic*, 40–6; G. May, *B. et Diderot critiques d'art*, passim; J. Seznec and J. Adhémar, ed. Diderot, *Salons*, I, 23; etc.), here appears rather as his philosophic adversary. For the more obvious 'quarrel' with Rousseau, cf. the passage from the *Notes nouvelles sur Edgar Poe* discussed below, pp. 155–6.

[3] For an analysis of the contradictions here arising within B.'s theory, see pp. 154–5, below.

La femme est bien dans son droit, et même elle accomplit une espèce de devoir en s'appliquant à paraître magique et surnaturelle; il faut qu'elle étonne, qu'elle charme; idole, elle doit se dorer pour être adorée. Elle doit donc emprunter à tous les arts les moyens de s'élever au-dessus de la nature pour mieux subjuguer les cœurs et frapper les esprits.

(*AR* 97–8)

Now this is scarcely the *comprehensive* aesthetic extension of Baudelaire's argument, that might seem to have been promised by his earlier assertion that everything he had said of the need to subordinate Nature to Reason, could be transferred from the sphere of morality to that of Art.[1] A certain continuity may none the less be discerned between the claim here made that by her 'magic' and '*super*natural' arts of self-adornment Woman raises herself *above* the Nature she thereby ('sublimely') re-forms,[2] and the criterion formulated, in the context of landscape painting, in the *Salon de 1859*, whereby Nature begins to 'exist' aesthetically only when 'purified' and interpreted by the artist.[3] And in the final section (which alone strictly answers to the title given to the chapter as a whole), Baudelaire while laying due stress on the purely decorative function of make-up, brings out strongly if briefly, by his rhetorical dismissal of *all* imitative art, the wider aesthetic implications of his subject:

Ainsi . . . la peinture du visage ne doit pas être employée dans le but vulgaire, inavouable, d'imiter la pure nature et de rivaliser avec la jeunesse. On a d'ailleurs observé que l'artifice n'embellissait pas la laideur et ne pouvait servir que la beauté. *Qui oserait assigner à l'art la fonction stérile d'imiter la nature?*[4]

---

[1] *AR* 97.

[2] It is intriguing to contrast this notion with that implied, as we have seen (pp. 22–3, above), in a text of B.'s earlier (and naturalist) period, the poem *Tu mettrais l'univers entier dans ta ruelle*: there, while rebuking the woman for the 'insolence' with which, by a 'pouvoir emprunté', she enhances the beauty of her eyes, the poet recognizes her to be, in this as in her other wiles, an *instrument* of Nature. Cf. also, in this connection (p. 63, above), *La Lune offensée*, ll. 12–14 (the mother 'artistically' repairing the ravages of the years); but conversely, cf. the somewhat perverse trait ('Eh! n'oubliez pas le rouge!') attributed to Cramer–B. in *La Fanfarlo*, pub. Jan. 1847 (ed. Pichois, 88).

[3] Cf. p. 133, above.

[4] *AR* 99–100, var. 463; my italics. In his preamble to a text published in 1857, the *Notes nouvelles sur Edgar Poe*, B. may be said to have obliquely anticipated the argument of the 'Éloge du maquillage' when drawing up, with somewhat heavy irony, his elaborate comparison between two imagined women representing respectively, on the one hand the dire tedium of classical literature,

This whole paradoxical extension of the theory of Art as artifice, whereby the woman making up her face becomes an 'artist' (i.e. a 'corrector' of Nature) in her own right, finds its echo in a series of anecdotes relating no doubt to the present period but recounted some twenty years later, under the pseudonym 'Maxime Rude', by the journalist Adolphe Perreau. I must first stress however, in this connection, the extreme prudence with which all testimonies of this kind should be treated. Quite apart from the distinctly variable reliability of the contemporary witnesses themselves, one must take into account all those impulses of pure mischief or sheer contra-suggestibility that so often led Baudelaire to provoke and scandalize (almost as a point of honour) the more gullible and impressionable of his acquaintances—to take automatically the exactly opposite view to that expected, or to that expressed by the previous speaker.[1] Moreover if it be true that the 'legend' constructed by Baudelaire during his own lifetime constitutes almost a 'work of art' in its own right,[2] this legend (one element of which is certainly an elaborately stylized hostility to Nature) must none the less be kept clearly subordinate for our purposes to what is after all the surer authenticity of Baudelaire's *written* pronouncements on Nature.

Of the various stories ('tall', or true, or a mixture of both) retailed by 'Maxime Rude', I must mention first those which are most closely related to the final paragraphs of the 'Éloge du maquillage'. Here then is Baudelaire's description, given to the journalist one evening at the Théâtre des Variétés, of the 'femme adorable' he had just chanced to see:

---

on the other the audacious and rewarding brilliance of so-called 'decadent' literature: '. . . il me semble que deux femmes me sont présentées: l'une, matrone rustique, répugnante de santé et de vertu, sans allure et sans regard, bref, *ne devant rien qu'à la simple nature*; l'autre, une de ces beautés qui dominent et oppriment le souvenir, unissant à son charme profond et originel toute l'éloquence de la toilette, maîtresse de sa démarche, consciente et reine d'elle-même . . .' (*NHE* v).

[1]Cf. Asselineau's amusing account, *EJC*, 282–3, of B.'s 'system' of astonishment ('Vous êtes étonné?', the poet would ask repeatedly)—a system further implied in certain prose texts of the present period (*Le Peintre de la vie moderne*, *AR* 89; *La Fausse monnaie*, *PPP* 98; *Une Mort héroïque*, *PPP* 92), with their references to 'le plaisir d'étonner'.

[2]Cf., for a searching discussion of this whole question, the essay by C. Pichois, 'Biographie ou légende?', prefacing the 1967 ed. of *BDC*, and especially this comment (p. 10): 'Cette légende est une *œuvre*; ce recueil doit prendre place à la suite des *Œuvres complètes*'.

11

Elle a les plus beaux sourcils du monde—qu'elle dessine à l'allumette,—
les yeux les plus provocants,—dont l'éclat n'existerait pas sans le kohl
de la paupière,—une bouche voluptueuse,—faite de carmin,—et, avec cela,
pas un cheveu qui lui appartienne.

To Rude's (predictable) exclamation: 'Mais c'est un monstre!',
Baudelaire was then able to retort: 'C'est une grande artiste!'[1] The
theme is further developed in the next anecdote, which concerns a
visit made to Versailles, in company with Hippolyte Babou:

Comme nous descendions de wagon, je remarquai, filant devant nous,
une jeune Anglaise dont la chevelure blonde ruisselait sur les épaules.
—Quelle jolie fille, m'écriai-je,—surtout si tous ses cheveux sont à elle!
—Pourquoi "surtout?", répliqua vivement Baudelaire. Elle ne serait que
plus curieuse et plus attrayante si cette chevelure, magnifiquement dis-
posée, n'était pas la sienne.[2]

The ensuing episode has a more particular interest, in that it introduces, within the context of the superiority of the artificial over
the real, the question of *external* Nature. Rude, having in this
instance replied to Baudelaire that he, for his part, preferred to
believe in Nature rather than in art or artifice, had exchanged with
Babou a meaning smile which Baudelaire had surprised, and for
which in due course he was able to take his 'revenge':

—Que tout cela est superbe! eus-je l'imprudence de murmurer au milieu
du parc de Versailles.
    Baudelaire m'entendait, et, me saisissant par le bras:
—Je vous y prends, me dit-il. Vous savez comme moi que rien de tout
cela n'est naturel, et vous admirez![3]

We must not of course make the mistake or taking too seriously
this purely circumstantial *riposte*; Rude's whole narrative does, however, serve to show something of the assiduity with which during
this period Baudelaire must have striven to build up, in his friends'
eyes, his *persona* of arch-enemy of all that was natural and real.

---

[1]*Confidences d'un journaliste*, 170 (cit. *AR* 463-4, *BDC* 211).
[2]Rude, op. cit., 170-1. As W. T. Bandy and C. Pichois have pointed out,
BDC, 211 n. 2, Rude may here simply be appropriating—and reversing—an
anecdote published some nine years earlier (a few weeks only after B.'s death)
by Francis Magnard: '—Voilà une femme qui a de beaux cheveux, lui disait
un de ses amis en lui montrant une anglaise au superbe chignon doré. Baudelaire regarda de près.—Vous vous trompez, dit-il, ces cheveux sont à elle;
elle n'a pas d'art, elle est atroce' (cit. ibid., 210).
[3]Rude, op. cit., 171.

Perhaps the most famous of all the anecdotes that have been handed down in this connection—certainly the one that has best lent itself to elegant philosophical variations![1]—is that recounted, in his *Memoirs*, by Alexandre Schanne, the 'Schaunard' of Murger's *Vie de Bohème*. The setting here is a train journey from Le Havre to Paris, the time an evening around 19 June 1859.[2] Having encountered Courbet and Schanne that same morning at Le Havre, Baudelaire had brought them home to dine with him at his mother's house at Honfleur (where he had been staying since the end of January[3]), and had then (according to Schanne) seized the opportunity offered by their departure, to make his own 'escape' with them to Paris—an escape, from what he had earlier described as an *enforced* sojourn in the country, which he now elaborately justifies in these terms:

—C'est que, nous dit-il, dans le wagon, la campagne m'est odieuse, surtout par le beau temps. La persistance du soleil m'accable; je me crois encore dans l'Inde où la continuité monotone de son rayonnement jette dans la torpeur plus de cent millions d'êtres humains . . . Ah! parlez-moi des ciels parisiens toujours changeants, qui rient et qui pleurent selon le vent, et sans que jamais leurs alternances de chaleur et d'humidité puissent profiter à de stupides céréales. Je froisserai peut-être vos convictions de paysagistes, mais je vous dirai que l'eau en liberté m'est insupportable; je la veux prisonnière, au carcan, dans les murs géométriques d'un quai.—Ma promenade préférée est la berge du canal de l'Ourcq . . . Quand je me baigne, c'est dans une baignoire; j'aime mieux une boîte à musique qu'un rossignol; et, pour moi, l'état parfait des fruits d'un jardin ne commence qu'au compotier! . . . Enfin, l'homme soumis à la nature m'a toujours semblé avoir refait un pas vers la sauvagerie originelle!

De paradoxes en paradoxes et de stations en stations, nous étions arrivés à la gare Saint-Lazare.[4]

From a purely biographical point of view, this whole story is somewhat suspect: to take but one small detail, it would appear that the

[1]Cf. J. P. Sartre, *B.*, 120–1.

[2]This date may be inferred from an exchange of letters, over the period 13–17 June 1859, between B. and Poulet-Malassis (*CG* II, 325–7; *EJC* 417–19), and from a text of Boudin's, cit. G. Jean-Aubry, *Boudin*, 39, dating Courbet's and Schanne's visits to him at Le Havre, as of 16–18 June.

[3]With an interruption of a few weeks during March and April; cf. p. 146, below.

[4]Schanne, *Souvenirs de Schaunard*, 231–2.

three travellers could in fact scarcely have left for Paris at the time
indicated by Schanne, since the last boat for Le Havre (making the
train connection to Paris) would by then already have left![1] Nor
can one really accept that the true reasons for Baudelaire's departure
(even assuming it in fact to have taken place in the manner indicated)
were those imputed to him by Schanne. Thus it must first be
observed that far from seeming to Baudelaire a tedious rural solitude
against which he had been obliged, even *forced*, to exchange the
fascination and vitality (both human and meteorological) of the
capital, Honfleur had on the contrary become for him a place of
refuge, of refreshment, of creative fulfilment, of *admired* (rather
than resented) natural beauty.[2] It is true that this had not prevented
him from snatching several weeks in Paris during March and April;
and no doubt having decided, in June, that he needed to make a
further journey to the capital,[3] he would have been only too ready
and glad to profit from the arrival at Honfleur of Schanne and
Courbet, by duly electing them his travelling-companions. Yet this
still leaves open the question of his actual motives for the departure
from Honfleur at the end of June, and these, in the event, would
seem certainly to have been of a more practical and circumstantial
than theoretical and dogmatic order: the pressing need to attend to
certain literary or financial problems that had arisen in the capital;[4]
the desire, perhaps, to be re-united with Marie Daubrun, on her
return to the Parisian theatrical scene after a (presumed) spell of
two years in the South of France;[5] the compulsion, finally (the word
would scarcely be too strong), to renew his depleted or exhausted
stocks of opium, and the accompanying resolve to assure himself, at
least for a while, of a more certain and substantial source of supply
than he could possibly count upon at Honfleur. In putting forward
this latter supposition, incidentally, I would cite in support not only
the letter to Poulet-Malassis written in mid-February 1859, with
its revealing conclusion:

[1]See J. Crépet and C. Pichois, *Figaro littéraire*, 12 April 1952, and G. Jean-
Aubry, *B. et Honfleur*, 27. For other implausibilities within Schaunard's
testimony, cf. ibid., 25–7; *CG* II, 327 n. 1; A. Feuillerat, *B. et sa mère*, 112.

[2]Cf., in this connection, my final chapter, pp. 254–5, below.

[3]See p. 145 n. 2, above; for the dates of the earlier trip to Paris, cf. *CG* II,
288 and 297.

[4]*CG* II, 325 (cf. ibid., 329); C. Pichois, *B.*, 265 n. 508.

[5]See A. Feuillerat, *B. et la Belle aux cheveux d'or*, 71–2, and *B. et sa mère*,
113—as also *CG* II, 327 n. 1.

Je suis bien noir, mon cher, et je n'ai pas apporté d'opium, et je n'ai pas d'argent pour payer mon pharmacien à Paris.

(*CG* II, 271)

—but also this testimony recorded many years later at Honfleur by Léon Lemonnier; the speaker (and 'reminiscer') is Mme Allais, mother of the famous humourist Alphonse Allais and widow of a Honfleur pharmacist who had served both Mme Aupick and her son:

'. . . De temps à autre, il avait avec mon mari de petites . . . querelles. Il avait pris l'habitude de l'opium, et il suppliait mon mari de lui en fournir. Mais M. Allais ne lui en a jamais donné qu'autant que le pouvait un pharmacien consciencieux.'[1]

These reservations need not oblige us, however, to refuse all credence to Schanne's account; this latter may well, for all its circumstantial implausibilities, reproduce accurately enough the actual words spoken by Baudelaire—the actual reasons he chose to give for his action, the familiar, even automatic, 'paradoxes' to which in the event he resorted. Certainly the whole speech, in the form transcribed by Schanne, catches authentically enough the calculated provocativeness as well as the dogmatic anti-naturalism of Baudelaire's 'public' utterances during this period.[2] It is amusing to note, incidentally, in the initial sentences quoted by Schanne, the almost symmetrical reversal of the theme and imagery of *Le Soleil*—or rather, of that poem's second section dating (as we have seen) from Baudelaire's earlier, 'naturalist' period. In those verses, it will be recalled, it is precisely *because* the sun 'profits' the 'cereals', here denounced as 'stupid', that it is revered as the benign 'foster-father' to all creation. . . .[3] Altogether more significant from out present standpoint, however, is the final sentence of the monologue recorded by Schanne: this in effect takes the general argument of the 'Éloge

[1] L. Lemonnier, *Enquêtes sur B.* ('B. à Honfleur'), 21. This explanation of B.'s visits to Paris from Honfleur has been admitted as a possibility by C. Pichois and R. Kopp, *Europe*, April–May 1967, p. 76, but with sole reference to the letter to Poulet-Malassis; the testimony of Mme Allais would seem to me to strengthen greatly the whole supposition. Cf. also A. Feuillerat, *B. et sa mère*, 220 n. 15 (n. to p. 110).

[2] P. Citron, *Poésie de Paris*, II, 360, justly remarks: '. . . ces phrases ont le ton mordant, glacé et péremptoire du dandy'—but adds: 'plus que la gravité esthétique du poète'.

[3] Cf. pp. 13–14, above.

du maquillage' a whole stage further, with the scope of Man's original sin now extended to include his subservience to external, as well as to inner, Nature.[1] What, conversely, is more difficult to reconcile with other texts of this period, is the distaste here voiced for all forms of 'free-flowing' water. Such an attitude, though it might seem to have indirect confirmation in the (admired) dream-imagery of *Rêve parisien*, with its vast expanses of explicitly 'channelled' water, can have but little weight when set beside the many contemporary expressions we shall later encounter, of Baudelaire's deep love for the unconfined and free-flowing *sea*.[2]

Reverting to the more purely aesthetic aspects of Baudelaire's anti-naturalism, we observe that after the *Salon de 1859* he has little further to add on the specific question of realism in Art. He does, it is true, deem it appropriate to return once more to the charge when sketching out, some four or five years later, that curious (and abortive) indictment of a whole national culture, *Pauvre Belgique*; here everything is grist to the anti-Belgian mill, and it is thus no surprise that the chapter headed 'Beaux-Arts' should begin its 'argument' in these terms:

En Belgique, pas d'Art; l'Art s'est retiré du pays.

Pas d'artistes, excepté Rops.

La composition, chose inconnue. Philosophie de ces brutes, philosophie à la Courbet.

Ne peindre que ce qu'on voit (Donc *vous* ne peindrez pas ce que *je* ne vois pas). Spécialistes.—Un peintre pour le soleil, un pour la lune, un pour les meubles, un pour les étoffes, un pour les fleurs,—et subdivisions de spécialités, à l'infini, comme dans l'industrie.—La collaboration devient chose nécessaire.

(*OP* III, 178)

The proposition recurs, in a slightly different form, in Baudelaire's 'Notes' for this same chapter:

PEINTURE BELGE MODERNE

L'art s'est retiré du pays.

Grossièreté dans l'art.

Peinture minutieuse de tout ce qui n'a pas vie.

Peinture des bestiaux.

---

[1]Cf., for the whole question of human nature and original sin, my next section, pp. 150–60, below.

[2]Cf. pp. 257–62, below, and for *Rêve parisien*, pp. 165–7, below.

Philosophie des peintres belges, philosophie de notre ami Courbet, l'empoisonneur intéressé (Ne peindre que ce qu'on voit! Donc *vous* ne peindrez que ce que *je* vois).

(ibid., 180)

To some extent Baudelaire is here renewing the rather oblique argument with which he had opened the third chapter of the *Salon de 1859*: since the artist who claims to be 'copying' Nature cannot in fact 'know' the *whole* of Nature (i.e. since he can reproduce only the particular fragment that chances to fall within his vision), it follows that the truest realism must lie, after all, in fidelity to one's *own* (rather than to external) Nature.[1] So too, when attributing, to the Belgian emulants of Courbet (for whom, incidentally, he seems to have conceived a new, or more specific, animosity[2]), the Realist contention 'One must paint only what one sees',[3] Baudelaire now explains this as meaning in effect: '*You* must paint only what *I* see' (or, in the alternative and negative formulation, '*You* must not be allowed to paint what *I* do NOT see'). But Baudelaire also goes on to imply, in this present attack on modern Belgian painters, two further and corollary strictures on naturalism: it encourages ever narrower and more restrictive 'specialization' among artists,[4] it favours the crude depiction of the inanimate or 'bestial'.[5] Finally

[1] *CE* 272–4. Cf. also (p. 130, above) the counter-claim made in *Puisque réalisme il y a* for the *true* reality captured by all good poets, when they equate impression and expression, object and 'hieroglyph'.

[2] Cf., in addition to the passages above-quoted (Courbet assimilated to 'ces brutes', Courbet 'l'empoisonneur intéressé'): *OP* III, 171, 167 (Léopold I 'élève de Courbet', 'amant de *la simple nature*'), 125 ('Victor Hugo domine [en Belgique] comme Courbet'), 101 (ironic comments on a painting by Courbet—inspired, as it happens, by B.'s own *Femmes damnées: Delphine et Hippolyte*! Cf. ibid., 328).

[3] Perhaps recalled in this instance from an article published by Asselineau in 1856; see *OP* III, 354.

[4] To the Belgian 'specialities' listed in the passage above-quoted, B. elsewhere adds: snow (*OP* III, 178 var.) and peonies (179: 'Il y a un artiste pour peindre les pivoines') . . . For previous attacks on specialization in modern art, cf. *L'Œuvre et la Vie d'Eugène Delacroix* (1863), *AR* 7; *Victor Hugo* (1861), *AR* 307; *Salon de 1846*, *CE* 162–4 (castigation of Horace Vernet: 'Qui sait mieux que lui combien il y a de boutons dans chaque uniforme . . .?', etc.).

[5] Cf. in this respect, in the *Salon de 1859* (*CE* 352), the comment on Clésinger's *Taureau romain* sculpture: a fine work, justly extolled—but surely a sculptor of Clésinger's quality should have other images in mind than those of mere *bulls*, should desire praise for something more worthy than the rendering of a mere *beast*, however splendid?

(and at a distinctly higher critical level), there is also the lively analysis of the paintings of Alfred Stevens, ending with the perhaps too-automatic equation of 'nothingness' with 'imitation of nature':

Le plus fort, dit-on, des peintres belges, celui que ces buveurs de faro et ces mangeurs de pommes de terre comparent volontiers à Michel-Ange, M. Alfred Stévens, peint d'ordinaire une petite femme (c'est sa tulipe, à lui) toujours la même, écrivant une lettre, recevant une lettre, cachant une lettre, recevant un bouquet, cachant un bouquet, bref, toutes les jolies balivernes que Devéria vendait 20 sols, sans plus grande prétention. Le grand malheur de ce peintre minutieux, c'est que la lettre, le bouquet, la chaise, la bague, la guipure, etc . . . deviennent, tour à tour, l'objet important, l'objet qui crève les yeux.—En somme, c'est un peintre *parfaitement* flamand, en tant qu'il y ait de la perfection dans le *néant*, ou dans *l'imitation de la nature*, ce qui est la même chose.[1]

3. HUMAN NATURE AND ORIGINAL SIN: THE INVETERATE PRIMITIVIST

We must now consider a series of texts revealing a rather different and indeed wholly contrasted aspect of Baudelaire's anti-naturalism. In the letter to Desnoyers, as in the chapter on landscape in the *Salon de 1859*, Baudelaire had taken up, it will be recalled, a broadly 'humanist' standpoint: Man has spiritual and aesthetic priority over Nature, Nature 'exists' only through and for Man. The doctrine of original sin, however, which from at least 1855 onwards was to become so integral an element of Baudelaire's moral thought,[2] implies

[1]*OCP* 1428; cf. *OP* III, 356.

[2]The first dated text in which B. explicitly appropriates to himself the doctrine (or *a* doctrine) of original sin, is the 1855 version of the essay *De l'essence du rire*; in its original draft, this essay goes back undoubtedly (as C. Pichois has shown *B.*, 80–94) to the period 1844–7, but it is by no means impossible that the specific references in question (*CE* 373-4, 376, 383, 385) were interpolated at some later date—perhaps at a date *after* 1852, since, as I have indicated already (p. 99 n. 1, above), the article *L'École païenne* (pub. Jan. 1852) shows no trace of these ideas (or of the corollary influence of J. de Maistre). But one may nevertheless suppose a strong *pre*disposition towards them on B.'s part, and this would have been fostered particularly, no doubt, by his reading, in Jan. –Feb. 1847, of Poe's *The Black Cat*—in a translation, moreover, which was introduced in terms that B., in his enthusiasm for Poe, may in retrospect have seen as a challenge or a provocation: 'Nous donnons cette nouvelle pour montrer à quels singuliers arguments sont réduits les derniers partisans de la *perversité native*' (*La Démocratie pacifique*, 27/1/1847—my italics; cit. L. Lemonnier, *Poe et la critique*, 12, and C. Pichois, *B.*, 121).

by definition the *degradation* of Man—even if also, as a corollary, the degradation of Nature viewed as the instinctive principle (i.e. 'human nature') working within each man; so far is this from being a humanist doctrine in any proper sense, that Daniel Vouga can speak, in this same context, of Baudelaire's 'pessimisme *anti*-humaniste'.[1] A glance at the main texts in question will illustrate this point clearly enough. Thus in the letter to Toussenel of 21 January 1856, Baudelaire poses a number of rhetorical questions bearing on various 'heresies' to which his correspondent had given expression in the third volume of his book *Le Monde des oiseaux*:[2]

> Qu'est-ce que le *Progrès indéfini*? qu'est-ce qu'une *société* qui n'est pas *aristocratique*! . . . Qu'est-ce que c'est que l'homme *naturellement* bon? où l'a-t-on connu? L'homme naturellement bon serait un *monstre*, je veux dire un *Dieu*.

> (*CG* I, 369)

A reference a few lines later to Joseph de Maistre: 'le grand génie de notre temps,—*un voyant*!', indicates the main intellectual source from which Baudelaire doubtless derived these strongly reactionary notions—which is not to say that they mirror in every respect his new mentor's philosophies.[3] But it is only in the final paragraphs of the letter that Baudelaire explicitly links, with the various 'heresies' incriminated, that ultimate heresy of all—the 'suppression' of the idea of original sin:

> Toutes les hérésies auxquelles je faisais allusion tout à l'heure ne sont, après tout, que la conséquence de la grande hérésie moderne, de la doctrine *artificielle*, substituée à la doctrine naturelle,—je veux dire la suppression de l'idée du *péché originel*.

---

[1] *B. et J. de Maistre*, 140 (my italics); cf. ibid., 122–3.

[2] For the identification (by J. Pommier) of this text, and for the question as to whether B. may have read also the *previous* volumes of Toussenel's work, see p. 221 and n. 2, below.

[3] Thus in the formulation of the last of the three (dismissively) rhetorical questions above-quoted ('Qu'est-ce que c'est que l'homme *naturellement* bon? où l'a-t-on connu?'), B. might seem to have discounted Maistre's postulate (*Soirées de Saint-Pétersbourg*, II⁰ 'Entretien', cit. D. Vouga, *B. et J. de Maistre*, 43–4) of a pre-lapsarian Golden Age; for another divergence from Maistre, cf. p. 154, below. In speaking here of Maistre as B.'s 'new mentor' in this sphere, I do not mean to imply that B. had no previous *knowledge* of Maistre's writings; cf. in this connection (Mother) Mary Alphonsus, *Influence of J. de Maistre on B.*, 7–14.

Votre livre réveille en moi bien des idées dormantes,—et à propos de *péché originel*, et de *forme moulée sur l'idée*, j'ai pensé bien souvent que les bêtes malfaisantes et dégoûtantes n'étaient peut-être que la vivification, corporification, éclosion à la vie matérielle, des *mauvaises pensées* de l'homme.—Ainsi la *nature* entière participe du péché originel.[1]

The 'Satanic' inflection here lent to the notion of original sin (maleficent and repulsive beasts viewed as the embodiment or materialization of Man's evil thoughts),[2] is directly voiced in a passage of the *Notes nouvelles sur Edgar Poe*, published later in the same year. The pretext on this occasion is an exposition of Poe's theory of the perverse; but in Baudelaire's hands this theory (as illustrated in the tales *The Black Cat* and *The Imp of the Perverse*) acquires a range of moral and theological connotation certainly unintended by Poe.[3] The latter, Baudelaire notes, having clearly perceived and 'imperturbably affirmed' the natural wickedness or perversity of Man, had found in this 'primitive and irresistible force' the motive for a whole host of otherwise inexplicable actions. The passage ends, after a reference to this 'primordial perversity of Man' as being the 'great forgotten truth' of our time,[4] with a scathing refutation of those whom Baudelaire calls

tous ces complimenteurs de l'humanité, . . . tous ces dorloteurs et endormeurs qui répètent sur toutes les variations possibles de ton: "Je suis né bon, et vous aussi, et nous tous, nous sommes nés bons!" oubliant, non! feignant d'oublier, ces égalitaires à contresens, que nous sommes tous nés marquis pour le mal![5]

---

[1]*CG* I, 370. In the final sentence here reproduced, I have ventured to substitute 'Ainsi' for 'Aussi', as being more plausible both logically and grammatically.

[2]B.'s sources here would appear to be Swedenborg and Fourier, rather than Maistre; see M. Milner, *Diable*, II, 456, and cf., for the 'Satanic inflection' aforementioned, ibid., 459–60.

[3]Cf. M. Gilman, *B. the Critic*, 94; P. F. Quinn, *French Face of Poe*, 131; G. Blin, *Sadisme de B.*, 48 n. 3 ('Baudelaire résume ici, ou s'annexe, l'auteur du *Chat noir* et du *Démon de la perversité*'). Poe had nevertheless already been assimilated, by certain of his early French critics, to the theorists of original sin; cf. the text of 1847 cit. p. 150 n. 2, above.

[4]By the phrase 'primordial perversity', B. (if not Poe) of course simply understands 'original sin'; cf. M. Gilman, loc. cit., as also M. Milner, *Diable*, II, 458, and the comment by G. Blin, *Le Sadisme de B.*, 48: 'Ainsi "Perversité naturelle" fait pléonasme'.

[5]*NHE*, ix. The reading 'marqués pour le mal', favoured by some critics, is in fact one that B. himself had *discarded* at the proof stage; see *NHE* 322 and

In a further passage of these *Notes*, Baudelaire returns once again, as we shall later see, to the question of 'natural depravity', while specifying (and admonishing) the historical precursor, i.e. Jean-Jacques Rousseau, of the 'egalitarians' here derided.

Passing over various other similar or complementary affirmations made over this whole period 1856–65,[1] I now return to the text in which for the first time the 'theological' condemnation of Nature[2] is invoked in respect of Art—i.e. to the 'Éloge du maquillage'. It will be recalled that Baudelaire begins this chapter of *Le Peintre de la vie moderne*, by refuting the (presumed) eighteenth-century belief in the natural goodness of Man; on the contrary, he maintains, Man's *natural* propensity (derived from original sin) is self-evidently towards evil and crime.[3] Hereafter follows the passage already briefly indicated, whereby Baudelaire extends this whole argument from the moral to the aesthetic sphere:

Tout ce que je dis de la nature comme mauvaise conseillère en matière de morale, et de la raison comme véritable rédemptrice et réformatrice, peut être transporté dans l'ordre du beau. Je suis ainsi conduit à regarder la parure comme un des signes de la noblesse primitive de l'âme humaine. Les races que notre civilisation, confuse et pervertie, traite volontiers de sauvages, avec un orgueil et une fatuité tout à fait risibles, comprennent, aussi bien que l'enfant, la haute spiritualité de la toilette. Le sauvage et le baby témoignent, par leur aspiration naïve vers le brillant, vers les

---

318–19. Yet in so doing he appears somewhat illogically to have confused the moral with the political aspects of naturalism; for is there not an implied principle of equality (and indeed of fraternity, if not of liberty!) in the very assumption that *all* men are born evil? Cf. the concluding line of *Au Lecteur* (first pub. June 1855): 'Hypocrite lecteur,—mon *semblable*,—mon *frère*!' (my italics). The inconsequence would remain, incidentally, even if one accepted that B. might possibly have intended, in the *Notes nouvelles* passage, a conscious or unconscious reference to the *Marquis* de Sade; cf. Milner, *Diable*, II, 459.

[1] Cf. *Fusées* XV, *JI* 34, l. 73–6; *Poëme du haschisch, PA* 57; *Le Fou raisonnable, OCP* 521 ('Il faut toujours en Revenir [sic] à De Sade, c'est-à-dire à *l'Homme Naturel*, pour expliquer le mal'); *Salon de 1859, CE* 318 (Fromentin's quest for beauty among 'les trivialités de la nature déchue'); *Mon Cœur mis à nu*, V and XLI, *JI* 56 and 97; *L'Œuvre et la vie d'Eug. Delacroix, AR* 37; *Pauvre Belgique, OP* III, 120. For texts relating (disparagingly) to 'natural woman', cf. p. 157 and n. 2, below.

[2] Cf. the comment by J. Crépet and G. Blin, *JI* 225–6: B. is here taking to their extreme limit 'les théories des Pères de l'Église, des Jansénistes et de Maistre'.

[3] *AR* 95–7; cf. p. 140, above.

plumages bariolés, les étoffes chatoyantes, vers la majesté superlative des formes artificielles, de leur dégoût pour le réel, et prouve ainsi, à leur insu, l'immatérialité de leur âme.   (*AR* 97)

Now at this point we encounter a significant inconsistency in Baudelaire's reasoning. He speaks of the 'primitive nobility of the human soul', as exhibited by the so-called 'savage' races, and of the 'spirituality' displayed by the savage and the baby in their spontaneous hankering after the brilliant and artificial (which is to say, the beautiful). 'Primitive' and 'natural' being here virtual synonyms, is this not a signal contradiction of the earlier statement that *everything* noble and beautiful comes from reason and calculation, and that from Nature comes nothing that is not ignoble or horrible?[1] If, as he now asserts, our modern civilization is so 'perverted' and 'confused', so absurd in its unjustified disdain for the primitive races, does this not argue that Man might after all have done better to remain in a state of nature, and that the benefits accruing from reason, calculation, religion, 'true philosophy', are a good deal less certain than Baudelaire has earlier claimed? Now this contradiction is of some importance, in that it shows Baudelaire's continuing fidelity—in this one respect at least—to the nostalgic primitivism of his youth.[2] Joseph de Maistre, arguing from the essential proposition that the *whole* of Mankind is in ever more rapid degradation as a consequence of original sin, had declared the savage to be still more deeply vicious and degenerate than 'civilized' Man;[3] Baudelaire, however—unable, as it were, to school himself to the relentless logic of this system— prefers to bolster his impeccably Maistrian denunciations of the cult of inevitable progress, with a wholly *un*-Maistrian protest against facile modern depreciations of the so-called 'barbarian' races.[4] The

[1]*AR* 96.

[2]The child being in the present context linked (by its unconscious 'spirituality') with the savage, one may note that in the almost exactly contemporary article on Banville (pub. 1861) B. refers, in the context of his friend's 'lyricism', to the 'lost Eden' of childhood (*AR* 355). Cf. for certain 'exotic' texts of the present period, p. 303 and n. 1, below.

[3]Maistre's own primitive ideal belongs, as we have noted (p. 151 n. 3, above), to a remote, Edenic past, and is thus on no account to be confused with the 'primitivism' of the present-day savage.

[4]B., in short, is here, in relation to Maistre, in something of the same position as Boswell arguing with Johnson in 1784—and earning from the stern Doctor the rebuke 'Don't cant in defence of savages' . . . (cit. H. N. Fairchild, *Noble Savage*, 338).

resulting dilemma may be still more clearly perceived if we turn for a moment from the 'Éloge du maquillage', to consider this (roughly contemporary) fragment from the 'intimate journal' *Mon Cœur mis à nu*:

Théorie de la vraie civilisation.

Elle n'est pas dans le gaz, ni dans la vapeur, ni dans les tables tournantes, elle est dans la diminution des traces du péché originel.

Peuples nomades, pasteurs, chasseurs, agricoles, et même anthropophages, *tous* peuvent être supérieurs, par l'énergie, par la dignité personnelles, à nos races d'Occident.

(XXXI, *JI* 87)

'. . . et même anthropophages': in other words, the very cannibals whom in the 'Éloge du maquillage' Baudelaire had singled out as the typically abominable products of 'infallible' Nature, i.e. as the salutary illustration of the workings of original sin,[1] are now offered, as potentially superior models of 'energy' and 'personal dignity', to a Western world requiring above all to 'diminish' in itself the 'traces' of that same original sin . . . Could it then be that we too (like the cannibals) would do best, after all, to *heed* rather than stifle the voice of Nature? But it is only fair to add that Baudelaire had previously shown some fleeting awareness of this whole unresolved contradiction, in another interesting passage of the *Notes nouvelles sur Edgar Poe*. Having here delivered himself of what was to become his ritual fulmination against the 'heresy' of 'unceasing progress', Baudelaire goes on to link Poe with Rousseau, in their common impatience with this whole 'perverse and mendacious' philosophy.[2] Yet Jean-Jacques, having (allegedly) incriminated Man as an 'animal dépravé',[3] must none the less earn reproach for having further presumed to 'invoke' mere (or brute) Nature—'la simple nature'. And Baudelaire duly continues:

La nature ne fait que des monstres, et toute la question est de s'entendre sur le mot *sauvages*. Nul philosophe n'osera proposer pour modèles ces

---

[1] *AR* 96.

[2] *NHE* x–xi.

[3] Rousseau's actual words show his denunciation to have been a good deal less comprehensive than B.'s context implies: '. . . j'ose presque assurer que l'état de réflexion est un état contre nature, et que *l'homme qui médite* est un animal dépravé' (*Discours sur . . . l'origine de l'inégalité*, Garnier, p. 45; my italics).

malheureuses hordes pourries, victimes des éléments, pâture des bêtes, aussi incapables de fabriquer des armes que de concevoir l'idée d'un pouvoir spirituel et suprême. Mais si l'on veut comparer l'homme moderne, l'homme civilisé, avec l'homme sauvage, ou plutôt une nation dite civilisée avec une nation dite sauvage, c'est-à-dire privée de toutes les ingénieuses inventions qui dispensent l'individu d'héroïsme, qui ne voit que tout l'honneur est pour le sauvage?

(*NHE* xi–xii)

Baudelaire here seems to imply three distinct stages of human development: an utterly primitive stage, in which Man lacks all means of self-defence, all true sense of religion; a (preferred) stage of strictly relative and freely 'heroic' 'primitivism', such as certain ancient or indigenous-American societies have attained;[1] a stage of 'full' civilization, finally, in the modern European (and degenerate) sense. Whether or not Baudelaire recognized the essential similarity between his scheme and that which underlies (somewhat more elaborately, it must be admitted!) Rousseau's *Discours sur . . . l'origine de l'inégalité*,[2] the fact remains that by the very terms he uses to describe his Noble Savages, he tacitly acknowledges their proximity to that same state of nature he must nevertheless by definition (and by Maistrian affiliation) condemn.[3]

Returning to the 'Éloge du maquillage', we find that in the ensuing paragraph Baudelaire's argument takes on a new (if paradoxical) subtlety and coherence, once transferred to the true subject of his chapter—to Woman, who by her sartorial fashions and (above all) her cosmetic arts, 'sublimely deforms' or rather *re*forms Nature, purging it of its inherent 'grossness' and thus truly serving the cause

[1]From certain later examples he gives (*NHE* xii–xiii), B. would seem especially to have Redskin or Aztec communities in mind; one thinks also of that pagan 'Great Tradition' he had invoked so admiringly in the *Salon de 1846*, *CE* 196.

[2]Thus to B.'s first two stages would correspond the first three of the 'four distinct cultural stages' into which Rousseau divides the 'juristic state of nature'; see the penetrating analysis by A. O. Lovejoy, *Essays*, ch. 2. It is true that for B., Rousseau (unlike Poe . . .!) was no true philosopher, but rather one of those 'intelligences obscures . . . à qui une sensibilité blessée et prompte à la révolte tient lieu de philosophie' (*NHE* xi).

[3]Cf. especially the admiring portrait of the 'sauvagesse, à l'âme *simple et enfantine, animal* obéissant et câlin' (*NHE* xii; my italics). And yet elsewhere Woman is denounced (as we shall see) for this same 'animality', the child declared (*AR* 37) to be closer than the man to the original sin shared by all three; the same differentiation (i.e. in man's favour, as against the woman and the child) is made in a letter of March 1862 (to Mme Aupick, *CG* IV, 70–1).

of Beauty and of the ideal; having received at birth (i.e. as a gift of Nature!) a spark of the sacred fire, she thereafter seeks to illumine her whole self by its light.[1] In tone if not in essential philosophy, this is at several removes from the Baudelaire who with stern theological rigour thunders in other writings of the period against the 'natural' viciousness of woman: 'La femme est *naturelle*, c'est-à-dire abominable', etc., etc.;[2] his repudiation of Woman, like his repudiation of external Nature, is essentially theoretical, provocative, dogmatic, and tends to falter before the specifically beautiful landscape, the specifically (or even generically) beautiful woman.[3]

In February 1859, writing (from Honfleur) to Asselineau, Baudelaire announces:

J'ai fait un long poëme dédié à Maxime du Camp, qui est à faire frémir la nature, et surtout les amateurs du progrès.

(*CG* II, 274)

The 'long poem' in question is *Le Voyage*, and not the least important or intriguing aspect of its composition is this curious dedication

[1] *AR* 97–8, 100.

[2] *Mon Cœur mis à nu*, III, *JI* 53; for other cognate texts, cf. the refs. given ibid. 226–7. But it should be noted that in his comments on the characters of Laclos' *Les Liaisons dangereuses* B., while noting of Cécile that she is 'tout près de l'ordure originelle' (or as he originally wrote, 'du péché originel'), at the same time concludes his admiring portrait of the Présidente de Tourvel with the words: 'Une femme *naturelle*. Une Ève touchante'—the latter trait contrasting with 'La Merteuil, une Ève satanique' (*OCP* 643, var. 1662; my italics). Cf. in this connection the just comment by J. P. Sartre, *B.*, 117: 'les passages abondent, dans les lettres de Baudelaire, où l'expression de "naturel" est synonyme de *légitime* et de *juste*'. (M. Sartre quotes one such passage, from L. Mme Aupick of 4/8/1860, *CG* III, 153.)

[3] Woman and Nature are indeed specifically linked, for their common nourishment and enrichment of the imagination, in an eloquent passage of the dedication (to 'J.G.F.'; completed in the first fortnight of Jan. 1860) of the *Paradis artificiels*: 'A des esprits niais il paraîtra singulier, et même impertinent, qu'un tableau de voluptés artificielles soit dédié à une femme, source la plus ordinaire des voluptés les plus naturelles. Toutefois il est évident que, comme le monde naturel pénètre dans le spirituel, lui sert de pâture, et concourt ainsi à opérer cet amalgame indéfinissable que nous nommons notre individualité, la femme est l'être qui projette la plus grande ombre ou la plus grande lumière dans nos rêves. La femme est fatalement suggestive; elle vit d'une autre vie que la sienne propre; elle vit spirituellement dans les imaginations qu'elle hante et qu'elle féconde' (*PA* v–vi). B.'s whole argument here in effect refutes the dogmatic proposition above-quoted from *Mon Cœur mis à nu*; one notes, however, the tacit postulation of an exclusively masculine readership!

—at once sincere and disingenuous, flattering and ironic—to Maxime
Du Camp.[1] The comment above-quoted applies strictly, however,
only to the powerful sixth section of the poem;[2] this, giving us the
further reply of the disabused 'Travellers' to the avid questions with
which they are assailed on their return ('Dites, qu'avez-vous vu?',
'Et puis, et puis encore?'), begins on this massively deflationary note:

> . . . O cerveaux enfantins!

> > Pour ne pas oublier la chose capitale,
> > Nous avons vu partout, et sans l'avoir cherché,
> > Du haut jusques en bas de l'échelle fatale,
> > Le spectacle ennuyeux de l'immortel péché . . .

> > > (1859 text, ll. 84–8)

There follows a scarifying indictment of human tyranny, perversity
and cruelty, in which the religions of the world, competing to scale
the Heavens, and the saint luxuriating in his own self-chastisement,
are no more spared than the ordinary run of men and women nor
the despot to whom they willingly submit.[3] A final group—forming
what in modern terms would no doubt be called 'the underground':
those bold enough (like Baudelaire himself) to seek oblivion in the
'vast' yet dangerous consolations of opium—lead us into this
wearily dismissive conclusion:

> Tel est du globe entier l'éternel bulletin.

> > (l. 108)

The epithet 'éternel', like the earlier 'immortel' ('Le spectacle
ennuyeux de l'*immortel* péché'), makes clear that what is here being
affirmed, over and above the inescapable present reality of human
iniquity, is the permanent reality of original sin; what equally by implication is being *denied*—or so it would seem from the comment to
Asselineau, above-quoted—is the contrary and conventional belief
at once in the natural goodness of Man, and in the inevitability of
Progress.[4] And thus it would seem that when setting down the words

[1] See, in this connection: *FMCB* 523–4; Y. Abé, 'B. et M. Du Camp', *RHLF*,
1967, pp. 273–82.
   [2] For a discussion of the remaining sections of the poem, see pp. 294–310, below.
   [3] I borrow this summary from my art. cit., 'B.: The Poet as Moralist', p. 212.
   [4] This double refutation is perhaps crystallized in the reference, in the previous
verse, to 'L'Humanité bavarde, ivre de son génie, / Et, folle maintenant comme
elle était jadis . . .' (ll. 101–2); cf., in this connection, *FMA* 431 n. 20.

'la nature' in the phrase in question ('un long poëme . . . à faire frémir la nature'), Baudelaire must clearly have had in mind not merely 'la nature *humaine*', but further (to balance the succeeding phrase: 'les amateurs du progrès') some such unformulated notion as 'les partisans de la bonté naturelle de l'homme'.[1] This whole comment to Asselineau makes plain, incidentally, that the Travellers are here (if not always elsewhere in the poem) directly voicing Baudelaire's *own* ideas—that it is indeed *he*, who through them, is here denouncing the 'eternal' ubiquity of human sin.

Within this denunciation is explicitly included, as I have indicated already, a disparagement of all established religions; to that extent, the doctrine of original sin is here emptied of its doctrinal or even dogmatic content. A more positive or orthodox counterpart to this attitude, however, is to be found in the concluding paragraphs of Baudelaire's review of Hugo's *Les Misérables*. This appeared in April 1862, some three years after the composition of *Le Voyage*, but within a few months only of the publication of the poem *L'Imprévu*; it may well mark, therefore, like this latter text, Baudelaire's (provisional?) return to the Catholic fold.[2] The 'appreciation' of Hugo in the article as a whole being avowedly insincere,[3] its interest lies, rather, in its revelation of Baudelaire's preoccupations at the time of writing the article. Would it not seem that in the phrases italicized hereunder, Baudelaire is in some measure harking back to the sixth section of *Le Voyage*, with its indictment of Man's 'furious' and presumptuous revolt against God?

Victor Hugo est pour l'Homme, et cependant il n'est pas contre Dieu. Il a confiance en Dieu, et pourtant il n'est pas contre l'Homme.

Il repousse *le délire de l'Athéisme en révolte*, et cependant il n'approuve pas les gloutonneries sanguinaires des Molochs et des Teutatès.

---

[1]There is certainly no question of an attack on *external* Nature in this poem; cf. my comments on the remaining sections, pp. 294–310, below.

[2]A note (in B.'s own hand) appended to *L'Imprévu*, on its republication in 1866 in *Les Epaves*, declares quite categorically if with a touch of irony: 'Ici l'auteur des *Fleurs du Mal* se tourne vers la Vie éternelle. Ça devait finir comme ça. Observons que, comme tous les nouveaux convertis, il se montre très-rigoureux et très-fanatique' (*FMCB* 566). For a further comment on this poem, see my art cit., pp. 212–13.

[3]'J'ai montré, à ce sujet, que je possédais l'art de mentir' (*CG* IV, 100); cf. *AR* 560–1—but cf. also, conversely, the extremely shrewd comments by J. Pommier, *RSH*, 1967, pp. 343–6. B.'s review, it should be added, bears only on the first 'instalment' of Hugo's novel (the two *Fantine* vols.).

Il croit que l'Homme est né bon, et cependant, même devant ses désastres permanents, *il n'accuse pas la férocité et la malice de Dieu.*[1]

Having gone on to imply—somewhat guardedly, it is true—a certain solidarity with those holding to the 'pure' Catholic doctrine, Baudelaire concludes with what in effect is a clear *refutation* of the very philosophy ('Il croit que l'Homme est né bon') summarized, with seeming approval, on the previous page:

Hélas! du Péché Originel, même après tant de progrès depuis si longtemps promis, il restera toujours bien assez de traces pour en constater l'immémoriale réalité!

(*AR* 392)

'True civilization', which as Baudelaire tells us in another text of this period, lies in the 'diminution of the traces of original sin',[2] would seem, on the evidence of this final sentence of the article on *Les Misérables*, to be distant indeed if not forever unattainable ... Certainly it is this sense of the 'immemorial reality' of original sin, that from at least 1855 onwards firmly determines Baudelaire's attitudes towards human nature—while not yet entirely forbidding him that primitivist nostalgia which assumes, conversely if tacitly, the reality of original *virtue*.

4. PARIS VERSUS NATURE?

It will be recalled that in his letter to Desnoyers, Baudelaire had implied that the two verse *Crépuscules* he had contributed to the Denecourt volume, were in some vague way the direct fruit of his musings within the twilit woods—that by a paradox, through his invincible preoccupation with Man, he had actually *conceived* these urban poems when in the midst of Nature. We need not take this claim too literally: we must remember that Baudelaire is concerned in this letter not only to expound his views on Nature and Nature-poetry but, more immediately, to rationalize his own determination to elude the 'bucolic' formula applied in the volume as a whole;[3]

[1] *AR* 391; cf. *Le Voyage*, ll. 101–4.
[2] *Mon Cœur mis à nu* XXXII, *JI* 87 (cit. p. 155, above).
[3] Cf. the similar technique of rationalization applied in the *Petits poëmes en prose*: 'Le poète semble avoir délibérément, et plus que de juste, coloré ses textes en les encadrant de déclarations parisiennes' (C. Pichois, *B. à Paris*, 28).

moreover, we have only to read the two poems in question to feel that they were surely woven out of the very fabric of Baudelaire's immediate, day-to-day experience. The antithesis posed in the letter to Desnoyers is none the less significant, in that it shows Baudelaire's increasing awareness of the essentially *urban* quality of his poetry; so specialized indeed, does he now regard himself as having become in this field, that he even expresses his doubt (when writing to his mother a year or so earlier) as to whether the two *Crépuscules* can truly be appreciated at all outside the Parisian *milieux* about which (and for which) they were written.[1] Yet is not the tacit claim he makes, in the letter to Desnoyers, to have opted for the unrecognized poetry of Mankind and of Mankind's cities, as against the conventional poetry of Nature—is this not immediately belied by the two further texts that conclude his contribution to the *Fontainebleau* volume: the prose poems *Le Crépuscule du soir* and *La Solitude*?[2] The first of these, with its characterization of the poet's two friends 'que le crépuscule rendait malades', brings what is almost a miniature 'pathology of twilight'; but this is preceded by a brief paragraph which specifically *assimilates* (rather than distinguishes) sylvan and urban *milieux*:

La tombée de la nuit a toujours été pour moi le signal d'une fête intérieure et comme la délivrance d'une angoisse. Dans les bois comme dans les rues d'une grande ville, l'assombrissement du jour et le scintillement des étoiles et des lanternes éclairent mon esprit.[3]

Again, in the second of these two prose poems the plea for solitude, though cautiously tempered by the recognition that it may for some ('idle souls' lacking the focus of a dominant 'active thought') be as dangerous as for others it is beneficial, is significantly justified in terms of the Solitary's enjoyment—or rather, his appropriation to himself—of the sublimities of *Nature*:

[1] L. of 27/4/1852 (*CG* I, 160). It is true that in its context Baudelaire's remark appears to cover not only the two poems, but the two articles, *Les Drames et les romans honnêtes* and *L'École païenne*, published (as we have seen) in this same journal, *La Semaine théâtrale*.

[2] Cf. my art. cit., 'A *Festschrift* of 1855', pp. 191–2.

[3] The text I reproduce (from *OCP* 1606–7 and notes), is that of the *proofs* for the *Fontainebleau* volume, as corrected by B. and conserved in the Bibliothèque littéraire Jacques Doucet; these corrections were not respected by the printer, but were incorporated when the text was republished two years later in *Le Présent*. For the 1864 text, see my next footnote.

Quant à la question de jouissance,—les plus belles agapes fraternelles, les plus magnifiques réunions d'hommes électrisés par un plaisir commun n'en donneront jamais de comparable à celle qu'éprouve le Solitaire, qui, d'un coup d'œil, a embrassé et compris toute la sublimité d'un paysage. Ce coup d'œil lui a conquis une propriété individuelle inaliénable.[1]

Yet although the two prose poems published with the letter to Desnoyers may seem in their context to belie Baudelaire's implicit claim to be exclusively the 'poet of Paris', he does of course during the ensuing period increasingly fulfil this promise—and in his prose poems no less than in his verse: thus not only does he constitute, for the 1861 *Fleurs du Mal*, a whole new chapter under the heading 'Tableaux parisiens', he also clearly intended to emphasize the specifically Parisian character of the *Petits poèmes en prose* when putting forward, as alternative titles for this collection, first 'Le Rôdeur *parisien*', and then, ultimately, 'Le Spleen de *Paris*'.[2] What is more open to question, however, is the extent to which Paris and Nature have indeed become for him wholly *opposed* notions; is it in fact true (as the letter to Desnoyers would appear to suggest) that the choice of urban themes now in effect continues or complements, for Baudelaire, the dogmatic repudiation of Nature? Of the two 'Parisian' texts that invite particular scrutiny from this point of view, the first, *Paysage [parisien]*, no doubt goes back in its original composition to the late 1840's and as such has already been discussed by me in an earlier chapter. It was only in 1861, however,

[1] *Fontainebleau* proofs; see *OCP* 1608 and notes. It must be added that this passage, although maintained in the 1857 and 1861 versions of *La Solitude*, disappears altogether from the ultimate (1864) text; the same is true of the passage previously cited from *Le Crépuscule du soir*.

[2] Four further alternatives he considered were: 'Le Promeneur solitaire', 'Poëmes nocturnes', 'La Lueur et la fumée', 'Petits poëmes lycanthropes'. An eighth possibility might seem, at first sight, to be suggested by a passage in the *Confidences* by 'Maxime Rude' (p. 169; cf. pp. 143–4, above) in which B. is declared to have been 'très-préoccupé . . . d'un volume de poésies en incubation avec le titre: "Paysages parisiens" '; it is likely, however, that Rude had simply misunderstood some reference of B.'s to the 'Tableaux parisiens' chapter of *FM*. (Cf. next footnote, below). I would add that on two distinct lists of projected prose poems, *OCP* 312, 315, 'Choses parisiennes' is given as the title of a main section of the new book; the *Petits poëmes en prose* would thus have followed in their structure the model established in *FM*. For a full account and discussion of B.'s two 'Parisian' projects, cf.: *FMCB* 259–61; *PPP* 222–47; G. Blin, *Le Sadisme de B.*, 168–71; P. Citron, *Poésie de Paris*, II, 337–43; C. Pichois, *B. à Paris*, 27–8.

that this poem finally took its place in *Les Fleurs du Mal*; having then chosen it as his opening text for the new 'Tableaux parisiens' chapter, Baudelaire for obvious reasons abridged its title to the single word *Paysage*.[1] Now in its earliest form especially this title (which we may perhaps assume to have been added only after 1852–3) brings, as Marcel Ruff has suggested,[2] a 'discreet renewal' of the very paradox implicit in the letter to Desnoyers: the *urban* 'landscape' which in its eloquent grandeur rivals that even of the mysterious forests of Nature.[3] One might here pertinently cite, by way of analogy, the reference in the *Salon de 1859* to certain etchings by Meryon: taking these as illustrations of a genre he describes, precisely, as 'le paysage des grandes villes', Baudelaire goes on to characterize them in terms that recall strikingly certain details of the opening section of *Paysage*: thus to Meryon's 'clochers *montrant du doigt le ciel*' and 'obélisques de l'industrie vomissant contre le firmament leurs coalitions de fumée',[4] correspond the steeples,

[1]In a letter to Bracquemond written during the summer of 1861 (and published recently by C. Pichois; see his *B.*, 196), B.'s publisher Poulet-Malassis refers, in the context of a projected de luxe edition of *FM*, to the 'Tableaux parisiens' as 'Paysages parisiens'; it would thus seem that B. had considered transferring the latter title from the poem of 1857 to the whole section in which it later appeared—and that it was this section that constituted what Rude, in the anecdote above-quoted, misremembered as a *volume* of 'poésies en incubation'.

[2]*L'Esprit du Mal*, 341.

[3]The paradox—if not the actual form of words—no doubt stems from Balzac: not only does the latter employ the phrase 'Un paysage parisien' as a chapter-heading in *Splendeurs et misères des courtisanes* (see *FMPP* 478), but his Parisian 'panoramas' are often built up on the model, or with the terminology, of landscape painting; cf., in this connection, P. Citron, *Poésie de Paris*, II, 192–4. B. himself, incidentally, in a letter to Feydeau of June 1858, recurs to the phrase almost as if compulsively, when praising (hypocritically) certain presumed qualities of style in his correspondent's novel *Fanny*: 'les élégances modernes, le *paysage* [sic] parisien, la forme de la souffrance et la forme de la jouissance chez un homme de notre temps' (*CG* II, 214–15, my italics; cf. ibid., 248). As a final instance, illustrating that 'grandeur' need not in itself be a necessary qualification for the urban 'landscape', I would mention that in the course of the anecdote aforementioned, B. and Rude find themselves in a district of Paris which offers to the view a cemetery, an undertaker's establishment, some dark workyards, and a building site with a few 'dismally new' houses; turning to his companion, B. blandly asks: 'N'est-ce pas que ce *paysage* est charmant?' (Rude, *Confidences*, 169).

[4]*CE* 342–3. The image of the 'spires pointing to Heaven' has an interesting history: Baudelaire got it from Gautier who got it from Régnier-Destourbet who got it from Wordsworth who got it from Coleridge! (See Asselineau, *Mélanges*,

factory-chimneys and workshops of the poem. And yet in their essential tone and atmosphere the two descriptions remain widely distinct: the city dreamingly contemplated from the poet's garret window lacks altogether the harsh nobility of Meryon's Paris,[1] and on the contrary takes on, from its context of reverie, a certain benign, idealized quality: 'melody' fills the air (the bells chime in the wind, the workshop 'sings' or hums), wide vistas open up to the view and in the mind. These, moreover, are only the opening lines of the poem; increasingly thereafter (as we have previously seen), the real Paris is abandoned in favour of imagined pastoral scenes, and the poem thus ends not at all as a Parisian but rather as an *anti*-Parisian landscape. I have yet to mention, however, Baudelaire's entire revision of the final six lines of the poem; here perhaps, after all, we may truly find some indirect echo of his changed attitude to Nature:

> L'Émeute, tempêtant vainement à ma vitre
> Ne fera pas lever mon front de mon pupitre;
> Car je serai plongé dans cette volupté
> D'évoquer le Printemps avec ma volonté,
> De tirer un soleil de mon cœur, et de faire
> De mes pensers brûlants une tiède atmosphère.
>
> (1861 text, ll. 21–6)

The 1857 version of these lines, it will be recalled, had consisted merely in a trivial reassertion of the author's bucolic (and elegiac) intentions; Baudelaire now seeks to point a specific moral, or at least to incline the reader towards a specific interpretation of the 'winter dreams' previously described. Does it not almost seem as if, in making this revision, Baudelaire had wished to insist on the personal and *imaginative* character of the landscapes he had conjured up—as if, having realised that these pastoral visions of distant horizons, of gardens and fountains and bird-song, might seem a tacit admission of the townsman's need to relieve, with thoughts of Nature, the winter bleakness of his surroundings, he had sought to

---

116, and J. Mayne, *AIP* 200 n. 1.) The phrase 'paysage des grandes villes' recurs, in a slightly varied form, in *Le Peintre de la vie moderne, AR* 63; so also, in an art. of 1862, *Peintres et aqua-fortistes, AR* 117, does the whole description of Meryon's etchings.

[1] Cf. J. Prévost, *B.*, 170–1.

temper this admission by the reminder that the dreams are at least of his own creation, are at least the product of the poet's own personal and *human* imagination and will? In this sense *Paysage*, in its revised version of 1861, might well be taken as a further reflection of that aesthetic expounded so strongly in the *Salon de 1859*, whereby Nature is brought firmly under the sway of the shaping and 'purifying' imagination.[1]

The second of these two 'Parisian pictures' has equally a somewhat misleading title: in *Rêve parisien*, as in *Paysage [parisien]*, the great city is not so much the subject of the poem as its starting-point and antithesis. But there the resemblance between the two poems ceases: *Rêve parisien* (first published in May 1860) describes a sleeping and not a waking dream, a haunting vision from which Baudelaire awakens (too soon!) to the brutal reality of a Parisian noon.[2] Nothing indeed could be more remote from the pastoral idyll of *Paysage*, or indeed from all 'natural' landscapes, than this strange dream-country with its clinical, metallic beauty, its unearthly, compelling and above all *artificial* glitter. For these perspectives stretching endlessly away are compounded solely of metal, marble and water; the 'irregular vegetable' is peremptorily banished, the sleeping pools are ringed round not by trees but by colonnades; the light that illumines the scene emanates not from the sun or the moon or any other planet, but from each individual object diffusing its strange 'personal' light:

> De ce terrible paysage,
> Tel que jamais mortel n'en vit,
> Ce matin encore l'image,
> Vague et lointaine, me ravit.

---

[1] Cf. pp. 131–3, above.

[2] The dream is thus not *of* Paris but *in* Paris; the title should be taken to signify simply 'rêve fait à Paris', since the only Parisian (if not *anti*-Parisian) element in the poem is brought by the second part, with its rude *awakening* from the dream. See p. 167, below, and cf. P. Citron, *Poésie de Paris*, II, 360; M. Ruff, *L'Esprit du mal*, 343. I cannot accept the contention by A. Feuillerat ('Architecture des *FM*', 310) that the title implies a dream that could only have existed in the mind of a Parisian, in view of the fact that numerous *non*-Parisian writers had previously given very similar descriptions of specifically *non*-Parisian scenes; cf. p. 170, below.

Le sommeil est plein de miracles!
Par un caprice singulier,
J'avais banni de ces spectacles
Le végétal irrégulier,

Et, peintre fier de mon génie,
Je savourais dans mon tableau
L'enivrante monotonie
Du métal, du marbre et de l'eau.

Babel d'escaliers et d'arcades,
C'était un palais infini,
Plein de bassins et de cascades
Tombant dans l'or mat ou bruni;

Et des cataractes pesantes,
Comme des rideaux de cristal,
Se suspendaient, éblouissantes,
A des murailles de métal.

Non d'arbres, mais de colonnades
Les étangs dormants s'entouraient,
Où de gigantesques naïades,
Comme des femmes, se miraient.

Des nappes d'eau s'épanchaient, bleues,
Entre des quais roses et verts,
Pendant des millions de lieues,
Vers les confins de l'univers;

C'étaient des pierres inouïes
Et des flots magiques; c'étaient
D'immenses glaces éblouies
Par tout ce qu'elles reflétaient!

Insouciants et taciturnes,
Des Ganges, dans le firmament,
Versaient le trésor de leurs urnes
Dans des gouffres de diamant.

Architecte de mes féeries,
Je faisais, à ma volonte,
Sous un tunnel de pierreries
Passer un océan dompté;

Et tout, même la couleur noire,
Semblait fourbi, clair, irisé;
Le liquide enchâssait sa gloire
Dans le rayon cristallisé.

Nul astre d'ailleurs, nuls vestiges
De soleil, même au bas du ciel,
Pour illuminer ces prodiges,
Qui brillaient d'un feu personnel!

Et sur ces mouvantes merveilles
Planait (terrible nouveauté!
Tout pour l'œil, rien pour les oreilles!)
Un silence d'éternité.

This vision, in its negation of all elements of landscape that are
spontaneously furnished by Nature, might seem the ultimate
realization of the intransigent humanist's ideal—the ultimate retort
to Nature's 'inhuman' arrogance, as denounced in the letter to
Desnoyers. But in that text, it will be remembered, Baudelaire had
turned in gratitude to the 'astonishing' cities of Man—whereas in
Rêve parisien, in the concluding verses, the urban reality is by implication resisted and condemned for its harsh banishment of the
'miraculous' dream, for the contrasting and sordid 'horror' it re-
inflicts upon him as with eyes still dazzled by all that he has 'seen',
he re-awakens to the numb and 'actual' misery of a Parisian noon:

En rouvrant mes yeux pleins de flamme
J'ai vu l'horreur de mon taudis,
Et senti, rentrant dans mon âme,
La pointe des soucis maudits;

La pendule aux accents funèbres
Sonnait brutalement midi,
Et le ciel versait des ténèbres
Sur le triste monde engourdi.

It is in fact only with these final words, 'le triste monde engourdi',
that the world of Man enters at all (and then obliquely) into the
poem; in the first part *all* forms of life, human and animal as well as
vegetable, are in effect excluded and by implication deemed 'irregular'.[1] How much importance should we properly attribute, however,
in the context of Baudelaire's anti-naturalism, to the avowedly
artificial character of this whole 'terrible paysage'? Gautier, in his

[1] The 'gigantesques naïades' of ll. 23–4 scarcely constitute an exception: they
are statuesque rather than living.

article of 1868 on Baudelaire, had deemed the 'sentiment de l'*artificiel*' here illustrated—further defined by him as 'une création due tout entière à l'Art et d'où la nature est complètement absente'— to be a tendency wholly characteristic of the poet.[1] Later critics, founding themselves on the further evidence (as it has seemed to them) of the 'Éloge du maquillage', and in the process going considerably beyond anything that Gautier can have intended, have (as we have seen) taken this 'sentiment de l'*artificiel*' to be of *determining* importance within Baudelaire's whole aesthetic thought. For my part, however, I feel this whole analogy between *Rêve parisien* and the 'Éloge du maquillage' to be a misleading one,[2] inasmuch as it lays a false emphasis on what within the former text is purely an incidental element; more important than any antithesis between Nature and ('man-made') artifice, is the truly essential contrast, reflected within the very structure of the poem, between Nature and 'super-Nature', real and 'surreal'.[3] The poet's dream creates for him—or, as he prefers to claim, he by his dream creates—a world purged not only of all natural forms but of all human contingencies; it is specifically to these latter that he is so 'brutally' returned on his awakening— this very word 'brutalement' serving indeed to underline a further and altogether more important analogy that one could draw, this time with a prose poem of the same period, *La Chambre double*. Here, too, the poet 'reawakens' (but from a 'chambre paradisiaque') to the squalid reality of his hovel—a resumption of Time's 'brutal dictatorship' that is marked not by the tolling of noon but by the importunate knock at the door that heralds the bailiff, the ignoble concubine, the office-boy in search of printer's 'copy'.[4] The similarity between the two poems extends even to their genesis: both, it would seem, transcribe first a hallucination induced by opium, and then its

[1] *FM* 1868, p. xxxvii (introductory 'Notice', reproduced from a long article published earlier that year in *L'Univers illustré*).

[2] It is true that *Rêve parisien* is inscribed to the very artist who had inspired the whole essay *Le Peintre de la vie moderne* (of which, of course, the 'Éloge du maquillage' forms a part). But B. was to explain this dedication, humorously, in his letter to Poulet-Malassis of 13 March 1860: 'Quant à la 2ᵉ pièce, celle dédiée à Guys [i.e. *Rêve parisien*], elle n'a pas avec lui d'autre rapport *positif et matériel* que *celui-ci*: c'est que comme le poëte de la pièce, *il se lève généralement à midi*' (*CG* III, 68).

[3] This whole distinction is explored more fully in the second section, 'Nature and Super-Nature', of my next chapter.

[4] *PPP* 11–14.

painful aftermath.[1] In this connection it should be noted that this same 'terrible lendemain' is elsewhere explicitly ascribed by Baudelaire to the hashish-eater, and moreover in terms that may seem particularly appropriate to out present purposes: '*La hideuse nature*, dépouillée de son illumination de la veille, ressemble aux mélancoliques débris d'une fete'.[2] But the term 'nature' of course here embraces the *whole* of reality—Man and his cities, the 'triste monde engourdi' of *Rêve parisien*, no less than purely external Nature. This brings me to a further aspect of the latter poem: the essentially *involuntary* character of its imagery—involuntary since necessarily predetermined by the actual recollected content of the dream itself. We must here be careful to assess at its true value Baudelaire's claim to be himself the inspired 'painter' of this 'picture' he proudly describes as his 'own' ('. . . peintre fier de mon génie,/Je savourais dans mon tableau . . .')—or again, to be the 'architect' (more strictly, the engineer!) of his own 'féeries', as he diverts 'at will', beneath its jewelled tunnel, the 'ocean' he himself has 'tamed':

> Architecte de mes féeries,
> Je faisais, à ma volonté,
> Sous un tunnel de pierreries
> Passer un océan dompté . . .

All this, if we relate it to its specifically 'oniric' context, is surely no more than the illusion of omnipotence familiar to the 'ordinary' nocturnal dreamer no less than to the hashish- or opium-addict;[3] only at a later and retrospective stage, when the poet arranges (or perhaps re-arranges) his dream-material into a poem, can one truly regard him as exercising conscious 'control'. Moreover it is at this stage only that one may allow the possible intervention within the poem of influences drawn from external sources—whether from

---

[1] In the case of *La Chambre double*, the 'phial of laudanum' is explicitly mentioned towards the end of the poem; in the case of *Rêve parisien*, the general assumption to this effect made by J. Prévost, *B.*, 104–5, has been specifically confirmed by the recent investigations of C. Pichois and R. Kopp: see their article 'B. et l'opium', *Europe*, April–May 1967, p. 77, where their observation that *Rêve parisien*, like *La Chambre double*, manifestly evokes 'un état d'ivresse et d'euphorie provoqué par la drogue', is based, Professor Pichois has kindly informed me, on the detailed study of the poem made by their eminent medical colleague at Bâle, Professor Marcel Monnier.

[2] *Poëme du haschisch* (first pub. 1858), *PA* 63; my italics.

[3] Cf. my similar comment on *Élévation*, p. 190, below.

artists such as Piranesi,[1] Kendall,[2] John Martin (*via* Gautier),[3] or writers such as Wordsworth (*via* De Quincey), the John of *Revelation* (*via* Swedenborg), Poe, Novalis, Banville[4]—whether again from descriptions of Lisbon,[5] or simply from recollections of visits to Versailles.[6] Now in several at least of these possible secondary 'sources', we encounter that selfsame 'exclusion of the vegetable' in favour of the mineral, that is so striking a feature of *Rêve parisien*. Taking this analogy into account, as well as the far greater likelihood that this whole characteristic of Baudelaire's 'paysage terrible' formed part, in any case, of his original dream experience, it would seem that only perhaps in the second verse of the poem (specifically, in the lines 'Par un caprice singulier,/J'avais banni de ces spectacles/ Le végétal irrégulier') is there to be found any true reflection of 'cult of the artificial' more fully declared in the 'Éloge du maquillage'; and even here, one might prefer to invoke the simple operation of the poet's analytical and rationalizing faculty: 'As I think back on that dream-landscape, one thing I strongly recall is the complete absence of trees or indeed of vegetable life of any kind'.

[1]Cf. the engraving (*Roman port*) reproduced by J. Pommier and C. Pichois, *FMPP* 484–5. In the context of B.'s poem, it is interesting to note this comment, on Piranesi's *Carceri*, by F. Salamon: 'In all the *Carceri* there is not a tree, not a tuft of grass: only the exaltation of his material in stone' (cit. M. F. M. Meiklejohn, in his notes to a Glasgow University exhibition of Piranesi prints).

[2]See my art., 'B. et Kendall', *RLC*, 1956, p. 63.

[3]In his 1862 article on B. (as again in his 1868 'Notice', *FM* 1868 p. xxxviii), Gautier describes *Rêve parisien* as 'un cauchemar splendide et sombre, digne des Babels à la manière noire de Martynn [sic]' (*Poëtes français,* ed. E. Crépet, IV, 600). But if B.'s poem owes anything at all to Martin (and it must be remembered that for Gautier, as J. Seznec has observed, *John Martin en France*, 26, 'Toute occasion ... est prétexte à évoquer Martin'), this can only have been at second-hand: thus the description of Cleopatra's palace given by Gautier in his novella *Une Nuit de Cléopâtre* (first pub. 1838)—a description which certainly in many of its details strikingly anticipates the 'paysage terrible' of *Rêve parisien* (see *FMCB* 478–9)—is itself the transposition of what Gautier had earlier written, in an article of 1837, concerning Martin's *Belshazzar's Feast* . . .; see J. Seznec, op. cit., 24–5.

[4]For these various references see *FMCB* 478–81, as also, respectively: G. T. Clapton, *B. et De Quincey*, 65; J. Pommier, *Mystique de B.*, 39–40, 173 n. 97; J. M. Bernard, *RHLF*, 1909, p. 792; R. Vivier, *Originalité de B.*, 157–8; J. Pommier, *Dans les chemins de B.*, 209, and E. Souffrin, in ed. Banville, *Stalactites,* 109–10.

[5]The analogy here is with the prose poem *Anywhere out of the world*; cf. p. 293, below.

[6]See A. Feuillerat, 'Architecture des *FM*', 310 n. 176.

The antithesis between Nature and Paris, country and town, we thus perceive to be of relatively minor importance within Baudelaire's thought during this period. As a final corrective here, I would cite a text which actually conciliates by analogy the second of these two (supposed) antagonisms. The text in question is extracted from a sheaf of miscellaneous notes bearing mainly on the unfinished article *L'Art philosophique,* and thus dating no doubt from the period 1857–60 when this work was in preparation.[1] The passage reproduced hereunder forms a short paragraph to itself:

Le vertige senti dans les grandes villes est analogue au vertige éprouvé au sein de la nature.—Délices du chaos et de l'immensité.—Sensation d'un homme sensible en visitant une grande ville inconnue.[2]

This interesting analogy may be further extended or deepened, if we bring it into relation with the following entry from the second (and no doubt contemporary) section of Baudelaire's 'intimate journal' *Fusées,* which begins in almost identical fashion:

Ivresse religieuse des grandes villes.—Panthéisme. Moi, c'est tous; tous, c'est moi.

Tourbillon.

(*JI* 9)

The sense of 'giddy' intoxication experienced within the great city thus shares with more conventional Nature-feelings not only what Baudelaire calls 'the delights of chaos and immensity', but also the idea of an 'objective' merging of the self within some vaster whole; the famous and essentially *urban* concept of the 'bain de multitude'— borrowed initially from Poe, developed subsequently in the prose poem *Les Foules* and in an important passage of *Le Peintre de la vie moderne*[3]—now takes on a curious continuity with that same

[1]See *OCP* 1705–6, and cf. M. Ruff, *Esprit du mal*, 454 n. 19.

[2]*OCP* 1107. B. had at first thought to write, as his opening phrase: 'Le vertige *des* grandes villes'; cf. the opening of the *Fusées* text cited below.

[3]For a discussion of these (and cognate) texts, see *JI* 205–7, and P. Citron, *Poésie de Paris*, II, 378–81; for other possible sources besides Poe, see also R. Vivier, *Originalité de B.*, 210–11. The image 'bain de multitude' itself implies a further analogy with Nature: in his art. of 1861 on Hugo, B. (like Maurice de Guérin before him; cf. H. J. Hunt, *Epic in 19th-Century France*, 234) speaks, in a similar image, of a 'bain de nature': 'Aucun artiste n'est plus universel que lui [Hugo], plus apte à se mettre en contact avec les forces de la vie universelle, plus disposé à prendre sans cesse un *bain de nature*' (*AR* 303–4; my italics).

pantheistic cult he had repudiated so trenchantly, only a few years
earlier, in the letter to Desnoyers.[1]

[1]B.'s perception of Nature continues in any case to be marked by a certain
'pantheistic' quality—as in those 'supernatural' moments when the self appears
to 'merge', or transpose itself, into the objects of Nature; cf. pp. 279–80, below.

VI

Nature and Symbol

1. A UNIVERSE OF ANALOGY: NATURE AND GOD

IT will be recalled that in several texts of 1848–52, Baudelaire had implied his sympathy for 'illuminist' and 'unitarian' theories,[1] and in the moral and aesthetic sphere at least had indicated, as a first article of faith, what he termed 'la croyance à l'*unité intégrale*'.[2] The first (dated) text, however, in which we find him explicitly professing the related doctrine of *universal analogy*, is the introductory paragraph (aforementioned) of the *Exposition universelle 1855*. Baudelaire is here mainly concerned (properly enough, in the context) to affirm a relativist and cosmopolitan, rather than absolutist and classical, aesthetic; but this is not altogether easy to reconcile with the notion that he at the same time declares, of a Providential hierarchy whereby within a scheme of universal and 'harmonious' analogy, certain plants, 'forms' and animals are deemed more holy, spiritual and sacred than others:

Il est peu d'occupations aussi intéressantes, aussi attachantes, aussi pleines de surprises et de révélations pour un critique, pour un rêveur dont l'esprit est tourné à la généralisation, aussi bien qu'à l'étude des détails, et, pour mieux dire encore, à l'idée d'ordre et de hiérarchie universelle, que la comparaison des nations et de leurs produits respectifs. Quand je dis hiérarchie, je ne veux pas affirmer la suprématie de telle nation sur telle autre. Quoiqu'il y ait dans la nature des plantes plus ou moins saintes, des formes plus ou moins spirituelles, des animaux plus ou moins sacrés, et qu'il soit légitime de conclure, d'après les instigations de l'immense analogie universelle, que certaines nations—vastes animaux dont l'organisme est adéquat à leur milieu,—aient été préparées et éduquées par la Providence pour un but déterminé, but plus ou moins élevé, plus ou moins rapproché du ciel,—je ne veux pas faire ici autre chose qu'affirmer leur *égale* utilité aux yeux de CELUI qui est indéfinissable, et le miraculeux secours qu'elles se prêtent dans l'harmonie de l'univers.   (*CE* 219–20)

---

[1]*Révélation magnétique*, HE 457; *Edgar Allan Poe, sa vie et ses ouvrages*, OP I, 292–3—cf. pp. 90–1, above.
[2]*Les Drames et les romans honnêtes*, AR 284; cf. *L'École païenne*, AR 294–6, and my comments on both texts, p. 98, above.

The long and elaborate sentence whereby Baudelaire concludes this preamble, has to my mind a fervour suggesting some recent 'conversion'. I have mentioned already the striking contradiction between his earlier sarcastic reference (in the letter to Desnoyers) to 'légumes sanctifiés', and the present passage in which the vegetable world is on the contrary expressly sanctified ('des plantes plus ou moins saintes') and related vaguely to the Godhead, even if not made (as by the derided pantheists) His direct and diffused 'habitation'. God is in fact here represented as the prime Mover or supreme Architect of a vast universal scheme whereby each element of creation—whether plant, 'form' (i.e. material object), animal or nation—is assigned not merely a distinct 'rank' within the 'hierarchy' of being, but also a certain providential *function* precisely appropriate to its hierarchical status. Since Baudelaire speaks of 'l'immense analogie universelle' as well as of 'l'harmonie de l'univers',[1] and indeed appears to regard the two notions as virtually interchangeable, we may suppose the providential function in question to be that of conveying or 'embodying', by some 'intrinsic' analogy with other corresponding objects, certain spiritual or moral truths—such, precisely, as Baudelaire himself demonstrates within this very passage, when describing particular nations as 'vast animals' which by their 'organisms' fulfil a pre-determined 'biological' (i.e. aesthetic, as well as social and political) role. Although, incidentally, Baudelaire goes on to imply, in his next sentence, that these 'vast contemplations' of his were the fruit of solitary meditation rather than of reading,[2] the paragraph above-quoted nevertheless awakens many literary echoes. Thus the conjoined terms 'analogie universelle' and 'harmonie de l'univers' both figure prominently within the Fourierist lexicon,[3] whilst the notion of a 'hierarchy' or 'scale' of being is common not only to several writers specifically admired by Baudelaire: Joseph de Maistre, Poe, Swedenborg, Fourier's disciple Toussenel,

---

[1] Another text from this period suggests, incidentally, that an occasional dissonance may after all come to disturb the universal 'harmony'; thus in the poem *L'Héautontimorouménos* (composed, perhaps, almost simultaneously with the present text), B. asks of himself: 'Ne suis-je pas un faux accord/Dans la *divine symphonie*...?'(ll. 13-14; my italics). But one must allow here for the resolutely ironic context.

[2] *CE* 220.

[3] See J. Pommier, *Mystique de B.*, 59-63, 179 n. 144; for B. and Fourier, see also C. Pichois, *B.*, 100-3.

Victor Hugo,[1] but also, more widely, to a whole host of eighteenth-
and nineteenth-century philosophers, scientists and poets.[2]

The notion of a divinely ordained and elaborately hierarchical
system of universal analogy, recurs, but briefly and incidentally, in
two subsequent texts. In the first of these, Baudelaire is concerned
to rebut the charge that Gautier lacked proper understanding of
religion; on the contrary, it is claimed, 'il [Gautier] possède, plus
qu'aucun autre, le sentiment d'universelle hiérarchie écrite du haut
en bas de la nature, à tous les degrés de l'infini'.[3] In the second of
these two passages, Baudelaire is affirming, in the context of Wagner's *Lohengrin* Prelude, the self-evident 'necessity' of inter-sensorial
analogy (or synaesthesia); before going on, however, to quote in
demonstration the first two quatrains of his sonnet *Correspondances*,
he interpolates this parenthetical assurance: 'les choses s'étant toujours exprimées par une analogie réciproque, depuis le jour où Dieu
a proféré le monde comme une complexe et indivisible totalité'.[4]

Now in all these various texts, the constant concept is of a scheme

[1]For Maistre, cf. M. Gilman, *B. the Critic*, 85–6 and 237–8 n. 38; for Poe, B.'s
own comment in his article of 1852, *OP* I, 291–2 (cit. p. 122, above); for Swedenborg, P. Laubriet, *Intelligence de l'art chez Balzac*, 293–4. For Toussenel, cf. this
passage (cit. L. Thomas, *Toussenel*, 64) summarizing his 'system': 'Les animaux
de tous les règnes sont, à l'instar des végétaux et des minéraux, des moules
particuliers de la passion humaine, des verbes inférieurs de Dieu destinés à an-
noncer le verbe typique supérieur de la création actuelle qui est l'homme'. As to
Hugo, the phrase 'végétation sainte' (cf. B.: 'des plantes plus ou moins saintes')
occurs in a similar context in his poem *Je lisais . . .*, ll. 46–7: 'Tout cet ensemble
obscur, végétation sainte,/Compose en se croisant ce chiffre énorme: DIEU'. But
this text was published only in April 1856, in *Les Contemplations*; see ed. J. Vianey, II, 167.

[2]See J. W. Beach, *Concept of Nature in 19th-Century English Poetry*, 330–2.

[3]*AR* 179.

[4]*AR* 206; for a further discussion of this text, cf. p. 211, below. The 'providential' harmony of Nature is more obliquely alluded to in the *Salon de 1859*, in
the opening paragraph of the chapter 'Du Paysage'—but in the specific context
this time, of the creative artist: 'Je sais bien que l'imagination humaine peut, par
un effort singulier, concevoir un instant la nature sans l'homme, et toute la masse
suggestive éparpillé dans l'espace, sans un contemplateur pour en extraire la
comparison, la métaphore et l'allégorie. Il est certain que tout cet ordre et toute
cette harmonie n'en gardent pas moins la qualité inspiratrice qui y est providentiellement déposée . . .' (*CE* 333). Cf. also, finally, in the letter to Toussenel
below-mentioned, the admiration expressed for this comment by his correspondent on the whole doctrine of analogy: '*comme l'esprit se repose dans une douce
quiétude à l'abri d'une doctrine si féconde et si simple, pour qui rien n'est mystère
dans les œuvres de Dieu!*' (*CG* I, 368).

of purely *terrestrial* analogies—i.e. analogies which, under God, link reciprocally one with another the different elements of His creation. A more ancient tradition, however—Platonic, Augustinian, Pauline, exemplarist, Swedenborgian—posits interrelationships of a distinctively transcendental kind, linking Earth with Heaven, the world of Nature with God. Baudelaire himself, it would seem, made little essential distinction between these two kinds of analogy, since in a striking passage of the letter to Toussenel of January 1856, he indifferently equates Fourierist (or terrestrial) with Swedenborgian (or transcendental) doctrines of analogy; thus he says, of the faculty of imagination, that it alone comprehends 'l'analogie universelle, ou ce qu'une religion mystique appelle *la correspondance*.'[1] Yet although Baudelaire's (perhaps superficial) interest in Swedenborg would appear to go back at least to 1846,[2] he in fact seems rarely, when writing of 'correspondences', to have had in mind those of a specifically transcendental and Swedenborgian kind. It is true that in a text of slightly earlier date than the letter to Toussenel, the unfinished article *Puisque réalisme il y a*, he had offered (as we have seen) this teasingly cryptic definition of poetry:

[1]*CG* I, 368; for a similarly oblique reference, cf. the prose poem *L'Invitation au voyage*, *PPP* 296 (1857–61 texts) or 55 (1862 text). 'L'analogie universelle' is of course the title given by Fourier himself to this aspect of his theory; see J. Pommier, *Mystique de B.*, 60. As for the 'mystical religion', 2 later texts serve to identify this as Swedenborgian : *Poëme du haschisch* (1858), *PA* 51; *Hugo* (1861), *AR* 305. In the 1st of these, incidentally, Fourier and Swedenborg are jointly and irreverently assimilated to the addict's hallucinatory vision of Nature; but this is no more than a somewhat elaborate reinforcement of the preceding phrase, 'le premier objet venu devient symbole parlant' (*PA* 51; cit. in extenso p. 208, below).

[2]See Champfleury, *Souvenirs*, 132–3, and *La Fanfarlo*, ed. Pichois, 52; for the whole question of Swedenborg's influence on B., cf. J. Pommier, op. cit., 28–41, and P. Mansell Jones, *BMFP*, 1–37. Champfleury stresses, be it noted, the ephemerality of these literary enthusiasms of B.'s: 'Un jour [il] se montrait avec un volume de Swedenborg sous le bras; rien dans aucune littérature ne pouvait, suivant lui, tenir à côté de Swedenborg . . . On rencontrait le poète avec un gros volume d'algèbre; il n'y avait plus de littérature, c'était l'algèbre qu'il fallait étudier et le polonais Wronski faisait oublier Swedenborg.' As to Samuel Cramer (who had a volume of Swedenborg for bedside reading), the references on other pages of *La Fanfarlo* to his atheism and 'matérialisme absolu', the statement (in the context of the pagans' preference for dancing over music) that 'le visible et le créé sont *au-dessus* de l'invisible et de l'incréé' (ed. Pichois, 50, 89, 82—my italics), hardly suggest B. at this period to have been a very convinced disciple of the Swedish mystic. Cf., in this connection, E. Starkie, *B.*, 226.

La Poésie est ce qu'il y a de plus réel, c'est ce qui n'est complètement vrai que dans *un autre monde*.

Ce monde-ci, dictionnaire hiéroglyphique. (*OP* I, 299)

Now it might well appear that in order to understand this passage, we need look no further than the oft-quoted paragraph from the *Notes nouvelles sur Edgar Poe* of 1857, in which, after inveighing strongly (as Poe had done) against 'the heresy of *The Didactic*'—after reaffirming the distinction (affirmed by Poe) between Pure Intellect, Taste and the Moral Sense—Baudelaire goes on to link the aesthetic perception of Beauty with the notion of correspondences:

C'est cet admirable, cet immortel instinct du Beau qui nous fait considérer la terre et ses spectacles comme un aperçu, comme une correspondance du Ciel. La soif insatiable de tout ce qui est au delà, et qui révèle la vie, est la preuve la plus vivante de notre immortalité. C'est à la fois par la poésie et *à travers* la poésie, par et *à travers* la musique que l'âme entrevoit les splendeurs situées derrière le tombeau; et quand un poëme exquis amène les larmes au bord des yeux, ces larmes ne sont pas la preuve d'un excès de jouissance, elles sont bien plutôt le témoignage d'une mélancolie irritée, d'une postulation des nerfs, d'une nature exilée dans l'imparfait et qui voudrait s'emparer immédiatement, sur cette terre même, d'un paradis révélé.

Ainsi le principe de la poésie est, strictement et simplement, l'aspiration humaine vers une beauté supérieure . . . (*NHE*, xx–xxi)

A certain continuity with the earlier text may here readily be perceived. If (as Baudelaire has stated in *Puisque Réalisme il y a*) this world of ours is 'hieroglyphic',[1] is this not because (as we now learn) its 'spectacles' correspond to, afford a glimpse of, Heaven? If Poetry is 'true only in *another world*', is this not because it testifies to the eternal human aspiration for what is not of this earth and thus lies 'beyond the tomb'? But this latter formulation has Platonic rather than Swedenborgian overtones,[2] and it must be remembered that in

[1]The terms 'hiéroglyphe', 'hiéroglyphique', are almost as widely favoured during this era, as are 'symbole' and 'symbolique'; numerous examples may be found in, e.g., the writings of Swedenborg, Ballanche, Jouffroy, Toussenel, etc. For two further uses by B., cf. pp. 220 n., 228, below.

[2]Cf., in this connection, the later comment, in the *Salon de 1859*, on Fromentin's 'faculté . . . de saisir *les parcelles du beau égarées sur la terre,* de suivre le beau à la piste partout où il a pu se glisser à travers les trivialités de la nature déchue' (*CE* 318). It will be observed that the Platonism of the phrase italicized (by me), is immediately and severely qualified by the ensuing reference to 'la nature déchue', i.e. to the notion of original sin; cf. p. 153 n. 1, above.

here reproducing almost textually, from his second sentence on-
onwards,[1] a passage from Poe's *The Poetic Principle*,[2] Baudelaire is
to some extent the prisoner of the American writer's vocabulary.
Indeed, the more one considers this whole passage, the more one
doubts whether Baudelaire here truly has in mind any specific
analogies *at all* of the presumed Swedenborgian type—the type represented, for instance, by Swedenborg's (specific) analogy between
the three realms of Heaven and the three parts (head, trunk, feet) of
the human anatomy.[3] Several years later, it is true, Baudelaire does
cite one such analogy ('Swedenborg . . . nous avait . . . enseigné que
le ciel est un très-grand homme') in his article of 1861 on *Victor
Hugo*.[4] Yet significantly enough the *general* doctrine thereafter
ascribed to Swedenborg: 'que tout, forme, mouvement, nombre,
couleur, parfum, dans le *spirituel* comme dans le *naturel*, est
significatif, réciproque, converse, *correspondant*',[5] is conceived
purely in terms of 'reciprocal', i.e. *terrestrial and material*
relationships (form, movement, number, colour, perfume); clearly
'spirituel' must here allude to the *human*, and not to the divine,

[1]The initial sentence, however (in which, precisely, B. affirms the notion of
'correspondence' between Heaven and Earth), has no counterpart in Poe who, as
P. F. Quinn points out (*French Face of Poe*, 151), was in general hostile to the
Swedenborgians; as to the two Poe texts adduced by Margaret Gilman in support
of her assertion that 'the mystic perception of correspondences . . . is the great
meeting place of Poe and Baudelaire' (*B. the Critic*, 132; cf. ibid., 243 n. 20 and
242 n. 15), neither of these in fact embodies a specific doctrine of analogy, and
moreover the first, from 'A Chapter of Suggestions', although published in 1845
in an American 'gift book', *The Opal*, was not to be reprinted in the 1850 edition
of the *Works* and is thus unlikely to have been seen by B.

[2]See, for this borrowing (which B. was not even indirectly to acknowledge,
incidentally, when he later repeated the whole passage in his 1859 article on
Gautier, *AR* 157–60), A. Ferran, *Esthétique de B.*, 186–7, and cf. Poe, *Literati,
etc.*, 1850, p. 7.

[3]*Heaven and Hell*, I, cit. J. Pommier, *Mystique de B.*, 36. It must be added that
in other, less arcane texts, Swedenborg descends to analogies of the 'moral' (i.e.
strictly mundane) type later to be developed by Fourier (the garden representing
wisdom and intelligence; precious jewels and perfumes representing particular
qualities of married love, etc.); cf. ibid., 37, and P. Laubriet, *Intelligence de l'art
chez Balzac*, 294.

[4]*AR* 305; for the (approximate) quotation from Swedenborg, see also J.
Pommier, op. cit., 33.

[5]Loc. cit. Earlier (*AR* 304), B. had spoken—in the context of Hugo's poetic
gifts—of the 'moral sensations' which are 'transmitted' to us by (supposedly)
inanimate objects.

element within the universal equation.[1]

All this is not to question the sincerity of Baudelaire's attitude in this matter, nor to suggest that he paid lip-service only to religious and 'mystical' doctrines of analogy. But his adherence to these doctrines would appear to be of the most general character; his true preoccupation lies quite elsewhere, and we shall see that in effect Baudelaire takes only, from Swedenborg, Fourier, Toussenel and other theorists of universal analogy, what little he needs for the elaboration of a personal theory of metaphor of his own. Thus Jean Pommier's remark is fully applicable to this period of Baudelaire's career:

. . . il était aussi peu porté que Pascal à voir Dieu dans la nature. Mais la nature est un livre qui s'interprète comme la Bible.

(*Mystique de B.*, 152)

'Like the Bible', but not, of course, according to the strict methods and principles of the Biblical exegetists. In the ensuing sections of this chapter, we shall see in what, precisely, this specifically Baudelairian 'interpretation of Nature' consists.

2. NATURE AND 'SUPER-NATURE'

But what (it may be objected), of Baudelaire's famous concept of 'surnaturalisme'? Does not this term imply, by common definition, the assumption that 'above' Nature (and controlling it) there lies some Divine order, or at least some mysterious and 'invisible' 'higher reality'—to be apprehended, perhaps, only through certain occult sciences?[2] Certainly in the prefatory Note to his translation, in 1848,

[1]Cf. equally this incidental comment in the dedicatory epistle 'A J.G.F.', prefacing the *Paradis artificiels* of 1860: '. . . le monde naturel pénètre dans le spirituel, lui sert de pâture, et concourt ainsi à opérer cet amalgame indéfinissable que nous nommons notre individualité' (*PA* v-vi)—'spirituel' directly equated, it will be noted, with 'notre individualité'. For the recurrent ambiguity of the term 'spirituel', cf. pp. 236–7 n. 3, below.

[2]Cf. the definition by M. Blondel in Lalande, *Vocabulaire de la philosophie*, II, 840 n.: 'Est *surnaturel* . . . ce qui, procédant d'une condescendance gratuite de Dieu, élève la créature intelligente à un état qui ne saurait être *l'état de nature* d'aucun être créé . . .' Cf. also the contemporary definitions by Hugo (*Post-Scriptum de ma vie*, cit. J. Roos, *Idées philosophique de Victor Hugo*, 32: '. . . qu'est-ce que le Surnaturalisme? C'est la partie de la Nature qui échappe à nos organes', and by B.'s unnamed adversary in the letter to Desnoyers, Laprade (cf. p. 122

of Poe's *Mesmeric Revelation*, Baudelaire had used the word in something like this conventional sense;[1] and so, it would seem, he does again in 1855, when enumerating, in his second article on the *Exposition universelle,* the essential qualities of an apotheosis—those very qualities, in fact, that he finds lacking in Ingres' *Apothéose de l'Empereur Napoléon I*er :

La caractère principal d'une apothéose doit être le sentiment surnaturel, la puissance d'ascension vers les régions supérieures, un entraînement, un vol irrésistible vers le ciel, but de toutes les aspirations humaines et habitacle classique de tous les grands hommes.[2]

On the other hand we have seen also that in its earliest (indirect) occurrence under Baudelaire's pen, in the *Salon de 1846,* the term had retained the rather specialized psychological and aesthetic sense that had been given to it by Heine;[3] and indeed we shall find still further variations of meaning, if we now turn from the second to the third (Delacroix) article of the *Exposition universelle* series. Initially, Baudelaire would here appear so to have broadened the scope of his concept, as to embrace within it everything that in any way appears mysteriously to 'reach out' beyond the immediate and real; the 'surnaturalisme' he had earlier sought in vain in Ingres'

n. 4, above; the passage figures in the volume *Le Sentiment de la nature chez les modernes,* 463): '. . . un monde invisible distinct de la matière, indépendant des lois physiques, se développant librement dans la sphère qui lui est propre, vivant et créateur par lui-même . . .'—or, again, the whole chapter of Carlyle's *Sartor Resartus* entitled 'Natural Supernaturalism' (see J. W. Beach, op. cit., 308–11). For the occultist (i.e. illuminist) 'deviation', see L. Lemonnier, *Poe et la critique française,* 13–15, 18–20. Other derived (and less rigorously defined) meanings are of course also to be encountered: thus 'surnaturel' may simply be used as a more impressive synonym for 'ideal', 'fantastic', 'mysterious', 'inexplicable', 'marvellous', 'miraculous'; cf. in this respect B.'s own reference, in *Le Poëme du haschisch,* to the absurd, unexpected, 'hieroglyphical' type of dream which represents 'le côté surnaturel de la vie' (*PA* 16).

[1]See pp. 90–1, above, and cf., more conventionally still, B.'s much later reference, in the context of the Anglo-American school of 'spiritualists', to 'les phénomènes surnaturels, tels que les apparitions de fantômes, les revenants, etc.' (*Poëme du haschisch, PA* 5).

[2]*CE* 240. Cf. also the linked comment on the same painter's *Jeanne d'Arc*: 'Ici, comme dans l'*Apothéose,* absence totale de sentiment et de surnaturalisme'.

[3]*CE* 108; cf. p. 90, above. What makes Heine a 'super-naturalist', in the passage quoted by B., is that 'above' Nature he sets Man, or the artist's self (rather than God, or 'another world'); there results a symbolism which being '*innate*', can thus scarcely be called 'supernatural' in the conventional sense.

Jeanne d'Arc or *Apothéose de l'Empereur*, he is now ready to discern in the unearthly beauty of Delacroix' Mary Magdalena, in the strange morbidity of glance shared by so many of the women in these paintings.[1] But in the penultimate paragraph of this article—as in the related text (published some nine months later) which I annex to it—we are offered something altogether more specific, distinctive and idiosyncratic.

Edgar Poe dit, je ne sais plus où, que le résultat de l'opium pour les sens est de revêtir la nature entière d'un intérêt surnaturel qui donne à chaque objet un sens plus profond, plus volontaire, plus despotique. Sans avoir recours à l'opium, qui n'a connu ces admirables heures, véritables fêtes du cerveau, où les sens plus attentifs perçoivent des sensations plus retentissantes, où le ciel d'un azur plus transparent s'enfonce comme un abîme plus infini, où les sons tintent musicalement, où les couleurs parlent, où les parfums racontent des mondes d'idées? Eh bien, la peinture de Delacroix me paraît la traduction de ces beaux jours de l'esprit. Elle est revêtue d'intensité et sa splendeur est privilégiée. Comme la nature perçue par des nerfs ultra-sensibles, elle révèle le surnaturalisme.[2]

Comme notre Eugène Delacroix, qui a élevé son art à la hauteur de la grande poésie, Edgar Poe aime à agiter ses figures sur des fonds violâtres et verdâtres où se révèlent la phosphorescence de la pourriture et la senteur de l'orage. La Nature dite inanimée participe de la nature des êtres vivants, et, comme eux, frissonne d'un frisson surnaturel et galvanique. L'espace est approfondi par l'opium; l'opium y donne un sens magique à toutes les teintes, et fait vibrer tous les bruits avec une plus significative sonorité.

(*Edgar Poe*, HE xxix)

The 'supernatural', then, is for Baudelaire that aspect of Nature which reveals itself to the sensitive observer at certain uniquely

[1] Cf., for these refs., CE 240, 246, 247–8. At some date later than 1855, when revising his Delacroix article for his projected volume of collected critical writings, B. interpolated a quotation of the relevant 'medallion' from *Les Phares* (ll. 29–32), adding the word 'surnaturalisme' by way of comment on the phrase 'hanté des mauvais anges' (l. 29); see CE 249, and cf. ibid. 486, 452–3, 459.

[2] CE 251. For B.'s earlier translation of the Poe passage in question (which in its original context bears a far more limited connotation than he here gives it; cf. L. J. Austin, *Univers poétique de B.*, 179–80), see *Les Souvenirs de M. Auguste Bedloe*, HE 289, and cf. *Poëme du haschisch*, PA 47. A landscape of Delacroix' which, in B.'s version (*Salon de 1859*, CE 297), would exactly induce this 'supernaturalist' effect, would be *Ovide chez les Scythes*.

privileged moments—here termed 'ces admirables heures' or 'ces beaux jours de l'esprit', but elsewhere described under a whole variety of similarly hyperbolical formulas.[1] This is, in fact, a theme to which Baudelaire recurs almost obsessively throughout the period 1855–1861; here, for instance, in a passage from the XIth section of *Fusées*, is a clear definition of *surnaturalisme*, taken as one of two 'fundamental literary qualities':

> Coup d'œil individuel, aspect dans lequel se tiennent les choses devant l'écrivain . . . Le surnaturel comprend la couleur générale et l'accent, c'est-à-dire intensité, sonorité, limpidité, vibrativité, profondeur et retentissement dans l'espace et dans le temps.
>
> Il y a des moments de l'existence où le temps et l'étendue sont plus profonds, et le sentiment de l'existence immensément augmenté.[2]

Relating this text to those previously quoted or referred to, we may specify, of the 'supernatural' state of mind, that it is distinguished in the first instance by an extreme precision and vividness of physical impression—each sound, each colour, each odour taking on, as it seems, a new sharpness and relief, a new vibrancy, a new depth of recession. But, further, the very intensity of these sensations confers upon the objects they illumine and 'isolate', a strange animistic quality of their own: they appear to take up a certain 'attitude' towards Man, to 'speak' to him through their colours and perfumes, to embody a whole world of ideas.[3] It is implicitly from this second aspect of the 'supernatural' experience that Baudelaire derives (as we shall see from certain texts to be examined in my next chapter) his conviction of the *symbolic* potentiality of such moments; explicitly, however, if in the most general terms, this

---

[1]Cf., e.g.: '[les] minutes heureuses' (*Le Balcon*, l. 21; *Notes nouvelles, NHE* xviii); 'de belles saisons, d'heureuses journées, de délicieuses minutes' (*Poëme du haschisch, PA* 3); 'les belles heures de la vie', 'ces merveilleux instants' (*Théodore de Banville, AR* 352, 353–4); 'les heures heureuses' (of Banville's poetry: *Fusées* IX, *JI* 19).

[2]*JI* 23. I have omitted, from the opening sentence of this passage, a phrase ('tournure d'esprit satanique') clearly relating to irony (the second of the two literary qualities in question) rather than to *surnaturalisme*.

[3]Cf., for a more direct (even abrupt) transition from the physical sensation to the moral idea, *Poëme du Haschisch, PA* 3–4: 'Il est des jours où . . . le monde extérieur s'offre à [l']homme] avec un relief puissant, une netteté de contours, une richesse de couleurs admirables. Le monde moral ouvre ses vastes perspectives, pleines de clartés nouvelles'.

conviction is already affirmed in that same XIth section of *Fusées*
from which I have already quoted above:

> Dans certains états de l'âme presque surnaturels, la profondeur de la
> vie se révèle tout entière dans le spectacle, si ordinaire qu'il soit, qu'on
> a sous les yeux. Il en devient le symbole.
>
> *(JI 24)*

In another and more elaborate text, the same observation is drawn
from the hallucinations whereby the hashish-addict (like his opium-
eating counterpart cited in the Delacroix article) accedes to the realm
of the 'supernatural':

> Cependant se développe cet état mystérieux et temporaire de l'esprit, où
> la profondeur de la vie, hérissée de ses problèmes multiples, se révèle
> tout entière dans le spectacle, si naturel et si trivial qu'il soit, qu'on a
> sous les yeux,—où le premier objet venu devient symbole parlant.
> Fourier et Swedenborg, l'un avec ses *analogies*, l'autre avec ses *corres-
> pondances*, se sont incarnés dans le végétal et l'animal qui tombent sous
> votre regard, et, au lieu d'enseigner par la voix, ils vous endoctrinent par
> la forme et par la couleur. L'intelligence de l'allégorie prend en vous des
> proportions à vous-même inconnues. . . . Le haschisch s'étend alors sur
> toute la vie comme un vernis magique; il la colore en solennité et en
> éclaire toute la profondeur. Paysages dentelés, horizons fuyants, perspec-
> tives de villes blanchies par la lividité cadavéreuse de l'orage ou illuminées
> par les ardeurs concentrées des soleils couchants,—profondeur de l'espace,
> allégorie de la profondeur du temps . . . tout enfin, l'universalité des
> êtres se dresse devant vous avec une gloire nouvelle non soupçonnée
> jusqu'alors.
>
> *(Poëme du haschisch, PA 51-2)*

There is a certain implied continuity, in these two texts, between
the *literal* 'depth' of the landscape (skies, horizons, perspectives of
various kinds), and the *symbolic* depth—the sense of some hidden,
inner 'meaning'—that is argued from the very intensity of the experience; consciously or unconsciously, Baudelaire seems here to
be playing on the two senses of the word 'profond'.[1] As for the

---

[1] As equally, no doubt, when observing, in *Edgar Poe, HE* xxix: 'L'espace est
approfondi par l'opium' (my italics—see p. 181, above). Cf., in this whole connection, the gloss by J. Crépet and G. Blin, *JI* 229: 'Dans cet état l'intensité que
revêt le sentiment de la vie se mesure très exactement sur l'élargissement que
présente l'univers extérieur, ou—si l'on préfère, l'accroissement présenté par
l'espace et le temps détermine un accroissement de la saisie spirituelle. Ici
Baudelaire rencontre l'idée forte que voir le monde en profondeur, c'est le voir

mention, in the second text, of Fourier and Swedenborg, with their 'analogies' and 'correspondences', this might seem at first to promise some specific mode of symbolic interpretation; but it is of course of the very essence of the hashish-eater's illusion, that the deep 'penetration' and limitless 'understanding' of the 'allegory' of life that he believes himself to have acquired, should remain wholly undefined and indeed irreducible to coherent explanation. As it happens, however, Baudelaire has elsewhere provided us, in his prose poem *Le Confiteor de l'artiste*, with a fully detailed illustration of the type of symbolism he must have had in mind when declaring, in the two texts quoted above, that in certain 'almost supernatural' or hallucinatory moments, the full 'profundity of life' seems to be disclosed and symbolized in the immediate spectacle before one's eyes.[1] The opening paragraphs of *Le Confiteor de l'artiste* record the poet's 'delicious' sense of 'immersion' within the vast seascape and skyscape opening out before him; and as he for his part 'thinks himself into' the diverse elements of the scene, these in return offer him—through the specific instance of the distant sail shimmering on the horizon—a *symbolic* reflection or 'imitation' of his own destiny:

Que les fins de journées d'automne sont pénétrantes! Ah! pénétrantes jusqu'à la douleur! car il est de certaines sensations délicieuses dont le vague n'exclut pas l'intensité; et il n'est pas de pointe plus acérée que celle de l'Infini.

Grand délice que celui de noyer son regard dans l'immensité du ciel et de la mer! Solitude, silence, incomparable chasteté de l'azur! une petite voile frissonnante à l'horizon, et qui, par sa petitesse et son isolement, imite mon irrémédiable existence, mélodie monotone de la

---

symboliquement'. For an instance where, by the juxtaposition of two distinct moments of time and space, B. lends to a Parisian 'landscape' an added dimension of figurative 'depth', cf. the final image of *A une Indienne* (ll. 27–8), and its later versions in *A une malabaraise* and *Le Cygne* (ll. 42–4)—or cf. equally the description of Meryon's etchings of the city: 'la profondeur des perspectives augmentée par la pensée de tous les drames qui y sont contenus' (*Salon de 1859*, *CE* 343). Cf., finally, in this whole connection, the sensitive comment by J. Pommier, *Mystique de B.*, 144–5, on a passage (to be discussed below) from the article on Hugo: 'Comme [Hugo], tout poète doit rendre, avec la silhouette des choses, cette *frange* mystérieuse dont leurs bords se revêtent soudain aux yeux du contemplateur en état de grâce'.

[1] Cf. also, in this respect, the incidental comment, in the *Salon de 1859*, on the artist's capacity (through his 'soul') to cast 'une lumière magique et *surnaturelle* sur l'obscurité naturelle des choses' (*CE* 310; my italics).

houle, toutes ces choses pensent par moi ou je pense par elles. . . .[1]

Here, clearly, we have the very process described in *Fusées* and in *Le Poëme du haschisch*: first, the 'supernatural' moment, with its piercing intensity of feeling and its vague sense of 'participation' in Nature;[2] next, the particular object (the 'petite voile frissonnante à l'horizon') disengaging itself from the general mass of impressions and assuming the privileged status of a symbol; finally, the conviction that in this one symbol is summed up the whole meaning and profundity of life—of one's *own* life, of one's *own* 'irremediable existence'. And thus we see that in its symbolic extension no less than in the immediate forms through which it manifests itself, the Baudelairian 'supernatural' requires wholly to be defined in *subjective* terms; while it may seem to be 'above' Nature in the sense that it goes *beyond* the reality of normal, everyday experience, beyond the limits of normal consciousness, it none the less remains firmly a part—a further dimension, a further region—of the poet's *interior* world of sensation, emotion, rêverie.[3] Rather than as a mystical or transcendent order of being, therefore—rather than as the manifestation of some 'higher' force or agency beyond natural law, and as such susceptible only of religious or metaphysical explanation—the Baudelairian 'supernatural' is perhaps best regarded simply as the substantial as well as etymological equivalent of our (wholly secular) modern 'surreal': 'above' Nature (in a certain sense), but yet clearly *within* Man.[4]

[1] *PPP*, ed. M. Zimmerman, 2. For a further discussion of this poem, see pp. 279–82, below.

[2] An illusion elsewhere noted by B. as characteristic of the hashish-trance; cf. *PA* 223–4 (*Du Vin et du hachish*) and 33–4 (*Poëme du haschisch*).

[3] Cf. the specific comment by L. J. Austin, *Univers poétique de B.*, 180–1, on the 1855 text (on Delacroix) cited above: ' "Intensité", "splendeurs", "nerfs ultra-sensibles": ce "surnaturalisme" n'implique pas de transcendance véritable. Au contraire, Baudelaire, quittant le domaine de la théologie ou de la métaphysique, parle ici en psychologue'—as also his more general definition, 'B. et l'énergie spirituelle', *RSH*, 1957, pp. 40–1: 'Le surnaturel baudelairien n'est pas la révélation d'un monde transcendant: c'est la nature portée à un degré supérieur d'intensité . . . Le surnaturel n'est pas dans les objets, mais dans le sujet lui-même'.

[4] This is not to imply that B. was a surrealist *avant la lettre*. On the contrary, in all the moments of heightened 'supernatural' (or surreal) experience he describes, the conscious mind appears still effectively to be 'in control', and there is in any case no question of his presenting, in its *unmodified* immediacy, the material dredged up from the unconscious. Cf., in this connection, B. Le Gall, *L'Imaginaire chez Senancour*, I, 611–12.

Before going on to consider what is undoubtedly Baudelaire's most complete (or elaborate) transcription of a 'supernatural' state, the poem *Élévation*, I must first briefly examine the related question of the actual *origin* of such experiences. From numerous other texts additional to those already cited, we may see that although for Baudelaire drugs (opium or hashish) may constitute a favoured mode of access to the 'supernatural',[1] these privileged 'minutes heureuses' may also occur quite spontaneously or in response to other and more 'natural' stimuli. They may, for instance, be the fruit of a rigorous moral 'hygiene', of assiduous prayer and constant spiritual aspiration; conversely, they may descend almost as a form of 'grace' or an angelic 'call to order', and thus by a paradox follow immediately upon a period of prolonged physical and mental abuse;[2] in retrospect, they may seem the special prerogative of childhood or youth;[3] they may, further, arise from the contemplation of a landscape,[4] from a moment of tender love,[5] from a benign fusion of the two at once;[6] finally, being part and parcel of the actual effort and wisdom of the creative imagination,[7] they may be conveyed to us through a specific work of art in whatever medium.[8] Yet when all these various

---

[1] *Du Vin et du hachish*, PA 223–6; *Poëme du haschisch*, PA 50–2; *Le Poison*, ll. 6–10; *Exposition universelle* III, CE 251 (cf. HE 289, PA 47); *Edgar Poe*, HE xxix; *Fusées* VIII, JI 17; *Mangeur d'opium*, PA 119–20; *La Chambre double* (cf. pp. 168–9, above); *Rêve parisien* (ibid.); *Le Confiteor de l'artiste* (cf. pp. 184–5, below). An interesting text in this connection is the long letter to Mme Aupick of 4/12/1847; having here confessed the powerlessness of laudanum and wine to help him 'remake his life', the anger he feels at his present mode of existence with its contrast between complete outward idleness and perpetual mental activity, B. adds: 'Le fait est que depuis quelques mois je vis dans un état *surnaturel*' (CG I, 93). Clearly the word italicized (by me) has in this context the meaning 'absurd' or 'fantastic'; one wonders, however, whether it does not carry also some covert association with the state of mind engendered by the drug?

[2] *PA* 3–5. For an analysis of this passage, see A. Fairlie, in: *The French Mind*, pp. 298–9.

[3] *Bénédiction*, ll. 21–8; *Peintre de la vie moderne*, AR 59–60; *Edgar Allan Poe*, OP I, 251; *Fanfarlo*, ed. C. Pichois, 60. (All these texts cit. pp. 4–5, above.)

[4] *Choix de maximes consolantes sur l'amour*, OP II, 3–4 (cit. p. 82, above).

[5] *Le Balcon*, ll. 12, 21 (cf. JI 230).

[6] *Harmonie du soir* (pp. 82–5, above).

[7] *Du Vin et du hachish*, PA 233; *Poëme du haschisch*, PA 68–9; *Salon de 1859*, CE 310; *Notes nouvelles sur Poe*, NHE xviii; *Fusées* XI, JI 23 (cit. p. 182, above). Cf. also *La Voix*, ll. 16–18, and for Balzac examples, P. Laubriet, *Intelligence de l'art chez Balzac*, 343.

[8] CE 251 and 298 (Delacroix); HE xxix–xxx and CG I, 382 (Poe); AR 165 (Gautier); CG II, 316 (Doré); AR 352, 353–4, and JI 19 (Banville); CG III,

texts have been enumerated, these various other avenues to the 'supernatural' explored, it is still to the *paradis artificiels* that one must return. For not only (in the book of that name) do opium and hashish furnish the main context within which Baudelaire develops his concept of the 'supernatural', but he tends also, almost as if compulsively, to introduce allusions to these drugs (and more especially to opium), even when speaking of quite other forms of 'supernaturalism'.[1] I would conclude that Baudelaire's experiences of opium and hashish remained for him the personal touchstone whereby he measured all 'supernatural' states of whatever kind;[2] moreover, I would go on to suggest that in *Le Poëme du haschisch* as in the earlier *Du Vin et du hachish*, the solemn warnings against the spiritual hazards of hashish-addiction, were perhaps obliquely aimed at Baudelaire's own *opium*-eating self.[3] Here once again therefore, on this assumption, we would encounter that note of covert self-admonition we have already noted in certain earlier texts;[4] and more particularly, we would find explained the almost identical concluding paragraphs to the two 'hashish' essays, with their specific exaltation (for the *poet* Baudelaire's benefit) of the true poet-philosopher's creative 'beatitude', over any other to be obtained through merely artificial means. In this respect it is perhaps significant that in both texts Baudelaire's final 'moral' should be conveyed through an

---

33-4 and *AR* 207-8 (Wagner). For the 'supernatural' effect of music in general, cf. *JI* 14, 95, as also the comment by L. J. Austin, *Univers poétique de B.*, 272-3, on these last four texts.

[1] Cf. *CE* 251 and 298 (Delacroix); *HE* xxix-xxx (Poe); *AR* 208 (Wagner). All these passages, it will be noted, concern artists whom B. particularly admired and had particularly assimilated to himself.

[2] Cf. the judicious comment by J. Pommier, *Mystique de B.*, 143: 'Quand Baudelaire essaie de traduire ces impressions singulières [de profondeur, etc.], c'est bien rare s'il ne se réfere pas, plus ou moins explicitement, à l'optique spéciale de l'intoxiqué.' B. is at pains to stress, however, that the drug merely exacerbates or heightens the normal 'poetic' response—that 'il n'y [a] rien de *positivement* surnaturel dans l'ivresse du haschisch' (*Poëme du haschisch, PA* 32; my italics); cf. also the comment, in the *Salon de 1859*, on the 'dream-like' quality of Delacroix' art: 'C'est le rêve! et je n'entends pas par ce mot les carpharnaüms de la nuit, mais la vision produite par une intense méditation, ou, *dans les cerveaux moins fertiles*, par un excitant artificiel' (*CE* 298; my italics).

[3] Cf. for a discussion of the extent and circumstances of B.'s addiction to this drug: *EJC* 192-4 n.; G. T. Clapton, *B. et De Quincey*, 6-11; C. Pichois and R. Kopp, 'B. et l'opium', art. cit., pp. 73-9.

[4] Cf. pp. 95, 97, above.

exterior spokesman. In *Du Vin et du hachish,* this spokesman is the musicographer Barbereau, who is approvingly quoted for his peremptory affirmation that Man has no need of artificial stimulants (such as hashish) in order to reach a state of beatitude: great poets, philosophers, prophets, all are able by sheer dint of 'enthusiasm' and will power to raise themselves to a higher and 'supra-natural' level of existence.[1] In *Le Poëme du haschisch,* Barbereau is replaced by an imaginary 'poetic' sage ('dirai-je un brahmane, un poëte ou un philosophe chrétien?') who, as he looks down (in both senses) on the world of men, from the Olympus of spirituality and pure art where he is enthroned, deplores their inability to perceive that the true path of 'redemption' and of 'supernaturalist' illumination, lies not in recourse to the 'black magic' of drugs, but in assiduous creative effort and purposive meditation:

Au-dessous de lui, au pied de la montagne, dans les ronces et dans la boue, la troupe des humains, la bande des ilotes, simule les grimaces de la jouissance et pousse des hurlements que lui arrache la morsure du poison; et le poëte attristé se dit: 'Ces infortunés qui n'ont ni jeûné, ni prié, et qui ont refusé la rédemption par le travail, demandent à la noire magie les moyens de *s'élever, d'un seul coup, à l'existence surnaturelle.* La magie les dupe et elle allume pour eux un faux bonheur et une fausse lumière; tandis que nous, poëtes et philosophes, nous avons régénéré notre âme par le travail successif et la contemplation; par l'exercice assidu de la volonté et la noblesse permanente de l'intention, nous avons créé à notre usage un jardin de vraie beauté. Confiants dans la parole qui dit que la foi transporte les montagnes, nous avons accompli le seul miracle dont Dieu nous ait octroyé la licence!'[2]

[1] *PA* 233. The word '*supra*-naturel' (later to be replaced, as we shall see, in the corresponding phrase of *Le Poëme du haschisch,* by the definitive '*sur*naturel') is here used in much the same implication and context as Nerval's term '*super*-naturaliste', as he applies it, some three years later, when describing the *Chimères* sequence of sonnets as 'composés dans cet état de rêverie *super-naturaliste,* comme diraient les Allemands' (*Les Filles du feu,* 1854, 'A Alexandre Dumas', Pléiade, 1, 158); it is, to this formula of Nerval's incidentally, that Breton recurs in his *Manifeste* of 1924, while continuing for practical reasons to prefer Apollinaire's more recent coinage 'surréalisme' (*Manifestes du surréalisme,* 36–7; cf. R. Pomeau, *RES,* 1959, p. 119). Finally, I would note that a similar technique (or theory) of 'supernaturalist rêverie', is to be found in Senancour and Balzac; cf., respectively, B. Le Gall, *Imaginaire chez Senancour,* 1, 611–13; P. Laubriet, *Intelligence de l'art chez Balzac,* 50–1.

[2] *PA* 69; my italics. B. here in effect returns to the theme of his opening pages (*PA* 3–5), while stressing more explicitly the special role of the poet-philosopher. In assigning to this figure the status of a 'sage', B. may perhaps

Is it some such 'miracle' as this that Baudelaire is concerned to convey in *Elévation*? Here also the squalor and misery of human existence have been left far behind—but so, too, have all the mountains of the world, even to the very highest Olympus; in the most literal as well as figurative sense the poet has here lifted himself 'above' Nature:

> Au-dessus des étangs, au-dessus des vallées,
> Des montagnes, des bois, des nuages, des mers,
> Par delà le soleil, par delà les éthers,
> Par delà les confins des sphères étoilées,
>
> Mon esprit, tu te meus avec agilité,
> Et, comme un bon nageur qui se pâme dans l'onde,
> Tu sillonnes gaiement l'immensité profonde
> Avec une indicible et mâle volupté.
>
> Envole-toi bien loin de ces miasmes morbides;
> Va te purifier dans l'air supérieur,
> Et bois, comme une pure et divine liqueur,
> Le feu clair qui remplit les espaces limpides.
>
> Derrière les ennuis et les vastes chagrins
> Qui chargent de leur poids l'existence brumeuse,
> Heureux celui qui peut d'une aile vigoureuse
> S'élancer vers les champs lumineux et sereins;
>
> Celui dont les pensers, comme des alouettes,
> Vers les cieux le matin prennent un libre essor,
> —Qui plane sur la vie, et comprend sans effort
> Le langage des fleurs et des choses muettes!

After the initial movement of bold 'ascension', the second verse takes us to the very heart of the experience Baudelaire is here re-enacting—without antecedents, without indications of any kind as to the particular circumstances whereby his mind, released from its body, thus finds itself transported into some higher region, there to traverse an infinite and luminous stratosphere. We may, of course, recognize the various associated sensations and emotions—levitation and flight, smooth and effortless movement, exhilaration and serene

---

be recalling his earlier essay *De l'essence du rire* (first pub. 1855); there, however, the context is specifically Christian: 'Le Sage, c'est-à-dire celui qui est animé de l'esprit du Seigneur, celui qui possède la pratique du formulaire divin . . .' (*CE* 372; cf. 371-4, 375, 380).

exaltation—to be of a type that figures constantly in almost all mystical texts;[1] but they belong equally to one of the commonest type of dream—the dream of flying, with its unmistakable erotic undertones and its deep sense of resistless mastery and omnipotence. Again, the vocabulary and imagery of the poem recall strongly certain descriptions furnished—by Baudelaire himself in 1851, by Gautier and Nerval in 1846 and 1847—of the effects of hashish;[2] equally, however, as has been suggested, the poet might here be rendering into words some powerful *musical* experience, such as he appears, for instance, to have undergone around 1845.[3] More simply,

---

[1]Cf. *FMCB* 292; among innumerable further instances that could be cited, I would note in passing the assertion made by a German/Tibetan monk to Dom Denys Routledge, that a state of contemplation can produce a sensation of flying, '*as though* the soul had soared aloft and were present somewhere else' (*In Search of a Yogi*, cit. Raymond Mortimer, *Sunday Times*, 4 Feb. 1962).

[2]I reproduce the passages in question in roughly chronological sequence: (a) Gautier, 'Le Club des Hachichins', *RDM*, 1/2/1846, p. 530: 'Je ne sentais plus mon corps; les liens de la matière et de l'esprit étaient déliés; je me mouvais par ma seule volonté dans un milieu qui n'offrait pas de résistance. . . . Je compris alors le plaisir qu'éprouvent, suivant leur degré de perfection, les esprits et les anges en traversant les éthers et les cieux, et à quoi l'éternité pouvait s'occuper dans les paradis. Rien de matériel ne se mêlait à cette extase; aucun désir terrestre n'en altérait la pureté' (in: *PA* ed. C. Pichois, 57, 58; the same notion of a 'beatitude' which separates mind from body, is found in Gautier's earlier essay, 'Le Hachich', 1843, in ibid., 38).

(b) Nerval, 'Scènes de la vie orientale', *RDM*, 15/8/1847, p. 598: '. . . l'esprit, dégagé du corps, son pesant geôlier, s'enfuit comme un prisonnier dont le gardien s'est endormi, laissant la clé à la porte du cachot. Il erre joyeux et libre dans l'espace et la lumière . . . Il traverse d'un coup d'aile facile des atmosphères de bonheur indicible et dans l'espace d'une minute qui semble éternelle' (*Voyage en Orient*, ed. G. Rouger, II, 306).

(c) Baudelaire, *Du Vin et du hachish*, 1851 (the effects of hashish, phase two): 'De temps en temps la personnalité disparaît. . . . Maintenant vous planez dans l'azur du ciel immensément agrandi' (*PA* 224; in the expanded version of 1858, *Le Poëme du haschisch*, *PA* 33, the final sentence becomes: '. . . l'oiseau qui plane au fond de l'azur *représente* d'abord l'immortelle envie de planer au-dessus des choses humaines; mais déjà vous êtes l'oiseau lui-même').

For analogous images of (winged) flight, arising from the effects of *wine*, cf. an earlier passage from this same text of B.'s (*Du Vin et du hachish*), *PA* 205 (wine is here speaking directly to Man): 'A nous deux nous ferons un Dieu, et nous voltigerons vers l'infini. . . .'—as also *Le Vin des amants* (comp. 1841–5?), ll. 3–4, 9–14.

[3]This interesting conjecture (which has a clear relevance to the date one might assign to the poem's original conception, if not to its ultimate composition) is made by L. J. Austin, *Univers poétique de B.*, 272—who argues both from a

Baudelaire may either, on the one hand, be giving a further imaginative extension to the specific emotions and sensations he himself associates with the 'supernatural' or 'lyrical' state—that state in which, precisely, as he tells us in his essay of 1861 on Banville, 'Tout l'être intérieur . . . s'élance en l'air par trop de légèreté et de dilatation, comme pour atteindre une region plus haute'[1]; or, on the other, he may be 'actualizing', or 'playing out' in fantasy, that aspiration to ascend ever higher into some purer realm, which since the middle of the previous century had so often crystallized the vagueness of Romantic (or pre-Romantic) *Sehnsucht*.[2] Finally, it may even

---

remark made in a letter of Feb. 1860 to Poulet-Malassis (*CG* III, 30), and from the striking analogy to be observed between *Elévation* and B's later accounts of his response to Wagner's music (ibid., 33 and *AR* 206–7; cf. *FMCB* 293 and n. 1.).

[1] *AR* 353–4. Cf. also the comment (arising out of Ingres' *Apothéose de l'Empereur Napoléon I*er): 'Le caractère principal d'une apothéose doit être le sentiment surnaturel, la puissance d'ascension vers les régions supérieures, un entraînement, un vol irrésistible vers le ciel' (*Exposition universelle*, II, *CE* 240).

[2] Cf. the 18th-century examples cited by Paul van Tieghem, *Sentiment de la nature dans le préromantisme*, 246–7. One of these, taken from Goethe's *Faust I*, may (in the 1840 or earlier translation by Nerval) have been a primary source for the present poem; Faust here speaks to Wagner, in the scene before the town gate: 'Oh! que n'ai-je des ailes pour m'élever de la terre, et m'élancer après lui [i.e. le soleil couchant] dans une clarté éternelle! Je verrais à travers le crépuscule tout un monde silencieux se dérouler à mes pieds, je verrais . . . toutes les vallées s'obscurcir. . . . La montagne et tous ses défilés ne pourraient plus arrêter mon essor divin. . . . C'est un beau rêve tant qu'il dure! Mais, hélas! le corps n'a point d'ailes pour accompagner le vol rapide de l'esprit! Pourtant il n'est personne au monde qui ne se sente ému d'un sentiment profond, quand, au-dessus de nous, perdue dans l'azur des cieux, l'alouette fait entendre sa chanson matinale; quand, au-delà des rocs couverts de sapins, l'aigle plane, les ailes immobiles, et qu'au-dessus des mers, au-dessus des plaines, la grue dirige son vol vers les lieux de sa naissance' (Nerval, *Faust de Goethe*, ed. F. Baldensperger, 273–4). Not only do we find here the general upward 'movement' ('Au-dessus', 'au-delà') of B.'s verses, but also nearly all its descriptive elements (valleys, mountains, etc.—even to the morning lark which of course for B. becomes purely metaphorical); indeed, one might almost regard B.'s positive assertion: 'Mon esprit, tu te meus', etc., as an *answer* to Faust's regret that the body should lack wings, whereby it might accompany the soul/mind in its desired and imagined ascension. This ascension had by 1845, however, already confidently been accomplished by the egregious abbé Constant, in his pretentiously entitled *La Gnose* (*Les Trois harmonies*, pp. 289–90, 292–3); here again the general 'movement', together with certain images, anticipates (feebly) those of B.'s poem. For other possible literary sources, cf. R. Vivier, *Originalité de B.*, 214–16 and 239; *FMCB* 292–4 and 292 n. 2; *FMA* 269–70; J. Pommier, *Dans les chemins de B.*, 98; M. Larroutis, *RHLF*, 1963, pp. 110–12.

be that Baudelaire is here transcribing and elaborating a personal experience of an altogether more humble kind. Thus one notes that the opening quatrain of the poem, by its syntactical progression and 'movement', its repeated adverbs linking one aspiring clause after another, recalls strongly the corresponding verses of the youthful *Incompatibilité*; a still more striking analogy, however, is between the whole content, tone and imagery of the latter poem, and a prose text of 1862, *Le Gâteau,* which at some twenty-three years' distance evokes the same mountain excursion that in 1838 had inspired *Incompatibilité*:[1]

Je voyageais. Le paysage au milieu duquel j'étais placé était d'une grandeur et d'une noblesse irrésistibles. Il en passa sans doute en ce moment quelque chose dans mon âme. Mes pensées voltigeaient avec une légèreté égale à celle de l'atmosphère; les passions vulgaires, telles que la haine et l'amour profane, m'apparaissaient maintenant aussi éloignées que les nuées qui défilaient au fond des abîmes sous mes pieds; mon âme me semblait aussi vaste et aussi pure que la coupole du ciel dont j'étais enveloppé; le souvenir des choses terrestres n'arrivait à mon cœur qu'affaibli et diminué. . . . Bref, je me sentais, grâce à l'enthousias-mante beauté dont j'étais environné, en parfaite paix avec moi-même et avec l'univers. . . .   (*PPP* 45–6)

And Baudelaire goes on to speak here of his 'perfect beatitude' and 'total forgetfulness of all earthly evil'. It might seem—unless we suppose Baudelaire in 1862 to be merely transposing into the language of *Elévation* his Pyrenean memories of 1838—that both poems (or all three, if we count *Incompatibilité*) refer back, in their different contexts, to a single, original youthful experience—but one that in the present instance has been enriched by the further image of the mind figuratively taking *wing*,[2] as the body reaches the highest point of its literal ascension.[3]

[1] See pp. 8–9, above, and cf. J. Prévost, *B.,* 23: 'le poète de dix-huit ans essaie gauchement l'élan de ce qui sera plus tard sa magnifique *Elévation*'. In a later chapter of his book (pp. 291–2), this excellent critic convincingly demonstrates, by a detailed analysis of its rhythmic structure, the said 'magnificence' of the poem.

[2] Cf. the passage from *Faust I,* cit. p. 191, n. 2, above.

[3] I reserve for a later chapter, pp. 230–1 n. 1, below, my comment on a yet further interpretation which has been put forward, and which argues (not from the actual text, but solely from the presumed 'architecture' of *FM,* i.e. from the grouping of certain poems) that the poet is here speaking throughout in his 'professional' capacity, i.e. as the generic or representative Poet (with a capital 'P').

The very diversity of these possibilities, the very difficulty that arises in determining the nature and origin of the experience described in *Elévation*—these are paradoxically an advantage from our present standpoint: they render the poem applicable, as it were, to any or every form of the Baudelairian 'supernatural', and thus lend a comprehensive or prototypical significance to the felicitous sequence of its images and ideas. Thus one observes that, in the opening verses, the poet's mind at first retains its awareness of the earthly landscapes swiftly receding from its view; then, as it penetrates into the immensities of the upper air, it gives itself up entirely to the delectable mobility, the 'virile', 'muscular' exhilaration of flight. The third and fourth verses bring, it is true, their reminders of the 'morbid miasmas', the sombre and oppressive tensions, of earth; but this is merely the better to convey by antithesis the sense of release and 'purification' experienced by the mind as it is borne upwards—much as, in that other poem of 'escape', *Moesta et errabunda*, the 'dark ocean' of the 'hideous' city, with its remorse, its crimes, its mud which is the very stuff of our tears, had been set in contrast with the distant paradise of joy and delight lying across the oceans under the translucent blue.[1] With the third verse of *Elévation*, however, a certain change of attitude and tone becomes discernible on the poet's part. This verse should not, I suggest, be regarded simply as a further elaboration of the opening description of the mind's privileged migration 'beyond the starry spheres'; its injunctions or exhortations (proceeding as if from a part of the poet's being that remains on earth) serve, rather, to give *moral* direction and purpose to what hitherto has been an essentially *sensual* experience, summed up in the words 'avec une indicible et mâle *volupté*'. Now, however, since the mind feels itself truly to have soared heavenwards, let it truly (Baudelaire urges) shake itself free from all the 'morbid miasmas' of earth, let it truly become 'purified' in these upper regions, let it truly and deeply drink of this radiance that by analogy at least, has in it some element of the divine ('bois, comme une pure et *divine* liqueur,/Le feu clair . . .'). A similarly purposive nuance seems implied in the prolonged exclamation of the final six lines, with their successive 'characterizations' hingeing on a vibrant 'Heureux celui

---

[1]Cf. pp. 38–40, above. Cf. also (p. 43, above) the reference in the essay *De l'essence du rire*, to Virginie's imagined arrival in a Paris exhaling these same 'morbid miasmas': 'Elle tombe . . . en pleine civilisation, turbulente, débordante et *méphitique* . . .' (*CE* 374; my italics).

qui . . .'[1] It might admittedly seem that by association of ideas—the
vigorous thrust of the wing, the free soaring flight as of a lark, the
poised hovering above the earth, now linked as symbols with the
purely descriptive imagery of the opening two verses—we were
being invited to identify with the personal experience initially conveyed through these images, the serene and joyful state of mind now
lauded in conclusion. Yet does this, can this mean that Baudelaire
is in effect *congratulating* himself on being that fortunate man?
('Happy he who can thus, *like me*,' etc.) A boast so complacent would
hardly be in character, nor would it accord with the strongly aspiring,
even ardent tone of these concluding verses. Should we not rather,
in the light of the concluding paragraphs (above-quoted) of the two
'hashish' essays, detect here an almost *envious* allusion to those other
and truly 'fortunate' men—poets, philosophers, prophets, mystics—
who by an 'assiduous exercise of the will', a 'constant nobility of
intention', are able to 'regenerate their souls' and raise themselves in
one fell swoop to a 'supernatural' level of existence—to those, in
short, whose thoughts may indeed be said to take flight 'each morning' towards the heavens ('Vers les cieux *le matin* prennent un libre
essor'), and whose felicity is thus not occasional merely, but miracu-
lously sustained or renewed?[2]

Some such ideally wise figure might seem particularly to be implied in the poem's concluding couplet. These two lines—the most
significant in the whole poem, as far as the development of Baudelaire's Nature-philosophy and Nature-symbolism are concerned—
make clear that the world earlier rejected by the poet, is solely the
'morbid' and anguished world of urban Man; the world of Nature,
by contrast—the innocent, inanimate and inarticulate Nature of
flowers and 'dumb things', as also by extension the valleys, mountains, woods, seas, of the opening lines—all this merits fully and
indeed solicits his 'effortless' understanding. Thus the fortunate man
is he who having (literally) 'risen above' the grim realities of existence, can then from this exalted vantage-point once more bend his
gaze earthwards, the better now to comprehend (in every sense) the
mystery of the universe, the more effortlessly and intuitively to 'read'

---

[1] Is this not the Horatian *Beatus ille* . . . (Epode 11, 'In Praise of Country
Life'), which set the pattern for so many eighteenth-century bucolic poems
launched on just such a didactic note? See Paul van Tieghem, op. cit., 214, 216.
  [2] Cf. (pp. 187–8, above) *Du Vin et du hachish*, *PA* 233; *Poëme du haschisch*,
PA 68–9.

the secret language of Nature. By the imagery of his poem, by its metaphoric 'geography' (above, the 'supernatural' world inhabited by the poet; below, spread out beneath him, visible and 'intelligible', the natural world), Baudelaire lends to the 'transported' mind, in its relationship with the objects it perceives with such heightened clarity, a certain privileged, even hierarchical status ('Qui *plane sur la vie*'), which at the same time does not exclude the sympathetic, almost kindly communion with Nature of one who

> . . . comprend sans effort
> Le langage des fleurs et des choses muettes![1]

3. THE 'LANGUAGE' OF NATURE: THE SONNET 'CORRESPONDANCES'

'The language of flowers and of dumb things'. But in what exactly does this 'language' consist? How is it conveyed, and what is the meaning of the individual 'words' that compose it? As if in answer to these questions Baudelaire, in the first edition of 1857 of *Les Fleurs du Mal,* took care to place immediately after *Élévation* the sonnet *Correspondances*—with the latter's opening lines thus as it were

[1]The phrase 'le langage des fleurs' no doubt carries an allusion, conscious or unconscious, to the numerous fashionable treatises thus entitled (one such, for instance: *Le Langage des fleurs, ou les Selams de l'Orient,* was published 'chez Rosa' in 1819). Cf. the explicit reference B. himself makes to them, some years later, in a letter of 1860 to Poulet-Malassis, concerning a projected frontispiece for the second edition of *FM*: 'Encore aurait-il fallu consulter les livres sur les analogies, le langage symbolique des Fleurs, etc.' (*CG* III, 177). For this popular tradition, see: B. Le Gall, *Imaginaire chez Senancour,* I, 332–3; M. Le Yaouanc, ed. Balzac, *Le Lys dans la vallée,* 115–16 n. 1, 116 n. 2, 121 n. 2, 235 n. 2; J. Pommier, *Mystique de B.,* 60–1 (Fourier). Among the many 18th- and 19th-century texts (additional to those cited by the above authorities) which draw upon the convention of the 'selam' or 'language of the flowers', may be mentioned the following: Bernardin de Saint-Pierre, *La Chaumière indienne,* in *Œuvres* (1825), VI, 274, 279; George Sand, *Consuelo,* III, ch. LXXVIII (ed. L. Cellier and L. Guichard, II, 246); Balzac, *Illusions perdues: Un grand homme de province à Paris* (ed. A. Adam, 265–8: the fictive sonnet-sequence, *Les Marguerites*); etc. Among innumerable earlier examples, one need only cite Ophelia's 'rosemary . . . for remembrance', 'pansies . . . for thoughts' (*Hamlet,* IV, 5)—or among later ones, our 'Flower People' of to-day. It should, however, be added that there is strictly a distinction to be made between a general symbolism of flowers, and the type of flower-language once used, as a more or less open 'code', among the feminine inmates of the Turkish harems; cf., in this latter connection, M. Hammer, *Annales des voyages,* 1809, pp. 346–60.

continuing and elaborating the final couplet of the preceding poem:

> Heureux celui . . .
> . . . Qui plane sur la vie, et comprend sans effort
> Le langage des fleurs et des choses muettes!
>
> *(Élévation,* ll. 15, 19–20)

> La Nature est un temple où de vivants piliers
> Laissent parfois sortir de confuses paroles;
> L'homme y passe à travers des forêts de symboles
> Qui l'observent avec des regards familiers.
>
> *(Correspondances,* ll. 1–4)

But before going on to examine this first quatrain (and the remaining verses) of *Correspondances,* I must first explain my reasons for postponing until the present chapter all discussion of a text widely agreed, and with good reason, to have been first composed during the period 1845–7.[1] Certainly this was the period when Baudelaire's interest in 'synaesthesia' was at its height.[2] But in the present sonnet this interest is evidenced solely in the second quatrain and in the tercets, and it is not until around 1855 or 1856 that we begin to encounter in Baudelaire's writings, ideas and images similar to those of the *first* quatrain (above-quoted).[3] Given the apparent logical hiatus (to be discussed shortly) between the first quatrain and the remainder of the poem, one might well conjecture that as in the case of *Le Soleil*[4] Baudelaire, when preparing the 1857 edition of *Les Fleurs du Mal,* here also chose to bring together two distinct fragments, of which one was of earlier date than the other.[5] Be this as it

[1] Cf. J. Pommier, *Mystique de B.,* vi, 6–10, and *Dans les chemins de B.,* 81–2; *FMCB* 298; M. Ruff, *Esprit du mal,* 176; L. J. Austin, *Univers poétique de B.,* 86; C. Pichois, *B.,* 114 and n. 237.

[2] See J. Pommier, *Mystique de B.,* 4–10.

[3] Cf., for these later texts, pp. 205–6, below. What might at first seem an echo, in the opening hemistich ('La Nature est un temple'), of B.'s youthful 'Religion of Nature', turns out when viewed in its proper context to have, as we shall see, a rather different implication.

[4] Cf. p. 108, above.

[5] Such a hypothesis would take into account what might otherwise seem B.'s curious reluctance to publish, or even to seek to publish, before 1856–7, a poem so striking and original as *Correspondances*; cf., in this connection, the shrewd observations by Enid Starkie, *B.,* 227, and by J. Pommier, who in the prefatory Note added to the 1967 reprint of his *Mystique de B.,* goes on to pose these specific and pertinent questions: '. . . [on] doit . . . se demander si cette poésie, si cet organisme est arrivé du premier coup à sa forme définitive. Peut-être quelques vers seulement ont-ils été jetés sur le papier en 1845–1846? . . . Où, à part la

may, since within the context of Baudelaire's developing Nature-philosophy it is above all the poem's opening quatrain that concerns us, it seems permissible to allow this latter verse to determine the relative chronology of our discussion of the sonnet as a whole.[1]

No poem of Baudelaire's, perhaps, has been more widely quoted or invoked than this sonnet; yet none, I suggest, has been more often misunderstood, or more often presented in a misleading perspective. Thus the opening quatrain has been assumed—quite without textual justification—to affirm the symbolic 'correspondence' of the material with the spiritual, of our world here below with the invisible world lying beyond.[2] Why? Firstly, no doubt, because the title *Correspondances* carries decided Swedenborgian overtones, and because Baudelaire, having previously represented himself as a reader and admirer of Swedenborg, once or twice from 1855 onwards refers to the mystical aspects of the latter's doctrine.[3] But it must be remembered that the word 'correspondences' had by this time gained considerable currency, even outside strictly Swedenborgian circles; why should not Baudelaire simply have appropriated it, as a title, for his own purposes—lending it in the process, as Jean Pommier has suggested, a quite personal meaning appropriate to the actual content of his poem?[4]

---

citation introduite par Baudelaire dans son article sur Wagner, l'idée de ces vers 1 à 4 est-elle représentée pendant la seconde époque?' To this latter challenge I have, as it happens, returned in the ensuing pages a positive (as also, I must hope, a convincing) answer.

[1]This does not, however, imply my entire acceptance of the argument by A. Adam (based on a rather different interpretation of the poem from my own) for 1855 as *sole* date of composition; see *FMA* 272–5, and cf. also E. Starkie, *B.*, 227, 236.

[2]The most influential version of this 'idealist' interpretation has been that furnished by G. Blin (*B.*, 108; cf. *FMCB* 295). Cf. also, inter alia, M. Ruff, *L'Esprit du mal*, 240, 290–1; M. Eigeldinger, *Le Platonisme de B.*, 65–6. I note, on the other hand, that four of the most perceptive critics of B.: J. Prévost (*B.*, 75–7), P. Mansell Jones (*BMFP*, 31–2), L. J. Austin (*Univers poétique de B.*, 195–8), A. Fairlie (*B: 'FM'*, 20–2), concur independently in stressing the aesthetic and psychological, rather than mystical, aspects of the poem and of its conjunct theory.

[3]Cf. pp. 176–8, above.

[4]'Ne serait-ce pas à ce moment [i.e. in 1855] que Baudelaire avisa ce mot de "correspondances" comme convenant au huitième vers de son Sonnet? Et ne l'aurait-il pas alors inscrit en titre, rompant l'attache du terme avec le système auquel il l'avait emprunté?' (*Mystique de B.*, 168 n. 64; cf. ibid., 27). Cf. also P. Mansell Jones, *BMFP*, 18: '... the only part of the language of the sonnet which

A further element within our sonnet, however, which has seemed greatly to favour a Swedenborgian or transcendental interpretation of the first quatrain, is the opening metaphorical statement: 'La Nature est un temple'. It is true that in this phrase or its variants (e.g. 'le temple de la nature') we have, as P. Mansell Jones has observed, 'one of the perennial romantic clichés produced by the diffusion of religious sentiment over the natural scene'.[1] And if one goes on to

---

can definitely be called "Swedenborgian" is the title . . .' Both these publications study in masterly fashion the whole question of Swedenborg's influence. At least two poems bearing analogous titles to Baudelaire's, were published during this period: C. P. Cranch's *Correspondences*, in 1839 (see W. T. Bandy, *RHLF*, 1953, 203–5); the abbé Constant's *Les Correspondances*, in 1845 (*Les Trois Harmonies*, 297–301; cit. *FMCB* 296); neither shows any significant resemblance to our sonnet (whether in content or quality), but together they testify to the wide diffusion the title-word was beginning to enjoy.

[1]*BMFP* 21. Since the phrase had become so much of a cliché, B. need not necessarily (as L. Cellier points out, *RU*, 1955, p. 28) have borrowed it from any one source; cf., however, for some of the innumerable antecedent versions: J. Pommier, *Mystique de B.*, 19–20 and 166–7 n. 51; *FMCB* 298–9; *MGC* xxvi (abbé Constant); (Mother) Mary Alphonsus, *Influence of J. de Maistre on B.*, 70; P. Mansell Jones, *BMFP* 20–1; L. Cellier, art. cit., 26–8; M. Ruff, *Esprit du Mal*, 176; *FMA* 275–6; A. Fongaro, *RSH*, 1957, p. 95 n. 3. To these I myself would add several further analogues which to my knowledge have not previously been remarked: Colardeau, *Ode sur la Poésie comparée à la Philosophie*: '. . . ce vaste Univers n'est qu'un Temple à ses yeux [i.e. aux yeux d'Homère]' (*Œuvres*, 1779, II, 101); Bernardin de Saint-Pierre, *La Chaumière indienne*: the Pariah declaring 'ma pagode c'est la nature' (*Œuvres*, 1825, VI, 225); Thomson, *The Seasons*, final hymn (later imitated by Kleist; see Paul van Tieghem, *Sentiment de la Nature dans le préromantisme*, 256); Erasmus Darwin, *The Temple of Nature* (1803), title and l. 66; the texts by Wordsworth, Southey and Coleridge below-mentioned; Hugo, *Pan*, l. 37: 'C'est Dieu qui remplit tout. Le monde, c'est son temple' (Pléiade, I, 804), and *Relligio*, passim (*Contemplations*, ed. J. Vianey, III, 356–7; cf. also Vianey's preliminary comments, ibid., 353–5); Laprade, *A la terre*: 'O chênes, ô forêts, ô lieux doux et sacrés,/ Temple où les premiers dieux à nous se sont montrés . . .' (*Odes et poëmes*, p. 180). In short, as C. Pichois wittily observes: 'Inutile . . . de chercher *la* source de ce premier hémistiche de *Correspondances*; elle nous inonde' (*B.*, 114; my italics). As to the reasons for the remarkable popularity of this image, these are not hard to understand: not only does it offer a natural extension of the conventional metaphor of the 'vaults of Heaven', but it implies also the whole notion of 'free' worship under the open sky (as against more formal worship within an institution-alized setting). Cf. in this connection the ironic comment by H. N. Fairchild, *The Romantic Quest*, 186 (in a chapter, 'The Religion of Nature', which cites incidentally several texts, by Wordsworth, Southey and Coleridge, in which may be found variants of our present image): 'Coleridge and Wordsworth, in their orthodox and conservative days, regard Nature chiefly as a temple in which God may be worshipped when no regular service of the Established Church is in progress'.

assume that Baudelaire must necessarily in his turn be giving to this
image the same meaning or thematic content as his predecessors—
most of whom, certainly, had employed it to mark the 'presence'
(whether diffused pantheistically, or attested by 'homage') of God in
Nature[1]—then no doubt one may argue that here too, as in the
opening paragraph of the *Exposition universelle* articles (albeit far
more obliquely), he is concerned to pay tribute to that guiding if
indefinable Creator who is at the same time the providential
'Instigator' of universal analogy;[2] as for the remainder of the first
quatrain, this would then be taken to imply (no less obliquely) that
what is conveyed by the symbolic, 'living' pillars of Nature, is
precisely the *fact* of their analogic relationship with God.

Yet so marked a degree of obliquity is surely somewhat surprising
—surprising in itself (since Baudelaire after all is not Mallarmé!),
and surprising by contrast with the (poetic) directness of the remaining verses of the poem. Moreover does not the 'mystical' interpretation of the first quatrain lend to its opening phrase an independent
meaning that in its context it is far from possessing? The syntax of
the whole first couplet, the metrical structure which forbids the
reader to pause after the word 'temple' but obliges him to run on,
from the caesura, to the end of the line:

> La Nature est un tem/ple où de vivants piliers[3]

—these surely limit considerably the image's range of distinctive
religious connotation, and suggest that its *primary* significance for
Baudelaire was emotive and picturesque: the vast pillars, the suggestion of arching vaults, the solemn and oracular sounds, the sense
of awe, mystery and the supernatural—the whole aesthetic of Chris-
tianity, in short, to which Chateaubriand had vibrated so influentially
in a famous passage (to be quoted hereunder) of the *Génie du
Christianisme*. Moreover, on another point of syntax, if we take the
opening quatrain (as we should) as a single proposition enunciated

[1]Most but not all; cf. Vigny, *La Maison du Berger*, l. 269 (the 'temple' of the
mountain and the wood is dedicated not to God, but specifically to 'Eva'; see J.
Pommier, op. cit., 166 n. 151), and the text by Erasmus Darwin, *The Temple of
Nature*, cited in my previous note.

[2]Cf. p. 174, above.

[3]In order to confer on the opening phrase a true 'religious' finality, Baudelaire
would have needed to recast the syntax in some such (clumsy) fashion as this: 'La
Nature est un temple; de vivants piliers . . .'

in two balanced clauses, does it not clearly emerge that the true
theme, here, is the relationship between Nature and *Man*? Thus of
the two questions one might pose concerning the mysterious 'voices'
of the first quatrain, the more important would seem to be not '*Of*
what are these voices speaking?' (unanswered, and perhaps un-
answerable), but rather '*To* whom?' (with its answer, 'To Man',
implying already the essential humanism we shall find to underlie
the sonnet as a whole). As to the exact nature of the symbolism
inherent in the objects (or 'pillars') of Nature, we shall see that this
can in fact be explained in terms of the actual text of the first
quatrain, without obligation to posit an external Agent nowhere
named (and doubtfully suggested) within the poem, and without
disturbing the latter's inner coherence of structure. For the Swedenborgian interpretation implies (and this is a further and signal
defect) a curious inconsequence of thought on Baudelaire's part—
since it is agreed that the remaining verses of the sonnet describe
and illustrate 'correspondences' of a quite different and purely
terrestrial (i.e. inter-sensorial) kind;[1] by abandoning this interpretation we shall moreover be freed from the somewhat barbarous jargon
that distinguishes between, on the one hand, 'horizontal' and
'reversible' correspondences, and, on the other, those that being
hierarchical, are therefore 'vertical' and '*ir*reversible'.[2] In short,
nothing within the first quatrain need lead us to suppose that these
'voices' which murmur so mysteriously to Man as he passes through
the temple of Nature, are in truth proclaiming (with Swedenborg)
the analogy of things material with things celestial—nor even, more
simply, that they are 'declaring' (with the Psalmist, or with Lamartine)[3] the glory or wisdom of God. The Baudelaire of *Correspondances*
is neither a Swedenborg nor a Lamartine,[4] nor is he even the

---

[1] Cf. *FMCB* 295. G. Blin (*Le Sadisme de B.*, 181–3), has attempted—ingeniously, but in my view gratuitously—to resolve this hiatus by invoking a con-
ceptual *tertium comparationis*.

[2] Cf. the gently witty devaluation of these coinages by P. Mansell Jones,
BMFP, 32.

[3] As equally, of course, with innumerable other writers of all centuries:
Chateaubriand, Hugo, the eighteenth-century Deists, etc., etc.

[4] Cf., for a particularly instructive comparison in this latter respect, Lamartine's
ode to Byron, *L'Homme*. The poet may here declare (in lines that have something
of the spirit of the present quatrain): 'Tantôt, pour deviner le monde inanimé,/
Fuyant avec mon âme au sein de la nature,/J'ai cru trouver un sens à cette langue
obscure'; but he later comes to the full and *explicit* realization that what he has

Baudelaire of the 1848–51 version of *Le Vin des chiffonniers*, with its incidental tribute to the infinite goodness of 'Celui que tout nomme'.[1]

Let us now therefore, setting aside all preconceptions, turn to examine once again this lapidary and (it might seem) elusive first quatrain,[2] while at the same time bringing into consideration certain of the 'borrowed' notions on which it draws:

> La Nature est un temple où de vivants piliers
> Laissent parfois sortir de confuses paroles;
> L'homme y passe à travers des forêts de symboles
> Qui l'observent avec des regards familiers.

Nature, so this image-sequence implies, is conceived at once as a temple and as a forest; these associated metaphors recall the passage (aforementioned) from the *Génie du Christianisme,* in which Chateaubriand explains how the Gothic architects constructed their first 'temples' in imitation of the shapes and the sounds of the forest:[3]

'everywhere seen', but not until that moment 'understood', is God (Pléiade, 7–8; cf. J. Pommier, *Mystique de B.,* 148). Another, equally illuminating comparison would be with the passage from the *MS.* version of Lamartine's *Voyage en Orient* (ed. L. S. Fam, 199), in which the poet speaks of 'cette langue sacrée et secrète des rapports des choses créées entre elles et de leur rapport avec le Créateur'— adding the (rhetorical) question: 'Qu'est-ce que cela prouve? Dieu et la nature. Voilà tout'. B. for his part, unlike Lamartine, limits himself purely (as we shall see) to the 'rapports des choses crées entre elles', leaving out of account the question of 'leur rapport avec Dieu'; in other words, while God may, for B. (in other texts, if not in the present sonnet; cf. pp. 173–5, above), be conceived as the Creator of terrestrial analogies as of all things, He is not Himself regarded as a transcendental element or term *within* the analogy.

[1]Cf. p. 92 and n. 2, above. In miniature, so to speak, B. after 1851 (with his later references to animals and plants which appear to 'embody' human ugliness or evil; cf. pp. 234–5, below) might here be said to have followed an evolution almost exactly parallel to that of Hugo; cf. this comment by Ch. Renouvier, *Hugo le philosophe,* 27, on the transformation in the latter's ideas after his exile: 'L'hymne banal des splendeurs de la nature et de l'immuable harmonie des cieux est remplacé par le tableau des phénomènes instables, des phénomènes subversifs, et des métamorphoses de la matière "affreuse" '.

[2]Cf. the comment by P. Mansell Jones, *B.,* 33: 'A density of suggestion is compressed within the first quatrain which might have been sufficient alone to launch the Symbolist movement'.

[3]A similar principle of (unconscious?) imitation, it is interesting to note, was later to be discerned by Shelley in the architecture of classical Greece; cf. this passage from the letter written in Jan. 1819 from Italy to his friend Peacock: 'They [the Greeks] lived in a perpetual commerce with external nature and nourished themselves upon the spirit of its forms. Their theatres were all open

Les forêts des Gaules ont passé à leur tour dans les temples de nos pères, et nos bois de chêne ont ainsi maintenu leur origine sacrée. Ces voûtes ciselées en feuillages, ces jambages qui appuient les murs et finissent brusquement comme des troncs brisés, la fraîcheur des voûtes, les ténèbres du sanctuaire, les ailes obscures, les passages secrets, les portes abaissées, tout retrace les labyrinthes des bois dans l'église gothique; tout en fait sentir la religieuse horreur, les mystères et la divinité. . . . L'architecte chrétien, non content de bâtir des forêts, a voulu, pour ainsi dire, en imiter les murmures, et, au moyen de l'orgue et du bronze suspendu, il a attaché au temple gothique jusqu'au bruit des vents et des tonnerres, qui roule dans la profondeur des bois.

(*Génie du Christianisme*, III, 1, Chap. 8)

Baudelaire for his part, however, reverses and extends this classic analogy:[1] for him (as equally for certain of his contemporaries), it is the forest that recalls the temples of Man,[2] and that itself becomes the one vast temple of Nature; the trees of the forest by implication form (one presumes) the 'pillars' of the temple,[3] and as such have not only a certain literal value, but additionally represent all those other objects of Nature by which Man feels himself to be 'observed'.[4]

---

to the mountains & the sky. *Their columns that ideal type of a sacred forest* with its roof of interwoven tracery admitted the light & wind . . .' (*Letters*, ed. F. L. Jones, II, 74, my italics; cit., in trans., U. Mengin, *L'Italie des romantiques*, 206). Cf. also, in this connection, the texts by P. Leroux (1831) and Toussenel (1846), cit., respectively, by M. Ruff, *Esprit du mal*, 176, and J. Pommier, op. cit., 21 and 167 n. 56.

[1] Cf., in this whole connection, J. Pommier, *Mystique de B.*, 19–20, and P. Mansell Jones, *BMFP* 23–4. To transpose Chateaubriand's image is not, of course, necessarily to assent to the aesthetic theory it illustrates; on the contrary, in his *Salon de 1846* (*CE* 108; cf. J. Pommier, loc. cit., as also, for the context, p. 90 and n. 3, above), B. quotes approvingly a passage of Heine's in which the latter affirms (contradicting Shelley) that the 'types' of primitive architecture were found not in Nature but in the human mind.

[2] Cf., e.g., Balzac, *Le Lys dans la Vallée*, ed. M. Le Yaouanc, 118: 'une longue allée de forêt semblable à quelque nef de cathédrale, où les arbres sont des piliers, où leurs branches forment les arceaux de la voûte', etc.—as also (*FMCB* 425; p. 121, above and p. 283, below) two further texts by B. himself: the letter to Desnoyers (final sentence); the sonnet *Obsession* (l. 1).

[3] As, explicitly, in the Balzac passage above-quoted (n. 2).

[4] J. Pommier and P. Mansell Jones (respectively) have stressed vividly this aspect of the sonnet's 4th line: 'Enfin ils [les piliers] regardent. Comme Baudelaire a bien retenu cette hantise du regard ouvert dans le mur et qui épie!' (*Mystique de B.*, 21); 'A notable line [of Nerval's] . . . warning us of the disquieting vigilance with which inanimate things are endowed . . . may have induced B. to charge the auditive imagery of his opening lines with a similar implication of *animistic watchfulness*' (*BMFP* 21; my italics).

Where Baudelaire ceases to follow (or perhaps even to adapt) Chateaubriand, is in the *sounds* that issue from his mysterious temple. It is of course possible that when assigning to his 'living pillars' the gift of muffled or imperfectly apprehended 'speech',[1] Baudelaire did indeed have in mind (like Chateaubriand explaining the Gothic cathedral's organ and 'suspended bronze') the crash of thunder in the forest, the myriad 'murmurs' and noises that issue from trees and other natural objects under the impact of wind and storm—or again, the roar of the waves, their gentle lapping against the shore, the no less eloquent rustling of the leaves or whispering of the grass[2]—in short, that whole vast repertory of sounds, which for so many writers has seemed, precisely, to constitute the (variously interpreted) 'language' of Nature.[3] Indeed, taking the present sonnet as a whole, one might well venture in this respect beyond the purely auditory domain. Thus the 'regards familiers' could be taken to suggest *visual* forms of 'communication': the endless colours of Nature (evoked in the second quatrain), the play of light in its various forms, what Laprade (in a poem we have already more than once encountered, *Hermia*) calls the 'signals' flashed by the clouds at sunset,[4] and so on. And as the tercets of Baudelaire's sonnet go on to remind us, *perfumes* also have their 'voice', and 'sing' within

[1]'Muffled', surely, rather than 'mumbled'! (or 'confused'); the phrase 'confuses *paroles*', taken in conjunction with the later epithet 'familiers', suggests the failure of communication to be on the hearer's rather than the 'speaker's' part—as if one were listening to a foreign language of which the sounds were disturbingly similar to a known tongue, but which nevertheless could not quite be fitted into a fully recognizable pattern of meaning.

[2]For evocations by Baudelaire himself of certain of these sounds of Nature, cf., in addition to the two texts above-cited (final sentence of letter to Desnoyers; *Obsession*, ll. 1-8), *Moesta et errabunda*, ll. 7-9 (the immense 'organ' of the waves, with its rough 'cradle song').

[3]Cf., e.g. (to take but two or three poets of whom we know B. to have had a close knowledge): Lamartine, *Poésie* (*Paysage dans le golfe de Gênes*), *Désir* (Pléiade, 330-1, 386-8); Hugo, *Ce que dit la bouche d'ombre* (ll. 10-48; *Contemplations*, ed. J. Vianey, III, 435-7); Laprade, *Hermia* (*Odes et poëmes*, 1843, pp. 105-7).

[4]Loc. cit.; cf. also p. 61 n. 1, above. For a similar extension of the 'voices' of Nature into other sensory domains, cf. the same poet's *Eleusis* (ibid., pp. 275-7), as also, from our other two poets: Hugo, *Pan* (Pléiade, 1, 804-5), and Lamartine, *La Chute d'un Ange*, VIII (Pléiade, 951-2). One could also cite, finally, in this connection, an interesting passage of Poe's *The Poetic Principle* (*Literati, etc.*, 1850, p. 19)—in which, however, it is a question, strictly, of the 'true poetical effect' (rather than the 'language') of Nature.

the universal harmony. Yet it is difficult to reconcile with such a
notion of a continual, wholly 'functional' Nature-symbolism, the
word 'parfois' in the second line ('Laissent *parfois* sortir de confuses paroles'), with its suggestion of a sporadic, even fortuitous
'eloquence'; moreover is there not implied, in the almost stifling
sense of mystery that envelops the whole first quatrain, something
considerably more recondite than this vast cosmic Esperanto
which all men may recognize, and some at least would claim to
understand?

At this point we may usefully pause to examine three later yet
wholly analogous texts of Baudelaire's in which is conveyed precisely (if more explicitly) this same conviction that in some obscure
way the objects of Nature *hold communication* with Man. The most
elaborate and comprehensive of these three texts is the famous
analysis, in an article of 1861, of the 'poetic faculties' of Victor
Hugo. Baudelaire begins, significantly for our purposes, by affirming
that very 'mysteriousness' of Nature which we have seen to be so
strikingly conveyed in our first quatrain—before going on to refer,
similarly, to those aspects of 'universal life' that are 'obscure and
confusedly revealed':

Victor Hugo était, dès le principe, l'homme le mieux doué, le plus
visiblement élu pour exprimer par la poésie ce que j'appellerai le *mystère
de la vie*. La nature qui pose devant nous, de quelque côté que nous nous
tournions, et qui nous enveloppe comme un mystère, se présente sous
plusieurs états simultanés dont chacun, selon qu'il est plus intelligible,
plus sensible pour nous, se reflète plus vivement dans nos cœurs: forme,
attitude et mouvement, lumière et couleur, son et harmonie. La musique
des vers de Victor Hugo s'adapte aux profondes harmonies de la nature;
sculpteur, il découpe dans ses strophes la forme inoubliable des choses;
peintre, il les illumine de leur couleur propre. Et, comme si elles venaient
directement de la nature, les trois impressions pénètrent simultanément
le cerveau du lecteur. De cette triple impression résulte la *morale des
choses*. Aucun artiste n'est plus universel que lui, plus apte à se mettre
en contact avec les forces de la vie universelle, plus disposé à prendre
sans cesse un bain de nature. Non-seulement il exprime nettement, il
traduit littéralement la lettre nette et claire; mais il exprime, avec
l'*obscurité indispensable*, ce qui est obscur et confusément révélé.[1]

---

[1] *AR* 303-4. Cf. *Salon de 1859*, *CE* 310; B. here refers, in the context of
paintings of 'fantasy', to 'l'obscurité naturelle des choses', and to the 'lumière
magique et surnaturelle' that a certain type of imagination may be able to cast
on this obscurity. For the texts by Hugo that B. may have in mind (*A Albert
Durer*, etc.), cf. p. 227 n. 3, below.

The reference here to the 'simultaneous penetration' of our minds by impressions from different senses, is clearly of considerable relevance to the present sonnet; I shall return to this observation of Baudelaire's when going on to discuss the second quatrain. What is of more immediate concern for our *first* quatrain, however, is the ensuing description of the diverse sensations (fugitive, complex, 'moral', as well as direct) that the human mind draws from the 'visible being', from 'so-called inanimate Nature':

. . . non-seulement, la figure d'un être extérieur à l'homme, végétal ou minéral, mais aussi sa physionomie, son regard, sa tristesse, sa douceur, sa joie éclatante, sa haine répulsive, son enchantement ou son horreur; enfin, en d'autres termes, tout ce qu'il y a d'humain dans n'importe quoi, et aussi tout ce qu'il y a de divin, de sacré ou de diabolique.

(*AR* 304)

Now this hallucinatory, symbolic and 'human' aspect that certain animals, plants, material objects may take on as we contemplate them, had already twice previously been defined by Baudelaire, but from the specific standpoint of the creative artist (rather than that of Mankind in general):

La Nature dite inanimée participe [chez Poe] de la nature des êtres vivants, et, comme eux, frissonne d'un frisson surnaturel et galvanique.

(*Edgar Poe*, 1856, *HE* xxix)

Manier savamment une langue, c'est pratiquer une espèce de sorcellerie évocatoire. C'est alors que la couleur parle, comme une voix profonde et vibrante; que les monuments se dressent et font saillie sur l'espace profond; que les animaux et les plantes, représentants du laid et du mal, articulent leur grimace non équivoque; que le parfum provoque la pensée et le souvenir correspondants; que la passion murmure ou rugit son langage éternellement semblable.

(*Gautier*, 1859, *AR* 165)

As we read here of these vivid colours which take on a *deepened* and vibrant 'eloquence' of their own—of these buildings which rear up or stand out against the *deepened* background of space—are we not clearly reminded of the 'supernatural' moments described in precisely such terms in the Delacroix article of 1855, or in the XIth section of *Fusées,* or again in *Le Poëme du haschisch*? These further analogies become the more significant if one recalls that it is at such moments of heightened perception especially that there occurs, according to Baudelaire, the impulse to transpose particular objects of Nature into personal *symbols*.[1]

The relationship to Nature implied in the opening quatrain of *Correspondances* (to which we may now return) is, I would suggest, essentially the same as in these cognate prose texts—which is not to say that it is presented in identical terms. Thus what in these other texts is affirmed solely of the representative Poet or of the particular poet Baudelaire, is here affirmed as a *general* truth, and explicitly extended to all Mankind: '*L'homme* y passe à travers des forêts de symboles. . . .'[2] Again, what Baudelaire elsewhere tacitly recognizes to be a *projection* of his own hallucinated or 'supernatural' state: the 'articulacy' and strangely independent vitality at times assumed by certain natural objects, here (as also in the Hugo article) becomes a property of the objects themselves, a defining characteristic of Nature as a whole[3]. No doubt these strange, unfamiliar glances, these 'muffled' voices, will be perceived by Man only at certain rare, privileged moments; hence the adverb 'parfois' in the opening line. Yet what is especially significant in the present text, is that the 'voices' and 'glances' are not here held to *originate* with Man. Rather are they the true elemental medium whereby the world of Nature 'chooses' to communicate with him, as if of its own volition; and thus, whether he becomes aware of them or not, these voices are (in principle, at least) already and expectantly 'there'.

Between the first quatrain, and the single long, expansive, sonorous sentence that makes up the second:

[1] Cf. pp. 182–5, above.

[2] B.'s text, as here quoted, clearly forbids us from reading 'l'homme' as meaning anything other than . . . 'l'homme'!—or indeed from importing anywhere into the poem (*pace* A. Ferran, ed. *Poésies choisies*, 16 n. 4–7; M. Ruff, *B.*, 103) a generic Poet nowhere named or even implied. It is true that in the 1861 edition of *FM*, B. did so arrange the order of his opening poems as to suggest a certain continuity between *Correspondances* and those two 'glorifications' of the Poet, *Bénédiction* and *L'Albatros*; cf. pp. 230–1 and n. s, below. But the very fact that B., when revising his poems for the 1861 edition, should have chosen to leave intact and wholly unmodified the original text of *Correspondances*, shows that he still wished it to make its *primary* impact on the reader as a universal statement of Man's relation to Nature.

[3] Cf., however (p. 182, above), the passage in *Fusées* XI, in which the two aspects, subjective and objective, are juxtaposed within the same sentence: 'Coup d'œil individuel, aspect dans lequel *se tiennent* les choses devant l'écrivain . . .' (*JI* 23; my italics). For the Hugo article, cf. p. 205, above.

> Comme de longs échos qui de loin se confondent
> Dans une ténébreuse et profonde unité,
> Vaste comme la nuit et comme la clarté,
> Les parfums, les couleurs et les sons se répondent,

the continuity of thought is not apparent; indeed the transition seems almost abrupt, as we move from the relationship between the objects of Nature and Man, to that between the various kinds of impression Man may receive from these objects. We can, I suggest, best understand (if not entirely bridge) this hiatus, if we invoke once again the various 'supernaturalist' prose texts above-quoted. Nature (as Baudelaire there affirms) displays itself variously before us, envelops us in its mystery, as it were 'solicits' our attention; this, precisely, is the situation described in the first quatrain of the present sonnet, with its image of Man wending his way through the obscurely eloquent 'forests of symbols' that surround him. But for certain men (an Hugo; any true poet who is master of the arts of 'evocative sorcery')—for all men, even, at certain rare and 'supernatural' moments of uniquely heightened perception—this confused bombardment of messages from the outside world can transform itself ('unscramble' itself, as we might say) into images of a singular clarity, depth and vividness, drawn specifically, and often simultaneously, from the domains of colour, perfume, sound. Now the account here given is, as will be recognized, a composite of certain passages from the articles on Hugo, on Gautier, on the *Exposition universelle 1855*;[1] a 'supernaturalist' text that has, however, a still closer relevance in our present context, is this description, in *Le Poëme du haschisch*, of the general effects of the drug:

C'est . . . à cette période de l'ivresse que se manifeste une finesse nouvelle, une acuité supérieure dans tous les sens. L'odorat, la vue, l'ouïe, le toucher participent également à ce progrès. Les yeux visent l'infini. L'oreille perçoit des sons presque insaisissables au milieu du plus vaste tumulte. C'est alors que commencent les hallucinations. Les objets extérieurs prennent lentement, successivement, des apparences singulières; ils se déforment et se transforment. Puis arrivent les équivoques, les méprises et les transpositions d'idées. Les sons se revêtent de couleurs, et les couleurs contiennent une musique. . . .

Il arrive quelquefois que la personnalité disparaît et que l'objectivité . . . se développe en vous si anormalement, que la contemplation des objets extérieurs vous fait oublier votre propre existence, et que vous vous

---

[1] Cf. pp. 204–5, 181, above.

15

confondez bientôt avec eux. Votre œil se fixe sur un arbre harmonieux courbé par le vent; dans quelques secondes, ce qui ne serait dans le cerveau d'un poëte qu'une comparaison fort naturelle deviendra dans le vôtre une réalité. Vous prêtez d'abord à l'arbre vos passions, votre désir ou votre mélancolie; ses gémissements et ses oscillations deviennent les vôtres, et bientôt vous êtes l'arbre. De même, l'oiseau qui plane au fond de l'azur *représente* d'abord l'immortelle envie de planer au-dessus des choses humaines; mais déjà vous êtes l'oiseau lui-même.   *(PA* 32-3)

In a later paragraph (already quoted, above, in its 'supernaturalist' context) Baudelaire is concerned to evoke the specific reactions of a type of subject he describes as 'une âme de mon choix', and who in fact is clearly modelled on himself. After an initial phase of hallucination, offering 'immense' scope for the 'innate' love of colour and form, comes this further and properly 'supernatural' state:

Cependant se développe cet état mystérieux et temporaire de l'esprit, où la profondeur de la vie, hérissée de ses problèmes multiples, se révèle tout entière dans le spectacle, si naturel et si trivial qu'il soit, qu'on a sous les yeux,—où le premier objet venu devient symbole parlant. Fourier et Swedenborg, l'un avec ses *analogies,* l'autre avec ses *correspondances,* se sont incarnés dans le végétal et l'animal qui tombent sous votre regard, et, au lieu d'enseigner par la voix, ils vous endoctrinent par la forme et par la couleur. L'intelligence de l'allégorie prend en vous des proportions à vous-même inconnues. . . .   *(PA* 51)

What is of particular interest here is that we re-encounter our title-word, *correspondances*—used interchangeably, be it noted, with the terms 'symbol', 'allegory' and 'analogy';[1] it will be remarked also that it is through the very properties of *form* and *colour* that the animal and vegetable world appear, during the process of hallucination, to 'speak' meaningfully to the hashish-eater—to enter into a

---

[1]The references to Fourier and Swedenborg serve of course in this context purely to lend humour (and a certain authority) to B.'s description: in declaring that these high priests of analogy have 'incarnated' themselves in the elements of the animal and vegetable world falling within one's gaze, he is in effect reformulating, more elaborately, his statement that 'le premier objet venu devient symbole parlant'—as if to add: 'a "speaking" symbol, or (if one prefers) an analogy à la Fourier, a correspondence à la Swedenborg'. Or one might say that the gift of symbolic interpretation having passed from Fourier and Swedenborg to the (provisionally) omniscient hashish-eater, is transposed onto the object itself— which then in turn, by a reversal characteristic of the drug's effects, is made to declare its own analogic meaning, to 'indoctrinate' the observer through the very 'eloquence' of its form and colour.

special and privileged relationship with him: a tree or a bird will
as it were 'draw' him into itself; within his mind colours and sounds
will merge into (or interchange with) one another. So too, in the
Gautier, Delacroix and Hugo articles, the very *colours, sounds,
scents, shapes* of Nature are felt to 'speak' and have 'meaning' for
the privileged observer. Now may we not presume a precisely
similar process to underlie the first quatrain of *Correspondances,* and
thereby to explain the progression from this quatrain to the second?[1]
Thus the 'obscure words' and the 'familiar glances' whereby the
objects of Nature vouchsafe to Man their quality as 'symbols', would
now reveal themselves to be in fact those same *colours, sounds* and
scents which in the cognate prose texts are described, precisely, as
'speaking' to the privileged observer and as holding for him some
mysterious 'depth' of (symbolic) meaning;[2] the term 'symbol' used
in the first quatrain ('des forêts de symboles'), the title-word *correspondances* as implied in the second—these would in effect become
(as in the passage from *Le Poëme du haschisch*) synonymous and
interchangeable.[3] At the same time we may now take the affirmation,
in the sixth and seventh lines, of the 'obscure and profound unity'
within which perfumes, colours and sounds distantly merge, as
applying comprehensively to the *whole* world of Nature as defined
in the first quatrain[4]—a world which thus constitutes a single, vast
unified system of interrelationships in which all things, near and
far, mysteriously come together and, in a word, *correspond.*[5] And
within this endless reciprocal interplay of all elements in creation,
this 'universe of mirrors', the objects of Nature 'communicate' by

[1]Or at least to have justified B. in bringing together the two parts of the poem
—if one agrees that they may indeed originally have been distinct from one
another; cf. p. 196, above.

[2]Cf. also the final line, with its perfumes *singing* the delights of the mind and
of the senses.

[3]Cf. (p. 225 n. 1, below) the general comment on B.'s 'freedom' of terminology in this domain.

[4]This 'unity' is for B. (l. 7) 'vast as night and as the light of day': indirectly,
by metaphor, he thus assimilates Man's perceptions of Nature to its two great
elemental aspects.

[5]A very similar continuity between the (secret) eloquence of Nature, and the
'invisible' interrelationships binding inanimate and animate things, is to be
found, curiously enough, in a quatrain by Delille, cited by Paul van Tieghem,
Sentiment de la nature dans le préromantisme, 235: 'Avez-vous donc connu ces
rapports invisibles/Des corps inanimés et des êtres sensibles?/Avez-vous
entendu des eaux, des prés, des bois,/La muette éloquence et la secrète voix?'

'word' and 'glance'—which is to say, by perfume, colour, shape or sound—with Man, who in turn 'reads' them as symbols; but equally, through these same properties (as apprehended, it is true, by Man), they 'answer' or 'echo' *one another:* 'Comme de longs échos qui de loin se confondent. . . . Les parfums, les couleurs et les sons se répondent'. One could thus with equal truth transfer to *both* quatrains of *Correspondances* the comment made by Margaret Gilman on Nerval's *Aurélia:* 'the correspondences express, not a relationship between two worlds, but the fundamental unity of a single world'.[1] By way of further (and, as it seems to me, decisive) confirmation of this whole interpretation, I would mention the significant fact that Baudelaire, in his 1861 article on Wagner, should have chosen precisely to cite *both* these quatrains, when asserting

---

[1] *Idea of Poetry in France*, 218. The whole passage of *Aurélia* from which Miss Gilman here quotes a part, has many striking analogies with *Correspondances*, which moreover gain added significance in the light of my interpretation given above; the narrator is here speaking of the various hallucinations which mark what he believes to be his 'sacred initiation': '. . . tout dans la nature prenait des aspects nouveaux, et des voix secrètes sortaient de la plante, de l'arbre, des animaux, des plus humbles insectes, pour m'avertir et m'encourager . . . les objets sans forme et sans vie se prêtaient eux-mêmes aux calculs de mon esprit;— des combinaisons de cailloux, des figures d'angles, de fentes ou d'ouvertures, des découpures de feuilles, des couleurs, des odeurs et des sons, je voyais ressortir des harmonies jusqu'alors inconnues. "Comment, me disais-je, ai-je pu exister si longtemps hors de la nature et sans m'identifier à elle? Tout vit, tout agit, tout se correspond; les rayons magnétiques émanés de moi-même ou des autres traversent sans obstacle la chaîne infinie des choses créés; c'est un réseau transparent qui couvre le monde, et dont les fils déliés se communiquent de proche en proche aux planètes et aux étoiles . . ." ' (Pléiade, 1, 403). This text was first published at the beginning of 1855; the same notions (and vocabulary) of terrestrial inter-relationship may, however, be found in earlier texts by other writers. Thus Laprade (or his spokesman) declares of the eponymous *Hermia*: '. . . les rapports secrets des natures vivantes,/Par quel lien sacré, mystérieux, profond,/Chaque degré de l'être aux autres correspond,/Elle avait tout senti . . .' (*Odes et poëmes*, 1843, pp. 106–7); whilst Thoré, in an article published in 1836, 'L'Art des parfums', affirms for his part that 'tous les êtres sont liés entre eux par des analogies intimes et des corrélations essentielles' (*Ariel*, 13/4/1836). My interpretation of B.'s quatrains would offer, incidentally, a new explanation of the word 'familiers' in l. 4 ('Qui l'observent avec des regards familiers'): if these glances seem 'familiar' to Man, may it not simply be because (within the context defined in the second quatrain) Man and the objects of Nature are together members of one vast, inter-communing *family*? For other interpretations of this epithet, cf. J. Pommier, *Mystique de B.*, 22; L. J. Austin, *Univers poétique de B.*, 91 n. 1; J. Barrère, *RHLF*, 1967, p. 336.

what he claimed to be the 'self-evident' principle of synaesthesia:

. . . ce qui serait vraiment surprenant, c'est que le son *ne pût pas* suggérer la couleur, que les couleurs *ne pussent pas* donner l'idée d'une mélodie, et que le son et la couleur fussent impropres à traduire des idées. . . .[1]

Now if, in the first of the two quatrains from *Correspondances* he goes on to quote, Baudelaire had truly been describing 'mystical' correspondences, why (in the purely synaesthetic context of the Wagner article) should he not simply have contented himself with quoting the second quatrain alone?[2] It is true that this whole passage of the Wagner article ends (as we have already seen) with a reference to God as the prime originator of all earthly things and therefore of all analogies; but the analogies themselves being (as Baudelaire terms them) 'reciprocal', remain specifically of *this* world.[3]

By its very complexity and systematization, the 'doctrine' affirmed in the second quatrain ('Les parfums, les couleurs et les sons se répondent') goes, of course, considerably beyond anything Baudelaire may have suggested in his descriptions in the prose texts above-quoted, of the 'supernatural' state: in these, no particular or specialized importance is attached either to 'synaesthesia proper' (i.e. the actual transposition of impressions from one sensory medium to another, as experienced, e.g., during the hashish trance), or to the type of 'associative' synaesthesia (various distinct impressions from different senses presenting themselves simultaneously to the mind) ascribed to Hugo's poetry, and which Baudelaire had himself illustrated both in *Harmonie du soir* and in *La Chevelure*.[4] Be this

[1] *AR* 206; B. is in process of 'deducing' this principle from the analogies discerned between three independent accounts (Liszt's; the composer's; his own) of the *Lohengrin* Prelude (*AR* 203–8). For a discussion of the aesthetic implications of this curious experiment of B.'s, cf. A. G. Lehmann, *Symbolist Aesthetic*, 264; L. J. Austin, *Univers poétique de B.*, 273–5.

[2] Cf. the pertinent comment by L. Guichard, *La Musique et les lettres en France au temps du wagnérisme*, 77: 'Quant aux *Correspondances*, Baudelaire ne les cite dans son article [sur Wagner] que pour justifier l'impression en partie *visuelle* qu'il avait ressentie à l'*audition* de ce Prélude'.

[3] *AR* 206 (loc. cit.); cf. p. 175, above.

[4] Cf. pp. 82–3, 34–5, above. The first of the two categories here mentioned (the synaesthetic experience undergone during the hashish trance) should strictly be termed 'clinical synaesthesia', i.e. the '*involuntary* awareness of a sensation, perception or "image" of one sense which accompanies . . . the stimulation of a different sense', and should be distinguished from what is really

as it may, Baudelaire having here established (as Jean Pommier has noted) a whole general 'law' of synaesthesia,[1] then goes on, in his tercets, to furnish a partial 'application' of this law:

a *third* category, the type of subjective *literary* synaesthesia presented, under the guise of objectivity, in the tercets of the present sonnet. B. himself, it should be added, from his essentially philosophical standpoint in this sonnet, would see no reason to distinguish these three categories which would seem to him (as to so many of his contemporaries) to be simply alternative manifestations of the same general principle or 'law'.—I borrow the term 'clinical synaesthesia', with its definition, from the searching and comprehensive account of 'Literary Synesthesia' by G. O'Malley, *JAAC*, 1956-7 (art. cit.), p. 392 and passim. Cf. also, for the general literary aspects of this question, S. Ullmann, *Principles of Semantics*, 266-89, and *Semantics*, 216-18; D. J. Mossop, *B.'s Tragic Hero*, 74-9; E. Noulet, *Le Premier visage de Rimbaud*, 115-16, 144-55.

[1]*Mystique de B.*, 8. This formulation of B.'s, as well as being echoed (as we have seen, p. 211, above) in the Wagner article, is so to speak transposed into amorous hyperbole in the final verse of *Tout entière*: ' "... O métamorphose mystique/De tous mes sens fondus en un!/Son haleine fait la musique,/Comme sa voix fait le parfum!" ' (ll. 21-4; for a comment on these lines, cf. J. Pommier, op. cit., 12, 14, as also my art. cit., 'The Amorous Tribute', p. 105). In enunciating such a general theory, it should be added, B. had been preceded, inter alia, by Mme de Staël (*De l'Allemagne*, cit. C. Pichois, *B.*, 116 n. 242: 'Les analogies des divers éléments de la nature physique entre eux servent à constater la suprême loi de la création, la variété dans l'unité, et l'unité dans la variété. Qu'y a-t-il de plus étonnant, par exemple, que le rapport des sons et des formes, des sons et des couleurs?'), by Ballanche (cit. *FMCB* 297: 'Tous les sens se réveillent réciproquement l'un l'autre'), by Balzac (cit. L. Guichard, *Musique et lettres au temps du romantisme*, 327 and n. 132), by Karr (cit. D. P. Scales, *Karr*, 100 n. 40, and L. B. Dillingham, *Gautier*, 307-8), but above all by Hoffmann, in a passage from the *Kreisleriana* cited by B., in the Loève-Veimars version, in his *Salon de 1846*—a passage which is described by G. O'Malley (art. cit., p. 406), as 'the first distinct description of "genuine" synesthesia which has any claim to objectivity', and which must certainly have been a primary source for our present sonnet, since it anticipates so many of its elements, including the specific image of the *oboe* linked with the *scent* of marigolds: 'Ce n'est pas seulement en rêve, ... c'est encore éveillé, lorsque j'entends de la musique, que je trouve une analogie et une réunion intime entre *les couleurs, les sons et les parfums*. Il me semble que toutes ces choses ont été engendrées par un même rayon de lumière, et qu'elles doivent se réunir dans un merveilleux concert. L'odeur des soucis bruns et rouges produit surtout un effet magique sur ma personne. Elle me fait tomber dans une profonde rêverie, et j'entends alors comme dans le lointain les sons graves et profonds du hautbois' (cit. *CE* 97-8—my italics; cf. J. Pommier, op. cit., 8 and 164 n. 20). I say 'in the Loève-Veimars version' advisedly: not only does the German original specify 'dark-red carnation' rather than 'brown and red marigolds', but the so-called 'oboe' is there a basset-horn! (Grisebach ed., 1, 46, cit. H. W. Hewett-Thayer, *Hoffmann*, 163-4 n. 25).

Il est des parfums frais comme des chairs d'enfants,
Doux comme les hautbois, verts comme les prairies,
—Et d'autres, corrompus, riches et triomphants,

Ayant l'expansion des choses infinies,
Comme l'ambre, le musc, le benjoin et l'encens,
Qui chantent les transports de l'esprit et des sens.

It will be seen that *perfumes* alone are here taken as starting-point for the demonstration of the 'unity' of the three senses (as proclaimed in the previous verse); it is true that in lines 9 and 10 the other two senses (colour and sound) are introduced, but only as 'corresponding' terms whereby the qualities of the perfumes may be better conveyed.[1] A more obvious illustration to have chosen would of course have been that of the perennial relationship between colour and sound; and indeed it was (as we have seen) precisely with such analogies in mind that Baudelaire was later, in his Wagner article, to cite the quatrains of the present sonnet. The whole Wagner episode, however, constituted something of a special circumstance; until then, i.e. until 1860-1, Baudelaire may well have felt that already in his earlier writings he had sufficiently explored an area of inter-sensorial correspondence which in any case had been extensively colonized by other French writers—most notably by two particular groups: art critics, and pictorially minded music-lovers, to both of which, as it happens, he himself belonged.[2] Not that it

[1]Or, to adopt the convenient and widely favoured—if slightly grotesque—terminology suggested by I. A. Richards (*Philosophy of Rhetoric*, 96-7), the 'tenors', in these two lines, are various kinds of perfumes, whilst the 'vehicles' are drawn from other sensory domains: colour, sound and (perhaps) touch.

[2]A keen interest in both these aspects of synaesthesia had been displayed already in the eighteenth century; see G. O'Malley, art. cit., 399-406. Among the innumerable nineteenth-century practitioners of the two genres, one might cite particularly, for their connections with B.: Hoffmann, Balzac, G. Sand, Gautier, Laprade (*Hermia, Odes et poëmes*, 1843, p. 132: the 'concert de couleurs' offered up by Nature to the sun). As to B.'s own writings, the main example of the first category (colour described in terms of sound) is of course the chapter 'De la Couleur' of the *Salon de 1846*, with its profusion of musical images and its declared criterion of 'melodiousness' (*CE* 96-7, 94; cf. pp. 79-80, above); other examples, mostly from the two early *Salons*, are noted by J. Pommier, *Mystique de B.*, 4 and 162-3 n. 10. For the converse process, cf., in addition to the Wagner article, the passage from Hoffmann's *Kreisleriana* cited in the *Salon de 1846* as expressing 'perfectly' B.'s own ideas (*CE* 97-8; reprod. in extenso p. 212 n. 1, above), and the significant comment made in the course of *La Fanarlof*

should be assumed that even within the present (olfactory) sphere, Baudelaire was by any means an innovator; Senancour, Hoffmann, George Sand, Thoré, were among previous writers who had argued the particular importance or significance of perfumes within the general scheme of inter-sensorial relationships.[1] It would seem nevertheless that for Baudelaire the olfactory sense held a more special imaginative potency than perhaps for any other writer before or since.[2] At all events it will be observed that Baudelaire, in these tercets, presents his perfumes in two distinct groups, which in turn imply two distinct forms of synaesthetic imagery. First, in lines 9 and 10, there are the perfumes specified only in terms of their

---

(first pub. Jan. 1847): 'Ceux-là seuls peuvent me comprendre à qui la musique donne des idées de peinture' (ed. C. Pichois, p. 82). Finally one must mention the special case of the hashish-experiences described both by B. and Gautier ('Les sons ont une couleur, les couleurs ont une musique', etc.); cf. *PA* ed. C. Pichois, 37–8, 57, 87, 120.

[1] For Senancour, cf. *Oberman*, ed. A. Monglond, II, 164 and n., and III, 80 n. For Hoffmann, cf. J. Pommier, *Mystique de B.*, 7. For George Sand, cf. *Consuelo*, ed. L. Cellier and L. Guichard, II, 246 and n. (but cf., in this respect, p. 195 n. 1, above: a limiting concept here is that of the 'language of flowers'). For Thoré, cf. 'L'Art des parfums', *Ariel*, 13/4/1836—an interesting and indeed prophetic essay which was to have its semi-humorous sequel in an anonymous article, 'Un nouvel Art—L'Osphrétique', which appeared in 1844 in *L'Illustration* (p. 294; cf. I. Massey, *MLN*, 1956, p. 204).

[2] 'Mon âme voyage sur le parfum comme l'âme des autres hommes sur la musique' (*Un Hemisphère dans une chevelure*, *PPP* 51). This is not, however, to say that perfume was necessarily the *dominant* sense for B.; cf. the sage comment by L. J. Austin (*Univers poétique de B.*, 294–5) on the wide range of B.'s sensibility, the richness of his 'gamut of sensations'. For the role played by perfume in B.'s writings, see the chapter 'Parfum, donc souvenir' of J. Prévost's book (pp. 217–23)—as also L. J. Austin, op. cit., 220–35, and my discussion, pp. 31–7, 82–5, above, of *Parfum exotique*, *La Chevelure* and *Harmonie du soir*. It is perhaps significant, from our present standpoint, that in the *Salon de 1846* the utilitarian and philistine Republican should be denounced specifically as an 'ennemi des roses et des parfums' (*CE* 192), and that one of B.'s (many) complaints against the Belgians, towards the end of his life, should have been that their flowers lacked all scent and that the sole and pervading odour of their capital was that of 'soft soap': 'jugez ce que j'endure dans un pays où les arbres sont noirs et *où les fleurs n'ont aucun parfum*!' (*CG* IV, 312); 'Les odeurs des villes . . . Bruxelles sent le savon noir . . . Peu de parfums' (*Pauvre Belgique*, *OP* III, 26; the same idea is repeated, on another page of this MS., ibid., 24, but within a context—further and contrasting examples of the topography of odours—which brings a reminiscence of the 'tropical paradise' and of ll. 29–30 of *La Chevelure*: 'Il y a des îles tropicales qui sentent la rose, le musc ou l'huile de coco'; cf., in this latter connection, p. 260 n. 1, below).

distinctive reminders of other senses:[1] perfumes having the sweet *sound* of oboes, the *colour* of green meadows, the cool *freshness* of children's skin;[2] these might be termed 'genuine', or 'authentic', synaesthesias.[3] And second, in the remaining four lines, there are those others—explicitly named this time: amber, musk, benjamin, incense—that evoke moral ideas as well as impressions of other senses: ideas of *corruption, richness, triumph, infinitude,* as well as various sensations inextricably bound up with these ideas (e.g. richness of colour, expansiveness felt as a 'growth' or measured in a vista[4]). This perhaps is what Baudelaire had in mind when he wrote in his articles on Delacroix and Gautier that at moments of supernaturally heightened sensibility, perfumes 'tell of whole worlds of ideas' or 'provoke corresponding thoughts and memories';[5] and indeed to the extent that such analogies partake of traditional moral symbolism, rather than of strict inter-sensorial transposition, one might well suggest that in the last four lines of *Correspondances,* Baudelaire is in effect sketching out a miniature 'symbolique des parfums', to match the 'symbolique des couleurs' fleetingly adumbrated in the *Salon de 1846* and in *La Fanfarlo.*[6]

Looking back over this whole intricate sonnet, we note that while in its progression or 'structure' it may show an increasing particularization or specialization of the theme announced at the outset, there is in fact no interruption or contradiction, no true 'hiatus', within the essentially continuous if somewhat cryptic poetic

[1]Cf. A. Fairlie, *B.: FM,* 21; J. Prévost, *B.,* 221–2; J. Pommier, *Mystique de B.,* 9.

[2]The 'freshness' may be visual rather than tactile; cf. J. Pommier, ibid.

[3]Cf. C. F. Roedig, 'B. and Synesthesia', *Kentucky Foreign Lang. Quarterly,* 1958, pp. 133–4.

[4]Cf., however, J. Pommier, *Mystique de B.,* 72: '. . . les parfums . . . ne traduisent-ils pas, quand il sont "riches" et "triomphants", les "transports de l'esprit" humain, dont ils ont, dirait-on, l'infinie "expansion"?' I would add that for A. Adam (*FMA* 271, 274), the moral division is on the contrary between the perfumes of ll. 9 and 10, on the one hand, which display a world of 'purity' and 'innocence', and those of ll. 11–14, on the other, which lead us into regions of 'sin' and 'corruption'. This main division, whatever its precise significance, is clearly indicated by B. ('il est des parfums . . . D'*autres* . . .'); I feel it unlikely that he can truly have intended any *further* discriminations or subdivisions within these perfumes, such as are ingeniously suggested, e.g., by C. F. Roedig, art. cit., p. 130.

[5]*CE* 251, *AR* 165; cf. pp. 181, 205, above.

[6]Cf. pp. 81–2, above.

argument. Thus in the opening quatrain we have the metaphoric description of an obscurely 'articulate', obscurely sentient universe standing in some mysteriously symbolic relationship with Man; and in this relationship we may discern, in the light of other cognate texts, the outward projection and dramatization of certain personal sensations and emotions, experienced at particular and 'privileged' moments, whereby external objects appear, in their sharpened vividness, to assume a positive 'attitude' towards the observer, to acquire for him a unique symbolic potential; in a word, we may here feel Baudelaire to be 'objectifying' the essential subjectivity of the 'supernatural' state. In the second quatrain (arguing, perhaps from the perceptions gained at such privileged moments), Baudelaire proclaims the inextricable and 'synaesthetic' inter-relationship of three specific qualities of external objects: perfume, colour, sound— but in terms that not only imply some vaster 'unity' embracing *all* forms and creatures within the 'temple' or 'forest' of Nature, but that also tacitly prolong the Man-centred symbolism of the first quatrain. This latter, 'humanist' bias emerges more clearly when we come to the tercets, with their singling-out of various perfumes to illustrate (as it would seem) the general 'law' proclaimed in the second quatrain ('Les parfums, les couleurs et les sons se répondent') Now if the successive analogies here invoked by Baudelaire were indeed purely and strictly of a synaesthetic order, then it could perhaps fairly be argued (as the second quatrain appears to suggest) that the experience of sense-transfer merely registers or confirms (or introjects) within the mind of Man, a relationship between objects that already exists, independently and objectively, in the external world. But it is in fact only in lines 9 and 10 that the perfumes are truly defined in terms of other sensory stimuli; thereafter, in the remaining four lines of the sonnet, the area of 'correspondence' is extended beyond the reciprocal domains of colour and sound, to embrace the whole complex of Man's sensuous and 'spiritual' experience: the analogies are now of a 'moral', abstract or emotive order, and what they record is a common *association* or *idea* ('corruption', 'richness', 'triumph'), which obviously demands for its realization the presence of a human observer, an *individual* man to whom, as he wends his way through the symbolic forest, the objects of Nature may confusedly 'speak' (or 'sing', if they are perfumes). In theory (i.e. according to the strict doctrine of universal analogy), Man may be but one participant within the vast harmonious concourse of all

things in Nature; in fact (i.e. in Baudelaire's version) it is through
Man or *within* Man alone that this harmony can be consciously
apprehended and 'recorded', by him alone that it can be transcribed.[1]
Thus we may here see Baudelaire moving some way towards the
notion he will later affirm in a passage of his *Salon de 1859*: that in
the absence of some human observer or interpreter, the whole
manifest order and harmony of Nature, would become as if non-
existent.[2] But in that text (as we have seen), this principle is linked,
in passing, with a specifically *literary* theory of 'correspondences';
and it is in this further direction also, as my next chapter will show,
that the present sonnet significantly leads.

4. A THEORY OF METAPHOR

Baudelaire's first mention of *correspondances* occurs, some two years
before the publication of the famous sonnet, in the first of the three
articles devoted to the *Exposition universelle 1855*. Having, in his
opening paragraph, affirmed the Providential 'hierarchy' reigning
within God's universe,[3] Baudelaire next applies himself, in the context of this '*Universal* Exhibition' of the products of *all* nations, to
refuting certain hidebound 'doctrinaires' and inveterate 'systematiz-
ers'.[4] More specifically, as he inveighs against the 'modern Winckel-
mann' whose 'rules' do not admit the existence of other than purely
classical forms of Beauty, Baudelaire goes on to categorize the
deficient learning of this 'sworn professor' in terms, precisely, of an
implied doctrine of 'correspondences':

. . . science barbouillée d'encre, goût bâtard, plus barbares que les
barbares, qui a oublié la couleur du ciel, la forme du végétal, le mouvement et l'odeur de l'animalité, et dont les doigts crispés, paralysés par la
plume, ne peuvent plus courir avec agilité sur l'immense clavier des
correspondances!

(*CE* 222)

---

[1]For the historical aspects of this (perennial) confusion between the objective
and the subjective, see G. O'Malley, art. cit., 400, 410–11.

[2]*CE* 333; cf. pp. 137–9, above.

[3]Cf. pp. 173–4, above.

[4]*CE* 220–4. For the personal significance of B.'s implicit denunciation here of
all aesthetic systems, see my art. cit., 'Les Esthétiques de B.', *RSH*, 1967, pp.
481–2, 495.

Baudelaire's arresting metaphor (probably adapted from a poem of
Hugo's) of the pedant whose 'writer's cramp' forbids him the truer
intuitive medium of the (musical) 'keyboard',[1] is significant less
perhaps for what it actually says, than for what it *suggests* in relation
to his other writings of the period. Certainly one finds tacitly implied a general context recalling that of the *Correspondances* sonnet;
here as there, within the general framework (established at the outset of the article) of a widely analogic universe, specific relationships
are hinted between, on the one hand, the colours, shapes, movements
and scents of the external world and, on the other, the observer who
apprehends and assimilates these in all their vivid immediacy. But
the observer is now no longer 'Man in general'; rather would it
seem that Baudelaire here has in mind, as the antithesis of his
dessicated pedant, some poet-critic able intuitively to respond to
the 'colour of the sky', the 'form of plants', the characteristic movement and odour of the animal world, but above all having un-
inhibited access to the wealth of analogies that Nature places, so to
speak, at his disposal. The image of the 'keyboard' clearly lends
itself particularly well to such a notion: as here fleetingly (if vividly)
sketched by Baudelaire, it invites us to imagine the gifted 'player'
seated before his 'vast' instrument, sounding the 'keys' which then
call up for him the exactly equivalent or *corresponding* 'notes', and
from these elements, as he performs his 'runs' with such agile

[1] Cf. *Pan* (*Feuilles d'automne,* 1831; concluding verse): 'Car, ô poètes saints!
l'art est le son sublime,/. . . Redit par un écho dans toute créature,/Que sous vos
doigts puissants exhale la nature,/Cet immense clavier!' (Pléiade, 1, 805; cit. M.
Gilman, *Idea of Poetry in France,* 212). This poem of Hugo's presents several
other analogies with texts of B.'s: the line above-quoted,'Redit par un écho dans
toute créature', is recalled, in a very similar context, in l. 35 of *Les Phares*: '. . .
un écho redit par mille labyrinthes'; the injunction 'Enivrez-vous de tout!',
together with the attendant natural imagery so comprehensively evoked by Hugo,
reappears (somewhat transformed in tone, it is true) in the prose poem *Enivrez-
vous, PPP* 123–4; finally, as already noted (p. 198 n. 1, above), we have in Hugo's
hemistich 'Le monde, c'est son temple', one of the many antecedents for the
opening hemistich of *Correspondances.* A. Adam, however, *FMA* 272–3, sees as
the 'direct source' for B.'s 'clavier' image, this translation of a passage from Hoffmann's *Das Sanctus*: 'Il m'a toujours semblé que la nature nous avait placés sur
un immense clavier dont nous touchons sans cesse les cordes'. Cf. also: (a) this
couplet from Laprade's *Eleusis*: 'La main qui de leurs nids chasse les vieux
Démons,/Va toucher le clavier des vagues et des monts' (*Odes et poëmes,* 1843, p.
284); (b) Toussenel's phrase 'le clavier passionnel humain'—explained in my n.
1 to p. 219, below.

bravura, creating (or re-creating) whole 'musical' compositions.[1] Thus by implication Baudelaire would here seem essentially to be positing an *art* of correspondences—an art of which the elected *practitioner* (here unspecified, since the context remains that of a generalized relativist aesthetic) is in subsequent texts revealed to be the Poet himself, and the elected *medium,* the traditional and time-honoured devices of poetic language (simile, metaphor, allegory, symbol, and the rest).

Baudelaire's initial concern, however, during the period 1855–1858, would seem to be with the first only of these two aspects. Thus it will be recalled that what preceded and led into the gnomic phrase in *Puisque Réalisme il y a:* 'Ce monde-ci, dictionnaire hiéroglyphique', was the unequivocal definition of Poetry as being 'ce qu'il y a de plus réel, . . . ce qui n'est complètement vrai que dans *un autre monde*';[2] the deliberate conjunction of the two sentences (what is true 'in another world' only, followed immediately by a statement about *this* world) implies that it is specifically the poet who holds the key to the 'hieroglyphs' of this world—who can 'read' it as a 'dictionary' and thus decipher its meanings.[3] Altogether

---

[1]For a more explicit adaptation of this image to the notion of 'correspondences', cf. the above-mentioned poem by Hugo, *Pan*: the 'sacred poets' are there specifically invited to 'interchange' or mingle, with the 'isolated notes' everywhere to be heard in the exterior and visible universe which surrounds them, the images, thoughts and emotions drawn from their own 'interior world'—Art being (as Hugo concludes, in the verse already cited, p. 218 n. 1, above) nothing more than the 'sublime sound' which their 'powerful fingers' draw from the 'vast keyboard' of Nature (Pléiade, 1, 803; cf. the comment on these verses by M. Shroder, *Icarus*, 81: 'the poet "plays nature" as he would play a musical instrument, giving voice to the voices of the water and the wind'). One may think also of Toussenel's so-called 'clavier passionnel humain' (L. Thomas, *Toussenel*, 64–7) —the analogic scheme obtained by setting 'l'échelle passionnelle des êtres inférieurs [i.e. animals]' in precisely calibrated relation to 'l'échelle passionnelle de l'homme'; it will be noted that here as in the B. text, the 'clavier' combines within itself both Nature *and* Man.

[2]*OP* I, 299; cf. p. 177, above.

[3]It will be noted that B. has here adapted to a new purpose the metaphor (external Nature as a 'dictionary') invoked in respect of Delacroix in 1846, and explained (in Delacroix' meaning) in 1859; in its present implication, the dictionary is 'consulted' for its actual (hieroglyphic) 'meanings', rather than for the means of expression it affords the artist; it is thus here, properly, a dictionary of 'definitions', rather than a 'translating', Nature-to-Man dictionary. (Cf. pp. 77 n. 2, and 131, above). For a further contemporary variant of this same analogy, cf. the text by Fromentin (*Une année dans le Sahel*, 1859) cit. B. Gheerbrant

more explicit, however, regarding the Poet's role, is the long letter to Toussenel of 21 January 1856, in which Baudelaire acknowledges the gift of a book by the latter—a book which Jean Pommier has identified for us as the third volume of *Le Monde des oiseaux*.[1] Here are the two passages from Baudelaire's letter which are most relevant from our present standpoint; first:

Ce qui est positif, c'est que vous êtes poëte. Il y a bien longtemps que je dis que le poëte est souverainement intelligent, qu'il est *l'intelligence* par excellence,—et que *l'imagination* est la plus *scientifique* des facultés, parce que seule elle comprend l'analogie universelle, ou ce qu'une religion mystique appelle *la correspondance*.

(*CG* I, 368)

And second, a page or so later, after questioning Toussenel's excessive deference to Fourier:

L'homme raisonnable n'a pas attendu que Fourier vînt sur la terre pour comprendre que la Nature est un *verbe*, une allégorie, un moule, un *repoussé*, si vous voulez. Nous savons cela, et ce n'est pas par Fourier que nous le savons; —nous le savons par nous-mêmes, et par les poëtes.

(*CG* I, 370)

One thing that is curious in these two passages is that they elaborate (for Toussenel's benefit) a point Toussenel himself had made in the opening pages of his previous and second volume (published at the very beginning of that same year 1855[2]). Toussenel had there spoken of the uncanny and significant resemblances (both physical and moral) supposedly linking birds and humans:

B. *Critique d'art*, 154 n.: 'Le monde extérieur est comme un dictionnaire: c'est un livre rempli de répétitions et de synonymès; beaucoup de mots équivalents pour la même idée. Les idées sont simples, les formes multiples; c'est à vous de choisir et de résumer'. B. himself, who seems to have had a quite particular fondness for this image (cf. the comment by W. T. Bandy and C. Pichois, *BDC* 68 n. 1), applies it, equally, in other spheres than the present one—i.e. to his own book of poems (original version of *FM* 'Dédicace', *FMCB* 276), and to mythology conceived as a repository of 'living hieroglyphs' (*Banville*, *AR* 354).

[1]See J. Pommier, *Mystique de B.*, 177–8 n. 137. All B.'s quotations and references are drawn, as Professor Pommier shows, from this third volume—which we may suppose from the entry date in *Bibliographie de la France* (15 Dec. 1855, s.v. No. 7784) to have been published around the beginning of Dec. 1855. It seems likely, however, that B. may, earlier, have received Toussenel's *second* volume; see p. 221, below.

[2]Cf. p. 241 and n. 3, below.

. . . cette similitude de traits et de caractères est si apparente, si parfaite, qu'elle a été entrevue dès l'origine par les poëtes de tous les climats et de toutes les littératures, et qu'elle a enfanté l'Apologue et la Comparaison.[1]

It will be seen that Toussenel does not merely credit poets with the perception of universal analogies, but suggests also an actual *continuity* between these analogies and certain forms of figurative language (apologue, simile); in this he goes beyond anything Baudelaire says in his letter, but in a direction which the latter was in fact to reach only (as we shall see) some two or three years later. Now this raises the question as to whether Baudelaire, at the time of writing his letter to Toussenel, may not previously have read the latter's second (as well as his third) volume. We shall see in a later chapter that there is in fact strong, if indirect, evidence to this precise effect;[2] but it would in any case have been natural enough that Baudelaire should have *received* a copy of the earlier volume, since the two writers shared certain common literary affiliations.[3] Moreover such a circumstance would serve to explain the slight embarrassment betrayed by Baudelaire in the opening sentences of his letter: having been reminded (one might thus suppose) by the arrival of the third volume, that he had not yet acknowledged the previous one, he hastens to repair the omission and to congratulate Toussenel on his 'book'—a term which could apply equally either to both volumes, or to the one last received, even though it may have been solely from the latter (this being the one he actually has to hand) that he is able to take his references . . .[4] Be this as it may, and although (as we have seen) Baudelaire may have found much to disagree with in Toussenel's fundamental moral and social assumptions,[5] the general Fourierist inspiration of the

[1]*Le Monde des oiseaux*, II, 4.

[2]See p. 241 and n. 3, below. I find no evidence, on the other hand, to suggest that B. had read the *first* volume, published some two years earlier, i.e. in 1853.

[3]See L. Badesco, *RSH*, 1957, p. 77.

[4]B.'s letter begins: 'Mon cher Toussenel, je veux absolument vous remercier du cadeau que vous m'avez fait. Je ne connaissais pas le prix de votre livre, je vous l'avoue ingénument et grossièrement' (*CG* I, 367). (Perhaps, if my suppositions are correct, we should, for 'ingenuously', read '*dis*ingenuously' . . .).

[5]As also perhaps in his specific analogies—with their inflexibly didactic and tendentiously ideological character: the shrike, symbolizing the gendarme; the magpie, the informer; the vulture, the high financier, etc. (Examples given by J. Pommier, op. cit., 65; cf. also the withal admiring characterization of

book, its whole underlying postulate of a vast, universal and 'hierarchical' system of analogies, would seem to have furnished a welcome opportunity or pretext for bringing together certain ideas which in their written formulation at least, had previously been dispersed or inchoate. More clearly, then, than the conjoined formulas of *Puisque Réalisme il y a,* the two passages from the letter to Toussenel show that for Baudelaire the poet has now acquired a highly significant status within the scheme of universal analogy or *correspondance;* if he is deemed to be supremely 'intelligent' (in the etymological sense of the word), it is precisely because, being gifted with *imagination,* he possesses the *science* of Nature's analogies, and thus alone perhaps can make fully known what other men (as the opening quatrain of *Correspondances* in effect tells us) only dimly perceive.[1]

I have quoted already the paragraph from the *Notes nouvelles sur Edgar Poe* of 1857 in which, paraphrasing the American author's *The Poetic Principle,* Baudelaire had linked the notion of correspond-ences with an explanation of the 'ideal' nature of poetic emotion. But a comment made on an earlier page of these same *Notes,* in the course of an eloquent paragraph on the primacy (for Poe, but also

---

Toussenel by Nadar, cit. C. Pichois, *B.,* 179; 'paradoxalement convaincu que la création animale se divise en bêtes à aimer et bêtes à ne pas aimer'). Yet disfigured though this nineteenth-century 'Catalogue des oiseaux' may be by certain irrational prejudices (e.g., a strident anti-semitism), it retains an engaging (and indeed Messiaen-like) enthusiasm and naivety, an exuberantly digressive elo-quence, a blunt frankness, which suffice to justify the no doubt genuine admira-tion expressed by B. ('Il y a bien longtemps . . . que je n'ai lu quelque chose d'aussi *absolument instructif et amusant*'). For his explicit disagreements with Toussenel, see p. 151, above.

[1]B. might indeed here be regarded as taking a stage further the implied 'argument' of the *Correspondances* quatrain, with its *'confuses* paroles' and 'regards familiers' vaguely 'beckoning' to Man *in general,* as he passes through Nature's symbolic forest. A significant analogy here is with a Jouffroy passage (cf. p. 229 n. 1) in which very similar notions are expressed through the same two words ('intelligent', 'savants'—cf. 'scientifique') taken in their etymological sense: 'La matière est un hiéroglyphe qui n'a de valeur que pour ce qu'il exprime . . . Cette intelligence naturelle . . . est d'abord confuse . . . les plus savants sont ceux qui ont déchiffré le plus grand nombre de symboles' (*Cours d'esthétique,* cit. L. J. Austin, *Univers poétique de B.,* 160–1). It is in this (again, etymological) sense (cf. Gilman, *Idea of Poetry in France,* 256) that the imagination is deemed the 'most scientific' of all the faculties—having already previously (in the *Exposition universelle, CE* 234: 'l'imagination, cette reine des facultés') been declared to be paramount among them.

for Baudelaire) of the imagination, affords a truer guide to Baudelaire's own personal thought; here once again, the creative or poetic
imagination is vested, in respect of 'correspondences and analogies',
with special and indeed 'quasi-divine' powers of intuition:

L'Imagination est une faculté quasi divine qui perçoit tout d'abord, en
dehors des méthodes philosophiques, les rapports intimes et secrets des
choses, les correspondances et les analogies.

(Notes nouvelles sur Edgar Poe, NHE xv*)*

In attributing this opinion to Poe (as also perhaps in speaking, some
years earlier in his essay of 1852, of the American writer's tendency
to 'assimilate the moral to the physical'[1]), Baudelaire may perhaps
have had in mind a passage in the *Marginalia* which is almost
exactly echoed in one of the very first of the *Tales—The Purloined
Letter*—that we know Baudelaire to have read:[2]

There are some facts in the physical world which have a really wonderful analogy with others in the world of thought, and seem thus to give
some color of truth to the (false) rhetorical dogma, that metaphor or
simile may be made to strengthen an argument, as well as to embellish
a description.[3]

Although Poe's concern here is with the dialectical rather than the
imaginative use of language, he does establish a certain provisional
relationship between the doctrine of correspondences and the
rhetorical devices of metaphor and simile, which may well have
prompted his French translator to speculate more comprehensively
along the same lines—to the extent, ultimately, of affirming (what
is of course nowhere to be found in the Poe texts[4]) that in metaphor
and simile we have the permanent *demonstration* (rather than simply
the occasional illustration) of the 'really wonderful analogy' affirmed
between the material world and the immaterial. In this connection,

[1] *Edgar Allan Poe, OP* I, 287.

[2] By virtue of the fact that it figures in the 1845 edition of the *Tales*, which
in turn was one of the few texts of Poe's of which B. had first-hand acquaintance
before writing his 1852 essay; see W. T. Bandy, *RHLF*, 1967, p. 333.

[3] *Marginalia* CCXV, *Literati etc.*, 1850, p. 588; cf. *The Purloined Letter, Works*,
1850, I, 276, and for B.'s (completely literal) translation of this latter passage,
HE 71.

[4] But which we *have* seen (p. 221, above) to be implied already in the 2nd
volume of Toussenel's *Le Monde des oiseaux;* cf. also, in this connection, the
Lamartine text (from the *Voyage en Orient) cit. p. 229 n. 3, below.

I would first cite a brief statement, figuring within the *Salon de 1859*, which in other respects might seem almost the reformulation of the earlier passage above-quoted (from the *Notes nouvelles sur Edgar Poe*), with its similar 'definition'of the creative imagination:

C'est l'imagination qui a enseigné à l'homme le sens moral de la couleur, du contour, du son et du parfum. Elle a créé, au commencement du monde, *l'analogie et la métaphore*.[1]

On a later page of this same *Salon,* the point is made once again, albeit in passing, when within his denunciation of 'Nature without Man',[2] Baudelaire interpolates, somewhat gratuitously, an allusion to simile, metaphor and allegory, i.e. to the tools of the writer rather than of the landscape painter who is strictly here in question:

Je sais bien que l'imagination humaine peut, par un effort singulier, concevoir un instant la nature sans l'homme, et toute la masse suggestive éparpillée dans l'espace, sans un contemplateur pour en extraire la comparaison, la métaphore et l'allégorie.

(*CE* 333)

Baudelaire goes on to stress that the whole inspirational quality of Nature, its whole 'order' and 'harmony', would be as if non-existent, if in fact (as well as in theory) one were to remove from the scene the human 'contemplator' aforementioned—from which it in turn follows that the true artist being unwilling merely to 'copy' Nature, will seek rather to express through his painting the actual *feelings* inspired in him by his chosen 'site'. Now it would clearly be inappropriate, on the strength merely of Baudelaire's use of the words 'metaphor' and allegory, to transfer bodily to the poet this whole 'code' here laid down for the artist in his relationship with Nature; there is after all an essential difference of kind— though both may be loosely grouped as varieties of aesthetic imagination—between the arts of literary analogy, and the emotive and 'poetic' qualities of a landscape. Thus the painter's primary subject remains the landscape itself—however much he may choose to manipulate his colour-harmonies and distribute his points of emphasis according to his 'feeling' about a landscape (rather than his photographic recollection of its details); whereas the poet-observer, 'extracting' similes, metaphors and allegories from Nature,

[1] *CE* 274; my italics.
[2] See my previous chap., pp. 137–9, above.

will in the last analysis be concerned mainly with the ideas and emotions which the objects of Nature convey or represent. This is not true, of course, of the purely descriptive poet (who would be the truer counterpart in literature of the landscape painter); but from Baudelaire's characterizations of Nature as a 'masse suggestive éparpillée dans l'espace', one infers that his (absent) observer would have utilized his similes, etc., for symbolist rather than impressionistic purposes.[1] Such certainly is the implication of an important passage of the article on Théophile Gautier—published a month or two before the *Salon de 1859*—in which for the first time Baudelaire *explicitly* links literary with universal analogies, *explicitly* relates the arts of metaphor to the wider 'philosophic' doctrine of *Correspondances*:

Si l'on réfléchit qu'à cette merveilleuse faculté de style, Gautier unit une immense intelligence innée de la *correspondance* et du symbolisme universels, ce répertoire de toute métaphore, on comprendra qu'il puisse sans cesse, sans fatigue comme sans faute, définir l'attitude mystérieuse que les objets de la création tiennent devant le regard de l'homme. Il y a dans le mot, dans le *verbe*, quelque chose de *sacré* qui nous défend d'en faire un jeu de hasard. Manier savamment une langue, c'est pratiquer une espèce de sorcellerie évocatoire. C'est alors que la couleur parle, comme une voix profonde et vibrante; que les monuments se dressent et font saillie sur l'espace profond; que les animaux et les plantes, représentants du laid et du mal, articulent leur grimace non équivoque; que le parfum provoque la pensée et le souvenir correspondants; que la passion murmure ou rugit son langage éternellement semblable.

(*AR* 164-5)

This passage (from which I have already had occasion to quote, in another context[2]) carries a stage further the notions adumbrated in the opening quatrain of *Correspondances*—or rather, adapts these to the specific standpoint of the creative artist. Thus when (as here)

---

[1] This is perhaps the place to stress that the terms 'symbole', 'allégorie', 'emblème', 'mythe', 'hiéroglyphe', 'image', etc., though sometimes given more precise and specialized connotations by B., are more often than not used by him quite interchangeably; cf. L. J. Austin, *Univers poétique de B.*, 162-70; M. Gilman, *Idea of Poetry in France*. 258-9—as also, for two specific examples, pp. 209, above, and 240 and n. 2, below. In this B. was not a pioneer; the same comprehensive standpoint had been adopted by Pierre Leroux in an article of 1834 (on 'Allegory') in the *Encyclopédie nouvelle*; see D. O. Evans, *Le Socialisme romantique*, 135.

[2] P. 205, above.

the man who passes through the temple of Nature is a poet, he is equipped in a special sense, Baudelaire implies, to interpret the 'confuses paroles' and 'regards familiers' of the objects of creation, the mysterious attitudes they assume under his glance; the obscure inter-relations which by metaphysical definition link all these objects, transpose themselves for him into metaphors which crowd into his mind and under his pen. Animals and plants accordingly become the symbolic representatives of human ugliness and evil; prefumes suggest the (human) ideas and memories which 'corres-pond' (subjectively) with them;[1] colours take on a vibrant and 'speaking' eloquence of their own; buildings assume, as they rear up or stand out against the background of space, a near-human vitality; certain sounds seem in their roar or murmur to be the language of human passion. It will be noted from this enumeration (in which I have intentionally stressed the *human* element common in varying degrees to all the examples cited) that Baudelaire has here chosen to represent the 'supernatural' state as being the par-ticular privilege of the poet, at the moment of creation—or rather, of those poets who are so fully masters of the arts of language that they can be said almost to be practising a kind of 'incantatory magic'. This 'sorcellerie évocatoire' of which Baudelaire speaks is surely, in the context, not simply the poet's power to 'conjure up', as if by 'incantation', the objects of Nature themselves, but rather his ability *to combine* this act of 'evocation' with the vivid and 'super-natural' revelation of the human and personal symbolism latent within each object; it is by this token above all that the poet's way of looking at Nature becomes an act of truly 'magical' re-creation.[2]

All this becomes fully explicit in a long passage, written some two years later, of the article on Victor Hugo. In the opening paragraph

[1] The word 'souvenir' indicates that B. here has in mind the *personal* emotions stirred up, through association of ideas, by a particular odour (cf. the poems discussed above: *Parfum exotique, La Chevelure),* as well as the more general type of analogy ('Il est des parfums frais comme des chairs d'enfants, etc.') asserted in the tercets of *Correspondances.*

[2] The phrase 'sorcellerie évocatoire'—which in this, or another analogous form, crops up in three other texts of this period: *Exposition universelle 1855, CE* 226; *Fusées* XI, *JI* 23, 24; *Poëme du haschisch, PA* 52—seems almost to have assumed, for B., a certain 'incantatory' power of its own! But in none of these contexts does the formula imply, for me, that continuity with occultist tradition, dis-cerned in it by J. Crépet and G. Blin, *JI* 221-2 (cf. G. Blin, *Sadisme de B.,* 97-100).

of this passage (as will be recalled from my previous section[1]),
Baudelaire begins his tribute to Hugo's rare 'poetic faculties' by
evoking in general terms Man's 'situation' in regard to Nature.
Thus Nature in its 'mysteriousness' (that 'mystery of life' which
Hugo is so uniquely qualified to convey in poetry) is declared to
impinge upon our minds through the various sense impressions at
our disposal (form, attitude, movement, light, colour, sound,
harmony), and in accordance with our relative sensitivity to these
impressions; in Hugo's case, however, his responsiveness is so
profoundly universal and sensitive that it allows him to convey
simultaneously in his poetry impressions derived from all senses, to
blend them into what Baudelaire calls 'la morale des choses', to
render (without robbing them of their 'indispensable obscurity') the
most fugitive and complex sensations.[2] Thus far, it might seem that
Baudelaire was concerned wholly with Hugo's descriptive or impressionistic talent, his ability to render into poetry the richness of
our immediate sensory perceptions of Nature; but as in the Gautier
article, the further development of Baudelaire's argument shows his
true preoccupation to be the symbolic and 'human' aspects of Nature
—that is, the way in which Nature may seem to Man to reflect, to
'correspond' with, his own human experience. Thus when Baudelaire praises Hugo's ability to transmit not only the most direct
sensations drawn from visible nature, but also the most fugitive,
the most complex, the most *moral* sensations conveyed by 'the
visible being', by 'so-called inanimate Nature', it transpires that he
has in mind, exactly as in the Gautier article, the hallucinatory,
symbolic and 'human' aspect that certain animals, plants or material
objects may take on as we contemplate them:

. . . non-seulement, la figure d'un être extérieur à l'homme, végétal ou
minéral, mais aussi sa physionomie, son regard, sa tristesse, sa douceur,
sa joie éclatante, sa haine répulsive, son enchantement ou son horreur;
enfin, en d'autres termes, tout ce qu'il y a d'humain dans n'importe
quoi, et aussi tout ce qu'il y a de divin, de sacré ou de diabolique.[3]

---

[1]Pp. 204–5, above.

[2]*AR* 303–4.

[3]*AR* 304. In thus describing Hugo's imagery, B. will no doubt have had
particularly in mind—as well as the earlier *A Albert Durer*—the elder poet's
two most recent collections, *Les Contemplations* (1856), the first series of *La
Légende des siècles* (1859). But it is interesting to record that as far back as 1829
Pierre Leroux (in an article later to be reprinted in the *Œuvres* of 1850–1) had

It is in the ensuing paragraph that Baudelaire for the first time explicitly formulates (and with a new and resolute *professionalism* of touch) the striking 'theory of metaphor'[1] towards which, as we have seen, he had been moving in several previous texts. He begins by reaffirming, in relation to such philosophers and mystics as Fourier, Swedenborg and Lavater, that special role, within the system of universal analogies, already imputed to poets in earlier texts—while here adding the consequential rider that 'only those who *are* poets can truly understand these things':

Ceux qui ne sont pas poëtes ne comprennent pas ces choses. Fourier est venu un jour, trop pompeusement, nous révéler les mystères de l'*analogie*. Je ne nie pas la valeur de quelques-unes de ses minutieuses découvertes, bien que je croie que son cerveau était trop épris d'exactitude matérielle pour ne pas commettre d'erreurs et pour atteindre d'emblée la certitude morale de l'intuition. Il aurait pu tout aussi précieusement nous révéler tous les excellents poëtes dans lesquels l'humanité lisante fait son éducation aussi bien que dans la contemplation de la nature. D'ailleurs Swedenborg, qui possédait une âme bien plus grande, nous avait déjà enseigné que *le ciel est un très-grand homme;* que tout, forme, mouvement, nombre, couleur, parfum, dans le *spirituel* comme dans le *naturel*, est significatif, réciproque, converse, *correspondant*. Lavater, limitant au visage de l'homme la démonstration de l'universelle verité, nous avait traduit le sens spirituel du contour, de la forme, de la dimension.

(*AR* 304–5)

'Extending the demonstration', Baudelaire arrives at another truth previously affirmed: 'tout est hiéroglyphique'[2]—but now goes on:

. . . nous savons que les symboles ne sont obscurs que d'une manière relative, c'est-à-dire selon la pureté, la bonne volonté ou la clairvoyance

---

noted, in the poems *Mazeppa* and *Fantômes,* Hugo's sense of 'la correspondance mystérieuse entre la forme des objets et leur essence intime' (cit. D. O. Evans, *Socialisme romantique,* 144). As to B.'s qualifying phrase here: 'la nature inanimée, ou dite inanimée', this recurs significantly in his obituary art. of 1863 on Delacroix; quoting anew, from the *Salon de 1859,* the explanation there given of Delacroix' metaphor 'La nature n'est qu'un dictionnaire', B. changes his original formula 'la nature extérieure' to 'la nature dite inanimée' (*AR* 10; cf. *CE* 280).

[1]This phrase, with its variant 'a doctrine of metaphor', I borrow from A. G. Lehmann's searching analysis (*The Symbolist Aesthetic,* 260–71) of this aspect of B.'s thought.

[2]Cf. p. 177, above.

native des âmes. Or qu'est-ce qu'un poëte (je prends le mot dans son acception la plus large), si ce n'est un traducteur, un déchiffreur?

(*AR* 305)

This latter question in itself poses nothing intrinsically new: the concept of the poet as the uniquely gifted interpreter of Nature, the 'seer' who perceives intuitively the hidden relationships binding the things of this world to another and 'truer' world beyond, goes back at least to the later eighteenth century,[1] and had only recently been given, by Victor Hugo himself in *Les Mages,* its most elaborate formulation of all.[2] What Baudelaire alone, however, seems fully to have perceived (perhaps, as I have suggested, through the speculations aroused in him by certain phrases of Poe's and Toussenel's) is that this special 'imaginative' gift of the poet could and should be related to *actual literary devices* of analogy, which thus become identical with the 'real' analogies already supposedly obtaining in the world of Nature outside:[3]

[1]Cf. the texts cited by M. Z. Shroder, *Icarus,* 81 (Joseph Warton, *The Enthusiast,* 1744; Mme de Staël); R. Vivier, *Originalité de B.,* 128 (Novalis), 129 (Sainte-Beuve, *Joseph Delorme,* Pensée XVIII—see ed. Antoine, 150), 239 (Sainte-Beuve, *Consolations: A mon ami Leroux*); by L. J. Austin, *Univers poétique de B.,* 160–1 (Jouffroy); by M. Gilman, *Idea of Poetry in France,* 136 (Soumet), 217 and 219 (La Morvonnais); by P. Laubriet, *Intelligence de l'art chez Balzac,* 305–7 and n. 99 (Ballanche, Balzac, Saint-Simon); by D. O. Evans, *Le Socialisme romantique,* 134 (Leroux).

[2]*Les Contemplations* (1856), Livre 6, XXIII; cf. especially ll. 425–6: 'A leur voix, l'ombre symbolique / Parle, le mystère s'explique' (ed. J. Vianey, III, 339; cit. M. Gilman, op. cit., 216). For a general comment on Hugo's 'Orphic mission', see M. Z. Shroder, *Icarus,* 67–9.

[3]Cf., however, in addition to the phrases above-quoted by Poe and Toussenel (*Le Monde des oiseaux,* II, 4), this strikingly prophetic passage from Lamartine's *Voyage en Orient* (first pub. 1835), to which I have referred already in connection with *Correspondances:* 'Il y a des harmonies entre tous les éléments, comme il y en a une générale entre la nature matérielle et la nature intellectuelle. Chaque pensée a son reflet dans un objet visible qui la répète comme un écho, la réfléchit comme un miroir, et la rend perceptible de deux manières: aux sens par l'image, à la pensée par la pensée; c'est la poésie infinie de la double création! Les hommes appellent cela comparaison: la comparaison c'est le génie. . . . Comparer c'est l'art ou l'instinct de découvrir des mots de plus dans cette langue divine des analogies universelles que Dieu seul possède, mais dont il permet à certains hommes de découvrir quelque chose. Voilà pourquoi le prophète, poète sacré et le poète, prophète profane, furent jadis et partout regardés comme des êtres divins' (ed. L. Fam, 199 and n.s.; cit. Y. Boeniger, *Lamartine et le Sentiment de la Nature,* 217).

Chez les excellents poëtes, il n'y a pas de métaphore, de comparaison ou
d'épithète qui ne soit d'une adaptation mathématiquement exacte dans la
ciconstance actuelle, parce que ces comparaisons, ces métaphores et ces
épithètes sont puisées dans l'inépuisable fonds de l'*universelle analogie*, et
qu'elles ne peuvent être puisées ailleurs.

(AR 305)

Thus literary analogy (and by extension, all aesthetic devices
involving some kind of expressive relation between things) become
the means whereby Man is able to apprehend the system of universal
correspondences, of 'hieroglyphic' truths, of which otherwise he
would only obscurely be aware; or, to put it another way, the master
poet who in a metaphor or simile ('Il est des parfums frais comme
des chairs d'enfants', for instance) embodies some newly discovered
analogic relationship, will in reality have drawn this correspondence
(which might have been thought to be of purely literary and subjective origin) from a vast, *pre-existing* system of analogies (an
'inexhaustible storehouse')—to which he gains access by forms of
intuition denied to other (and lesser) men. It is this second formulation that gives us, I believe, the truer insight into Baudelaire's
underlying preoccupations when framing this whole 'theory of
metaphor'. We must first, however, discount the continuing influence, as a determining factor in Baudelaire's thought, of the sonnet
Correspondances, which perhaps furnishes in this respect a somewhat
misleading antecedent. It may well be that in the 1861 edition of
Les Fleurs du Mal, Baudelaire did indeed so arrange the opening
poems of his first ('Spleen et Idéal') chapter, as to suggest by their
sequence that had the traveller through the forests of Nature been
the Poet, rather than Man in general, he would have found no
difficulty in understanding and interpreting those 'muffled' words,
those strangely 'familiar' glances, that issue from the 'living' and
symbolic 'pillars';[1] moreover since no such implication can be taken

---

[1]The necessary supposition here is that by the continuity of imagery between
the first and third, the second and third, and the third and fourth poems
respectively (i.e. *Bénédiction—Élévation, L'Albatros—Élévation, Élévation—
Correspondances)*, B. will have intended to convey to the reader a continuity
of *theme* similar to that which already links the first poem *(Bénédiction)* with
the second *(L'Albatros).* Thus from the fact that certain lines from the first
part of *Bénédiction* ('L'Enfant déshérité s'enivre de soleil, / Et dans tout ce
qu'il boit et dans tout ce qu'il mange / Retrouve l'ambroisie et le nectar
vermeil. / Il joue avec le vent, cause avec le nuage . . .') could be transferred
almost bodily to *Élévation;* that in both *L'Albatros* and *Élévation* the motif of

from the corresponding poem-sequence in the 1857 *Fleurs du Mal*,[1]
we might further legitimately conclude that the 1861 arrangement
truly mirrors the clear development in Baudelaire's ideas during
the period separating the two editions. Yet all this scarcely justifies
the common assumption that the present text (i.e. the passage from
the Hugo article) is simply the belated demonstration, within the
aesthetic sphere, of a *general* theory of analogy previously declared
only in a cryptic poetic version. It will be recalled that from the
outset of the present phase—or at least from 1855 onwards—
Baudelaire has been above all concerned to exalt the status of the
Poet within the scheme of correspondences as he now defines it.
Viewed in this light the final theory as expounded in the article on
Hugo, provides not so much an illustration (through the poet's
gift of metaphor) of the general doctrine of analogy, as an illustration
(through this general doctrine) of the supreme importance of the
Poet; it thus serves to complement more subtly Baudelaire's earlier
personal contribution (through such poems as *Bénédiction, Les
Phares, Sur 'Le Tasse en Prison', L'Albatros)* to the collective con-
solidation of the Romantic myth of the Artist ('Seer', 'Prophet',
'Demiurge', 'Unacknowledged Legislator', etc.), with his 'Orphic'
mission to lead or guide Mankind.[2] As for the logical contradictions
patent within Baudelaire's theory—the fact that it lends itself less

---

flight into a purer sky represents a privileged escape from the trammels of
earth; that the 'langage des fleurs et des choses muettes' of the final couplet of
Élévation, is by implication that precisely into which the 'confuses paroles' of
Correspondances resolve themselves—from all this one might argue a single
common theme, that of the Poet finding, through his ascension into the Ideal,
not only a release from the persecution and suffering he suffers in our world
here below, but also the power to interpret the true symbolic 'mysteries' of that
world. Cf., for certain of these presumed interconnections: *FMCB* 294; A.
Feuillerat, 'Architecture des *FM*', 226–7; M. Ruff, *Esprit du mal*, 290; D. J.
Mossop, *B.'s Tragic Hero*, 57, 63—but cf. also, for his sagacious reservations
concerning this whole question of 'l'architecture des *FM*' (a question I hope
myself to discuss fully in a forthcoming publication), the excellent introduction
by A. Adam to his recent edition of *FM, FMA* xiv–xv.

[1]The implicit connection between *Élévation* and *Correspondances* is admittedly
(as we have seen, pp. 195–6, above) to be found already in the 1857 text; there is,
however, no similar continuity, whether of imagery or of theme, between
Élévation and the poem originally preceding, i.e. *Le Soleil*, and the 1857 reader
thus has no reason to link the theme of the 'language' of Nature, with that of
the *generic* Poet.

[2]Cf. M. Z. Shroder, *Icarus*, 46–8.

well to the original and creative type of metaphor he clearly here has in mind, than to conventional symbols and myths;[1] the failure to allow for subjective variation such as would necessarily arise not only between one poet and another (however 'excellent', and even when working within the identical circumstance or context), but also within the work of a *single* poet, according to his mood[2]—these fall perhaps into a truer perspective if one allows that Baudelaire may have been concerned less with finding a place for poetic metaphor within a coherent universal system of analogy, than with extracting from that system an additional, almost hyperbolical justification for poetic metaphor in particular and poetic activity in general.

5. THE PRACTICAL SYMBOLIST:
MODES OF NATURE-SYMBOLISM

Such, then, in its various aspects, is Baudelaire's *theory* of Nature-symbolism; what, however, of its implications in practice? Which particular modes of symbolism will he have had in mind when formulating his theory, and which, in his own poetic practice, does he consciously favour? On the latter point, it must be said at once that since the theory was elaborated so relatively late in his career, its direct illustrations in his writings are relatively few; it is in any case rare with him—as indeed with most writers—for aesthetic theory to precede and determine actual literary practice. (The reverse is more often true: theory rationalizes practice retrospectively —where it does not compensate, unconsciously, for the latter's felt deficiencies.) There are, nevertheless, a few texts of this period, in which the images chosen by Baudelaire betray, in their formulation, a clear reference to some predetermined doctrine of analogy (which is not to say that in the first instance they did not arise quite spontaneously). I shall also refer briefly, hereafter, to certain of Baudelaire's earlier and less 'systematic' Nature-symbols— taking these, however, purely as illustrations or anticipations of his

[1] Inasmuch as the Poet, if drawing upon a *universal* 'fund' of analogies, in effect *re*discovers rather than discovers—thereby making manifest to all something of which all, vaguely or potentially, have 'knowledge'.

[2] For further discussion of certain of these contradictions, cf. J. Pommier, *Mystique de B.*, 98-9; M. Gilman, *RR*, 1948, pp. 31-2; A. G. Lehmann, *Symbolist Aesthetic*, 265-9; L. J. Austin, *Univers poétique de B.*, 165.

later theory, and not at all as indications, in themselves, of his attitudes towards external Nature.[1]

I must first stress an important distinction which needs clearly to be kept in mind in any discussion of Nature-symbols (i.e. of those symbols in which the analogy centres on some specific aspect— a landscape, an animal, a plant—of external Nature). Although Baudelaire in his article on Hugo, may have implied that the metaphors, similes and epithets drawn by the poet-'decipherer' from the 'inexhaustible storehouse of universal analogy', are specifically of the type which discerns symbols *in* Nature, he never-theless must equally have had in mind that other and converse type which draws symbols *from* Nature, in order to convey some human idea, some reality of inner human experience;[2] certainly in his own poetry we may find (as will be seen) copious examples of both types of symbolism.

I have already indicated one important respect in which Baude-laire as a Nature-symbolist differs from certain of his contemporaries (e.g. Lamartine and Hugo): while he may in principle appear to subscribe to both main theories of universal analogy—'mystical' no less than terrestrial, Swedenborgian no less than Fourierist—in practice he seems rarely indeed to be thinking in terms of specific analogies of the Swedenborgian type, i.e. linking Earth with Heaven; indeed, of such analogies we have so far encountered only the one instance furnished by the 1848–1851 version of *Le Vin des chiffon-niers*.[3] Almost equally rare in *Les Fleurs du Mal*, is overtly *didactic*

---

[1]Perhaps I should here make clear that I regard as entirely fallacious the view that from the mere classification of a writer's images (e.g. into sea-metaphors, forest-metaphors, etc.), one can make valid deductions as to his tastes, opinions, temperament, etc.; cf. in this connection the excellent article by Lillian H. Hornstein, 'Analysis of Imagery', *PMLA*, 1942, pp. 638–53. The proper approach in this domain is shown, on the contrary, in the complementary studies by J. Pommier and L. J. Austin, of the whole range and detail of B.'s symbolism: respectively, *La Mystique de B.* (Parts 3 and 4, 'L'Herméneutique' and 'L'Écriture figurative') and *L'Univers poétique de B.* (296–331, 'L'imagination de Baudelaire'). Cf. also M. Gilman, *RR*, 1948, pp. 32–5, and *Idea of Poetry in France*, 259–60; G. Hess, *Die Landschaft in Bs 'FM'*, 43–86.

[2]In the first type (to apply the terminology coined by I. A. Richards; cf. p. 213 n. 1, above), Nature supplies the 'tenor' of the metaphor; in the second, it supplies the 'vehicle' (the 'tenor' being, in this latter case, some aspect of human reality).

[3]Final lines, beginning 'Grandeur de la bonté de *Celui que tout nomme*' (my italics; cf. p. 92, above).

symbolism of the kind encountered, for instance, in the earlier Hugo—with Nature made to offer to Man sage precepts, 'sermons in stones' and the like; the sole examples in Baudelaire of such 'lessons' drawn from external Nature would seem to be the two poems *Les Hiboux* and *L'Homme et la mer*.[1] It is true that in his article on Hugo, Baudelaire speaks of the 'moral sensations' conveyed to us by 'so-called inanimate Nature'; but what he understands by this, as we have already seen, is simply the power of certain animals and plants to embody or 'incarnate' specific characteristics of Mankind, specific human qualities such as 'tenderness', 'joy' and 'enchantment' on the one hand, 'sadness', 'hatred' and 'horror' on the other[2]—a notion we should perhaps relate to that more positively affirmed in the sonorous preamble to the *Exposition universelle* 1855, with its vision of a securely hierarchical universe in which are to be found 'des plantes plus ou moins saintes, des formes plus ou moins spirituelles, des animaux plus ou moins sacrés'.[3] Other texts of this period nevertheless make clear that for Baudelaire himself the bias is decidedly towards the representation of ugliness and evil; thus in the essay on Gautier he declares that in those inspired

---

[1]For *L'Homme et la mer*, cf. pp. 104–6, above; for *Les Hiboux*, cf. my art. cit., 'B.: The Poet as Moralist', pp. 200–1. Among Hugo texts, one could cite particularly *A un riche* (*Les voix intérieures*, 1837), with its dead tree and herdsman's burnt-out fire reminding of passion one day to be spent, and its affirmation that 'Tout objet dont le bois se compose répond / A quelque objet pareil dans *la forêt de l'âme*' (Pléiade, I, 979, my italics; cf. ibid., 1467–8)—or, again, *Que la musique date du XVIᵉ siècle* (*Les Rayons et les ombres*, 1840), with its recommendation to the infant genius: 'Écoute la nature aux vagues entretiens. / Entends sous chaque objet sourdre la parabole. / Sous l'être universel vois l'éternel symbole . . .' (Pléiade, I, 1101–2; cf. ibid., 1575). Cf., for some earlier (eighteenth-century) examples of this specifically didactic interpretation of Nature, Paul van Tieghem, *Sentiment de la nature dans le préromantisme*, 258–60.

[2]*AR* 304; cf. p. 205, above.

[3]*CE* 219–20; cf. pp. 173–4, above, as also, for a detailed analysis of B.'s 'animal and vegetable symbolism', J. Pommier, op. cit., 74–9. We must here no doubt allow for the influence of those fully developed *systems* of (terrestrial) analogy evolved by Fourier and his disciple Toussenel. B. continues also, during this period, to invoke that 'symbolique des couleurs' which, as we have seen (pp. 81–2, above) had particularly excited his attention around 1846; cf. in this connection (as noted by J. Pommier, op. cit., 72–4), *Salon de 1859*, *CE* 278, 281; *Fusées* II, *JI* 9; *Le Peintre de la vie moderne*, *AR* 99, 102–3—as also, in the tercets of *Correspondances*, what I have suggested (p. 215, above) to be a miniature 'symbolique des parfums'.

moments when the masters of (poetic) language practise their 'sorcellerie évocatoire', 'les animaux et les plantes, *représentants du laid et du mal,* articulent leur grimace non équivoque'[1]—having already previously implied, in the letter to Toussenel written several years earlier, in 1856, that his own propensity to the 'Satanic' interpretation of Nature, is of long standing:

. . . j'ai pensé bien souvent que les bêtes malfaisantes et dégoûtantes n'étaient peut-être que la vivification, corporification, éclosion à la vie matérielle, des *mauvaises pensées* de l'homme.[2]

In all these cases, the poet-'decipherer' has already been confronted, as it were, with the spectacle of Nature, to which he then lends (through metaphor, etc.) a moral interpretation of his own; it may happen, however (and this is our converse type of symbolism), that Man rather than Nature is the starting-point for the image, with the poet now summoning up aspects of Nature the better to characterize forms of human behaviour. As a striking example of this tendency, one might take the final verses of the poem *Au Lecteur* (first published 1855), with its nameless monster representing *Ennui* and exceeding in hideousness and viciousness all the 'jackals', 'panthers', 'hound bitches', 'monkeys', 'scorpions' 'vultures', 'snakes', that similarly infest the loathsome 'menagerie' of human vices; or again, the actual title *Les Fleurs du Mal*—of which, however, the full symbolic (and theological) implications were to be realized only in the frontispiece designed by Félicien Rops for the 1866 volume, *Les Épaves,* with its accompanying commentary:

Sous le Pommier fatal dont le *tronc-squelette* rappelle la déchéance de la race humaine, s'épanouissent les *Sept Péchés capitaux,* figurés par des plantes aux formes et aux attitudes symboliques. Le Serpent, enroulé au bassin du squelette, rampe vers ces *Fleurs du Mal* . . .[3]

---

[1] *AR* 165—my italics.

[2] *CG* I, 370; cf. p. 152, above. Cf. also the reference, in *Les Bienfaits de la lune, PPP* 134, to the fondness of all 'lunatics' for 'les animaux sauvages et voluptueux qui sont les *emblèmes* de leur folie' (my italics). For a further analogy with Hugo, cf. this comment by A. Viatte, *Hugo,* 221, on the elder poet's far more comprehensive preoccupation with evil in (external) Nature: 'La nature, qu'ils [les romantiques] adorent, devient à ses yeux une géhenne. . . . Il a partout rencontré le Mal. . . .'

[3] Cit. *BDI,* 119; for the whole history of this frontispiece, and of the (abortive) project for a similar frontispiece to the second edition of *FM,* see ibid., 100-21, and illustrations nos. 108-18; cf. also J. Pommier, *Mystique de B.,* 74-5.

In coming now to those symbols which arise from whole landscapes (rather than from the fauna and flora which inhabit them),
I shall take first that type of (extended) metaphor which may be
considered the most authentically Baudelairian of all; the starting-
point here is the poet's own (or another's) state of mind, for which
is then evoked some equivalent and *imagined* aspect of Nature.[1]
Baudelaire was not, of course, the inventor of this (on the contrary)
highly traditional mode of symbolism, which had even (as L. J.
Austin has pointed out) received its formal 'consecration' in a
prophetic article of 1794 by Schiller.[2] An important Baudelaire text
here is the elaborate paragraph with which he concludes his article
of 1861 on the poetess Marceline Desbordes-Valmore. Although
the word 'symbol' is nowhere here pronounced, the use of the
epithet 'spirituel',[3] as well as the type of metaphor illustrated, show

---

[1]L. J. Austin *(Univers poétique de B.,* 19–20; cf. ibid., 172), has proposed that
the term 'symbolisme' be reserved for this type of imagery, which would thus
be clearly distinguished from what he would call 'la symbolique'—i.e. that
more traditional symbolism in which a transcendental or divine 'reality' is
expressed through a 'fixed' and conventional system of analogies with Nature.

[2]See L. J. Austin, *Univers poétique de B.,* 142–3, and cf. ibid., 327–30
(illuminating comparison between B.'s *L'Ennemi* and Shakespeare's Sonnet
LXXIII, *That time of year thou may'st in me behold . . .*), 152–3 (Coleridge).
Among numerous nineteenth-century examples the most pertinent, perhaps,
would be the brief six-line poem published by Hugo in 1840 in *Les Rayons et
les Ombres* (X): 'Comme dans les étangs assoupis sous les bois, / Dans plus
d'une âme on voit deux choses à la fois, / Le ciel . . . / Et la vase . . .' (Pléiade,
I, 1052), and the various Balzac texts cited in this connection by P. Laubriet,
Intelligence de l'art chez Balzac, 500–1.

[3]In the sense of 'moral' or 'mental'; cf., for an analogous use, this observation
assigned by Balzac, in *Honorine,* to his narrator the Consul-General: 'Les
drames de la vie ne sont pas dans les circonstances, ils sont dans les sentiments,
ils se jouent dans le cœur, ou, si vous voulez, dans ce monde immense que nous
devons nommer le *Monde Spirituel*' (*OCC,* [IV], 373; cit. P. Laubriet, op, cit.,
50). This is perhaps the place to stress the perennial and insidious ambiguity
of the term 'spirituel', which so often is allowed illegitimately to retain all its
mystical and religious overtones, when in fact denoting simply a subjective
state—a mental or even a physical event—an idea, a moral attitude or an
emotion; thus to classify a realm of experience as 'spiritual' may mean nothing
more than to identify it as a function of the human mind, without regard for
that mind's relation with God or with any other 'ultimate reality'. I would
add that although the ambiguity is rendered doubly treacherous in French by
the very fact that the cognate term 'esprit' combines within itself the two
distinct if related meanings 'spirit' *and* 'mind', it nevertheless can arise equally
in the corresponding English vocabulary—as may be seen from this paragraph

clearly that we are within the sphere of the general doctrine of
correspondences declared in other texts of this period. The passage
begins with a remark that is of high interest for its relation to
Baudelaire's own poetic development:

> Je me suis *toujours* plu à chercher dans la nature extérieure et visible des
> exemples et des métaphores qui me servissent à caractériser les jouissances
> et les impressions d'un ordre spirituel.

(AR 329; my italics)

'Toujours', as we know with Baudelaire, may mean anything from
ten years to a few months! But in this case, many instances spring
to mind which would justify at least the chronological implications
of his assertion—if not necessarily its suggestion of a conscious and
deliberate *selection* of imagery.[1] Thus one might cite those imagined
landscapes (Saharan or Polar, autumnal or wintry, crepuscular or
nocturnal), extending sometimes over a whole poem, whereby he
had earlier rendered the desolation and horror of his 'spleen', the
inhuman indifference or disquieting inscrutability of his mistress.[2]

---

by M. Z. Shroder, *Icarus*, 80, in which the word 'spirit' is carried over with a
changed meaning from one sentence to the next, precisely in the context of the
Romantic attitude to Nature: 'The Romantic association of nature and spirit
expressed itself in one of two ways. The landscape was, on the one hand,
regarded as an extension of the human personality, capable of sympathy with
man's emotional state. . . . On the other hand, nature was regarded as a
vehicle for spirit just as man was: the breath of God fills both man and the earth.'
In effect, the writer is saying, in his final formula: 'the spirit (i.e. "the breath
of God") fills both spirit (i.e. "human personality" or "man's emotional state")
and the earth'. Cf., in this whole connection, the excellent comments by
J. W. Beach, *Concept of Nature in 19th-Century English Poetry*, 479, 480.

[1]B. liked to represent himself as the coldly calculating artist, always in full
command of his material and of the 'tricks of the trade' ('Le mécanisme des
trucs', as he himself puts it, in his 'Projets de Préface' for *FM, FMCB* 214);
but how far was this ever true? Cf., however, the comment, on the present text,
by M. Gilman, *B. the Critic*, 195: 'the fundamental idea of the imagination
as an active agent, as held by Delacroix and Baudelaire, controls the discovery of
the correspondences, prevents the poet from accepting them passively'.

[2]Cf. *De profundis clamavi* (which on its second publication, in 1855, was given
the title *Le Spleen*); *Spleen: J'ai plus de souvenirs que si j'avais mille ans; La
Destruction*, ll. 9–11; *Chant d'automne*, ll. 5–8; *Le Voyage*, ll. 111–12; *Chanson
d'après-midi*, ll. 37–40; *Avec ses vêtements ondoyants et nacrés . . .*, ll. 5–8; *Ciel
brouillé*. For an excellent analysis of these and other cognate texts, see L. J.
Austin, *Univers poétique de B.*, 305–21; for the last three, see also my art. cit.,
'The Amorous Tribute', in *FRH*, pp. 99–100, 107–8, 111–12.

The particular example that Baudelaire now goes on to offer, however, is an elaborate comparison between the poetry of Marceline Desbordes-Valmore (or its effects upon him) and an informal 'English' garden; and here we recall that it was with a very different kind of garden—autumnal, flooded, ravaged—that he had identified his own declining or uncertain creativity, in that tragic sonnet of 1855, *L'Ennemi*.[1] It is interesting to note that while, in this second version of his 'garden' symbol, Baudelaire is at some pains to specify, at various points, the correspondences between image and theme—between the 'jardin anglais' and the poetess's naive and delicately effusive verses—he none the less clearly abandons himself, at other moments, to the pleasures of purely picturesque or 'decorative' elaboration:[2]

C'est un simple jardin anglais, romantique et romanesque. Des massifs de fleurs y représentent les abondantes expressions du sentiment. Des étangs, limpides et immobiles, qui réfléchissent toutes choses s'appuyant à l'envers sur la voûte renversée des cieux, figurent la profonde résignation toute parsemée de souvenirs. Rien ne manque à ce charmant jardin d'un autre âge, ni quelques ruines gothiques se cachant dans un lieu agreste, ni le mausolée inconnu qui, au détour d'une allée, surprend notre âme et lui commande de penser à l'éternité. Des allées sinueuses et ombragées aboutissent à des horizons subits. Ainsi la pensée du poëte, après avoir suivi de capricieux méandres, débouche sur les vastes perspectives du passé ou de l'avenir; mais ces ciels sont trop vastes pour être généralement purs, et la température du climat trop chaude pour n'y pas amasser des orages. Le promeneur, en contemplant ces étendues voilées de deuil, sent monter à ses yeux les pleurs de l'hystérie, *hysterical tears*. Les fleurs se penchent vaincues, et les oiseaux ne parlent qu'à voix basse. Après un éclair précurseur, un coup de tonnerre a retenti: c'est l'explosion lyrique; enfin un déluge inévitable de larmes rend à toutes ces choses, prostrées, souffrantes et découragées, la fraîcheur et la solidité d'une nouvelle jeunesse![3]

For our converse (and still more traditional) mode of symbolism, we may conveniently borrow the term *paysage d'âme*—adapted from a famous (if usually misquoted) saying of Amiel's, which needs to be restored to its true context:

[1] Cf. in this connection L. J. Austin, op. cit., 297 n. 1.
[2] For an examination, from this standpoint, of four specified types of metaphoric intention ('illustrative', 'evocative', 'emotive', as well as 'decorative'), see my art., 'Intention in Metaphor', *Essays in Criticism*, 1954, pp. 191–8.
[3] *AR* 329–30, var. 546.

Paysage d'automne. Ciel tendu de gris et plissé de diverses nuances, brouillards traînant sur les montagnes de l'horizon; nature mélancolique. Les feuilles tombaient de tout côté comme les dernières illusions de la jeunesse sous les larmes de chagrins incurables ... tous ces innombrables et merveilleux symboles que les formes, les couleurs, les végétaux, les êtres vivants, la terre et le ciel fournissent à toute heure à l'œil qui sait les voir, m'apparaissaient charmants et saisissants. Je tenais la baguette poétique et n'avais qu'à toucher un phénomène pour qu'il me racontât sa signification morale. *Un paysage quelconque est un état de l'âme,* et qui lit dans tous deux est émerveillé de retrouver la similitude dans chaque détail.[1]

Thus the true *paysage d'âme,* unlike the 'symbolic landscape' previously discussed (to which incidentally, reversing the terminology, one might well apply the description *âme-paysage*), has its point of departure in a real setting or situation whose 'harmony' with the writer's state of mind may then—if his surrender to the 'Pathetic Fallacy' is not too complete—be crystallized into a specific metaphor or symbol.[2] (Of equal psychological importance, of course,

[1]*Fragments d'un journal intime,* I, 55–6 (entry of 31 October 1852). Almost a century earlier, however, the theory of the *paysage d'âme* had been expounded by Saint-Lambert, in the Preface to his long descriptive poem, *Les Saisons,* in which he observes: 'Il y a de l'analogie entre nos situations, les états de notre âme, et les sites, les phénomènes de la nature' (cit. Paul van Tieghem, *Sentiment de la nature dans le préromantisme,* 235). As to the actual *practice* of the genre, Petrarch, on the authority of J. A. Scott, 'Petrarch and B.', *RLC,* 1957, p. 561 (cf. G. Charlier, *Sentiment de la nature chez les romantiques,* 293), would seem to be 'the first poet in European literature to see Nature as reflecting "un état d'âme"'; for another early instance, cf. the *chanson* by Charles d'Orléans, cit. L. J. Austin, *Univers poétique de B.,* 330–1 n. For more recent (eighteenth- and nineteenth-century) examples, cf. D. Mornet, *Sentiment de la nature en France,* 188, 197–9 (Rousseau); Paul van Tieghem, op. cit., 232–5; G. Charlier, op. cit., 73, 156, 243–56, 293 and 304 (Lamartine); P. Laubriet, *Intelligence de l'art chez Balzac,* 339–41; etc. Of all nineteenth-century specimens of the genre, incidentally, perhaps the finest and most elaborate (as I hope to have the opportunity of showing on another occasion) is Lamartine's *L'Occident* (*Harmonies poétiques et religieuses,* 1830).

[2]One might, for complete clarification, represent diagrammatically the distinction between the two kinds of Nature-symbols—the first unit in each case being the one *chronologically* prior: (a) âme→paysage (the poet, noting his state of mind, seeks in his imagination for an analogy drawn from Nature); (b) paysage→âme (or *paysage d'âme:* the poet observes a particular landscape, then relates it to his state of mind). I would add, concerning the 'Pathetic Fallacy', that although the actual phrase may have been coined by Ruskin (*Modern Painters,* III, Part 4) to denote that 'falseness in all our impressions of

17

is the reverse phenomenon, where the two elements are in *dis*-harmony—as in the perennial complaint against the 'indifference' or 'irony' of Nature.[1]) An intermediate category is represented by a type of poem of which we find two examples in Baudelaire: in both, by the fiction of an imaginary 'voyage', the poet transposes himself (and his beloved, in the second case) into a setting with which a symbolic relationship is then established. The two texts differ violently, however, in the nature of the two situations imagined: wholly malign, in *Un Voyage à Cythère*:

> Dans ton île, ô Vénus! je n'ai trouvé debout
> Qu'un gibet symbolique où pendait mon image . . .[2]

—wholly benign, in the prose poem *L'Invitation au voyage*. This latter text (dating probably from 1855–6[3]) merits our particular attention, in that Baudelaire here specifically invokes, in justification of his symbolism, a doctrine of correspondences derived, as he himself says, from 'the mystics'. In the first part of the poem, however, his primary concern is to evoke, for his 'sœur d'election' (i.e. Marie Daubrun[4]), that ideal country to which he 'invites' her

---

external things' which leads us to attribute sympathetic human sentiments to inanimate objects, the human tendency itself had already been analysed a full century earlier by Rousseau: 'Forêt sans bois, marais sans eaux, genêts, roseaux, tristes bruyères, êtres insensibles et morts, ce charme n'est point en vous, il n'y saurait être, il *est dans mon propre cœur qui veut tout rapporter à lui*' (posth. text, cit. Paul van Tieghem, op. cit., 234, my italics; cf. D. Mornet, *Sentiment de la nature en France*, 188). For a Baudelairian instance (the 'Pathetic Fallacy' satirized in the poet himself), cf. *La Béatrice*, ll. 1–2, 19–20 (p. 111, above). I. Babbitt, it should be noted finally, has discerned a historical ambiguity within this whole concept—turning on the distinction between the Greek, who 'humanized nature', and the Rousseauist, who 'naturalizes man' *(Rousseau and Romanticism, 269–71)*.

[1]Perhaps one should call this an *'anti*-paysage d'âme'? For an extreme instance of such 'disharmony' between landscape and poet, cf. the text cited hereunder, *Un Voyage à Cythère;* for other examples taken both from B. and from other writers, cf. p. 110 and n. 1, above.

[2]ll. 57–8. The epithet 'symbolique' appears for the first time (replacing 'dégoutant' [sic]) in the 1855 text; but the (for B.) synonymous term 'allégorie' is to be found already in the immediately preceding line of the 1851–2 MS. ('. . . j'avais, comme en un suaire épais, / Le cœur enseveli dans cette allégorie'); cf., for the synonymity of these two terms, p. 225 n. 1, above.

[3]See, for this dating, n. 3 to p. 241, below.

[4]See A. Feuillerat, *B. et la Belle aux cheveux d'or*, 94 n. 71, and cf. the prior and corollary demonstration, ibid., 11–12, 54–8, that the verse poem of the same title was also inspired by this same Marie.

to journey—that 'pays singulier, noyé dans les brumes de notre Nord, et qu'on pourrait appeler l'Orient de l'Occident, la Chine de l'Europe',[1] which we know (from evidence both internal and external) to be in fact Holland.[2] Yet already here we encounter a phrase (twice-repeated, and moreover having its analogue in the parallel verse text) premonitory of what is to come: 'un pays . . . où tout vous ressemble', 'Il est une contrée qui te ressemble'.[3]

[1]*PPP* 53.

[2]Cf., within the present text, *PPP* 55 (with the comment by J. Crépet, *PPP* 295-6), and in another prose poem (to be discussed in my chapter VIII), *Any where out of the World, PPP* 166, the related passage beginning 'Puisque tu aimes tant le repos'. Cf. also, in the article by J. B. Barrère, *RLC,* 1957, 481-5, the searching discussion of the 'geography' of the linked verse poem.

[3]*PPP* 53-4; cf. the verse text, ll. 1-6: 'Mon enfant, ma sœur, / Songe à la douceur / D'aller là-bas vivre ensemble! / Aimer à loisir, / Aimer et mourir / *Au pays qui te ressemble!*' (my italics). Not only the phrase italicized (by me), but also the other lines of this stanza, have their echo within the prose poem; cf.: 'C'est là qu'il faut aller vivre, c'est là qu'il faut aller mourir! Oui, c'est là qu'il faut aller respirer, rêver et allonger les heures par l'infini des sensations!' (PPP 54; the formula 'il faut aller vivre, etc.' recurs a third time in a later paragraph, *PPP* 55, to be quoted hereunder). A more unexpected analogy here, however, is that which obtains between both these texts, and a passage, from the second volume of Toussenel's *Le Monde des oiseaux,* which sings the virtues of that other 'ideal' country, America: 'Il n'y a eu depuis six mille ans, dans les deux continents, dans les deux hémisphères, qu'un peuple heureux et libre, un seul, celui de l'Amérique du Nord. L'Amérique du Nord est le seul pays de la terre où la femme soit reine! *C'est là qu'il faut aimer, c'est là qu'il faut mourir*' (p. 11). The similarity between the phrase italicized, and those quoted from the two versions of *L'Invitation au voyage,* is in my view so striking as to indicate that we may here have a specific source; and this, in turn, would have important consequences for the chronology of the two B. texts. Thus the Toussenel book (i.e. Vol. II of *Le Monde des oiseaux*) is noted in the *Bibliographie de la France* under the date 27 January 1855 (No. 501), and will thus have appeared in print around the beginning of that month; since by 7 April 1855, Victor de Mars, the then editor of *RDM,* seems already to have had in his possession all the poems of B.'s from which he was to choose the 18 to be published by him on 1 June (see *CG* I, 330), it follows that *L'Invitation au voyage* (which was among these 18) must, if it did indeed derive in part from Toussenel's text, have been written in its final form between Jan. and April 1855—i.e. a few months later than the date, end-1854, argued implicitly, on biographical grounds, by A. Feuillerat, *B. et la belle,* 54 (as also, more positively, by A. Adam, *FMA* 340-1). As to the prose version, which is likely in any case to have been composed *after* the verse text (cf., in this connection, *FMCB* 387; G. Blin, *Sadisme de B.*, 162), I would suggest this to have been written (as a further variation on a theme already treated in verse) between May 1855 and the end of 1856; the (ensuing) seven months which preceded the prose poem's

But it is in the concluding paragraphs—introduced by the poet's retort to those 'alchemists of horticulture' who seek in the rarest flowers the ultimate 'limits of their happiness'—that we see the full development of the 'correspondence' theme proper:

... Moi, j'ai trouvé ma *tulipe noire* et mon *dahlia bleu*!

Fleur incomparable, tulipe retrouvée, allégorique dahlia, c'est là, n'est-ce-pas, dans ce beau pays si calme et si rêveur, qu'il faudrait aller vivre et fleurir? Ne serais-tu pas encadrée dans ton analogie, et ne pourrais-tu pas te mirer, pour parler comme les mystiques, dans ta propre *correspondance*?

Des rêves! toujours des rêves! ... Vivrons-nous jamais, passerons-nous jamais dans ce tableau qu'a peint mon esprit, ce tableau qui te ressemble?

Ces trésors, ces meubles, ce luxe, cet ordre, ces parfums, ces fleurs miraculeuses, c'est toi. C'est encore toi, ces grands fleuves et ces canaux tranquilles. Ces énormes navires qu'ils charrient, tout chargés de richesses, et d'où montent les chants monotones de la manœuvre, ce sont mes pensées qui dorment ou qui roulent sur ton sein. Tu les conduis doucement vers la mer qui est l'Infini, tout en réfléchissant les profondeurs du ciel dans la limpidité de ta belle âme;—et quand, fatigués par la houle et gorgés des produits de l'Orient, ils rentrent au port natal, ce sont encore mes pensées enrichies qui reviennent de l'Infini vers toi.

(*PPP* 55-6)

The epithet 'allégorique', the apparently systematic correspondences of the final paragraph, should not mislead us into supposing that we have here any such fully-fledged and fully-detailed scheme of 'equivalences' as Baudelaire admittedly offers us in another poem dedicated to Marie Daubrun, *A une Madone*;[1] rather than the tradition of mediaeval allegory, Baudelaire in the present poem renews, more simply, that of amorous hyperbole. Thus in this final section, having declared himself to have discovered what others vainly seek: the 'incomparable flower' (black tulip or blue dahlia) of his dreams, the poet goes on to reiterate, but more explicitly than hitherto, his notion of the mysterious 'resemblance' linking the girl's admired person with the ideal setting imagined for her— his sense, perfectly captured in three brief lines of the verse doublet,

---

publication in Aug. 1857 in *Le Présent*, having been largely given over to the preparation by the poet first of *FM* and then of his legal defence at the 'trial', would scarcely, perhaps, have been favourable to wider literary composition.

[1]Still less does this apply, I would add to the *verse* poem *L'Invitation au voyage*—where the analogy between 'pays' and 'sœur' is abandoned altogether after the first stanza.

of the vague sympathetic affinity, the secret 'language of the heart', that 'speaks' from the one to the other:

> Tout y parlerait
> A l'âme en secret
> Sa douce langue natale.[1]

By his adjective 'allégorique,' therefore, Baudelaire denotes here a relationship essentially of 'affinity' but from which 'resemblance' is argued—a relationship that on another occasion he might well have preferred to call 'symbolique'.[2] So, too, when in the opening sentences of the final paragraph, he assimilates directly to his mistress ('c'est toi') all the different elements of the Dutch interior and landscape (treasures, furniture, luxury, order, perfumes, flowers, rivers, canals), he implies not that each corresponds symmetrically with some particular part of her anatomy or character,[3] but rather that each 'belongs' to her by right of temperamental affinity—as if to say 'not only are these "you", but they are *yours*', 'c'est toi et c'est à toi'. Even the concluding two sentences of the prose poem are in my view more truly hyperbolical than allegorical in intention. For when Baudelaire, with such seeming exactness of correlation, goes on to explain the movements of the great ships in terms of the 'journeyings' of his own thoughts (the ones borne along the Dutch rivers and canals, the others 'sleeping' within her breast; the ones guided towards the sea, the others towards Infinity; the ones returning lashed by the waves and laden

---

[1] ll. 24–6. Cf., for this postulated *affinity* with a distant scene, firstly, the prose poem *Les Projets*, with its comment on a print showing, within a tropical landscape, a 'belle case en bois' which with its surrounding trees, would constitute the lovers' 'petit domaine' (an imagined situation very similar to that of the present text): '"Non! ce n'est pas dans un palais que je voudrais posséder sa chère vie. Nous n'y serions pas *chez nous*. . . . Décidément, c'est *là* qu'il faudrait demeurer pour cultiver le rêve de ma vie. . . . Oui, en vérité, c'est bien *là* le décor que je cherchais. Qu'ai-je à faire de palais?"' (*PPP* 79–80; Dec. 1864 text)—and, secondly, the sonnet *La Vie antérieure* (pp. 44–8, above).

[2] For the interchangeability, for B., of these two terms, see p. 225 n. 1, above.

[3] It is true that in a further Marie Daubrun poem, *Le Beau navire*, we encounter just such a specific analogy between an item of furniture and an item of her person! 'Ta gorge triomphante est une belle armoire / Dont les panneaux bombés et clairs / Comme les boucliers accrochent des éclairs' (ll. 18–20). But this metaphor is incidental to the main poetic argument, and moreover does not derive from the exterior setting; see my discussion of this whole poem in my art. cit., 'The Amorous Tribute', pp. 93–7.

with all the stuffs of Orient, the others returning likewise 'enriched',
but from Infinity and to her)—when he adds that her soul, as it
bears his thoughts onwards, 'reflects' (sea-like) the 'profundity' of
the sky (again, one recognizes the Petrarchan theme: the beauty of
the beloved's soul, surpassing that even of her body and matching
that of external Nature)—is he in fact doing more than ingeniously
platonicize a sensual reverie ('mes pensées qui dorment ou qui
roulent sur ton sein'), much as he had earlier done in a letter of
explicitly Petrarchan inspiration addressed to this same Marie,[1] while
at the same time combining a further nostalgic glimpse of that
'elsewhere' (the ships 'fatigués par la houle et gorgés des produits
de l'Orient') to which he had before been 'guided', as we have seen,
in the arms of another mistress?[2]

In his article of 1859–61 on Pierre Dupont,[3] Baudelaire makes
this comment on his friend's 'barcarolle', *La Promenade sur l'eau:*

> Grâce à une opération d'esprit toute particulière aux amoureux quand
> ils sont poëtes, ou aux poëtes quand ils sont amoureux, la femme s'embellit
> de toutes les grâces du paysage, et le paysage profite occasionnellement
> des grâces que la femme aimée verse à son insu sur le ciel, sur la terre et
> sur les flots.

(AR 369)

Baudelaire does not here specifically declare the poet-lover's
assimilation of woman and landscape to be of analogic type—for the
good reason that this does not happen to be the case with the
Dupont poem from which he is arguing. But with this qualification
borne in mind, one might well choose to regard the prose version
of *L'Invitation au voyage* as being the application of the first at

---

[1] Cf. *CG* I, 102: '. . . vous ne pourrez empêcher mon esprit d'errer autour
de vos bras, de vos si belles mains, de vos yeux où toute votre vie réside, de toute
votre adorable personne charnelle; non, je sais que vous ne le pourrez pas;
mais, soyez tranquille, vous êtes pour moi un objet de culte et il m'est impossible
de vous souiller; je vous verrai toujours aussi radieuse qu'avant . . . vos
yeux . . . ne peuvent inspirer au poëte qu'un amour immortel'. This letter is
dated by A. Feuillerat, *B. et la Belle*, 13, as of 1847–9, and by C. Pichois, ed.
Fanfarlo, 11, as of early May 1846 at the latest; cf., however, W. T. Bandy,
RLM, 1959, pp. 73–4.

[2] Cf. my discussion, pp. 31–7, above, of *Parfum exotique* and *La Chevelure*.
But in the present poem the 'elsewhere' belongs essentially to a hypothetical
future, rather than to a remembered past.

[3] Not to be confused with his earlier essay on the same writer, published in
1851 and discussed pp. 94–5, above.

least of the two processes described ('la femme s'embellit de toutes les grâces du paysage'); as for the second (the landscape 'profiting' in turn from the woman's graces), this could scarcely be better illustrated than by these lines from the parallel verse text:

> Les soleils mouillés
> De ces ciels brouillés
> Pour mon esprit ont les charmes
> Si mystérieux
> De tes traîtres yeux,
> Brillant à travers leurs larmes.[1]

In short, if we take into account the biographical situation out of which both verse and prose texts arise[2]—if, simply, we agree to regard them as being above all *love* poems—we are then, I think, obliged to conclude that the notion of correspondences, for all the 'mystical' overtones it may carry in the prose poem, is in fact exploited by Baudelaire mainly for amorous and sentimental purposes; and even if, turning aside from all such considerations, we view the latter text purely in its aesthetic implications, we must still note that the specific correspondences invoked remain purely subjective and hence terrestrial in their scope—'spiritual', perhaps (since this term, as we have seen, is conveniently ambiguous), but in no proper sense transcendental or Swedenborgian.

Although more numerous in Baudelaire's poetry are those symbols drawn from a 'present', rather than a 'potential' and imagined, landscape.[3] Of particular interest in this connection are two linked sonnets, *Alchimie de la douleur* and *Horreur sympathique* (published for the first time, side by side, in October 1860, nine months before the Hugo article), which take as their actual subject-matter the poet's attitude to Nature and the ensuing process of symbolization;

---

[1] ll. 7–12. The first process could equally be illustrated from another poem of B.'s, *Le Jet d'eau*—which curiously enough has several close points of resemblance with the Dupont text cited by B.; cf. *FMCB* 580, and D. Higgins, *FS*, 1949, pp. 133–4.

[2] Cf., in this connection, A. Feuillerat, *B. et la Belle*, 54–8.

[3] Cf., e.g., the following poems discussed in other chapters of the present book: *Moesta et errabunda*, ll. 6–10: *Harmonie du soir; Chant d'automne; Obsession; Le Confiteor de l'artiste*. Cf. also *Spleen* [IV] (*Quand le ciel bas et lourd . . .*), and *Les Sept vieillards*, ll. 8–9: 'Un matin, cependant que . . ., *décor semblable à l'âme de l'acteur*, / Un brouillard sale et jaune inondait tout l'espace' (my italics); for a comment on this latter analogy, my art. cit., 'Intention in Metaphor', pp. 197–8.

significantly enough, Baudelaire seems at one stage to have contemplated giving to one or other or both of the poems, a title, *Similia Similia*,[1] which would have served, somewhat self-consciously, to stress this same analogic element.

Alchimie de la douleur opens on a deceptively impersonal note; in a cryptic, declamatory style,[2] Baudelaire here contrasts two kinds of temperament, two alternative attitudes to Nature:

> L'un t'éclaire avec son ardeur,
> L'autre en toi met son deuil, Nature!
> Ce qui dit à l'un: Sépulture!
> Dit à l'autre: Vie et splendeur!

The remainder of the sonnet makes clear, if the title had not sufficiently forewarned us, to which of the two camps Baudelaire himself belongs: he is of those who are alert only to the funereal aspects of Nature, who seek only, in Nature, the reflection of their own sorrow; not for him the positive and optimistic response, which 'irradiates' with its own ardour a Nature perceived as splendid and vital. And so he now turns, abruptly, to apostrophize the 'unknown Hermes' who seemingly prompts these morose, and perverse, transmutations of reality:

> Hermès inconnu qui m'assistes
> Et qui toujours m'intimidas,
> Tu me rends l'égal de Midas,
> Le plus triste des alchimistes;
>
> Par toi je change l'or en fer
> Et le paradis en enfer;
> Dans le suaire des nuages

---

[1]See *FMCB* 618, and *CG* III, 136 and n. 1.

[2]Deriving, perhaps (as L. J. Austin has suggested, *Univers poétique de B.*, 104), from a poem of Lamartine's, *Désir (Harmonies poétiques et religieuses*, 1830), to which I have already previously referred (p. 203 n. 3, above). In the particular passage in question, Lamartine asks how many, among the ignorant 'children of men', have hearkened to the 'voices' of the different elements of Nature (winds, sea, thunder); then follow these lines: 'L'un a dit: Magnificence! / L'autre: Immensité! puissance! / L'autre: Terreur et courroux! / L'un a fui devant sa face, / L'autre a dit: Son ombre passe: / Cieux et terre, taisez-vous!' (Pléiade, 386). Among the further elements common to both poems, I would note: first, the idea of an 'interpretation of Nature' by Man; second, the reference to the clouds and heavens ('Son ombre passe: / Cieux et terre, taisez vous!'—cf. *Alchimie de la douleur*, ll. 11–14); third, the rapid metre (heptasyllabic, in *Désir;* octosyllabic, in the B. text).

Je découvre un cadavre cher,
· Et sur les célestes rivages
Je bâtis de grands sarcophages.

The influence Baudelaire here attributes to Hermes is something akin to that exerted by the insidious 'yellow serpent' whose obstructive and 'nay-saying' empire over the mind he describes in another sonnet of this period, L'Avertisseur.[1] Why Hermes? Because Hermes by tradition is the patron of all occult science, and the poet's response to Nature suggests a comparison with one such occult science, i.e. alchemy. But what the alchemists sought to do was to change base metal into gold, and what Baudelaire (subjectively) achieves is the reverse transformation: in his eyes, gold (the gold of Nature) turns to iron; the paradises of Nature become infernos; the clouds, with their dark trails, suggest only shrouds and the memory of the dear departed—and thus even the shores of Heaven become for him a place of mourning. Midas, too, as well as the alchemists, is invoked, and this further comparison is so cryptic as to demand some further explanation. The poet is strictly the *opposite* of Midas: whereas under Midas's hands all things changed to gold, for this still sadder 'alchemist' even gold itself turns to iron. But both, Midas and poet alike, share the same power of transmutation, and are equals also in the 'ironic' intensity of their sadness.[2]

This sonnet is to my mind terse and laconic to a fault; not only is the meaning at times elusive (as, e.g., in the mythological references to Hermes and Midas), but what is more serious, the images pass almost too swiftly to allow of any effective visualization or even

[1]'Tout homme digne de ce nom / A dans le cœur un Serpent jaune, / Installé comme sur un trône, / Qui, s'il dit: "Je veux!" répond: "Non!" ' (ll. 1–4; first pub. 1861). Cf. also L'Héautontimorouménos, ll. 13–16.

[2]Cf. the comparison between Midas and the opium-eater in Un Mangeur d'Opium, PA 134: 'Midas changeait en or tout ce qu'il touchait, et se sentait martyrisé par cet ironique privilége'. (The second part of this sentence was added by B. himself, when adapting De Quincey's 1822 text; cf. Confessions, ed. M. Elwin, 420.) The alchemical image recurs also, but without irony and in the context of the poet's 'saintly' performance of his 'quintessentializing' duty, in the final lines of the projected Épilogue (addressed to the city of Paris) for the second edition of 1861 of FM: 'Comme un parfait chimiste et comme une âme sainte . . . / . . . j'ai de chaque chose extrait la quintessence, / Tu m'as donné ta boue et j'en ai fait de l'or' (FMCB 216; cf. also Bribes, OP 1, 3, and the further texts cited in this connection by L. J. Austin, Univers poétique de B., 345 and n. 1).

decisive impact. Within an identical compass (the octosyllable sonnet), the companion poem *Horreur sympathique* is altogether more successful. We here start, more graphically and immediately than in *Alchimie de la douleur,* from a particular aspect of Nature, a particular cloudscape whether real or pictured,[1] into which the poet reads his own demeanour and state of mind—or in which, rather (as the paradoxical title suggests) he finds these 'sympathetically' reflected.[2] Thus we stand with him, looking up into the strange 'tormented' sky, and hear his peremptory injunction to himself to *declare* the thoughts that float down into a mind that is as 'empty' as his 'libertine' soul:

> De ce ciel bizarre et livide,
> Tourmenté comme ton destin,
> Quels pensers dans ton âme vide
> Descendent? réponds, libertin.[3]

The remainder of the sonnet gives us the poet's reply—with the tercets bringing, more particularly, his elaboration and defiant acceptance of the analogy posed in the second line:

> —Insatiablement avide
> De l'obscur et de l'incertain,
> Je ne geindrai pas comme Ovide
> Chassé du paradis latin.

---

[1] B. may here be recalling, it has been suggested, certain specific works of art he had described in his *Salon de 1859*: Delacroix' painting *Ovide en exil chez les Scythes (CE* 295–7); the Boudin pastels seen at Honfleur *(CE* 340–1; cf. pp. 134–6, above). Cf., for these 'plastic sources', J. Prévost, *B.,* 139–40; *FMCB* 430; *FMPP* 475–7.

[2] By his title at least, therefore, B. would seem here to be subscribing, however sardonically, to the 'Pathetic Fallacy'; cf. p. 239 and n. 2, above.

[3] My comment on ll. 3–4 assumes that B. may have intended to play on the ambiguity of 'âme': not only is the poet's *mind* 'empty' (because simply, like Wordsworth recalling the daffodils, he finds himself 'in vacant or in pensive mood'?); so also is his *soul*, because of the 'void' created by his unbelief. (For a similar use of 'libertin' in the sense of 'free-thinker', cf. *Le Couvercle*—pub. 1862—l. 12). In the previous line, we have, of course, a more obviously calculated ambiguity, in the word 'tourmenté' (='turbulent' or 'storm-tossed' when applied to the sky, 'troubled' or 'tormented' when applied to the poet's destiny; cf. J. D. Hubert, *Esthétique des 'FM',* 137). It must be stressed, however, that word-play of this kind is relatively rare in B., and that there is no evidence whatsoever of his having subscribed to any thorough-going 'aesthetic of ambiguity'; cf., on this whole question, my review, *FS,* 1958, 171–3, of the above-mentioned book by J. D. Hubert.

Cieux déchirés comme des grèves,
En vous se mire mon orgueil;
Vos vastes nuages en deuil

Sont les corbillards de mes rêves,
Et vos lueurs sont le reflet
De l'Enfer où mon cœur se plaît.

These lines might in effect be seen as the specific demonstration of the process described in more general terms in *Alchimie de la douleur*: 'Par toi je change l'or en fer / Et le paradis en enfer'. But the dark vision of the world there imposed by temperament, is here accepted, even welcomed; the bleak alchemist is now *proud* to declare himself such. The allusion to Ovid, although less cryptic than those to Hermes and Midas in the companion sonnet, needs for its full understanding to be set in relation with a passage in the *Salon de 1859*. Baudelaire is here introducing, graphically but somewhat obliquely, his appreciation of Delacroix' painting *Ovide chez les Scythes*:

Le voilà couché sur des verdures sauvages, avec une mollesse et une tristesse féminines, le poëte illustre qui enseigna l'*art d'aimer*. Ses grands amis de Rome sauront-ils vaincre la rancune impériale? Retrouvera-t-il un jour les somptueuses voluptés de la prodigieuse cité? Non, de ces pays sans gloire s'épanchera vainement le long et mélancolique fleuve des *Tristes*; ici il vivra, ici il mourra.[1]

Thus to Ovid's 'Latin paradise'—those 'sumptuous pleasures' of Rome, from which he has been so peremptorily banished—must correspond, in Baudelaire's case, some other 'paradise', earthly or celestial, from which he for his part has *chosen* to exclude himself. Not for him, therefore, the 'whinings' of the languid and effeminate Ovid—nor even the note of complaint voiced fleetingly in *Alchimie de la douleur*. On the contrary, driven by that inveterate *curiosity* to which he has more than once confessed,[2] he enters with 'avidity' into all that is dark and uncertain in his destiny. The lowering, ravaged skies, with their tossing 'breakers', thus reflect his obstinate

---

[1] *CE* 295. For a comment on this aspect of the *Tristia* (with full quotation and translation of III, x), see A. O. Lovejoy and G. Boas, *Primitivism in Antiquity*, 333–6.
[2] Cf. p. 67 and n. 1, above.

pride;[1] the clouds, in the blackness of their mourning 'livery', recall
the funereal imagery of his dreams;[2] the lightning flashes, finally,
piercing the heavens and bathing the whole scene in a strange
unearthly 'lividity', bring also a nuance of Satanism that is altogether
absent from the companion poem, and that in its tone of perverse
delectation as well as in its hint of an irretrievable predicament,
reminds one rather of the concluding quatrains of *L'Irrémédiable :*[3]

> Tête-à-tête sombre et limpide
> Qu'un cœur devenu son miroir!
> Puits de Vérité, clair et noir,
> Où tremble une étoile livide,
>
> Un phare ironique, infernal,
> Flambeau des grâces sataniques,
> Soulagement et gloire uniques,
> —La conscience dans le Mal!

The self-admonition of the fourth line of *Horreur sympathique*
('réponds, *libertin*') is now explained, the dramatic (or melodramatic) aspects of the skyscape find, now, their moral complement:
this Hell is not the mere inferno of suffering of *Alchimie de la
douleur,* but a private universe of sin and (perhaps) unbelief. The
final word of the sonnet ('. . . l'Enfer où mon cœur se *plaît*') has
a most telling and appropriate incisiveness of sound: more perhaps
than at any other moment in Baudelaire's poetry, we seem to catch
here the very tone and quality of his actual speaking voice: brittle,
mordant, sardonic, curt.

[1]This type of symbolic characterization of a skyscape in terms of human
passions, seems to have been much favoured by B. during the present period;
we find it not only in the present two sonnets, but also in the *Salon de 1859*
(CE 343, of Meryon's Parisian skies: 'le ciel tumultueux, chargé de colère et de
rancune'), and again, in a more cryptic version, in the Delacroix 'medallion'
of *Les Phares* (ll. 31–2: '. . . sous un ciel chagrin, des fanfares étranges /
Passent . . .'); in *Fusées* VI, finally, it forms the chosen illustration to one of
B.'s rare stylistic comments: '*Ciel tragique.* Epithète d'un ordre abstrait
appliqué à un être matériel' *(JI* 14; cf. J. Pommier, *Mystique de B.,* 85–6, and
M. Gilman, *Idea of Poetry in France,* 263).

[2]Cf., in the fourth *Spleen* poem *(Quand le ciel bas et lourd pèse comme un
couvercle),* ll. 17–20, those other 'hearses' which by their slow procession
through the poet's mind announce the defeat of Hope.

[3]Cf., in this connection, J. Prévost, *B.,* 215–16.

VII

Nature without Man:
The Intrusions of Misanthropy

A HUMANISM such as Baudelaire had declared in the letter to Desnoyers, could scarcely (we have seen) be sustained in face of his more
strongly dogmatic commitment to the doctrine of original sin.[1]
Still less, however, inasmuch as it implies by definition a certain
measure of philanthropy, could such a humanism be reconciled
with the deepening *mis*anthropy that descended on him after 1857.
I have already commented on what is perhaps the most flagrant
Baudelairian instance of a contradiction of this kind: in the very
paragraph of the *Salon de 1859* in which he initially asserts the
aesthetic 'necessity' of Man's presence in Nature, its aesthetic
nullity in the absence of Man, he is led tacitly to *approve* this same
'absence' within Boudin's pastels, and to depreciate, almost sneeringly, Man's liking for the society of his fellows:

Chose assez curieuse, il ne m'arriva pas une seule fois, devant ces magies
liquides ou aériennes, de me plaindre de l'absence de l'homme. Mais je me
garde bien de tirer de la plénitude de ma jouissance un conseil pour qui
que ce soit, non plus que pour M. Boudin. Le conseil serait trop dangereux. Qu'il se rappelle que l'homme, comme dit Robespierre, qui avait
soigneusement fait ses *humanités*, ne voit jamais l'homme sans plaisir; et
s'il veut gagner un peu de popularité, qu'il se garde bien de croire que le
public soit arrivé à un égal enthousiasme pour la solitude.[2]

[1]Cf. pp. 150-1, above.

[2]*CE* 341-2. Referring to this judgement of B.'s, Ruth Benjamin, *Boudin*, 34,
makes this interesting comment: 'To Boudin men and women were always
secondary considerations in a picture. When he did introduce them, it was not
as individuals, but as spots of colour. He handled them as he did the masts
of sail-boats, or poles stuck in the sand, simply to vary the lines of sea and sky'.
For an explicit *refutation* of humanism by B., cf. the concluding section of the
article on Gautier of 1859; answering the critics of Gautier's supposed 'coldness'
and 'lack of humanity', B. observes: 'Tout amoureux de l'humanité ne manque
jamais, en de certaines matières qui prêtent à la déclamation philanthropique,
de citer la fameuse parole: *Homo sum; nihil humani a me alienum puto*. Un
poète aurait le droit de répondre: "Je me suis imposé de si hauts devoirs, que
quidquid humani a me alienum puto. Ma fonction est extra-humaine!"' *(AR* 179).
Cf. also, in this whole connection, the further texts adduced and discussed in
my art. cit., 'B.: The Poet as Moralist', pp. 210-12.

It might almost seem that Baudelaire's feigned reluctance to endorse Boudin's 'banishment' of Man from his landscapes, concealed a deeper reluctance to accept the full implications of such an attitude, as far as his own Nature-philosophy was concerned. But his final words here, concerning 'enthusiasm for solitude', remind us that this theme had already been explored by him in his prose poem of 1855, *La Solitude*—published, in the *Fontainebleau* volume, within a few pages of the (humanist) letter to Desnoyers. It is true that this apologia for solitude lacks any true (or explicit) misanthropic element, even in the ultimate and drastically remodelled version of 1864—from which, moreover, are equally excluded all such traces of the external world as the 'sublime landscape' which in the 1855–61 texts the fortunate Solitary appropriates to himself at a single glance;[1] and indeed it might perhaps be thought, from the fact that in 1861–2 Baudelaire was to put forward the Rousseauesque phrase 'Le Promeneur solitaire' as the title for two distinct sequences of largely 'urban' texts,[2] that he now conceived himself purely as the solitary wanderer through *Parisian* landscapes. To any such notion the following passage from the *Salon de 1859*, with its reference (exactly recalling the concluding sentences of the 1855 prose poem) to the privileged delights to be gained from the solitary contemplation of *Nature*, provides a ready corrective:

[1]Cf. p. 162 and n. 1, above.

[2]The first of these two sequences, we learn from an 1861 MS. of *Le Couvercle* (see *FMCB* 620–1), would have included the latter poem, together with *Recueillement* and several other (unnamed) sonnets; as for the second sequence, this—as we have seen already (p. 162 n. 2, above)—was ultimately to become the collected *Petits poëmes en prose*. I say 'the Rousseauesque phrase', since it is clearly from the *Rêveries d'un promeneur solitaire* that B.'s own title must derive; cf. G. Blin, *Sadisme de B.*, 146 n. 1, and for a general comment on Rousseau's love of solitude, D. Mornet, *Sentiment de la nature*, 188–9. For a more recent precedent, cf. (*FMC* 225 n. 2; G. Blin, loc. cit.) the *Livre du Promeneur* (likewise composed of prose poems) by Lefèvre-Deumier. In the dedicatory preface ('A.J.G.F.') to the *Paradis artificiels* of 1860, *PA*, vi, B. describes himself (by assimilation) as 'un promeneur sombre et solitaire, plongé dans le flot mouvant des multitudes,' and he reappears in this role (i.e. as 'notre promeneur') in the prose poem *Le Tir et le cimetière* (*PPP* 155; pub. 1867); cf. also, in *Les Foules*, *PPP* 34, the reference to the 'promeneur solitaire et pensif' who nevertheless 'espouses' the crowd. Finally, one may recall his admiring description, in the introductory article to the *Exposition universelle 1855*, of the 'voyageurs solitaires qui ont vécu pendant des années au fond des bois, au milieu des vertigineuses prairies, sans autre compagnon que leur fusil . . .' (*CE* 221).

Il y a de [M. Lavieille] un paysage fort simple: une chaumière sur une lisière de bois, avec une route qui s'y enfonce. La blancheur de la neige fait un contraste agréable avec l'incendie du soir qui s'éteint lentement derrière les innombrables mâtures de la forêt sans feuilles. Depuis quelques années, les paysagistes ont plus fréquemment appliqué leur esprit aux beautés pittoresque de la saison triste. Mais personne, je crois, ne les sent mieux que M. Lavieille. Quelques-uns des effets qu'il a souvent rendus me semblent des extraits du bonheur de l'hiver. Dans la tristesse de ce paysage, qui porte la livrée obscurément blanche et rose des beaux jours d'hiver à leur déclin, il y a une volupté élégiaque irrésistible que connaissent tous les amateurs de promenades solitaires.[1]

The *Salon de 1859* was written, as we have seen, from Honfleur— Honfleur, where Baudelaire had made the acquaintance of Boudin, and had fallen under the spell of the latter's studies of sea and sky;[2] Honfleur, with its 'maison-joujou' in which Mme Aupick had come to settle in 1857, after the death of her husband (Baudelaire's stepfather). There, at this retreat by the sea, Baudelaire joined her towards the end of January 1859, for a visit extending, with one interruption of a few weeks, over the next five months. This visit was fruitful to him poetically: it was from Honfleur that he sent

---

[1]*CE* 338. For one such 'solitary walk' of B.'s, see the letter of 13 Dec. 1862, to his mother: 'Il y a déja longtemps . . . je suis allé, *tout seul, bien entendu*, à Versailles. J'adore Versailles et les Trianons. Ce sont de bonnes solitudes' *(CG* IV, 133; cf. p. 113 and n. 1, above). There is of course no necessary contradiction, but on the contrary an implied continuity, between the solitude enjoyed in Nature and that experienced (paradoxically) in the great city; cf. my comments, p. 171 above, on the text of 1857-60 beginning 'Le vertige senti dans les grandes villes est analogue au vertige éprouvé au sein de la nature' (Notes for *L'Art philosophique*, *OCP* 1107). We shall see also that where the life of the city encroaches too oppressively upon the poet's 'solitude', Nature (in the form of Honfleur) may furnish a desired refuge; thus in May 1862, he writes to his mother: '. . . *je veux absolument me retremper dans la solitude*. Je fuis Paris, surtout pour fuir toute compagnie. Donc je ne veux pas retrouver à Honfleur le supplice parisien . . .' *(CG* IV, 89; cf. P. Citron, *Poésie de Paris*, II, 333-5). At such moments B. seems ready to exclaim, with Lamartine *(Nouvelles confidences*, I, XLI, cit. Y. Boeniger, *Lamartine et le sentiment de la Nature*, 24): 'Je hais les villes comme les plantes du Midi haïssent l'ombre humide d'une cour de prison'—or to echo, more simply, Rousseau's repeated denunciations of Paris (see P. Citron, op. cit., I, 99-103). Finally, it is perhaps significant in this respect that B. should, a few years earlier, in the letter to Toussenel of Jan. 1856, have cited approvingly the latter's 'amour de la vie en plein air' *(CG* I, 368).

[2]Cf. pp. 134-6, above.

out to his friends, in February 1859, a leaflet offering the first printed versions of *L'Albatros* and *Le Voyage*—with the comment, in one instance: 'Vous voyez que la *Muse de la Mer* me convient'.[1] The sea figures directly, of course—though as a background rather than as a dominant theme—in both these poems; in a more immediate and *local* sense, the 'Muse de la Mer' (i.e. the Honfleur seascape) would seem to have inspired not only the prose poem *Le Confiteor de l'artiste,* but also these exquisitely cadential lines from *Chant d'automne:*

> J'aime de vos longs yeux la lumière verdâtre,
> Douce beauté, mais tout aujourd'hui m'est amer,
> Et rien, ni votre amour, ni le boudoir, ni l'âtre,
> Ne me vaut le soleil rayonnant sur la mer.[2]

Chant d'automne was in all probability written in Paris, in the early autumn of that same year 1859; Baudelaire's entranced recollection of the sun streaming over the sea, as he had seen it a few months before at Honfleur, is here woven into a subtly elegiac structure which combines both the reality and the symbolism of the seasons, with a last poignant appeal to Marie Daubrun, the whole pierced by the premonition and apprehension of death.

We glimpse something, in this poem, of the deep personal significance that Honfleur had acquired in the poet's mind. More

---

[1]Letter to Calonne *(CG* II, 283); the phrase is varied in another letter, to Poulet-Malassis, despatched the same day (ibid.) For further details concerning the house at Honfleur, and B.'s visits there, see G. Jean-Aubry, *B. et Honfleur,* 13–34; A. Feuillerat, *B. et sa mère,* 100–12 and 129–30; C. Pichois, *B.,* 265–9; pp. 145–7, above.

[2]ll. 17–20; in the earlier (1859) text, the final line of this verse lacks the haunting cadence aforementioned: '(Rien) . . . . Ne vaut l'ardent soleil rayonnant sur la mer'. Consciously or unconsciously, B. would seem here to be transposing to a more intimate context the notion previously expressed by Maxime Du Camp, in this couplet from his poem *Le Voyageur (Les Chants modernes,* 1855), cited by Y. Abé, *RHLF,* 1967, p. 277: 'Je ne veux pas aimer; j'aime mieux, sur les ondes,/ Regarder le soleil descendre et s'abîmer . . . .' It is true that Du Camp goes on to say: 'J'aime mieux m'en aller par les forêts profondes:/L'amour me fait trop peur; je ne veux pas aimer'—but are the sentiments of this last line so very different from those expressed by B. in other texts of this period, e.g. his (similarly entitled) *Sonnet d'automne?* These particular verses of Du Camp's were well known to B., since as M. Abé has clearly shown (loc. cit.), they furnished several 'motifs de réflexion' for that other Honfleur poem, *Le Voyage.* For a full discussion of this latter poem and of Part II of *Chant d'automne,* cf., respectively, pp. 294–310 and 271–2, below.

comprehensively, from his letters, we perceive that the 'maison-joujou' had become, even before he first visited it, a symbolic haven, a refuge, a 'true home' in which at last, he felt, he might hope to bring his life's work to fruition—and this not only because of the beauty of its setting ('perched' directly over the sea, to borrow Baudelaire's own description), but because here alone, in a life harassed by debts, illness, amorous infidelities, could he find secure affection and warmth (in even the most literal sense), an escape from what he savagely termed 'l'horreur de la face humaine'.[1] And yet, through certain contradictions within his temperament—perhaps also through the artist's suspicion of any too-exigent emotional dependence, or the opium-addict's fear of being cut off for long from his main 'sources of supply'[2]—perhaps even through the persisting ambivalence of his feeling towards Nature—he was to defer indefinitely the fulfilment of his longing, and to place continual, almost gratuitous obstacles in the way of his so-long-desired establishment at Honfleur.[3]

Honfleur, however, in the context of Baudelaire's renewed sensitivity to Nature, signified still more, even, than the 'maison-joujou' itself, and the wide vistas it commanded over the sea. There was the port, for instance, offering a spectacle which in itself, in its turmoil and bustle, in the intricate 'architecture' and the subtle rhythms of the sailing vessels, had always captivated him,[4] and which at the same time stirred vivid memories of his own departure from a port of France some eighteen years before, thereby reviving and quickening old sensations and nostalgias. And there was also the happy coincidence, as we have seen, of a neighbour, Boudin, whose studio was crowded with innumerable sketches and impressions of

---

[1] *CG* IV, 99 (cf. p. 285 and n. 2, below); for the other references in question, see notably *CG* II, 127, 130, 203–4, 231, 243, IV, 288, 320, V, 194, 304, as also *Fusées* XVI, *JI* 39. In a letter to Asselineau, Mme Aupick movingly recalls the times B. had spent with her at Honfleur: 'Je vous montrerai la place où, en étendant les bras devant le ciel et la mer, il m'a dit maintes et maintes fois: "Oh! si je n'avais pas de dettes, comme je serais heureux ici!"' (cit. *EJC* 134).

[2] Cf. p. 146, above.

[3] Cf., for the very numerous references that could here be adduced, *CG* VI, 219–21, Index s.v. 'Honfleur', and G. Jean-Aubry, op. cit., 17–34.

[4] Cf. in this connection the prose poem *Le Port, PPP* 141–2, and the comment by G. Jean-Aubry, op. cit., 54–5; for B.'s other references to sailing ships, etc., cf. the art. by H. Peyre, *MLN*, 1929, pp. 447–50, and my art. cit., 'The Amorous Tribute', in *FRH*, pp. 114–15.

18

sun, sea and ships. It is interesting to speculate how far Baudelaire's encounter with Boudin may have served to 'open his eyes' to the beauties that surrounded him[1], or how far these would in any case have claimed his response—through their very immediacy, or through their harmony (as in *Chant d'automne*) with his inner mood; certainly it would be altogether appropriate and characteristic if Baudelaire were in fact to have re-apprehended Nature through the intermediary of Art!

Be this as it may, Baudelaire around 1859 seems to have been most strongly attracted towards those aspects of Nature (whether directly experienced, as at Honfleur, or imagined) which by definition are most remote from Man: sea, sky, clouds, sun, moon, desert, mountains, lakes; so much, indeed, is this the case that on the strength of certain texts of this period one might almost apply to Baudelaire himself the description he gives, in 1861, of Victor Hugo —that illustrious exile to whom he had recently dedicated his magnificent poem of all exiles, *Le Cygne,* with its final verse stressing, precisely, his own (self-imposed) alienation from other men:[2]

Quand aujourd'hui nous parcourons les poésies récentes de Victor Hugo, nous voyons que tel il était, tel il est resté: un promeneur pensif, un homme solitaire mais enthousiaste de la vie, un esprit rêveur et interrogateur. Mais ce n'est plus dans les environs boisés et fleuris de la grande ville . . . qu'il fait errer ses pieds et ses yeux. Comme Démosthènes, il converse avec les flots et le vent; autrefois, il rôdait solitaire dans des lieux bouillonnant de vie humaine; aujourd'hui, il marche dans des solitudes peuplées par sa pensée. Ainsi est-il peut-être encore plus grand et plus singulier. Les couleurs de ses rêveries se sont teintées en solennité, et sa voix s'est approfondie en rivalisant avec celle de l'Océan.[3]

[1]For another influence possibly exerted by Boudin, cf. pp. 281–2 n. 2, below.
[2]ll. 49–50: 'Ainsi dans la forêt où mon esprit s'exile/Un vieux Souvenir sonne à plein souffle du cor!' It is interesting, incidentally, to note that in an earlier verse B. juxtaposes the epithets 'ridicule et sublime' (applied to the swan) with a reference to exiles in general: 'Je pense à mon grand cygne, avec ses gestes fous,/ Comme les exilés, ridicule et sublime . . .' (ll. 34–5). 'Ridicule et sublime': does not this paradox exactly convey—and perhaps unconsciously betray—the essential ambivalence of B.'s attitude to the *exiled* Hugo during this period?
[3]*Hugo, AR* 301. The phrase 'il converse avec les flots et le vent', would seem an echo, conscious or unconscious, of the line describing the infant Poet in *Bénédiction*: 'Il joue avec le vent, cause avec le nuage . . .' (l. 25; cf. p. 4, above). As to the further phrase 'enthousiaste de la vie', it must be admitted that this (alone) scarcely fits the B. of 1861!

... Aucun artiste n'est plus universel que lui, plus apte à se mettre en contact avec les forces de la vie universelle, plus disposé à prendre sans cesse un bain de nature.[1]

Thus in the *Salon de 1859*, towards the end of the chapter 'Le Paysage' to which I have already several times referred, we find Baudelaire complaining of contemporary landscape painters that they are altogether too 'herbivorous', that they seem 'terrified' of the sky and the desert—whereas he for his part *regrets* the Romantic landscapes of yesteryear:

Je regrette ces grands lacs qui représentent l'immobilité dans le bonheur et dans le désespoir, les immenses montagnes, escaliers de la planète vers le ciel, d'où tout ce qui paraissait grand paraît petit, les châteaux forts ... les abbayes crénelées qui se mirent dans les mornes étangs, les ponts gigantesques, les constructions ninivites, habitées par le vertige, et enfin tout ce qu'il faudrait inventer, si tout cela n'existait pas![2]

This 'regret' is moreover not merely aesthetic in origin: in evoking, in conjunction with the 'vast mountains', these 'despairingly' immobile lakes favoured by the Romantic landscape painters, Baudelaire would seem to be thinking back also to that Pyrenean excursion which at 17 had left so deep an impression on him, and which is recorded not only in the youthful *Incompatibilité*, but also in a prose poem of 1862, *Le Gâteau*.[3] As to the implied preference for the desert and the sky, this in the poem *La Voix* becomes (with the sea added as immediate 'partner' to the desert) the very sign and definition of the poet's whole temperament:

[1]Ibid., 303–4. In the contemporary article on Leconte de Lisle, these forces de la vie universelle' become, still more impressively, 'les forces imposantes, écrasantes de la nature' (*AR* 375). For the phrase 'bain de nature', cf. p. 171, n. 3, above.

[2]1859 text, *CE* 344, var. 498. (After 1859, B. significantly deletes the initial phrase 'dans le bonheur'.) B. Gheerbrant, *B. critique d'art*, 168, suggests that this passage may refer specifically to Rodolphe Bresdin; may not B. equally have had in mind, however, such artists as John Martin ('les constructions ninivites') and H. E. Kendall, Jun. ('les ponts gigantesques'; cf. *CE* 257, *AR* 173, as also my art. cit., *RLC*, 1956, pp. 62–3)? For this general Romantic and pre-Romantic feeling for 'wild' Nature, see C. A. Moore, *Studies in Philology*, 1917, pp. 243–4; Paul van Tieghem, *Sentiment de la nature dans le préromantisme*, 242; J. W. Beach, *Concept of Nature in 19th-Century English Poetry*, 34–6 (Byron).

[3]Cf. pp. 6–9 and 192, above. For further possible allusions to this voyage, cf. p. 6 n. 4, above.

Et c'est depuis ce temps que, pareil aux prophètes,
J'aime si tendrement le désert et la mer;
Que je ris dans les deuils et pleure dans les fêtes,
Et trouve un goût suave au vin le plus amer;

Que je prends très-souvent les faits pour des mensonges,
Et que, les yeux au ciel, je tombe dans des trous.

(*La Voix*, 1861 text, ll. 21–6)

The context here is the poet's compulsion, from infancy, to hearken
to the second of the two 'voices' that speak to him as he lies in his
cradle—to the voice of imagination and dream, rather than to the
voice of reality which invites him ('La Terre est un gâteau plein
de douceur') to taste to the full the sweets of the earth. As in
Alchimie de la douleur (though the antithesis is there framed in
rather different terms), the poet's choice is made to argue a certain
perversity of temperament; to this, however, there is now added,
in the concluding couplet which follows immediately upon the
verses quoted above, a needlessly explicit and disappointingly conventional justification:

Mais la Voix me console et dit: "Garde tes songes:
Les sages n'en ont pas d'aussi beaux que les fous!"

(ll. 27–8)

Idiosyncratic perversity has here been generalized to a Romantic
cliché not unlike that formulated on the generic Poet's behalf in
the equally (and appropriately!) lame conclusion to *L'Albatros*:

Le Poëte est semblable au prince des nuées
Qui hante la tempête et se rit de l'archer;
Exilé sur le sol au milieu des huées,
Ses ailes de géant l'empêchent de marcher.[1]

A text published a year or so later (in 1863), the prose poem
Déjà!, links in a more subtle fashion the poet's 'tender love' for
the sea, and his rejection of the material world. Recalling perhaps
an episode of his youthful voyage (if not the exact mood of those
days), Baudelaire describes how he alone, of all the passengers on
a ship, feels sad, deeply sad, when land is at last sighted. This is not

---

[1] ll. 13–16. Cf., however, for a more favourable judgement on *La Voix*, the
persuasive J. Prévost, *B.*, 196–7.

because the shores at which they touch are in any way displeasing
or disappointing; on the contrary:

... nous vîmes, en approchant, que c'était une terre magnifique, éblouis-
sante. Il semblait que les musiques de la vie s'en détachaient en un vague
murmure, et que de ces côtes, riches en verdures de toute sorte, s'exhalait,
jusqu'à plusieurs lieues, une délicieuse odeur de fleurs et de fruits.

(1863 text, *PPP* 126)

These lines might seem the exotic translation of all the 'sweetness'
so insidiously promised in *La Voix:* 'La Terre est un gâteau plein
de douceur . . .'—even more so when at the end of the prose poem,
the same description returns (as we shall see) in a still more haunting
and seductive form. And yet here again, as in *La Voix,* Baudelaire
prefers the sea—not only for the magnificence of the spectacles it
affords, the endless dramas evoked in the opening sentence of the
poem:

Cent fois déjà le soleil avait jailli, radieux ou attristé, de cette cuve immense de la mer dont les bords ne se laissent qu'à peine apercevoir; cent
fois il s'etait replongé, étincelant ou morose, dans son immense bain du
soir.

(*PPP* 125)

—but also for the strange and altogether 'human' fascination of its
endlessly variable moods. Here are the closing paragraphs of this
prose poem; their 'music' (the harmonious 'phrasing' of the
elaborate sentences, the delicate balance of the 'inner parts', the
graceful cadences) is surely as mellifluous as any that can have
wafted out from the beckoning shores, and testifies to the unerring
sureness of Baudelaire's ear for prose rhythms:

Moi seul j'étais triste, inconcevablement triste. Semblable à un prêtre à
qui on arracherait sa divinité, je ne pouvais, sans une navrante amertume,
me détacher de cette mer si monstrueusement séduisante, de cette mer si
infiniment variée dans son effrayante simplicité, et qui semble contenir en
elle et représenter par ses jeux, ses allures, ses colères et ses sourires, les
humeurs, les agonies et les extases de toutes les âmes qui ont vécu, qui
vivent et qui vivront!
En disant adieu à cette incomparable beauté, je me sentais abattu
jusqu'à la mort; et c'est pourquoi, quand chacun de mes compagnons dit:
"Enfin!" je ne pus crier que: " *Déjà!* "

Cependant c'était la terre, la terre avec ses bruits, ses passions, ses commodités, ses fêtes; c'était une terre riche et magnifique, pleine de promesses, qui nous envoyait un mystérieux parfum de rose et de musc, et d'où les musiques de la vie nous arrivaient en un amoureux murmure.[1]

Now one may here be reminded, by Baudelaire's assimilation of the sea to all the human souls that ever have been, are or will be, of that earlier analogy between Man and sea that he had sustained in the sonnet *L'Homme et la mer*; or, again, of those continuing thoughts of mankind that had pursued him (in the letter to Desnoyers) into the very depths of the forest; or even, in a more general sense, of the largely 'Man-centred' system of analogies favoured by him during this period. And yet can one truly, in this instance, speak without paradox of Baudelaire's 'humanism'? The sea may, for him, owe something of its charm to the images of Mankind it arouses in his mind; on the other hand, in opting for the sea as against the delights of the land, has he not consciously set himself apart from those fellow-passengers whom he clearly despises for their trivial grievances and bickerings, and whose 'absurd' yearnings for land he had scathingly mocked in an earlier paragraph?

Il y en avait qui pensaient à leur foyer, qui regrettaient leurs femmes infidèles et maussades, et leur progéniture criarde. Tous étaient si affolés par l'image de la terre absente, qu'ils auraient, je crois, mangé de l'herbe avec plus d'enthousiasme que les bêtes.[2]

Indeed, in closing his ears to the ravishing music of the shores, is he not in effect turning his back altogether on the world of men,

---

[1]*PPP* 126-7. The two conjoined perfumes, musk and rose, seem for B. during this last phase to have come to symbolize or represent all that is benign and smiling and idyllic in life, by implied or explicit contrast with any too grim reality: cf., in this connection, the prose poem *Les Projets*, with its imagined 'setting' for the poet and his beloved: ' "Au bord de la mer, une belle case en bois . . . dans l'atmosphère, une odeur enivrante, indéfinissable . . ., dans la case un puissant parfum de rose et de musc . . ." ' (*PPP* 80; in the earliest, 1857 version, the 'musk' stands alone: 'partout un parfum indescriptible de musc')—or, again, the letter to Nadar of 14 May 1859, with its protest against the 'B. legend' which had already begun to spring up during the poet's lifetime: 'Il m'est pénible de passer pour le Prince des Charognes. Tu n'as sans doute pas lu une foule de choses de moi, qui ne sont que musc et que roses' (*CG* II, 310).

[2]*PPP* 126. This last phrase reminds us of the ironic comment in the *Salon de 1859*: 'Nos paysagistes sont des animaux beaucoup trop *herbivores*' (*CE* 344—my italics; cf. p. 257, above).

declaring once again for solitude as against fellowship? In marvelling at the immensity, the endless variety, the *infinitude* of the sea, is he not indirectly voicing his dissatisfaction with that same, all-too finite world of men?

These references to the protean multiformity and expansive symbolism (as well as to the eternal fascination) of the sea, are echoed in a number of other texts of this period—thus giving the lie, incidentally, to the Schanne anecdote cited in an earlier chapter, where Baudelaire is credited, on the contrary, with a dogmatic preference for *contained* and *channelled* water.[1] Perhaps the most striking (certainly the most closely analytical) of these various texts, is the famous passage from *Mon Cœur mis à nu* (xxx):

> Pourquoi le spectacle de la mer est-il infiniment et si éternellement agréable?
>
> Parce que la mer offre à la fois l'idée de l'immensité et du mouvement. Six ou sept lieues représentent pour l'homme le rayon de l'infini. Voilà un infini diminutif. Qu'importe s'il suffit à suggérer l'idée de l'infini total? Douze ou quatorze lieues (sur le diamètre), douze ou quatorze de liquide en mouvement suffisent pour donner la plus haute idée de beauté qui soit offerte à l'homme sur son habitacle transitoire.[2]

Conversely, in its relation to human aspirations, the sea may become a symbol not of the infinite but rather of the *finite*—as in these lines, from the opening section of *Le Voyage,* evoking the restless 'ardour' of the departing Travellers:

> Un matin nous partons, le cerveau plein de flamme,
> Le cœur gros de rancune et de désirs amers,
> Et nous allons, suivant le rhythme de la lame,
> Berçant notre infini sur le fini des mers . . .　　　　(ll. 5–8)

---

[1] Cf. p. 145, above.

[2] *JI* 85. Cf. also the comment on Hugo, in the article of 1861: 'Ainsi est-il emporté irrésistiblement vers tout symbole de l'infini, la mer, le ciel . . .' (*AR* 309); the singling-out, as 'une grande allégorie naturelle', of De Quincey's meditation on the city of L[iverpool] and its sea, ending: 'L'Océan, avec sa respiration éternelle, mais couvé par un vaste calme, personnifiait mon esprit et l'influence qui le gouvernait alors' (*PA* 119–20; cf. *Confessions* ed. Elwin, 398–9 and 275, and G. T. Clapton, *B. et De Quincey*, 54); the mysterious phrase 'Réthorique [sic] de la mer' which occurs in the 'Notes' for *L'Art philosophique* (*OCP* 1107). In all this (as in so many other respects)', B. could be deemed almost the lineal descendant of that Jean-Jacques Rousseau to whom he is so often (and too automatically) opposed; cf., for Rousseau's 'passionate' love of water in all its forms, D. Mornet, *Sentiment de la nature*, 190.

In the concluding verses, however—as will be seen when, in my next chapter, I come to discuss this poem more fully—there is affirmed a more traditional symbolism: the sea then becomes simply the *after*-life, on which (under the 'captaincy' of Death) one may at last 'joyfully' set sail, leaving behind the tedious 'country' in which one has so long been condemned to dwell.[1]

Among the wonders of the world seen (and dismissed) by the returning Travellers of *Le Voyage,* none (they declare) can match, in its 'mysterious charm', the capricious pageant of the clouds.[2] In this preference, the 'étonnants voyageurs' show themselves to be the true kindred of the Baudelaire who in his *Salon de 1859* had confessed the hypnotic spell cast over him by Boudin's cloudscapes, and who in *Horreur sympathique* had gazed up at the turbulent, tempestuous sky, seeking (and finding) therein the 'sympathetic' reflection of his own temperament.[3] Two further, and linked, prose poems explore still more intensively this almost obsessive pre-occupation, and at the same time convey the sense of alienation from his fellows that seems the almost inevitable accompaniment of Baudelaire's response to Nature during this last phase of his life, when he so often assumed the posture (both literal and figurative) of the man 'lost in the clouds'. The first of these two poems, *L'Étranger,* takes the form of a dialogue—best quoted in full, since wholly self-explanatory:

[1] ll. 122–44; cf. pp. 306–8, below.

[2] ll. 65–8 (cit. p. 301, below).

[3] Cf. pp. 136, 248–9, above. Cf. also, in this connection, *Alchimie de la douleur* ll. 11–14 (pp. 246–7, above); *Bénédiction*, l. 25 (p. 61, above); *Recueillement*, ll. 9–14 (p. 269, below); the anecdote, recounted by Asselineau (p. 12 and n. 2, above) concerning B.'s 'frosting' of his windows at the Hôtel Pimodan; the comment by G. Jean-Aubry, *B. et Honfleur*, 55–7, on the particular interest and opportunities afforded by Honfleur to the 'connoisseur of clouds'. For analogous preoccupations in other writers, cf. the passage from De Quincey's *Suspiria* (*Confessions*, ed. Elwin 475) describing the 'visions' prompted in him, in church, by his grief at his sister's death, and thus summarized by B. *PA* 172: ' . . . ses yeux, fixés sur la partie non coloriée des vitraux, voyaient sans cesse les nuages floconneux du ciel se transformer en rideaux et en oreillers blancs, sur lesquels reposaient des têtes d'enfants, souffrants, pleurants, mourants'; the section beginning 'Où vont ces rapides nuages . . . ?', of Lamartine's *Poésie, ou Paysage dans le golfe de Gênes* (Pléiade, 326–7; cf. *FMCB* 430); the lines from Wordsworth's *The Excursion*, quoted by De Quincey and summarized by B., *PA* 137–8 (*Confessions*, ed. M. Elwin, 423; cf. G. T. Clapton, *B. et De Quincey*, 65).

—Qui aimes-tu le mieux, homme énigmatique, dis? tes parents, ta
sœur ou ton frère?

—Je n'ai ni parents, ni sœur, ni frère.

—Tes amis?

—Vous vous servez là d'une parole dont le sens m'est resté jusqu'à
ce jour inconnu.

—Ta patrie?

—J'ignore sous quelle latitude elle est située.

—La beauté?

—Je l'aimerais volontiers, déesse et immortelle.

—L'argent?

—Je le hais comme vous haïssez Dieu.

—Eh! qu'aimes-tu donc, extraordinaire étranger?

—J'aime les nuages ... les nuages qui passent ... là-bas ... là-bas ...
les merveilleux nuages![1]

How far is Baudelaire himself the 'Stranger', or 'Outsider', of this
poem? *L'Étranger* was the text chosen (by him? or by his posthumous editors, Banville and Asselineau?) to open the first published
edition, in 1869, of the collected *Petits Poëmes en prose*; this in
itself, perhaps, implies a certain measure of self-projection or self-
identification.[2] More conclusive, however, is the evidence of *La
Soupe et les nuages,* which forms in a sense the ironic pendant to
L'Étranger, and in which Baudelaire speaks directly in the first
person:

Ma petite folle bien aimée me donnait à dîner, et par la fenêtre ouverte
de la salle à manger je contemplais les mouvantes architectures que Dieu
fait avec les vapeurs, les merveilleuses constructions de l'impalpable; — et
je me disais, à travers ma contemplation: '—Toutes ces fantasmagories
sont presque aussi belles que les vastes yeux de ma bien aimée, la petite
folle monstrueuse aux yeux verts.'

Et tout à coup je reçus un violent coup de poing dans le dos, et j'entendis
une voix rauque et charmante, une voix hystérique et comme enrouée par
l'eau de vie, la voix de ma chère petite bien aimée, qui disait: 'Allez-
vous bientôt manger votre soupe, sacré bougre de marchand de nuages!'[3]

---

[1] 1862 text, *PPP* 3–4, var. 272.

[2] Cf. also the concluding words of Champfleury's *Les Amis de la Nature*, in
which is anticipated, as we have seen (pp. 120–1 n. 3, above), the final riposte of
our present prose poem; if Bigle, with his 'Monsieur Gorenflot ... donnez-moi
le nuage qui passe!' (p. 141), is indeed modelled on B., then this would imply
that Champfleury, before 1859, must have heard his friend giving vent precisely
to such preferences as these.

[3] MS. Godoy (c. 1863), *PPP* 153–4, var. 333–4.

In another prose poem of this period, *Les Bienfaits de la lune,* the Moon, descending her 'staircase of clouds' to penetrate within the room she then pervades 'comme une atmosphère phosphorique, comme un poison lumineux', defines in these terms the 'gifts' (in the fairy-tale sense) that she brings to the cradle of her elected godchild, the poet's 'pampered' mistress:

'Tu subiras éternellement l'influence de mon baiser. Tu seras belle à ma manière. Tu aimeras ce que j'aime et ce qui m'aime: l'eau, les nuages, le silence et la nuit; la mer immense et verte; l'eau informe et multiforme; le lieu où tu ne seras pas; l'amant que tu ne connaîtras pas . . .

'Et tu seras aimée de mes amants, courtisée par mes courtisans. Tu seras la reine des hommes aux yeux verts dont j'ai serré aussi la gorge dans mes caresses nocturnes; de ceux-là qui aiment la mer, la mer immense, tumultueuse et verte, l'eau informe et multiforme, le lieu où ils ne sont pas, la femme qu'ils ne connaissent pas . . .'

(PPP 134)

It will be seen that the girl's supposed lovers are themselves also accorded, by symmetrical repetition, precisely those attributes and predilections bestowed upon her in her infancy by the Moon— the 'redoubtable Divinity' having resolved, as it were, to draw together infallibly, under her sign, all those she has marked with her impress, all those 'lunatics' she deems fatally 'hers'.[1] Baudelaire's passion for the sea and for the clouds is thus here linked with a certain 'Moon-worship' that recalls the early *Tristesses de la lune,*[2] and that likewise has the solemnity if not of a true 'religion', at least of a personal mythology.

It might well seem, from certain of the examples above-quoted, that the prose poem had become for Baudelaire almost the elected medium within which to renew certain earlier 'characterizations' of elemental Nature. Thus if *Le Gâteau* harks back to *Incompatibilité,* and *Les Bienfaits de la lune* to *Tristesses de la lune,* we may similarly

---

[1] In what may be regarded as the companion poem to *Les Bienfaits de la lune, Le Désir de peindre*—the two are grouped together, side by side, in the (posthumous) *Petits poëmes en prose* and had previously both been published in periodical form within the same year 1863—B. again portrays a woman of whom he can say: 'elle fait . . . penser à la lune, qui sans doute l'a marquée de sa redoutable influence'. But here it is the second of the two 'faces' of the moon—sinister and tormented, rather than serene and discreet—that he invokes as patron for this other (and 'fugitive') beauty.

[2] Cf. pp. 15–16, above, as also pp. 62–8 (*La Lune offensée*).

find in *Le Tir et le cimetière* (composed 1864–5) a return to the theme so powerfully interpolated within *Une Charogne*: the traditional concept of the endless cycle of creation, figured, for Baudelaire, by the image of the hot sun beating down on the putrefying carcase which in turn is destined to give 'nourishment' to other (and still living) forms.[1] It will be recalled that Banville, in his 'companion' poem to his friend's *Une Charogne* (i.e. *Dans le vieux cimetière*), had likewise chosen what is perhaps indeed the obvious setting for such a theme: the cemetery with its constant reminder of death-in-life, and life-in-death.[2] But what for Baudelaire, in his prose poem, adds a quite particular 'piquancy' to the scene, is, firstly, that the cemetery is overlooked by an *estaminet* which unexpectedly advertises itself to its customers in these very terms, i.e. by a signboard reading '*A la vue du cimetière, Estaminet*';[3] secondly, that (as the poem's title forewarns us) the cemetery adjoins a *rifle-range* which accordingly punctuates the vast and pervading hum of insect life with its muffled explosions, its 'muted symphony':[4]

... la lumière et la chaleur ... faisaient rage, et l'on eût dit que le soleil ivre se vautrait tout de son long sur un tapis de fleurs magnifiques engraissées par la destruction. Un immense bruissement de vie remplissait l'air,—la vie des infiniment petits,—coupé à intervalles réguliers par la crépitation des coups de feu d'un tir voisin, qui éclataient comme l'explosion des bouchons de champagne dans le bourdonnement d'une symphonie en sourdine.

The 'humanist' Baudelaire of the letter to Desnoyers would no doubt—like the Vigny of *La Maison du berger*—have found deeply insulting or inimical this 'enrichment', through the very destruction of Man, of Nature's prolific growth.[5] And certainly he is here no

[1] For *Une Charogne*, cf. pp. 21–2, above.

[2] Cf. loc. cit., above. Among latter-day variations on this symbolism, one need only instance Valéry's *Le Cimetière marin*.

[3] *PPP* 154. This 'singulière enseigne' equally furnishes the theme for the two quatrains dedicated to Monselet and published in *Les Épaves* (1866) under the title *Un Cabaret folâtre*; cf. *PPP* 335, and for the germ of both texts in *Pauvre Belgique*, *OP* III, 212, 378, and *OCP* 1576.

[4] *PPP* 156; not the happiest of musical analogies!

[5] Cf. *La Maison du berger*, ll. 303–5: 'Et dans mon cœur alors je la hais [i.e. la Nature], et je vois/Notre sang dans son onde et nos morts sous son herbe/Nourissant de leurs sucs la racine des bois'—as also Lamartine, *Le Dernier chant du pèlerinage d'Harold*, XLII (Pléiade, 237–8; cit. Y. Boeniger, *Lamartine et le sentiment de la nature*, 67).

longer content simply to affirm, as in *Une Charogne,* the sovereign
'greatness' of Nature. But the true 'lesson' he derives from this
bizarre conjunction of urban 'amenities' (bar, cemetery, rifle range),
is revealed—in the imagined (and whispered) dialogue which concludes the poem—to be that same misanthropic nihilism that so
constantly informs his writings during this period;[1] here as in *Le
Voyage,* with its joyful 'embarkation' on the 'ship' of Death, Baudelaire takes as his symbol the immediate image with which his literal
context supplies him—that ultimate 'Target' which (as the dead in
their hindsight know) is the sole 'aim' truly worthy to be pursued in
life:

Alors, sous le soleil qui lui chauffait le cerveau et dans l'atmosphère des
ardents parfums de la Mort, il entendit une voix chuchoter sous la tombe
où il s'était assis. Et cette voix disait: "Maudites soient vos cibles et vos
carabines, turbulents vivants, qui vous souciez si peu des défunts et de
leur divin repos! . . . Si vous saviez comme le prix est facile à gagner,
comme le but est facile à toucher, et combien tout est néant, excepté la
Mort, vous ne vous fatigueriez pas tant, laborieux vivants, et vous trouble-
riez moins souvent le sommeil de ceux qui depuis longtemps ont mis dans
le But, dans le seul vrai but de la détestable vie!"[2]

The stress laid by Baudelaire, in *Le Tir et le cimetière,* on what
might be called the 'aggressive' aspect of the sun's radiance, should
not be taken as implying in any sense a *denunciation* of Nature
(for its presumed 'hostility' to Man), such as we have noted in
certain earlier texts of the 1852–4 period;[3] on the contrary, even
when presented as 'cruel' or 'ironic',[4] the sun is tacitly or openly
admired for its elemental power and 'dynamic' influence. Thus in the
opening paragraphs of another prose poem, *Le Fou et la Vénus*
(first published 1862), the description of the vast park 'swooning'
amorously and 'ecstatically' under the 'burning eye' of the sun—
a 'swoon' which induces not passivity, but rather (as in *Le Tir et le
cimetière*) a massive surge of vitality, an 'energy' of brilliance, colour

---

[1] Cf. my final chapter, below. I here use the word 'nihilism'—for want of a
better, and in what is admittedly not quite the established sense—to denote a
reasoned and philosophic aspiration towards Death; cf. *FMCB* 265.

[2] *PPP* 136. In *La Mort des pauvres,* l. 2, B. had likewise presented Death as 'le
but de la vie'—but without, of course, giving the word the specific metaphorical
connotations it here carries.

[3] Cf. pp. 108–10, 125, above.

[4] Cf., in this connection, the texts cited pp. 106–7 n. 3, above.

and perfume—is no less expansively lyrical than the chapter 'De la couleur' of the *Salon de 1846*, and moreover as an expression of the 'sun-cult' far surpasses in vigour and conviction the youthful verses of *Le Soleil:*[1]

Quelle admirable journée! Le vaste parc se pâme sous l'œil brûlant du soleil, comme la jeunesse sous la domination de l'Amour.

L'extase universelle des choses ne s'exprime par aucun bruit; les eaux elles-mêmes sont comme endormies. Bien différente des fêtes humaines, c'est ici une orgie silencieuse.

On dirait qu'une lumière toujours croissante fait de plus en plus étinceler les objets; que les fleurs excitées brûlent du désir de rivaliser avec l'azur du ciel par l'énergie de leurs couleurs, et que la chaleur, rendant visibles les parfums, les fait monter vers l'astre comme des fumées.

(*PPP* 17–18)

Of all these aspects of Nature, however, it is the setting sun which seems, during this period, to have held the deepest emotional significance for Baudelaire. Such a response, whether aesthetic or affective, was not of course in itself new; indeed, the very earliest Baudelaire text quoted in the present volume is, it will be recalled, a description of a sunset seen at the age of ten,[2] and we have seen that in subsequent years the spectacle continues to move him not only by its beauty, but above all by the *elegiac* overtones it appears almost infallibly to carry.[3] In *Harmonie du soir,* in particular, Baudelaire draws from certain elements of the evening scene a melancholy inflection (the violin with its 'sad' waltz, the vast sky that again is both beautiful and 'sad', the sun 'dying' in its dramatic, blood-red glow) that in part, no doubt, derives from his own mood, but that has become also (by association of ideas, through the play of nostalgia) a constant, almost a *physical* 'component' of the actual spectacle itself.[4] Yet because these memories are in themselves

[1]Cf. pp. 13–14, 106–8, above.

[2]See p. 3, above. The most elaborate such description is, of course, that which concludes the long 'colour symphony' in the chapter 'De la couleur' of the *Salon de 1846*; cf. pp. 79–80, above.

[3]This elegiac note may be discerned already within the mainly descriptive context of *Je n'ai pas oublié, voisine de la ville* (p. 13, above); cf. also, in this connection, *La Vie antérieure* (pp. 44–8, above).

[4]Cf. pp. 82–5, above; a similar genesis is inferred by A. Adam, *FMA* 319, for *Le Balcon* (pub. 1857). In another text of the period 1845–51, the essay *Du Vin et du hachish*, *PA* 213, we may find an instance of a purely metaphorical

benign, the sunset, the evening scene, nevertheless take on for the poet a consolatory as well as an elegiac quality: 'Un cœur tendre, qui hait le néant vaste et noir, / Du passé lumineux recueille tout vestige. . . .' An exactly similar process may be observed in a poem of our present period, *Recueillement,* which to some extent may be regarded as the ulterior counterpart of *Harmonie du soir.* Before, however, one can fully discuss *Recueillement* from this (or indeed from any other) point of view, it is necessary to 'see' clearly the 'real' landscape (with its figures) which is implied throughout the sonnet as a whole, but which in the tercets is no more than lightly sketched in or suggested. In the first quatrain, the poet having in his role as 'Promeneur solitaire' climbed to some high vantage-point above the city, stands looking down over it;[1] 'beside' him is his imagined and by now constant 'companion', his Suffering. Night is coming on—the benison for which 'she' has craved. He bids her 'take his hand', and turn away with him from the spectacle they can dimly discern, or divine, in the teeming streets below, and which is described in the second quatrain: the 'vile multitude', driven by the scourge of Pleasure, launching itself upon a hectic nocturnal round that is no more than a laying-up (on earth) of future remorse:[2]

> Sois sage, ô ma Douleur, et tiens-toi plus tranquille.
> Tu réclamais le Soir; il descend; le voici:
> Une atmosphère obscure enveloppe la ville,
> Aux uns portant la paix, aux autres le souci.

---

sunset, which the immediate *elegiac* theme has sufficed, I suggest, to call into being: cf., for a discussion of this passage in relation to *Harmonie du soir* and to the whole associative nexus to which both texts belong, my art. cit., 'Pour une étude chronologique des *FM*', *RHLF*, 1967, pp. 351–2.

[1] It will be recalled that it was under the title 'Le Promeneur solitaire' that B. had at first intended—on the evidence of an 1861 MS. of *Le Couvercle*; cf. p. 252 n. 2, above—to group several sonnets which would have included *Recueillement* as well as *Le Couvercle.*

[2] Cf. (p. 188, above) the concluding paragraph of *Le Poëme du haschisch* (first pub. 1858), with its picture of the 'saddened' philosopher-poet: 'Au-dessous de lui, au pied de la montagne, . . . la troupe des humains, la bande des ilotes, simule les grimaces de la jouissance et pousse des hurlements que lui arrache la morsure du poison' (*PA* 69); or again, in the 1864 version of the prose poem *La Solitude,* the reference to that other sage, Pascal, 'rappelant . . . dans la cellule du *recueillement* tous ces affolés qui cherchent le bonheur dans le mouvement . . .' (*PP* 77; my italics).

> Pendant que des mortels la multitude vile,
> Sous le fouet du Plaisir, ce bourreau sans merci,
> Va cueillir des remords dans la fête servile,
> Ma Douleur, donne-moi la main; viens par ici,
>
> Loin d'eux . . .
>
> (ll. 1–9)

In their elected solitude, the 'two' thus turn, instead, towards the west; there, far from the multitude, far from Mankind, may be descried just such a sunset 'architecture' of clouds as serves, in the exactly contemporary article on Banville, to convey by analogy the magnificence of the lyric poet's 'apotheosis':[1] terraced clouds forming 'balconies' in the sky, cloud-shapes rising up from the water, the sun sinking to rest (or to its 'death') behind an 'arch' of clouds, the whole cloudscape beginning to darken, with the almost audible onset of night, into long shroud-like forms 'trailing towards the east':

> . . . Ma Douleur, donne-moi la main; viens par ici,
>
> Loin d'eux. Vois se pencher les défuntes Années,
> Sur les balcons du ciel, en robes surannées;
> Surgir du fond des eaux le Regret souriant;
>
> Le Soleil moribond s'endormir sous une arche,
> Et, comme un long linceul traînant à l'Orient,
> Entends, ma chère, entends la douce Nuit qui marche.
>
> (ll. 8–14)

The element of consolation of which I have spoken, is here expressed not directly but through stylized yet graceful personification: the 'bygone Years' lean out from the balconies of Heaven in their quaintly charming dresses; 'smiling Règret' emerges like some Ondine from her native depths; the poet's 'companion' gazes with

---

[1]"Il [the lyric poet] ne peut se reposer que dans de verdoyants Élysées, ou dans les palais plus beaux et plus profonds que *les architectures de vapeur bâties par les soleils couchants*' (*AR* 356; my italics). B. may here be recalling certain verses from Hugo's cycle, *Soleils couchants*, in the *Feuilles d'automne* of 1831 (Pléiade, 1, 785–6, 788–9). For other cloud 'constructions' or 'fancies' in B., cf. the youthful *Incompatibilité*, ll. 25–8, as also, more especially (p. 263, above), *La Soupe et les nuages*; among innumerable instances from earlier writers, could be cited, as well as Shakespeare's 'cloud that's dragonish', those noted by P. Albouy, in ed. Hugo, Pléiade, 1, 1384.

him at the scene, and all her agitation (so one presumes) is gently
stilled. Or in other words (transposing back into directly personal
terms this outward projection of emotion onto a landscape), the
poet under the spell cast by the evening sky—having already, so
one senses from the opening line ('Sois sage, ô ma Douleur, et
tiens-toi plus tranquille'), 'come to terms' in some measure with
his suffering, to the extent of achieving, almost beyond the ultimate
limits of endurance, a certain stoic serenity of despair—now seeks
further to abate this suffering, to soften its still harsh asperities,
by turning his thoughts (as in *Harmonie du soir*) towards the
regretted happiness of the past, by 'withdrawing' meditatively (the
'recueillement' of his title) into the interior solitude that Night itself
fashions for him.[1] Yet in the final couplet Night appears as a still
further, still more soothing balm—with the faint implication,
indeed, that to see Night's gathering darkness as a *shroud,* is to
desire from it some more complete oblivion;[2] thus a better analogy,
here, than with *Harmonie du soir* (where the 'tender heart' on the
contrary fears, or 'hates', the 'dark nothingness' to come), would
perhaps be with these final paragraphs of *Le Crépuscule du soir,*
in its 1864 version:

Crépuscule, comme vous êtes doux et tendre! Les lueurs roses qui
traînent encore à l'horizon comme l'agonie du jour sous l'oppression
victorieuse de sa nuit, les feux des candélabres qui font des taches d'un

---

[1] Cf. in this connection the concluding section of the verse *Crépuscule du soir*
('Recueille-toi, mon âme, en ce grave moment', etc.) in which the poet similarly
'closes his ears' to the distracting and vicious clamour of the city. Cf. also the
prose poem *Les Veuves* (pub. 1862), *PPP* 37: the *afternoon* sky, in autumn, is
held to induce in the mind a similar profusion of 'memories' and 'regrets'.

[2] This most fundamental of all analogies ('Death's twin-brother, Sleep') is
implied more strongly in another poem of this period, *La Fin de la journée*, and
is explicitly if hyperbolically formulated in an earlier text, *Le Léthé*: 'Je veux
dormir! dormir plutôt que vivre!/Dans un sommeil aussi doux que la mort . . .'
(ll. 9–10). As to the 'shroud' itself, this may perhaps derive, as A. G. Engstrom
has suggested, *MLN*, 1959, pp. 697–8, from the opening verse of Longfellow's
Hymn to the Night; cf. also, however, the first of Hugo's six *Soleils couchants*
poems aforementioned, where this image likewise figures the evening 'veils'
of the sky (but of the winter sky); see final verse, Pléiade I, 786. Curiously enough,
B. in his article on Hugo, published during this same year 1861, seems consciously or unconsciously to have had the final couplet of *Recueillement* (and its
title) in mind, when declaring, of the exile of Guernsey: 'toujours il nous apparaît comme la statue de la Méditation qui marche' (*AR* 301).

rouge opaque sur les dernières gloires du couchant, les lourdes draperies qu'une main invisible attire des profondeurs de l'Orient, imitent tous les sentiments compliqués qui luttent dans le cœur de l'homme aux heures solennelles de la vie.

On dirait encore d'une des ces robes étranges de danseuses, où une gaze transparente et sombre laisse entrevoir les splendeurs amorties d'une jupe éclatante, comme sous le noir présent transperce le délicieux passé; et les étoiles vacillantes d'or et d'argent, dont elle est semée, représentent ces feux de la fantaisie qui ne s'allument bien que sous le deuil profond de la Nuit.

(PPP 73, var. 302)

Here, shorn of allegorical stylization, we re-encounter certain images from *Recueillement* (the heavy draperies drawn, as it were, 'from East to West', and, a little later, the 'mourning garb' which Night puts on), while the telling phrase 'sous le noir présent transperce le délicieux passé' could be extended equally to *Harmonie du soir,* as indeed to more than one elegiac poem of Baudelaire's.[1]

However indirectly conveyed, however charged with symbolic overtones may seem the sunset of *Recueillement,* it still remains, like that of *Harmonie du soir,* a 'real' sunset; in other texts of the period, the symbolism becomes more explicit and it is this figurative intensification of the image that lends it a new importance. I quoted at the beginning of this chapter the verse from *Chant d'automne* in which Baudelaire exclaims to Marie Daubrun, in the harsh duress of his winter mood, that for him nothing—not her beauty, even, nor her love—can now match that other brightness of the sun shining out over the sea.[2] But he goes on:

> Et pourtant aimez-moi, tendre cœur! soyez mère,
> Même pour un ingrat, même pour un méchant;
> Amante ou sœur, soyez la douceur éphémère
> D'un glorieux automne ou d'un soleil couchant.
>
> Courte tâche! La tombe attend; elle est avide!
> Ah! laissez-moi, mon front posé sur vos genoux,
> Goûter, en regrettant l'été blanc et torride,
> De l'arrière-saison le rayon jaune et doux!

(ll. 21–8)

---

[1]Cf. *Moesta et errabunda* (pp. 37–40, above), *Un Fantôme* I (1860).
[2]Cf. p. 254, above.

19

The symbolism of this 'song of autumn'—one of several texts in which Baudelaire declares his (sometimes ambivalent) fondness for the two 'sad seasons'[1]—is here complex and subtly personal in its reference. The autumn sunset, in its consoling quality, its 'douceur éphémère', is at first linked, pleadingly, with Marie herself; then, however, by a traditional symbolism, it is brought obliquely into relation with the present, troubled moment of the poet's life, at which he stands poised on the threshold of a chill winter which presages only death, looking back on a 'summer' that has fled all too swiftly by.[2]

The melancholy that for the Romantic artist seems intrinsic in the spectacle of the setting sun,[3] need not, of course, exclude majesty or splendour; on the contrary, it is these qualities especially that are invoked by Baudelaire, for emotive and symbolic purposes, during this period. Thus at the purely literal level we find him, in the *Salon de 1859*, commending a landscape by Jadin (a view of Rome from the *Arco di Parma*) in terms that echo distantly the chapter 'De la couleur' of an earlier *Salon:*

C'est l'impression glorieuse et mélancolique du soir descendant sur la cité sainte, un soir solennel, traversé de bandes pourprées, pompeux et ardent comme la religion romaine.[4]

In another passage of this same *Salon de 1859*, it is an earlier Rome that is brought briefly into relation with the ('imperial') majesty of

[1]Cf. *Brumes et pluies; Edgar Poe, HE* xxviii–xxix; *Ciel brouillé; Salon de 1859, CE* 338 (Lavieille; cf. p. 253, above). For B.'s precursors in this particular sphere of Nature-feeling, cf. Paul van Tieghem, in *Mélanges Baldensperger*, II, 337–41; G. Charlier, *Sentiment de la nature chez les romantiques*, 246 (Senancour). A model he is perhaps more likely to have had in mind, however, is Sainte-Beuve's *La Plaine* (*Joseph Delorme*, ed. G. Antoine, 125–6).

[2]Cf. ll. 2, 15: 'Adieu, vive clarté de nos étés trop courts!/. . . C'était hier l'été; voici l'automne!' Cf. also this passage translated from De Quincey: 'Nos yeux voient l'été, et notre pensée hante la tombe; la glorieuse clarté est autour de nous, et en nous sont les ténèbres' (*Mangeur d'opium, PA* 168; cf. De Quincey, *Confessions*, ed. M. Elwin, 465)—as also, for a more explicit seasonal symbolism, the two sonnets *L'Ennemi*, ll. 1–5 ('Voilà que j'ai touché l'automne des idées . . .'), *Sonnet d'automne*, ll. 13–14 (and here one might speak of an 'automne des émotions'). For an alternative symbolism, finally, cf. *Le Balcon*: here, within a similar elegiac context, the remembered sunsets ('Que les soleils sont beaux dans les chaudes soirées!') suggest in conclusion, as an image of consolation or hope, a corresponding yet purely figurative sun*rise* (ll. 28–9).

[3]Cf., e.g., Lamartine's *L'Occident* (*Harmonies poétiques et religieuses*, 1830).

[4]*CE* 339–40; cf. *Salon de 1846, CE* 94.

the sunset when before a painting of Gérôme's *(La Mort de César)* Baudelaire is led to exclaim: 'Jules César! quelle *splendeur de soleil couché* le nom de cet homme jette dans l'imagination!'[1] Altogether more elaborate and detailed, however, are the descriptions given in other texts of this period, of sunsets which none the less remain purely symbolic in character.[2] Thus when seeking to refute, in his *Notes nouvelles sur Edgar Poe* of 1857, the automatic condemnation by the classical aestheticians of so-called 'decadent' literature, Baudelaire launches himself upon a sunset-description which in its vividness no less than in its general formulation, recalls strongly the equivalent paragraph of the aforementioned chapter 'De la couleur' in the *Salon de 1846*. But the present description adds (as befits its symbolic function) a new elegiac cadence:

Ce soleil qui, il y a quelques heures, écrasait toutes choses de sa lumière droite et blanche, va bientôt inonder l'horizon occidental de couleurs variées. Dans les jeux de ce soleil agonisant, certains esprits poétiques trouveront des délices nouvelles; ils y découvriront des colonnades éblouissantes, des cascades de métal fondu, des paradis de feu, une splendeur triste, la volupté du regret, toutes les magies du rêve, tous les souvenirs de l'opium. Et le coucher du soleil leur apparaîtra en effet comme la merveilleuse allégorie d'une âme chargée de vie, qui descend derrière l'horizon avec une magnifique provision de pensées et de rêves.

(*NHE* vi)

A more specific literary association informs a no less eloquent passage of the article of 1859 on Gautier; here, Baudelaire looks back 'proudly and regretfully' to the early heyday of Romanticism, and by way of epitomizing his feeling, quotes (or adapts) the elegiac final lines of a poem by Hugo:

Tout écrivain français, ardent pour la gloire de son pays, ne peut pas, sans fierté et sans regrets, reporter ses regards vers cette époque de crise féconde où la littérature romantique s'épanouissait avec tant de vigueur. . . . Quelle ardeur chez l'homme de lettres de ce temps, et quelle

---

[1] *CE* 304; my italics.
[2] Cf. among earlier texts, the second *Spleen* poem (*J'ai plus de souvenirs que si j'avais mille ans . . .*), with its concluding, 'Memnon' image. In the passage from *La Fanfarlo* (ed. C. Pichois, 62), cited in *FMCB* 558, as an instance of the 'motif symbolique du soleil couchant', the sunset is surely but one incidental detail within a wider symbolic landscape.

curiosité, quelle chaleur dans le public! *O splendeurs éclipsées, ô soleil descendu derrière l'horizon!*[1]

This last-quoted text leads us to another which at first scrutiny might seem almost its logical complement or extension, but which in fact, as we shall see, constitutes something of a 'special case'. The text in question is a sonnet, first published in January 1862:

> Que le Soleil est beau quand tout frais il se lève,
> Comme une explosion nous lançant son bonjour!
> —Heureux encor celui qui peut avec amour
> Saluer son coucher plus glorieux qu'un rêve!
>
> Je me souviens! . . . J'ai vu tout, fleur, source, sillon,
> Se pâmer sous son œil comme un cœur qui palpite . . .
> —Courons vers l'horizon, il est tard, courons vite,
> Pour attraper au moins un oblique rayon!
>
> Mais je poursuis en vain le Dieu qui se retire;
> L'irrésistible Nuit établit son empire,
> Noire, humide, funeste et pleine de frissons;
>
> Une odeur de tombeau dans les ténèbres nage,
> Et mon pied peureux froisse, au bord du marécage,
> Des crapauds imprévus et de froids limaçons.

(1862 text)

As here reproduced, without its title, this sonnet might seem a Nature-poem of a more or less conventional Romantic type. The addition of the title, however: 'Le Coucher du soleil romantique', transforms its meaning entirely—or rather, since obviously the title is the first thing in a poem that we (normally) apprehend, let us say that it here deters us from the purely literal, purely sensory and emotive response, that the text alone would elicit. Now the reader alert for symbolic meanings—a modern intellectual reader, for instance, duly conditioned by the New Criticism—would

---

[1]*OCP* 682. The complete final couplet from Hugo's poem (*Passé*, from the *Voix intérieures* of 1837) runs: 'O temps évanouis! ô splendeurs éclipsées!/O soleils descendus derrière l'horizon!' (Pléiade I, 971); the 'vanished epoch' in this case is that of Louis XIII. Cf. also the parenthetical comment in the *Salon de 1859* when, having described Paul Huet as '*un vieux de la vieille*', B. interpolates: '. . . je puis appliquer aux débris d'une grandeur militante comme le *Romantisme*, déjà si lointaine, cette expression familière et grandiose . . .' (*CE* 339).

presumably infer, from the mere title,[1] some vague underlying literary theme whereby the sonnet as a whole becomes a lament for the passing of Romanticism, for the setting of its 'sun'. But, as it happens, Baudelaire himself has furnished us with a more specific and authoritative gloss, in the form of an explanatory footnote appended to the poem on its re-publication in February or March 1866 in *Les Épaves*:

Le mot: *Genus irritabile vatum*, date de bien des siècles avant les querelles des Classiques, des Romantiques, des Réalistes, des Euphuistes, etc. . . . Il est evident que par *l'irrésistible Nuit* M. Charles Baudelaire a voulu caractériser l'état actuel de la littérature, et que les *crapauds imprévus* et les *froids limaçons* sont les écrivains qui ne sont pas de son école.[2]

Thus Baudelaire's sonnet is explicitly presented as a poem not of Nature but of (literary) nurture: an expression, as he explained in a letter to Vigny accompanying a copy of the poem, of his 'piety',

[1] Or from the general context, if he were confronted with the poem in the version later to be published in December 1866—the version which in fact fulfils B.'s original intention, which was to furnish for a Romantic 'Miscellany' by his friend Asselineau (*Mélanges tirés d'une petite Bibliothèque romantique*), a 'Sonnet-Épilogue' corresponding to a similarly conceived 'prologue' by Banville; on this latter occasion—the more so since Banville's poem, under the specific title *L'Aube romantique*, already offered an elaborate roll-call of all the various literary and artistic figures deemed to have inspired or assisted at the Romantic 'dawn'— B. could afford to discard all direct symbolic 'pointers', and to entitle his sonnet simply *Soleil couché*. See Asselineau, *Mélanges*, p. 208 and cf. ibid., i–viii. For the date of publication of this volume, see *FMCB* 237 n. 2; for a further comment on the cryptic symbolism of the present sonnet, cf. L. J. Austin, *Univers poétique de B.*, 303–4.

[2] *FMCB* 558. A further paragraph (which in the manuscript is in Poulet-Malassis' handwriting) adds various items of bibliographical information nearly all of which, as it happened, were to prove inaccurate. Thus Banville's poem for the Asselineau volume neither bears the title *Le Lever du soleil romantique*, nor is a sonnet; cf. previous n. As to the statement: 'Ce sonnet a été composé en 1862', this one can scarcely accept in any primary sense of the word 'composé', since the poem had actually appeared *in print* within the first fortnight of January 1862. B. and/or Poulet-Malassis must therefore simply have misremembered— unless, of course, we have here a deliberate or an unconscious ambiguity: 'composé' in the sense of 'set up in type'! I would add that Poulet-Malassis' reference in the 1866 edition of *Les Épaves* to 'un livre de M. Charles Asselineau qui n'a pas paru', was maintained in the later, 1874 edition—by which time the Asselineau volume had not only duly 'appeared' (some nine months, in fact, after *Les Épaves*), but had itself run into a second edition! (under the revised title, *Bibliographie romantique*).

which is to say his nostalgic admiration for the aesthetic movement to which (at least intermittently) he owed allegiance[1]—an admiration he had previously expressed, as we have seen, in two texts of 1859.[2] And yet . . . when one turns back to Baudelaire's sonnet, it becomes strangely hard to reconcile its actual text with the detailed interpretations put forward in the *Épaves* footnote. Can one really credit that behind the chilling image of the final couplet ('Et mon pied peureux froisse, au bord du marécage, / Des crapauds imprévus et de froids limaçons'), there really stood for Baudelaire, as he wrote, the figures of his literary opponents? Why, if these creatures of night are (in symbolic terms) so contemptible, should he feel *fear* as his (presumably contemptuous) foot brushes against them? Where, in the tercets, is that nuance of mockery and scorn, that satirical and polemical intention, which should surely be felt in a poem in which the coming of night supposedly symbolizes 'the present state of literature'? Again, if (as the *Épaves* footnote directs us to do) we are to take the sonnet, in its full allegorical detail, as a *personal* elegy for Romanticism, are we not justified in pointing out that Baudelaire could scarcely with strict accuracy claim to have *seen* the actual Romantic 'sunrise', since at the time of the famous 'bataille d'*Hernani*' (1830), he was not yet nine years old?[3] And finally, is not the half-flippant tone of the *Épaves* footnote, in itself such as to deter us from taking too seriously its interpretation of the poem?[4] What I would myself suggest is that Baudelaire was here responding to some challenge—from Poulet-Malassis, or Asselineau,

[1]Letter of 26 Jan. 1862, *CG* IV, 54: 'Vous n'avez peut-être pas deviné la raison pour laquelle je vous ai adressé un petit journal contenant quelques vers de moi: c'était simplement à cause d'un sonnet sur un *certain coucher de soleil*, où j'avais essayé d'exprimer *ma piété*!'

[2]See pp. 273–4, above.

[3]The analogous reminiscence (cit. above) in the Gautier article, speaks of 'carrying one's glance back' to those early glories; this is a little different from claiming (symbolically) to have actually witnessed this scene: 'Je me souviens! . . . *J'ai vu tout* . . .' (l. 5). 1830 is the date chosen by Banville for his Romantic 'dawn'; indeed it constitutes in itself almost the whole of his opening hexasyllable line ('Mil huit cent trente! Aurore', etc.)!

[4]This collection, *Les Épaves*, was composed of poems that B. had made over or abandoned to Poulet-Malassis; the notes, though for the most part composed by B. himself, were given as being the work of his publisher, whose 'manner' B. is known to have amused himself by imitating. See *FMCB* 235–6, n. 6. All this argues a certain caution in assessing the strict relevance of the particular footnote in question.

or another of his friends—to elucidate the presumed symbolism of the tercets (the quatrains being sufficiently explained already by the adjective 'romantique' in the title). Such an explanation would have been easy enough to devise: if the sunset symbolizes the passing of Romanticism, then 'obviously' the night which follows 'must' represent the literary sequel to Romanticism, i.e. 'the present state of literature'; and from this, for a determined symbolist (or a sardonic poet hard pressed by symbolist readers), it would be but a short step to equate the more disagreeable creatures of night with whatever the poet happened specifically to disapprove of in the literary sphere.[1] Indeed, I would go further than this in my speculations on the genesis of the poem, and hazard the supposition that it may originally have been conceived as a pure Nature-impression, or rather as a 'landscape' conceived in the style recommended in both the 1846 and 1859 *Salons*:[2] for surely the essential effect upon us of this sonnet is to make us re-experience not only the scene itself in all its physical detail, but beyond this the full range of emotions (admiration and awe, regret tinged with apprehension, sudden fear) that it originally inspired in the poet. The literary theme would thus have been brought in strictly as an afterthought—whether prompted by a natural association of ideas (the image of a sunset linked once again, as in the Gautier article and the *Notes nouvelles sur Poe*, with the notion of literary decline), or whether simply by Asselineau's request for a contribution of some kind to his book; in the latter event, bethinking himself of his sonnet, Baudelaire might have reflected that by the addition of a suitable title (and of a few personifying capital letters) he could conveniently transform his verse 'landscape' into a symbolic 'Sonnet-Épilogue'. · · ·

[1] Cf. A. Adam, *FMA* 450–1, who shrewdly declares B.'s 'extravagant commentary' to be 'malicious in intention', and to reveal his 'taste for mystification'. I cannot, however, follow Professor Adam when he goes on to superimpose on B.'s explicit *general* symbolism (cf. p. 278, below), a further and personal symbolism analogous to that of *Chant d'automne*, but in *this* text nowhere stated or implied.

[2] Cf. pp. 75–9, 131–4, above; unlike the 'historical-landscape' painters derided in the *Salon de 1846*, B. has not felt obliged to banish the irregular (or unexpected) *toad* from his composition! Cf. on the one hand, 'toute mare à crapauds et à têtards est impitoyablement enterrée' (*CE* 179), and on the other, 'mon pied peureux froisse, au bord du marécage, / Des crapauds imprévus . . .' (ll. 13–14).

I do not mean to imply by these speculations regarding the sonnet's (putative) genesis, that we are in any way entitled to read it, in the form in which it has been presented to us by Baudelaire, as a pure Nature-description; to do so would be to disregard the patently symbolic intention conveyed through the title. What I would venture to suggest, however, is that we can best appreciate the poem's essential aesthetic qualities if we place ourselves in the situation *not* of the reader of *Les Épaves:* invited (as his eye travels down the page to a footnote we have seen to be of somewhat suspect authority) to construe the tercets as a detailed and incongruous allegory—but rather of the 'plain-text' reader of 1862 or of December 1866[1]: free, while duly recognizing the poem to be in its main theme a simple elegy for the past glories of Romanticism, to respond, without didactic impediments or distractions, to the expressive and dramatic detail of its imagery.[2] This detail is moreover such, in its sharp vividness, as to suggest strongly that whatever the general *conception* of the poem—whether or not it was in fact conceived from the outset as a meditation on the declining fortunes of Romanticism—it will in its descriptive *imagery* have derived from some actual and remembered experience; to that extent we may further take it as attesting Baudelaire's renewed or enhanced sensitivity to external Nature around 1859. The poem cannot however be regarded, like *Chant d'automne*, as a direct fruit of his seminal visits to Honfleur: at Honfleur (as *Chant d'automne* obliquely reminds us) the sun sets over the sea, whereas this sonnet takes us inland; its sun shines over flowers, streams, ploughland, a marsh. It may, however, have been the spell cast by the sunsets of Honfleur, that set the poet's mind travelling back over the years to other remembered sunsets—to whole days spent in the sun (at Creil, for instance, in the spring of 1841[3]), or even to that youthful 'sun-cult' to which in *Le Soleil,* he had once given such awkward and prosaic

[1]i.e. of the original version in *Le Boulevard*, or the 'Epilogue' version in the Asselineau *Mélanges*.

[2]I am thus in full agreement with L. J. Austin, *Univers poétique de B.*, 304, when he asks rhetorically: '. . . le poème n'aurait-il pas eu une plus grande force suggestive s'il n'avait pas eu de clef?' The desired response would then be precisely of the kind elicited by the prose poem *Chacun sa Chimère*, *PPP* 15–16, in which it is solely the ambiguity of the word 'Chimères' that indicates to the reader that in the strange scene depicted by the poet, the creatures each man carries on his back are something more than merely literal 'monsters'.

[3]Cf. p. 4 and n. 3, above.

expression. Indeed the third couplet of *Le Coucher du soleil romanti-que* ('. . . . J'ai vu tout, fleur, source, sillon, / Se pâmer sous son œil comme un cœur qui palpite . . .') seems almost a reminiscence of that earlier poem, with its similarly personified sun shining beneficently over the fields and over the harvests which it 'com-mands' to grow and ripen 'Dans le cœur immortel qui toujours veut fleurir'.[1]

A landscape (or seascape) more certainly inspired by Baudelaire's visits to Honfleur,[2] is that of the prose poem *Le Confiteor de l'artiste,* published in August 1862, a few months after *Le Coucher du soleil romantique,* and from which I have already quoted the opening lines in another connection.[3] Here more than in any other text of Baudelaire's, the ambivalence and complexity of his attitude to Nature become fully articulate:

Que les fins de journées d'automne sont pénétrantes! Ah! pénétrantes jusqu'à la douleur! car il est de certaines sensations délicieuses dont le vague n'exclut pas l'intensité; et il n'est pas de pointe plus acérée que celle de l'Infini.

Grand délice que celui de noyer son regard dans l'immensité du ciel et de la mer! Solitude, silence, incomparable chasteté de l'azur! une petite voile frissonnante à l'horizon, et qui, par sa petitesse et son isolement, imite mon irrémédiable existence, mélodie monotone de la houle, toutes ces choses pensent par moi, ou je pense par elles (car dans la grandeur de la rêverie, le *moi* se perd si vite!); elles pensent, dis-je, mais musicale-ment et pittoresquement, sans arguties, sans syllogismes, sans déductions.

Toutefois, ces pensées, qu'elles sortent de moi ou s'élancent des choses, deviennent bientôt trop intenses. L'énergie dans la volupté crée un malaise et une souffrance positive. Mes nerfs trop tendus ne donnent plus que des vibrations criardes et douloureuses.

Et maintenant la profondeur du ciel me consterne; sa limpidité m'exaspère. L'insensibilité de la mer, l'immuabilité du spectacle me révoltent . . . Ah! faut-il éternellement souffrir, ou fuir éternellement

---

[1]Cf. p. 13, above. Cf. also *Bénédiction,* l. 22: 'L'Enfant déshérité *s'enivre* de soleil' (my italics); *Le Fou et la Vénus* (1862), *PPP* 17 (cit. p. 267, above).

[2]More specifically, if we are to judge from the internal evidence of the text, by one of his two *autumn* visits—both lasting a few days only—in Oct. 1858 and Oct. 1860 respectively; see *CG* II, 224-5, 231, and III, 196-9, and cf. *PPP* 274. (If I am right in supposing B.'s prose poem to owe something to his conver-sations with Boudin, the latter of these dates would be the more probable; cf. pp. 281-2 n. 1, below.)

[3]Cf. pp. 184-5, above.

le beau? Nature, enchanteresse sans pitié, rivale toujours victorieuse, laisse-moi! Cesse de tenter mes désirs et mon orgueil! L'étude du beau est un duel où l'artiste crie de frayeur avant d'être vaincu.[1]

The initial mood is one of utter surrender to the beauty of the scene. Yet how far does this imply a total surrender of *self*? The second paragraph suggests an 'immersion', within the immensity of sky and sea, so complete that all sense of personal identity seems lost; is it he who thinks through the objects of Nature, or they who 'think' through him? But in fact he has already given his answer, in the very analogy which precedes (and provokes) his question: the tiny sail quivering on the horizon 'imitates' by its littleness and isolation his own 'irremediable existence'—which is to say that he projects onto it his own constant and despairing *awareness* of self; and thus even before this vast, almost empty sea, he cannot escape that 'langage connu' of human symbols of which he complains (as we shall see) in *Obsession*.[2] Yet what excites his eventual protest here, is not so much the inescapable (and paradoxical) 'humanity' of Nature, but the too great intensity of feeling, the ultimately unbearable *pressure* of delight, that the beauty of the scene engenders. Once before, in that earliest of all his poems: *Incompatibilité*, Baudelaire had expressed, but fleetingly and obliquely, the sense of disquiet aroused by the very grandeur of Nature, by the all-pervading, eternal silence of the mountains: 'Le silence qui fait qu'on voudrait se sauver'.[3] The general psychological condition described in the present text, however, is one with which he had been more constantly familiar: the exalted sensations of extreme sharpness and vividness and yet of immeasurable expansiveness (the 'état surnaturel'),[4] followed in turn by the violent contrast of depression, unease and even horror—this sequence inclines one to suppose that here at elsewhere, Baudelaire may in fact be describing the specific effects of opium.[5] A new element, perhaps, is the

[1] 1862 text, *PPP*, ed. M. Zimmerman, 2–3, var. 159.

[2] Cf. pp. 283–8, below. M. Raymond, in ed. Rousseau, *Rêveries*, has equally questioned, but from a philosophical standpoint, the completeness of B.'s 'self-surrender' in this passage.

[3] Cf. pp. 7–8, above. Cf. also (p. 82, above) the 'poètes hoffmaniques' of the early *Choix de maximes consolantes sur l'amour*, with their 'extases *dangereuses*'.

[4] Cf. p. 182, above.

[5] Cf. in this respect my comments on *Rêve parisien* and *La Chambre double* (pp. 168–9, above), as also the more explicit descriptions given in *Le Poison*, ll. 6–10; in the letter to Armand Fraisse of Aug. 1860, *CG* III, 168; in

unpredictable sequence of ideas that develops from this initial stimulus. Thus we observe that his malaise springs at first from the very intensity, or over-intensity, of his pleasure, and is, therefore, by a familiar paradox, expressed in terms almost of physical pain: 'Mes nerfs trop tendus ne donnent plus que des vibrations criardes et douloureuses'. But, thereafter, his dissatisfaction takes on increasingly a moral or emotional colouring: he is dismayed by the 'depth' of the sky, exasperated by its limpidity, outraged by the indifference of the sea and by the very unchangeability of the spectacle confronting him. The complaint of indifference, the sense of outrage, hint at a renewal of the old, humanist grievance against Nature; but at this point, in justification of his title ('The Confiteor of the *Artist*'),[1] Baudelaire modulates from the broadly human to the 'professionally' aesthetic sphere. He does not, I think, mean to imply that his standpoint has *throughout* been that of the creative artist—except in so far as such a standpoint would of itself explain the exceptional refinement and intensity of his response to the spectacle before him; rather should we suppose that at this final stage of the poem, the experience undergone has suggested to him, by a natural associative sequence—reinforced, perhaps, by certain conversations he may have held with Boudin during his stay at Honfleur in 1859—the *analogy* of the creative artist's struggle (or 'duel') with the intractability or elusiveness of his material.[2] There

---

Edgar Poe, HE xxix. For the effect of 'intensification' only, cf. the passage from Poe's *A Tale of the Ragged Mountains* translated in *HE* 289, reproduced in *Le Poëme du haschisch, PA* 47, and paraphrased in *Exposition universelle 1855* (*CE* 251; cf. p. 181 and n. 2). For the analogous effects of hashish (including, precisely, the sense of 'participation' in Nature), cf. *PA* 223-4, 32-4, 50-2, 63. By the very intensity (and bitterness) of their 'aftermath', both drugs in effect accentuate the essential 'precariousness' (recorded in *Le Confiteor de l'artiste*) of the 'supernatural' state.

[1]Cf., for a cognate borrowing from this same 'ecclesiastical' context, the poem *Confession,* with its final 'confidence horrible chuchotée / Au *confessional* du cœur' (ll. 39-40); my italics.

[2]Cf. especially in this respect the poems *La Beauté* and *La Mort des artistes.* The image of the poet 'duelling' with words occurs, as we have seen (p. 106, above) in *Le Soleil,* ll. 5-8; cf. also *La Lune offensée,* l. 7. In his *Salon de 1846,* B. had similarly spoken of a 'contest' between Nature and the artist; but he had then allowed, significantly, for the possibility that the *artist* might triumph: 'Le dessin est une lutte entre la nature et l'artiste, où l'artiste triomphera d'autant plus facilement qu'il comprendra mieux les intentions de la nature' (*CE* 144; cf. p. 78, above). As to the presumed influence of Boudin, it is

is indeed an almost imperceptible gliding from one idea to another: from the discomfort that any hypersensitive observer might feel before the too-exquisite beauty of Nature, to this same 'suffering' transposed to the creative artist that the poet, in the act of writing, has consciously become; from the artist in particular, to the artist in general—condemned by the law of his vocation to pursue an ideal of Beauty which he can never adequately encompass; from this Beauty as embodied in Nature, to the wider Beauty that the artist's ideal necessarily implies and comprehends. The poem taken as a whole ranges over what is almost the full gamut of Baudelaire's attitudes to Nature: an extreme sensitivity to natural beauty; the recognition of Nature's 'apartness' and self-sufficiency, in relation to Man; a sense of personal affinity (or 'familiarity') so great as to submerge all feeling of separate identity, while allowing the perception of subjective human symbols or 'correspondences'; disquiet and protest; the notion of an unending conflict, an unequal duel, between Man and Nature, transposed to the professional context of the artist seeking (in vain!) to assimilate the forms of Nature to his own imaginative or emotional needs.

---

interesting to note that in a passage quoted by G. Jean-Aubry *(Boudin,* 29), the painter, in 1854, consigns to his intimate notebooks this 'confiteor' which strangely anticipates our present text, even to certain shared phrases: 'Perfection qui fuis, fuis toujours! . . . Nature que je regarde sans cesse, sans la voir. . . . Parfois en me promenant mélancolique, je regarde cette lumière qui inonde la terre, qui frémit sur l'eau, qui joue sur les vêtements et j'ai des défaillances de voir combien il faut de génie pour saisir tant de difficultés. . . . J'entrevois parfois ce qu'il faudrait exprimer'. That these preoccupations were still in the forefront of Boudin's mind at the very time when he was making the acquaintance of B. (see, in this connection, G. Jean-Aubry, op. cit., 39–41, and *B. et Honfleur,* 26–7), is shown by this later entry, dated 28 May 1859, i.e. a few weeks before B.'s return from Honfleur to Paris (see pp. 145–6, above): 'La nature est si belle, si splendide que c'est toujours là mon tourment secret, quand la misère lâche un peu prise. C'est un bien grand bonheur pour nous de voir, d'admirer sans cesse toutes [ces] splendeurs du ciel et de la terre; s'il n'y avait qu'à les admirer, mais ne s'y mêle-t-il pas sans cesse le tourment de les reproduire, les impossibilités de la peinture à créer à son tour par des moyens si bornés . . .' (cit. G. Jean-Aubry, *Boudin,* 35). For other possible sources for the final paragraph of B.'s prose poem, cf. Balzac, *Le Chef-d'œuvre inconnu* (Frenhofer's despairing cry: 'O! nature! nature! qui t'a jamais saisie dans tes fuites?'—cit. P. Laubriet, '*Chef-d'œuvre inconnu*' *de Balzac,* 171), and the passage by Jouffroy cit. L. J. Austin, *Univers poétique de B.,* 160.

VIII

The Nihilist Solution

In Nature, so it would seem from certain of the texts cited in the previous chapter, Baudelaire can still during this period find a consolation which is the very reverse of all that he had professed in the letter of 1853–4 to Desnoyers; the obstinately 'urban' poet whose thoughts, even in the depths of the forest, were turned always towards Man,[1] can now on the contrary, only a few years later, gratefully seek out those forms of Nature which by their indifferent grandeur seem most *remote* from Man. Yet even within the heart of elemental Nature, there remains the one inescapable human presence which resists all exorcism: the observer's *self* which in all things discerns, as if compulsively, its own reflected image. Thus to the newly misanthropic poet, the situation described in the closing sentence of the letter to Desnoyers ('Dans le fond des bois, enfermé sous ces voûtes semblables à celles des sacristies et des cathédrales, je pense à nos étonnantes villes, et la prodigieuse musique qui roule sur les sommets me semble la traduction des lamentations humaines'[2]) may seem malign rather than benign, may provoke consternation rather than a renewed conviction of human solidarity.

It is this contradiction, precisely, that is explored in what is perhaps the most profoundly nihilistic of all Baudelaire's texts, the sonnet *Obsession* (first published—perhaps only a few months after its composition—in May 1860):

> Grands bois, vous m'effrayez comme des cathédrales;
> Vous hurlez comme l'orgue; et dans nos cœurs maudits,
> Chambres d'éternel deuil où vibrent de vieux râles,
> Répondent les échos de vos *De profundis*.
>
> Je te hais, Océan! tes bonds et tes tumultes,
> Mon esprit les retrouve en lui; ce rire amer
> De l'homme vaincu, plein de sanglots et d'insultes,
> Je l'entends dans le rire énorme de la mer.

---

[1] Cf. pp. 125–6, above.
[2] *Fontainebleau*, p. 74; cf. pp. 121–2, above.

Comme tu me plairais, ô nuit! sans ces étoiles
Dont la lumière parle un langage connu!
Car je cherche le vide, et le noir, et le nu!

Mais les ténèbres sont elles-mêmes des toiles
Où vivent, jaillissant de mon œil par milliers,
Des êtres disparus aux regards familiers.

The first quatrain of this sonnet, with its (similar) adaptation of the
famous passage by Chateaubriand on the Gothic cathedrals,[1] might
seem at first merely the elaboration of the concluding sentence
(above-quoted) of the letter to Desnoyers—with the 'prodigious
music' of the winds, roaring through the 'cathedral vaults' of the
forest, now specifically linked, however, by their echo of the *De
profundis* psalm, to the 'human lamentations' which they translate,
and which issue from hearts that are themselves places of eternal
mourning, filled with the sounds of death. Yet if the forests now
inspire fear in the poet, it is not so much because their sound is in
itself lugubrious or threatening, but rather because they carry a
reminder which in the context of the letter to Desnoyers would (on
the contrary) have been reassuring rather than frightening—the
reminder of Man and of the curse of sorrow which he bears.[2] So,
too, in the second quatrain, the analogy between Man and the sea
is no longer (as in *L'Homme et la mer, Moesta et errabunda* and
Déjà!) a source of consolation or delight; now, on the contrary,
only hatred is aroused in the poet by his recognition, in the sound
and swell of the ocean, in its huge and ironic laughter, of his own
'vanquished' human likeness.[3] This hatred of Nature is a very
different one, be it noted, from that confessed (by analogy) in *A
Celle qui est trop gaie:* it lacks all ambivalence, it is inspired not

[1]Cf., in this connection, A. Ferran, ed. B., *Poésies choisies,* 51 n. 7—as also
p. 202 and n. 2, above. L. J. Austin, *Univers poétique de B.,* 93, makes the further
suggestion that we may here have a reminiscence of a passage from Balzac's
Les Chouans.

[2]The formula 'dans nos cœurs maudits, / Chambres d'éternel deuil . . . /
Répondent les échos de vos *De profundis*', corresponds almost exactly to the
final phrase of the letter: 'la prodigieuse musique qui roule sur les sommets
me semble la traduction des lamentations humaines'.

[3]Cf., for the descriptive elements of this quatrain, the comment on Wagner's
Flying Dutchman Overture—which B. had heard (at the Théâtre Italien concerts
in Jan.-Feb. 1860), at the very moment when, perhaps, he was composing
Obsession: 'lugubre et profonde comme l'Océan, le vent et les ténèbres' (*Wagner,*
AR 237).

by Nature's 'insolent' disregard of the poet's distress, but by its all too pointedly allusive 'echo' of his predicament.[1] The tercets accentuate still more strongly the note of personal affliction; they reveal a Baudelaire wholly possessed by that terrible 'desire for nothingness' declared more fully (as we shall see) in another poem of this period, *Le Goût du néant,* and for which the preferred setting is the utter darkness, emptiness and bareness of night—the annihilating 'bain de ténèbres' so ardently invoked and welcomed, in the prose poem *A une heure du matin,* for the blessed release it brings from 'la tyrannie de la face humaine'.[2] But not alas! to the poet of *Obsession:* for him, even night spells out, by its stars, an all too intelligible 'language'; for him, a darkness lit by stars is a darkness onto which the mind 'projects' the images of departed beings, ideograms of memory in each of which is crystallized some facet of past experience, some inveterate trace of past human relationships;[3] no less disturbingly, therefore, than the ocean or the forests, this darkness 'speaks'

[1]In short, this is a repudiation not of Nature, but of Man (or self) *through* Nature. Cf. the vivid comment by J. Prévost, *B.,* 215: 'Il s'agit de renoncer aux dernières forces de l'être vaincu et de les maudire: maudire dans la voix de l'Océan le dernier sanglot et le dernier défi du vaincu, maudire dans les étoiles tous les yeux et ses propres yeux, et la faculté de voir elle-même. . . .'

[2]*PPP* 25 (first pub. 1862). Cf. also two further texts of this same period: *La Fin de la journée (FM* 1861, ll. 8–14), the prose poem *Le Crépuscule du soir* (1864 text, *PPP* 73)—both of which describe the poet's grateful surrender to the night's 'rafraîchissantes ténèbres'. For other references to the dreaded 'tyranny' (or 'horror') of the human face, cf. *Mangeur d'opium, PA* 118, 138 (De Quincey, *Confessions,* ed. M. Elwin, 397, 424); *Pauvre Belgique, OP* III, 81; letter to Mme Aupick of 11 Aug. 1862, *CG* IV, 99.

[3]Inveterate but unspecified; the analogy, however, with *Le Voyage,* ll. 133–4 (p. 307, below), and with the Poe 'Parable' from which both texts perhaps derive (*Shadow,* final sentence, *Works,* 1850, II, 294; trans. B., *NHE* 284), has suggested to J. Crépet and G. Blin, *FMCB* 426, that B. may here be remembering departed *friends.* This suggestion could be reinforced by various further analogies: with the question posed in *Mon Cœur mis à nu,* VIII, *JI* 59, 'Où sont nos amis morts?' (to which the present answer, metaphorically speaking, would be: 'In the stars!'); with the phrase prompted, in the Poe art. of 1856 (*Edgar Poe, HE* xviii), by the recent (presumed) suicide of B.'s friend, Nerval: 'Et ainsi se forme une compagnie de fantômes déjà nombreuse, qui nous hante familièrement'; with the second of the four *Spleen* poems, with its opening line 'J'ai plus de souvenirs que si j'avais mille ans', and its later reference to the 'morts les plus chers' which people the 'graveyard' of the poet's mind (ll. 8–10); with the third verse of Hugo's *La Pente de la rêverie (Feuilles d'automne,* 1831, Pléiade I, 771), with its similar vision of absent friends, within a context of Nature. The metaphor of the mind painting or projecting

of the ubiquitous and inescapable self.[1] The obsession has now, however, become entirely visual (where in the quatrains it was largely auditory: the tumult of woods and sea, resounding with their 'echo' of Man), and here again the comparison with an earlier text, *Correspondances,* imposes itself, indeed is almost forced upon us by the exact reiteration, within a similar context of Nature, of the phrase 'regards familiers'. It is as if the poet, at this later stage of his career, had discovered himself to be in fact, and in the most deeply personal sense, in the precise situation ascribed to Man in general in *Correspondances;* he too now looks out at the objects of Nature (specifically, here, the stars in the night sky), and in their 'glances' discerns a meaningful 'language'. But this language has now lost all the intrinsic vagueness of the earlier poem ('de confuses paroles'), has on the contrary become for the poet all too exactly 'known' and understood.[2] Moreover what in *Correspondances* was proclaimed as a universal truth, is here feared as a subjective threat; the image of the final tercet implies a totally solipsistic universe, in which the elements of Nature are scrutinized solely for their intimate relation to the onlooker.[3] It also illustrates graphically the self-defeating psychology of obsession: like Hugo's Cain, Baudelaire is *pursued* by his obsession even into the ultimate refuge of darkness.[4] Indeed

---

images on to a 'screen' of some kind (darkness, literal or figurative; memory; the imagination) is one that recurs in numerous texts of B.'s, mostly of the present period: *Confession,* ll. 3–4; *Mangeur d'opium, PA* 134 (De Quincey, *Confessions,* ed. M. Elwin, 419); *Un Fantôme* I, ll. 5–6; *Wagner, AR* 208; *Le Gouffre,* ll. 7–8; *Le Voyage,* ll. 54–6 (cf. p. 299, below).

[1] Cf., on the other hand, the opening lines of the 1855–62 version of the prose poem aforementioned (*Le Crépuscule du soir*): there, as night falls, the radiance of the stars is *welcomed* by the poet for the 'illumination' it brings to his mind (*OCP* 1607 and n.: 'l'assombrissement du jour et le scintillement des étoiles et des lanternes éclairent mon esprit').

[2] Cf. L. J. Austin, *Univers poétique de B.,* 91 n. 1, 92–3, who excellently notes (p. 93) these still further symmetrical 'oppositions' between the two texts: 'les "longs échos" qui se confondaient dans la "ténébreuse et profonde unité" sont remplacés par des "echos" plus sinistres: les "hurlements" des bois ne sont que l'écho des malédictions de l'homme; car ce "temple" est devenu une cathédrale où l'on célèbre éternellement l'office des morts . . .'

[3] Cf. the penetrating comment by J. Pommier, *Mystique de B.,* 150: 'Le sonnet "Obsession" traduit la souffrance du poète qui ne peut voir sans lire, et écouter sans entendre'. Thus the poet is victimized above all by his own ceaselessly analytical temperament.

[4] 'L'œil était dans la tombe et regardait Caïn' (*La Conscience,* l. 68, *Légende des siècles,* ed. P. Berret, I, 51. Restated in less pathological and less dramatic

one might even take the final tercet to imply that having banished from reality all potentially symbolic images, the poet still felt the compulsion to conjure up their equivalents from *within* his own mind; in his frantic search for 'le vide, et le noir, et le nu', he would thus in fact confront, in the twelfth line, a night wholly black and starless, wholly void of natural objects; no matter—the darkness instantly becomes for him a 'screen', an obsessive phantom-show, onto which his eye projects countless flickering 'stars' *of his own creation*. But whatever our interpretation of the final tercet, the impression with which it leaves us is one of unnerving disquiet, almost of claustrophobia; the vast, infinitely ramifying universe of *Correspondances* has become a prison, within which at every turn Man (in the person of the poet) feels bearing down upon him the *oppression* of his analogic likeness.[1] This change of attitude is implicit even within the phrase that in its form is exactly reiterated (as we have seen) from the one sonnet to the other. Thus the reader sensitive to the tone and dramatic quality of *Obsession,* will pause for an instant after the word 'regards', and by this hesitation confer on the last word of all: 'familiers', a note of sinister apprehension wholly absent from the smooth and confident delivery of the same words in *Correspondances*. There, the glances merely 'observe' Man, and their familiarity seems, in the context, almost kindly; here, these same glances *pursue,* and their familiarity is that of the hunter glimpsed, ever more frequently, by his fleeing prey.

Each section of this poem refutes, in effect, some earlier 'humanist' text; through the violence and bitterness of personal despair, a whole Man-centred philosophy of Nature, a whole 'system' of Nature-symbolism, are momentarily set at naught. Certainly the poet who here aspires only after 'le vide, et le noir, et le nu', would willingly exchange the universe of symbols for a universe of phenomena; far from denouncing (as in the letter to Desnoyers) Nature's presumed 'insolence' or indifference to Man, far from

---

terms, the dilemma posed in *Obsession* could be reduced simply to our perennial human inability to 'stop thinking'; cf. *De profundis clamavi,* ll. 12–13: 'Je jalouse le sort des plus vils animaux / Qui peuvent se plonger dans un sommeil stupide . . .', and L. Mme Aupick of 26/3/1853: 'Il y a des moments où il me prend le désir de dormir infiniment; mais je ne peux plus dormir, parce que je pense toujours' *(CG* I, 193; cit. *FMA* 364).

[1] This 'oppression' is what J. Prévost, *B.,* 234, has interestingly termed a 'pantheism in reverse': 'l'intrusion de la nature jusqu'au fond de l'être, des sentiments brutalement et intimement imposés par le monde à l'être intérieur'.

seeking out (as in *Horreur sympathique*) the image of his own self, he here on the contrary repudiates and dreads this image, deplores its massive pervasion of Nature, could delight in Nature only if it were somehow divested of its implacable and *obsessive* 'familiarity': 'Comme tu me plairais, ô nuit! *sans* ces étoiles / Dont la lumière parle un langage connu. . . .' It is true that a year or so earlier Baudelaire had appeared to discern (and savour), in Boudin's pastel sketches, a Nature free of all human imprint and association; but this the symbolic cloudscapes of *Horreur sympathique*, no less than the explicit denials of *Obsession*, quickly reveal to have been an illusion.[1] Sooner or later, it would seem, all aspects of Nature—the clouds, the forest, the sea, the night sky itself—come to impose on the tormented poet the obsessive image of his own kind.

At other moments, or in other texts, Baudelaire may be thought nevertheless to have found some measure of fulfilment of his craving for 'le vide, et le noir, et le nu'—at least in so far as this latter state corresponds with the brute insensibility 'envied' in an earlier sonnet, *De profundis clamavi*.[2] Such, certainly, is the implication to be taken from these opening verses of the poem, *Le Goût du néant,* which in the *Fleurs du Mal* of 1861 Baudelaire chose to place immediately after *Obsession*:

> Morne esprit, autrefois amoureux de la lutte,
> L'Espoir, dont l'éperon attisait ton ardeur,
> Ne veut plus t'enfourcher! Couche-toi sans pudeur,
> Vieux cheval dont le pied à chaque obstacle butte.
>
> Résigne-toi, mon cœur; dors ton sommeil de brute.
>
> Esprit vaincu, fourbu! Pour toi, vieux maraudeur,
> L'amour n'a plus de goût, non plus que la dispute;
> Adieu donc, chants du cuivre et soupirs de la flûte!
> Plaisirs, ne tentez plus un cœur sombre et boudeur!
>
> Le Printemps adorable a perdu son odeur!
>
> (ll. 1–10)

In the sombre inertia of the state here described, all purpose, will and vitality are stifled, all feelings and sensations numbed; even the

---

[1]Cf. pp. 136, 248–50, above.

[2]'Je jalouse le sort des plus vils animaux / Qui peuvent se plonger dans un sommeil stupide . . .' (ll. 12–13).

simple fragrance of spring—what Baudelaire elsewhere during this period (admittedly in the more genial context of the poetry of Pierre Dupont) consents to call the 'immortal freshness' of Nature[1]—now lies beyond the ever-narrowing range of his perceptions. ('Il n'y a pas *jusqu'au* Printemps adorable qui n'ait perdu pour moi son odeur': such is the ultimate avowal implicit in this poignantly memorable line.) And so, dully withdrawn from all that diversifies the sameness of existence, the poet listlessly assents to the slow paralysis of all his faculties; surrendering himself already to the remorseless invasions of time (as might some marooned traveller who in sleep yields to the embrace of the snows), he allows himself, in a last flicker of energy, what is almost a prayer for the coming, or the hastening on, of the 'avalanche':

> Et le Temps m'engloutit minute par minute,
> Comme la neige immense un corps pris de roideur;
> Je contemple d'en haut le globe en sa rondeur
> Et je n'y cherche plus l'abri d'une cahute.
>
> Avalanche, veux-tu m'emporter dans ta chute?
>
> (ll. 11–15)

In these concluding lines, the images of Time and Death seem to shade into one another: the oppressive consciousness of Time is already a living petrification, but the avalanche of the last line no doubt prefigures the ultimate and total 'nothingness' of death. Yet if we take the poem as a whole, we see that its title implies a condition still more negative than the at least active (even if frustrated) *desire* for nothingness of *Obsession* ('Car je *cherche* le vide, et le noir, et le nu!'); here, by contrast, for the completely incurious because dulled and desensitized palate, the 'goût du néant' is merely what remains when all other appetites have been lost, and when from life itself—from love, from Nature, from the very act of disputation—all savour, as it seems, has drained heedlessly away.

Baudelaire's attitude to Death, even during this last nihilistic phase of his life, remains a complex one. We have seen, from such texts as *Chant d'automne*, that the simple apprehension of death may reassert itself in him even against the darkest 'winter' background of the mind;[2] at other times, however, the fear is not so

---

[1] *Dupont* II, *AR* 366–7.
[2] Cf. pp. 271–2, above.

much of the actual *coming* of death, as that *when* it comes, it may
bring not the 'promised slumber', but a 'treacherous' prolongation
of the travail of life. (Which is to say, in religious terms, that
Baudelaire's nihilism is at times uneasily agnostic rather than
firmly atheistic.[1]) This is the disquieting possibility Baudelaire
infers from the anatomical drawings which are the starting-point of
Le Squelette laboureur, and which show skeletal figures condemned,
by the convention of the genre, endlessly to till, with vigorous spades
and arms 'stripped' to the sinew, some unknown and harsh terrain:

> De ce terrain que vous fouillez,
> Manants résignés et funèbres,
> De tout l'effort de vos vertèbres,
> Ou de vos muscles dépouillés,
>
> Dites, quelle moisson étrange,
> Forçats arrachés au charnier,
> Tirez-vous, et de quel fermier
> Avez-vous à remplir la grange?
>
> Voulez-vous (d'un destin trop dur
> Épouvantable et clair emblème!)
> Montrer que dans la fosse même
> Le sommeil promis n'est pas sûr;
>
> Qu'envers nous le Néant est traître;
> Que tout, même la Mort, nous ment,
> Et que sempiternellement,
> Hélas! il nous faudra peut-être
>
> Dans quelque pays inconnu
> Écorcher la terre revêche
> Et pousser une lourde bêche
> Sous notre pied sanglant et nu?
>
> (ll. 13–32)

The same anxious question ('Will Death prove a cheat?') is posed,
but in a very different form, in *Le Rêve d'un curieux*. Here, with the
'avidity' of the child at the theatre, the dreaming poet waits for the
'curtain' to rise, for the 'terrible dawn' to break; it comes, yet
'without surprise', as the 'cold truth' stands revealed. What happens
after death is that *nothing* happens; the curtain rises, but upon an
empty stage, and still the spectator waits ...

[1] Cf., in this connection, p. 291 n. 1, below.

Enfin la verité froide se révéla:

J'étais mort sans surprise, et la terrible aurore
M'enveloppait.—Eh quoi! n'est-ce donc que cela?
La toile était levée et j'attendais encore.[1]

More authentic, perhaps, than either of these two 'distrustful' attitudes towards Death, is one, finally, that by its note of eager *aspiration* (if not by its persisting nihilism), recalls the three 'Death' sonnets that had formed the original conclusion of the (1857) *Fleurs du Mal*.[2] I would first cite, in this connection, as well as the prose poem *Le Tir et le cimetière* already discussed,[3] a brief passage from one of Baudelaire's various projected 'Prefaces' for the second and third editions of *Les Fleurs du Mal*; I here italicize the phrase in which the 'aspiring' quality in question is most clearly to be discerned:

J'aspire à un repos absolu et à une nuit continue. Chantre des voluptés folles du vin et de l'opium, *je n'ai soif que d'une liqueur inconnue sur la terre*, et que la pharmaceutique céleste elle-même ne pourrait pas m'offrir; d'une liqueur qui ne contiendrait ni la vitalité, ni la mort, ni l'excitation, ni le néant. Ne rien savoir, ne rien enseigner, ne rien vouloir, ne rien sentir, dormir, et encore dormir, tel est aujourd'hui mon unique vœu. Vœu infâme et dégoûtant, mais sincère.

(*FMCB* 214)

But the two texts of this period in which, within a context of Nature, Baudelaire's nihilism assumes its most strongly (if paradoxically) 'positive' character, are first, the prose poem *Any where out of the world*, and second, the verse poem which to some extent may seem its earlier counterpart, *Le Voyage*. In the former of these two texts, the English title is borrowed, somewhat inappropriately, from Thomas Hood's highly sentimental and pedestrian, yet withal affecting ballad, *The Bridge of Sighs*.[4] Baudelaire's own (prose) poem

---

[1] ll. 11–14. For a comment on the religious questionings implicit in this sonnet, and the presumed attitude of Nadar (to whom it was dedicated), see J. Crépet, *Manuscrit autographe*, 1927 (Special B. No.), pp. 122–3.

[2] *La Mort des amants, La Mort des pauvres, La Mort des artistes.*

[3] Pp. 265–6, above.

[4] In this original context the phrase sums up, rather than any temperamental longing, the 'wild insanity' (the description is Poe's) to which the young girl suicide has been driven as, cast out by her family for some 'sin' unspecified (yet clearly hinted at), she stands on the river bank: 'The bleak wind of March/

begins with a statement, in symbolic terms, of the notion elaborated more discursively (as we shall see) in *Le Voyage,* that of the illusions (and implied disillusions) of travel; but this is quickly adapted to the poet's own case:

> Cette vie est un hôpital où chaque malade est possédé du désir de changer de lit. Celui-ci voudrait souffrir en face du poêle, et celui-là croit qu'il guérirait à côté de la fenêtre.
>
> Il me semble que je serais toujours bien là où je ne suis pas, et cette question de déménagement en est une que je discute sans cesse avec mon âme.[1]

Thereafter the poem resolves itself into an interior dialogue, a

---

Made her tremble and shiver; / But not the dark arch, / Or the black flowing river. / Mad from life's history, / Glad to death's mystery, / Swift to be hurled—/ Anywhere, anywhere, / Out of the world!' (Hood, *Poetical Works,* Hampstead library edition, p. 528). During his final period in Brussels (to be exact, on 8 April 1865), B. dictated to his friend the art critic Arthur Stevens, a literal translation of Hood's poem (see *OP* II, 129–32, and cf. ibid., 285–6, and J. Crépet, *MF* 1/4/1949, pp. 599–601). No inference can be drawn from this, however, as to the date of composition of B.'s prose poem; Hood's ballad, since it is quoted in full by Poe in the course of *The Poetic Principle* (*Literati, etc.,* 1850, pp. 15–16; cf. the comment cit. above), must have been familiar to B. at least since 1853—the year in which, in the 1850 (Redfield) edition, he will have read Poe's essay for the first time. See W. T. Bandy, 'B. and Poe', art. cit., pp. 31–2; for the borrowing from Hood, cf. M. Gilman, *RR,* 1935, p. 243 n. 5. From internal evidence, I would myself date B.'s prose poem as of 1859–62.

[1] *PPP* 165. Cf., for the second sentence quoted, the description in *Les Bienfaits de la lune* of the girl's predestined lovers (who include, of course, the poet himself): 'ceux-là qui aiment . . . le lieu où ils ne sont pas . . .' (*PPP* 134; cf. p. 264, above); or again, the remark by the fourth young boy in *Les Vocations* (whom B. feels to be a 'frère à moi-même inconnu'): 'Je ne suis jamais bien nulle part, et je crois toujours que je serais mieux ailleurs que là où je suis' (*PPP* 116; cf. 118). This notion goes back at least to Rousseau; cf. the passage from *La Nouvelle Héloïse,* cit. G. Charlier, *Sentiment de la nature chez les romantiques,* 56: 'Le goût des points de vue et des lointains [i.e. in the landscaping of gardens] vient du penchant qu'ont la plupart des hommes à ne se plaire qu'où ils ne sont pas'—as also the more personal avowal in the eighth 'Promenade' of the *Rêveries:* '. . . j'avais sans cesse besoin de changer de place et je n'étais bien nulle part' (ed. M. Raymond, p. 126; cit., in another context, by M. Zimmerman, ed. *PPP,* 119); more recent instances would include those cited by G. T. Clapton, *RHLF,* 1931, pp. 243–4 n. (Balzac, *Le Curé de Tours*), and by M. Zimmerman, op. cit., 128 (Z. Werner, *Le Voyageur,* pub. 1841). For a full enumeration of the various B. texts in which is proclaimed what he calls 'l'horreur du domicile', see G. T. Clapton, loc. cit.

series of 'invitations to a journey', addressed by the poet to his own soul.[1] Thus turn by turn he proposes Lisbon, Holland, the extreme Baltic, the North Pole itself; but to each suggestion, the soul returns an unnerving silence. (Thus far, it would be more accurate to speak of an interior monologue than of a true dialogue.) What is particularly interesting from our point of view is that each successive landscape described, embodies a distinct and characteristc conception of Nature; it is as if Baudelaire were here testing out anew—and rejecting—a whole sequence of his attitudes to Nature. Thus Lisbon, that most purely 'artificial' of all cities—set beside waters that reflect back the mineral and the light of which it is compounded, stripped (according to Baudelaire) of all trees—is almost the analogue of the fabulous dream-landscape of *Rêve parisien*; in its supposed exclusion of the 'irregular vegetable', we recognize the humanist's rebuff to the 'insolence' of Nature.[2] Holland in its turn, with its crowded masts bringing their (man-made) 'forest' within the very streets of Rotterdam, would marry (as in the two versions of *L'Invitation au voyage*) beatitude and calm on the one hand, with the spectacle of movement on the other. Batavia would offer a brief glimpse of the 'tropical beauty' so ardently evoked in other poems—but here intriguingly wedded to 'the spirit of Europe'. In the far polar landscapes, finally, with their slow and barely distinguishable alternations of day and night, varied inter-mittently by the pyrotechnic (and 'Satanic') splendours of the northern lights, the poet's soul would find a grimly consoling simulacrum of Death.[3] But this same inertia is at last galvanized into articulacy, in a final sentence which brings the single, 'explosive' utterance of the exasperated soul:

Enfin, mon âme fait explosion, et sagement elle me crie: "N'importe où! n'importe où! pourvu que ce soit hors de ce monde!"

(*PPP* 167)

This 'sage' answer implies, of course, not weary assent but passionate protest: 'anywhere' means in effect 'nowhere that you have mentioned

[1]On the model, G. T. Clapton suggests (art. cit., 243) of a passage from Seneca's letters to Serenus.

[2]Cf. p. 170, above.

[3]Such imagery had already previously been exploited by B. for symbolic (i.e. subjective) purposes, in the two poems *De profundis clamavi* and *Chant d'automne* (ll. 5–8); cf. p. 237 and n. 2, above.

or could mention', and thus all countries of the world are rejected in favour of the one country truly *not* of this world—that country which (as we shall now see) is likewise the ardently desired goal of the 'Travellers' of *Le Voyage*.

This latter poem, although in its composition it goes back to the early months (spent in Honfleur) of 1859, may well be considered Baudelaire's ultimate, since most authoritative and comprehensive, utterance on Nature; it will thus afford an appropriate (as well as majestic) conclusion to the long series of texts we have examined in the course of this study. The structure of the poem is elaborate, even devious: four middle sections of question and answer, of eager interrogation and disabused response, flanked on each side by two sections of a more meditative and less obviously dramatic nature; whilst from one section to another, and often within individual sections, the tone and manner shift continually in the most fluid manner and by the most subtle transitions.[1] The poem is cast throughout in the first person plural; from a reference Baudelaire himself makes to 'Le Voyageur', in the course of the letter in which he solicits, somewhat defensively, Du Camp's endorsement of the poem's dedication,[2] we may assume that he has in mind, as the presumed speaker of these verses, some Olympian and much-travelled Sage (a composite figure based variously, perhaps, on certain personal myths,[3] on literary models such as Byron's 'Childe

---

[1]Cf. the comment by J. Prévost, *B.*, 321, who says (of *Le Voyage*) : 'Ce n'est point une suite rhétorique et logique; c'est une suite de pensées, suite naturelle jusqu'en ses écarts et ses bizarreries; nulle part ailleurs dans les *Fleurs du Mal* nous n'allons si avant dans l'âme du poète; nulle part nous ne nous sentons aussi près de devenir nous-mêmes Baudelaire'. 'Nowhere else' save (I would add) in one or two other longish poems of this same period: *Le Cygne* (especially), *Danse macabre*, *L'Imprévu*; cf., in this connection, my art. cit., 'B.: The Poet as Moralist', pp. 214–15. In its original, 1859 version, *Le Voyage* was divided into six sections only—sections IV to VI forming a single (IVth) section.

[2]L. of 23/2/1859, *CG* II, 278–9: 'Si le ton systématiquement byronien de ce petit poëme vous déplaisait, si, par exemple, vous étiez choqué de mes plaisanteries contre le progrès, ou bien de ce que le Voyageur avoue n'avoir vu que la banalité, ou enfin de n'importe quoi, dites-le-moi sans vous gêner; je ferai pour vous autre chose avec tout autant de joie'. For the whole question of this dedication to Du Camp, see the excellent article by Y. Abé, *RHLF*, 1967, pp. 273–85, and cf. pp. 157–8, above.

[3]Cf., e.g. (p. 188, above), the 'poëte attristé' of the almost exactly contemporary *Poëme du haschisch*, *PA* 68–9.

Harold',[1] on personal friends such as Gautier[2] or Du Camp himself[3]), who would at the same time be speaking in the collective
name of other, no less seasoned travellers, on whose experiences,
attitudes and motivations he would draw for the meditation of his
own deeply disabused and pessimistic philosophy. This philosophy,
as we have previously noted, is in many respects Baudelaire's own;[4]
it would, nevertheless, be a dire simplification to regard the
Travellers as being merely the spokesmen for the poet himself—
the more so, indeed, since the latter could equally well be identified
with the very different group of travellers—or rather, of *would-be*
travellers—who are introduced in the middle sections of the poem.

The opening quatrain has (as L. J. Austin has remarked[5]) a
telling 'vastness of sweep'—its first three lines so richly evocative
of the world of childhood (of Baudelaire's own childhood, as he
elsewhere describes it[6]), its contrasting fourth so eloquently (if as
yet vaguely) prophetic of the whole future course of the poem:[7]

[1]In his letter to Du Camp, B. (as we have seen, n. 2, above) had spoken of the
poem's 'ton systématiquement byronien'; in what way he regarded it as
'Byronic', we may perhaps gauge from this phrase he extracts from Villemain's
Chateaubriand (p. 51): 'Caractère oriental de Byron, "le *sceptique* voyageur" '
(OP I, 327; B.'s, and not Villemain's, italics). Cf. the analogies with Byron's
poem noted by G. de Reynold, *B.,* 269—with the comment: '*Le Voyage . . .*
est presque un résumé du *Pèlerinage de Childe Harold*'.

[2]Cf. the comment by A. Lebois, *Admirable XIX*ᵉ *siècle,* 95–6, prompted by
the analogy between ll. 17–18 of *Le Voyage* and a passage from Gautier's
Voyage en Espagne: 'Je serais fort surpris si l'on me prouvait que tout le poème
du *Voyage,* bien que dédié à Maxime du Camp, ne traduit pas quelque entretien
avec Théo. Il est le véritable voyageur de cette époque. . . . Lui seul [sic]
pouvait "documenter" Baudelaire le sédentaire, qu'une équipée avait gorgé'.

[3]The author, precisely, of a poem entitled *Le Voyageur,* as of certain other
texts from which B. here borrows elements; see Y. Abé, art. cit., pp. 276–82.

[4]See pp. 158–9, above.

[5]In his very full and penetrating account of the poem (from which, however,
I diverge on a few points of interpretation), 'B.: Poet or Prophet?', in *SMFL,*
pp. 25–6.

[6]Cf. the texts cit. p. 3 and n. 1, above: the youthful letters to his half-brother
(LS 45–6, 77–8), the prose poem *Les Vocations (PPP* 116). Y. Abé, art. cit.,
p. 280, has remarked that in this verse B. in effect sums up the whole theme of a
poem by Du Camp, *L'Enclos (Les Convictions,* 1858); cf. also the analogy noted
by E. Drougard, *RHLF,* 1932, pp. 446–7, with a passage from Nerval's *Voyage
en Orient.*

[7]See p. 304, below, and cf. the comment by L. J. Austin, art. cit., p. 25:
'. . . before the first stanza is over, we are warned that this world, so vast in
imagination in the golden glow of the lamplight, will shrink to insignificance
in the eyes of memory. Experience will give the lie to these childish dreams'.

> Pour l'enfant, amoureux de cartes et d'estampes,
> L'univers est égal à son vaste appétit.
> Ah! que le monde est grand à la clarté des lampes!
> Aux yeux du souvenir que le monde est petit!

In the succeeding quatrain, the Travellers as it were cast back to the moment of departure which all have known, with its strange compound of exaltation, rancour and 'bitter desire'—emotions that are more fully explained in the remaining verses of the section, with their subtle differentiation of motive:

> Un matin nous partons, le cerveau plein de flamme,
> Le cœur gros de rancune et de désirs amers,
> Et nous allons, suivant le rhythme de la lame,
> Berçant notre infini sur le fini des mers:[1]
>
> Les uns, joyeux de fuir une patrie infâme;
> D'autres, l'horreur de leurs berceaux, et quelques-uns,
> Astrologues noyés dans les yeux d'une femme,
> La Circé tyrannique aux dangereux parfums.
>
> Pour n'être pas changés en bêtes, ils s'enivrent
> D'espace et de lumière et de cieux embrasés;
> La glace qui les mord, les soleils qui les cuivrent,
> Effacent lentement la marque des baisers.
>
> Mais les vrais voyageurs sont ceux-là seuls qui partent
> Pour partir; cœurs légers, semblables aux ballons,
> De leur fatalité jamais ils ne s'écartent,
> Et, sans savoir pourquoi, disent toujours: Allons!
>
> Ceux-là dont les désirs ont la forme des nues,
> Et qui rêvent, ainsi qu'un conscrit le canon,
> De vastes voluptés, changeantes, inconnues,
> Et dont l'esprit humain n'a jamais su le nom!

> (ll. 5–24)

The departing travellers here distinguished are, it will be noted, of two main kinds. On the one hand, there are what might be called the 'refugees': the self-exiled from home or native land, the

---

[1] For a comment on this striking antithesis, and on its relationship to the preceding verse, see p. 304 and n. 1, below; cf. also p. 261, above.

'victims' of love;[1] on the other, the true (the sole true) travellers who depart simply for the *sake* of departing,[2] or in pursuit of some vast, nameless desire. Here, in the process of analysis, the dramatic mode of presentation has seemingly yielded place to something more objective, with the Travellers momentarily forgotten as the poet in effect takes over from them to speak directly to the reader. It might admittedly appear, at first glance, that with the reversion to the collective pronoun in the opening quatrain of the second section, the original mode of address had been restored; but this 'nous', it soon becomes apparent, refers, rather, to Humanity in general:

[1]By temperament and *potential* motive, B. himself could be said to belong to each of these categories—as could be amply demonstrated from his writings; cf., e.g., the exalted tributes, discussed in an earlier chapter, to that 'pagan elsewhere' which B. so often relives (or conjures up in his imagination) precisely for the intoxication of its 'espace', its 'lumière', its 'cieux embrasés'. But I must content myself, in the present context, with noting one further and curious analogy, with a poem which though having certain autobiographical implications, is presented, explicitly, in purely imaginative terms. In that perverse masterpiece, *Une Martyre,* B. describes in these terms the 'hot-house atmosphere in the bedroom in which lies the decapitated corpse: 'Dans une chambre tiède où, comme en une serre, / *L'air est dangereux et fatal . . .*'; later, speaking of the 'revengeful' husband we presume to be the woman's assassin, the poet with studied complicity questions her 'cadavre impur': 'L'homme vindicatif que tu n'as pu, vivante, / Malgré tant d'amour, assouvir, / Combla-t-il sur ta chair inerte et complaisante / *L'immensité de son désir?'*— while finally declaring of him: 'Ton époux court le monde . . .' (ll. 5–6, 45–8, 57; my italics). It would thus seem that in evoking, in the 1st section of *Le Voyage,* his third and fourth group of travellers: those who flee the 'dangerous perfumes' which sum up the 'tyrannies' of love, those whose desires are vast and boundless, B. wittingly or unwittingly was echoing the terms and psychology of this considerably earlier poem (comp. in first draft 1842?), while at the same time harking back, perhaps, to the personal experiences from which it may have arisen. (Cf., in this connection, the commentary on *Une Martyre* in *FMCB* 493–4.)

[2]The slight pause imposed here by the line-ending, heightening as it does the effect of the repetition of 'partir', admirably conveys the ironical yet at the same time admiring tone of the explanation: 'ceux-là seuls qui partent . . .' (a shrug, a gesture of both hands) '. . . *pour partir!'* ('et rien que pour cela!'). As a further but perhaps accidental felicity, one might note that this run-over from the one line to the next, 'imitates' in advance by its very sound the balloon-like volatility of the 'cœurs légers'; I say 'perhaps accidental', since one should always be extremely wary, in my opinion, of attributing to a poet's deliberate calculation, subtleties of expression that are often quite implausible by the very nature of the creative situation (in which happy chance, considerations of pure euphony dictated by the poet's 'ear' rather than his mind, etc., play so important, though so often unrecognized, a part).

Nous imitons, horreur! la toupie et la boule
Dans leur valse et leurs bonds; même dans nos sommeils
La Curiosité nous tourmente et nous roule,
Comme un Ange cruel qui fouette des soleils.

Singulière fortune où le but se déplace,
Et, n'étant nulle part, peut être n'importe où!
Où l'Homme, dont jamais l'espérance n'est lasse,
Pour trouver le repos court toujours comme un fou!

(ll. 25–32)

One may here discern a certain inconsistency in Baudelaire's argument. He has posited what might be called a *general* psychology
of travel: the two things, he declares, that drive Man endlessly on
as he journeys hither and thither, are, firstly, *curiosity*—that same
tormenting curiosity he had earlier singled out as the representative
malady of the age;[1] and secondly, an unwearying *hope* that in some
strange paradoxical way Man may, by sheer frenzy of movement,
somewhere achieve a point of rest, if not the actual fulfilment of
what in any case is an undefined and perhaps undefinable ambition.[2]
Yet in the previous (first) section, this thirst for the unknown had
seemingly been confined to the 'true travellers' alone—to one group
rather than to all. The 'generalizing' process is pursued still further
in the succeeding verses of this second section: through images of
travel that are now purely symbolic (the look-out man with his
visionary gaze, deaf to the voice which warns from the bridge of
rocks lying ahead, and for whom every reef sighted is a 'promised'
Eldorado), the argument from human self-delusion is extended to
cover the whole field of imagination working upon desire to fashion
therefrom dreams of love, fame and happiness.[3] The final verse
of this section, however, returns us to the literal world of the

[1]Cf. pp. 66–7, above. The particular nature of the 'torment' is clarified in
the 4th section of the poem, ll. 69–74; cf. p. 302, below.
[2]This paradox is further explored in the 7th section, ll. 113–20; cf. p. 305,
below.
[3]ll. 33–44. What B. (through his Travellers) is here affirming, is thus the very
opposite of the consoling self-admonitions proffered in that other, almost exactly
contemporary poem, *La Voix* (cf. p. 258, above)—as also in the concluding
paragraph of the 1864 text of the prose poem *Les Projets* (*PPP* 81). And yet,
in the 1857–61 version of this same passage (*PPP* 308), the 'lesson' drawn had
been (as in *Le Voyage*, but more explicitly) a *condemnation* of dreams . . .

Parisian (?) tramp, while evoking a voyage that is now purely of
the imagination:

> Tel le vieux vagabond, piétinant dans la boue,
> Rêve, le nez en l'air, de brillants paradis;
> Son œil ensorcelé découvre une Capoue
> Partout où la chandelle illumine un taudis.
>
> (ll. 45-8)

It is this 'imaginary voyage' which furnishes the unspoken
transition to the second main part of the poem — into which, with
the third section and by an apparently complete hiatus, we now
move:

> Étonnants voyageurs! quelles nobles histoires
> Nous lisons dans vos yeux profonds comme les mers!
> Montrez-nous les écrins de vos riches mémoires,
> Ces bijoux merveilleux, faits d'astres et d'éthers.
>
> Nous voulons voyager sans vapeur et sans voile!
> Faites, pour égayer l'ennui de nos prisons,
> Passer sur nos esprits, tendus comme une toile,
> Vos souvenirs avec leurs cadres d'horizons.
>
> Dites, qu'avez-vous vu?
>
> (ll. 49-57)

This clearly is a new voice not previously heard in the poem, but
addressing itself to the familiar Travellers whom it salutes as
'étonnants voyageurs'. The new speakers are for their part 'armchair
travellers': unable (or unwilling for some reason?) to depart themselves, they nevertheless seek relief, from the tedium of the 'prisons'
within which they live, in the 'travellers' tales' they 'read' into the
deeply experienced eyes that confront them. This whole image,
developed over two verses, is an interesting one that repays careful
analysis. The richly filled jewel-case stands for the memories the
Travellers are invited to display — or rather, more strictly, for the
faculty of memory, which may be awakened or dormant, open or
closed. It is when the box is opened, the train of reminiscence set
going, that the individual jewels of memory are revealed: 'Ces
bijoux merveilleux, faits d'astres et d'éthers' — the descriptive
complement, which is both hyperbolical and evocative, calling to
mind the exotic skies and climes under which the travellers have

journeyed. (In the ensuing section, in reply to the question 'Dites, qu'avez-vous vu?,' the Travellers will reply: 'Nous avons vu des *astres*/Et des flots . . .') In the next quatrain, the luminosity of these remembered images serves as it were to *project* them on to the receptive screen of the listeners' imaginations ('Faites . . ./Passer sur nos esprits, tendus comme une toile,/Vos souvenirs . . .')—as in some magic-lantern show well calculated to delight these 'cerveaux enfantins', as they will be described (by the Travellers) in the next section. And as a final touch, with the phrase 'avec leurs cadres d'horizons', we have the filling-in of the exotic background, the provision of the 'frame' within which and against which each individual image of memory stands out. What the new speakers are in reality soliciting from the Travellers is of course a stimulus for their *own* imaginations—a stimulus more direct than that which sufficed the exalted tramp of the previous section, with his 'bewitched eye' which could, of itself, transmute the candle-lit hovel into a Capuan garden of delight. But tramp and 'armchair travellers' are none the less alike members of the same vast family of 'imaginatives' (and this, precisely, is the unspoken transition between the two sections of which I earlier spoke)—a family which, moreover, clearly includes Baudelaire himself: Baudelaire who after all only once truly 'departed', and then under duress rather than through any imperious choice of his own;[1] Baudelaire with his frustrated 'rage de voyage' that had possessed him since childhood, Baudelaire with his voracious reading of travel books and his susceptibility to their 'charm', Baudelaire the perpetual dreamer of new settings (or 'cadres d'horizons') for his beloved, and who indeed has elevated this form of 'voyage . . . sans vapeur et sans voile' almost into a new amorous strategy.[2]

With the fourth section we hear once again the voice of the Travellers, which in effect had been stilled since the second verse; now, to the eager question 'Dites, qu'avez-vous vu?'—to the plea that they should bring forth from their 'caskets' the 'jewelled' treasures of memory—they reply, indulgently enough:[3]

[1] Cf., for this voyage of 1841–2, pp. 26–7, above.

[2] Cf. L.s of 1/2/1832, 12/7/1833, 8/12/1848, 28/3/1857 and 6/5/1861 *(LS* 45–6, 77–8; *CG* I, 110, II, 35, 36, and III, 284); *Salon de* 1846, *CE* 183; the poems *Moesta et errabunda* and *L'Invitation au voyage*; the prose poems *Les Projets*, *L'Invitation au voyage*, *Any where out of the world*, *Les Vocations* (final section, *PPP* 116–18)—as also my comments, above, on certain of these texts.

[3] And within inverted commas, marking their entry into the actual dialogue.

. . . "Nous avons vu des astres
Et des flots; nous avons vu des sables aussi;
Et, malgré bien des chocs et d'imprévus désastres,
Nous nous sommes souvent ennuyés, comme ici.

La gloire du soleil sur la mer violette,
La gloire des cités dans le soleil couchant,
Allumaient dans nos cœurs une ardeur inquiète
De plonger dans un ciel au reflet alléchant.

Les plus riches cités, les plus grands paysages,
Jamais ne contenaient l'attrait mystérieux
De ceux que le hasard fait avec les nuages.
Et toujours le désir nous rendait soucieux![1]

The (unheeded) qualification in the fourth line above-quoted, may be thought to take up the very reference the naive questioners have just made to the 'tedium' of their lives. 'No doubt' (so the Travellers' retort would imply), 'no doubt we may succeed, by our "tales", in enlivening your boredom for a while; but do not imagine that travel in itself provides any cure for such a condition; we too, many times, have been bored!' But in their further comments on their experiences, the Travellers return, insistently, to the theme of Man's unassuageable curiosity—a confirmation (if confirmation were needed) that they were indeed describing their own motives when they earlier spoke of the 'vrais voyageurs . . . qui partent/Pour partir'. More specifically, the marvels of exotic Nature no less than the marvels created by Man, are shown as being alike powerless to quench the insatiable thirst for novelty that drives him forever onwards, to the ends of the earth and (ultimately) beyond. From this observation the Travellers develop, digressively, an elaborate homily which in metaphoric and rhetorical terms recognizes how powerfully

[1] ll. 57-68. There are curious echoes here—as in certain ensuing lines (77, 128-30) of B.'s poem—of a passage in Ménard's *Prométhée delivré* of 1843, in which the so-called 'Révélateurs' describe their vision of the Orient: '*Nous avons aperçu* les mers asiatiques . . . / *Nous avons salué* les royaumes antiques . . . / L'Inde seule . . . / Fait résonner encor des hymnes de ses dieux / *Les îles de lotus,* les rivières ambrées, / Et les *mers empourprées* / Aux flots mélodieux . . . / Orient parfumé, tout peuplé de chimères, / Ton soleil de pourpre est si doux . . .' (pp. 77, 78, 80; my italics). It would be ironic indeed if, at some thirteen years' distance, B. had harked back even fleetingly and unwittingly to the 'philosophical poem' he had so summarily dismissed in 1846! (Cf. p. 24, above.)

curiosity feeds upon curiosity, desire upon desire[1]—while leaving its hearers suspended upon an interrogation to which (as L. J. Austin has noted[2]) the answer comes only in the concluding verses of the poem:

> —La jouissance ajoute au désir de la force.
> Désir, vieil arbre à qui le plaisir sert d'engrais,
> Cependant que grossit et durcit ton écorce,
> Tes branches veulent voir le soleil de plus près!
>
> Grandiras-tu toujours, grand arbre plus vivace
> Que le cyprès? . . .

                                                                (ll. 69–74)

The description is nevertheless resumed; the Travellers consent, after all, to display a few of the 'sketches' they have culled for the 'voracious albums' of these incurable (and 'fraternal') seekers after the exotic:

> . . .—Pourtant nous avons, avec soin,
> Cueilli quelques croquis pour votre album vorace,
> Frères qui trouvez beau tout ce qui vient de loin!
>
> Nous avons salué des idoles à trompe;
> Des trônes constellés de joyaux lumineux;
> Des palais ouvragés dont la féerique pompe
> Serait pour vos banquiers un rêve ruineux;
>
> Des costumes qui sont pour les yeux une ivresse;
> Des femmes dont les dents et les ongles sont teints,
> Et des jongleurs savants que le serpent caresse.

                                                                (ll. 74–83)

There is certainly here implied a critique of exoticism—but of a superficial and purely 'pictural' exoticism,[3] such as delights in the

---

[1] The underlying psychological mechanism is neatly summed up in this gloss by A. Fairlie, *B.: 'FM'*, 34: '. . . achievement gives way to satiety which intensifies further longing. . . .'

[2] Art. cit., pp. 27–8; cf. ibid., p. 26.

[3] As represented, e.g., in certain writings by Gautier (from whom, precisely, B. seems to have borrowed one detail at least of his Travellers' description; see *FMA* 430 n. 14), Flaubert, the Goncourt brothers; cf., in this connection, A. Cassagne, *Théorie de l'art pour l'art,* 376–84. But the same critic notes equally, ibid., 397–8, the note of idealistic pessimism in Flaubert's exoticism—as in that of Leconte de Lisle and B.

strangeness of idols armed (or 'nosed') with elephantine trunks, of jewelled thrones, of snake-charmers, of women with painted nails and [sic] teeth, etc., rather than of that purer and deeper nostalgia for the 'pays chauds et bleus', which continued to pursue Baudelaire throughout this period; indeed, if there is one category of travellers that is unrepresented or unnamed in *Le Voyage*, it is precisely those who return, not disabused, but on the contrary forever *haunted* by the memory of an ideally primitive, ideally consoling way of life.[1]

So naively single-minded, however, is the questioners' pursuit of the exotic, so entranced are they by the intrinsic vividness of the Travellers' descriptions, that they fail entirely to perceive the irony that underlies the reply; they return to the charge with still further, still more avid questioning: 'Et puis, et puis encore?' This brief phrase forms a whole section to itself (the fifth); when, in the sixth section, the Travellers resume their account, it is with an exclamation: 'O cerveaux enfantins!', which completes, and ironically annuls, the line that had been left suspended after the questioners' renewed prompting—an exclamation which not only bespeaks a massive disdain but at the same time reminds us (continuing the characterization that had already been sketched in the previous section: 'Frères qui trouvez beau tout ce qui vient de loin!') that the insatiable appetite for 'tales of other lands' is precisely that of the *child* with whom the poem began. And it is from this perspective of a whole human life now viewed in retrospect as it draws to a close, that the Travellers—having completed, in the sixth section (to the final discomfiture, we presume, of their questioners, who now disappear from the poem[2]), their long and savage catalogue of human iniquity[3]—look back reflectively, from the bitter wisdom they have gained, on the 'lessons' of Travel. Thus, at the opening of this

---

[1]Cf., in this connection my Chap. III, above ('The Nostalgic Primitivist'). J. Pommier, *Dans les chemins de B.*, 346, has noted the 'reviviscence de l'inspiration exotique' during the present period; cf., in addition to the texts there cited (*Un Hémisphère dans une chevelure, La Chevelure* in its 1859 text, the prose poem *La Belle Dorothée*, the sonnet *Bien loin d'ici*), the descriptions, vivified by B.' personal nostalgia, both of the paintings of Fromentin, and of the poems of Leconte de Lisle (*Salon de 1859, CE* 317–18—cit. p. 45, above; *Leconte de Lisle, AR* 375–6).

[2]The closing of the inverted commas at the end of the 6th section, marks the end of the dialogue proper, and the resumption of the 'meditation' on past experiences of travel, which the Travellers had begun in the second verse.

[3]Cf., for a comment on this sixth section of the poem, pp. 158–9, above.

21

seventh section, we hark back almost textually to the opening lines of the poem. For the child (we were there told) the world is boundless and infinite in its scope and promise; for the reminiscent adult (we were in effect warned) it would narrow to an all too finite littleness: 'Aux yeux du souvenir que le monde est petit!'[1] Now, however, this observation is extended to the whole of present as well as remembered reality, and is presented in terms no longer of simple regret but of explicit pessimism:

> Amer savoir, celui qu'on tire du voyage!
> Le monde, monotone et petit, aujourd'hui,
> Hier, demain, toujours, nous fait voir notre image:
> Une oasis d'horreur dans un désert d'ennui![2]

In this verse, with its final, desolating image, the Travellers might seem at first simply to be reaffirming that one arid discovery they had previously reported (and retorted) to their questioners: sin is universal, boredom is unrelieved, and indeed in its very repetitiveness sin is itself boredom.[3] And yet the final wisdom offered by the Travellers, proves in effect to run counter to the moral seemingly implicit in the second and fourth sections of the poem—a moral which several critics have too hastily assumed to be that of the poem as a whole: the Pascalian lesson ('tout le malheur des hommes vient d'une seule chose, qui est de ne savoir pas demeurer en repos, dans une chambre') which Baudelaire had previously enshrined in his sonnet Les Hiboux:

> L'homme ivre d'une ombre qui passe
> Porte toujours le châtiment
> D'avoir voulu changer de place.[4]

---

[1] A similar and related antithesis (the adult's *infinite* aspirations continuing those of the child, the sea imaging the contrasted *finiteness* of the external world) is offered in the ensuing, 8th line of the poem: 'Et nous allons . . . / Berçant notre infini sur le fini des mers'.

[2] ll. 109-12. For the relation with the first verse, cf. L. J. Austin, art. cit., p. 29, who goes on to make an interesting comparison with Macbeth's 'Tomorrow and tomorrow and tomorrow. . . .'

[3] 'Le spectacle *ennuyeux* de l'immortel péché' (l. 88). Cf. ll. 60 and 54, as also B.'s observation to Du Camp: '. . . le Voyageur avoue n'avoir vu que la banalité' (*CG* II, 278; p. 294 n. 2, above). For the *universality* of sin, cf. ll. 85-108.

[4] ll. 12-14; cf. also (pp. 41-2, above) the final section of *A une Indienne* (1846), and the later texts cit. p. 268 and n. 2, above. For a further comment on *Les Hiboux,* see my art. cit., 'B.: The Poet as Moralist', pp. 200-2. In the

In *Le Voyage*, however, the wise man's solution (as learnt, in *Les Hiboux*, from the wise owls: 'shun movement, be content to stay at home'), becomes a solution valid for the wise man alone; in the last analysis, as the Travellers recognize, there *is* no one universal solution, and the sole counsel that can be proffered ('Stay, if you can; go, if you must') is one simply of 'laisser-faire': [1]

> Faut-il partir? rester? Si tu peux rester, reste;
> Pars, s'il le faut. L'un court, et l'autre se tapit
> Pour tromper l'ennemi vigilant et funeste,
> Le Temps! Il est, hélas! des coureurs sans répit,
>
> Comme le Juif errant et comme les apôtres,
> A qui rien ne suffit, ni wagon ni vaisseau,
> Pour fuir ce rétiaire infâme; il en est d'autres
> Qui savent le tuer sans quitter leur berceau. [2]

With this final reference to those who while abstaining from all 'movement', are yet able to 'kill' Time, Baudelaire may seem after all to be reintroducing a quietist condemnation of travel. But it is at this very moment that the poem deftly changes its whole character and direction, the hinge or mechanism for the transition being precisely the idea of Time. By a play on words, by a logical sleight of hand, Time's enmity is transformed in character from one line to the next: from the Time whose 'slowness' drags out and intensifies

---

1864 text of *La Solitude* (*PPP* 76-7), B. was to quote—or rather, misquote—the Pascal phrase in question, but in the specific context indicated by his title. For the 'Pascalian' interpretation of *Le Voyage*, cf., especially, E. Drougard, *RHLF*, 1932, pp. 448-50. To the numerous other writers cited by E. Drougard (ibid.), by J. Crépet and G. Blin (*FMCB* 526-7), by G. T. Clapton (*RHLF*, 1931, pp. 242-7), by R. Vivier (*Originalité de B.*, 205), as sharing this condemnation of needless movement from one place to another, should be added Vigny; cf. the texts cit. E. Lauvrière, *Vigny*, 286-7.

[1] Cf. the comment by J. Pommier, *Dans les Chemins de B.*, 343: 'Le poète tourne en dérision le voyageur et ses mirages, sans que sa propre philosophie soit celle de l'immobilité à tout prix. . . .'

[2] ll. 113-20. The same basic classification of Mankind is made, more tersely, in a line of *Le Couvercle*: 'Citadin, campagnard, *vagabond, sédentaire*, / . . . Partout l'homme subit la terreur du mystère . . .' (ll. 5, 7); cf. also this contrast of attitudes in the concluding sentence of the prose poem *Le Port* (first pub. 1864): '. . . il y une sorte de plaisir mystérieux et aristocratique pour celui qui n'a plus ni curiosité ni ambition, à contempler . . . tous ces mouvements de ceux qui partent et de ceux qui reviennent, de ceux qui ont encore la force de vouloir, le désir de voyager ou de s'enrichir' (*PPP* 141-2).

the tedium of life—whom some can 'kill', by their own inner strength, without leaving their birthplace, but whom others must seek to 'cheat' by ceaseless movement from one place to another, by a restless search for new pleasures and diversions—it becomes, with the succeeding line ('Lorsque enfin il mettra le pied sur notre échine . . .'), that *other* Time whose relentless (and in this case all too rapid) progress brings us each day nearer to Death, and whom we can thus never truly 'cheat';[1] 'kill' Time in one sense though we may, in the truer sense it is Time which of course kills *us*—pinning us to the ground, 'press-ganging' us (as it were) for that last voyage which none can elude.

And yet it is precisely at this point of the poem, as the perspectives deepen and widen and the context shifts from the literal voyages of life to the last symbolic voyage of Death, that the prospect lightens, paradoxically, to one of joy and hope:

> Lorsque enfin il mettra le pied sur notre échine,
> Nous pourrons espérer et crier: En avant!
> De même qu'autrefois nous partions pour la Chine,
> Les yeux fixés au large et les cheveux au vent,
>
> Nous nous embarquerons sur la mer des Ténèbres
> Avec le cœur joyeux d'un jeune passager. (ll. 121-6)

The wheel has indeed come full circle; in the words of L. J. Austin:

. . . once again we set out on a voyage, as at the beginning of the poem. And we set out with the same eager anticipation. Here the power of the archetypal image strikes home with overwhelming force. Just as we once set sail for China with our eyes gazing over the open sea and our hair streaming in the wind, even so we shall embark upon the Sea of Darkness with the joyous heart of a young passenger. We shall have become once more like the child who pored lovingly over his maps and prints at the opening of the poem. Or rather, that child, with his vast appetite, has never died within us.[2]

---

[1]Both these contrasting attitudes to Time are of course fully represented elsewhere in Baudelaire's poetry. Cf., e.g., on the one hand, *L'Ennemi, L'Horloge;* on the other, *De profundis clamavi, Spleen* [II] (*J'ai plus de souvenirs . . .*), and more particularly the concluding sentence of *Portraits de maîtresses, PPP* 149: 'Ensuite on fit apporter de nouvelles bouteilles, pour tuer le Temps qui a la vie si dure, et accélérer la Vie qui coule si lentement'. (The image 'tuer le Temps' recurs, equally, in the punning context of *Le Galant Tireur, PPP* 152: 'tirer quelques balles pour *tuer* le Temps').

[2] Art. cit., pp. 29-30.

As 'young passengers' the Travellers were mainly driven, it will be recalled, by an unassuageable and indeed self-frustrating curiosity. What of their present desires, as they prepare to depart on yet another 'journey'? What are these 'hopes' they now at last declare themselves free to voice ('. . . enfin . . . nous pourrons *espérer* . . .')? One answer is given in the verses which immediately follow: their hope, their *expectation,* is to see again those 'dear departed ones'— those Electras and Pylades—whose voices they seem already to hear calling to them across the water, singing a siren song that is wholly benign; their hope, equally, is to be freed at last from the tyranny or 'enmity' of Time, in that Lotus-land of *eternal* afternoon to which these same voices sweetly 'beckon' them on.[1] But this of course is not the whole answer: the true nature, the profound significance, of the Travellers'—of Baudelaire's—hopes, is disclosed only in the two verses forming the poem's eighth and final section, its magnificent, so justly praised *envoi.*[2] The symbolism sketched in the previous section ('Nous nous embarquerons sur la mer des Ténèbres . . .'), is here fully established: the captain (Death himself) is on the bridge, the urgent plea goes forth to weigh anchor at last and to set sail—however black the sea and sky, however treacherous the passage, whatever the country of destination, Heaven or Hell, no matter! Here surely, in these verses which carry so vivid an accent of personal longing, we may feel the poet to have wholly identified himself with his Travellers: he too now embarks with them, in imagination, on the ship of Death; in the same spirit of reckless bravado but with a more bracing, even Promethean sense of challenge, he now lends a convincing 'reality' to the heartfelt cry we have heard in the prose poem:[3] 'n'importe où! pourvu que ce soit *hors* de ce monde!'

---

[1] ll. 127–36. Cf. L. J. Austin, art. cit., p. 30: 'Mysterious voices promise that in the world beyond the travellers will find the fragrant Lotus, symbolizing the miraculous fruit that can alone allay their hunger, and the strange sweetness of an everlasting afternoon, symbolizing escape from the ravages of Time'.

[2] Cf. the characteristically sensitive comment by P. Mansell Jones, *B.,* 53, on B.'s 'fusion of strange serenity of feeling with mastery of the long, nervous, solemn yet exultant rhythm'; of the earlier verses, the same critic notes, ibid., with equal felicity: 'A noble exhilaration carries the quatrains on with a fine swing of controlled rapture towards the unknown, even if the unknown proves to be "Le spectacle ennuyeux de l'immortel péché" '.

[3] P. 293, above.

> O Mort, vieux capitaine, il est temps! levons l'ancre!
> Ce pays nous ennuie, ô Mort! Appareillons!
> Si le ciel et la mer sont noirs comme de l'encre,
> Nos cœurs que tu connais sont remplis de rayons!
>
> Verse-nous ton poison pour qu'il nous reconforte!
> Nous voulons, tant ce feu nous brûle le cerveau,
> Plonger au fond du gouffre, Enfer ou Ciel, qu'importe?
> Au fond de l'Inconnu pour trouver du *nouveau!*

What has not yet, I think, been sufficiently emphasized is the extent to which the Travellers here *contradict* by implication the whole philosophy they have set forth in previous sections of the poem. Not only is the frame of mind in which they depart identical with that of the 'jeunes passagers' they once were, but have now disavowed; so, also, are their motives and expectations. Are they not here once again seeking escape, a diversion, from the tedium of their existence, its stale routine of boredom and horror?[1] Are they not here, once again, with unwearying hope ('. . . enfin . . . nous pourrons *espérer* . . .'), pursuing the dream of some ultimate haven of rest, some eternal Lotus-land (or Eldorado)?[2] Above all, are they not here once again driven on by curiosity, by the appetite for the new, by the unwearying desire to explore the unknown— be it even the *Great* Unknown: 'Au fond de l'*Inconnu* pour trouver du *nouveau!*'?[3] Thus for all the 'bitter wisdom' they have learned

---

[1] l. 138: 'Ce pays nous *ennuie*, ô Mort! Appareillons!' Cf. ll. 60, 88, 112.

[2] ll. 121–2, 128–32; cf. ll. 31–2 ('. . . l'Homme, dont jamais l'espérance n'est lasse, / Pour trouver le repos court toujours comme un fou!'), ll. 37–8: ('Chaque ilôt signalé par l'homme de vigie / Est un Eldorado promis par le Destin').

[3] l. 144; cf. ll. 2, 21–4, 26–8 ('. . . même dans nos sommeils / La Curiosité nous tourmente et nous roule, / Comme un Ange cruel qui fouette des soleils'), ll. 68–74 ('Et toujours le désir nous rendait soucieux'). Cf. also the comment on this poem (arising from a phrase of M. Ruff's) by J. Pommier, *RHLF*, 1958, p. 45: 'Délivrance, si l'on veut, mais . . .d'un billet pour l'Inconnu. Par *Le Rêve d'un Curieux*, par *Le Voyage*, *Les Fleurs du Mal* se terminent sur une poussée de Curiosité. . . . Et cet appétit du *nouveau* dévore la pensée du salut: "Enfer ou Ciel, qu'importe?"'. Here specifically (as G. de Reynold has noted, *B.*, 269), B.'s Travellers show themselves to be the lineal descendants of Byron's 'Childe Harold': 'With pleasure drugg'd, he almost long'd for woe, / And e'en for change of scene would seek the shades below' (*Childe Harold's Pilgrimage*, Canto 1, verse vi). Cf. also B.'s exclamation in the unfinished *Lettre à Jules Janin* (1865): 'Quoi! jamais vous n'avez eu envie de *vous en aller,* rien que pour changer de spectacle!' (*OP* 1, 230; there follows, in the next paragraph, a reference to Byron).

(and are so ready to impart), the Travellers show themselves to be essentially unchanged from the child, the 'young passengers', of the earlier sections of the poem; their earlier condemnation of human curiosity and restlessness and self-delusion, is in effect undermined by their own unregenerate eagerness to revert to these same attitudes, when at last they find themselves again confronted with an experience that promises utter novelty and total *dépayse-ment*. In short, the sole element of the Travellers' moral analysis that retains its validity to the end, is their denunciation of human sin; and thus no single group of travellers—not even the would-be travellers who most nearly represent the poet himself—stands finally condemned, but only Man in his most general and endemic sinfulness. The poem taken as a whole is thus in no sense a condemnation of Travel (or of any one traveller, e.g. Maxime du Camp); in its faithful rendering of the diverse psychologies of Travel, its unwillingness to 'conclude' (save in respect of the axiomatic universality of sin), it shows on the contrary a proper recognition of the complex diversity of human experience.

I spoke earlier (and as it might seem, paradoxically) of the *aspiring* quality of Baudelaire's nihilism in this poem—suggesting almost a prolongation of the idealism of the three 'Death' sonnets with which he chose to conclude the 1857 *Fleurs du Mal* (*La Mort des amants, La Mort des pauvres, La Mort des artistes.*) And indeed even though, in *Le Voyage,* the concept of Death may no longer entail the fulfilment of specific earthly aspirations, it nevertheless remains, still, the expression of a 'heart's desire'—the desire to be released from the boredom of life and the tyranny of Time, the desire above all to experience 'something new', 'du nouveau'; for the Baudelaire of *Le Voyage,* no less than for the paupers of *La Mort des pauvres,* Death is 'le portique ouvert sur les Cieux in-connus!'[1] Yet clearly, in its relation to external Nature, this philosophy cannot be viewed as other than wholly negative. For if, in the perspective of Death, the poet of *Le Voyage* turns so eagerly towards the new, is this not simply because he has lost all taste for life and conserves only the 'taste for nothingness'? Are not these hearts that fill with radiance as they sail out under a black sky over a black sea, the same that ardently crave 'le vide, et le noir, et le nu'?[2] In the final verses of *Le Voyage,* the poet (as Jean Prévost has

[1] L. 14; my italics.
[2] *Obsession,* l. 11.

observed) 'closes his eyes' to the external world, and to all save the interior vision which possesses him:

Une fois de plus, ce Monde qu'il a vu se déroule devant nos yeux, cette fois tout entier en un seul poème, et la vie comme la mer nous fatiguent de leur éblouissement monotone. Fermons les yeux—pour les reposer d'abord, puis pour demander éperdument *du nouveau;* la flamme spirituelle a comme éteint l'éblouissant spectacle de la nature, et le soleil n'est plus qu'intérieur. . . .[1]

Man also, with all his works, is here denied and condemned; and thus in this ultimate text (ultimate not in the chronological sense, but in the authority and grandeur of its conception), misanthropy and nihilism combine to supersede *all* prior attitudes to Nature—whether pious or impious, admirative or disdainful, humane or inhumane.

[1] *B.,* 124.

IX

Conclusion

THE foregoing survey has shown that Baudelaire's Nature-philosophy, far from being fixed and uniform throughout his career (as has so widely been assumed[1]) presents on the contrary a highly complex pattern of shifting and variously interrelated ideas. An initial phase sees him subscribing to something very like a 'cult' or 'religion' of Nature, which at times appears almost as a naturalist *counter*-ethic, owing much to eighteenth-century philosophic 'models'. By 1846, however, these ideas have begun to change their direction: the tendency is now on the one hand towards the (didactic) 'moralization' of Nature, on the other towards its aesthetic 'idealization'—Baudelaire's essential subjectivism, as a disciple of Delacroix, serving additionally, in this latter (aesthetic) sphere, to restrain any inclination he might feel towards purely descriptive or objective forms of naturalism. During this whole period we find him pursuing, equally, the nostalgic and elusive ideal of a pagan or primitivist 'elsewhere', a world of primal, uncorrupted felicity and of instinctive communion with Nature—here, actively remembered by the poet, from childhood or from the tropical 'paradise' briefly visited in 1841–2; there, drawing upon Romantic and pre-Romantic versions of an ideal and stylized classical antiquity. In its personal aspects, i.e. in the first two of these forms, the primitivist vision will continue to haunt Baudelaire throughout his life; the pagan-classical affiliation, on the other hand, will by 1851 yield its place under the pressures of two distinct forms of modernism: aesthetic, on the one hand, as proclaimed already in the *Salon de 1846* and as maintained, in various forms, throughout his life; social and utilitarian, on the other, arising directly from the poet's 'involvement' in the political events of 1848–51, but quickly and decisively abandoned thereafter.

The winter of 1851–2 marks, as we have seen, a decisive turning-point in Baudelaire's Nature-philosophy. From that point onwards

[1]E.g. (to take only the two most illustrious examples) by J. Crépet himself (*FMCB* 274, *PPP* 274, *AR* 463, *OP* I, 489, etc.), by J. Prévost *(B.*, 232), etc.

we may discern, within this philosophy, four main and intercrossing strands that are often in clear contradiction with one another, but which yet retain as their common basis (or starting-point) a defining *subjectivism*. (This latter, as we have seen, was already during the preceding period a feature of Baudelaire's aesthetic theory of Nature.) The first of these strands corresponds to what is no doubt the best-known (and indeed for some, the sole) attitude to Nature professed by Baudelaire: a dogmatic and trenchant hostility to Nature (usually antedated by critics by some six years, on the strength of a single phrase from the *Salon de 1846*, taken out of context[1])—in short a philosophy of *anti*-naturalism. In the form in which it occurs in the famous letter to Desnoyers of 1853–4— which is to say, directed against external Nature and its 'sanctified vegetables', and argued from a humanist and subjective standpoint —Baudelaire's anti-naturalism would seem to be more superficial than profound: a deliberately provocative or 'contra-suggestible' reaction (shared in common with several other equally articulate fellow-members of the Bohemian group: Boyer, Champfleury, Babou) against the fashionably pantheistic Nature-cult, as (supposedly) exemplified within the pages of the *Fontainebleau* volume of 1855. Certainly Baudelaire's humanism cannot be compared, either in eloquence or in comprehensiveness, with that of Vigny, and moreover one might well argue that certain of his earlier texts such as the 1848–51 version of *Le Vin des chiffonniers*, or the essay of 1851 on Pierre Dupont, are more genuinely humanistic—because humanitarian—than any written during the present period. A more significant aspect of Baudelaire's anti-naturalism, however, might seem to be his condemnation (from around 1859 onwards) of realism in art; yet this in turn we have seen to derive essentially from the criterion of 'idealization' elaborated some thirteen years earlier in the *Salon de 1846*, but now replaced by the analogous concept of the guiding creative *imagination*. As for the seemingly related 'cult of the artificial', this notion is never in fact given any true aesthetic extension by Baudelaire, but is presented simply within the moral and theological context of the doctrine of original sin. It is here that we encounter our main contradiction within Baudelaire's (supposedly coherent) philosophy of 'anti-Nature'. The letter to Desnoyers had implied the elevation of Man above Nature; but the doctrine of original sin (as expounded, notably, in the

[1] Cf. pp. 78–9, above.

'Éloge du maquillage') implies, on the contrary, the *degradation* of Man—both external Nature *and* human Nature now being subsumed within a common reprobation. Nor can a systematic repudiation of Nature be argued from Baudelaire's increasing 'specialization' of his talent, as the 'poet of *Paris*'; his attitudes to the city and to the countryside are if anything parallel rather than opposed, and display on occasion a like ambivalence. Thus we perceive that when replaced within their contemporary context, and studied in all their diverse and sometimes contradictory manifestations, Baudelaire's much-publicized diatribes against Nature reveal a far more limited and inconsistent attitude than is commonly supposed; his anti-naturalism (as manifested intermittently during this period 1852–1865) would appear certainly to lack the rigour and stern (poetic) logic variously displayed in this domain by such other nineteenth-century 'critics of Nature' as Vigny, Matthew Arnold, Tennyson, Hardy or even (in his later years) Laprade.[1]

The second of these four main preoccupations within Baudelaire's Nature-philosophy after 1852, brings what is no doubt his most original and influential contribution in this sphere: a theory (and practice) of Nature-symbolism that, while founded on the scattered intuitions of many previous writers, for the first time is made to constitute in itself a whole (modernist) aesthetic. Here again it is important to examine closely, and within the appropriate context, the detailed implications of Baudelaire's texts—implications which prove, when thus scrutinized, to be very different from those of the more traditional theories he so often invokes. Thus when citing, in support of his own theories, the authority of a Swedenborg or a Fourier, Baudelaire seems above all to have in mind the common *principle* of analogy which links their systems with his, rather than any similarity in the exact *nature* or *range* of the analogy; furthermore, when we pass to the specific illustrations of Baudelaire's doctrine to be found within his writings, we find that where Swedenborg had posited *transcendental* 'correspondences' between Earth and Heaven, and Fourier (and his disciples) *terrestrial* analogies between the objects of Nature disposed (by God) in a certain

---

[1]For Vigny and Laprade, see pp. 125 and n. 2, and 123–4 n. 1, above; for Tennyson, Hardy and Arnold (the latter having, it must be admitted, something of Baudelaire's inconsistency), see J. W. Beach, *Concept of Nature in Nineteenth-Century English Poetry*, 407–13, 504–9, 397–400 (respectively).

'hierarchy' of interrelationships whereby are conveyed spiritual or moral truths, Baudelaire for his part, while he may on occasion offer a moral symbolism of broadly Fourierist type, is nevertheless mainly concerned (both in his theory and in his practice) with a *subjective* symbolism which discerns in these same objects of Nature a reflection of a human (or personal) state of mind. Thus if one consents to discard in this connection the ambiguous word 'spiritual'—with its confusion between what is properly religious or divine, and what is merely a function of the human mind conceived as the antithesis of 'material' or 'real'—one perceives that Baudelaire's universe of analogy (like that of Fourier, but unlike that of Swedenborg) remains firmly confined within the universe of Nature. This restriction applies equally, moreover, to the notion (frequently invoked by Baudelaire in this context) of the 'supernatural': the Baudelairian 'supernatural' reveals itself to be in fact simply a state of mind—an exceptional state of mind, it is true, to which one may accede only at certain privileged or 'poetic' moments, and which favours strongly the perception of significantly symbolic relationships between the objects of Nature and one's own self. The 'supernatural', in short (like our modern 'surreal'), is for Baudelaire to be found *within* Man rather than without: an extension of his consciousness into realms which while being clearly distinct from the exterior or natural world, are in no proper sense 'mystical' or transcendent. But what lends Baudelaire's whole doctrine of 'correspondences' its particular individuality and cogency, is the specific 'theory of metaphor' he extracts from his general intuition of the 'meaningfulness' of Nature. By this theory, the actual devices of poetic language (simile, metaphor in the more restricted sense, allegory, symbol, etc.) are seen as the means whereby the Poet transcribes for other men the analogic intuitions he is especially (and as it were, *professionally*) gifted to perceive. What in practice this implies, of course, is that through his mastery of these devices, the Poet (holding, as he does, the 'keys' to Nature's symbols) acquires a status and authority which it may precisely (as I suggested) have been Baudelaire's primary intention to affirm. But he himself perhaps best summarizes his whole theory and practice of Nature-symbolism, in the answer that in his unpublished essay of 1857–60, *L'Art philosophique,* he goes on to give to the question he propounds, rhetorically, at the outset, 'Qu'est-ce que l'art pur suivant la conception moderne?'

C'est créer une magie suggestive contenant à la fois l'objet et le sujet,
le monde extérieur à l'artiste et l'artiste lui-même.

(*AR* 119)

My findings in this sphere thus, from their different standpoint, fully
confirm L. J. Austin's contention that Baudelaire's poetic 'correspondences', far from continuing traditional and transcendental modes
of analogy, are on the contrary 'at the service' of an essentially
personal and human (which is to say, *subjective*) symbolism;[1] where,
for a Lamartine, the poet's 'reflection' of Nature merely 'repeats'
Nature's prior reflection of God:

> Ame de l'univers, Dieu, père, créateur,
> Sous tous ces noms divers je crois en toi, Seigneur . . .
> . . . L'univers tout entier réfléchit ton image,
> Et mon âme à son tour réfléchit l'univers.[2]

—for a Baudelaire the first alone of these two 'equations' effectively subsists, to become indeed the determining symbolic principle
in a universe that for all practical poetic purposes is centred, not on
God, but on Man or on the poet's self.

Baudelaire's theory of correspondences, although it may in a sense
subordinate Nature to Man, as the mere 'dictionary' which awaits
the creative transformations to be wrought by the artist, is nevertheless not altogether easy to reconcile with his humanistic repudiation
of Nature; for how can he preserve his hostility towards a Nature
which at the same time, as the repository of latent analogies
'providentially' placed there by God Himself, must by definition
compel his awe and reverence? A still more radical discrepancy,
however, is with the terrible and withering *misanthropy* that increasingly possessed him after 1857 (and this is the third of the four
main strands which go to form his mature Nature-philosophy). For
how, again, can the theoretical or ostensible 'humanist' sustain his

[1] *Univers poétique de B.*, 55; cf. ibid., 172, 19-20. Cf. also, in this connection,
J. Prévost, *B.*, 75-6; M. Gilman, *Idea of Poetry*, 258, 260; M. Raymond,
De B. au Surréalisme, 24. For the further (modernist) development of this
'lyrisme subjectif', cf. ibid., 128-9: 'Il importait que la nature devînt, suivant
le mot de Baudelaire, un dictionnaire de formes, une forêt de symboles; que
l'univers entier plongeât ses racines dans le cœur du poète de façon que des
liens invisibles, sortes de nerfs sensibles, pussent rattacher les images au point
vif, au point central du *moi*'.
[2] *La Prière* (Pléiade, 46; cit. L. J. Austin, op. cit., 103).

championship of a mankind that appears to him ever more fla-grantly vile? Turning away, then, from Man, Baudelaire—who in his role as 'Promeneur *solitaire*' had in any case never abated his sensitive response to the beauties of landscape and of the changing seasons—is led to reaffirm strongly his (Byronic) admiration for certain elemental forms which display Nature in its vastest, most awe-inspiring, least tamed, least *humanized* aspect: sea, clouds, sun, moon, desert, mountains, lakes.[1] Yet this love (or admiration) lacks all sentimental effusiveness: unlike his Romantic precursors, Baudelaire in his solitude seeks no mitigating 'consolation'—whether from Nature herself, or from God-in-Nature,[2] or from some other and sympathetic human presence[3]—nor does he presume to hold 'private conference with the infinite';[4] perhaps, in the genuineness both of his misanthropy and of his feeling for Nature, as in his essential subjectivism, he comes nearest of all to the original 'Pro-meneur solitaire'—to Jean-Jacques Rousseau. At all events, even though he may continue, in his *Salon de 1859*, to denounce the type of 'positivist' artist who in his 'objectivity' dares to depict Nature 'in the absence of Man': 'l'univers sans homme',[5] in personal and

[1]Cf., for the analogy with Byron, the comments by H. N. Fairchild, *Romantic Quest*, 135–7 (' . . . Byron prizes Nature for her glorious *in*humanity', etc.). But Byron's Childe Harold, exulting in his 'interviews' with elemental Nature, goes on to add this reassurance which the misanthropic B. of the present period could scarcely have endorsed: 'I love not Man the less, but Nature more . . . ' (*Childe Harold's Pilgrimage,* canto IV, verse clxxviii; cf. also the lines from the previous verse, cit. below).

[2]Both these aspects of solitude could be illustrated from Lamartine: cf., respectively, *Le Vallon:* 'Mais la nature est là qui t'invite et qui t'aime; / Plonge-toi dans son sein qu'elle t'ouvre toujours . . .' (Pléiade, 20); *La Solitude:* 'Mais ton image, ô Dieu, dans ces grands traits épars, / En s'élevant vers toi grandit à nos regards. . . . Chaque pas te révèle à l'âme solitaire . . .' (Pléiade, 137).

[3]This is the Romantic 'solitude à deux'—as craved, e.g., by both Vigny (*La Maison du berger*) and Byron: 'Oh! that the Desert were my dwelling-place, / With one fair Spirit for my minister, / That I might all forget the human race, / And, hating no one, love but only her!' (*Childe Harold's Pilgrimage,* Canto IV, verse clxxvii).

[4]This phrase (which could equally be applied to Hugo) is used by H. N. Fairchild of Coleridge, when comparing him with Wordsworth: 'With Words-worth, love of nature led to love of man; but with Coleridge, love of nature tended gradually to draw him away from man into private conference with the infinite' (*Noble Savage,* 223).

[5]CE 284; cf. p. 138 n. 1, above.

philosophical contexts he is now ready to declare his preference for a Nature from which, precisely, Man has been excluded. . . . Thus by a paradox common enough in human experience, and by a process of development that is not so much circular as 'cyclic',[1] Baudelaire reverts, towards the end of his life, to a relationship with Nature which recalls, but at a more chastened and cynical remove, the 'honeymoon' phase of his youth.

Yet all this—and it might seem, all else—is negated by a further and complementary aspect of Baudelaire's pessimism, the *nihilism* that constitutes the fourth and final element of his Nature-philosophy. To the man who having forsworn his fellows, now forswears his own self, the very habit of analogy may by its sub-jectivism transform into torment the most remotely elemental spectacles of Nature—even to the forest, sea or starless night of *Obsession*. But a still further and indeed ultimate torment lies in wait for the nihilist. By the very reliance he places on the totality of his annihilation, he renders himself uniquely vulnerable to self-tormenting doubts and apprehensions: could it thus be (Baudelaire asks in *Le Squelette laboureur* and *Le Rêve d'un curieux*) that in death we are condemned to find only an endless prolongation of life —of its travail and toil, of its (frustrated) aspiration after the un-known? Yet it is precisely from this last expectancy—transformed into an infectious, almost 'optimistic' *conviction*—that Baudelaire wrests, in *Le Voyage,* a paradoxical nobility and ardour, and thus fittingly crowns (aesthetically, if not by strict chronology) his whole achievement as a Nature-poet and indeed as a poet of any kind.

Yet however complex and shifting the pattern of Baudelaire's Nature-philosophy may appear—however self-contradictory at times its diversity[2]—however much, in its individual elements, it may seem to owe to the influence of earlier or contemporary thinkers[3]—for all this, it retains none the less certain broadly constant and distinctively idiosyncratic features which I shall attempt in con-clusion to define. I earlier, for convenience, termed Baudelaire a

[1] Cf. especially, in this respect (p. 280, above), my comment on the analogy between the prose poem *Le Confiteor de l'artiste* and the youthful *Incompatibilité*.

[2] I would here recall, once again, that B. has so to speak armed himself in advance against any criticisms on this score, by proclaiming (for all and thus by implication for himself) the privilege and right of self-contradiction! Cf. p. 124 and n. 3, above.

[3] Cf. the footnotes accompanying my commentaries throughout this volume.

'Nature-poet'; but it is clear that he could never properly be described as such in any conventional sense of the word, and could, for instance, find no place—except by contradiction—in any history of 'Nature-feeling' pure and simple. Not only does he lack entirely the exalted Nature-mysticism of a Wordsworth or a Lamartine, but Nature-description itself is virtually absent from his poetry:[1] we may look in vain, in *Les Fleurs du Mal,* for the type of poem (represented only, within his writings, by the youthful—and discarded—*Incompatibilité*) in which a specific 'landscape' is fixed for us in its distinctive physical detail, and in which any subsequent emotional or philosophical response proceeds directly from the antecedent word-painting.[2] Where Nature does figure directly in Baudelaire's poetry, it is almost always in its more general and elemental aspects (mountains, sea, sun, moon, forests);[3] more often than not, the natural scene is invoked for some ulterior imaginative purpose—as an 'elsewhere', a vague, dream-like antithesis to immediate reality, or, again, as a symbol or 'correspondence' for the poet's mood or ideas. All this does not mean that Baudelaire was insensitive to the beauties of Nature; numerous passages, both in his poems and in his prose writings, attest the contrary. But Nature is at the periphery rather than at the centre of his universe; at the centre is Man (or a particular man: himself), and Nature is seen almost always in some human relation, is viewed through the screen of some remembered personal emotion, idea or sensation[4]—

[1]Such descriptions are, it is true, to be found in his art-criticism; but cf., in this connection, pp. 319-20, below.

[2]Lamartine's *L'Occident,* Leconte de Lisle's *La Ravine Saint-Gilles,* are two examples among many that spring to mind. Cf., concerning the relative absence in *FM* of 'tableaux de nature composés', H. Peyre, *Connaissance de B.,* 83.

[3]Cf. the comment made (with some exaggeration) by J. Prévost, *B.,* 125: 'Baudelaire nous montre dans la Nature le soleil, la mer, quelques trous d'ombre, quelques lambeaux d'une laideur et d'une pourriture compliquées. Ses peintures, si réalistes dans le détail, restent le plus souvent, dans l'ensemble, anonymes et presque universelles; nul n'a moins nommé de lieux. Elles font songer aux portraits d'inconnus, aux paysages dont le cadre ne porte point de nom'. A similar generality has been remarked in B.'s Parisian settings; cf. P. Citron, *Poésie de Paris,* II, 358.

[4]Here as elsewhere the past may often seem more vivid to the poet, more highly prized by him, than the present; such a demeanour is in fact precisely that dramatized in *Le Cygne.* Cf. my comments on *Paysage* (pp. 17-19, 162-5, above: the pastoral 'Idyll' to which the poet—abortively—dedicates himself, is a product of dream rather than of reality) and on *La Chevelure* (pp. 32-7;

if not indeed, during the final creative phase of his life, through the self-'enhancing' haze of opium.[1] We must also reckon here, to some extent, with the accidents of personal experience. It is a fact that for most of his adult life, Baudelaire hardly stirred from Paris;[2] his mistrust of Nature—while it may have been fostered on occasion by that strange inhibition or tension, before the beauty of a landscape, that he twice confesses, in two texts standing at some twenty years' distance from one another: the youthful *Incompatibilité,* the prose poem *Le Confiteor de l'artiste*—stems also no doubt, quite simply, from the defensive inertia, the fear of 'boredom', of the inveterate townsman. Certainly, of the three major excursions he made from Paris during the twenty-eight years (1836–1864) that he lived there continuously: the holiday trip to the Pyrenees at the age of seventeen, the long voyage to the Indian Ocean some four years later (in 1841–1842), the stay of four to five months at Honfleur in 1859—the first alone was fully and freely 'consented'.[3] And yet each of these journeys was in turn to prove, as we have seen, notably influential from a creative point of view. A final factor of some importance was Baudelaire's early training as an art critic: more often perhaps than at first hand, Baudelaire saw Nature in its aesthetic reproductions and transmutations—selected and

it is significant that of the various 'landscapes' sketched in *FM,* so many should—like this one—be 'exotic', and therefore distant both in place *and* time).

[1] I have mentioned already the dominant influence exerted by opium in B.'s personal concept of the 'surnaturel', as also the specific traces of its action that one may detect in certain later texts (e.g. especially *Le Confiteor de l'artiste*); cf. pp. 187, 280 and n. 5. It would be interesting to examine systematically the possible effect on B.'s perception of landscape of his addiction to opium; cf., in this connection, *Mangeur d'opium, PA* 28, the reference to the 'paysage opiacé' supposedly illustrated in a couplet from Shelley's *Revolt of Islam* (as quoted, in epigraph, by De Quincey; cf. *Confessions,* ed. M. Elwin, 413), as also the suggestive observations by E. Starkie, *B.,* 377, and C. Pichois, ed. *PA,* 19.

[2] Cf. C. Pichois, *B. à Paris,* 11; G. Jean-Aubry, *B. et Honfleur,* 20-1; P. Citron, *Poésie de Paris,* II, 332.

[3] Cf. my comments on these three journeys, pp. 6 and n.s, 26-7, 254-6, above—as also this judicious observation by B. L. O. Richter, *LM,* 1956, p. 288: 'L'épisode du voyage de 1841 nous montre—comme plus tard les irrésolutions entre Paris et Honfleur—que, malgré ses imprécations, Baudelaire restait foncièrement attaché à son ambiance. Ce qui devint une évasion nette, à but précis, pour Gauguin, la coupure nette qu'osa faire un Rimbaud, ces fuites vers des plages lointaines restaient des fictions pour notre Baudelaire'. One might here cite, additionally (cf. p. 26 n. 2, above), B.'s attitude to the nervously aired project of a return to Mauritius in 1847.

fragmented, bounded within a frame, refracted through an artist's temperament.[1] Moreover since the painter offers so much closer an approximation to the actual forms of Nature, than does the artist in any other medium, his art may well be seen (by an art critic such as Baudelaire, if not by the painter himself) as offering a kind of rivalry with Nature—as obliging the philosophically-minded on-looker to a choice between Nature-in-itself and Nature-as-art.

This brings me, finally, to the essential *ambivalence* of Baudelaire's attitude to Nature. 'Je te hais autant que je t'aime'—'Je t'aime autant que je te hais': these alternative formulations (the first figuring, of course, in the poem *A Celle qui est trop gaie*) might well, as I suggested in an earlier chapter, be transferred to our present context, so well do they characterize the poet's whole complex love-hate relationship with Nature.[2] In this respect it is surely significant that at the end of *Le Confiteor de l'artiste,* Baudelaire should have declared the study of Beauty in Nature to be a *duel,* in which the artist is eternally vanquished. Yet by the very act of memorably recording that failure, the artist (in whatever medium: poetry, prose, painting, music) contrives, in spite of all, to wrest a paradoxical and enduring victory. In tracing the vicissitudes of Baudelaire's running duel with Nature—in lending an attentive ear to the successive quarrels and reconciliations that punctuate the dialogue between them—I hope, by this very token, to have made clear the ultimate creative triumph that lies behind so many outward or self-imputed 'defeats'.

[1] B.'s spiritual precursor here (as in so much else) would seem to be Diderot; cf. the comments by Paul van Tieghem, *Sentiment de la Nature dans le pré-romantisme,* 153, 201: '. . . Diderot aime peindre la nature, mais au second degré, d'après un tableau'; '. . . beaucoup plus touché par l'art qui choisit et met en relief que par la nature observée directement dans sa complexité, persuadé que celui-là peut et doit embellir celle-ci, il montre en toute occasion qu'entre son âme ardente et la beauté du monde il a besoin de l'artiste comme intermédiaire et comme interprète'. But as I have shown (pp. 139–40, 168, above; *pace* A. Cassagne, *Théorie de l'art pour l'art,* 325–6), B. goes much *less* far in this direction than do certain contemporaries such as Gautier, Flaubert and the Goncourt brothers; cf. the respective declarations cit. F. Luitz, *Ästhetik von Gautier,* 135 n. 35, and A. Cassagne, op. cit., 324 (Flaubert), 325 (Goncourt).

[2] B., in short, loved Nature 'in his fashion'—the fashion equally demonstrated in his love (and hatred) for the city of Paris, or again for Jeanne Duval, for Marie Daubrun, for the 'heroine' of *A Celle qui est trop gaie.* . . .

Analytical Bibliography

Note : This Bibliography includes only those items, consulted at first hand, to which direct reference is made in the text.

A

EDITIONS OF BAUDELAIRE'S WRITINGS, ETC.

Complete works

Œuvres complètes, Paris, Conard. [*OCC*]
  Volumes edited by JACQUES CRÉPET:
  Les Fleurs du Mal. Les Épaves, 1930 (reprint of 1922 edition). [*FMC*]
  Quelques-uns de mes contemporains. Curiosités esthétiques, 1923. [*CE*]
  Quelques-uns de mes contemporains. L'Art romantique, 1925. [*AR*]
  Petits Poëmes en prose (Le Spleen de Paris). Le Jeune enchanteur, 1926.
  [*PPP*]
  Les Paradis artificiels. La Fanfarlo, 1928. [*PA*]
  Histoires extraordinaires, par Edgar Poe [translation], 1932. [*HE*]
  Nouvelles histoires extraordinaires, par Edgar Poe [translation], 1933.
  [*NHE*]
  Juvenilia. Œuvres posthumes. Reliquiæ, vol. I, 1939. [*OP*]
  Correspondance générale, vols. I–V, 1947–9. [*CG*]
  Volumes edited by JACQUES CRÉPET and CLAUDE PICHOIS:
  Juvenilia. Œuvres posthumes. Reliquiæ, vols. II–III, 1952. [*OP*]
  Correspondance générale, vol. VI, 1953. [*CG*]

Œuvres complètes. Edition définitive précédée d'une Notice par
THÉOPHILE GAUTIER, Paris, Lévy ('Bibliothèque contemporaine').
  I. *Les Fleurs du Mal*, 1868.
  II. *Curiosités esthétiques*, 1868.
  III. *L'Art romantique*, 1869.
  IV. *Petits poëmes en prose. Les Paradis artificiels.* [*La Fanfarlo. Le
      Jeune Enchanteur*], 1869.

Œuvres complètes. Edition critique par F. F. GAUTIER continuée par
Y. G. LE DANTEC, Paris, NRF (Editions de la Nouvelle Revue
française).
  II. (Ed. Y. G. LE DANTEC). *Les Fleurs du Mal. Documents—Variantes
      —Bibliographie*, 1934. [*FMLD*]

Œuvres complètes. Edition presentée dans l'ordre chronologique . . .,
Paris, Le Club du meilleur livre ('Le Nombre d'or' series), vols. I–II,
1955. [*CML*]
Œuvres complètes. Texte établi et annoté par Y. G. LE DANTEC; édition
révisée, complétée et présentée par CLAUDE PICHOIS, Paris, NRF
('Bibliothèque de la Pléiade'), 1966. [*OCP*]

Verse texts (other editions)

Douze poèmes [facsimile reproductions], ed. ADOLPHE VAN BEVER, Paris,
Crès, 1917. [*DP*]
*Les Épaves. Pièces condamnées. Galanteries. Épigraphes. Pièces diverses.
Bouffonneries,* Brussels, 'chez tous les libraires' [i.e. Poulet-Malassis],
1874 [reprint of 1866 edition].
Les Fleurs du Mal, Paris, Poulet-Malassis and De Broise, 1857 (original
edition; facsimile reprint: Geneva, Slatkine Reprints, 1968).
*Les Fleurs du Mal. Les Épaves. Bribes. Poèmes divers. Amœnitates
Belgicæ,* ed. ANTOINE ADAM, Paris, Garnier ('Classiques Garnier'
series), [1961]. [*FMA*]
Les Fleurs du Mal, ed. JACQUES CRÉPET and GEORGES BLIN, Paris,
Corti, [1950]. [*FMCB*]
*Les Fleurs du Mal. Les Épaves. Sylves, avec certaines images qui ont pu
inspirer le poëte,* ed. JEAN POMMIER and CLAUDE PICHOIS, Paris, Club
des Libraires de France, [1959]. [*FMPP*]
Poésies choisies, ed. ANDRÉ FERRAN, Paris, Hachette ('Classiques
illustrés Vaubourdolle' series), [1936].
Selected Verse, ed. and trans. FRANCIS SCARFE, Harmondsworth,
Penguin Books, ('The Penguin Poets' series), [1961].
Vers retrouvés (Juvenilia—Sonnets). Manoël, ed. JULES MOUQUET,
Paris, Émile-Paul, 1929. [*VR*]

Prose texts (other editions)

Art in Paris 1845–1862. Salons and other Exhibitions, trans. and ed.
JONATHAN MAYNE, London, Phaidon Press, [1965].
*Baudelaire critique d'art. 'Curiosités esthétiques', poèmes, œuvres diverses,
lettres,* ed. BERNARD GHEERBRANT, Club des Libraires de France, [1956].
Baudelaire en 1848. 'La Tribune nationale'. Texts introd. and ed. JULES
MOUQUET and W. T. BANDY, Paris, Émile-Paul, 1946.
Curiosités esthétiques. Édition intégrale illustrée, Introduction et notes
de JEAN ADHÉMAR, Lausanne, L'Œil ('L'Œil des maîtres' series), [1956].
Critique d'art, ed. CLAUDE PICHOIS, Paris, Colin ('Bibliothèque de
Cluny'), vols. I–II, [1965].
Critique littéraire et musicale, ed. CLAUDE PICHOIS, Paris, Colin ('Biblio-
thèque de Cluny'), [1961]. [*CLM*].

La Fanfarlo, ed. CLAUDE PICHOIS, Monaco, Éditions du Rocher ('Grands et petits chefs-d'œuvre'), [1957].

Journaux Intimes. Fusées—Mon Cœur mis à nu—Carnet, ed. JACQUES CRÉPET and GEORGES BLIN, Paris, Corti, [1949]. [*JI*]

Lettres inédites aux siens, ed. PHILIPPE AUSERVE, Paris, Grasset, [1966]. [*LS*]

[Baudelaire and ***], *Mystères galans des théâtres de Paris*, ed. JACQUES CRÉPET, Paris, NRF—Gallimard, [1938]. [*MGC*]

Les Paradis artificiels, précédé de *La pipe d'opium. Le hachich. Le club des hachichins* par THÉOPHILE GAUTIER, ed. CLAUDE PICHOIS, Paris, [Gallimard—Librairie générale française], 'Le Livre de poche classique', [1964].

Petits Poèmes en prose (*Le Spleen de Paris*), ed. HENRI LEMAITRE, Paris, Garnier ('Classiques Garnier' series), [1958].

Petits Poèmes en prose, ed. MELVIN ZIMMERMAN, Manchester University Press ('French Classics' series), [1968].

Le Salon de 1845, ed. ANDRÉ FERRAN, Toulouse, Aux Éditions de l'Archer, 1933. [*S45F*]

Miscellaneous

Baudelaire. Documents iconographiques (*Iconographie de Charles Baudelaire*), ed. CLAUDE PICHOIS and FRANÇOIS RUCHON, Geneva, Cailler, 1960. [*BDI*]

BIBLIOTHÈQUE NATIONALE. *Charles Baudelaire. Exposition organisée pour le centenaire des 'Fleurs du Mal'* [Exhibition Catalogue], Paris, 1957. [*BNE*]

Note: For contemporary publications by Baudelaire, see s.v. Chronological Index of Texts, as also s.v. Section B: ASSELINEAU, *Mélanges;* CRÉPET (Eugène), *Les Poëtes français;* and DENECOURT, *Fontainebleau*.

B

EARLIER OR CONTEMPORARY TEXTS

ANON. *Le Langage des fleurs, ou les Selams de l'Orient*, Paris, chez Rosa, 1819.

ANON. 'Un nouvel art.—L'Osphrétique', *L'Illustration*, III, 1844, p. 294.

ASSELINEAU, CHARLES. *Mélanges tirés d'une petite bibliothèque romantique . . .*, Paris, Pincebourde, 1866.[1]
—See also s.v. Section C.

AUDEBRAND, PHILIBERT. 'Le Dernier chapitre', in: *Fontainebleau* [q.v., s.v. DENECOURT, below], pp. 357–66.

[1]For B.'s contribution to this volume, see s.v. Chronological Index of Texts: *Coucher du soleil romantique (Le)*.

BABOU, HIPPOLYTE. [Review of] *Fontainebleau* [q.v., s.v. DENECOURT, below], *L'Athenæum français*, IV, No. 27, 7 July 1855, pp. 562–3.

BALZAC, HONORÉ DE. *Œuvres complètes*, ed. MARCEL BOUTERON and HENRI LONGNON, Paris, Conard. [*OCC*].

    [XL] *Œuvres diverses, III (1836–1848)*, 1940.

    [IV] *Études de mœurs: Scènes de la vie privée, IV: ... Honorine*, 1947.

    [XXIII] *Études philosophiques, II. Le Chef-d'œuvre inconnu...*, 1963.

—*Illusions perdues*, ed. ANTOINE ADAM, Paris, Garnier ('Classiques Garnier' series), [1956].

—*Le Lys dans la vallée*, ed. MOÏSE LE YAOUANC, Paris, Garnier ('Classiques Garnier' series), [1966].

BANVILLE, THÉODORE DE. *Les Cariatides*, Paris, Pilout, 1842.

—*Les Stalactites* [1846], ed. E. M. SOUFFRIN, Paris, Didier, [1942].

—'A la forêt de Fontainebleau', in: *Fontainebleau* [q.v., s.v. DENECOURT, below], pp. 34–6.

—'L'Aube romantique', in: ASSELINEAU, *Mélanges* [q.v., above], pp. i-viii.

—See also s.v. Section D.

BERNARDIN DE SAINT-PIERRE, JACQUES-HENRI. *Œuvres complètes*, ed. L. AIMÉ-MARTIN, Vol. VI: *Paul et Virginie, La Chaumière indienne . . .*, Paris, Dupont, 1825.

BOYER, PHILOXÈNE. *Les Deux Saisons*, Paris, Lemerre, 1867.

BYRON, GEORGE GORDON (Sixth Lord). *Poems*, ed. V. de Sola PINTO, London, Dent ('Everyman's Library'), [1963] (revised edition), Vol. II.

CASTILLE, HIPPOLYTE. 'Sur la solitude', in: *Fontainebleau* [q.v., s.v. DENECOURT, below], pp. 84–9.

CHAMPFLEURY. *Contes vieux et nouveaux*, Paris, Lévy, 1852.

—'Vision dans la forêt', in: *Fontainebleau* [q.v., s.v. DENECOURT, below], pp. 102–6.

—*La Succession Le Camus. Les Amis de la Nature*, Paris, Poulet-Malassis and De Broise ('Œuvres illustrées de Champfleury'), 1861.

—*Souvenirs et portraits de jeunesse*, Paris, Dentu, 1872.

CHATEAUBRIAND, (vicomte) FRANÇOIS-RENÉ DE. *Génie du Christianisme, ou: Beautés de la religion chrétienne*, Paris, Le Normant, 1816 (6th edition), vols. I–V.

COLARDEAU, CHARLES-PIERRE. *Œuvres*, Vols. I–II, Paris, 1779.

CONSTANT DE BAUCOUR, M. A. ('l'abbé Constant'). *Les Trois Harmonies. Chansons & Poésies*, Paris, Fellens and Dufour, 1845.

CRÉPET, EUGÈNE (ed.). *Les Poëtes français . . .* [Anthology, with critical notices by BAUDELAIRE, etc.], Paris, Hachette, 1862: Vol. IV, *Les Contemporains*.[1]

---

[1] For B.'s contributions to this volume, see s.v. Chronological Index: *Leconte de Lisle; Marceline Desbordes-Valmore; Pierre Dupont* II; *Théodore de Banville; Victor Hugo*.

Darwin, Erasmus. *The Temple of Nature; or, The Origin of Society*, London, Jones, 1824 (reprint of 1803 edition).

Delacroix, Eugène. *Correspondance générale*, ed. André Joubin, Paris, Plon, Vols. i–v, [1935–8].

—*Journal*, ed. André Joubin, Paris, Plon, Vols. i–iii, revised edition, [1950].

—*Œuvres littéraires*, ed. Élie Faure, Paris, Crès ('Bibliothèque dionysienne'), Vols. i–ii, [1923].

—See also s.v. Section D, Sérullaz, below.

Denecourt, C. F. *Hommage à C. F. Denecourt. Fontainebleau. Paysages—Légendes—Souvenirs—Fantaisies*, par Charles Asselineau . . . Baudelaire, etc., Paris, Hachette, 1855.[1]

—*Le Palais et la forêt de Fontainebleau, guide historique et descriptif* [16th edition of the *Indicateurs-Denecourt*], Fontainebleau, l'auteur, 1856.

De Quincey, Thomas. *Confessions of an English Opium-Eater*, ed. Malcolm Elwin, London, Macdonald ('Illustrated Classics' series), [1956].

Diderot, Denis, *Supplément au Voyage de Bougainville*, ed. Gilbert Chinard, Paris, Droz, 1935.

—*Œuvres*, vol. xxi: *Le Neveu de Rameau . . .*, Paris, Brière, 1821.

—*Le Neveu de Rameau*, ed. Jean Fabre, Geneva/Lille, Droz/Giard ('Textes littéraires français'), 1950.

—*Salons*, ed. Jean Seznec and Jean Adhémar, Oxford, Clarendon Press, Vol. i, 1957 (*1759, 1761, 1763*); Vol. ii, 1960 (*1765*).

—[See also s.v. Encyclopédie, below.]

Encyclopédie. *The Encyclopédie of Diderot and D'Alembert. Selected Articles*, ed. J. Lough, Cambridge, University Press, 1954.

Gautier, Théophile. 'Francisco Goya y Lucientes', *Le Cabinet de l'amateur et de l'antiquaire*, i, 1842, pp. 337–45.

—'Le Club des Hachichins', *Revue des Deux Mondes*, xvi⁰ année, N.S. xiii, 1 February 1846, pp. 520–35.

—*Salon de 1847*, Paris, Hetzel and Warnod, 1847.

—*Histoire de l'art dramatique en France depuis vingt-cinq ans*, Brussels, Hetzel: vol. i, 1858; vols. ii–vi, 1859.

—*España*, ed. René Jasinski, Paris, Vuibert, 1929.

—*Poésies complètes*, ed. René Jasinski, Paris, Firmin-Didot, Vols. i–iii, [1932.]

—[See also s.v. Sections A, C, and D (Bergerat, Spoelberch de Lovenjoul).]

Gérard de Nerval. [See s.v. Nerval.]

[1]For full details of this publication, see my art. cit., 'A *Festschrift* of 1855', pp. 195–6 n. 1, and passim. For B.'s contributions to the volume, see s.v. Chronological Index: *Crépuscule du matin (Le); Crépuscule du soir (Le;* prose and verse); Letter to Desnoyers; *Solitude (La)*.

HOLBACH, (Baron) PAUL-HENRI D' [under pseudonym of MIRABAUD]. *Système de la Nature, ou Des Loix du Monde Physique et du Monde Moral,* London, 1770, Vols. I–II.

HOOD, THOMAS. *Poetical Works,* London, Finch ('Hampstead Library' edition), n.d.

HUGO, VICTOR. *Œuvres poétiques,* ed. PIERRE ALBOUY, Paris, NRF, 'Bibliothèque de la Pléiade', Vol. I: *Avant l'exil, 1802–1851,* [1964].

—*Les Contemplations,* ed. JOSEPH VIANEY, Paris, Hachette ('Les Grands Écrivains de la France' series), 1922, Vols. I–III.

—*La Légende des Siècles,* ed. PAUL BERRET, Paris ('Les Grands Écrivains de la France' series), Vols. I–III, 1921.

LACAUSSADE, AUGUSTE. *Poèmes et paysages,* Paris, Ducloux-Garnier, 1852.

LAMARTINE, ALPHONSE DE. *Œuvres poétiques complètes,* ed. MARIUS-FRANÇOIS GUYARD, Paris, NRF, 'Bibliothèque de la Pléiade', [1966].

—*Voyage en Orient,* ed. LOTFY FAM, Paris, Nizet, [1960].

LAPRADE, VICTOR DE. *Odes et poëmes,* Paris, Labitte, 1843.

—*Le Sentiment de la nature chez les modernes,* Paris, Didier, 1868.

—See also s.v. Section D, SÉCHAUD.

LARGENT, A. [Review of] *Fontainebleau* [q.v., s.v. DENECOURT, above], *L'Artiste,* 5e série, XV, No. 11, 15 July 1855, pp. 151–2.

LIMAYRAC, PAULIN. 'La Poésie symbolique et socialiste: *Odes et poëmes,* par M. V. de Laprade', *Revue des Deux Mondes,* XIVe année, N.S. V, 15 February 1844, pp. 669–82.

LUCHET, AUGUSTE. 'Pour qui ce livre est fait', in: *Fontainebleau,* [q.v., s.v. DENECOURT, above], pp. 1–23.

MAISTRE, JOSEPH DE. *Les Soirées de Saint-Pétersbourg,* ed. PIERRE MARIEL, Paris, La Colombe ('Littérature et Tradition' series), [1960].

—[See also s.v. Section C, below, ALPHONSUS and VOUGA.]

MÉNARD, LOUIS. [Under pseudonym of 'L. de Senneville'], *Prométhée délivré,* Paris, Au Comptoir des Imprimeurs unis, 1844.

—See also s.v. Section D, PEYRE.

MIRABAUD. [See s.v. HOLBACH.]

MUSSET, ALFRED DE. *Œuvres complètes en prose,* ed. MAURICE ALLEM and PAUL-COURANT, Paris, NRF, 'Bibliothèque de la Pléiade', [1960].

—*Poésies complètes,* ed. MAURICE ALLEM, Paris, NRF, 'Bibliothèque de la Pléiade', [1962].

NERVAL, GÉRARD DE. 'Voyage à Cythère: III', *L'Artiste,* 4e série, I, 11 August 1844, pp. 225–8.

—'Les Druses, Le Kalife Hakem, Scènes de la vie orientale', *Revue des Deux Mondes,* XVIIIe année, N.S. XIX, 15 August 1847, pp. 577–626.

—*Œuvres complètes,* ed. ARISTIDE MARIE, etc., Paris, Champion. *Les Deux 'Faust' de Goethe* [translation], ed. FERNAND BALDENSPERGER, 1932.

—*Œuvres*, ed. ALBERT BÉGUIN and JEAN RICHER, Paris, NRF, 'Bibliothèque de la Pléiade', [1966], Vols. I–II.

—*Voyage en Orient*, ed. GILBERT ROUGER, Paris, Imprimerie nationale de France ('Collection nationale des classiques français'), [1950], Vols. I–IV.

PIOT, EUGÈNE. 'Catalogue raisonné de l'œuvre gravé de Francisco Goya y Lucientes', *Le Cabinet de l'amateur et de l'antiquaire*, I, 1842, pp. 346–66.

PLOUVIER, ÉDOUARD. 'L'Ami Soleil', in: *Chants et Chansons de la Bohème*, Paris, Bry, 1853.

POE, EDGAR ALLAN. *Works*, with Notices . . . by N. P. WILLIS, J. R. LOWELL and R. W. GRISWOLD, New York, Redfield, Vols. I–II, 1850.

—*The Literati . . . together with Marginalia, Suggestions and Essays*, with a Sketch of the Author by R. W. GRISWOLD, New York, Redfield, 1850.

—See also s.v. Section C, below, BANDY and QUINN.

PORTAL, FRÉDÉRIC. *Des Couleurs symboliques dans l'antiquité, le moyen âge et les temps modernes*, Paris, Treuttel and Würtz, 1837.

PRAROND, ERNEST. *De quelques écrivains nouveaux*, Paris, Lévy, 1852.

—*Les Impressions et Pensées d'Albert*, Paris, Lévy, 1854.

—[See also s.v. Section C, below.]

RONSARD, PIERRE DE. *Œuvres complètes*, ed. GUSTAVE COHEN, Paris, NRF, 'Bibliothèque de la Pléiade', [1966,] vol. II.

ROUSSEAU, JEAN-JACQUES. *Du Contrat Social ou Principes du droit politique . . . Discours sur l'origine de l'inégalité parmi les hommes . . .*, Paris, Garnier ('Classiques Garnier' series), [1962].

—*Émile ou de l'éducation*, ed. FRANÇOIS and PIERRE RICHARD, Paris, Garnier ('Classiques Garnier'), [1964].

—*Les Rêveries du Promeneur solitaire*, ed. MARCEL RAYMOND, Lille/ Geneva, Giard/Droz ('Textes littéraires français'), 1948.

SAINTE-BEUVE, CHARLES-AUGUSTIN DE. *Chateaubriand et son groupe littéraire sous l'Empire. Cours professé à Liège en 1848-9*, Paris, Garnier, 1861 (2nd edition), vols. I–II.

—*Vie, Poésies et Pensées de Joseph Delorme*, ed. GÉRALD ANTOINE, Paris, Nouvelles éditions latines, [1956].

SAINT-PIERRE, BERNARDIN DE. [See s.v. BERNARDIN].

SAND, GEORGE. *Consuelo. La Comtesse de Rudolstadt*, ed. LÉON CELLIER and LÉON GUICHARD, Paris, Garnier ('Classiques Garnier' series), Vols. I–III, [1959].

—*Lettres d'un Voyageur* (*Œuvres complètes*, IX), Paris, Perrotin, 1843.

SENANCOUR. *Oberman, etc.*, ed. ANDRÉ MONGLOND, Grenoble, Arthaud, 1947, vols. I–III.

SHELLEY, PERCY BYSSHE. *Letters*, Vol. II: *Shelley in Italy*, ed. FREDERICK L. JONES, Oxford, Clarendon Press, 1964.

THORÉ, THÉOPHILE. 'L'Art des parfums', *L'Ariel*, No. 13, 13 April 1836.

TOUSSENEL, ALPHONSE. *L'Esprit des bêtes. Le Monde des oiseaux. Ornithologie passionnelle*, Paris, Librairie phalanstérienne: Vol. I, 1853; Vol. II, 1855; Vol. III, 1855.

—See also s.v. Section D, THOMAS.

TRAHERNE, THOMAS. *Centuries of Meditations*, ed. BERTRAM DOBELL, London, the Editor, 1908.

VIGNY, ALFRED DE. 'La Maison du Berger . . .', *Revue des Deux Mondes*, XIVe année, N.S. VII, 15 July 1844, pp. 302–13.

—*Les Destinées*, ed. VERDUN L. SAULNIER, Geneva/Lille, Droz/Giard, (Textes littéraires français'), 1955.

VILLEMAIN, FRANÇOIS. *La Tribune moderne, I: M. de Chateaubriand. Sa vie, ses écrits, son influence politique et littéraire sur son temps*, Paris, Lévy, 1858.

C.

BOOKS, ARTICLES, ETC. ON BAUDELAIRE

ABÉ, YOSHIO. 'Baudelaire et Maxime Du Camp', *Revue d'histoire littéraire de la France*, LXVII, April–June 1967, pp. 273–85.

ALPHONSUS, (Mother) MARY (S.H.C.J.). *The Influence of Joseph de Maistre on Baudelaire* (Dissertation for degree of Doctor of Philosophy, Bryn Mawr College), Bryn Mawr, Pennsylvania, 1943.

ASSELINEAU, CHARLES. *Baudelaire et Asselineau*, textes recueillis et commentés par JACQUES CRÉPET and CLAUDE PICHOIS, Paris, Nizet, 1953.

—[See also s.v. Section B.]

AUSTIN, LLOYD JAMES. *L'Univers poétique de Baudelaire. Symbolisme et Symbolique*, Paris, Mercure de France, 1956.

—'Baudelaire et l'énergie spirituelle', *Revue des sciences humaines*, XXII, fasc. 85, January–March 1957, pp. 35–42.

—'Baudelaire: Poet or Prophet?', in: *Studies in Modern French Literature presented to P. Mansell Jones by Pupils, Colleagues and Friends*, ed. L. J. AUSTIN, GARNET REES and EUGÈNE VINAVER, Manchester University Press, [1961]. pp. 18–34.

BADESCO, LUC. 'Baudelaire et la revue *Jean Raisin*', *Revue des sciences humaines*, XXII, fasc. 85, January–March 1957, pp. 55–88.

BANDY, W. T. *Baudelaire Judged by his Contemporaries (1845–1867)*, New York, Publications of the Institute of French Studies, Columbia University, 1933.

—'Baudelaire et Croly. La Vérité sur *Le Jeune Enchanteur*', *Mercure de France*, CCCVIII, No. 1038, 1 February 1950, pp. 233–47.

—'Trois études baudelairiennes. 1, A propos de *Correspondances*: Un précurseur américain de Baudelaire', *Revue d'histoire littéraire de la France*, LIII, 1953, pp. 203–5.

—'New Light on Baudelaire and Poe', *Yale French Studies*, V, No. 10, 1953, pp. 65–9.

—'Le Chiffonnier de Baudelaire', *Revue d'histoire littéraire de la France*, LVII, 1957, pp. 580–4.

—'Baudelaire and Poe', in: *The Centennial Celebration of Baudelaire's 'Les Fleurs du Mal'*, Austin, University of Texas Press, 1958, pp. 28–35.

—'What's in a Name? (Variant Signatures in Baudelaire's Letters)', *Rivista di Letterature Moderne e Comparate*, XII, March 1959, pp. 71–4.

—'Baudelaire et Poe: vers une nouvelle mise au point', *Revue d'histoire littéraire de la France*, LXVII, April–June 1967, pp. 329–34.

—[See also s.v. Section A.]

BANDY, W. T. and PICHOIS, CLAUDE (eds.). *Baudelaire devant ses con temporains. Témoignages . . .*, Paris, Union générale d'édition ('Le Monde en 10:18' series), [1967.]

BARRÈRE, JEAN-BERTRAND. ' Chemins, échos et images dans *l'Invitation au voyage* de Baudelaire', *Revue de littérature comparée*, XXXI, 1957, pp. 481–90.

—'En marge d'un "Baudelaire" de poche', *Revue d'histoire littéraire de la France*, LXVII, April–June 1967, pp. 335–42.

BERNARD, JEAN-MARC. 'A propos d'un sonnet de Baudelaire', *Revue d'histoire littéraire de la France*, XVI, October 1909, pp. 792–3.

BILLY, ANDRÉ. *La Présidente et ses amis*, Paris, Flammarion, [1945.]

—See also s.v. Section D.

BLIN, GEORGES. *Baudelaire*, Paris, NRF-Gallimard, [1939].

—*Le Sadisme de Baudelaire*, Paris, Corti, 1948.

—See also s.v. Section A.

BUISSON, JULES. 'Lettre réfutant un article de Banville', [1882], in: BAUDELAIRE, *Œuvres complètes*, Club du meilleur livre [q.v., above], Vol. II, pp. 1162–6.[1]

CASSAGNE, ALBERT. *Versification et métrique de Ch. Baudelaire*, Paris, Hachette, 1906.

—See also s.v. Section D, below.

CASTEX, PIERRE-GEORGES. 'Balzac et Baudelaire', *Revue des sciences humaines*, XXIII, fasc. 89, January–March 1958, pp. 139–51.

CAUSSY, FERNAND. 'Chronologie des *Fleurs du Mal* (esquisse)', *L'Ermitage*, XVIIe année, II, no. 12, 15 December 1906, pp. 328–38.

[1]For a more fully annotated version of this text, see C. Pichois, *B.*, 37–43.

CELLIER, LÉON. ' "La Nature est un temple" ou l'apprenti sourcier', *Revue universitaire*, LXIV, 1955, pp. 26–8.

—'Baudelaire et George Sand', *Revue d'histoire littéraire de la France*, LXVII, April-June 1967, pp. 239–59.

—[See also s.v. Section B, SAND.]

CHÉRIX, ROBERT-BENOIT. *Essai d'une critique intégrale. Commentaire des 'Fleurs du Mal'*, Geneva, Cailler, ' Collection d'études et de documents littéraires', 1949.

CITRON, PIERRE. [See s.v. Section D.]

CLAPTON, G.T. *Baudelaire et De Quincey*, Paris, Les Belles Lettres, [1931].

—'Baudelaire, Sénèque et Saint Jean Chrysostome', *Revue d'histoire littéraire de la France*, XXXVIII, April 1931, pp. 235–61.

—'Lavater, Gall et Baudelaire', *Revue de littérature comparée*, XIII, 1933, pp. 259–98 and 429–56.

CRÉPET, EUGÈNE and JACQUES. *Charles Baudelaire*, Paris, Vanier-Messein, 1906. [*EJC*]

—[For EUGÈNE CRÉPET, see also s.v. Section B.]

CRÉPET, JACQUES. 'Causerie du Scoliaste', *Le Manuscrit Autographe*, Special Baudelaire Number, 1927, pp. 117–33.

—[Prefatory Note to] '*Le Pont des Soupirs* de Thomas Hood. Traduction inédite par Baudelaire', *Mercure de France*, CCCV, No. 1028, 1 April 1949, pp. 599–601.

—[See also s.v. Section A, passim.]

CRÉPET, JACQUES and PICHOIS, CLAUDE. ' Baudelaire à Honfleur', *Le Figaro littéraire*, 12 April 1952.

—[See also s.v. Section A.]

DROUGARD, E. 'En marge de Baudelaire. *Le Voyage* et ses sources', *Revue d'histoire littéraire de la France*, XXXIX, 1932, pp. 444–59.

EIGELDINGER, MARC. *Le Platonisme de Baudelaire*, Neuchâtel, A la Baconnière, [1951.]

ENGSTROM, ALFRED G. ' Baudelaire and Longfellow's *Hymn to the Night*', *Modern Language Notes*, LXXIV, 1959, pp. 695–8.

FAIRLIE, ALISON. 'Some Remarks on Baudelaire's *Poème du Haschish*', in: *The French Mind. Studies in Honour of Gustave Rudler*, ed. WILL MOORE, RHODA SUTHERLAND and ENID STARKIE, Oxford, Clarendon Press, 1952, pp. 291–317.

—*Baudelaire: 'Les Fleurs du Mal'*, London, Arnold ('Studies in French Literature', No. 6), [1960].

FERRAN, ANDRÉ. *L'Esthétique de Baudelaire*, Paris, Hachette, 1933.

—[See also s.v. Section A, above.]

FEUERLICHT, IGNACE. 'Baudelaire's *Harmonie du soir*', *French Review*, XXXIII, October 1959, pp. 17–26.

FEUILLERAT, ALBERT. *Baudelaire et la Belle aux cheveux d'or*, New Haven, Yale University Press, 1941.

—'L'Architecture des *Fleurs du Mal*', in: *Studies by Members of the French Department of Yale University* (*Decennial Volume*), ed. ALBERT FEUILLERAT, New Haven, Yale University Press (Yale Romanic Studies, XVIII), 1941, pp. 221–330.

—*Baudelaire et sa mère*, Montreal, Variétés, [1944].

FONGARO, ANTOINE. 'Sources de Baudelaire', *Revue des sciences humaines*, XXII, 1957, fasc. 85, pp. 89–96.

FRANÇOIS, C. R. '*La Vie antérieure* de Baudelaire', *Modern Language Notes*, LXXIII, 1958, pp. 194–200.

GALLAS, K. R. 'Plastische en graphische inspiratie bij Baudelaire', *Neophilologus*, XVIII, 1943, pp. 171–81.

GAUTIER, THÉOPHILE. 'Charles Baudelaire', in *Les Poëtes français*, ed. EUGÈNE CRÉPET, Paris, Hachette, 1862, Vol. IV, pp. 594–600.

—'Charles Baudelaire', in: BAUDELAIRE, *Œuvres complètes, I. Les Fleurs du Mal*, Paris, Lévy, [1868], pp. i–lxxiii.

—[See also s.v. Sections A, B and D (BERGERAT and SPOELBERCH DE LOVENJOUL)].

GENDREAU, GEORGES and PICHOIS, CLAUDE. 'Autour d'un billet inédit de Charles Baudelaire. Par qui le poète fut-il présenté à Delacroix?', *Revue d'histoire littéraire de la France*, LVII, 1957, pp. 574–8.

GILMAN, MARGARET. 'Baudelaire and Thomas Hood', *Romanic Review*, XXVI, 1935, pp. 240–44.

—*Baudelaire the Critic*, New York, Columbia University Press, 1943.

—'*L'Albatros* again', *Romanic Review*, XLI, 1950, pp. 96–107.

—See also s.v. Section D, below.

GILMAN, MARGARET and SCHENCK, EUNICE MORGAN. '*Le Voyage* and *L'Albatros*: the first text', *Romanic Review*, XXIX, 1938, pp. 262–77.

GUIRAL, PIERRE and PICHOIS, CLAUDE. '*L'Albatros* de Polydore Bounin', *Revue d'histoire littéraire de la France*, LVII, 1957, pp. 570–4.

HÉRISSON, CHARLES D. 'Le voyage de Baudelaire dans l'Inde. Histoire d'une légende', *Mercure de France*, CCCXXVIII, No. 1118,1 October 1956, pp. 273–95.

—'A propos de Baudelaire en 1841 et 1842', *Mercure de France*,CCCXXXVIII, No. 1159, 1 March 1960, pp. 449–75.

HESS, GERHARD. *Die Landschaft in Baudelaires 'Fleurs du Mal'*, Heidelberg, Winter (Sitzungsberichte der Heidelberger Akademie der Wissenschaften, Philosophisch-historiche Klasse, Jahrgang 1953, 1. Abhandlung), 1953.

HORNER, LUCIE. *Baudelaire critique de Delacroix*, Geneva, Droz, 1956.

—'Alphonse Karr or Victor Fournel? A needed Clarification', *Modern Language Notes*, LXXIII, 1958, pp. 432–4.

HUBERT, J. D. *L'Esthétique des 'Fleurs du Mal'. Essai sur l'ambiguïté poétique*, Geneva, Cailler (Collection d'études et de documents littéraires), 1953.

JEAN-AUBRY, G. *Un paysage littéraire. Baudelaire et Honfleur*, Paris, Maison du livre, 1917.

—[See also s.v. Section D, below.]

JONES, P. MANSELL. *The Background of Modern French Poetry. Essays and Interviews*, Cambridge, University Press, 1951 (Chap. I: 'Swedenborg, Baudelaire and their Intermediaries').

—*Baudelaire*, Cambridge, Bowes and Bowes (Studies in Modern European Literature and Thought), [1952].

KOPP, ROBERT. '*L'Albatros* de Baudelaire', *Bulletin annuel de la Fondation suisse*, XI, 1962, pp. 9–19.

—[See also s.v. PICHOIS.]

LARROUTIS, M. 'Le Sujet d'une "Fleur du Mal" chez Ballanche. Source ou préfiguration?', *Revue d'histoire littéraire de la France*, LXIII, 1963, pp. 110–13.

LEAKEY, F. W. 'Baudelaire et Kendall', *Revue de littérature comparée*, XXX, January–March 1956, pp. 53–63.

—'Two Poems of Baudelaire: A Problem of Ambiguity', *Letterature moderne*, VI, 4, July–August 1956, pp. 482–9.

—[Review of] Jean Prévost, *Baudelaire* [q.v., below], *Modern Language Review*, L, January 1955, pp. 85–8.

—[Review of] J. D. Hubert, *L'Esthétique des 'Fleurs du Mal'* [q.v., above], etc., *French Studies*, XII, April 1958, pp. 171–6.

—'Baudelaire: The Poet as Moralist', in: *Studies in Modern French Literature, presented to P. Mansell Jones by Pupils, Colleagues and Friends*, ed. L. J. AUSTIN, GARNET REES and EUGÈNE VINAVER, Manchester University Press, [1961,] pp. 196–219.

—'Pour une étude chronologique des *Fleurs du Mal*: *Harmonie du soir*', *Revue d'histoire littéraire de la France*, LXVII, 2, April–June 1967, pp. 343–56.

—'Les Esthétiques de Baudelaire: le "système" des années 1844–47', *Revue des sciences humaines*, XXXII, fasc. 127, July–September 1967, pp. 481–96.

—'*A Festschrift* of 1855: Baudelaire and the *Hommage à C. F. Denecourt*', in: *Studies in French Literature presented to H. W. Lawton by Colleagues, Pupils and Friends*, ed. J. C. IRESON, I. D. MCFARLANE and GARNET REES, Manchester University Press, [1968,] pp. 175–202.

—'The Amorous Tribute: Baudelaire and the Renaissance Tradition', in: *The French Renaissance and its Heritage. Essays presented to Alan Boase by Colleagues, Pupils and Friends*, ed. D. R. HAGGIS, S. JONES, F. W. LEAKEY, G. M. SUTHERLAND and E. G. TAYLOR, London, Methuen, 1968, pp. 93–116.

—See also s.v. Section D.

LE DANTEC, YVES-GÉRARD. 'Un Secret de Baudelaire. L'Héautontimorouménos et l'énigme de J.G.F.', Mercure de France, CCCXXXII, No. 1136, 1 April 1958, pp. 676–90.

—[See also s.v. Section A.]

LEMONNIER, LÉON. Les Traducteurs d'Edgar Poe en France de 1845 à 1875: Charles Baudelaire, Paris, Presses universitaires de France, 1928.

—Enquêtes sur Baudelaire, Paris, Crès, 1929.

—See also Section D below.

MAY, GITA. Diderot et Baudelaire critiques d'art, Geneva/Paris, Droz/Minard, 1957.

MENEMENCIOGLU, MEÂLHAT. 'Le Thème des Bohémiens en voyage dans la peinture et la poésie, de Cervantes à Baudelaire', Cahiers de l'Association internationale des Études françaises, March 1966, no. 18, pp. 227–38.

MILNER, MAX. Le Diable dans la littérature française: de Cazotte à Baudelaire, 1772–1861, Paris, Corti, Vols. I–II, 1960 (Vol. II, Chap. XXVII: 'Baudelaire').

MOREAU, PIERRE. 'Le Symbolisme de Baudelaire', Symposium, V, May 1951, pp. 89–102.

MOSSOP, D. J. Baudelaire's Tragic Hero: A Study of the Architecture of 'Les Fleurs du Mal', London, Oxford University Press, 1961.

PATTY, JAMES S. 'Baudelaire et Hippolyte Babou', Revue d'histoire littéraire de la France, LXVII, April-June 1967, pp. 260–72.

PEYRE, HENRI. 'L'Image du navire chez Baudelaire', Modern Language Notes, XLIV, November 1929, pp. 447–50.

—Connaissance de Baudelaire, Paris, Corti, 1951.

—[See also s.v. Section D, below.]

PICHOIS, CLAUDE. 'Le beau-père de Baudelaire: le général Aupick', Mercure de France, CCCXXIV, Nos. 1102, 1103, 1104, 1 June, 1 July, 1 August 1955, pp. 261–81, 472–90, 651–74.

—'Sur le prétendu voyage aux Indes', Revue d'histoire littéraire de la France, LVII, October-December 1957, pp. 568–70.

—Baudelaire à Paris, Paris, Hachette ('Albums littéraires de la France'), [1967].

—Baudelaire. Études et témoignages, Neuchâtel, Editions de la Baconnière '(Langages' series), [1967].

—See also s.v. ASSELINEAU, BANDY, CRÉPET, GENDREAU, GUIRAL, above, and s.v. Sections D and A (passim).

PICHOIS, CLAUDE and KOPP, ROBERT. 'Baudelaire et l'opium: une enquête à reprendre', Europe, XLV, No. 456–7, April-May 1967, pp. 61–79.

POMMIER, JEAN. La Mystique de Baudelaire, Geneva, Slatkine Reprints,

1967 (reprint, with Prefatory Note on loose leaf, of Paris edition, Les Belles Lettres, 1932).

—*Dans les chemins de Baudelaire*, Paris, Corti, [1945].

—'Baudelaire et Musset', in: *Mélanges d'histoire littéraire et de bibliographie offerts à Jean Bonnerot . . . par ses Amis et ses Collègues*, Paris, Nizet, 1954, pp. 353–64.

—'Baudelaire devant la critique théologique', *RHLF*, LVIII, 1958, pp. 35–46.

—'Baudelaire et Hugo: nouvelles glanes', *Revue des sciences humaines*, XXXII, fasc. 127, July–September 1967, pp. 337–49.

PORCHÉ, FRANÇOIS. *Baudelaire et la Présidente*, Geneva, Éditions du milieu du monde ('Les Amitiés amoureuses' series), [1941].

—*Baudelaire. Histoire d'une âme*, Paris, Flammarion, [1945].

PRAROND, ERNEST. [Letter to Eugène Crépet, October 1886] in: BAUDELAIRE, *Œuvres complètes*, Club du meilleur livre [q.v., above], Vol. II, pp. 1147–62.[1]

PRÉVOST, JEAN. *Baudelaire. Essai sur l'inspiration et la création poétiques*, Paris, Mercure de France, 1953.

QUENNELL, PETER. *Baudelaire and the Symbolists. Five Essays*, London, Chatto and Windus, 1929.

QUINN, PATRICK F. *The French Face of Edgar Poe*, Carbondale, Southern Illinois University Press, 1957.

REYNOLD, GONZAGUE DE. *Charles Baudelaire*, Paris/Geneva, Crès/Georg ('Collection Franco-Suisse'), 1920.

RICHTER, BODO L. O. 'Baudelaire, poète de l'évasion', *Letterature moderne*, VI, 1956, pp. 285–301.

ROEDIG, CHARLES F. 'Baudelaire and Synesthesia', *Kentucky Foreign Language Quarterly*, V, 1958, pp. 128–35.

RUFF, MARCEL A. *L'Esprit du mal et l'esthétique baudelairienne*, Paris, Colin, 1955.

—*Baudelaire: l'homme et l'œuvre*, Paris, Hatier-Boivin ('Connaissance des Lettres' series), 1955.

SARTRE, J.-P. *Baudelaire*, Paris, NRF-Gallimard ('Les Essais' series, XXIV), [1947].

SCHENCK, EUNICE M. [See s.v. GILMAN, above.]

SCOTT, J. A. 'Petrarch and Baudelaire', *Revue de littérature comparée*, XXXI, 1957, pp. 550–62.

STARKIE, ENID. *Baudelaire*, London, Faber and Faber, [1957.]

—[See also s.v. Section D.]

TABARANT, A. [See s.v. Section D.]

TURNELL, MARTIN. *Baudelaire. A Study of his Poetry*, London, Hamish Hamilton, [1953].

[1]For a more fully annotated version of this text, see C. Pichois, *B.*, 12-36.

VIVIER, ROBERT. *L'Originalité de Baudelaire*, Brussels, Palais des Académies (Académie royale de langue et de littérature françaises de Belgique), 1952 [reprint of 1926 edition].

VOUGA, DANIEL. *Baudelaire et Joseph de Maistre*, Paris, Corti, 1957.

D

BOOKS, ARTICLES, etc. ON OTHER SUBJECTS

ALAZARD, JEAN. *L'Orient et la peinture française au XIXᵉ siècle, d'Eugène Delacroix à Auguste Renoir*, Paris, Plon ('1830–1930: Collection du Centenaire de l'Algérie, Vie intellectuelle et artistique'), 1930.

AMIEL, HENRI-FRÉDÉRIC. *Fragments d'un journal intime*, précédés d'une étude par Edmond SCHÉRER, Paris/Neuchâtel—Geneva, Sandoz and Thuillier/Librairie générale, 2nd edition, 1884, Vol. I.

ATKINSON, GEOFFROY. *Les Relations de voyages du XVIIᵉ siècle et l'évolution des idées. Contribution à l'étude de la formation de l'esprit du XVIIIᵉ siècle*, Paris, Champion, [1924].

BABBITT, IRVING. *Rousseau and Romanticism*, Boston and New York, Houghton Miflin, [1919].

BANVILLE, THÉODORE DE. *Petit traité de poésie française*, Paris, Charpentier, 1883.

—[See also s.v. Section B.]

BEACH, JOSEPH WARREN. *The Concept of Nature in Nineteenth-Century English Poetry*, New York, Pageant Book Co., 1956 [reprint of 1936 edition, New York, Macmillan].

BENJAMIN, RUTH. *Eugène Boudin*, New York, Raymond and Raymond, [1937].

BERGERAT, ÉMILE. *Théophile Gautier. Entretiens, souvenirs et correspondance* (with Preface by EDMOND DE GONCOURT), Paris, Charpentier, 1879.

BILLY, ANDRÉ. *Fontainebleau délices des poètes. De la Renaissance à nos jours*, Paris, Horizons de France, [1949].

—[See also s.v. Section C.]

BOAS, GEORGE. [See s.v. LOVEJOY, below.]

BOENIGER, YVONNE. *Lamartine et le Sentiment de la Nature*, Paris, Nizet et Bastard, 1934.

BOUVIER, ÉMILE. *La Bataille réaliste (1844–1857)*, Paris, Fontemoing, [1914].

BRETON, ANDRÉ. *Manifestes du surréalisme*, Paris, NRF—Gallimard ('Collection Idées'), [1963].

CANAT, RENÉ. *L'Hellénisme des romantiques*, Paris, Didier, Vols. I–III, [1951–5].

23

CASSAGNE, ALBERT. *La théorie de l'art pour l'art en France chez les derniers romantiques et les premiers réalistes,* Paris, Dorbon, [1959] (reprint of 1906 edition).

CHARLIER, GUSTAVE. *Le sentiment de la nature chez les romantiques français,* Paris, Fontemoing, 1912.

CHARPIER, JACQUES. *Saint-John Perse,* Paris, NRF—Gallimard ('La Bibliothèque idéale'), [1962].

CHENNEVIÈRES, PHILIPPE DE. 'Souvenirs d'un directeur des Beaux-Arts: les poésies de jeunesse d'un Préfet', *L'Artiste,* 59ᵉ année, March 1889, pp. 204–30.

CHINARD, GILBERT. *L'Exotisme américain dans la littérature française au XVIe siècle, d'après Rabelais, Ronsard, Montaigne, etc.,* Paris, Hachette, 1911.

—*L'Amérique et le rêve exotique dans la littérature française au XVIIᵉ et au XVIIIᵉ siècle,* Paris, Droz, 1934.

—[See also s.v. Section B, DIDEROT.]

CITRON, PIERRE. *La Poésie de Paris dans la littérature française de Rousseau à Baudelaire,* Paris, Éditions de Minuit, [1961], Vols. I–II.

CROCKER, LESTER G. *Nature and Culture. Ethical Thought in the French Enlightenment,* Baltimore, Johns Hopkins Press, [1963].

DILLINGHAM, LOUISE B. *The Creative Imagination of Théophile Gautier. A. Study in Literary Psychology,* Princeton (N.J.) and Albany (N.Y.), Psychological Review Company (Psychological Monographs, Vol. XXXVII, No. 1), 1927.

DORBEC, PROSPER. *L'Art du paysage en France. Essai sur son évolution, de la fin du XVIIIᵉ siècle à la fin du Second Empire,* Paris, Laurens, 1925.

EVANS, DAVID OWEN. *Le Socialisme romantique. Pierre Leroux et ses contemporains,* Paris, Rivière (Bibliothèque d'histoire économique et sociale), 1948.

FAIRCHILD, HOXIE NEALE. *The Noble Savage. A Study in Romantic Naturalism,* New York, Columbia University Press, 1928.

—*The Romantic Quest,* Philadelphia, Saifer, [1931].

GILMAN, MARGARET. 'From Imagination to Immediacy in French Poetry', *Romanic Review,* XXXIX, 1948, pp. 30–49.

—*The Idea of Poetry in France, from Houdar de la Motte to Baudelaire,* Cambridge (Mass.), Harvard University Press, 1958.

—[See also s.v. Section C.]

GONCOURT, EDMOND DE. [See s.v. BERGERAT, above.]

GUICHARD, LÉON. *La Musique et les lettres au temps du romantisme,* Paris, Presses universitaires de France (Université de Grenoble: Publications de la Faculté des Lettres, 12), 1955.

—*La Musique et les lettres en France au temps du wagnérisme,* Paris, Presses universitaires de France (Université de Grenoble: Publications de la Faculté des Lettres et Sciences humaines, 29), 1963.

HAMMER, M. 'Sur le langage des fleurs', *Annales des voyages de la géographie et de l'histoire*, IX, 1809, pp. 346–60.

HEISS, HANNS. 'Die Pantouns Malais. Bemerkungen zu Leconte de Lisles Technik und Verskunst', in: *Vom Geiste neuer Literaturforschung. Festchrift für Oskar Walzel . . .*, ed. JULIUS WAHLE and VICTOR KLEMPERER, Wildpark-Potsdam, Akademische Verlagsgesellschaft Athenaion, [1924], pp. 144–61.

HERMAND, PIERRE. *Les Idées morales de Diderot*, Paris, Presses universitaires de France (Université de Paris: Bibliothèque de la Faculté des Lettres, 2e série, I), 1923.

HEWETT-THAYER, HARVEY W. *Hoffmann: Author of the Tales*, Princeton (N.J.), Princeton University Press, 1948.

HIGGINS, D. 'Pierre Dupont: A Chansonnier of the 1848 Revolution', *French Studies*, III, April 1949, pp. 122–36.

HOOG, ARMAND (trans. Beth Brombert). 'Who invented the *Mal du siècle*?', *Yale French Studies*, 1954, No. 13 ('Romanticism Revisited'), pp. 42–51.

HORNSTEIN, LILLIAN H. 'Analysis of Imagery: A Critique of Literary Method', *PMLA*, LVII, September 1942, pp. 638–53.

HUNT, HERBERT J. *The Epic in Nineteenth-Century France*, Oxford, Blackwell, 1941.

JEAN-AUBRY, G. *Eugène Boudin, d'après des documents inédits. L'homme et l'œuvre*, Paris, Bernheim-Jeune, 1922.
—[See also s.v. Section C].

LALANDE, ANDRÉ. *Vocabulaire technique et critique de la philosophie . . .*, Paris, Alcan (for Société française de philosophie), 1928, Vols. I–II.

LAUBRIET, PIERRE. *Un Catéchisme esthétique. Le 'Chef-d'œuvre inconnu' de Balzac*, Paris, Didier, 1961.
—*L'Intelligence de l'art chez Balzac. D'une esthétique balzacienne*, Paris, Didier, [1961].

LAUVRIÈRE, ÉMILE. *Alfred de Vigny. Sa vie et son œuvre*, Paris, Colin, 1909.

LEAKEY, F. W. 'Intention in Metaphor', *Essays in Criticism*, IV, April 1954, pp. 191–8.
—[See also s.v. Section C, above.]

LEBOIS, ANDRÉ. *Admirable XIXe siècle*, Paris, L'Amitié par le livre, [1958].

LE GALL, BÉATRICE. *L'Imaginaire chez Senancour*, Paris, Corti, Vols. I–II, 1966.

LEHMANN, A. G. *The Symbolist Aesthetic in France 1885–95*, Oxford, Blackwell (Modern Language Studies), 1950.

LEMONNIER, LÉON. *Edgar Poe et la critique française de 1845 à 1875*, Paris, Presses universitaires de France, 1928.
[See also s.v. Section C.]

LEVALLOIS, JULES. *Milieu de siècle. Mémoires d'un critique*, Paris, Librairie illustrée, [1895].

LINDEN, J. P. VAN DER. [See s.v. VAN DER LINDEN].

LOVEJOY, ARTHUR O. *Essays in the History of Ideas*, Baltimore, Johns Hopkins Press, 1948 (II, 'The Supposed Primitivism of Rousseau's *Discourse on Inequality*'; V, ' "Nature" as Aesthetic Norm').

LOVEJOY, ARTHUR O. and BOAS, GEORGE. *Primitivism and Related Ideas in Antiquity*, New York, Octagon Books, 1965 [reprint of 1935 edition, Baltimore, Johns Hopkins Press].

LOVENJOUL, SPOELBERCH DE. [See s.v. SPOELBERCH, below].

LUITZ, FRIEDRICH. *Die Ästhetik von Théophile Gautier* (Doctoral Dissertation), Freiburg i.B., Günter and Renner, [1912].

MASSEY, IRVING. 'A Note on the History of Synaesthesia', *Modern Language Notes*, LXXI, March 1956, pp. 203–6.

MENGIN, URBAIN. *L'Italie des romantiques*, Paris, Plon, 1902.

MOORE, C. A. 'The Return to Nature in English Poetry of the Eighteenth Century', *Studies in Philology*, XIV, 1917, pp. 242–91.

MORNET, DANIEL. *Le Sentiment de la nature en France de J. J. Rousseau à Bernardin de Saint-Pierre. Essai sur les rapports de la littérature et des mœurs*, New York, Burt Franklin, n.d. (reprint of Paris edition of 1907).

NOULET, ÉMILIE. *Le Premier visage de Rimbaud. Huit poèmes de jeunesse. Choix et commentaire*, Brussels, Palais des Académies (Académie Royale de langue et de littérature françaises de Belgique), 1953.

O'MALLEY, GLENN. 'Literary Synesthesia', *The Journal of Aesthetics and Art Criticism*, XV, June 1957, pp. 391–411.

PERREAU, ADOLPHE. [See s.v. RUDE, below].

PEYRE, HENRI. *Louis Ménard*, New Haven, Yale University Press, 1932.
—[See also s.v. Section C.]

PICHOIS, CLAUDE. 'Le Premier Pantoum français', *Mercure de France*, CCCXXIII, No. 1099, 1 March 1955, pp. 548–51.
—'Autour du Premier Pantoum français', ibid., CCCXXIV, No. 1102, 1 June 1955, pp. 369–71.
—*L'Image de Jean-Paul Richter dans les lettres françaises*, Paris, Corti, [1963].
—[See also s.v. Sections A and C.]

POMEAU, RENÉ, 'De la Nature: essai sur la vie littéraire d'une idée', *Revue de l'Enseignement Supérieur*, January-March 1959, pp. 107–19.

RAYMOND, MARCEL. *De Baudelaire au Surréalisme*, Paris, Corti, 1966 (revision of 1933 edition).

RENOUVIER, CHARLES. *Victor Hugo le philosophe*, Paris, Colin, 1921.

RICHARDS, I. A. *The Philosophy of Rhetoric*, New York, Oxford University Press (The Mary Flexner Lectures on the Humanities, III), [1936].

ROGER-MARX, CLAUDE. *Le Paysage français de Corot à nos jours, ou: le dialogue de l'homme et du ciel,* Paris, Plon; Éditions d'histoire et d'art ('Messages' series, 2), 1952.

ROOS, JACQUES. *Les Idées philosophiques de Victor Hugo. Ballanche et Victor Hugo,* Paris, Nizet, 1958.

RUDE, MAXIME. *Confidences d'un Journaliste,* Paris, Sagnier, 1876.

SCALES, D. P. *Alphonse Karr. Sa vie et son œuvre (1809–1890),* Geneva/ Paris, Droz/Minard, 1959.

SCARFE, FRANCIS. *André Chénier. His Life and Work (1762–94),* Oxford, Clarendon Press, 1965.

SCHANNE, ALEXANDRE. *Souvenirs de Schaunard,* Paris, Charpentier, 1887.

SÉCHAUD, P. *Victor de Laprade. L'homme. Son œuvre poétique,* Paris, Picard, 1934.

SÉRULLAZ, MAURICE. *Delacroix. Aquarelles du Maroc,* Paris, Hazan (Bibliothèque Aldine des Arts, XXIII), 1951.

SEZNEC, JEAN. *John Martin en France,* London, Faber and Faber (All Souls Studies, IV), [1964].

SHRODER, MAURICE Z. *Icarus. The Image of the Artist in French Romanticism,* Cambridge (Massachusetts), Harvard University Press (Harvard Studies in Romance Languages, XXVII), 1961.

SPOELBERCH DE LOVENJOUL, (vicomte) CHARLES DE. *Histoire des œuvres de Théophile Gautier,* Paris, Charpentier, Vols. I–II, 1887.

STARKIE, ENID. *Petrus Borel the Lycanthrope. His Life and Times,* London, Faber, [1954].
—[See also s.v. Section C.]

STEELE, A. J. (Ed. and introd.), *Three Centuries of French Verse, 1511–1819,* Edinburgh, University Press, 1956.

TABARANT, A. *La Vie artistique au temps de Baudelaire,* Paris, Mercure de France, [1963] (reprint, with Index, of 1942 edition).

THOMAS, LOUIS. *Les Précurseurs. Alphonse Toussenel. Socialiste national antisémite (1803–1885),* Paris, Mercure de France, 1941.

TIEGHEM, PAUL VAN. [See s.v. VAN TIEGHEM, below.]

ULLMANN, STEPHEN. *The Principles of Semantics,* Glasgow, Jackson (Glasgow University Publications LXXXIV), 1951.
—*Semantics. An Introduction to the Science of Meaning,* Oxford, Blackwell, 1962.

VAN DER LINDEN, J. P. *Alphonse Esquiros. De la Bohème romantique à la République sociale,* Paris/Heerlen, Nizet/Uitgeverij Winants ('Bibliothèque de Parcival', 2), 1948.

VAN TIEGHEM, PAUL. 'L'Automne dans la poésie ouest-européenne, de Brockes à Lamartine (1720–1820)', in: *Mélanges offerts à Fernand Baldensperger,* Paris, Champion, 1930, vol. II, pp. 327–43.
—*Le Sentiment de la Nature dans le Préromantisme européen,* Paris, Nizet, 1960.

VIATTE, AUGUSTE. *Victor Hugo et les Illuminés de son temps,* Montreal, Éditions de l'Arbre, [1942].

WAGNER, R. L. '"Langue poétique" (du quantitatif au qualificatif)', in: *Studia Romanica. Gedenkschrift für Eugen Lerch,* ed. CHARLES BRUNEAU and PETER M. SCHON, Stuttgart, Port Verlag, [1955], pp. 416–30.

WILLEY, BASIL. *The Eighteenth Century [sic] Background. Studies on the Idea of Nature in the Thought of the Period,* London, Chatto and Windus, 1940.

WILSON, D. B. *Ronsard, Poet of Nature,* Manchester University Press, [1961].

WIMSATT, WILLIAM K. (Jr.) *The Verbal Icon. Studies in the Meaning of Poetry.* [With] two preliminary essays written in collaboration with MONROE C. BEARDSLEY, Lexington (Kentucky), Noonday Press, [1960], 2nd edition. ('The Intentional Fallacy', pp. 3–18; 'The Structure of Romantic Nature Imagery', pp. 103–16).

Chronological Index of Texts
by Baudelaire

Note: (1) Page-references to the present volume are given in roman type in column 1, s.v. Title.

(2) I have been able to take account in this Index (but not in my main text) of two important publications which appeared at the end of 1968: Baudelaire, *Les Fleurs du Mal,* édition critique par Jacques Crépet et Georges Blin, refondue par Georges Blin et Claude Pichois, Paris, Corti (hereafter abbreviated: *FMCB* 1968); Baudelaire, *Petit Palais, 23 novembre 1968 – 17 mars 1969,* Paris, Réunion des Musées Nationaux (hereafter abbreviated: Catalogue of B. Exhibition 1968).

Title	First extant text(s)	Select list of subsequent texts	Date of original composition	Select list of chronological references
A Celle qui est trop gaie 107, n.3 to p. 106; 108–9 and 109 n. 1; 111–12; 124; 284–5; 320 and n. 2	1852, MS. in letter to Mme Sabatier of 9 Dec. (title: *A une femme trop gaie*; *CG* I, 181–2)	1857, *FM* proofs (see *FMCB* 1968); 1857, *FM*;	→1852	A. Feuillerat, *B. et la Belle aux cheveux d'or,* 28–31; J. Pommier, *Dans les chemins de B.,* 188; *FMA* 434
A Ivonne Pen-Moore [attrib.] 29–30; 38 n. 2; 61 n. 1	1845, *L'Artiste,* 26 Jan., p. 60 (under name of Privat d'Anglemont; *OP* I, 40–1)	1861, etc., in: *Paris inconnu* (by Privat)	→1845	*VR* 44–50; *OP* I, 419–20, 407, 413–14 and n. 1. (But cf. J. Pommier, *Dans les chemins de B.,* 38–9)
Albatros (L') 206 n. 2; 230 n. 1; 231; 254; 258	1859, c. 15 Feb., privately printed leaflet (M. Gilman and E. M. Schenck, *RR,* 1938, pp. 276–7; facsimile, 271)	1861, *FM*;	1841–3	Prarond, *CML,* II, 1154, 1148; *FMCB,* 289–90; M. Gilman and E. M. Schenck, *RR,* 1938, p. 273; M. Gilman, *RR,* 1950, pp. 96–107; P. Guiral and C. Pichois, *RHLF,* 1957, pp. 570–4; *FMA* 266–8; R. Kopp, *Bull. de la Fondation suisse,* 1962, pp. 9–19; *FMCB* 1968, p. 491 and n. 1. (But cf. J. Pommier, *Dans les chemins de B.,* 348–52)
Alchimie de la douleur 14 n. 2; 245–8 and notes; 249; 250; 258; 262 n. 3	1860, *L'Artiste,* 15 Oct.	1861, *FM*;	1857–60	*FMCB* 428–30 (De Quincey); *FMA* 366–7
Allégorie 23–4; 57 n. 1; 99; 100 n. 1	1857, *FM* proofs (see *FMCB* 1968)	1857, *FM*;	→1843	Prarond, *CML* II, 1155; *VR* 12; *FMCB* 499

Title	First extant text(s)	Select list of subsequent texts	Date of original composition	Select list of chronological references
Ame du vin (L') 92–3	l. 1 only: March 1846, cit. as epigraph to Banville, *La Chanson du vin,* in *Les Stalactites* (ed. E. Souffrin, 194; cf. ibid., 14)	1848, *R. de Belgique,* cit. 'Retchezken', art. on Banville and Vacquerie (see C. Pichois, *MF,* March 1955, p. 549, and June 1955, p. 370)	→1843	Prarond, *CML* II, 1155; *FMCB* 483–4; E. Souffrin, in ed. Banville, *Stalactites,* 198 n. 1; *CML* I, 1250–1; Asselineau, in *B. et Asselineau,* 174–5; *FMA* 400–1
	Complete text: 1850, *Magasin des familles,* June, pp. 336–7 (title: *Le Vin des honnêtes gens)*	.... 1857, *FM;*		
Amour du mensonge (L') 64 n. 2	1860, [March?], MS. in letter to Poulet-Malassis (title: *Le Décor; CG* III, 74 and n. 4)	1860, *RC,* 15 May; 1861, *FM;*	→1860	*FMA* 392–4
Any where out of the world 170 n. 5; 241 n. 2; 291–4 and notes; 300 n. 2	1867, *R.nationale,* 28 Sept.	1869, *PPP*	→1865 (1859–62?)	P. 292, n. 4 to p. 291, above
Art philo- sophique (L') 123 n. 1, 314–15	1857–60, MS. (posth.)	1869, *AR*	1857–60 (1858–9?)	*AR* 470–1; *OCP* 1705–6
—[Notes diverses sur] 105 n. 1; 171 and notes; 253 n. 1; 261 n. 2	1857–60, MS. (posth.; *OCP* 1106–7)		1857–60 (1858–9?)	*OCP* 1705–6; M. Ruff, *Esprit du mal,* 454 n. 19
Au Lecteur 153, n. 5 to p. 152; 235	1855, *RDM,* 1 June, pp. 1079–80 (ll. 17–20 omitted)	1857, *FM* proofs (see *FMCB* 1968); 1857, *FM;*	→1855	M. Ruff, op. cit., 276; *FMA* 259 (cf. ibid., 460–1)
A une Créole	See s.v. *A une Dame créole*			

Title	First extant text(s)	Select list of subsequent texts	Date of original composition	Select list of chronological references
↑ une Dame ↑éole iii n. 3; 29; 30	1841, MS. in letter to M. Autard de Bragard, 20 Oct. (untitled; *CG* I, 16)	1845, *L'Artiste*, 25 May, p. 60 (title: *A une Créole*); 1857, *FM* proofs (see *FMCB* 1968); 1857, *FM*;	1841, Sept.–Oct.	
↑ une femme ↑op gaie	See s.v. *A Celle qui est trop gaie*			
↑ une heure du ↑atin ↑5	1862, *La Presse*, 27 Aug.	1869, *PPP*	→1862	
↑ une Indienne	See s.v. *A une Malabaraise*			
↑ une Madone ↑2	1860, *La Causerie*, 22 Jan.	1861, *FM*;	→15 Dec. 1859 (early Dec. 1859?)	*CG* II, 385; J. Pommier, *Dans les chemins de B.*, 213; A. Feuillerat, *B. et la Belle*, 75, 96 n. 92
↑ une ↑alabaraise ↑; 40–2 and ↑otes; 50; 55; ↑4, n. 1 to p. ↑3; 304 n. 4	1846, *L'Artiste*, 13 Dec., p. 92 (title: *A une Indienne*)	1857, *Le Présent*, 15 Nov.; .... 1868, *FM*	→1843	Pp. 40–1, n. 1, above. (But cf. C. Pichois, *B.*, 75 n. 150; *FMA* 440–1)
↑ une ↑endiante ↑usse iii n. 3; 29 n. 4	→1850 (c. 1843?), MS. (*FMPP* 479–80)	1851–2, MS. (*DP*; cf. *FMCB* 1968, p. 504 n. 2; 1857, *FM* proofs; 1857, *FM*;	→1842 (1841–2?)	Ch. Cousin, cit. *FMCB* 446 (cf. C. Pichois, *B. à Paris* 15 – but cf. Nadar, cit. *FMCB* 446); *FMA* 378–9; *FMCB* 1968, p. 164
↑vec ses ↑êtements 2 n. 1; 57 n. 1; 10 n. 1; 237 . 2	1857, *RF*, 20 April; 1857, *FM* proofs (see *FMCB* 1968)	1857, *FM*;	→1856 (1842–6?)	Cf. *FMCB* 345; *FMA* 309–10; p. 57 n. 1, above (inspired by Jeanne; theme of 'sterility')
↑vertisseur (L') ↑47 and n. 1	1861, *R. européenne*, 15 Sept.	.... 1868, *FM*	→1861	*FMCB* 1968, p. 350
↑alcon (Le) ↑82 n. 1; 186 ↑nd n.5; 267 ↑. 4; 272 n.2	1857, *Journal d'Alençon*, 17 May; 1857, *FM* proofs (see *FMCB* 1968)	1857, *FM*;	→1856 (c. Sept. 1856?)	*FMCB* 357–8; E. Starkie, *B.*, 275–6; *FMA* 319–20

Title	First extant text(s)	Select list of subsequent texts	Date of original composition	Select list of chronological references
Banville	See s.v. *Théodore de Banville*			
Béatrice (La) 110–11; 240, n. 2 to p. 239	1857, *FM* proofs (see *FMCB* 1968)	1857, *FM*;	→1856 (1842–8?)	P. 110 and n. 3, above; cf. also *FMA* 415 n. 4
Beau navire (Le) 243 n. 3	1857, *FM* proofs (see *FMCB* 1968)	1857, *FM*;	→1856 (1854–5?)	A Feuillerat, *B. et la Belle*, 48 (cf. 34, 45); *FMA* 339
Beauté (La) 281 n. 2	1857, *RF*, 20 April	1857, *FM* proofs (see *FMCB* 1968); 1857, *FM*;	→1856 (1842–5?)	*FMCB* 325; M. Ruff *Esprit du mal*, 180–1, 197, 428 n. 61. (But cf. *FMA* 294–6)
Belle Dorothée (La) 40 n. 1; 107, n. 3 to p. 106; 303 n. 1	1863, *R. nationale*, 10 June	1869, *PPP*	→End-Dec. 1861 (1859–61?)	*CG* II 385, 388, III 66, 135, IV, 33; *PPP* 310, 282; *FMC* 578; J. Pommier, *Dans les chemins de B.* 346
Bénédiction 4–5; 10; 60–2 and notes; 186 and n. 3; 206 n. 2; 230 n. 1; 231; 256 n. 3; 262 n. 3; 279 n. 1	1857, *FM* proofs (see *FMCB* 1968)	1857, *FM*;	→1856 (1844–6?)	Prarond, *CML* II, 1155; my art. cit., *RHLF*, 1967, pp. 344–5. (But cf. *FMA* 264)
Bienfaits de la lune (Les) 14 n. 3; 235 n. 2; 264 and n. 1; 292 n. 1	1863, *Le Boulevard*, 14 June (without title)	1869, *PPP*	→1863 (1862–3?)	*OCP* 1567–8; C. Pichois, *B.*, 77
Bien loin d'ici 40 n. 1; 303 n. 1	1864, *R. nouvelle*, 1 March	1868, *FM*	→1863 (1859–63?)	*FMCB* 578; *PPP* 28 J. Pommier, op. cit., 346; *FMA* 446
Bijoux (Les) 32 n. 1	1857, *FM* proofs (see *FMCB* 1968)	1857, *FM*;	→1856 (1842–8?)	*FMCB* 531; J. Pommier, *Dans les chemins de B.*, 201–2, 216–17; *FMA* 432–3
Bohémiens en voyage 20; 51; 53–5 and notes	1851–2, MS. (*DP*; title: *La Caravane des Bohémiens*)	1857, *FM* proofs (see *FMCB* 1968); 1857, *FM*;	→1851	E. Starkie, *B.*, 111; *FMA* 290

Title	First extant text(s)	Select list of subsequent texts	Date of original composition	Select list of chronological references
...ribes ...4 n. 2); 16 ..., 2; 247 n. 2	[1864–6?], MS. (*FMCB* 1968, pp. 379–81; part-facsimile, *CML* II, pl. xix)		→1864 (1844–55?)	Y.G. Le Dantec, *OCP* 1582–3; *OP* I, 370; *FMA* 460
...rumes et ...luies ...72 n. 1	1857, *FM* proofs (see *FMCB* 1968)	1857, *FM*;	→1856	
...abaret folâtre ...Un)	See s.v. *Un Cabaret folâtre*			
...aravane des ...ohémiens (La)	See s.v. *Bohémiens en voyage*			
...auserie ...8 n. 1	1857, *FM* proofs (see *FMCB* 1968)	1857, *FM*;	→1856 (1854?)	A. Feuillerat, *B. et la Belle*, 58–9 (cf. 34); *FMA* 346
...auseries [in ...ollaboration ...ith Banville ...nd Vitu] ...46 n. 1); 97 n. 1	1846–7, *Le Tintamarre*, 13 Sept. to 3 April (*OP* I, 118–190)		1846–7	*OP* I 494–5
...hacun sa ...himère ...78 n. 2	1862, *La Presse*, 26 Aug. (title: *Chacun la sienne*)	1869, *PPP*	→1862	
...hambre ...ouble (La) ...68–9 and 169 ..., 1; 186 n. 1; ...80 n. 5	1862, *La Presse*, 26 Aug.	1869, *PPP*	1859–62	*PPP* 275; G. Blin, *Sadisme de B.*, 161 n. 3; C. Pichois and R. Kopp, 'B. et l'opium' (*Europe*, 1967), p. 77
...hanson ...'après-midi ...37 n. 2	1860, *L'Artiste*, 15 Oct.	1861, *FM*;	→1860	*FMA* 350
...hant ...'automne ...8 n. 1; 237 ..., 2; 245 n. 3; ...54 and n. 2; ...56; 271–2; 278; ...89; 293 n. 3	1859, *RC*, 30 Nov.	1861, *FM*;	Sept. – Oct. 1859	A. Feuillerat, *B. et la Belle*, 72–5, 96 n. 89; *FMA* 346–7
...harogne (Une)	See s.v. *Une Charogne*			
...hâtiment de ...'orgueil ...92 and n. 3; ...99–100 and ...100 n. 1	1850, *Le Magasin des familles*, June, pp. 335–6	.... 1857, *FM*;	→1850 (→1847?)	W. T. Bandy, cit. *FMA* 293; F. Caussy, *L'Ermitage*, 1906, p. 333; *FMCB* 1968, p. 52

Title	First extant text(s)	Select list of subsequent texts	Date of original composition	Select list of chronological references
Chats (Les) xiii n. 3; 48 n. 1	1847, *Le Corsaire*, 14 Nov. (cit. Champfleury)	1851, *Le Messager de l'Assemblée*, 9 April; .... 1857, *FM*;	→1847	*FMCB* 1968, p. 534
Chevelure (La) 31 and n. 1; 32–7 and notes; 38 n. 3; 50; 85; 211; 214 n. 2; 226 n. 1; 303 n. 1; 318–19 n. 4	1859, *RF*, 20 May	1861, *FM*;	→1859	P. 31 n. 1, above. (But cf. *FMA* 305)
Choix de maximes consolantes sur l'amour 20–1; 22; 67 n. 1; 69 n. 4; 82 and n. 1; 110 n. 3; 186 n. 4; 280 n. 3	1846, *Le Corsaire-Satan*, 3 March (*OP* II, 3–11)		→Feb. 1846	
Ciel brouillé 237 n. 2; 272 n. 1	1857, *FM* proofs (see *FMCB* 1968)	1857, *FM*;	→1856 (1854?)	A. Feuillerat, *B. et la belle*, 60–1 (cf. 34, 45)
Confession 15 n. 1; 281 n. 1; 286, n. 3 to p. 285	1853, MS. (untitled), in letter to Mme Sabatier, 9 May (*CG* I, 210–11)	1855, *RDM*, 1 June, pp. 1082–3 (title: *La Confession*); 1857, *FM* proofs (see *FMCB* 1968); 1857, *FM*;	1851–3	A. Billy, *La Présidente et ses amis*, 123–4; F. Porché, *B. et la Présidente*, 157, 159
Confiteor de l'artiste (Le) 184–5; 186 n. 1; 245 n. 3; 254; 279–82 and notes; 317 n. 1; 319 and n. 1; 320	1862, *La Presse*, 26 Aug.	1869, *PPP*	Oct. 1858–Dec. 1862 (Oct. 1860?)	*PPP* 274; *CG* IV, 33; p. 279 n. 2, above
Conseils aux jeunes littérateurs 20; (46 n. 1)	1846, *L'Esprit public*, 15 April (*AR* 267–78)	1869, *AR*	→April 1846	

Title	First extant text(s)	Select list of subsequent texts	Date of original composition	Select list of chronological references
Contes de Champfleury (Les) 5 n. 1; 71 n. 2); 85-8 and notes	1848, *Le Corsaire-Satan*, 18 Jan. (*OP* II, 242-5)		1847	*OP* I, 563-4; pp. 85-6 n. 6, above
Contes normands et Historiettes baguenaudières (Les) 1 and n. 2; 6 and n. 2	1845, *Le Corsaire-Satan*, 4 Nov. (*OP* I, 237)		1845	*OP* I, 560; C. Pichois, *B.*, 88
Correspondances 4 n. 2; 175; 95-217 and notes; 218 and n. 1; 225-6; 226 n. 1; 229 n. 3; 230-1 and notes; 234 n. 3; 286 and n. 2; 87	1857, *FM* proofs (see *FMCB* 1968, p. 34)	1857, *FM*;	→1856 (ll. 1-4: 1851-6? ll. 5-14: 1845-7?)	Pp. 196-7 and notes, above
Coucher du soleil romantique (Le) 0 n. 1; 274-9 and notes	1862, *Le Boulevard*, 12 Jan.	1862, [Sept.-Oct.; see *FMCB* 1968, p. 558], *Almanach parisien pour* 1863; 1866, Feb.-March, *Les Épaves*; 1866, Dec., in Asselineau, *Mélanges*, p. 208 (title: *Soleil couché*)	→1861	Pp. 275-9 and notes, above
Couvercle (Le) 248 n. 3; 252 n. 2; 268 n. 1; 305 n. 2	Autumn 1861, MS. (see *FMCB* 1968, p. 345)	1862, *Le Boulevard*, 12 Jan.; .... 1868, *FM*	→1861	*FMCB* 620-1

Title	First extant text(s)	Select list of subsequent texts	Date of original composition	Select list of chronological references
Crépuscule du matin (Le) 117 and n. 1; 121; 160-1	1851-2, MS. *(DP)*	1852, *La Semaine théâtrale*, 1 Feb., p. 26; [1853-4?], MS. acc. letter to Desnoyers (facsimile, *BDI* no. 199, c); 1855, *Fontaine-bleau*, pp. 76-7; 1857, *FM* proofs; 1857, *FM*;	1841-3	Prarond, *CML* II, 1155; Asselineau, in *B. et Asselineau*, 174-5; *FMCB* 1968, p. 203
Crépuscule du soir (Le) (in verse) 108 n. 1; 117 and n. 1; 121; 160-1; 270 n. 1	1851-2, MS. *(DP)*	1852, *La Semaine théâtrale*, 1 Feb., pp. 26-7; [1853-4?], MS. acc. letter to Desnoyers (facsimile, *BDI* nos. 199, a-b); 1855, *Fontaine-bleau*, pp. 74-6; 1857, *FM* proofs (see *FMCB* 1968); 1857, *FM*;	→1849	Asselineau, loc. cit.; P. Citron, *Poésie de Paris*, II, 337; F. Caussy, *L'Ermitage*, 1906, p. 333
Crépuscule du soir (Le) (in prose) 120 n. 3; 161 and n. 3; 162 n. 1; 270-1; 285 n. 2; 286 n. 1	1855, *Fontainebleau* proofs (see *OCP* 1606-7)	1855, May, *Fontaine-bleau*, pp. 78-9; 1857, *Le Pré-sent*, 24 Aug.; 1861, *R. fan-taisiste*, 1 Nov.; 1864, *Figaro*, 7 Feb.; 1869, *PPP*	→May 1855 (1853-5?)	G. Blin, *Sadisme de B.*, 161-2

Title	First extant text(s)	Select list of subsequent texts	Date of original composition	Select list of chronological references
Cygne (Le) 07, n. 3 to p. 106; 110 n. 1; 256 and n. 2; 294 n. 1; 318 n. 4	1860, *La Causerie*, 22 Jan.	1861, *FM*;	→1859	*CG* VI, 82 n. 1 (letter to Hugo of 7 Dec. 1859, extract); *FMCB* 449-50
Danse macabre 294 n. 1	1859, *RC*, 15 March (for lost MS., [end-1858], see *FMCB* 1968)	.... 1861, *FM*;	Dec. 1858	*CG* II, 251 (cf. ibid., 250); *FMCB* 468; my art. cit., 'B.: The Poet as Moralist', p. 210
Dedications: a) *Les Fleurs du Mal*, to Théophile Gautier 220, n. 3 to p. 219	Original version: 1857, 25 Jan., MS. (see *FMCB* 1968, pp. 372-3)		Jan. 1857	*CG* II, 15, 18-19; *FMCB* 1968, pp. 502-3, 18-19
	Revised version: 1857, [8 March], MS. (see *FMCB* 1968, p. 18)	1857, *FM* proofs (see *FMCB* 1968, pp. 18-19); 1857, *FM*;	March 1857	
b) *Les Paradis artificiels*, to 'J.G.F.' 157 n. 3; 179 n. 1; 252 n. 2	1860, May, *PA*	1869, *PPP*	1-13 Jan. 1860	*CG* III, 3, 5, 10
c) *Petits poëmes en prose*, to Arsène Houssaye (107 and n. 3)	1862, *La Presse*, 26 Aug.	1869, *PPP*	Dec. 1861– Aug. 1862	*PPP* 223-5
Déjà! 258-61, 284	1863, *R. nationale*, 10 Dec.	1869, *PPP*	→ 1863	*PPP* 325
Delacroix	See s.v. *Exposition universelle*, III; *Œuvre et la vie d'Eugène Delacroix (L')*			
De l'Essence du rire	See s.v. *Essence du rire (De l')*			
De profundis clamavi 110 n. 3; 237 n. 2; 287, n. 4 to p. 286; 288 and n. 2; 293 n. 3; 306 n. 1	1851, *Le Messager de l'Assemblée*, 9 April (title: *La Béatrix*)	1855, *RDM*, 1 June, pp. 1090-1 (title: *Le Spleen*); 1857, *FM* proofs (see *FMCB* 1968); 1857, *FM*;	→1851	

Title	First extant text(s)	Select list of subsequent texts	Date of original composition	Select list of chronological references
Desbordes-Valmore	See s.v. *Marceline Desbordes-Valmore*			
Désir de peindre (Le) 14 n. 3; 65 n. 1; 264 n. 1	1863, *R. nationale*, 10 Oct.	1869, *PPP*	→1863	
Destruction (La) 237 n. 3	1855, *RDM*, pp. 1083–4 (title: *La Volupté*)	1857, *FM* proofs (see *FMCB* 1968); 1857, *FM*;	→1855 (→1846?)	Prarond, *CML* II, 1155; *FMA* 408–9
Deux bonnes sœurs (Les) 57 n. 1	1857, *FM* proofs (see *FMCB* 1968)	1857, *FM*;	→Dec. 1842	Prarond, *CML* II, 1155; *VR* 11–12; *FMCB* 496; my art. cit., *RHLF* 1967, p. 344
Don Juan aux enfers xiii n. 3	1846, *L'Artiste*, 6 Sept., p. 158 (title: *L'Impénitent*)	1857, *FM* proofs (see *FMCB* 1968); 1857, *FM*;	1841–3	Prarond, *CML* II, 1154. Cf. J. Pommier, *Dans les chemins de B.*, 295–6, and *FMPP* 20–1, 466–7 (S. Guérin lithograph, 1841, as source)
'Double Vie' par Charles Asselineau ('La') 141 n. 2	1859, *L'Artiste*, 9 Jan.	1869, *AR*	1858	*OCP* 1663–4
Drames [list of projected plays] 54 n. 1	[1859–61?], MS. (*OP* I, 101)		1853–63 (1859–61?)	*OP* I, 479; cf. ibid., 472–6
Drames et les romans honnêtes (Les) 96–8 and notes; 100; 161 n. 1; 173 and n. 2	1851, *La Semaine théâtrale*, 27 Nov., pp. 26–8	1869, *AR*	1851	M. Gilman, *B. the Critic*, 69–70, 236 n. 26, 27
Drame sur les Bohémiens (Un)	See s.v. *Drames*			
Dupont (Pierre)	See s.v. *Pierre Dupont* [I], [II]			

le	First extant text(s)	Select list of subsequent texts	Date of original composition	Select list of chronological references
Vin et du hish n. 2; 91 and 5; 105 n. 2; –3 n. 5; 185 2; 186 n. 1, 187–8; 190 2; 194 n. 2; 4, n. 2 to 213); 267–8 4; (281, n. 5 p. 280)	1851, *Le Messager de l'Assemblée*, 7, 8, 11, 12 March (*PA*, ed. C. Pichois, 67–93)	1869, *PPP*	→1851	*PA* 283–6; *PA*, ed. C. Pichois, 246–7
le païenne *)* and n. 1, 2; 97–9 and es; 100; n. 1; 123; n. 3; 150 2; 161 n. 1; and n. 2	1852, *La Semaine théâtrale*, 22 Jan., pp. 17–18 (*AR* 289–97)	1869, *AR*	Dec. 1851–Jan. 1852	*AR* 292 (internal evidence: ref. to political events of 2 Dec. 1851); *CG* I, 159 and n. 1, 160; M. Gilman, *B. the Critic*, 69–70, 236 n. 27
gar Allan Poe, vie et ses rages nd n. 3; 67; 103 and 1; 122; 124 3; 173 and 1; 175 n. 1; n. 3; 223	1852, *RPa*, March and April (*OP* I, 246–93)		1851–2	W. T. Bandy, *YFS* no. 10, [1953], pp. 66–8, and 'B. and Poe' (1958), pp. 31–2
gar Poe, sa et ses res . 3; 9 n. 2; 4 n. 3; 181; 3 n. 1; 186 1, (8); (187 1); 205; 272 1; 280–1 5; 285 n. 3	1856, *Le Pays*, 25 Feb. (in part); 1856, 12 March, *HE*		1855–6	*HE* 372–3, 393–4
vation . 3; 9 n. 1; n. 3; 186; –95 and es; 230–1 1; 231 n. 1	1857, *FM* proofs; 1857, *Journal d'Alençon*, 17 May	1857, *FM*;	→1856	Pp. 190–1 and n. 2, 3; E. Starkie, *B.*, 111; *FMCB* 1968, p. 32
ge du quillage	See s.v. *Peintre de la vie moderne (Le)*			
ivrez-vous 8 n. 1	1864, *Figaro*, 7 Feb.	1869, *PPP*	→1863	

24

Title	First extant text(s)	Select list of subsequent texts	Date of original composition	Select list of chronological references
Ennemi (L') 48 n. 1; 236 n. 2; 238 and n. 1; 272 n. 2; 306 n. 1	1855, *RDM*, 1 June, pp. 1089-90	1857, *FM* proofs (see *FMCB* 1968); 1857, *FM*;	→1855 (1854-5?)	*FMA* 286; my art. cit., *RSH*, 1967, p. 482 and n. 4
Épilogue [II] (draft) for *FM* 1861 14 n. 2; 247 n. 2	MS. (*FMCB* 1968, pp. 383-4)		→1860	(For *Épilogue* [I], cf. R. Kopp, ed. *PPP*, 1969, cit. *FMCB* 1968, p. 382
Esprit et le style de M. Villemain (L') xv n. 2; 27 n. 3; (295 n. 1)	MS. (posth.; *OP* I, 302-27)		1862	*OP* I, 587-8
Essence du rire (De l') 42-4 and 42 n. 4; 78 n. 3; 150 n. 2; 188-9 n. 2; 193 n. 1	1851, *L'Événement*, 20 April (one fragment only, cit. Champfleury); 1855, *Le Portefeuille*, 8 July (*in toto*)	1868, *CE*	1844-6	C. Pichois, *B.*, 80-9
Étranger (L') 121, n. 3 to p. 120; 262-3 and 263 n. 2	1862, *La Presse*, 26 Aug.	1869, *PPP*	→1862 (1859?)	*PPP* 272; G. Jean-Aubry, *B. et Honfleur*, 56; p. 121, n. 3 to p. 120 above (Champfleury cit.)
Exposition universelle 1855 I. *Méthode de critique* xii-xiii n. 2; 26-7; 66 n. 1; 126 and n. 4; 127 and n. 2; 129 and n. 3; 173-4; 199; 217-19 and notes; 226 n. 2; 234; 252 n. 2	1855, *Le Pays*, 26 May	1868, *CE*	May 1855	*CE* 482-3; *CG* I, 332-3
II. *Ingres* 127-9 and notes; 180-1 and notes; 191 n. 1; (222 n. 1)	1855, *Le Portefeuille*, 12 Aug.			

itle	First extant text(s)	Select list of subsequent texts	Date of original composition	Select list of chronological references
I. *Eugène* *elacroix* ·7 and n. 2; ·8;129 and n.3; ·o-1 and 181 1; 185 n. 3; ·6 n. 1, (8); ·87 n. 1); 205; ·7; 209; 215; ·1, n. 5 to ·280	1855, *Le Pays,* 3 June			
anfarlo (La) and n. 4; 14 ·2; 16 n. 1; 31 ·1; 51; 53 n. 1; ·7 n. 1; 59; 67; ·, n. 5 to p. 69; ·) n. 1; 82; 85; ·3 n. 2; 142 ·2; 176 n. 2; ·6 n. 3; 213-14 ·2; 215; 273 ·, 2	1847, *Bull. de la Société des Gens de lettres,* Jan.	.... 1869, *PPP*	1843-6 (1843-4?)	*Fanfarlo,* ed. C. Pichois, 9
antôme (Un)	See s.v. *Un Fantôme*			
ausse *onnaie (La)* ·43 n. 1	1864, *L'Artiste,* 1 Nov.	.... 1869, *PPP*	→1864 (c. 1852?)	*AR* 537; *PPP,* ed. M. Zimmerman, 123-4
emmes *amnées: A la ·île clarté* ... ·8 n. 1; 149 ·, 2	1857, *FM* proofs (see *FMCB* 1968)	1857, *FM*;	ll. 1-84: →1853 (→ Oct. 1845?); ll. 85-104: 1857	*FMCB* 538, 271-2 (cf. *BNE* p. 52 no. 212); my art. cit., *RHLF* 1967, p. 345; *FMCB* 538 (Poulet-Malassis cit.; cf. *FMCB* 1968, p. 276, re proof *a*)
in de don *uan(La)* ·4 n. 1	[1853?], MS. (posth.; *OCP* 563-4)		→1854 (1853?)	*OP* I, 459-60; *OCP* 1563
in de la *urnée (La)* ·70 n. 2; 285 ·, 2	1861, *FM*	.... 1868, *FM*	→1861	
leurs du Mal *Les)*	See s.v. Dedications, (a); *Préface* (draft)			
ontaine de *ang (La)* ·6-7 n. 5; ·9 n. 1	1851-2, MS. (*DP*)	1857, *FM* proofs (see *FMCB* 1968); 1857, *FM*;	→1851	

Title	First extant text(s)	Select list of subsequent texts	Date of original composition	Select list of chronological references
Fou et la Vénus (Le) 107, n. 3 to p. 106; 266–7; 279 n. 1	1862, La Presse, 26 Aug.	1869, PPP	→1862 (1861–2?)	
Foules (Les) 171 and n. 3; 252 n. 2	1861, R. fantaisiste, 1 Nov.	.... 1869, PPP	→1861	
Fou raisonnable et la belle adventurière (Le) 153 n. 1	[1858–9], MS. (OCP 520–1)		1858–9	CG I, 191 and n. 2; FMCB 400 (B.'s acquaintance with 'Sisina', mentioned in this text)
Fusées 153 n. 1; 171 and n. 2; 182–3 and notes; 185; 186 n. 1, 7; 186–7 n. 8; 205; 206 n. 3; 226 n. 2; 234 n. 3; 250 n. 1; 255 n. 1	MS. (posth.; JI)		1855–62	JI 182. (But cf. M. Ruff, Esprit du mal, 353–6)
Galant Tireur (Le) 306 n. 1	1869, PPP		→1865 (1858–60?)	PPP 246 and n. 1, 333; JI 182, 284, 287, 288 (dating of Fusées XI → first draft of present poem)
Gâteau (Le) 6 n. 3; 8–9; 9 n. 1; 192; 257; 264	1862, La Presse, 24 Sept.	1869, PPP	→1862	
Gautier (Théophile) See s.v. Théophile Gautier, [I]				
Géante (La) 20; 51–2	1857, RF, 20 April; 1857, FM proofs (see FMCB 1968)	1857, FM;	→1843	Prarond, CML II, 1154; FMA 298
Gouffre (Le) 286, n. 3 to p. 285	1862, L'Artiste, 1 March	.... 1868, FM	→1862	
Goût du néant (Le) 124; 285; 288–9	1859, RF, 20 Jan.	1861, FM;	→1858	

itle	First extant text(s)	Select list of subsequent texts	Date of original composition	Select list of chronological references
armonie du ir 8–5 and notes; 6 n. 6; 211; 4 n. 2; 245 3; 267–8 d n. 4; 271	1857, *FM* proofs; 1857, *Le Présent*, 20 April	1857, *Journal d'Alençon*, 17 May; 1857, *FM*;	→1856 (1845–6?)	My art. cit., *RHLF*, 1967, pp. 346–56; *FMCB* 1968, p. 102
éauton-norouménos L') 4 n. 1; 7 n. 1	1855, 7 April, summary in letter to V. de Mars (*CG* I, 331); 1855, MS. (facsimile, Y.G. Le Dantec, *MF*, April 1958, pp. 678–9)	.... 1857, *FM*;	April 1855 – May 1857	*FMCB* 431–2; *FMCB* 1968, pp. 152, 514–15
élas! qui a gémi . . . n. 1; 12 and 3	1839–45, MS. (*OP* I, 14)		1839–45 (1839–40?)	P. 12 n. 3, above
émisphère dans e chevelure Un)	See s.v. *Un Hémisphère dans une chevelure*			
libou philo-phe (Le)' Notes pour la daction et la mposition du urnal] o n. 1	MS. (posth.; *OP* I, 209–11)		Jan.–Feb. 1852	*OP* I, 536–7
iboux (Les) 4 and n. 1; 4–5 and n. 4	1851, *Le Messager de l'Assemblée*, 9 April	1857, *FM* proofs (see *FMCB* 1968); 1857, *FM*;	→1851	*FMA* 357; my art. cit., *SMFL*, p. 200
omme et la er (L') 4–6 and tes; 112; 4 and n. 1; 0; 284	1852, *RPa*, Oct. (title: *L'Homme libre et la mer*)	1857, *FM* proofs (see *FMCB* 1968); 1857, *FM*;	→1852	
orloge (L') 6 n. 1	1860, *L'Artiste*, 15 Oct.	1861, *FM*;	→1860	*FMA* 373
orreur mpathique 1 n. 1; 135 2; 245–6; 8–50 and tes; 262; 7–8	1860, *L'Artiste*, 15 Oct.	1861, *FM*;	→July 1860 (1859–60?)	*CG* III, 136 and n. 1; p. 248 n. 1, above

Title	First extant text(s)	Select list of subsequent texts	Date of original composition	Select list of chronological references
Hugo	See s.v. *Victor Hugo*			
Idéal (L') 58; 65 n. 4; 69 n. 4	1851, *Le Messager de l'Assemblée*, 9 April	1857, *FM* proofs (see *FMCB* 1968); 1857, *FM*;	→1851 (1842–6?)	Prarond, *CML* II, 1155; my art. cit., *RHLF*, 1967, pp. 344–5; *FMCB* 327; *FMA* 296–8
Imprévu (L') 159 and n. 2; 294 n 1	[1862–3], MS. (see *FMCB* 1968)	1863, *Le Boulevard*, 25 Jan.; 1868, *FM*	→1862	
Incompatibilité 6–10 and notes; 192 and n. 1; 257; 264; 269 n. 1; 280; 317 n. 1; 319	MS. (*OP* I, 8–9)		End –Aug. to end – Sept. 1838	P. 6 and n. 1, above
Ingres	See s.v. *Exposition universelle*, II			
Invitation au voyage (L') (in verse) 38 n. 1; 240 n. 4; 241 and n. 2, 3; 242 n. 1; 245; 293; 300 n. 2	1855, *RDM*, 1 June, pp. 1087–8	1857, *FM* proofs (see *FMCB* 1968); 1857, *FM*;	→1855 (Jan. – March 1855?)	P. 241, n. 3, above
Invitation au voyage (L') (in prose) 133 n. 1; 139 and n. 3; 176 n. 1; 240–5 and notes; 293; 300 n. 2	1857, *Le Présent*, 24 August	1861, *R. fantaisiste*, 1 Nov.; 1862, *La Presse*, 24 Sept.; 1869, *PPP*	1855–7 (1855–6?)	Pp. 241–2 n. 3, above. Cf. also *PPP* 295–6, and *PPP*, ed. H. Lemaitre, 90 n. 1 (Houssaye text of 1856 as 'source')
Irrémédiable (L') 96; 250	1857, *FM* proofs (see *FMCB* 1968); 1857, *L'Artiste*, 10 May (title: *L'Irrémédiable*)	1857, *FM*;	→1856	
Irréparable (L') 38 n. 1; 96	1855, *RDM*, 1 June, pp. 1085–7 (title: *A la Belle aux cheveux d'or*)	1857, *FM* proofs (see *FMCB* 1968); 1857, *FM*;	→1855 (1853–4?)	A. Feuillerat, *B. et la Belle*, 45–6 (but cf. also 26–7); *FMA* 344; *FMCB* 392

Title	First extant text(s)	Select list of subsequent texts	Date of original composition	Select list of chronological references
J'aime le souvenir de ces époques nues . . . 5; 18; 20; 49–50 and notes; 51; 52; 53; 55–60 and notes; 69 and n. 2, 4; 108	1857, *FM* proofs (see *FMCB* 1968)	1857, *FM*;	→1856 (1841–5?)	Prarond, *CML* II, 1155; my art. cit., *RHLF*, 1967, pp. 344–5; *FMCB* 300; M. Ruff, *Esprit du mal*, 180–1; *FMA* 278; *Fanfarlo*, ed. C. Pichois, 104–6; pp. 58–60, above
Je n'ai pas oublié, voisine de la ville . . . 4; 13; 267 n. 3	1857, *FM* proofs (see *FMCB* 1968)	1857, *FM*;	1841–3	Prarond, *CML* II, 1155; *FMCB* 474
Jet d'eau (Le) 15 n. 1; 245 n. 1	1853, title only (see *FMCB* 1968, p. 522); [→June 1865], MS. (see ibid., 291)	1865, *La Petite R.*, 8 July; .... 1868, *FM*	→1853	*FMCB* 580; *FMCB* 1968, pp. 291, 522
Je te donne ces vers . . . 48 n. 1	1857, *RF*, 20 April	1857, *FM* proofs (see *FMCB* 1968); 1857, *FM*;	→1856 (1842–8?)	Inspired by Jeanne in her heyday? (But cf. *FMA* 323)
Jeune enchanteur (Le) 69 n. 5	1846, *L'Esprit public*, 20–22 Feb.	1869, *PPP*	1845–6	W. T. Bandy, *MF*, Feb. 1950, pp. 238–9; G. Gendreau and C. Pichois, *RHLF*, 1957, pp. 574–6
Je vis, et ton bouquet . . . 140 n. 3	MS., in letter dated 'mardi 3 novembre' (posth.; *OP* I, 22)		1846 or 1857 or 1863	*OCP* 1589
Joueur généreux (Le) 47 n. 1	1864, *Figaro*, 7 Feb.	.... 1869, *PPP*	→1863 (1858–61?)	Y. G. Le Dantec, *OCP* 1583 (MS. cit.; for date, cf. *FMCB* 1968, p. 124); *CG* III, 135 and n. 2, IV, 33 and n. 2
Laclos	See s.v. *Notes sur 'Les Liaisons dangereuses'*			
Leconte de Lisle (28 and n. 4); 257 n. 1; 303 n. 1	1861, *R. fantaisiste*, 15 Aug.	1862, *Les Poëtes français*, IV, 571–4; 1869, *AR*	→1861	
Lesbos 16 n. 2	[June–July] 1850, in: *Les Poëtes de l'Amour*, ed. J. Lemer, pp. 469–72 (see *FMCB* 1968, 535)	1857, *FM*;	→1850 (→1845?)	*FMCB* 271–2 (cf. *BNE* p. 52 no. 212); my art. cit., *RHLF*, 1967, p. 345

Léthé (Le) 270 n. 2 | 1857, *FM* proofs (see *FMCB* 1968) | 1857, *FM*; .... | →1856 (1842–8?) | Inspired by Jeanne in her heyday? (But cf. *FMA* 433)

Letters:[1]
(a) to Fern. Desnoyers 110 n. 1; 112; 115 n. 2; 117; 119 n. 1; 120 n. 3; 121–6 and notes; 127 and n. 1; 150; 160–1; 162; 163; 167; 172; 174; 179 n. 2; 202 n. 2; 203 n. 2; 251; 252; 260; 265; 283; 284; 287; 312 | [1853–4?], MS. (facsimile, *BDI* no. 199, a; *CG* I, 321–3) | 1855, May, *Fontaine-bleau*, pp. 73–4 | →1855 (1853–4?) | My art. cit., 'A *Festschrift* of 1855', pp. 189 and 199–200 n. 33

(b) to Alph. Toussenel 151–2 and notes; 175 n. 4; 176; 220–2 and notes; 235; 253 n. 1 | 1856, 21 Jan., MS. (*CG* I, 367–71) | Jan. 1856

(c) to Richard Wagner 139 n. 2; (191, n. 3 to p. 190) | 1860, 17 Feb., MS. (*CG* III, 31–5) | Feb. 1860

Lettre à Jules Janin [projected article] 308 n. 3 | Feb. – March 1865, MS. (*OP* I, 223–33) | Feb. – March 1865 | *OP* I, 548–50

'*Liaisons dangereuses (Les)*' | See s.v. [*Notes sur 'Les Liaisons dangereuses*']

Lune offensée (La) 30 n. 1; 62–8 and notes; 264 n. 2; 281 n. 2 | 1862, *L'Artiste*, 1 March | 1868, *FM* | →1861 (1844–6?) | Pp. 62–4, notes, above; *FMA* 458–9. (But cf. M. Ruff, *Esprit du mal*, 448 n. 11)

Mangeur d'opium (Un) | See s.v. *Un Mangeur d'opium*

Marceline Desbordes-Valmore 236–8 | 1861, *R. fantaisiste*, 1 July | 1862, *Les Poëtes français*, IV, 147–50; 1869, *AR* | 1859–61 | *CG* II, 329 n. 4, 330, III, 315

[1] I include here only certain letters having a particular significance for the development of B.'s thought.

Title	First extant text(s)	Select list of subsequent texts	Date of original composition	Select list of chronological references
Mort héroïque (Une)	See s.v. *Une Mort héroïque*			
Musée classique du Bazar Bonne-Nouvelle (Le) 24 n. 1; 50 n. 2; 76 n. 4; 77 and n. 4; 127	1846, *Le Corsaire-Satan*, 21 Jan.	1868, *CE*	Jan. 1846	*CE* 481; *CE*, ed. J. Adhémar, 91; A. Tabarant, *Vie artistique*, 84–6; my art. cit., *RSH*, 1967, p. 487
Muse malade (La) 14; 50–3 and 51 n. 2; 69 and n. 2	1857, *FM* proofs (see *FMCB* 1968)	1857, *FM*;	→1856 (1841–5?)	*FMCB* 307; M. Ruff, *Esprit du mal*, 180–1; *FMA* 283–4; J. Prévost, *B.*, 207–8. Cf. also p. 51, above (analogy with *Fanfarlo*)
Mystères galans des théâtres de Paris [anon., in collaboration] 21 n. 1	1844, Feb. (*MGC*)		1843–4	*MGC* 121–7
Noble femme au bras fort . . . 57 n. 1	[1844–7], MS. (posth.; *FMCB* 1968)		1844–7 (1844?)	*OP* I, 383–4 (Laffont cit.); *FMA* 465; *FMCB* 1968, p. 395
[*Notes diverses sur*] *L'Art philosophique*	See s.v. *Art philosophique (L')*			
Notes nouvelles sur Edgar Poe 141 n. 2; 142–3 n. 4; 152–3 and n. 3, 4, 5; 155–6 and notes; 177–8 and 178 n. 1, 2; 182 n. 1; 186 n. 7; 222–4; 273; 277	1857, 26 Jan., proofs for *NHE*	1857, early March, *NHE*	1856–7	*NHE* 317–19, 309
[*Notes pour la rédaction et la composition du journal*] '*Le Hibou philosophe*'	See s.v. *Hibou philosophe (Le)*			
[*Notes sur 'Les Liaisons dangereuses'*] 157 n. 2	MS. (posth.; *OCP* 638–46)		1856–7⎫ 1865–6⎭	*OP* I, 598–9

Title	First extant text(s)	Select list of subsequent texts	Date of original composition	Select list of chronological references
Notes . . . sur sa vie et ses ouvrages] (for Duranty) 5 n. 3	[c. 1861], MS. (*OP* II, 136)		c. 1861	*CG* III, 198, 190 and n. 3; *OP* II, 287–9
Obsession 202 n. 2; 203 n. 2; 245 n 3; 280; 283–8 and notes; 289; 309 and n. 2; 317	[1860, c. 10 Feb.?], MS., in letter to Poulet-Malassis (*CG* III, 22); [1860, Feb.?], MS., in letter to Asselineau [?] (*CG* III, 25)	1860, *RC*, 15 May; 1861, *FM*;	→1860 (early 1860?)	*CG* III, 22 n. 1 and 25 n. 2–3; *FMCB* 1968, p. 148; p. 284 n. 3, above
Œuvre et la vie d'Eugène Delacroix (L') 133 n. 1; 149 n. 4; 153 n. 1; (156 n. 3); 228, n. 3 to p. 227	1863, *L'Opinion nationale*, 2 Sept., 14 and 22 Nov.	1869, *AR*	End–Aug. 1863	*CG* IV, 183; *OCP* 1144; *CE*, ed. J. Adhémar, 463; A. Tabarant, *Vie artistique*, 321–3
Ombre [trans. of Poe, *Shadow*] 285 n. 3	1854, *Le Pays*, 5 Aug. (title: *L'Ombre*)	.... 1857, *NHE*	1853–4	*NHE* 491. Cf. W. T. Bandy, *YFS* no. 10, [1953], pp. 68–9, and 'B. and Poe' (1958), pp. 31–2
Paradis artificiels (Les)	See s.v. Dedications (b); *Poëme du haschisch (Le)*; *Un Mangeur d'opium*			
Parfum exotique 31–2 and 31 n. 1; 39; 50; 85; 214 n. 2; 226 n. 1	1857, *Journal d'Alençon*, 17 May; 1857, *FM* proofs (see *FMCB* 1968)	1857, *FM*;	→1856 (1842–6?)	P. 31 n. 1, above (but cf. *FMA* 305); *FMCB* 1968, p. 61
Pauvre Belgique 130; 148–50 and notes; 153 n. 1; 214 n. 2; 265 n. 3; 285 n. 2	[1864–5], MS. (*OP* III)		1864–5	*OP* III, 265–76
Paysage 6; 15 n. 1; 17–19 and notes; 60; 162–5 and notes; 318 n. 4	1857, *Le Présent*, 15 Nov. (title: *Paysage parisien*)	1861, *FM*;	→1852 (1841–5?)	P. 17 and n. 1, above. Cf. also: *FMC* 451; *FMCB* 443; A. Feuillerat, 'Architecture des *FM*', 304 n. 163; M. Ruff, *Esprit du mal*, 455 n. 27; *FMA* 375–7; *FMPP* 477–8; F. Scarfe, *Chénier*, 37–8, and ed., B., *Selected Verse*, 13

Title	First extant text(s)	Select list of subsequent texts	Date of original composition	Select list of chronological references
Peintre de la vie moderne (Le) 5 and n. 2; 27 n. 3; 106 n. 3; 128 n. 1; 140–2 and notes; 143 n. 1; 153–7 and notes; 164, n. 4 to p. 163; 168 n. 2; 171 and n. 3; 186 n. 3; 234 n. 3; 312–13	1863, *Figaro*, 26 and 29 Nov., 3 Dec.	1869, *AR*	Nov. 1859–Feb. 1860	*AR* 453; *OCP* 1711
Peintres et aqua-fortistes 164, n. 4 to p. 163	1862, *R. anecdotique*, 2nd fortnight of April (= anon., earlier and shorter version, without title; *OCP* 1150–1)	1862, *Le Boulevard*, 14 Sept.; 1869, *AR*		*AR* 465–6; *OCP* 1710; A. Tabarant, *Vie artistique*, 295
Peintures murales d'Eugène Delacroix à Saint-Sulpice 139 n. 1	1861, *R. fantaisiste*, 15 Sept.	1869, *AR*	July–Sept. 1861	*AR* 452; L. Horner, *B. critique de Delacroix*, 164–6
[*Petits poëmes en prose*: list of] *Poëmes à faire* 162 n. 2	[1859–62?], MS. (*OCP* 312–13)		→1865 (1859–62?)	Anterior to '*Spleen de Paris*': *à faire* (q.v., below)?
Phares (Les) 93 n. 1; 181 n. 1; 218 n. 1; 250 n. 1	1857, *FM* proofs (see *FMCB* 1968)	1857, *FM*;	→1856 (1845–7?)	P. 93 n. 1, above; K. R. Gallas, *Neophilologus*, 1943, 179 n. 6. (But cf. *FMCB* 303; C. Pichois, *B.*, 125–9)
Pierre Dupont, [I] 94–5 and notes; 97; 100; 244 n. 3; 312	1851, end – Aug., = part 20 of Pierre Dupont, *Chants et Chansons*	1851, as Pref. to ibid. in vol. form; 1869, *AR*	→Aug. 1851	*AR* 502–3; *OCP* 1658
Pierre Dupont, [II] 244–5 and 245 n. 1; 289	1861, *R. fantaisiste*, 15 Aug.	1862, *Les Poëtes français*, IV, 609–15; 1869, *AR*	1859–61	*CG* II, 329 n. 4, 330, 359, etc.

Title	First extant text(s)	Select list of subsequent texts	Date of original composition	Select list of chronological references
Poe	See s.v. *Edgar Allan Poe, sa vie et ses ouvrages*; *Edgar Poe, sa vie et ses œuvres*; *Notes nouvelles sur Edgar Poe*			
Poëme du Haschisch (Le) 53 n. 1; 169 and n. 2; 176 n. 1; 181 n. 2; 182 n. 1, 2, 3; 183–4; 185 and n. 2; 186 n. 1, 7; 187–8 and 188 n. 1, 2; 190 n. 2; 194 n. 2; 205; 207–9 and 208 n. 1; (214, n. 2 to p. 213); 226 n. 2; 268 n. 2; 281, n. 5 to p. 280; 294 n. 3	1858, *RC*, 30 Sept., pp. 274–307 (title: *De l'Idéal artificiel – Le Haschisch*)	1860, *PA*; 1869, *PPP*	1857–8	*PA* 288–9; *OCP* 1623–4
Poison (Le) 186 n. 1; 280 n. 5	1857, *FM* proofs (see *FMCB* 1968); 1857, *RF*, 20 April	1857, *FM*;	→1856 (1854?)	A. Feuillerat, *B. et la Belle*, 53 (cf. 34); *FMA* 336
Port (Le) 255 n. 5; 305 n. 2	[1864?], MS. (facsimile, *CML* II, pl. xx)	1864, *Nouvelle RPa*, 25 Dec.; 1869, *PPP*	→1864 (1859?)	P. 255 and n. 5, above; M. Zimmerman, ed. *PPP*, 179
Portraits de maîtresses 306 n. 1	[1865?], MS. (facsimile, *Manuscrit autographe*, 1927, pp. 95–9; see *PPP* 333 and *PPP* ed. M. Zimmerman, 179–80)	.... 1869, *PPP*	→1865	*PPP* 246 and n. 1, 332; *PPP*, ed. M. Zimmerman, 142–3
Préface (draft) for *Les Fleurs du Mal* 237 n. 1; 291	[1859–60, 1862–3?], MSS. (*FMCB* 1968, pp. 361–71)		1859–60	*FMCB* 588–90; *OCP* 1584
Première et la Dernière (La) [anon., attrib.] 291 n. 5	1848, *Le Salut public*, 1 March (*OP* I, 204–5)		26–29 Feb. 1848	*OP* I, 534; cf. ibid., 528–30
Projets (Les) 34 n. 2; 36 n. 1; 243 n. 1; 260 n. 1; 298 n. 3; 300 n. 2	1857, *Le Présent*, 24 Aug.	1861, *R. fantaisiste*, 1 Nov.; 1864, *Vie parisienne*, 13 Aug.; 1864, *Nouvelle RPa*, 25 Dec.; 1869, *PPP*	→1857 (1855–6?)	M. Zimmerman, ed. *PPP*, 120

Title	First extant text(s)	Select list of subsequent texts	Date of original composition	Select list of chronological references
'Prométhée délivré' par L. de Senneville 24 and n. 2; 25; 69 n. 4; 99; (122); 301 n. 1	1846, Le Corsaire-Satan, 3 Feb. (OP I, 238–41)		1844–6	OP I, 561; my art. cit., RHLF, 1967, p. 354 n. 2
Puisque Réalisme il y a 129–30; 176–7; 219; 222	[end–1855], MS. (OP I, 296–9)		end–1855	OP I, 579–80
Quelques caricaturistes étrangers 63, n. 3 to p. 62	1857, Le Présent, 15 Oct.	1868, CE	1844–6	C. Pichois, B., 80–6, 92–4
Quelques caricaturistes français 71 n. 2; 77 n. 2; 78 n. 2; 107, n. 3 to p. 106; 110 n. 1	1857, Le Présent, 1 Oct.	1868, CE	1844–6	Ibid.
Recueillement 48 n. 2; 252 n. 2; 262 n. 3; 268–71 and notes	[1861], MS. (facsimile, CML II, pl. xvi); [1861?], MS. [?] (see BNE no. 253 – but cf. FMCB 1968, pp. 356, 525)	1861, R. européenne, 1 Nov.; .... 1868, FM	→1861 (1860–1?)	FMLD 436; BNE p. 71, no. 318; FMCB 1968, p. 356
Reniement de Saint Pierre (Le) 103 n. 1	1851–2, MS. (DP)	1852, RPa, Oct.; .... 1857, FM;	→1851–2 (Dec. 1851 –April 1852?)	P. 103 n. 1, above; FMCB 1968, p. 237
Rêve d'un curieux (Le) 290–1; 308 n. 3; 317	1860, MS., in letter of 13 March to Poulet-Malassis (title: Le Rêve du Curieux; CG III, 68); 1860, [March–May?], MS. (facsimile, CML II, pl. xi)	1860, RC, 15 May; 1861, FM;	→1860 (1859–60?)	FMCB 522; J. Crépet, MS. Autographe, 1927, pp. 122–3. (But cf.: J. Mouquet, VR 16–17; E. Starkie, B. 114–15; FMA 428)

Title	First extant text(s)	Select list of subsequent texts	Date of original composition	Select list of chronological references
Révélation magnétique (trans. of Poe, *Mesmeric Revelation*): [Prefatory Note] 67 n. 1; 88–91 and notes; 173 and n. 1; 179–80	1848, *La Liberté de Penser*, 15 July (*HE* 456–8)		→June 1848 (End–1847 or early 1848?)	Pp. 88–9 and notes, above; *HE* 456, 458
Rêve parisien 18 n. 1; 140; 148; 165–70 and notes; 186 n. 1; 280 n. 5; 293	1860, 13 March, MS., in letter to Poulet-Malassis (part-facsimile, Catalogue of Hôtel Drouot Sale, 29 May 1968, [1] s.v. no. 11; see also *FMCB* 1968, p. 199); 1860 [March–May?], MS. (facsimile, *CML* II, pl. xii-xiv)	1860, *RC*, 15 May; 1861, *FM*;	1859–60?	*FMA* 396; *FMCB* 481; *FMCB* 1968, p. 199
Réversibilité 38 n. 1	1853, MS. sent to Mme Sabatier, 3 May (*CG* I, 207–9; title: *A A.*)	1855, *RDM*, 1 June, pp. 1080–1; 1857, *FM* proofs (see *FMCB* 1968); 1857, *FM*;	→1853 (1852–3?)	*CG* I, 207–8 n. 3; *FMA* 329
Richard Wagner et 'Tannhaüser' à Paris 37 n. 2; 175; 187, n. 8 to p. 186, and n. 1; (191, n. 3 to p. 190); 210–11 and 211 n. 1, 2; 212 n. 1; 213 n. 2; 284 n. 3; 286, n. 3 to p. 285	1861, *R. européenne*, 1 April	.... 1869, *AR*	April 1860– March 1861	*CG* III, 101; ibid. 261, 264–5; A. Ferran, *Esthétique de B.*, 327
Romans [Notes relating to projected novels]: [XIV] 82 n. 1	[1859–60?], MS. (posth.; *OCP* 519)		1859–60?	Opening sentence: cf. *PA* 166, *AR* 94, *CG* III 96–7 (all texts of 1859–60)

---

[1]*Collection d'autographes littéraires. Lettres et Manuscrits des XVII*ᵉ*, XVIII*ᵉ*, XIX*ᵉ*, XX*ᵉ *siècles.*

Title	First extant text(s)	Select list of subsequent texts	Date of original composition	Select list of chronological references
Salon de 1845 xiii and n. 1; 71–3 and notes; (74 and n. 4); 75–6 n. 4; 76 and n. 4; 78 n. 2; 124; (213 n. 2)	1845, early May	1868, *CE*	March 1845	*CE* 465; *S45F* 137; A. Tabarant, *Vie artistique*, 78–9; *CE*, ed. J. Adhémar, 34
Salon de 1846 20 and n. 3; 28 n. 2, 4; 38 n. 2; (46 n. 1); 49 and n. 2; 56 n. 1; 58 and n. 1; 70, n. 5 to p. 69; 71 and n. 1, 2; 73–81 and notes; 83 and n. 2; 86–7 and 87 n. 1; 88; 89; 90 and n. 1, 3; 127; 128 n. 1; 129 and n. 2; 131 and n. 1; 133 n. 2; (134); 139 n. 1; 149 n. 4; 156 n. 1; 202 n. 1; 212 n. 1; 213 n. 2; 214 n. 2; 215; (219 n. 3); 267 and n. 2; 272 n. 4; 273; 277 and n. 2; 281 n. 2; 300 n. 2; 311; 312	1846, early May	1868, *CE*	April 1846 (1844–6?)	*CE* 474, 475, 450; A. Tabarant, op. cit., 90; *CE*, ed. J. Adhémar, 106; my art. cit., *RSH*, 1967, pp. 495 n. 81, 484
Salon de 1859 9 n. 2; 45; 47 n. 1; 77 n. 2; 106 n. 3; 113 n. 2; 123 n. 1; 130–9 and notes; 142; 148, 149 and n. 5; 153 n. 1; 163–4 and n. 4; 175 n. 4; 177 n. 2; 181 n. 2; 184, n. 1 to p. 183, and n. 1; 186 n. 7, (8); 187 n. (1), 2; 204 n. 1; 217; (219	1859, *RF*, 10 and 20 June, 1 and 20 July	1868, *CE*	1859, May	*CE* 487–8; *OCP* 1701; A. Tabarant, op. cit., 261–2; *CE*, ed. J. Adhémar, 306

[contd. over]

Title	First extant text(s)	Select list of subsequent texts	Date of original composition	Select list of chronological references
n. 3); 224–5; 228, n. 3 to p. 227; 234 n. 3; 248 n. 1; 249; 250 n. 1; 251–2; 252–3; 257 and n. 2; 260 n. 2; 272 n. 1; 272–3; 274 n. 1; 277; 303 n. 1; 316				
Le Salut Public	See s. v. *Première et la Dernière (La)* ; *Réouverture des théâtres* (see p. 373)			
Sept vieillards (Les) 245 n. 3	1859, [June], MS. (*CG* II, 321–3); 1859, two further MSS. (see *FMCB* 1968; title in all three MSS.: *Fantômes parisiens*)	1859, *RC*, 18 Sept. .... 1861, *FM*;	→June 1859	*CG* II, 346 (letter to Hugo, end–Sept. 1859: '[ces] vers . . . se jouaient depuis longtemps dans mon cerveau'); ibid., 323–4; *FMCB* 1968, pp. 170–1
Serpent qui danse (Le) 32 n. 1; 34 n. 1; 36 n. 1; 38 n. 2	1857, *FM* proofs (see *FMCB* 1968)	1857, *FM*;	→1856 (1842–8?)	Inspired by Jeanne in her heyday? Cf. *FMCB* 345, *FMA* 310
Servante au grand cœur . . . (La) 17 n. 1	1857, *FM* proofs (see *FMCB* 1968)	1857, *FM*;	1841–3	Prarond, *CML* II, 1155; *FMCB* 474
Siècle . . . par Bathild Bouniol (Le) 69 n. 4	1846, Le Corsaire-Satan, 1 Feb. (*OP* I, 241)		→1846	*OP* I, 562–3
Sisina 30 n. 1	1858–9, MS. (see *FMCB* 1968, p. 124)	1859, *RF*, 10 April; 1861, *FM*;	→1859 (1858–9?)	*FMCB* 400
Soleil (Le) 13–14 and notes; 15; 106–8 and notes; 119 n. 1; 122 and n. 2; 147; 196; 231 n. 1; 267; 278–9; 281 n. 2	1857, *FM* proofs (see *FMCB* 1968)	1857, *FM*;	→1856 (Part I: 1852–5? Parts II, III: 1841–5?)	Pp. 13 and n. 2 (cf. 4 n. 3), 14 n. 2, 108 and n. 1, above. Cf. also *FMCB* 444; *FMA* 377; F. Caussy, *L'Ermitage*, 1906, p. 333
Soleil couché	See s.v. *Coucher du soleil romantique (Le)*			

Title	First extant text(s)	Select list of subsequent texts	Date of original composition	Select list of chronological references
Solitude (La) 120 n. 3; 161–2 and 162 n. 1; 252; 268 n. 2; 304–5 n. 3	1855, *Fontainebleau* proofs (see *OCP* 1608–9)	1855, May, *Fontaine-bleau*, pp. 79–80; 1857, *Le Présent*, 24 Aug.; 1861, *R. fantaisiste*, 1 Nov.; 1864, proofs for *Nouvelle RPa* (see *OCP* 1608, 1609); 1864, *Nouvelle RPa*, 25 Dec.; 186, *PPP*	→1855 (1853–5?)	*OCP* 1606–9
Sonnet d'automne 38 n. 1; 254 n. 2; 272 n. 2	1859, *RC*, 30 Nov.	1861, *FM*;	→1859	
Soupe et les nuages (La) 121, n. 3 to p. 120; 263; 269 n. 1	[c. 1863], MS. (facsimile, *Manuscrit autographe*, 1927, p. 94; see *OCP* 1617)	1869, *PPP*	c. 1863	*OCP* 1567–8; C. Pichois, *B.*, 77; *PPP* 246 and n. 1
Souvenirs de M. Auguste Bedloe (Les) (trans. of Poe, *A Tale of the Ragged Mountains*) 181 n. 2; (281, n. 5 to p. 280)	1852, *L'Illustration*, 11 Dec. (title: *Une Aventure dans les Montagnes Rocheuses*)	.... 1856, *HE*	1851–2	W. T. Bandy, 'B. and Poe' (1958), pp. 31–2; *HE* 466
Spleen [II]: *J'ai plus de souvenirs . . .* 237 n. 2; 273 n. 2; 285 n. 3; 306 n. 1	1857, *FM* proofs (see *FMCB* 1968)	1857, *FM*;	→1856	
Spleen [IV]: *Quand le ciel bas et lourd . . .* 245 n. 3; 250 n. 2	1857, *FM* proofs (see *FMCB* 1968)	1857, *FM*;	→1856	*FMA* 364

Title	First extant text(s)	Select list of subsequent texts	Date of original composition	Select list of chronological references
*'Spleen de Paris': à faire [projected prose poems] 5 n. 2; (162 n. 2)	[1863–5?], MS. (*OCP* 313–15)		(1863–5?)	Title 'Le Spleen de Paris' given by B. to his prose poems, from 1863 (cf. *CG* IV, 152–3, etc.)
*Squelette laboureur (Le) 290; 317	1859, 15 Dec., MS. in letter to Poulet-Malassis (*CG* II, 388 and n. 1)	.... 1861, *FM*;	→1859 (1859?)	*FMA* 387, *FMCB* 1968; p. 182
*Sur 'Le Tasse en prison' d'Eugène Delacroix 40 n. 1; 231	Original version: 1844, Feb., MS. (title: *Sur le Tasse à l'hôpital des fous de Mr Delacroix...*; copy by La Fizelière, *FMPP* 492, 494 – cf. *FMCB* 1968)		Feb. 1844	*CG* III 155, IV 223, 224; *FMCB* 577; *FMPP* 22, 492–5; *FMCB* 1968, pp. 310, 526, 528
	Revised version: 1864, Jan.–Feb., MS. (see *FMCB* 1968)	1864, *R. Nouvelle*, 1 March; 1866, *Les Épaves*; 1868, *FM*		
*Théodore de Banville 52–3; 61 n. 1; 154 n. 2; 182 n. 1; (186 n. 8); 220, n. 3 to p. 219; 269 and n. 1	1861, *R. fantaisiste*, 1 Aug.	1862, *Les Poëtes français*, IV, 580–6; .... 1869, *AR*	→1861	*AR* 551–2
*Théophile Gautier [I] (175); 178 n. 2; 186 n. (8); 205; 207; 209; 215; 225–6 and 226 n. 1; 227; 234–5; 251 n. 2; (257 n. 2); 273–4; 276 n. 3; 277	1859, *L'Artiste*, 13 March	1859, [Aug.–Oct.], proofs for booklet (see *OCP* 1668); 1859, Oct.–Nov., as booklet; 1869, *AR*	1858–9 (Early Feb. 1859?)	*CG* II, 223–4, 268, 271, 331, 352, 358; *OCP* 1666
*Tir et le Cimetière (Le) 107, n. 3 to p. 106; 252 n. 2; 265–7; 291	1867, *R, nationale*, 11 Oct.	1869, *PPP*	1864–5	*PPP* 335, 268; *PPP*, ed. M. Zimmerman, 180; p. 265 and n. 3, above
*Tous imberbes alors... 10 n. 2; 16 n. 2; 44–5	[1843–5], in letter to Sainte-Beuve (*OCP* 198–200; *FMCB* 1968, pp. 392–4)		1843–5 (1843?)	*FMCB* 1968, p. 392; C. Pichois, *B.*, 33 n. 55

Title	First extant text(s)	Select list of subsequent texts	Date of original composition	Select list of chronological references
Tout entière 19 n. 2; 48 n. 1; 212 n. 1	1857, *RF*, 20 April; 1857, *FM* proofs (see *FMCB* 1968)	1857, *FM*;	→1856 (1852–4?)	*CG* II, 87 (letter to Mme Sabatier of 18 Aug. 1857: this poem 'composed for' her); F. Porché, *B. et la Présidente*, 130. But cf. M. Ruff, *Esprit du mal*, 300–1
Tristesses de la lune 15–16 and notes; 63; 65 n. 1; 264	1850, 10 Jan., in letter to Ancelle, title only: *Tristesse de la lune* (*CG* I, 116); 1857, *FM* proofs (see *FMCB* 1968)	1857, *FM*;	→1850 (c. 1846?)	*CG* I, 115–16; p. 16 n. 2, above (Champfleury allusion?); *FMA* 356
Tu mettrais l'univers entier dans ta ruelle . . . 22–3 and 23 n. 1; 64 n. 2; 142 n. 2	1857, *FM* proofs (see *FMCB* 1968)	1857, *FM*;	1840–6 (1840–2?)	Prarond, *CML* II, 1155, 1156; my art. cit., *RHLF*, 1967, p. 344. (But cf. *FMA* 307–8)
Un Cabaret folâtre 265 n. 3	1865–6, MS. (see *FMCB* 1968)	1866, *Les Épaves*	1864–5	P. 265 and n. 3, above
Une Charogne 21–2 and n. 3; 107, n. 3 to p. 106; 110 n. 1; 265–6	Undated, 2 MSS. [?]: (A) ll. 1–44 (title: *La Charogne*; see *FMCB* 31–3 and 349, *BNE* no. 253 – but cf. *FMCB* 1968); (B) ll. 45–8 (*CML* I, 1208 – but cf. *FMCB* 1968); 1853, list, title only: *La Charogne* (see *FMCB* 1968, pp. 70, 522); 1857, *FM* proofs (see *FMCB* 1968)	1857, *FM*;	→1843	Prarond, *CML* II, 1154; *FMCB* 348; *FMA* 311; *FMCB* 1968 p. 70
Une Martyre 83 n. 2; 297 n. 1	1857, *FM* proofs (see *FMCB* 1968)	1857, *FM*;	→1856 (1842–6?)	*FMCB* 493–4 (Banville cit.); Prarond, *CML* II, 1155
Une Mort héroïque 143 n. 1	1863, *R. nationale*, 10 Oct.	.... 1869, *PPP*	→1863	Cf. M. Zimmerman, ed. *PPP*, 122
Un Fantôme 271 n. 1; 286, n. 3 to p. 285	1860, March, MS. sent to Poulet-Malassis (see *CG* III, 66–7 and n. 2; *FMCB* 1968, p. 84)	1860, *L'Artiste*, 15 Oct.; 1861, *FM*;	→March 1860	*FMCB* 360; *FMA* 321

Title	First extant text(s)	Select list of subsequent texts	Date of original composition	Select list of chronological references
Un Hemisphère dans une chevelure 31 n. 1; 34–5 n. 2; 36 n. 1; 214 n. 2; 303 n. 1	1857, Le Présent, 24 Aug. (title: La Chevelure)	1861, R. fantaisiste, 1 Nov. (title: La Chevelure); 1862, La Presse, 24 Sept. (Subtitle: 'Poème exotique'); 1869, PPP	→1857	P. 31 n. 1, above; G. Blin, Sadisme de B., 161; PPP 265–6, 291; PPP, ed. M. Zimmerman, 162
Un Mangeur d'opium 10 n. 2; 82 n. 2; 107, n. 3 to p. 106; 186 n. 1; 247 n. 2; (261 n. 2); 272 n. 2; 285 n. 2; 286, n. 3 to p. 285; 319 n. 1	1860, RC, 15 and 31 Jan., pp. 24–55 and 304–32 (title: Enchantements et Tortures d'un Mangeur d'opium)	1860, May, PA	1857–9	PA 290–2, 295–9; G. T. Clapton, B. et De Quincey, 12–13
Un Voyage à Cythère 69 and n. 2; 240 and n. 1, 2	1851–2, MS. (DP; title: Voyage à Cythère); →1855, MS. (title: Voyage à Cythère; part-facsimile in Catalogue of B. Exhibition 1968, p. 77 – see also FMCB 1968 p. 230)	1855, RDM 1 June, pp. 1084–5 (title: Voyage à Cythère); 1857, FM proofs (see FMCB 1968); 1857, FM;	1844–51 (1844–6?)	Prarond, CML II, 1155; my art. cit., RHLF, 1967, p. 345 and n. 1; FMCB 501–2; FMA 416, 417 n. 2
Vampire (Le) 110 n. 3	[→1855], MS. (untitled; see FMCB 1968)	1855, RDM, 1 June, pp. 1092–3 (title: La Béatrice); 1857, FM proofs (see FMCB 1968); 1857, FM;	→1855 (1842–8?)	P. 110 n. 3, above; cf. also E. Starkie, B., 95 (cf. 110)
Veuves (Les) 270 n. 1	1861, R. fantaisiste, 1 Nov.	1862, La Presse, 27 Aug.; 1869, PPP	Aug. 1857 – Oct. 1861 (c. May 1861?)	OCP 1601–2 (J. Vier cit.); PPP 284

Title	First extant text(s)	Select list of subsequent texts	Date of original composition	Select list of chronological references
Victor Hugo 149 n. 4; 171 n. 3; 176 n. 1; 178–9 and n. 4, 5; 204–5; 206; 207; 209; (211); 226–31 and 227–8 n. 3; 233; 234; 256 and n. 3; 261 n. 2; 270 n. 2	1861, *R. fantaisiste*, 15 June	1862, *Les Poëtes français*, IV, 265–75; 1869, *AR*	May 1860 – June 1861	*CG* III, 109, 309, 314
Villemain	See s.v. *Esprit et le style de M. Villemain (L')*			
Vin des amants (Le) 190 n. 2	1857, *FM* proofs	1857, *FM*;	→1856 (1841–5?)	Cf. C. Pichois, ed. *Fanfarlo*, 106, n. 3 to p. 61 (analogy with *Fanfarlo* – q.v., above)
Vin des chiffonniers (Le) xiii n. 3; 92 and n. 1, 2; 201; 233 and n. 3; 312	1848–51, MS. *(OCP* 1551; facsimile, *CML* II, pl. i – see p. 92 n. 1, above)	.... 1857, *FM*;	→1843	Prarond, *CML* II, 1155; Asselineau, in *B. et Asselineau*, 174–5; *FMCB* 1968, p. 209; L. Badesco, *RSH*, 1957, pp. 59–61; W. T. Bandy, *RHLF*, 1957, pp. 580–4; *FMA* 402–3. (But cf. J. Pommier, *Mystique de B.*, 189–91)
Vin des honnêtes gens (Le)	See s.v. *Ame du vin (L')*			
Vin du solitaire (Le) 15 and n. 1	1857, *FM* proofs (see *FMCB* 1968)	1857, *FM*;	→1856 (1841–5?)	*FMA* 406–7
Vocations (Les) 3 n. 1; 10 and n. 1; 54 n. 1; 292 n. 1; 295 n. 6; 300 n. 2	1864, *Figaro*, 14 Feb.	1869, *PPP*	→end– 1863 (→Aug. 1862?)	*PPP* 229, 234–5
Voix (La) 186 n. 7; 257–8 and 258 n. 1; 259; 298 n. 3	1861, *RC*, 28 Feb.	.... 1868, *FM*	→1860	*FMA* 442–3

Title	First extant text(s)	Select list of subsequent texts	Date of original composition	Select list of chronological references
Vous avez, compagnon . . . 12 n. 3	1840, MS. for Antony Bruno (*OP* I, 11–12); [1840?], MS. for Félicité B. (see P. Auserve, *Figaro littéraire*, 2–8 Oct. 1967, p. 16)		1840	*OP* I, 378–9; P. Auserve, loc. cit.; Catalogue of B. Exhibition 1968, p. 8 no. 40
Voyage (Le) 3 n. 1; 157–9 and notes; 160 n. 1; 237 n. 2; 254 and n. 2; 261–2; 266; 285 n. 3; 285–6 n. 3; 291; 292; 294–309 and notes; 317	1859, c. 15 Feb., privately printed leaflet (M. Gilman and E. M. Schenck, *RR*, 1938, 274–6 and 271, facsimile)	1859, *RF*, 10 April; 1861, *FM*;	Jan.– Feb. 1859	*CG* II, 274; M. Gilman and E. M. Schenck, art. cit., 273; Y. Abé, *RHLF*, 1967, 273–82
Voyage à Cythère	See s.v. *Un Voyage à Cythère*			
Wagner	See s.v. *Richard Wagner*			

ADDENDUM, P. 364

Réouverture des théâtres [anon., attrib.] 53 n. 2	1848, *Le Salut public*, 27 Feb. (*OP* I, 198)		24–26 Feb. 1848	*OP* I, 529, 531

Index of Persons